HIGHER LEVEL

PEARSON BACCALAUREATE

HIGHER LEVEL

Physics

2nd Edition

CHRIS HAMPER

Supporting every learner across the IB continuum

Published by Pearson Education Limited, Edinburgh Gate, Harlow, Essex, CM20 2JE.

www.pearsonglobalschools.com

Text © Pearson Education Limited 2014

Edited by Gwynneth Drabble
Proofread by Fern Watson
Designed by Astwood Design
Typeset by Ken Vail Graphic Design
Original illustrations © Pearson Education 2014
Illustrated by Tech-Set Ltd and Ken Vail Graphic Design
Cover design by Pearson Education Limited

The right of Chris Hamper to be identified as author of this work has been asserted by him in accordance with the Copyright, Designs and Patents Act 1988.

First published 2014

20 19 18 17
IMP 10 9 8 7 6 5

British Library Cataloguing in Publication Data
A catalogue record for this book is available from the British Library

ISBN 978 1 447 95902 1
eBook only ISBN 978 1 447 95903 8

Printed in Italy by Lego S.p.A.

Acknowledgements
I would like to thank my family for supporting me through the ups and downs of the writing process. The physics students of UWCRCN for unknowingly testing my ideas, Mitch Campbell for help with astrophysics, my dog Ben for insisting that I take some fresh air breaks and Per for making me go rock climbing when I thought I didn't have time.

The author of this book has received financial support from the Norwegian Non-fiction Literature Fund.

The author and publisher would like to thank the following individuals and organisations for permission to reproduce photographs:

(Key: b-bottom; c-centre; l-left; r-right; t-top)

Alamy Images: Aerial Archives 208c, Bill Grant 419tr, Julie Edwards 130c, Noam Armonn 150bl; **Chris Hamper:** 11cr, 12tc, 38bl, 445c; **Corbis:** Bodo Marks / dpa 161cl, Christophe Boisvieux 34c, George Steinmetz 344bl, Martial Trezzini / epa 9t, Ocean 288tc, Pierre Jacques 417bl, Richard Du Toit / Minden Pictures 148c, Stocktrek Images 530c, 549tl; **Fotolia.com:** EcoPim-studio 307tr, gekaskr 241c, Gudellaphoto 430bc, nikkytok 476c, TEK IMAGE 334bl; **Getty Images:** DAJ 436t, Hulton Archive 51bc, Image Source 168bl, Pegasus / Visuals Unlimited, Inc. 68c, Rachel Husband 428tc, Trout55 172bc; **Glow Images:** 65c, 70bc, 92c; **Ole Karsten Birkeland:** 72tl; **PASCO scientific (www.pasco.com):** 44cl, 133br, 449tr, 489t; **Science Photo Library Ltd:** A. Bolton / H-s Cfa / Slacs / Nasa / Esa / Stsci 404cl, 143bc, 521bl, Alex Bartel 173t, Andrew Lambert Photography 175tr, 175cr, 242tr, 288cl, 466c, 469tr, Antoine Rosset 516cl, B. Mcnamara (university Of Waterloo) / Nasa / Esa / Stsci 576tr, Babak Tafreshi, Twan 533cr, 535c, Bernhard Edmaier 345bl, Carlos Munoz Yague / Look At Sciences 229cr, Charles D. Winters 96tc, 120bc, David Nunuk 124c, David Parker 188tr, 504bc, Dept. Of Physics, Imperial College 281tl, Dr Najeeb Layyous 519br, Dr. Arthur Tucker 106tl, Drs A. Yazdani & D.j. Hornbaker 294c, Edward Kinsman 49tl, Erich Schrempp 187tr, European Southern Observatory 563tr, Giphotostock 31bc, 288bl, Goronwy Tudor Jones, University Of Birmingham 301bc, Gustoimages 515br, John Beatty 107bl, John Heseltine 197cr, John Sanford 538bc, K. H. Kjeldsen 576br, Kaj R. Svensson 129br, Lawrence Berkeley Laboratory 246cr, 293tr, Lawrence Livermore National Laboratory 276c, Leonard Lessin 320cl, Mark Clarke 131c, Mark Sykes 105tc, 199cr, Mark Williamson 461tc, Martin Bond 163t, 350cl, Martin Rietze / Westend61 332c, Maximilien Brice, Cern 366c, Mehau Kulyk 293tc, Nasa 401b, 504tl, Nasa / Bill Ingalls 562tl, Nasa / Esa / Stsci / J.hester & P.scowen, Asu 531bc, Nasa / Esa / Stsci / W.colley & E.turner, Princeton 555bc, Nasa / Jpl-caltech 552cl, Nasa / Wmap Science Team 565tc, Pasieka 416c, Pasquale Sorrentino 179tl, Peter Muller 258tl, Philippe Plailly 60bl, Photostock-israel 336br, Physics Dept., Imperial College 542t, Ria Novosti 340cl, Ronald Royer 535tr, Royal Astronomical Society 404tl, 503bc, Seymour 311tr, Sheila Terry 343cr, 372tr, Simon Fraser / Dept. Of Neurology, Newcastle General Hospital 521bl, Ted Kinsman 100bc, Tek Image 2c

Cover images: *Front:* **Corbis:** Don Hammond / Design Pics *Inside front cover:* **Shutterstock.com:** Dmitry Lobanov

All other images © Pearson Education

We are grateful to the following for permission to reproduce copyright material:

Screenshots
Screenshot on page 176 from http://www.falstad.com/ripple/, with permission from Paul Falstad; Screenshots on page 181 from http://audacity.sourceforge.net/, Audacity with permission.

Text
Quote on page 3 from http://www.bipm.org/en/si/si_brochure/ Bureau International des Poids et Mesures, organisation intergouvernementale de la Convention du Mètre, The International System of Units (SI), Bureau International des Poids et Mesures, March 2006. Web: 21 May 2012, reproduced with permission of the BIPM, which retains full internationally protected copyright; Quote on page 351 from the IPCC website: http://www.ipcc.ch/organization/organization.shtml#.Uc6QPJw8lXY Intergovernmental panel on climate change (IPCC); Quote on page 999 from *The Ultimate Quotable Einstein* (Alice Calaprice), with permission: The Albert Einstein Archives, The Hebrew University of Jerusalem; Quote on page 1004 from http://www.aphorismsgalore.com/aphorists/Albert%20Einstein, with permission: The Albert Einstein Archives, The Hebrew University of Jerusalem; Quote on page 1007 from Carl Sagan http://www.carlsagan.com/ with permission.

Every effort has been made to trace the copyright holders and we apologise in advance for any unintentional omissions. We would be pleased to insert the appropriate acknowledgement in any subsequent edition of this publication.

The Understandings, Applications and Skills, Guidance, Essential ideas, past exam questions, corresponding mark schemes provided on the eBook, and assessment criteria have been reproduced from IB documents and past examination papers. Our thanks go to the International Baccalaureate for permission to reproduce its intellectual copyright.

This material has been developed independently by the publisher and the content is in no way connected with or endorsed by the International Baccalaureate (IB).

International Baccalaureate® is a registered trademark of the International Baccalaureate Organization.

There are links to relevant websites in this book. In order to ensure that the links are up to date and that the links work we have made the links available on our website at www.pearsonhotlinks.co.uk. Search for this title or ISBN 9781447959021.

Contents

Contents

Introduction

Author's introduction to the second edition

Welcome to your study of IB Higher Level physics! This second edition has been completely rewritten to match the specifications of the new IB physics curriculum, and gives thorough coverage of the entire course content. While there is much new and updated material, we have kept and refined the features that made the first edition so successful.

Content

The book covers the three parts of the IB syllabus: the core, the AHL (additional higher level) material and the options, of which you will study one. The AHL material is integrated with the core material and the sequence in which the sub-topics are covered is given in the Contents list. Each chapter starts with a list of the Essential ideas from the IB physics guide, which summarize the focus of each sub-topic.

Essential ideas

3.1 Thermal concepts
Thermal physics deftly demonstrates the links between the macroscopic measurements essential to many scientific models with the microscopic properties that underlie these models.

This is followed by an introduction, which gives the context of the topic and how it relates to your previous knowledge. The relevant sections from the IB physics guide for each sub-topic are then given as boxes showing Understanding, applications and skills, with notes for Guidance shown in italics where they help interpret the syllabus. The headings above the Understandings, applications and skills boxes refer to the numbering within the IB guide.

1.1 Measurements in physics

> ### Understandings, applications, and skills:
>
> **Fundamental and derived SI units**
> - Using SI units in the correct format for all required measurements, final answers to calculations and presentation of raw and processed data.
>
>   **Guidance**
>   *SI unit usage and information can be found at the website of Bureau International des Poids et Mesures. Students will not need to know the definition of SI units except where explicitly stated in the relevant topics. Candela is not a required SI unit for this course.*
>
> **Scientific notation and metric multipliers**
> - Using scientific notation and metric multipliers.
> **Significant figures**
> **Orders of magnitude**
> - Quoting and comparing ratios, values, and approximations to the nearest order of magnitude.
> **Estimation**
> - Estimating quantities to an appropriate number of significant figures.

The text covers the course content using plain language, with all scientific terms explained and shown in *bold* as they are first introduced. We have been careful also to apply the same terminology you will see in IB examinations in all worked examples and questions.

The nature of science

Throughout the course you are encouraged to think about the nature of scientific knowledge and the scientific process as it applies to physics. Examples are given of the evolution of physical theories as new information is gained, the use of models to conceptualize our understanding, and the ways in which experimental work is enhanced by modern technologies. Ethical considerations, environmental impacts, the importance of objectivity, and the responsibilities regarding scientists' code of conduct are also considered here. The emphasis is not on learning any of these examples, but rather appreciating the broader conceptual themes in context. We have included at least one example in each sub-section, and hope you will come up with your own as you keep these ideas at the surface of your learning.

Key to information boxes

A popular feature of the book is the different coloured boxes interspersed through each chapter. These are used to enhance your learning as explained below.

 Nature of science

This is an overarching theme in the course to promote concept-based learning. Through the book you should recognize some similar themes emerging across different topics. We hope they help you to develop your own skills in scientific literacy.

 Newton's three laws of motion are a set of statements, based on observation and experiment, that can be used to predict the motion of a point object from the forces acting on it. Einstein showed that the laws do not apply when speeds approach the speed of light. However, we still use them to predict outcomes at the lower velocities achieved by objects travelling in the lab.

 In cold countries houses are insulated to prevent heat from escaping. Are houses in hot countries insulated to stop heat entering?

 International-mindedness

The impact of the study of physics is global, and includes environmental, political and socio-economic considerations. Examples of this are given here to help you to see the importance of physics in an international context.

 Utilization

Applications of the topic through everyday examples are described here, as well as brief descriptions of related physical industries. This helps you to see the relevance and context of what you are learning.

 Although the first ever engine was probably a steam turbine, cylinders of expanding gas are the basis of most engines.

People sweat to increase the rate at which they lose heat. When you get hot, sweat comes out of your skin onto the surface of your body. When the sweat evaporates, it cools you down. In a sauna there is so much water vapour in the air that the sweat doesn't evaporate.

 ## Interesting fact

These give background information that will add to your wider knowledge of the topic and make links with other topics and subjects. Aspects such as historic notes on the life of scientists and origins of names are included here.

 ## Laboratory work

These indicate links to ideas for lab work and experiments that will support your learning in the course, and help you prepare for the Internal Assessment. Some specific experimental work is compulsory, and further details of this are in the eBook.

 Specific heat capacity of a metal

A metal sample is first heated to a known temperature. The most convenient way of doing this is to place it in boiling water for a few minutes; after this time it will be at 100°C. The hot metal is then quickly moved to an insulated cup containing a known mass of cold water. The hot metal will cause the temperature of the cold water to rise; the rise in temperature is measured with a thermometer. Some example temperatures and masses are given in Figure 3.34.

We perceive how hot or cold something is with our senses but to quantify this we need a measurement.

 ## TOK

These stimulate thought and consideration of knowledge issues as they arise in context. Each box contains open questions to help trigger critical thinking and discussion.

 ## Key fact

These key facts are drawn out of the main text and highlighted in bold. This will help you to identify the core learning points within each section. They also act as a quick summary for review.

 Solid → liquid
Specific latent heat of fusion
Liquid → gas
Specific latent heat of vaporization

There are two versions of the equation for centripetal force
Speed version:
$F = \frac{mv^2}{r}$
Angular speed version:
$F = m\omega^2 r$

 ## Hints for success

These give hints on how to approach questions, and suggest approaches that examiners like to see. They also identify common pitfalls in understanding, and omissions made in answering questions.

Challenge yourself

These boxes contain open questions that encourage you to think about the topic in more depth, or to make detailed connections with other topics. They are designed to be challenging and to make you think.

Towards the end of the book, there are three appendix chapters: Theory of Knowledge as it relates to physics, and advice on the Extended Essay and Internal Assessment.

eBook

In the eBook you will find the following:

- Interactive glossary of scientific words used in the course
- Answers and worked solutions to all exercises in the book
- Summary and labs worksheets
- Interactive quizzes
- Animations
- Videos

For more details about your eBook, see the following section.

Questions

There are three types of question in this book:

1. Worked example with solution

These appear at intervals in the text and are used to illustrate the concepts covered. They are followed by the solution, which shows the thinking and the steps used in solving the problem.

Worked example

Referring to Figure 4.21 if a body is moved from A to B what is the change in potential?

Solution

$V_A = 30\,\mathrm{J\,kg^{-1}}$

$V_B = 80\,\mathrm{J\,kg^{-1}}$

Change in potential = $80 - 30 = 50\,\mathrm{J\,kg^{-1}}$

2. Exercises

These questions are found throughout the text. They allow you to apply your knowledge and test your understanding of what you have just been reading.

The answers to these are given on the eBook at the end of each chapter.

Exercises

7 Calculate the mass of air in a room of length 5 m, width 10 m, and height 3 m.

8 Calculate the mass of a gold bar of length 30 cm, width 15 cm, and height 10 cm.

9 Calculate the average density of the Earth.

3. Practice questions

These questions are found at the end of each chapter. They are mostly taken from previous years' IB examination papers. The mark-schemes used by examiners when marking these questions are given in the eBook, at the end of each chapter.

Practice questions

1. This question is about energy sources.

(a) Fossil fuels are being produced continuously on Earth and yet they are classed as being non-renewable. Outline why fossil fuels are classed as non-renewable. (2)

(b) Some energy consultants suggest that the solution to the problem of carbon dioxide pollution is to use nuclear energy for the generation of electrical energy. Identify **two** disadvantages of the use of nuclear fission when compared to the burning of fossil fuels for the generation of electrical energy. (2)

(Total 4 marks)

Worked solutions

Full worked solutions to all exercises and practice questions can be found in the eBook, as well as regular answers.

 Hotlinks boxes can be found throughout the book, indicating that there are weblinks available for further study. To access these links go to www.pearsonhotlinks.com and enter the ISBN or title of this book. Here you can find animations, simulations, movie clips and related background material, which can help to deepen your interest and understanding of the topic.

I hope you enjoy your study of IB physics.

Chris Hamper

How to use your enhanced eBook

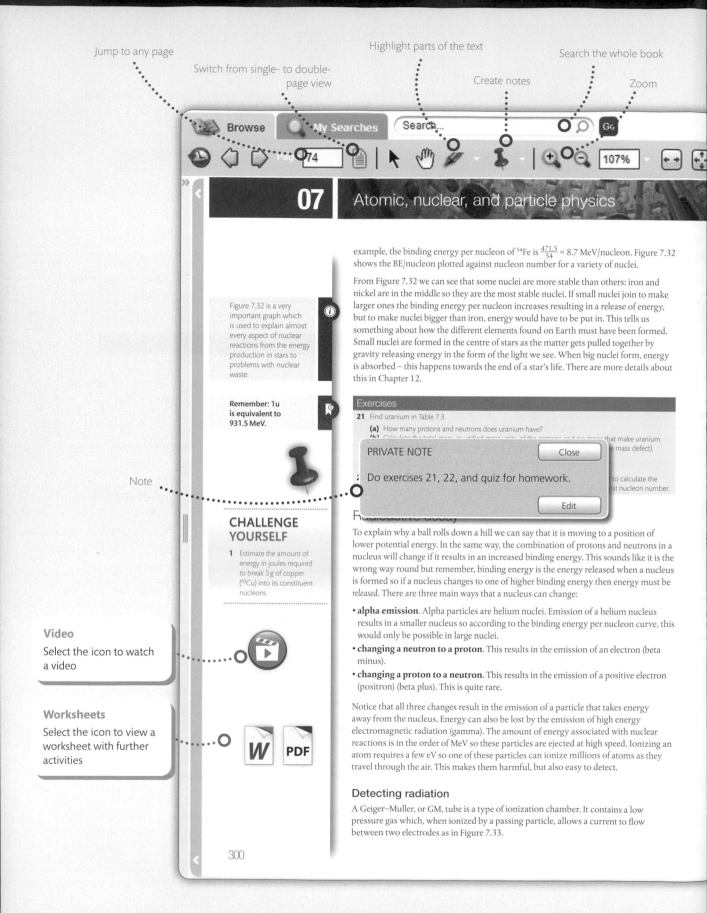

Jump to any page

Switch from single- to double-page view

Highlight parts of the text

Create notes

Search the whole book

Zoom

Note

Video

Select the icon to watch a video

Worksheets

Select the icon to view a worksheet with further activities

07 Atomic, nuclear, and particle physics

example, the binding energy per nucleon of ^{54}Fe is $\frac{471.5}{54}$ = 8.7 MeV/nucleon. Figure 7.32 shows the BE/nucleon plotted against nucleon number for a variety of nuclei.

From Figure 7.32 we can see that some nuclei are more stable than others: iron and nickel are in the middle so they are the most stable nuclei. If small nuclei join to make larger ones the binding energy per nucleon increases resulting in a release of energy, but to make nuclei bigger than iron, energy would have to be put in. This tells us something about how the different elements found on Earth must have been formed. Small nuclei are formed in the centre of stars as the matter gets pulled together by gravity releasing energy in the form of the light we see. When big nuclei form, energy is absorbed – this happens towards the end of a star's life. There are more details about this in Chapter 12.

Figure 7.32 is a very important graph which is used to explain almost every aspect of nuclear reactions from the energy production in stars to problems with nuclear waste.

Remember: 1u is equivalent to 931.5 MeV.

Exercises

21 Find uranium in Table 7.3.

(a) How many protons and neutrons does uranium have?
(b) Calculate the total mass, in unified mass units, of the protons and neutrons that make uranium.

PRIVATE NOTE   Close

Do exercises 21, 22, and quiz for homework.

Edit

to calculate the nst nucleon number.

CHALLENGE YOURSELF

1 Estimate the amount of energy in joules required to break 3 g of copper (^{63}Cu) into its constituent nucleons.

Radioactive decay

To explain why a ball rolls down a hill we can say that it is moving to a position of lower potential energy. In the same way, the combination of protons and neutrons in a nucleus will change if it results in an increased binding energy. This sounds like it is the wrong way round but remember, binding energy is the energy released when a nucleus is formed so if a nucleus changes to one of higher binding energy then energy must be *released*. There are three main ways that a nucleus can change:

• **alpha emission**. Alpha particles are helium nuclei. Emission of a helium nucleus results in a smaller nucleus so according to the binding energy per nucleon curve, this would only be possible in large nuclei.
• **changing a neutron to a proton**. This results in the emission of an electron (beta minus).
• **changing a proton to a neutron**. This results in the emission of a positive electron (positron) (beta plus). This is quite rare.

Notice that all three changes result in the emission of a particle that takes energy away from the nucleus. Energy can also be lost by the emission of high energy electromagnetic radiation (gamma). The amount of energy associated with nuclear reactions is in the order of MeV so these particles are ejected at high speed. Ionizing an atom requires a few eV so one of these particles can ionize millions of atoms as they travel through the air. This makes them harmful, but also easy to detect.

Detecting radiation

A Geiger–Muller, or GM, tube is a type of ionization chamber. It contains a low pressure gas which, when ionized by a passing particle, allows a current to flow between two electrodes as in Figure 7.33.

300

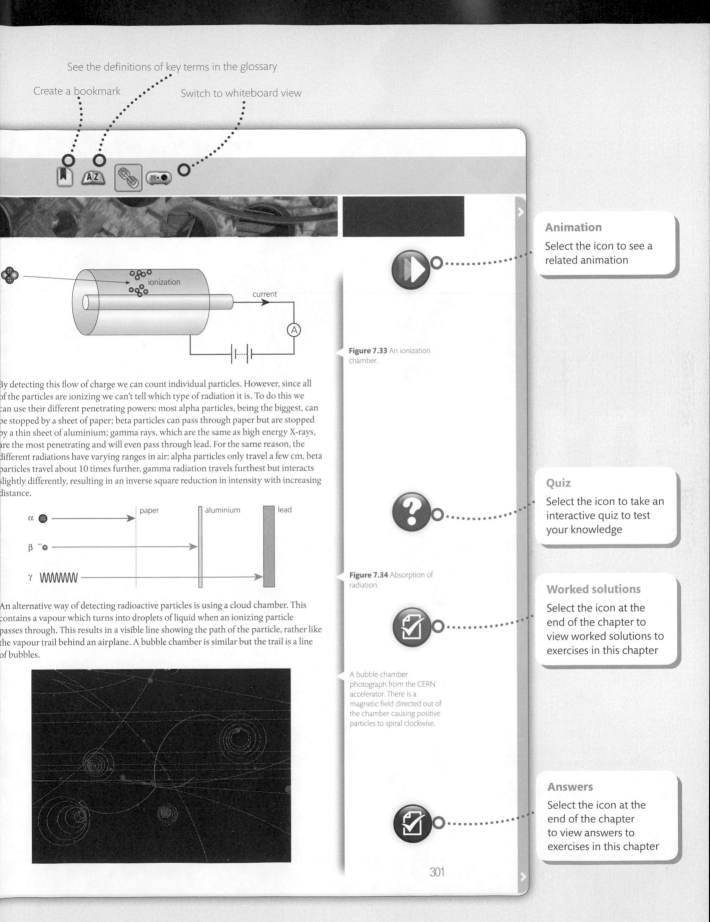

See the definitions of key terms in the glossary

Create a bookmark

Switch to whiteboard view

Animation

Select the icon to see a related animation

ionization

current

Figure 7.33 An ionization chamber.

By detecting this flow of charge we can count individual particles. However, since all of the particles are ionizing we can't tell which type of radiation it is. To do this we can use their different penetrating powers: most alpha particles, being the biggest, can be stopped by a sheet of paper; beta particles can pass through paper but are stopped by a thin sheet of aluminium; gamma rays, which are the same as high energy X-rays, are the most penetrating and will even pass through lead. For the same reason, the different radiations have varying ranges in air: alpha particles only travel a few cm, beta particles travel about 10 times further, gamma radiation travels furthest but interacts slightly differently, resulting in an inverse square reduction in intensity with increasing distance.

α

β

γ

paper   aluminium   lead

Figure 7.34 Absorption of radiation.

An alternative way of detecting radioactive particles is using a cloud chamber. This contains a vapour which turns into droplets of liquid when an ionizing particle passes through. This results in a visible line showing the path of the particle, rather like the vapour trail behind an airplane. A bubble chamber is similar but the trail is a line of bubbles.

A bubble chamber photograph from the CERN accelerator. There is a magnetic field directed out of the chamber causing positive particles to spiral clockwise.

Quiz

Select the icon to take an interactive quiz to test your knowledge

Worked solutions

Select the icon at the end of the chapter to view worked solutions to exercises in this chapter

Answers

Select the icon at the end of the chapter to view answers to exercises in this chapter

301

01

Measurements and uncertainties

Essential ideas

1.1 Measurements in physics
Since 1948, the Système International d'Unités (SI) has been used as the preferred language of science and technology across the globe and reflects current best measurement practice. A common standard approach is necessary so units 'are readily available to all, are constant through time and space, and are easy to realize with high accuracy' – France: Bureau International des Poids et Mesures, organisation intergouvernementale de la Convention du Mètre, *The International System of Units (SI),* Bureau International des Poids et Mesures, March 2006. Web: 21 May 2012.

1.2 Uncertainties and errors
Scientists aim towards designing experiments that can give a 'true value' from their measurements, but due to the limited precision in measuring devices they often quote their results with some form of uncertainty.

1.3 Vectors and scalars
Some quantities have direction and magnitude, others have magnitude only, and this understanding is key to correct manipulation of quantities. This subtopic will have broad applications across multiple fields within physics and other sciences.

NATURE OF SCIENCE

Physics is about modelling the physical Universe so that we can predict outcomes but before we can develop models we need to define quantities and measure them. To measure a quantity we first need to invent a measuring device and define a unit. When measuring we should try to be as accurate as possible but we can never be exact, measurements will always have uncertainties. This could be due to the instrument or the way we use it or it might be that the quantity we are trying to measure is changing.

1.1 Measurements in physics

1.1 Measurements in physics

Understandings, applications, and skills:

Fundamental and derived SI units
- Using SI units in the correct format for all required measurements, final answers to calculations and presentation of raw and processed data.

  Guidance
  - *SI unit usage and information can be found at the website of Bureau International des Poids et Mesures. Students will not need to know the definition of SI units except where explicitly stated in the relevant topics. Candela is not a required SI unit for this course.*

Scientific notation and metric multipliers
- Using scientific notation and metric multipliers.

Significant figures

Orders of magnitude
- Quoting and comparing ratios, values, and approximations to the nearest order of magnitude.

Estimation
- Estimating quantities to an appropriate number of significant figures.

If used properly a Vernier calliper can measure small lengths to within ±0.02 mm.

3

Making observations

Before we can try to understand the Universe we have to observe it. Imagine you are a cave man/woman looking up into the sky at night. You would see lots of bright points scattered about (assuming it is not cloudy). The points are not the same but how can you describe the differences between them? One of the main differences is that you have to move your head to see different examples. This might lead you to define their position. Occasionally you might notice a star flashing so would realize that there are also differences not associated with position, leading to the concept of time. If you shift your attention to the world around you you'll be able to make further close-range observations. Picking up rocks you notice some are easy to pick up while others are more difficult; some are hot, some are cold, and different rocks are different colours. These observations are just the start: to be able to understand how these quantities are related you need to measure them but before you do that you need to be able to count.

Figure 1.1 Making observations came before science.

Numbers

Numbers weren't originally designed for use by physics students: they were for counting objects.

$$2 \text{ apples} + 3 \text{ apples} = 5 \text{ apples}$$

$$2 + 3 = 5$$

$$2 \times 3 \text{ apples} = 6 \text{ apples}$$

$$\frac{6 \text{ apples}}{2} = 3 \text{ apples}$$

So the numbers mirror what is happening to the apples. However, you have to be careful: you can do some operations with numbers that are not possible with apples. For example:

$$(2 \text{ apples})^2 = 4 \text{ square apples}?$$

TOK

If the system of numbers had been totally different, would our models of the Universe be the same?

Standard form

In this course we will use some numbers that are very big and some that are very small. 602 000 000 000 000 000 000 000 is a commonly used number as is 0.000 000 000 000 000 000 16. To make life easier we write these in standard form. This means that we write the number with only one digit to the left of the decimal place and represent the number of zeros with powers of 10.

So

602 000 000 000 000 000 000 000 = 6.02×10^{23} (decimal place must be shifted right 23 places)

0.000 000 000 000 000 000 16 = 1.6×10^{-19} (decimal place must be shifted left 19 places).

Exercise

1 Write the following in standard form.
  (a) 48 000
  (b) 0.000 036
  (c) 14 500
  (d) 0.000 000 48

Measurement

We have seen that there are certain fundamental quantities that define our Universe. These are position, time, and mass.

Distance

Before we take any measurements we need to define the quantity. The quantity that we use to define the position of different objects is *distance*. To measure distance we need to make a scale and to do that we need two fixed points. We could take one fixed point to be ourselves but then everyone would have a different value for the distance to each point so we take our fixed points to be two points that never change position, for example the ends of a stick. If everyone then uses the same stick we will all end up with the same measurement. We can't all use the same stick so we make copies of the stick and assume that they are all the same. The problem is that sticks aren't all the same length, so our unit of length is now based on one of the few things we know to be the same for everyone: the speed of light in a vacuum. Once we have defined the unit, in this case the metre, it is important that we all use it (or at least make it very clear if we are using a different one). There is more than one system of units but the one used in this course is the SI system (International system). Here are some examples of distances measured in metres.

The distance from Earth to the Sun = 1.5×10^{11} m
The size of a grain of sand = 2×10^{-4} m
The distance to the nearest star = 4×10^{16} m
The radius of the Earth = 6.378×10^{6} m

Exercise

2 Convert the following into metres (m) and write in standard form:
  (a) Distance from London to New York = 5585 km.
  (b) Height of Einstein was 175 cm.
  (c) Thickness of a human hair = 25.4 µm.
  (d) Distance to furthest part of the observable Universe = 100 000 million million million km.

It is also acceptable to use a prefix to denote powers of 10.

Prefix	Value
T (tera)	10^{12}
G (giga)	10^{9}
M (mega)	10^{6}
k (kilo)	10^{3}
c (centi)	10^{-2}
m (milli)	10^{-3}
µ (micro)	10^{-6}
n (nano)	10^{-9}
p (pico)	10^{-12}
f (femto)	10^{-15}

If you set up your calculator properly it will always give your answers in standard form.

Realization that the speed of light in a vacuum is the same no matter who measures it led to the speed of light being the basis of our unit of length.

The metre

The metre was originally defined in terms of several pieces of metal positioned around Paris. This wasn't very accurate so now one metre is defined as the distance travelled by light in a vacuum in $\frac{1}{299\,792\,458}$ of a second.

Time

When something happens we call it an *event*. To distinguish between different events we use time. The time between two events is measured by comparing to some fixed value, the second. Time is also a fundamental quantity.

Some examples of times:

Time between beats of a human heart = 1 s
Time for the Earth to go around the Sun = 1 year
Time for the Moon to go around the Earth = 1 month

Exercise

3 Convert the following times into seconds (s) and write in standard form:

(a) 85 years, how long Newton lived.
(b) 2.5 ms, the time taken for a mosquito's wing to go up and down.
(c) 4 days, the time it took to travel to the Moon.
(d) 2 hours 52 min 59 s, the time for Concord to fly from London to New York.

Mass

If we pick different things up we find another difference. Some things are easy to lift up and others are difficult. This seems to be related to how much matter the objects consist of. To quantify this we define mass measured by comparing different objects to a piece of metal in Paris, the standard kilogram.

Some examples of mass:

Approximate mass of a man = 75 kg
Mass of the Earth = 5.97×10^{24} kg
Mass of the Sun = 1.98×10^{30} kg

Exercise

4 Convert the following masses to kilograms (kg) and write in standard form:

(a) The mass of an apple = 200 g.
(b) The mass of a grain of sand = 0.00001 g.
(c) The mass of a family car = 2 tonnes.

Volume

The space taken up by an object is defined by the volume. Volume is measured in cubic metres (m^3). Volume is not a fundamental unit since it can be split into smaller units (m × m × m). We call units like this derived units.

Exercises

5 Calculate the volume of a room of length 5 m, width 10 m, and height 3 m.
6 Using the information from page 5, calculate:

(a) the volume of a human hair of length 20 cm.
(b) the volume of the Earth.

Density

By measuring the mass and volume of many different objects we find that if the objects are made of the same material, the ratio mass/volume is the same. This quantity is called the *density*. The unit of density is kg m^{-3}. This is another derived unit.

Examples include:

$$\text{Density of water} = 1.0 \times 10^3 \, \text{kg m}^{-3}$$
$$\text{Density of air} = 1.2 \, \text{kg m}^{-3}$$
$$\text{Density of gold} = 1.93 \times 10^4 \, \text{kg m}^{-3}$$

Exercises

7 Calculate the mass of air in a room of length 5 m, width 10 m, and height 3 m.

8 Calculate the mass of a gold bar of length 30 cm, width 15 cm, and height 10 cm.

9 Calculate the average density of the Earth.

Displacement

So far all that we have modelled is the position of objects and when events take place, but what if something moves from one place to another? To describe the movement of a body, we define the quantity *displacement*. This is the distance moved in a particular direction.

The unit of displacement is the same as length: the metre.

Example:
Refering to the map in Figure 1.2:
If you move from B to C, your displacement will be 5 km north.
If you move from A to B, your displacement will be 4 km west.

Angle

When two straight lines join, an angle is formed. The size of the angle can be increased by rotating one of the lines about the point where they join (the vertex) as shown in Figure 1.3. To measure angles we often use degrees. Taking the full circle to be 360° is very convenient because 360 has many whole number factors so it can be divided easily by e.g. 4, 6, and 8. However, it is an arbitrary unit not related to the circle itself.

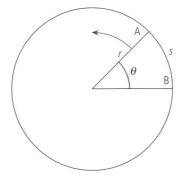

If the angle is increased by rotating line A the arc lengths will also increase. So for this circle we could use the arc length as a measure of angle. The problem is that if we take a bigger circle then the arc length for the same angle will be greater. We therefore define the angle by using the ratio $\frac{s}{r}$ which will be the same for all circles. This unit is the radian.

For one complete circle the arc length is the circumference $= 2\pi r$ so the angle 360° in radians $= \frac{2\pi r}{r} = 2\pi$.

So 360° is equivalent to 2π.

Since the radian is a ratio of two lengths it has no units.

Summary of SI units

The International System of units is the set of units that are internationally agreed to be used in science. It is still OK to use other systems in everyday life (miles, pounds, Fahrenheit) but in science we must always use SI. There are seven fundamental (or base) quantities.

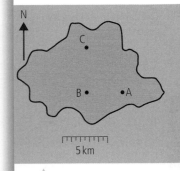

Figure 1.2 Displacements on a map.

Figure 1.3 The angle between two lines.

Base quantity	Unit	Symbol
length	metre	m
mass	kilogram	kg
time	second	s
electric current	ampere	A
thermodynamic temperature	kelvin	K
amount of substance	mole	mol
luminous intensity	candela	cd

The candela will not be used in this course.

All other SI units are derived units; these are based on the fundamental units and will be introduced and defined where relevant. So far we have come across just two.

Table 1.2 Some SI derived quantities.

Derived quantity	Symbol	Base units
volume	m^3	m × m × m
density	$kg\,m^{-3}$	$\dfrac{kg}{m \times m \times m}$

1.2 Uncertainties and errors

1.2 Uncertainties and errors

Understandings, applications, and skills:

Random and systematic errors
• Explaining how random and systematic errors can be identified and reduced.
Absolute, fractional, and percentage uncertainty
• Collecting data that include absolute and/or fractional uncertainties and stating these as an uncertainty range (expressed as: [best estimate] ± [uncertainty range]).

> *Guidance*
> • *Analysis of uncertainties will not be expected for trigonometric or logarithmic functions in examinations.*

Error bars
• Propagating uncertainties through calculations involving addition, subtraction, multiplication, division, and raising to a power.
Uncertainty of gradient and intercepts
• Determining the uncertainty in gradients and intercepts.

In physics experiments we always quote the uncertainties in our measurements. Shops also have to work within given uncertainties and will be prosecuted if they overestimate the weight of something.

NATURE OF SCIENCE

When counting apples we can say there are exactly 6 apples but if we measure the length of a piece of paper we cannot say that it is exactly 21 cm wide. All measurements have an associated uncertainty and it is important that this is also quoted with the value. Uncertainties can't be avoided but by carefully using accurate instruments they can be minimized. Physics is all about relationships between different quantities. If the uncertainties in measurement are too big then relationships are difficult to identify. Throughout the practical part of this course you will be trying to find out what causes the uncertainties in your measurements. Sometimes you will be able to reduce them and at other times not. It is quite alright to have big uncertainties but completely unacceptable to manipulate data so that it appears to fit a predicted relationship.

Uncertainty and error in measurement

The SI system of units is defined so that we all use the same sized units when building our models of the physical world. However, before we can understand the relationship between different quantities, we must measure how big they are. To make measurements we use a variety of instruments. To measure length, we can use a ruler and to measure time, a clock. If our findings are to be trusted, then our measurements must be accurate, and the accuracy of our measurement depends on the instrument used and how we use it. Consider the following examples.

Even this huge device at CERN has uncertainties.

Measuring length using a ruler

Example 1

A good straight ruler marked in mm is used to measure the length of a rectangular piece of paper as in Figure 1.4.

The ruler measures to within 0.5 mm (we call this the *uncertainty* in the measurement) so the length in cm is quoted to 2 dp. This measurement is precise and accurate. This can be written as 6.40 ± 0.05 cm which tells us that the actual value is somewhere between 6.35 and 6.45 cm.

Figure 1.4
Length = 6.40 ± 0.05 cm.

Example 2

Figure 1.5 shows how a ruler with a broken end is used to measure the length of the same piece of paper. When using the ruler, you fail to notice the end is broken and think that the 0.5 cm mark is the zero mark. This measurement is precise since the uncertainty is small but is not accurate since the value 6.90 cm is wrong.

Figure 1.5
Length ≠ 6.90 ± 0.05 cm.

Estimating uncertainty

When using a scale such as a ruler the uncertainty in the reading is half of the smallest division. In this case the smallest division is 1 mm so the uncertainty is 0.5 mm. When using a digital device such as a balance we take the uncertainty as the smallest digit. So if the measurement is 20.5 g the uncertainty is ±0.1 g.

If you measure the same thing many times and get the same value, then the measurement is precise.

If the measured value is close to the expected value, then the measurement is accurate. If a football player hit the post 10 times in a row when trying to score a goal, you could say the shots are precise but not accurate.

Example 3

A cheap ruler marked only in $\frac{1}{2}$ cm is used to measure the length of the paper as in Figure 1.6.

These measurements are precise and accurate, but the scale is not very sensitive.

Figure 1.6
Length = 6.5 ± 0.25 cm.

Example 4

In Figure 1.7, a good ruler is used to measure the maximum height of a bouncing ball. Even though the ruler is good it is very difficult to measure the height of the bouncing ball. Even though you can use the scale to within 0.5 mm, the results are not precise (may be about 4.2 cm). However, if you do enough runs of the same experiment, your final answer could be accurate.

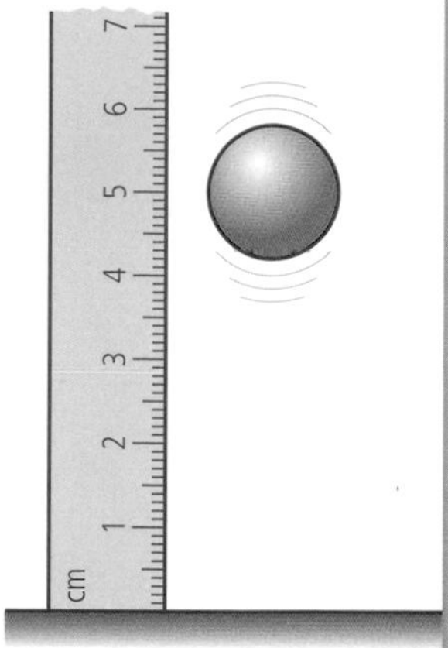

Figure 1.7
Height = 4.2 ± 0.2 cm

Precision and accuracy

To help understand the difference between precision and accuracy, consider the four attempts to hit the centre of a target with 3 arrows shown in Figure 1.8.

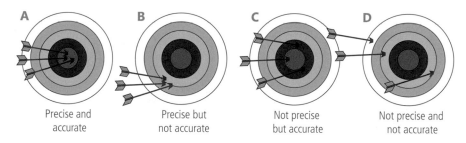

| Precise and accurate | Precise but not accurate | Not precise but accurate | Not precise and not accurate |

Figure 1.8 Precise or accurate?

A The arrows were fired accurately at the centre with great precision.

B The arrows were fired with great precision as they all landed near one another, but not very accurately since they are not near the centre.

C The arrows were not fired very precisely since they were not close to each other. However, they were accurate since they are evenly spread around the centre. The average of these would be quite good.

D The arrows were not fired accurately and the aim was not precise since they are far from the centre and not evenly spread.

So *precision* is how close to each other a set of measurements are and the *accuracy* is how close they are to the actual value.

Errors in measurement

TOK

There are two types of measurement error – random and systematic.

Random error

If you measure a quantity many times and get lots of slightly different readings then this called a random error. For example, when measuring the bounce of a ball it is very difficult to get the same value every time even if the ball is doing the same thing.

It is not possible to measure anything exactly. This is not because our instruments are not exact enough but because the quantities themselves do not exist as exact quantities.

Systematic error

This is when there is something wrong with the measuring device or method. Using a ruler with a broken end can lead to a 'zero error' as in Example 2 on page 9. Even with no random error in the results, you'd still get the wrong answer.

Reducing errors

To reduce random errors you can repeat your measurements. If the uncertainty is truly random, they will lie either side of the true reading and the mean of these values will be close to the actual value. To reduce a systematic error you need to find out what is causing it and correct your measurements accordingly. A systematic error is not easy to spot by looking at the measurements, but is sometimes apparent when you look at the graph of your results or the final calculated value.

Adding uncertainties

If two values are added together then the uncertainties also add. For example, if we measure two lengths $L_1 = 5.0 \pm 0.1$ cm and $L_2 = 6.5 \pm 0.1$ cm then the maximum value of L_1 is 5.1 cm and the maximum value of L_2 is 6.6 cm so the maximum value of $L_1 + L_2 = 11.7$ cm. Similarly, the minimum value is 11.3 cm. We can therefore say that $L_1 + L_2 = 11.5 \pm 0.2$ cm.

If $\quad\quad y = a \pm b \quad\quad\quad$ then $\quad \Delta y = \Delta a + \Delta b$

If you multiply a value by a constant then the uncertainty is also multiplied by the same number.

So $\quad\quad 2L_1 = 10.0 \pm 0.2$ cm $\quad$ and $\quad \frac{1}{2}L_1 = 2.50 \pm 0.05$ cm.

Example of measurement and uncertainties

Let us consider an experiment to measure the mass and volume of a piece of plasticine (modelling clay). To measure mass we can use a top pan balance so we take a lump of plasticine and weigh it. The result is 24.8 g. We can repeat this measurement many times and get the same answer; there is no variation in the mass so the uncertainty in this measurement is the same as the uncertainty in the scale. The smallest division on the balance used is 0.1 g so the uncertainty is ±0.1 g.

So $\quad\quad\quad\quad\quad\quad\quad\quad\quad\quad$ mass = 24.8 ±0.1 g.

To measure the volume of the plasticine we first need to mould it into a uniform shape: let's roll it into a sphere. To measure the volume of the sphere we measure its diameter ($V = \frac{4\pi r^3}{3}$).

Making an exact sphere out of the plasticine isn't easy; if we do it many times we will get different shaped balls with different diameters so let's try rolling the ball 5 times and measuring the diameter each time with a ruler.

Using the ruler, we can only judge the diameter to the nearest mm so we can say that the diameter is 3.5 ± 0.1 cm. It is actually even worse than this since we also have to line up the zero at the other end, so 3.5 ± 0.2 cm might be a more reasonable estimate. If we turn the ball round we get the same value for d. If we squash the ball and make a new one we will still get a value of 3.5 ± 0.2 cm. This is not because the ball is perfect sphere every time but because our method of measurement isn't *sensitive* enough to measure the difference.

Ball of plasticine measured with a ruler.

Let us now try measuring the ball with a vernier calliper.

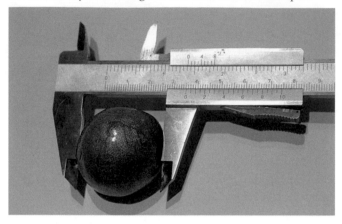

A vernier calliper has sliding jaws which are moved so they touch both sides of the ball.

The vernier calliper can measure to the nearest 0.002 cm. Repeating measurements of the diameter of the same lump of plasticine might give the results in Table 1.3.

Table 1.3 Measurements of the diameter of a lump of plasticine.

Diameter/cm								
3.640	3.450	3.472	3.500	3.520	3.520	3.530	3.530	3.432
3.540	3.550	3.550	3.560	3.560	3.570	3.572	3.582	3.582

The reason these are not all the same is because the ball is not perfectly uniform and if made several times will not be exactly the same. We can see that there is a spread of data from 3.400 cm to 3.570 cm with most lying around the middle. This can be shown on a graph but first we need to group the values as in Table 1.4.

Distribution of measurements

Figure 1.9 Distribution of measurements of diameter.

Range/cm	No. of values within range
3.400–3.449	1
3.450–3.499	2
3.500–3.549	6
3.550–3.599	8
3.600–3.649	1

Table 1.4.

Even with this small sample of measurements you can see in Figure 1.9 that there is a spread of data: some measurements are too big and some too small but most are in the middle. With a much larger sample the shape would be closer to a 'normal distribution' as in Figure 1.10.

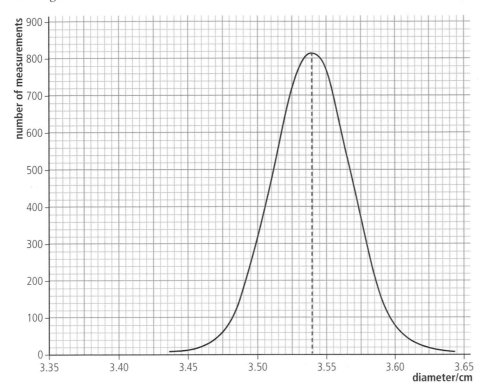

Figure 1.10 Normal distribution curve.

The mean

At this stage you may be wondering what the point is of trying to measure something that doesn't have a definite value. Well, we are trying to find the volume of the plasticine using the formula $V = \frac{4\pi r^3}{3}$. This is the formula for the volume of a perfect sphere. The problem is we can't make a perfect sphere; it is probably more like the shape of an egg so depending on which way we measure it, sometimes the diameter will be too big and sometimes too small. Now it is just as likely to be too big as too small so if we take the mean of all our measurements we should be close to the 'perfect sphere' value which will give us the correct volume of the plasticine.

The mean or average is found by adding all the values and dividing by the number of values. In this case the mean = 3.537 cm. This is the same as the peak in the distribution. We can check this by measuring the volume in another way; for example, sinking it in water and measuring the volume displaced. Using this method gives a volume = 23 cm³. Rearranging the formula gives $r = \sqrt[3]{\frac{3V}{4\pi}}$.

Substituting for V gives $d = 3.53$ cm which is fairly close to the mean. Calculating the mean reduces the random error in our measurement.

There is a very nice example of this that you might like to try with your friends. Fill a jar with jellybeans and get your friends to guess how many there are. Assuming that they really try to make an estimate rather than randomly saying a number, the guesses are just as likely to be too high as too low. So, if after you collect all the data you find the average value, it should be quite close to the actual number of beans.

Standard deviation

The standard deviation tells us how spread out the data is from the mean. It is calculated by using the following formula:

$$d = \sqrt{\frac{(\Delta x_1)^2 + (\Delta x_2)^2 + \dots + (\Delta x_N)^2}{N-1}}$$

The Δx terms are the difference between the value and the mean and N is the total number of values. This has been calculated in Table 1.5.

The standard deviation gives us an idea of the size of the random variations in the data enabling us to estimate the uncertainty in the measurement. In this case we could say that the uncertainty is ±0.05 cm so we can only quote the value to 2 decimal places:

$$d = 3.54 \pm 0.05 \text{ cm}.$$

Note: This is quite a lot more than the uncertainty in the measuring device, which was ±0.002 cm. If the calculated uncertainty is smaller than the uncertainty in the measuring instrument we use the larger value.

In Excel the function STDEV(A2:A19) will do all the calculations for you where (A2:A19) is the range of values you want to find the standard deviation for. In this example the range is from A2 to A19, but this would depend on your table.

x/cm	Δx/cm	Δx^2/cm²
3.432	−0.105	0.01096
3.450	−0.087	0.00751
3.472	−0.065	0.00418
3.500	−0.037	0.00134
3.520	−0.017	0.00028
3.520	−0.017	0.00028
3.530	−0.007	0.00004
3.530	−0.007	0.00004
3.540	0.003	0.00001
3.550	0.013	0.00018
3.550	0.013	0.00018
3.560	0.023	0.00054
3.560	0.023	0.00054
3.570	0.033	0.00111
3.572	0.035	0.00125
3.582	0.045	0.00206
3.582	0.045	0.00206
3.640	0.103	0.01068

Mean value	Standard deviation
3.537 cm	0.05043 cm

Table 1.5

> If the data follows a normal distribution 68% of the values should be within one standard deviation of the mean. In the example given this would mean that 68% of the measurements should be between 3.49 and 3.59 cm.

Smaller samples

You will be collecting a lot of different types of data throughout the course but you won't often have time to repeat your measurements enough to get a normal distribution. With only 4 values the uncertainty is not reduced significantly by taking the mean so *half* the range of values is used instead. This often gives a slightly exaggerated value for the uncertainty – for the example above it would be ± 0.1 cm – but it is an approach accepted by the IB.

Relationships

In physics we are very interested in the relationships between two quantities; for example, the distance travelled by a ball and the time taken. To understand how we represent relationships by equations and graphs, let us consider a simple relationship regarding fruit.

Linear relationships

To make this simple let us imagine that all apples have the same mass, 100 g. To find the relationship between number of apples and their mass we would need to measure the mass of different numbers of apples. These results could be put into a table as in Table 1.6.

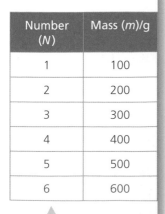

Number (N)	Mass (m)/g
1	100
2	200
3	300
4	400
5	500
6	600

Table 1.6 The relationship between the mass and the number of apples.

In this example we can clearly see that the mass of the apples increases by the same amount every time we add an apple. We say that the mass of apples is *proportional* to the number. If we draw a graph of mass *vs* number we get a straight line passing through the origin as in Figure 1.11.

The gradient of this line is given by $\frac{\Delta y}{\Delta x} = 100\,\text{g/apple}$. The fact that the line is straight and passing through the origin can be used to test if two quantities are proportional to each other.

The equation of the line is $y = mx$ where m is the gradient so in this case $m = 100\,\text{g apple}^{-1}$.

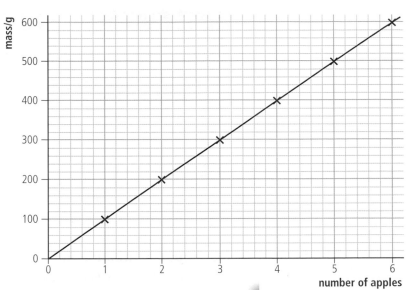

Figure 1.11 Graph of mass *vs* number of apples.

This equation can be used to calculate the mass of any given number of apples. This is a simple example of what we will spend a lot of time doing in this course.

To make things a little more complicated let's consider apples in a basket with mass 500 g. The table of masses is shown in Table 1.7.

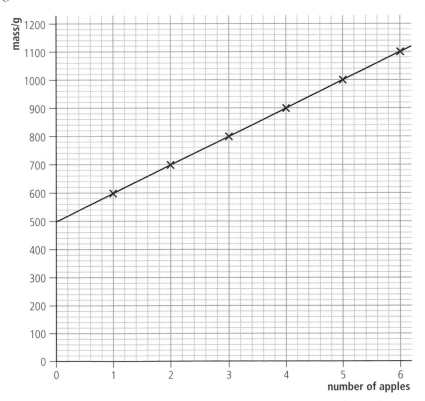

Number (N)	Mass (m)/g
1	600
2	700
3	800
4	900
5	1000
6	1100

Table 1.7

Figure 1.12 Graph of mass *vs* number of apples in a basket.

The slope in Figure 1.12 is still 100 g/apple indicating that each apple still has a mass of 100 g, but the intercept is no longer (0, 0). We say that the mass is linearly related to the number of apples but they are *not* directly proportional.

The equation of this line is $y = mx + c$ where m is the gradient and c the intercept on the *y*-axis. The equation in this case is therefore $y = 100x + 500$.

It is much easier to plot data from an experiment without processing it but this will often lead to curves that are very difficult to draw conclusions from. Linear relationships are much easier to interpret so worth the time spent processing the data.

10 What conclusions can you make about the data displayed in the graphs in Figure 1.13?

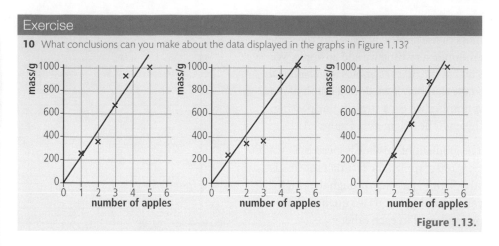

Figure 1.13.

Nonlinear relationships

Moving away from fruit but keeping the round theme, let us now consider the relationship between radius and the area of circles of paper as shown in Figure 1.14.

Figure 1.14 Five circles of green paper.

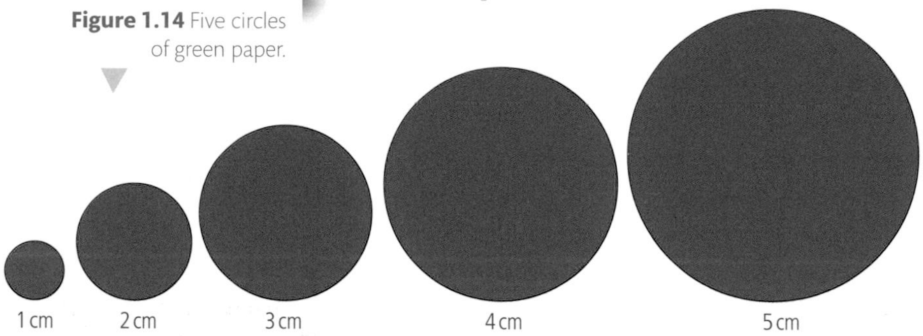

The results are recorded in Table 1.8.

1 cm   2 cm   3 cm   4 cm   5 cm

Radius/m	Area/m²
1	3.14
2	12.57
3	28.27
4	50.27
5	78.54

Table 1.8

If we now graph the area *vs* the radius we get the graph shown in Figure 1.15.

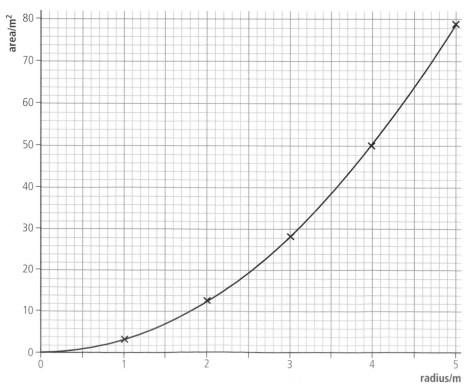

Figure 1.15 Graph of area of green circles *vs* radius.

This is not a straight line so we cannot deduce that area is linearly related to radius. However, you may know that the area of a circle is given by $A = \pi r^2$ which would mean that A is proportional to r^2. To test this we can calculate r^2 and plot a graph of area vs r^2. The calculations are shown in Table 1.9.

This time the graph is linear, confirming that the area is indeed proportional to the radius^2. The gradient of the line is $3.14 = \pi$. So the equation of the line is $A = \pi r^2$ as expected.

Radius/m	r^2/m^2	Area/m^2
1	1	3.14
2	4	12.57
3	9	28.27
4	16	50.27
5	25	78.54

Table 1.9.

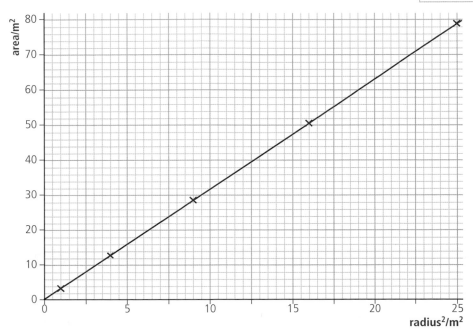

Figure 1.16 Graph of area of green circles vs radius^2.

Using logs

It may be a bit early in the course to start using logs but it might be a useful technique to use in your practical work so here we go. In the previous exercise we knew that $A = \pi r^2$ but if we hadn't known this we could have found the relationship by plotting a log graph. Let's pretend that we didn't know the relationship between A and r, only that they were related. So it could be $A = kr^2$ or $A = kr^3$ or even $A = k\sqrt{r}$.

We can write all of these in the form $A = kr^n$

Now if we take logs of both sides of this equation we get $\log A = \log kr^n = \log k + n\log r$.

This is of the form $y = mx + c$ so where $\log A$ is y and $\log r$ is x.

So if we plot $\log A$ vs $\log r$ we should get a straight line with gradient n and intercept $\log k$. This is all quite easy to do if using a spreadsheet, resulting in Table 1.10 and the graph in Figure 1.17.

Table 1.10.

Radius/m	Area/m^2	Log A	Log r
1	3.14	0.4969	0.0000
2	12.57	1.0993	0.3010
3	28.27	1.4513	0.4771
4	50.27	1.7013	0.6021
5	78.54	1.8951	0.6990

Figure 1.17 Log A vs log r for the green paper discs.

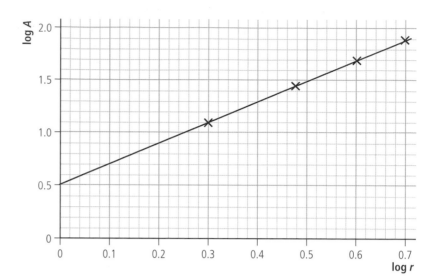

A	B
1.1	0.524
3.6	0.949
4.2	1.025
5.6	1.183
7.8	1.396
8.6	1.466
9.2	1.517
10.7	1.636

Table 1.11.

This has gradient = 2 and intercept = 0.5 so if we compare it to the equation of the line

$$\log A = \log k + n\log r$$

we can deduce that $n = 2$ and $\log k = 0.5$.

The inverse of $\log k$ is 10^k so $k = 10^{0.5} = 3.16$ which is quite close to π.

Substituting into our original equation $A = kr^n$ we get $A = \pi r^2$.

Exercise

11 Use a log–log graph to find the relationship between A and B in Table 1.11.

Relationship between the diameter of a plasticine ball and its mass

So far we have only measured the diameter and mass of one ball of plasticine. If we want to know the relationship between the diameter and mass we should measure many balls of different size. This is limited by the amount of plasticine we have, but should be from the smallest ball we can reasonably measure up to the biggest ball we can make.

Table 1.12.

Mass/g ±0.1 g	Diameter/cm ± 0.002 cm			
	1	2	3	4
1.4	1.296	1.430	1.370	1.280
2.0	1.570	1.590	1.480	1.550
5.6	2.100	2.130	2.168	2.148
9.4	2.560	2.572	2.520	2.610
12.5	2.690	2.840	2.824	2.720
15.7	3.030	2.980	3.080	2.890
19.1	3.250	3.230	3.190	3.204
21.5	3.490	3.432	3.372	3.360
24.8	3.550	3.560	3.540	3.520

In Table 1.12 the uncertainty in diameter d is given as 0.002 cm. This is the uncertainty in the vernier calliper: the actual uncertainty in diameter is *more* than this as is revealed by the spread of data which you can see in the first row, which ranges from 1.280 to 1.430, a difference of 0.150 cm. Because there are only 4 different measurements we can use the approximate method using $\Delta d = \frac{(d_{max} - d_{min})}{2}$. This gives an uncertainty in the first measurement of ±0.08 cm. Table 1.13 includes the uncertainties and the mean.

Table 1.13.

Mass/g ±0.1 g	Diameter/cm ± 0.002 cm					
	1	2	3	4	d_{mean}/cm	Uncertainty Δd/cm
1.4	1.296	1.430	1.370	1.280	1.34	0.08
2.0	1.570	1.590	1.480	1.550	1.55	0.06
5.6	2.100	2.130	2.168	2.148	2.14	0.03
9.4	2.560	2.572	2.520	2.610	2.57	0.04
12.5	2.690	2.840	2.824	2.720	2.77	0.08
15.7	3.030	2.980	3.080	2.890	3.00	0.10
19.1	3.250	3.230	3.190	3.204	3.22	0.03
21.5	3.490	3.432	3.372	3.360	3.41	0.07
24.8	3.550	3.560	3.540	3.520	3.54	0.02

Now, to reveal the relationship between the mass m and diameter d we can draw a graph of m *vs* d as shown in Figure 1.18. However, since the values of m and d have uncertainties we don't plot them as points but as lines. The length of the lines equals the uncertainty in the measurement. These are called *error bars*.

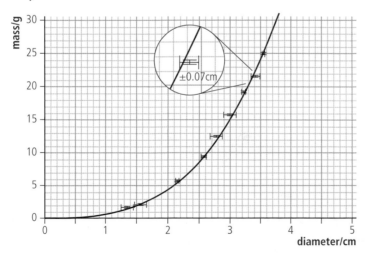

Figure 1.18 Graph of mass of plasticine ball *vs* diameter with error bars.

Relationship between mass and diameter of a plasticine sphere

Full details of how to carry out this experiment with a worksheet are available online.

The curve is quite a nice fit but very difficult to analyse; it would be more convenient if we could manipulate the data to get a straight line. This is called *linearizing*. To do this we must try to deduce the relationship using physical theory and then test the relationship by drawing a graph. In this case we know that density, $\rho = \frac{mass}{volume}$ and the volume of a sphere $= \frac{4\pi r^3}{3}$ where r = radius

so
$$\rho = \frac{3m}{4\pi r^3}.$$

01 | Measurements and uncertainties

Rearranging this equation gives

$$r^3 = \frac{3m}{4\pi\rho}$$

but

$$r = \frac{d}{2} \text{ so } \frac{d^3}{8} = \frac{3m}{4\pi\rho}$$

$$d^3 = \frac{6m}{\pi\rho}$$

Since $\left(\frac{6}{\pi\rho}\right)$ is a constant this means that d^3 is proportional to m. So, a graph of d^3 vs m should be a straight line with gradient $= \frac{6}{\pi\rho}$. To plot this graph we need to find d^3 and its uncertainty. The uncertainty can be found by calculating the difference between the maximum and minimum values of d^3 and dividing by 2: $\frac{(d_{max}^3 - d_{min}^3)}{2}$. This has been done in Table 1.14.

Table 1.14.

Mass/g ±0.1 g	Diameter/cm ± 0.002 cm						
	1	2	3	4	$d_{mean}/$ cm	$d^3_{mean}/$ cm^3	$d^3_{unc.}/$ cm^3
1.4	1.296	1.430	1.370	1.280	1.34	2.4	0.4
2.0	1.570	1.590	1.480	1.550	1.55	3.7	0.4
5.6	2.100	2.130	2.168	2.148	2.14	9.8	0.5
9.4	2.560	2.572	2.520	2.610	2.57	17	1
12.5	2.690	2.840	2.824	2.720	2.77	21	2
15.7	3.030	2.980	3.080	2.890	3.00	27	3
19.1	3.250	3.230	3.190	3.204	3.22	33	1
21.5	3.490	3.432	3.372	3.360	3.41	40	2
24.8	3.550	3.560	3.540	3.520	3.54	44	1

Figure 1.19 Graph of diameter^3 of a plasticine ball *vs* mass.

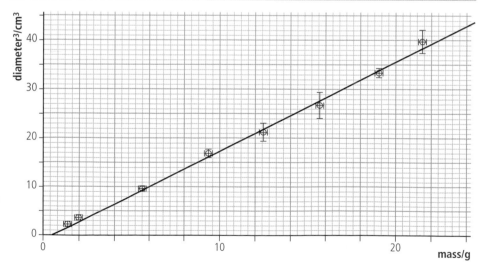

Looking at the line in Figure 1.19 we can see that due to random errors in the data the points are not exactly on the line but close enough. What we expect to see is the line touching all of the error bars which is the case here. The error bars should reflect the random scatter of data; in this case they are slightly bigger which is probably due to the approximate way that they have been calculated. Notice how the points furthest from the line have the biggest error bars.

According to the formula, d^3 should be directly proportional to m; the line should therefore pass through the origin. Here we can see that the y intercept is $-0.3 \, \text{cm}^3$ which is quite close and probably just due to the random errors in d. If the intercept had been more significant then it might have been due to a *systematic error* in mass. For example, if the balance had not been zeroed properly and instead of displaying zero with no mass on the pan it read 0.5 g then each mass measurement would be 0.5 g too big. The resulting graph would be as in Figure 1.20.

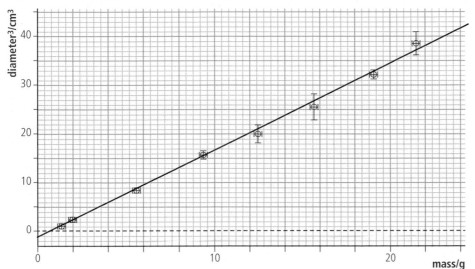

Figure 1.20 Graph of diameter³ of a plasticine ball *vs* mass with a systematic error.

A systematic error in the diameter would not be so easy to see. Since diameter is cubed, adding a constant value to each diameter would cause the line to become curved.

Outliers

Sometimes a mistake is made in one of the measurements; this is quite difficult to spot in a table but will often lead to an outlier on a graph. For example, one of the measurements in Table 1.15 is incorrect.

Table 1.15

Mass/g ±0.1 g	Diameter/cm ± 0.002 cm			
	1	2	3	4
1.4	1.296	1.430	1.370	1.280
2.0	1.570	1.590	1.480	1.550
5.6	2.100	2.130	2.148	3.148
9.4	2.560	2.572	2.520	2.610
12.5	2.690	2.840	2.824	2.720
15.7	3.030	2.980	3.080	2.890
19.1	3.250	3.230	3.190	3.204
21.5	3.490	3.432	3.372	3.360
24.8	3.550	3.560	3.540	3.520

This is revealed in the graph in Figure 1.21.

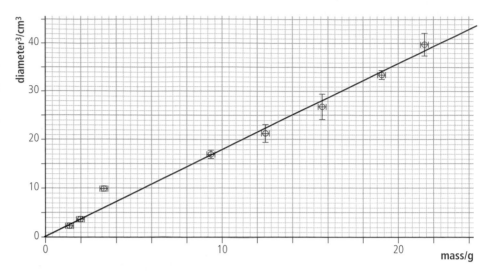

When you find an outlier you need to do some detective work to try to find out why the point isn't closer to the line. Taking a close look at the raw data sometimes reveals that one of the measurements was incorrect: this can then be removed and the line plotted again. However, you can't simply leave out the point because it doesn't fit. A sudden decrease in the level of ozone over the Antarctic was originally left out of the data since it was an outlier. Later investigation of this 'outlier' led to a significant discovery.

Uncertainty in the gradient

The general equation for a straight-line graph passing through the origin is $y = mx$. In this case the equation of the line is $d^3 = \frac{6m}{\pi\rho}$ so if d^3 is y and m is x and the gradient is $\frac{6}{\pi\rho}$. You can see that the unit of the gradient is cm³/g. This is consistent with it representing $\frac{6}{\pi\rho}$.

From the graph we see that gradient = $1.797\,\text{cm}^3\,\text{g}^{-1} = \frac{6}{\pi\rho}$ so $\rho = \frac{6}{1.797\pi}$

$\frac{6}{1.797\pi} = 1.063\,\text{g}\,\text{cm}^{-3}$ but what is the uncertainty in this value?

There are several ways to estimate the uncertainty in a gradient. One of them is to draw the steepest and least steep lines through the error bars as shown in Figure 1.22.

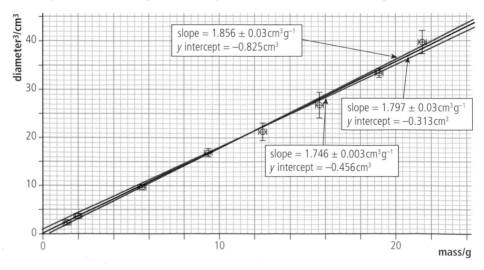

slope = $1.856 \pm 0.03\,\text{cm}^3\,\text{g}^{-1}$
y intercept = $-0.825\,\text{cm}^3$

slope = $1.797 \pm 0.03\,\text{cm}^3\,\text{g}^{-1}$
y intercept = $-0.313\,\text{cm}^3$

slope = $1.746 \pm 0.003\,\text{cm}^3\,\text{g}^{-1}$
y intercept = $-0.456\,\text{cm}^3$

This gives a steepest gradient = $1.856\,\text{cm}^3\,\text{g}^{-1}$ and least steep gradient = $1.746\,\text{cm}^3\,\text{g}^{-1}$.

So the uncertainty in gradient $= \frac{(1.856 - 1.746)}{2} = 0.06\,\text{cm}^3\,\text{g}^{-1}$.

Note that the program used to draw the graph (LoggerPro®) gives an uncertainty in the gradient of $\pm 0.03\,\text{cm}^3\,\text{g}^{-1}$. This is a more correct value but the steepest and least steep lines method is accepted at this level.

The steepest and least steep gradients give max and min values for the density of:

$$\rho_{max} = \frac{6}{1.746\pi} = 1.094\,\text{g}\,\text{cm}^{-3}$$

$$\rho_{min} = \frac{6}{1.856\pi} = 1.029\,\text{g}\,\text{cm}^{-3}$$

So the uncertainty is $\quad \frac{(1.094 - 1.029)}{2} = 0.03\,\text{g}\,\text{cm}^{-3}$.

The density can now be written $1.06 \pm 0.03\,\text{g}\,\text{cm}^{-3}$.

Fractional uncertainties

So far we have dealt with uncertainty as $\pm\Delta x$. This is called the *absolute uncertainty* in the value. Uncertainties can also be expressed as fractions. This has some advantages when processing data.

In the previous example we measured the diameter of plasticine balls then cubed this value in order to linearize the data. To make the sums simpler let's consider a slightly bigger ball with a diameter of 10 ± 1 cm.

So the measured value $d = 10$ cm and the absolute uncertainty $\Delta d = 1$ cm.

The fractional uncertainty $= \frac{\Delta d}{d} = \frac{1}{10} = 0.1$ (or, expressed as a percentage, 10%).

During the processing of the data we found $d^3 = 1000\,\text{cm}^3$.

The uncertainty in this value is not the same as in d. To find the uncertainty in d^3 we need to know the biggest and smallest possible values of d^3; these we can calculate by adding and subtracting the absolute uncertainty.

$$\text{Maximum } d^3 = (10 + 1)^3 = 1331\,\text{cm}^3$$

$$\text{Minimum } d^3 = (10 - 1)^3 = 729\,\text{cm}^3$$

So the range of values is $\quad (1331 - 729) = 602\,\text{cm}^3$

The uncertainty is therefore $\pm 301\,\text{cm}^3$ which rounded down to one significant figure gives $\pm 300\,\text{cm}^3$.

This is not the same as $(\Delta d)^3$ which would be $1\,\text{cm}^3$.

The fractional uncertainty in $d^3 = \frac{300}{1000} = 0.3$. This is the same as 3 × the fractional uncertainty in d. This leads to an alternative way of finding uncertainties in raising data to the power 3.

If $\frac{\Delta x}{x}$ is the fractional uncertainty in x then the fractional uncertainty in $x^3 = \frac{3\Delta x}{x}$.

More generally, if $\frac{\Delta x}{x}$ is the fractional uncertainty in x then the fractional uncertainty in $x^n = \frac{n\Delta x}{x}$.

So if you square a value the fractional uncertainty is 2 × bigger.

Another way of writing this would be that, if $\frac{\Delta x}{x}$ is the fractional uncertainty in x, then the fractional uncertainty in $x^2 = \frac{\Delta x}{x} + \frac{\Delta x}{x}$. This can be extended to any multiplication.

So if $\frac{\Delta x}{x}$ is the fractional uncertainty in x and $\frac{\Delta y}{y}$ is the fractional uncertainty in y then the fractional uncertainty in $xy = \frac{\Delta x}{x} + \frac{\Delta y}{y}$.

It seems strange but, when dividing, the fractional uncertainties also add; so if $\frac{\Delta x}{x}$ is the fractional uncertainty in x and $\frac{\Delta y}{y}$ is the fractional uncertainty in y then the fractional uncertainty in $\frac{x}{y} = \frac{\Delta x}{x} + \frac{\Delta y}{y}$.

If you divide a quantity by a constant with no uncertainty then the fractional uncertainty remains the same.

This is all summarized in the data book as:

If $\qquad\qquad\qquad\qquad\qquad y = \frac{ab}{c}$ then $\frac{\Delta y}{y} = \frac{\Delta a}{a} + \frac{\Delta b}{b} + \frac{\Delta c}{c}$

And if $\qquad\qquad\qquad\qquad\quad y = a^n$ then $\frac{\Delta y}{y} = n\frac{\Delta a}{a}$

Example

If the length of the side of a cube is quoted as 5.00 ± 0.01 m what is its volume plus uncertainty?

The fractional uncertainty in $\quad$ length $= \frac{0.01}{5} = 0.002$

$$\text{Volume} = 5.00^3 = 125 \text{ m}^3$$

When a quantity is cubed its fractional uncertainty is $3 \times$ bigger so the fractional uncertainty in volume $= 0.002 \times 3 = 0.006$.

The absolute uncertainty is therefore $0.006 \times 125 = 0.75$ (approx. 1) so the volume is 125 ± 1 m^3.

Exercises

12 The length of the sides of a cube and its mass are quoted as:
    length $= 0.050 \pm 0.001$ m.
    mass $= 1.132 \pm 0.002$ kg.
    Calculate the density of the material and its uncertainty.

13 The distance around a running track is 400 ± 1 m. If a person runs around the track 4 times calculate the distance travelled and its uncertainty.

14 The time for 10 swings of a pendulum is 11.2 ± 0.1 s. Calculate the time for one swing of the pendulum and its uncertainty.

1.3 Vectors and scalars

1.3 Vectors and scalars

Understandings, applications, and skills:

Vector and scalar quantities
Combination and resolution of vectors
● Solving vector problems graphically and algebraically.

  Guidance
  ● *Resolution of vectors will be limited to two perpendicular directions.*
  ● *Problems will be limited to addition and subtraction of vectors, and the multiplication and division of vectors by scalars.*

NATURE OF SCIENCE

We have seen how we can use numbers to represent physical quantities. Representing those quantities by letters we can derive mathematical equations to define relationships between them, then use graphs to verify those relationships. Some quantities cannot be represented by a number alone so a whole new area of mathematics needs to be developed to enable us to derive mathematical models relating them.

Vector and scalar quantities

So far we have dealt with six different quantities:

- Length
- Time
- Mass
- Volume
- Density
- Displacement

All of these quantities have a size, but displacement also has a direction. Quantities that have size and direction are *vectors* and those with only size are *scalars*; all quantities are either vectors or scalars. It will be apparent why it is important to make this distinction when we add displacements together.

Example

Consider two displacements one after another as shown in Figure 1.23.

Starting from A walk 4 km west to B, then 5 km north to C.

The total displacement from the start is not 5 + 4 but can be found by drawing a line from A to C.

We will find that there are many other vector quantities that can be added in the same way.

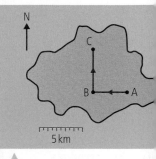

Figure 1.23 Displacements shown on a map.

Addition of vectors

Vectors can be represented by drawing arrows. The *length* of the arrow is proportional to the magnitude of the quantity and the *direction* of the arrow is the direction of the quantity.

To add vectors the arrows are simply arranged so that the point of one touches the tail of the other. The resultant vector is found by drawing a line joining the free tail to the free point.

Example

Figure 1.23 is a map illustrating the different displacements. We can represent the displacements by the vectors in Figure 1.24.

Calculating the resultant:

If the two vectors are at right angles to each other then the resultant will be the hypotenuse of a right-angled triangle. This means that we can use simple trigonometry to relate the different sides.

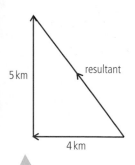

Figure 1.24 Vector addition.

Some simple trigonometry

You will find *cos*, *sin* and *tan* buttons on your calculator. These are used to calculate unknown sides of right-angled triangles.

$$\sin \theta = \frac{\text{opposite}}{\text{hypotenuse}} \rightarrow \text{opposite} = \text{hypotenuse} \times \sin \theta$$

$$\cos \theta = \frac{\text{adjacent}}{\text{hypotenuse}} \rightarrow \text{adjacent} = \text{hypotenuse} \times \cos \theta$$

$$\tan \theta = \frac{\text{opposite}}{\text{adjacent}}$$

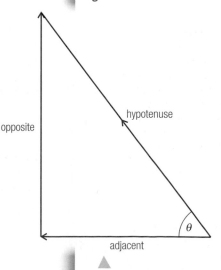

Figure 1.25.

Worked example

Find the side X of the triangle.

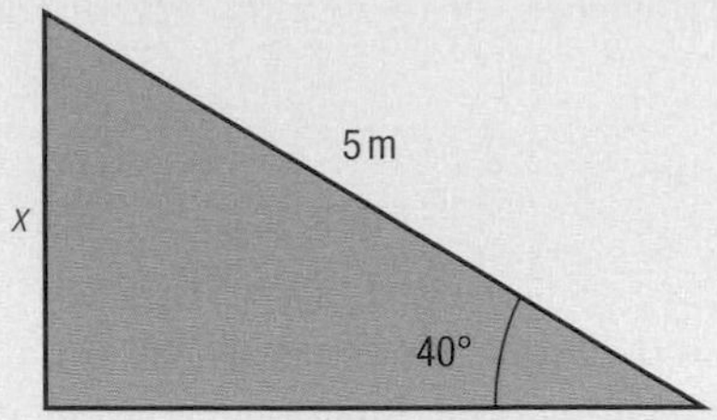

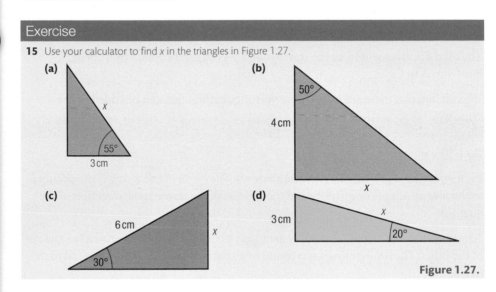

Figure 1.26.

Solution

Side X is the opposite so $X = 5 \times \sin 40°$

$\sin 40° = 0.6428$ so $X = 3.2$ m

Vector symbols

To show that a quantity is a vector we can write it in a special way. In textbooks this is often in bold (A) but when you write you can put an arrow on the top. In physics texts the vector notation is often left out. This is because if we know that the symbol represents a displacement, then we know it is a vector and don't need the vector notation to remind us.

Exercise

15 Use your calculator to find x in the triangles in Figure 1.27.

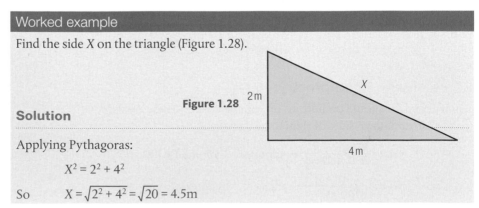

Figure 1.27.

Pythagoras

The most useful mathematical relationship for finding the resultant of two perpendicular vectors is Pythagoras' theorem.

$$\text{hypotenuse}^2 = \text{adjacent}^2 + \text{opposite}^2$$

Worked example

Find the side X on the triangle (Figure 1.28).

Figure 1.28

Solution

Applying Pythagoras:

$$X^2 = 2^2 + 4^2$$

So $X = \sqrt{2^2 + 4^2} = \sqrt{20} = 4.5$m

Exercise

16 Use Pythagoras' theorem to find the hypotenuse in the triangles in Figure 1.29.

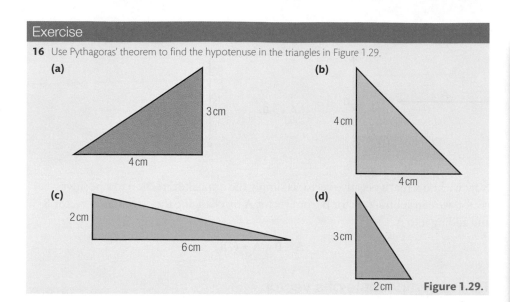

(a)

3 cm

4 cm

(b)

4 cm

4 cm

(c)

2 cm

6 cm

(d)

3 cm

2 cm

Figure 1.29.

Using trigonometry to solve vector problems

Once the vectors have been arranged point to tail it is a simple matter of applying the trigonometrical relationships to the triangles that you get.

Exercises

Draw the vectors and solve the following problems using Pythagoras' theorem.

17 A boat travels 4 km west followed by 8 km north. What is the resultant displacement?

18 A plane flies 100 km north then changes course to fly 50 km east. What is the resultant displacement?

Vectors in one dimension

In this course we will often consider the simplest examples where the motion is restricted to one dimension, for example a train travelling along a straight track. In examples like this there are only two possible directions – forwards and backwards. To distinguish between the two directions, we give them different signs (forward + and backwards –). Adding vectors is now simply a matter of adding the magnitudes, with no need for complicated triangles.

−ve   +ve

▷ **Figure 1.30** The train can only move forwards or backwards.

Worked example

If a train moves 100 m forwards along a straight track then 50 m back, what is its final displacement?

Solution

Figure 1.32 shows the vector diagram.

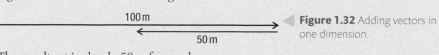

100 m

50 m

▷ **Figure 1.32** Adding vectors in one dimension.

The resultant is clearly 50 m forwards.

Which direction is positive?

You can decide for yourself which you want to be positive but generally we follow the convention in Figure 1.31.

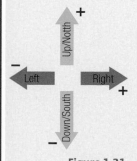

+
Up/North

−
Left   Right
+

Down/South
−

Figure 1.31.

27

Subtracting vectors

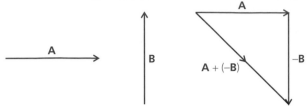

Figure 1.33 Subtracting vectors.

Now we know that a negative vector is simply the opposite direction to a positive vector, we can subtract vector **B** from vector **A** by changing the direction of vector **B** and adding it to **A**.

$$\mathbf{A} - \mathbf{B} = \mathbf{A} + (-\mathbf{B})$$

Taking components of a vector

Consider someone walking up the hill in Figure 1.34. They walk 5 km up the slope but want to know how high they have climbed rather than how far they have walked. To calculate this they can use trigonometry.

Figure 1.34 5 km up the hill but how high?

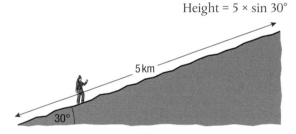

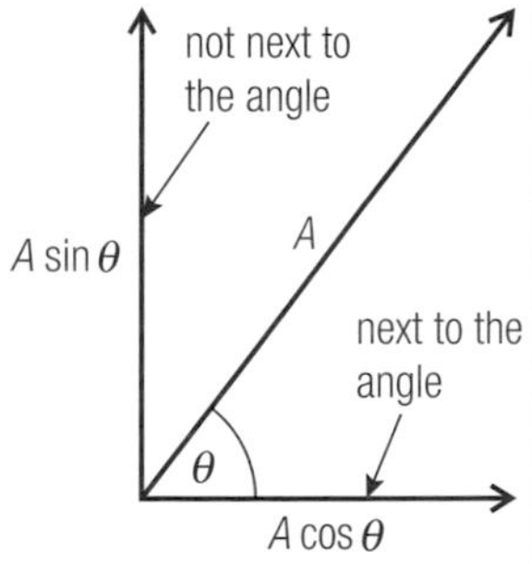

Height = 5 × sin 30°

The height is called the vertical component of the displacement.

The horizontal displacement can also be calculated.

Horizontal displacement = 5 × cos 30°

This process is called 'taking components of a vector' and is often used in solving physics problems.

Figure 1.35 An easy way to remember which is cos is to say that 'it's becos it's next to the angle'.

Exercises

19 If a boat travels 10 km in a direction 30° to the east of north, how far north has it travelled?

20 On his way to the South Pole, Amundsen travelled 8 km in a direction that was 20° west of south. What was his displacement south?

21 A mountaineer climbs 500 m up a slope that is inclined at an angle of 60° to the horizontal. How high has he climbed?

1. This question is about measuring the permittivity of free space ε_0.

Figure 1.36 shows two parallel conducting plates connected to a variable voltage supply. The plates are of equal areas and are a distance d apart.

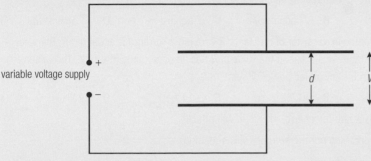

variable voltage supply

Figure 1.36

> This question is about processing data. You don't have to know what 'permittivity of free space' means to be able to answer it.

The charge Q on one of the plates is measured for different values of the potential difference V applied between the plates. The values obtained are shown in Table 1.16. The uncertainty in the value of V is not significant but the uncertainty in Q is $\pm 10\%$.

V / V	Q / nC $\pm$ 10%
10.0	30
20.0	80
30.0	100
40.0	160
50.0	180

Table 1.16.

(a) Plot the data points in Table 1.16 on a graph of V (x-axis) against Q (y-axis). (4)

(b) By calculating the relevant uncertainty in Q, add error bars to the data points (10.0, 30) and (50.0, 180). (3)

(c) On your graph, draw the line that best fits the data points and has the maximum permissible gradient. Determine the gradient of the line that you have drawn. (3)

(d) The gradient of the graph is a property of the two plates and is known as *capacitance*. Deduce the units of capacitance. (1)

The relationship between Q and V for this arrangement is given by the expression

$$Q = \frac{\varepsilon_0 A}{d} V \text{ where } A \text{ is the area of one of the plates.}$$

In this particular experiment $A = 0.20 \pm 0.05\,\mathrm{m^2}$ and $d = 0.50 \pm 0.01\,\mathrm{mm}$.

(e) Use your answer to (c) to determine the maximum value of ε_0 that this experiment yields. (4)

(*Total 15 marks*)

2. A student measures a distance several times. The readings lie between 49.8 cm and 50.2 cm. This measurement is best recorded as

A $49.8 \pm 0.2\,\mathrm{cm}$ **B** $49.8 \pm 0.4\,\mathrm{cm}$ **C** $50.0 \pm 0.2\,\mathrm{cm}$ **D** $50.0 \pm 0.4\,\mathrm{cm}$ (1)

3. The time period T of oscillation of a mass m suspended from a vertical spring is given by the expression

$$T = 2\pi\sqrt{\frac{m}{k}}$$ where k is a constant.

Which **one** of the following plots will give rise to a straight-line graph?

    A T^2 against m **B** $\sqrt{T}$ against $\sqrt{m}$ **C** T against m **D** $\sqrt{T}$ against m (1)

4. The power dissipated in a resistor of resistance R carrying a current I is equal to I^2R. The value of I has an uncertainty of $\pm2\%$, and the value of R has an uncertainty of $\pm10\%$. The value of the uncertainty in the calculated power dissipation is

    A $\pm8\%$ **B** $\pm12\%$ **C** $\pm14\%$ **D** $\pm20\%$ (1)

5. An ammeter has a zero offset error. This fault will affect

    A neither the precision nor the accuracy of the readings.

    B only the precision of the readings.

    C only the accuracy of the readings.

    D both the precision and the accuracy of the readings.   (1)

6. When a force F of $(10.0 \pm 0.2)\,\text{N}$ is applied to a mass m of $(2.0 \pm 0.1)\,\text{kg}$, the percentage uncertainty attached to the value of the calculated acceleration $\frac{F}{m}$ is

    A 2% **B** 5% **C** 7% **D** 10% (1)

7. Which of the following is the best estimate, to one significant digit, of the quantity shown below?

$$\frac{\pi \times 8.1}{\sqrt{(15.9)}}$$

    A 1.5   **B** 2.0   **C** 5.8   **D** 6.0   (1)

8. Two objects X and Y are moving away from the point P. Figure 1.37 shows the velocity vectors of the two objects.

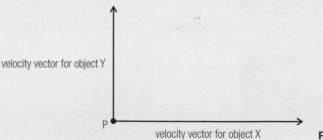

velocity vector for object Y

P velocity vector for object X

Figure 1.37.

Which of the velocity vectors in Figure 1.38 best represents the velocity of object X relative to object Y?

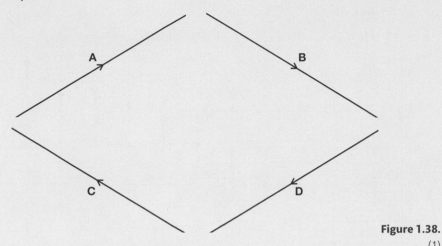

Figure 1.38.

(1)

9. The order of magnitude of the weight of an apple is

A 10^{-4} N   B 10^{-2} N   C 1 N   D 10^2 N   (1)

10. Data analysis question.

The photograph shows a magnified image of a dark central disc surrounded by concentric dark rings. These rings were produced as a result of interference of monochromatic light.

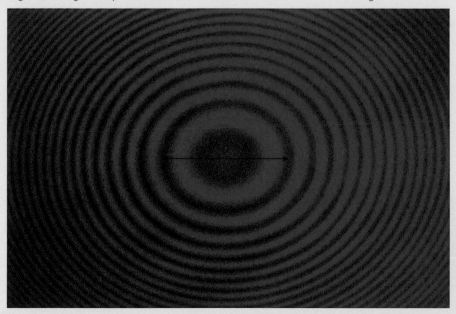

Figure 1.39 shows how the ring diameter D varies with the ring number n. The innermost ring corresponds to $n = 1$. D is the diameter of the first ring. Error bars for the diameter D are shown.

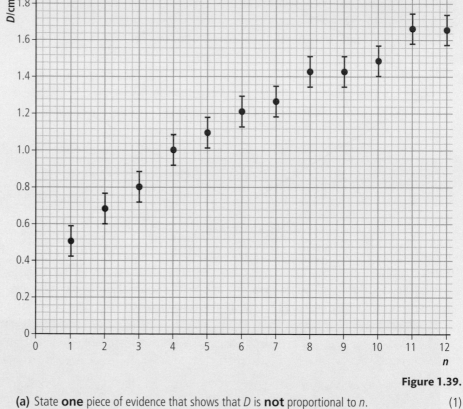

Figure 1.39.

(a) State **one** piece of evidence that shows that D is **not** proportional to n. (1)

(b) Copy the graph in Figure 1.39 and on your graph draw the line of best fit for the data points. (2)

(c) It is suggested that the relationship between D and n is of the form

$$D = cn^p$$

where c and p are constants.

Explain what graph you would plot in order to determine the value of p. (3)

(d) Theory suggests that $p = \dfrac{1}{2}$ and so $D^2 = kn$ (where $k = c^2$).

A graph of D^2 against n is shown in Figure 1.40. Error bars are shown for the first and last data points only.

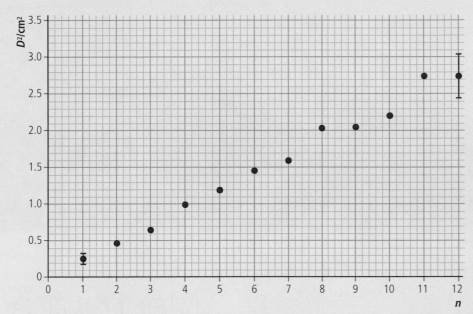

Figure 1.40.

(i) Using the graph in Figure 1.39, calculate the percentage uncertainty in D^2, of the ring $n = 7$. (2)

(ii) Based on the graph in Figure 1.40, state one piece of evidence that supports the relationship $D^2 = kn$. (1)

(iii) Use the graph in Figure 1.40 to determine the value of the constant k, as well as its uncertainty. (4)

(iv) State the unit for the constant k. (1)

(Total 14 marks)

02

Mechanics

Essential ideas

2.1 Motion
Motion may be described and analysed by the use of graphs and equations.

2.2 Forces
Classical physics requires a force to change a state of motion, as suggested by Newton in his laws of motion.

2.3 Work, energy, and power
The fundamental concept of energy lays the base upon which all areas of science are built.

2.4 Momentum and impulse
Conservation of momentum is an example of a law which is never violated.

NATURE OF SCIENCE

From the definitions of velocity and acceleration we can use mathematics to derive a set of equations that predict the position and velocity of a particle at any given time. We can show by experiment that these equations give the correct result for some examples, then make the generalization that the equations apply in all cases.

2.1 Motion

2.1 Motion

Understandings, applications, and skills:

Distance and displacement
Speed and velocity
• Determining instantaneous and average values for velocity, speed, and acceleration.
Acceleration
• Determining the acceleration of free fall experimentally.
Graphs describing motion
• Sketching and interpreting motion graphs.
Equations of motion for uniform acceleration
• Solving problems using equations of motion for uniform acceleration.
Projectile motion
• Analysing projectile motion, including the resolution of vertical and horizontal components of acceleration, velocity, and displacement.

Guidance
• *Calculations will be restricted to those neglecting air resistance.*
• *Projectile motion will only involve problems using a constant value of g close to the surface of the Earth.*
• *The equation of the path of a projectile will not be required.*

Fluid resistance and terminal speed
• Qualitatively describing the effect of fluid resistance on falling objects or projectiles, including reaching terminal speed.

In Chapter 1, we observed that things move and now we are going to mathematically model that movement. Before we do that, we must define some quantities that we are going to use.

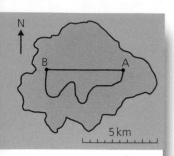

Displacement and distance

It is important to understand the difference between distance travelled and displacement. To explain this, consider the route marked out on the map shown in Figure 2.1

Displacement is the shortest path moved in a particular direction.

The unit of displacement is the metre (m).

Displacement is a vector quantity.

On the map, the displacement is the length of the straight line from A to B, a distance of 5 km west. (Note: since displacement is a vector you should always say what the direction is.)

Distance is how far you have travelled from A to B.

The unit of distance is also the metre.

Distance is a scalar quantity.

In this example, the distance travelled is the length of the path taken, which is about 10 km.

Sometimes this difference leads to a surprising result. For example, if you run all the way round a running track you will have travelled a distance of 400 m but your displacement will be 0 m.

In everyday life, it is often more important to know the distance travelled. For example, if you are going to travel from Paris to Lyon by road you will want to know that the distance by road is 450 km, not that your final displacement will be 336 km SE. However, in physics, we break everything down into its simplest parts, so we start by considering motion in a straight line only. In this case it is more useful to know the displacement, since that also has information about which direction you have moved.

Velocity and speed

Both speed and velocity are a measure of how fast a body is moving, but velocity is a vector quantity and speed is a scalar.

Velocity is defined as the displacement per unit time.

$$\text{velocity} = \frac{\text{displacement}}{\text{time}}$$

The unit of velocity is m s^{-1}.

Velocity is a vector quantity.

Speed is defined as the distance travelled per unit time.

$$\text{speed} = \frac{\text{distance}}{\text{time}}$$

The unit of speed is also m s^{-1}.

Speed is a scalar quantity.

Exercise

1 Convert the following speeds into m s^{-1}.

   (a) A car travelling at 100 km h^{-1}.

   (b) A runner running at 20 km h^{-1}.

Average velocity and instantaneous velocity

Consider travelling by car from the north of Bangkok to the south – a distance of about 16 km. If the journey takes 4 hours, you can calculate your velocity to be $\frac{16}{4} = 4$ km h^{-1} in a southwards direction. This doesn't tell you anything about the journey, just the difference between the beginning and the end (unless you managed to travel at a constant speed in a straight line). The value calculated is the *average velocity* and in this example it is quite useless. If we broke the trip down into lots of small pieces, each lasting only one second, then for each second the car could be considered to be travelling in a straight line at a constant speed. For these short stages we could quote the car's *instantaneous velocity* – that's how fast it's going at that moment in time and in which direction.

Figure 2.2 It's not possible to take this route across Bangkok with a constant velocity.

The bus in the photo has a constant velocity for a very short time.

Exercise

2 A runner runs around a circular track of length 400 m with a constant speed in 96 s starting at the point shown. Calculate:

(a) the average speed of the runner.
(b) the average velocity of the runner.
(c) the instantaneous velocity of the runner after 48 s.
(d) the displacement after 24 s.

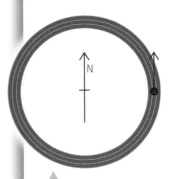

Figure 2.3.

Constant velocity

If the velocity is constant then the instantaneous velocity is the same all the time so instantaneous velocity = average velocity.

Since velocity is a vector this also implies that the direction of motion is constant.

Measuring a constant velocity

From the definition of velocity we see that velocity = $\frac{\text{displacement}}{\text{time}}$.

Rearranging this gives displacement = velocity × time.

So, if velocity is constant, displacement is proportional to time. To test this relationship and find the velocity we can measure the displacement of a body at different times. To do this you either need a lot of clocks or a stop clock that records many times. This is called a *lap timer*. In this example a bicycle was ridden at constant speed along a straight road past 6 students standing 10 m apart, each operating a stop clock as in Figure 2.4. The clocks were all started when the bike, already moving, passed the start marker and stopped as the bike passed each student.

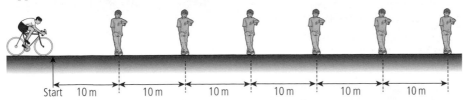

Start   10 m   10 m   10 m   10 m   10 m   10 m

Figure 2.4 Measuring the time for a bike to pass.

The results achieved have been entered into Table 2.1.

Distance/m ±0.1 m	Time/s ±0.02 s
10.0	3.40
20.0	5.62
30.0	8.55
40.0	12.21
50.0	14.17
60.0	17.21

Table 2.1.

The uncertainty in position is quoted as 0.1 m since it is difficult to decide exactly when the bike passes the marker.

The digital stop clock had a scale with 2 decimal places so the uncertainty was 0.01 s. However, the uncertainty quoted is 0.02 s since the clocks all had to be started at the same time.

Since s is proportional to t, then a graph of s vs t should give a straight line with gradient = velocity as shown in Figure 2.5.

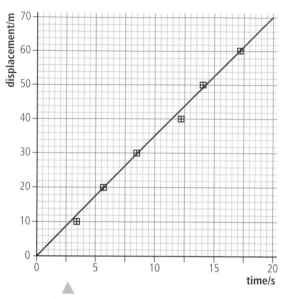

Figure 2.5 Graph of displacement vs time for a bike.

Notice in this graph the line does not quite hit all the dots. This is because the uncertainty in the measurement in time is almost certainly bigger than the uncertainty in the clock (±0.02 s) due to the reaction time of the students stopping the clock. To get a better estimate of the uncertainty we would have to have several students standing at each 10 m position. Repeating the experiment isn't possible in this example since it is very difficult to ride at the same velocity several times.

The gradient indicates that the velocity = 3.4 m s^{-1}.

Laboratory example

Most school laboratories aren't big enough to ride bikes in so when working indoors we need to use shorter distances. This means that the times are going to be shorter so hand-operated stop clocks aren't going to be accurate enough. One way of timing in the lab is by using photogates. These are connected to the computer via an interface and record the time when a body passes in or out of the gate. So to replicate the bike experiment in the lab using a ball we would need 7 photogates as in Figure 2.6, one extra to represent the start.

Figure 2.6 How to measure the time for a rolling ball if you've got 7 photogates.

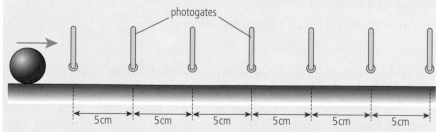

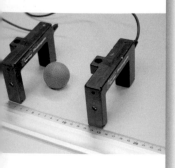

This is would be quite expensive so we compromise by using just two photogates and a motion that can be repeated. An example could be a ball moving along a horizontal section of track after it has rolled down an inclined plane. Provided the ball starts from the same point it should have the same velocity. So instead of using seven photogates we can use two, one is set at the start of the motion and the other is moved to different positions along the track as in Figure 2.7.

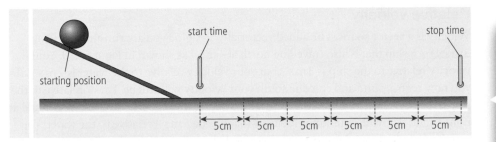

Figure 2.7 Measuring the velocity of a ball with 2 photogates.

Table 2.2 shows the results were obtained using this arrangement.

Table 2.2.

Displacement/cm ±0.1 cm	Time(*t*)/s ±0.0001 s					Mean *t*/s	Δ*t*/s
5.0	0.0997	0.0983	0.0985	0.1035	0.1040	0.101	0.003
10.0	0.1829	0.1969	0.1770	0.1824	0.1825	0.18	0.01
15.0	0.2844	0.2800	0.2810	0.2714	0.2779	0.28	0.01
20.0	0.3681	0.3890	0.3933	0.3952	0.3854	0.39	0.01
25.0	0.4879	0.5108	0.5165	0.4994	0.5403	0.51	0.03
30.0	0.6117	0.6034	0.5978	0.6040	0.5932	0.60	0.01

Notice the uncertainty calculated from $\frac{(max - min)}{2}$ is much more than the instrument uncertainty. Graphing displacement *vs* time gives Figure 2.8.

From this graph we can see that within the limits of the experiment's uncertainties the displacement was proportional to time, so we can conclude that the velocity was constant. However, if we look closely at the data we see that there seems to be a slight curve indicating that perhaps the ball was slowing down. To verify this we would have to collect more data.

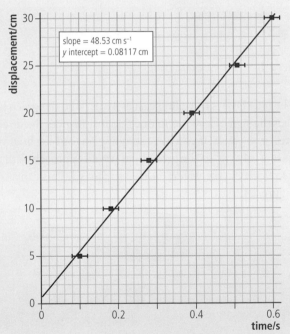

slope = 48.53 cm s^{-1}
y intercept = 0.08117 cm

Figure 2.8 Graph of displacement *vs* time for a rolling ball.

Measuring the constant velocity of a ball rolling across a flat table

A worksheet with full details of how to carry out this experiment is available on your eBook.

Measuring instantaneous velocity

To measure instantaneous velocity, a very small displacement must be used. This could be achieved by placing two photogates close together or attaching an obstructer such as a piece of card to the moving body as shown in Figure 2.9. The time taken for the card to pass through the photogate is recorded and the instantaneous velocity calculated from the $\frac{\text{length of card}}{\text{time taken}}$ $\left(\frac{d}{t}\right)$.

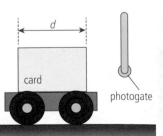

Figure 2.9 A card and photogate used to measure instantaneous velocity.

Relative velocity

Velocity is a vector so must be added vectorially. Imagine you are running north at $3\,\mathrm{m\,s^{-1}}$ on a ship that is also travelling north at $4\,\mathrm{m\,s^{-1}}$ as shown in Figure 2.10. Your velocity relative to the ship is $3\,\mathrm{m\,s^{-1}}$ but your velocity relative to the water is $7\,\mathrm{m\,s^{-1}}$. If you now turn around and run due south your velocity will still be $3\,\mathrm{m\,s^{-1}}$ relative to the ship but $1\,\mathrm{m\,s^{-1}}$ relative to the water. Finally, walking towards the east the vectors add at right angles to give a resultant velocity of magnitude $5\,\mathrm{m\,s^{-1}}$ relative to the water. You can see that the velocity vectors have been added.

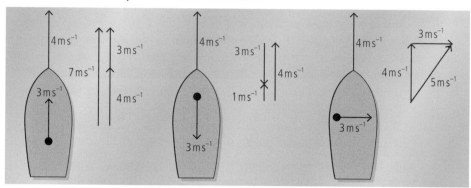

Figure 2.10 Running on board a ship.

Imagine now that you are floating in the water watching two boats travelling towards each other as in Figure 2.11.

Figure 2.11 Two boats approach each other.

The blue boat is travelling east at $4\,\mathrm{m\,s^{-1}}$ and the green boat west at $-3\,\mathrm{m\,s^{-1}}$. Remember that the sign of a vector in one dimension gives the direction, so if east is positive then west is negative. If you were standing on the blue boat you would see the water going past at $-4\,\mathrm{m\,s^{-1}}$ so the green boat would approach with the velocity of the water plus its velocity in the water: $-4 + -3 = -7\,\mathrm{m\,s^{-1}}$. This can also be done in 2 dimensions as in Figure 2.12.

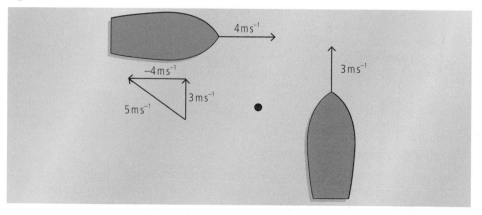

Figure 2.12 Two boats travelling perpendicular to each other.

According to the swimmer floating in the water, the green boat travels north and the blue boat travels east. but an observer on the blue boat will see the water travelling towards the west and the boat travelling due north; adding these two velocities gives a velocity of $5\,\mathrm{m\,s^{-1}}$ in an approximately northwest direction.

Exercises

3 An observer standing on a road watches a bird flying east at a velocity of $10\,\mathrm{m\,s^{-1}}$. A second observer, driving a car along the road northwards at $20\,\mathrm{m\,s^{-1}}$ sees the bird. What is the velocity of the bird relative to the driver?

4 A boat travels along a river heading north with a velocity $4\,\mathrm{m\,s^{-1}}$ as a woman walks across a bridge from east to west with velocity $1\,\mathrm{m\,s^{-1}}$. Calculate the velocity of the woman relative to the boat.

Acceleration

In everyday usage, the word *accelerate* means to go faster. However, in physics, acceleration is defined as the rate of change of velocity.

$$\text{acceleration} = \frac{\text{change of velocity}}{\text{time}}$$

The unit of acceleration is $\mathrm{m\,s^{-2}}$.

Acceleration is a vector quantity.

This means that whenever a body changes its velocity, it accelerates. This could be because it is getting faster, slower, or just changing direction. In the example of the journey across Bangkok, the car would have been slowing down, speeding up, and going round corners almost the whole time, so it would have had many different accelerations. However, this example is far too complicated for us to consider in this course (and probably any physics course). For most of this chapter we will only consider the simplest example of accelerated motion, constant acceleration.

Constant acceleration in one dimension

In one-dimensional motion, the acceleration, velocity, and displacement are all in the same direction. This means they can simply be added without having to draw triangles. Figure 2.13 shows a body that is starting from an initial velocity u and accelerating at a constant rate a to velocity v in t seconds. The distance travelled in this time is s. Since the motion is in a straight line, this is also the displacement.

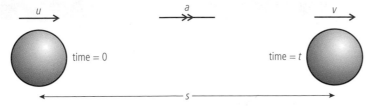

Figure 2.13 A red ball is accelerated at a constant rate.

Using the definitions already stated, we can write equations related to this example.

Average velocity

From the definition, the average velocity $= \dfrac{\text{displacement}}{\text{time}}$.

So
$$\text{average velocity} = \frac{s}{t} \qquad (1)$$

Since the velocity changes at a constant rate from the beginning to the end, we can also calculate the average velocity by adding the velocities and dividing by two.

$$\text{Average velocity} = \frac{(u + v)}{2} \qquad (2)$$

Acceleration

Acceleration is defined as the rate of change of velocity.

So
$$a = \frac{(v - u)}{t} \qquad (3)$$

We can use these equations to solve any problem involving constant acceleration. However, to make problem solving easier, we can derive two more equations by substituting from one into the other.

Equating equations (1) and (2)

$$\frac{s}{t} = \frac{(u + v)}{2}$$

so
$$s = \frac{(u + v)\,t}{2} \qquad (4)$$

Rearranging (3) gives $v = u + at$.

If we substitute for v in equation (4) we get $s = ut + \frac{1}{2}at^2$ (5)

Rearranging (3) again gives $t = \frac{(v - u)}{a}$

If t is now substituted in equation (4) we get $v^2 = u^2 + 2as$ (6)

These equations are sometimes known as the *suvat* equations. If you know any 3 of s, u, v, a, and t you can find either of the other two in one step.

> **suvat equations**
> $a = \frac{(v - u)}{t}$
> $s = \frac{(v + u)t}{2}$
> $s = ut + \frac{1}{2}at^2$
> $v^2 = u^2 + 2as$

Worked example

A car travelling at $10\,\mathrm{m\,s^{-1}}$ accelerates at $2\,\mathrm{m\,s^{-2}}$ for $5\,\mathrm{s}$. What is its displacement?

Solution

The first thing to do is draw a simple diagram like Figure 2.14.

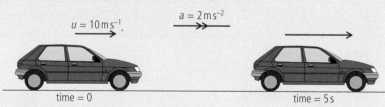

$u = 10\,\mathrm{m\,s^{-1}}$ $a = 2\,\mathrm{m\,s^{-2}}$

time = 0   time = 5 s

Figure 2.14 A simple diagram is always the best start.

This enables you to see what is happening at a glance rather than reading the text. The next stage is to make a list of *suvat*.

$$s = ?$$

$$u = 10\,\mathrm{m\,s^{-1}}$$

$$v = ?$$

$$a = 2\,\mathrm{m\,s^{-2}}$$

$$t = 5\,\mathrm{s}$$

To find s you need an equation that contains *suat*. The only equation with all 4 of these quantities is $s = ut + \frac{1}{2}at^2$

Using this equation gives:
$$s = 10 \times 5 + \frac{1}{2} \times 2 \times 5^2$$

$$s = 75\,\mathrm{m}$$

> You don't need to include units in all stages of a calculation, just the answer.

The signs of displacement, velocity, and acceleration

We must not forget that displacement, velocity, and acceleration are vectors. This means that they have direction. However, since this is a one-dimensional example, there are only two possible directions, forward and backward. We know which direction the vector is in from its sign.

A positive displacement means that the body has moved to the right.

A positive velocity means the body is moving to the right.

A positive acceleration means that the body is either moving to the right and getting faster or moving to the left and getting slower. This can be confusing, so consider the following example.

Figure 2.15

The car is travelling in a negative direction so the velocities are negative.

$$u = -10 \, \text{m s}^{-1}$$
$$v = -5 \, \text{m s}^{-1}$$
$$t = 5 \, \text{s}$$

The acceleration is therefore given by

$$a = \frac{(v - u)}{t} = \frac{-5 - -10}{5} = 1 \, \text{m s}^{-2}$$

The positive sign tells us that the acceleration is in a positive direction (right) even though the car is travelling in a negative direction (left).

Example

A body with a constant acceleration of $-5 \, \text{m s}^{-2}$ is travelling to the right with a velocity of $20 \, \text{m s}^{-1}$. What will its displacement be after $20 \, \text{s}$?

$$s = ?$$
$$u = 20 \, \text{m s}^{-1}$$
$$v = ?$$
$$a = -5 \, \text{m s}^{-2}$$
$$t = 20 \, \text{s}$$

To calculate s we can use the equation $s = ut + \frac{1}{2}at^2$

$$s = 20 \times 20 + \frac{1}{2}(-5) \times 20^2 = 400 - 1000 = -600 \, \text{m}$$

This means that the final displacement of the body is to the left of the starting point. It has gone forward, stopped, and then gone backwards.

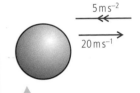

Figure 2.16 The acceleration is negative so pointing to the left.

g

The acceleration due to gravity is not constant all over the Earth. $9.81 \, \text{m s}^{-2}$ is the average value. The acceleration also gets smaller the higher you go. However we ignore this change when conducting experiments in the lab since labs aren't that high.

To make the examples easier to follow, $g = 10 \, \text{m s}^{-2}$ is used throughout; you should only use this approximate value in exam questions if told to do so.

Exercises

5 Calculate the final velocity of a body that starts from rest and accelerates at $5 \, \text{m s}^{-2}$ for a distance of $100 \, \text{m}$.

6 A body starts with a velocity of $20 \, \text{m s}^{-1}$ and accelerates for $200 \, \text{m}$ with an acceleration of $5 \, \text{m s}^{-2}$. What is the final velocity of the body?

7 A body accelerates at $10 \, \text{m s}^{-2}$ reaching a final velocity of $20 \, \text{m s}^{-1}$ in $5 \, \text{s}$. What was the initial velocity of the body?

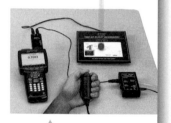

Apparatus for measuring g.

Table 2.3 Measuring g.

Free fall motion

Although a car was used in one of the previous illustrations, the acceleration of a car is not usually constant, so we shouldn't use the *suvat* equations. The only example of constant acceleration that we see in everyday life is when a body is dropped. Even then the acceleration is only constant for a short distance.

Acceleration of free fall

When a body is allowed to fall freely we say it is in free fall. Bodies falling freely on the Earth fall with an acceleration of about 9.81 m s^{-2}. (It depends where you are.) The body falls because of gravity. For that reason we use the letter g to denote this acceleration. Since the acceleration is constant, we can use the *suvat* equations to solve problems.

Exercises

In these calculations use $g = 10 \text{ m s}^{-2}$.

8 A ball is thrown upwards with a velocity of 30 m s^{-1}. What is the displacement of the ball after 2 s?

9 A ball is dropped. What will its velocity be after falling 65 cm?

10 A ball is thrown upwards with a velocity of 20 m s^{-1}. After how many seconds will the ball return to its starting point?

Measuring the acceleration due to gravity

When a body falls freely under the influence of gravity it accelerates at a constant rate. This means that time to fall, t, and distance, s, are related by the equation $s = ut + \frac{1}{2}at^2$. If the body starts from rest then $u = 0$ so the equation becomes $s = \frac{1}{2}at^2$. Since s is directly proportional to t^2, a graph of s vs t^2 would therefore be a straight line with gradient $\frac{1}{2}g$. It is difficult to measure the time for a ball to pass different markers but if we assume the ball falls with the same acceleration when repeatedly dropped we can measure the time taken for the ball to fall from different heights. There are many ways of doing this. All involve some way of starting a clock when the ball is released, and stopping it when it hits the ground. Table 2.3 shows a set of results from a 'ball drop' experiment.

Height(h)/m ±0.001	Time(t)/s ±0.001					Mean t/s	t^2/s²	Δt^2/s²
0.118	0.155	0.153	0.156	0.156	0.152	0.154	0.024	0.001
0.168	0.183	0.182	0.183	0.182	0.184	0.183	0.0334	0.0004
0.218	0.208	0.205	0.210	0.211	0.210	0.209	0.044	0.001
0.268	0.236	0.235	0.237	0.239	0.231	0.236	0.056	0.002
0.318	0.250	0.254	0.255	0.250	0.256	0.253	0.064	0.002
0.368	0.276	0.277	0.276	0.278	0.276	0.277	0.077	0.001
0.418	0.292	0.293	0.294	0.291	0.292	0.292	0.085	0.001
0.468	0.310	0.310	0.303	0.300	0.311	0.307	0.094	0.003
0.518	0.322	0.328	0.330	0.328	0.324	0.326	0.107	0.003
0.568	0.342	0.341	0.343	0.343	0.352	0.344	0.118	0.004

Notice the uncertainty in t^2 is calculated from $\frac{(t_{max}^2 - t_{min}^2)}{2}$.

Notice how the line in Figure 2.17 is very close to the points, and that the uncertainties reflect the actual random variation in the data. The gradient of the line is equal to $\frac{1}{2}g$ so $g = 2 \times$ gradient.

$$g = 2 \times 4.814 = 9.624 \text{ m s}^{-2}$$

The uncertainty in this value can be estimated from the steepest and least steep lines.

$$g_{max} = 2 \times 5.112 = 10.224 \text{ m s}^{-2}$$
$$g_{min} = 2 \times 4.571 = 9.142 \text{ m s}^{-2}.$$
$$\Delta g = \frac{(g_{max} - g_{min})}{2} = \frac{(10.224 - 9.142)}{2} = 0.541 \text{ m s}^{-2}$$

So the final value including uncertainty is $9.6 \pm 0.5 \text{ m s}^{-2}$.

This is in good agreement with the accepted average value which is 9.81 m s^{-2}.

Measuring the acceleration due to gravity by timing a freefalling object

A worksheet with full details of how to carry out this experiment is available on your eBook.

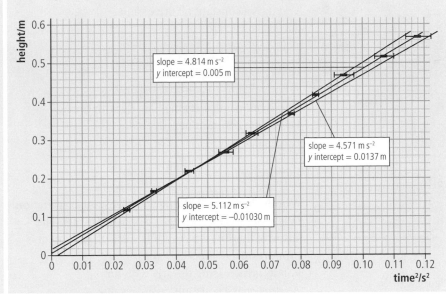

slope = 4.814 m s^{-2}
y intercept = 0.005 m

slope = 4.571 m s^{-2}
y intercept = 0.0137 m

slope = 5.112 m s^{-2}
y intercept = −0.01030 m

Figure 2.17 Height *vs* time^2 for a falling object.

Graphical representation of motion

Graphs are used in physics to give a visual representation of relationships. In kinematics they can be used to show how displacement, velocity, and acceleration change with time. Figure 2.18 shows the graphs for four different examples of motion. They are placed vertically since they all have the same time axis.

The best way to go about sketching graphs is to split the motion into sections then plot where the body is at different times; joining these points will give the displacement–time graph. Once you have done that you can work out the *v–t* and *a–t* graphs by looking at the *s–t* graph rather than the motion.

Gradient of displacement–time

The gradient of a graph is $\frac{\text{change in } y}{\text{change in } x} = \frac{\Delta y}{\Delta x}$

In the case of the displacement–time graph this will give

$$\text{gradient} = \frac{\Delta s}{\Delta t}$$

This is the same as velocity.

You need to be able to
- figure out what kind of motion a body has by looking at the graphs
- sketch graphs for a a given motion.

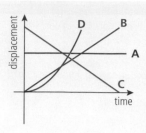

Line A

A body that is not moving.
Displacement is always the same.
Velocity is zero.
Acceleration is zero.

Line B

A body that is travelling with a constant positive velocity.
Displacement increases linearly with time.
Velocity is a constant positive value.
Acceleration is zero.

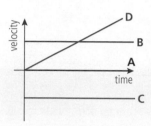

Line C

A body that has a constant negative velocity.
Displacement is decreasing linearly with time.
Velocity is a constant negative value.
Acceleration is zero.

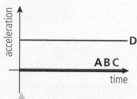
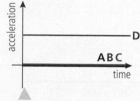

Line D

A body that is accelerating with constant acceleration.
Displacement is increasing at a non-linear rate. The shape of this line is a parabola since displacement is proportional to t^2 ($s = ut + \frac{1}{2}at^2$).
Velocity is increasing linearly with time.
Acceleration is a constant positive value.

Figure 2.18 Graphical representation of motion.

So the gradient of the displacement–time graph equals the velocity. Using this information, we can see that line A in Figure 2.19 represents a body with greater velocity than line B and that since the gradient of line C is increasing, this must be the graph for an accelerating body.

Instantaneous velocity

When a body accelerates its velocity is constantly changing. The displacement–time graph for this motion is therefore a curve. To find the instantaneous velocity from the graph we can draw a tangent to the curve and find the gradient of the tangent as shown in Figure 2.20.

Area under velocity–time graph

The area under the velocity–time graph for the body travelling at constant velocity v shown in Figure 2.21 is given by

$$\text{area} = v\Delta t$$

But we know from the definition of velocity that $v = \dfrac{\Delta s}{\Delta t}$

Rearranging gives $\Delta s = v\Delta t$ so the area under a velocity–time graph gives the displacement.

This is true not only for simple cases such as this but for all examples.

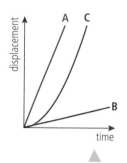

Figure 2.19.

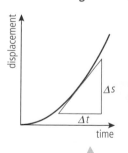

Figure 2.20.

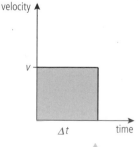

Figure 2.21.

Gradient of velocity–time graph

The gradient of the velocity–time graph is given by $\frac{\Delta v}{\Delta t}$. This is the same as acceleration.

Area under acceleration–time graph

The area under an acceleration–time graph in Figure 2.22 is given by $a\Delta t$. But we know from the definition of acceleration that $a = \frac{(v - u)}{t}$

Rearranging this gives $v - u = a\Delta t$ so the area under the graph gives the change in velocity.

If you have covered calculus in your maths course you may recognize these equations:

$$v = \frac{ds}{dt}, \; a = \frac{dv}{dt} = \frac{d^2s}{d^2t}, \text{ and } s = \int v\,dt, \; v = \int a\,dt$$

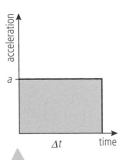

Figure 2.22.

Exercises

11 Sketch a velocity-time graph for a body starting from rest and accelerating at a constant rate to a final velocity of $25\,\text{m s}^{-1}$ in 10 seconds. Use the graph to find the distance travelled and the acceleration of the body.

12 Describe the motion of the body whose velocity-time graph is shown in Figure 2.23. What is the final displacement of the body?

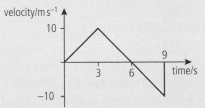

Figure 2.23

13 A ball is released from rest on the hill in Figure 2.24. Sketch the s–t, v–t, and a–t graphs for its horizontal motion.

Figure 2.24.

14 A ball rolls along a table then falls off the edge landing on soft sand. Sketch the s–t, v–t, and a–t graphs for its vertical motion.

Example 1: the *suvat* example

As an example let us consider the motion we looked at when deriving the *suvat* equations.

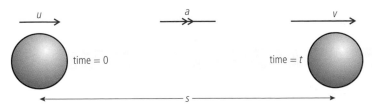

 Figure 2.25 A body with constant acceleration.

Negative time

Negative time doesn't mean going back in time – it means the time before you started the clock.

Displacement–time

The body starts with velocity u and travels to the right with constant acceleration, a for a time t. If we take the starting point to be zero displacement, then the displacement–time graph starts from zero and rises to s in t seconds. We can therefore plot the two

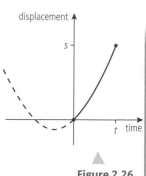

Figure 2.26.

points shown in Figure 2.26. The body is accelerating so the line joining these points is a parabola. The whole parabola has been drawn to show what it would look like – the reason it is offset is because the body is not starting from rest. The part of the curve to the left of the origin tells us what the particle was doing before we started the clock.

Velocity–time

Figure 2.27 is a straight line with a positive gradient showing that the acceleration is constant. The line doesn't start from the origin since the initial velocity is u.

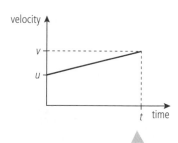

Figure 2.27.

The gradient of this line is $\frac{(v-u)}{t}$ which we know from the *suvat* equations is acceleration.

The area under the line makes the shape of a trapezium. The area of this trapezium is $\frac{1}{2}(v+u)t$. This is the *suvat* equation for s.

Acceleration–time

The acceleration is constant so the acceleration–time graph is simply a horizontal line as shown in Figure 2.28. The area under this line is $a \times t$ which we know from the *suvat* equations equals $(v-u)$.

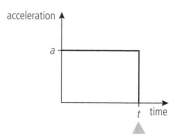

Figure 2.28.

Example 2: The bouncing ball

Consider a rubber ball dropped from some position above the ground A onto a hard surface B. The ball bounces up and down several times. Figure 2.29 shows the displacement–time graph for 4 bounces. From the graph we see that the ball starts above the ground then falls with increasing velocity (as deduced by the increasing negative gradient). When the ball bounces at B the velocity suddenly changes from negative to positive as the ball begins to travel back up. As the ball goes up, its velocity gets less until it stops at C and begins to fall again.

Figure 2.29.

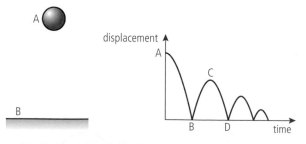

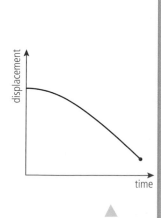

Figure 2.30.

Exercise

15 By considering the gradient of the displacement–time graph in Figure 2.29, plot the velocity–time graph for the motion of the bouncing ball.

Example 3: A ball falling with air resistance

Figure 2.30 represents the motion of a ball that is dropped several hundred metres through the air. It starts from rest and accelerates for some time. As the ball accelerates, the air resistance gets bigger, which prevents the ball from getting any faster. At this point the ball continues with constant velocity.

Projectile motion

A stroboscopic photograph of a projected ball.

We all know what happens when a ball is thrown; it follows a curved path like the one in the photo. We can see from this photo that the path is parabolic, and later we will show why that is the case.

Modelling projectile motion

All examples of motion up to this point have been in one dimension but projectile motion is two-dimensional. However, if we take components of all the vectors vertically and horizontally, we can simplify this into two simultaneous one-dimensional problems. The important thing to realize is that the vertical and horizontal components are independent of each other; you can test this by dropping a stone off a cliff and throwing one forward at the same time: they both hit the bottom together. The downward motion is not altered by the fact that one stone is also moving forward.

Consider a ball that is projected at an angle θ to the horizontal, as shown in Figure 2.31. We can split the motion into three parts, beginning, middle, and end, and analyse the vectors representing displacement, velocity, and time at each stage. Note that the path is symmetrical so the motion on the way down is the same as on the way up.

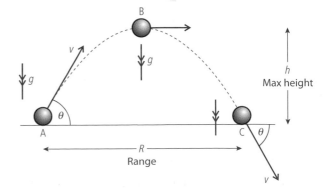

Figure 2.31 A projectile launched at an angle θ.

49

Horizontal components

Table 2.4 Horizontal components.

At A (time = 0)	At B (time = $\frac{t}{2}$)	At C (time = t)
Displacement = zero	Displacement = $\frac{R}{2}$	Displacement = R
Velocity = $v\cos\theta$	Velocity = $v\cos\theta$	Velocity = $v\cos\theta$
Acceleration = 0	Acceleration = 0	Acceleration = 0

Vertical components

Table 2.5 Vertical components.

At A	At B	At C
Displacement = zero	Displacement = h	Displacement = zero
Velocity = $v\sin\theta$	Velocity = zero	Velocity = $-v\sin\theta$
Acceleration = $-g$	Acceleration = $-g$	Acceleration = $-g$

We can see that the vertical motion is constant acceleration and the horizontal motion is constant velocity. We can therefore use the *suvat* equations.

suvat for horizontal motion

Since acceleration is zero there is only one equation needed to define the motion.

Table 2.6 *suvat* for horizontal motion.

suvat	A to C
Velocity = $v = \frac{s}{t}$	$R = v\cos\theta t$

suvat for vertical motion

When considering the vertical motion it is worth splitting the motion into two parts.

Table 2.7 *suvat* for vertical motion.

suvat	At B	At C
$s = \frac{1}{2}(u + v)t$	$h = \frac{1}{2}(v\sin\theta)\frac{t}{2}$	$0 = \frac{1}{2}(v\sin\theta - v\sin\theta)t$
$v^2 = u^2 + 2as$	$0 = v^2\sin^2\theta - 2gh$	$(-v\sin\theta)^2 = (v\sin\theta)^2 - 0$
$s = ut + \frac{1}{2}at^2$	$h = v\sin\theta t - \frac{1}{2}g(\frac{t}{2})^2$	$0 = v\sin\theta t - \frac{1}{2}gt^2$
$a = \frac{v - u}{t}$	$g = \frac{v\sin\theta - 0}{\frac{t}{2}}$	$g = \frac{v\sin\theta - -v\sin\theta}{t}$

Parabolic path

Since the horizontal displacement is proportional to *t* the path has the same shape as a graph of vertical displacement plotted against time. This is parabolic since the vertical displacement is proportional to t^2.

Some of these equations are not very useful since they simply state that 0 = 0. However we do end up with three useful ones (highlighted):

$$R = v\cos\theta t \tag{1}$$

$$0 = v^2\sin^2\theta - 2gh \quad \text{or} \quad h = \frac{v^2\sin^2\theta}{2g} \tag{2}$$

$$0 = v\sin\theta t - \frac{1}{2}gt^2 \quad \text{or} \quad t = \frac{2v\sin\theta}{g} \tag{3}$$

Solving problems

In a typical problem you will be given the magnitude and direction of the initial velocity and asked to find either the maximum height or range. To calculate *h* you can use equation (2) but to calculate *R* you need to find the time of flight so must use

(3) first (you could also substitute for t into equation (1) to give a fourth equation but maybe we have enough equations already).

You do not have to remember a lot of equations to solve a projectile problem. If you understand how to apply the *suvat* equations to the two components of the projectile motion, you only have to remember the *suvat* equations (and they are in the databook).

Worked example

A ball is thrown at an angle of 30° to the horizontal at a speed of $20\,\mathrm{m\,s^{-1}}$. Calculate its range and the maximum height reached.

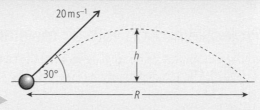

Figure 2.32. ▶

Solution

First, as always, draw a diagram, including labels defining all the quantities known and unknown.

Now we need to find the time of flight. If we apply $s = ut + \frac{1}{2}at^2$ to the whole flight we get

$$t = \frac{2v \sin \theta}{g} = \frac{(2 \times 20 \times \sin 30°)}{10} = 2\,\mathrm{s}$$

We can now apply $s = vt$ to the whole flight to find the range:

$$R = v \cos \theta t = 20 \times \cos 30° \times 2 = 34.6\,\mathrm{m}$$

Finally to find the height, we use $s = ut + \frac{1}{2}at^2$ to the vertical motion, but remember, this is only half the complete flight so the time is $1\,\mathrm{s}$.

$$h = v \sin \theta t - \frac{1}{2}gt^2 = 20 \times \sin 30° \times 1 - \frac{1}{2} \times 10 \times 1^2 = 10 - 5 = 5\,\mathrm{m}$$

Worked example

A ball is thrown horizontally from a cliff top with a horizontal speed of $10\,\mathrm{m\,s^{-1}}$. If the cliff is $20\,\mathrm{m}$ high what is the range of the ball?

Solution

This is an easy one since there aren't any angles to deal with. The initial vertical component of the velocity is zero and the horizontal component is $10\,\mathrm{m\,s^{-1}}$. To calculate the time of flight we apply $s = ut + \frac{1}{2}at^2$ to the vertical component. Knowing that the final displacement is $-20\,\mathrm{m}$ this gives

$$-20\,\mathrm{m} = 0 - \frac{1}{2}gt^2 \text{ so } t = \sqrt{\frac{(2 \times 20)}{10}} = 2\,\mathrm{s}$$

We can now use this value to find the range by applying the formula $s = vt$ to the horizontal component: $R = 10 \times 2 = 20\,\mathrm{m}$

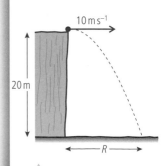

▲ Figure 2.33.

Exercises

17 Calculate the range of a projectile thrown at an angle of 60° to the horizontal with velocity $30\,m\,s^{-1}$.

18 You throw a ball at a speed of $20\,m\,s^{-1}$.

(a) At what angle must you throw it so that it will just get over a wall that is 5 m high?

(b) How far away from the wall must you be standing?

19 A gun is aimed so that it points directly at the centre of a target 200 m away. If the bullet travels at $200\,m\,s^{-1}$ how far below the centre of the target will the bullet hit?

20 If you can throw a ball at $20\,m\,s^{-1}$ what is the maximum distance you can throw it?

CHALLENGE YOURSELF

1 A projectile is launched perpendicular to a 30° slope at $20\,m\,s^{-1}$. Calculate the distance between the launching position and landing position.

Projectile motion with air resistance

In all the examples above we have ignored the fact that the air will resist the motion of the ball. The actual path of a ball including air resistance is likely to be as shown in Figure 2.34.

Figure 2.34.

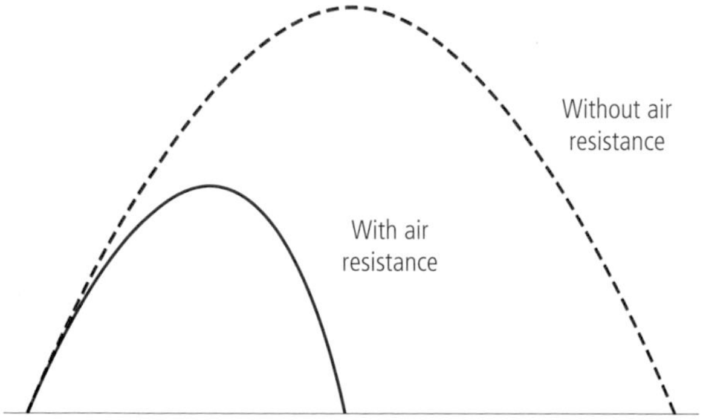

Notice both the height and range are less. It is also no longer a parabola – the way down is steeper than the way up.

To learn more about motion, go to the hotlinks site, search for the title or ISBN and click on Chapter 2.

2.2 Forces

2.2 Forces

Understandings, applications, and skills:

Objects as point particles
Free body diagrams
- Representing forces as vectors.
- Sketching and interpreting free body diagrams.

Guidance
- *Students should label forces using commonly accepted names or symbols. e.g. Weight.*
- *Free body diagrams should show scaled vector lengths acting from the point of application.*

Translational equilibrium
Newton's laws of motion
- Describing the consequences of Newton's first law for translational equilibrium.
- Using Newton's second law quantitatively and qualitatively. Identifying force pairs in the context of Newton's third law. Solving problems involving forces and determining resultant force.

Guidance
- *Examples and questions will be limited to constant mass.*
- mg *should be identified as weight.*
- *Calculations relating to the determination of resultant forces will be restricted to one and two dimensional situations.*

Solid friction
- Describing solid friction (static and dynamic) by coefficients of friction.

NATURE OF SCIENCE

Newton's three laws of motion are a set of statements, based on observation and experiment, that can be used to predict the motion of a point object from the forces acting on it. Einstein showed that the laws do not apply when speeds approach the speed of light. However, we still use them to predict outcomes at the lower velocities achieved by objects travelling in the lab.

Force (*F*)

We can now model the motion of a constantly accelerating body but what makes it accelerate? From experience we know that to make something move we must push or pull it. We call this *applying a force*. One simple way of applying a force to a body is to attach a string and pull it. Imagine a sphere floating in space with two strings attached; the sphere will not start to move unless one of the astronauts pulls the string as in Figure 2.35.

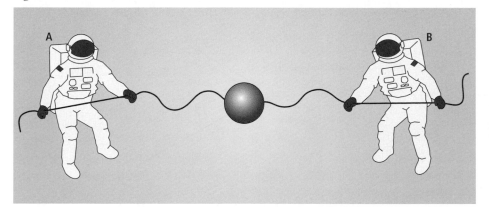

If A pulls the string then the body will move to the left, and if B pulls it will move to the right. We can see that force is a *vector* quantity since it has *direction*.

Addition of forces

Since force is a vector we must add forces vectorially, so if A applies a force of 50 N and B applies a force of 60 N the resultant force will be 10 N towards B, as can be seen in Figure 2.36.

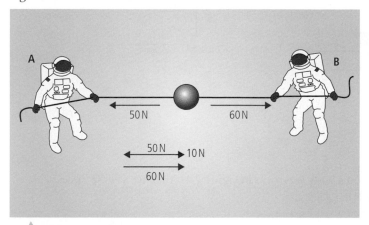

Figure 2.36 Astronaut A pulls harder than B.

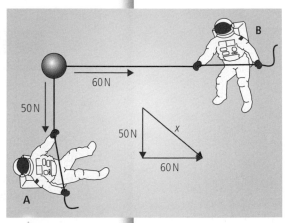

Figure 2.37 Astronauts pulling at right angles.

Or, in two dimensions, we can use trigonometry as in Figure 2.37.

In this case we can use Pythagoras to find *x*

$$x = \sqrt{50^2 + 60^2} = 78\,\text{N}$$

A force is a push or a pull.

The unit of force is the newton.

Figure 2.35 Two astronauts and a red ball.

The size of one newton
If you hold an object of mass 100 g in your hand then you will be exerting an upward force of about one newton (1 N).

Astronauts in space are considered here so that no other forces are present. This makes things simpler.

Taking components

As with other vector quantities we can calculate components of forces, for example we might want to know the resultant force in a particular direction.

In Figure 2.38 the component of the force in the x direction is $F_x = 60 \times \cos 30° = 52\,\text{N}$.

This is particularly useful when we have several forces.

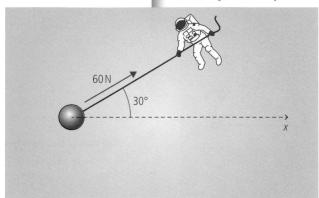

Figure 2.38 Pulling at an angle.

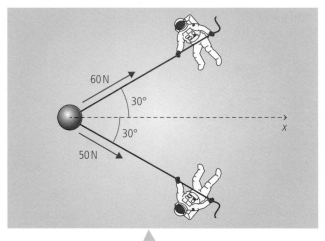

Figure 2.39 Astronauts not pulling in line.

In the example shown in Figure 2.39 we can use components to calculate the resultant force in the x direction $= 60 \times \cos 30° + 50 \times \cos 30° = 52 + 43 = 95\,\text{N}$.

Exercise

21 Find the resultant force in the following examples:

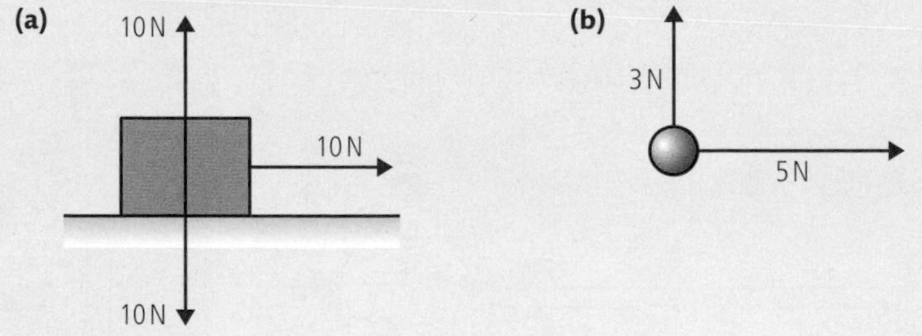

(a)

10 N

10 N

10 N

(b)

3 N

5 N

Figure 2.40.

Equilibrium

If the resultant force on a body is zero, as in Figure 2.41, then we say the forces are *balanced* or the body is in *equilibrium*.

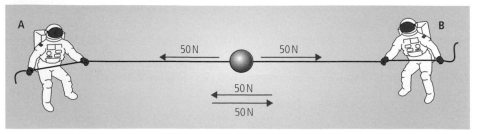

A   50 N   50 N   B

50 N

50 N

Figure 2.41 Balanced forces.

Or with three forces as in Figure 2.42.

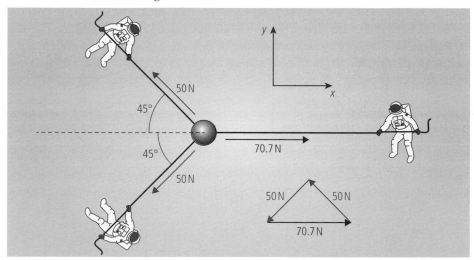

Figure 2.42 Three balanced forces.

In this example the two blue forces are perpendicular making the trigonometry easy. Adding all three forces gives a right-angled triangle. We can also see that if we take components in any direction then the forces must be balanced.

Taking components in the x direction:

$-50 \times \cos 45° - 50 \times \cos 45° + 70.7 = -35.35 - 35.35 + 70.7 = 0$

Taking components in the y direction:

$50 \times \sin 45° - 50 \times \sin 45° = 0$

Free body diagrams

Problems often involve more than one body; for example, the previous problem involved four bodies, three astronauts, and one red ball. All of these bodies will experience forces but if we drew them all on the diagram it would be very confusing, For that reason we only draw forces on the body we are interested in, in this case the red ball. This is called a free body diagram as shown in Figure 2.43. Note that we treat the red ball as a point object by drawing the forces acting on the centre. Not all forces actually act on the centre but when adding forces it can be convenient to draw them as if they do.

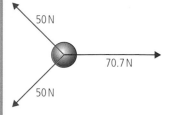

Figure 2.43 A free body diagram of the forces in Figure. 2.42.

Exercises

22 In the following examples calculate the force F required to balance the forces.
Figure 2.44.

23 Calculate the resultant force for the following.
Figure 2.45.

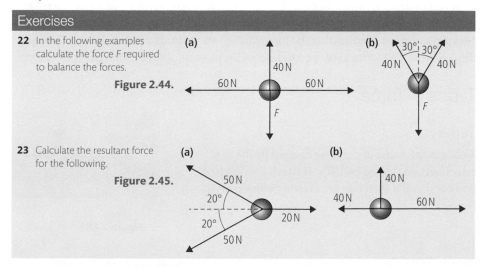

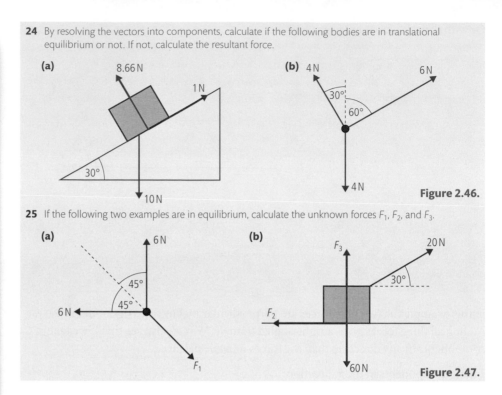

24 By resolving the vectors into components, calculate if the following bodies are in translational equilibrium or not. If not, calculate the resultant force.

(a)
8.66 N
1 N
30°
10 N
(b)
4 N
6 N
30°
60°
4 N

Figure 2.46.

25 If the following two examples are in equilibrium, calculate the unknown forces F_1, F_2, and F_3.

(a)
6 N
45°
45°
6 N
F_1
(b)
F_3
20 N
30°
F_2
60 N

Figure 2.47.

Using laws in physics

TOK

A law in physics is a very useful tool. If applied properly, it enables us to make a very strong argument that what we say is true. If asked 'will a box move?' you can say that you think it will and someone else could say it won't. You both have your opinions and you would then argue as to who is right. However, if you say that Newton's law says it will move, then you have a much stronger argument (assuming you have applied the law correctly).

Newton's first law of motion

From observation we can conclude that to make a body move we need to apply an unbalanced force to it. What isn't so obvious is that once moving it will continue to move with a constant velocity unless acted upon by another unbalanced force. Newton's first law of motion is a formal statement of this:

A body will remain at rest or moving with constant velocity unless acted upon by an unbalanced force.

The reason that this is not obvious to us on Earth is that we don't tend to observe bodies travelling with constant velocity with no forces acting on them; in space it would be more obvious. Newton's first law can be used in two ways. If the forces on a body are balanced then we can use Newton's first law to predict that it will be at rest or moving with constant velocity. If the forces are unbalanced then the body will not be at rest or moving with constant velocity. This means its velocity changes – in other words, it accelerates. Using the law the other way round, if a body accelerates then Newton's first law predicts that the forces acting on the body are unbalanced. To apply this law in real situations we need to know a bit more about the different types of force.

Types of force

Tension

Tension is the name of the force exerted by the astronauts on the red ball. If you attach a string to a body and pull it then you are exerting tension, as in Figure 2.48.

T

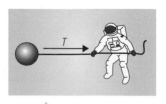

Figure 2.48 Exerting tension with a string.

Normal reaction

Whenever two surfaces are in contact with (touching) each other there will be a force between them. This force is perpendicular to the surface so it is called the *normal reaction force*. If the astronaut pushes the ball with his hand as in Figure 2.49, then there will be a normal reaction between the hand and the ball.

Note that the force acts on both surfaces so the astronaut will also experience a normal force. However, since we are interested in the ball, not the astronaut, we take the ball as our 'free body' so only draw the forces acting on it.

Gravitational force (weight)

Back on Earth, if a body is released above the ground as in Figure 2.50, it accelerates downwards. According to Newton's first law there must be an unbalanced force causing this motion; this force is called the *weight*. The weight of a body is directly proportional to its mass: $W = mg$ where $g = 9.81 \, \text{N kg}^{-1}$. Note that this is the same as the acceleration of free fall. You will find out why later on.

Note that the weight acts at the *centre* of the body.

If a block is at rest on the floor then Newton's first law implies that the forces are balanced. The forces involved are weight (because the block has mass and is on the Earth) and normal force (because the block is in contact with the ground). Figure 2.51 shows the forces.

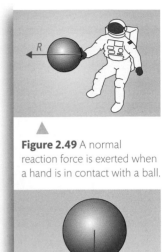

▲ **Figure 2.49** A normal reaction force is exerted when a hand is in contact with a ball.

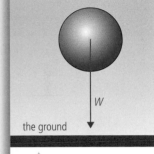

▲ **Figure 2.50** A ball in free fall.

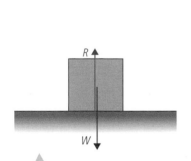

▲ **Figure 2.51** A free body diagram of a box resting on the ground.

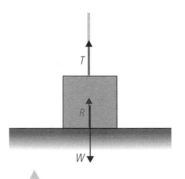

▲ **Figure 2.52** A string applies an upward force on the box.

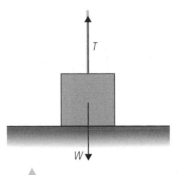

▲ **Figure 2.53** The block is lifted as the tension is bigger than its weight.

These forces are balanced so $-W + R = 0$ or $W = R$.

If the mass of the block is increased then the normal reaction will also increase.

If a string is added to the block then we can exert tension on the block as in Figure 2.52.

The forces are still balanced since $T + R = W$. Notice how W has remained the same but R has got smaller. If we pull with more force we can lift the block as in Figure 2.53. At this point the normal reaction R will be zero. The block is no longer in contact with the ground; now $T = W$.

The block in Figure 2.54 is on an inclined plane (slope) so the weight still acts downwards. In this case it might be convenient to split the weight into components, one acting down the slope and one into the slope.

The component of weight perpendicular to the slope is $W \cos \theta$. Since there is no movement in this direction the force is balanced by R. The component of weight

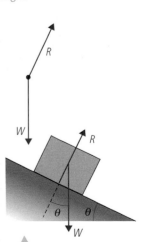

▲ **Figure 2.54** Free body diagram for a block on a slope.

57

parallel to the slope is $W \sin \theta$. This force is unbalanced, causing the block to accelerate down the slope. If the angle of the slope is increased then $\sin \theta$ will also increase, resulting in a greater force down the slope.

Friction

There are two types of friction: *static friction*, which is the force that stops the relative motion between two touching surfaces and *dynamic friction*, which opposes the relative motion between two touching surfaces. In both cases the force is related to both the normal force and the nature of the surfaces, so pushing two surfaces together increases the friction between them.

$F = \mu R$ where μ is the coefficient of friction (static or dynamic).

Dynamic friction

In Figure 2.55 a block is being pulled along a table at a constant velocity.

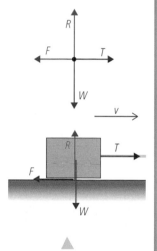

Figure 2.55 The force experienced by a block pulled along a table.

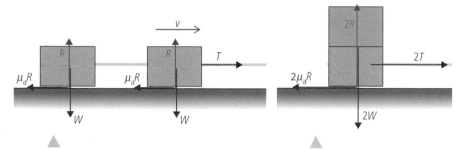

Figure 2.56 Two blocks joined with a rope.

Figure 2.57 Two blocks on top of each other.

Since the velocity is constant, Newton's first law implies that the forces are balanced so $T = F$ and $W = R$. Notice that friction doesn't depend on the area of contact. We can show this by considering two identical blocks sliding at constant velocity across a table top joined together by a rope as in Figure 2.56. The friction under each cube is $\mu_d R$ so the total friction would be $2\mu_d R$.

If the one cube is now placed on top of the other as in Figure 2.57, the normal force under the bottom cube will be twice as much so the friction is now $2\mu_d R$. It doesn't matter if the blocks are side by side (large area of contact) or on top of each other (small area of contact); the friction is the same.

If this is the case, then why do racing cars have wide tyres with no tread pattern (slicks)? There are several reasons for this but one is to increase the friction between the tyres and the road. This is strange because friction is not supposed to depend on area of contact. In practice friction isn't so simple. When one of the surfaces is sticky like the tyres of a racing car the force *does* depend upon the surface area. The type of surfaces we are concerned with here are quite smooth, non-sticky surfaces like wood and metal.

Static friction

If a very small force is applied to a block at rest on the ground it won't move. This means that the forces on the block are *balanced* (Newton's first law): the applied force is balanced by the static friction.

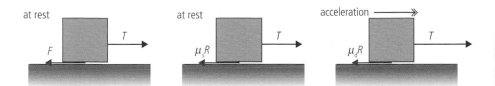

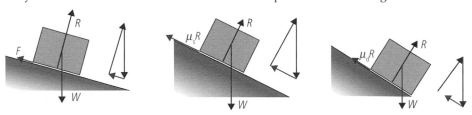

Figure 2.58 μR is the maximum size of friction.

In this case the friction simply equals the applied force: $F = T$. As the applied force is increased the friction will also increase. However, there will be a point when the friction cannot be any bigger. If the applied force is increased past that point the block will start to move; the forces have become *unbalanced* as illustrated in Figure 2.58. The maximum value that friction can have is $\mu_s R$ where μ_s is the coefficient of static friction. The value of static friction is always *greater* than dynamic friction. This can easily be demonstrated with a block on an inclined plane as shown in Figure 2.59.

Figure 2.59 A block rests on a slope until the forces become unbalanced.

In the first example the friction is balancing the component of weight down the plane which equals $W \sin \theta$, where θ is the angle of the slope. As the angle of the slope is increased, the point is reached where the static friction $= \mu_s R$. The forces are still balanced but the friction cannot get any bigger so if the angle is increased further the forces become unbalanced and the block will start to move. Once the block moves the friction becomes dynamic friction. Dynamic friction is less than static friction, so this results in a bigger resultant force down the slope, causing the block to accelerate.

Friction doesn't just slow things down, it is also the force that makes things move. Consider the tyre of a car as it starts to drive away from the traffic lights. The rubber of the tyre is trying to move relative to the road. In fact, if there wasn't any friction the wheel would spin as the tyre slipped backwards on the road. The force of friction that opposes the motion of the tyre slipping backwards on the road is therefore in the *forwards* direction.

If the static friction between the tyre and the road is not big enough the tyre will slip. Once this happens the friction becomes dynamic friction which is less than static friction, so once tyres start to slip they tend to continue slipping.

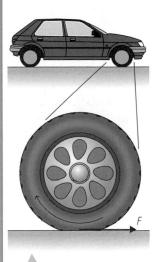

Figure 2.60 Friction pushes the car forwards.

Buoyancy

Buoyancy is the name of the force experienced by a body totally or partially immersed in a fluid (a fluid is a liquid or gas). The size of this force is equal to the weight of fluid displaced. It is this force that enables a boat to float and a helium balloon to rise in the air. Let us consider a football and a bucket full of water.

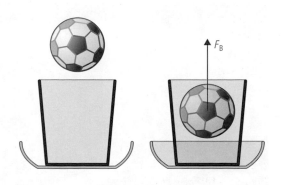

Figure 2.61 A football immersed in a bucket of water.

Figure 2.62 A football floats in a bucket of water.

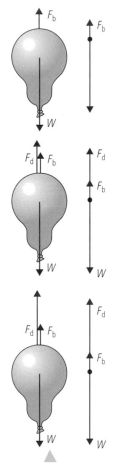

Figure 2.63 A balloon reaches terminal velocity as the forces become balanced. Notice the buoyant force is also present.

Speed skiers wear special clothes and squat down like this to reduce air resistance.

If you take the football and push it under the water then water will flow out of the bucket, (luckily a big bowl was placed there to catch it). The weight of this displaced water is equal to the upward force on the ball. To keep the ball under water you would therefore have to balance that force by pushing the ball down.

The forces on a floating object are balanced so the weight must equal the buoyant force. This means that the ball must have displaced its own weight of water as in Figure 2.62.

Air resistance

Air resistance, or *drag force*, is the force that opposes the motion of a body through the air. The size of this force depends on the speed, size and shape of the body. At slow speeds the drag force experienced by a sphere is given by Stoke's law:

$$F = 6\pi \eta v r$$
$$\text{where } \eta = \text{viscosity (a constant)}$$
$$v = \text{velocity}$$
$$r = \text{radius}$$

When a balloon is dropped it accelerates downwards due to the force of gravity. As it falls through the air it experiences a drag force opposing its motion. As the balloon's velocity gets bigger so does the drag force, until the drag force balances its weight at which point its velocity will remain constant (Figure 2.63). This maximum velocity is called its *terminal velocity*.

The same thing happens when a parachutist jumps out of a plane. The terminal velocity in this case is around 54 m s⁻¹ (195 km h⁻¹). Opening the parachute increases the drag force which slows the parachutist down to a safer 10 m s⁻¹ for landing.

As it is mainly the air resistance that limits the top speed of a car, a lot of time and money is spent by car designers to try to reduce this force. This is particularly important at high speeds when the drag force is related to the square of the speed.

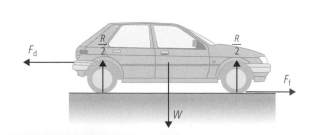

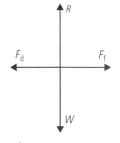

Figure 2.64 The forces acting on a car travelling at constant velocity.

Exercises

26 A ball of weight 10 N is suspended on a string and pulled to one side by another horizontal string as shown in Figure 2.65. If the forces are balanced:

(a) write an equation for the horizontal components of the forces acting on the ball
(b) write an equation for the vertical components of the forces acting on the ball
(c) use the second equation to calculate the tension in the upper string, T
(d) use your answer to (c) plus the first equation to find the horizontal force F.

27 The condition for the forces to be balanced is that the sum of components of the forces in any two perpendicular components is zero. In the 'box on a ramp' example the vertical and horizontal components were taken. However, it is sometimes more convenient to consider components parallel and perpendicular to the ramp.

Consider the situation in Figure 2.66. If the forces on this box are balanced:

(a) write an equation for the components of the forces parallel to the ramp
(b) write an equation for the forces perpendicular to the ramp
(c) use your answers to find the friction (F) and normal force (N).

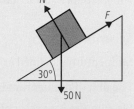

Figure 2.66.

28 A rock climber is hanging from a rope attached to the cliff by two bolts as shown in Figure 2.67. If the forces are balanced

(a) write an equation for the vertical component of the forces on the knot
(b) write an equation for the horizontal forces exerted on the knot
(c) calculate the tension T in the ropes joined to the bolts.

The result of this calculation shows why ropes should not be connected in this way.

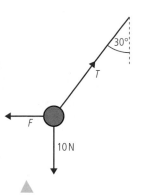

Figure 2.65.

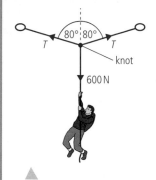

Figure 2.67.

2.3 Momentum and impulse

2.4 Momentum and impulse

Understandings, applications, and skills:

Newton's second law expressed as a rate of change of momentum
- Applying conservation of momentum in isolated systems including (but not limited to) the motion of rockets, collisions, explosions, or water jets.
- Using Newton's second law quantitatively and qualitatively in cases where mass is not constant.

  Guidance
  - *Students should be aware that* F = ma *is equivalent to* F = Δp/Δt *only when mass is constant.*

Impulse and force-time graphs
- Sketching and interpreting force–time graphs.
- Determining impulse in various contexts including (but not limited to) car safety and sports.

Conservation of linear momentum

Elastic collisions, inelastic collisions, and explosions
- Qualitatively and quantitatively comparing situations involving elastic collisions, inelastic collisions, and explosions.

  Guidance
  - *Solving simultaneous equations involving conservation of momentum and energy in collisions will not be required.*
  - *Calculations relating to collisions and explosions will be restricted to one-dimensional situations.*
  - *A comparison between inelastic collisions (in which kinetic energy is not conserved) and the conservation of (total) energy should be made.*

The relationship between force and acceleration

Newton's first law states that a body will accelerate if an unbalanced force is applied to it. Newton's second law tells us how big the acceleration will be and in which direction.

Before we look in detail at Newton's second law we should look at the factors that affect the acceleration of a body when an unbalanced force is applied. Let us consider the example of catching a ball. When we catch the ball we change its velocity, Newton's first law tells us that we must therefore apply an unbalanced force to the ball. The size of that force depends upon two things, the mass and the velocity. A heavy ball is more difficult to stop than a light one travelling at the same speed, and a fast one is harder to stop than a slow one. Rather than having to concern ourselves with two quantities we will introduce a new quantity that incorporates both mass and velocity: *momentum*.

Momentum (*p*)

Momentum is defined as the product of mass and velocity: $\mathbf{p} = \mathbf{mv}$

The unit of momentum is $\mathrm{kg\,m\,s^{-1}}$.

Momentum is a vector quantity.

Impulse

When you get hit by a ball the effect it has on you is greater if the ball bounces off you than if you catch it. This is because the change of momentum is greater when the ball bounces, as shown in Figure 2.68.

The unit of impulse is $\mathrm{kg\,m\,s^{-1}}$.

Impulse is a vector.

Red ball

Momentum before = mv
Momentum after = $-mv$ (remember momentum is a vector)
Change in momentum = $-mv - mv = -2mv$

Blue ball

Momentum before = mv
Momentum after = 0
Change in momentum = $0 - mv = -mv$

The impulse is defined as the change of momentum.

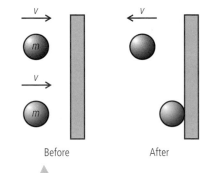

Before   After

Figure 2.68 The change of momentum of the red ball is greater.

Exercises

29 A ball of mass 200 g travelling at $10\,\mathrm{m\,s^{-1}}$ bounces off a wall as in Figure 2.68. If after hitting the wall it travels at $5\,\mathrm{m\,s^{-1}}$, what is the impulse?

30 Calculate the impulse on a tennis racket that hits a ball of mass 67 g travelling at $10\,\mathrm{m\,s^{-1}}$ so that it comes off the racket at a velocity of $50\,\mathrm{m\,s^{-1}}$.

Newton's second law of motion

The rate of change of momentum of a body is directly proportional to the unbalanced force acting on that body and takes place in same direction.

Let us once again consider a ball with a constant force acting on it as in Figure 2.69.

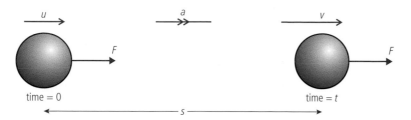

time = 0   time = t

Figure 2.69.

Unit of momentum

If F = change in momentum/time then momentum = force × time.
So the unit of momentum is N s. This is the same as $kg\,m\,s^{-1}$.

Newton's first law tells us that there must be an unbalanced force acting on the ball since it is accelerating.

Newton's second law tells us that the size of the unbalanced force is directly proportional to the rate of change of momentum. We know that the force is constant so the rate of change of momentum is also constant, which, since the mass is also constant, implies that the acceleration is uniform so the *suvat* equations apply.

If the ball has mass m we can calculate the change of momentum of the ball.

Initial momentum = mu

Final momentum = mv

Change in momentum = $mv - mu$

The time taken is t so the rate of change of momentum = $\dfrac{mv - mu}{t}$

This is the same as $\dfrac{m(v-u)}{t} = ma$

Newton's second law states that the rate of change of momentum is proportional to the force, so $F \propto ma$.

To make things simple the newton is defined so that the constant of proportionality is equal to 1 so:

$$F = ma$$

So when a force is applied to a body in this way, Newton's second law can be simplified to:

The acceleration of a body is proportional to the force applied and inversely proportional to its mass.

Not all examples are so simple. Consider a jet of water hitting a wall as in Figure 2.70. The water hits the wall and loses its momentum, ending up in a puddle on the floor.

Newton's first law tells us that since the velocity of the water is changing, there must be a force on the water,

Newton's second law tells us that the size of the force is equal to the rate of change of momentum. The rate of change of momentum in this case is equal to the amount of water hitting the wall per second multiplied by the change in velocity; this is not the same as ma. For this reason it is best to use the first, more general statement of Newton's second law, since this can always be applied.

Figure 2.70.

However, in this course most of the examples will be of the $F = ma$ type.

Example 1: Elevator accelerating upwards

An elevator has an upward acceleration of $1\,m\,s^{-2}$. If the mass of the elevator is $500\,kg$, what is the tension in the cables pulling it up?

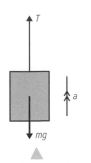

Figure 2.71 An elevator accelerating upwards. This could either be going up getting *faster* or going down getting *slower*.

First draw a free body diagram as in Figure 2.71. Now we can see what forces are acting. Newton's first law tells us that the forces must be unbalanced. Newton's second law tells us that the unbalanced force must be in the direction of the acceleration (upwards). This means that T is bigger than mg.

Newton's second law also tells us that the size of the unbalanced force equals ma so we get the equation

$$T - mg = ma$$

Rearranging gives

$$T = mg + ma$$
$$= 500 \times 10 + 500 \times 1$$
$$= 5500\,\text{N}$$

Example 2: Elevator accelerating downwards

The same elevator as in example 1 now has a downward acceleration of $1\,\text{m s}^{-2}$ as in Figure 2.72.

This time Newton's laws tell us that the weight is bigger than the tension so $mg - T = ma$

Rearranging gives

$$T = mg - ma$$
$$= 500 \times 10 - 500 \times 1$$
$$= 4500\,\text{N}$$

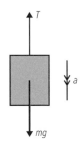

Figure 2.72 The elevator with downward acceleration.

Example 3: Joined masses

Two masses are joined by a rope. One of the masses sits on a frictionless table, the other hangs off the edge as in Figure 2.73.

M is being dragged to the edge of the table by m.

Both are connected to the same rope so T is the same for both masses. This also means that the acceleration a is the same.

We do not need to consider N and Mg for the mass on the table because these forces are balanced. However the horizontally unbalanced force is T.

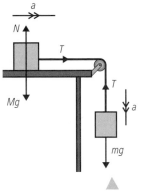

Figure 2.73.

Applying Newton's laws to the mass on the table gives

$$T = Ma$$

The hanging mass is accelerating down so mg is bigger than T. Newton's second law implies that $mg - T = ma$

Substituting for T gives $mg - Ma = ma$ so $a = \dfrac{mg}{M + m}$

Example 4: The free fall parachutist

After falling freely for some time, a free fall parachutist whose weight is 60 kg opens his parachute. Suddenly the force due to air resistance increases to 1200 N. What happens?

Looking at the free body diagram in Figure 2.74 we can see that the forces are unbalanced and that according to Newton's second law the acceleration, a, will be upwards.

The size of the acceleration is given by

$$ma = 1200 - 600 = 60 \times a$$

so
$$a = 10\,\mathrm{m\,s^{-2}}$$

The acceleration is in the opposite direction to the motion. This will cause the parachutist to slow down. As he slows down, the air resistance gets less until the forces are balanced. He will then continue down with a constant velocity.

Figure 2.74 The parachutist just after opening the parachute.

Even without a parachute base jumpers reach terminal velocity.

Exercises

31 The helium in a balloon causes an upthrust of 0.1 N. If the mass of the balloon and helium is 6 g, calculate the acceleration of the balloon.

32 A rope is used to pull a felled tree (mass 50 kg) along the ground. A tension of 1000 N causes the tree to move from rest to a velocity of 0.1 m s⁻¹ in 2 s. Calculate the force due to friction acting on the tree.

33 Two masses are arranged on a frictionless table as shown in Figure 2.75. Calculate:
  (a) the acceleration of the masses
  (b) the tension in the string.

Figure 2.75.

34 A helicopter is lifting a load of mass 1000 kg with a rope. The rope is strong enough to hold a force of 12 kN. What is the maximum upward acceleration of the helicopter?

35 A person of mass 65 kg is standing in an elevator that is accelerating upwards at 0.5 m s⁻². What is the normal force between the floor and the person?

36 A plastic ball is held under the water by a child in a swimming pool. The volume of the ball is 4000 cm³.
  (a) If the density of water is 1000 kg m⁻³, calculate the buoyant force on the ball (remember buoyant force = weight of fluid displaced).
  (b) If the mass of the ball is 250 g, calculate the theoretical acceleration of the ball when it is released. Why won't the ball accelerate this quickly in a real situation?

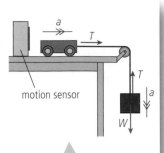

Experiment to test the relationship between acceleration and force

It isn't easy to apply a constant, known force to a moving body: just try pulling a cart along the table with a force meter and you will see. One way this is often done in the laboratory is by hanging a mass over the edge of the table as shown in Figure 2.76.

If we ignore any friction in the pulley or in the wheels of the trolley then the unbalanced force on the trolley = T. Since the mass is accelerating down then the weight is bigger than T so $W - T = ma$ where m is the mass hanging on the string. The tension is therefore given by $T = mg - ma = m(g - a)$.

There are several ways to measure the acceleration of the trolley; one is to use a motion sensor. This senses the position of the trolley by reflecting an ultrasonic pulse off it. Knowing the speed of the pulse, the software can calculate the distance between the trolley and sensor. As the trolley moves away from the sensor the time taken for the pulse to return increases; the software calculates the velocity from these changing times. Using this apparatus, the acceleration of the trolley for different masses was measured, and the results are given in the Table 2.8.

Figure 2.76 Apparatus for finding the relationship between force and acceleration.

Table 2.8 Results from the force and acceleration experiment.

Mass/kg ±0.0001	Acceleration/m s⁻² ±0.03	Tension $(T = mg - ma)$/N	Max T/N	Min T/N	ΔT/N
0.0100	0.10	0.097	0.098	0.096	0.001
0.0500	0.74	0.454	0.453	0.451	0.001
0.0600	0.92	0.533	0.532	0.531	0.001
0.1000	1.49	0.832	0.830	0.828	0.001
0.1500	2.12	1.154	1.150	1.148	0.001

The relationship between force and acceleration

Full details of how to carry out this experiment with a worksheet are available online.

Figure 2.77 Graph of tension against acceleration.

The uncertainty in mass is given by the last decimal place in the scale, and the uncertainty in acceleration by repeating one run several times. To calculate the uncertainty in tension the maximum and minimum values have been calculated by adding and subtracting the uncertainties.

These results are shown in Figure 2.77.

Applying Newton's second law to the trolley the relationship between T and a should be $T = Ma$ where M is the mass of the trolley. This implies that the gradient of the line should be M. From the graph we can see that the gradient is 0.52 ± 0.02 kg which is quite close to the 0.5 kg mass of the trolley.

According to theory the intercept should be (0, 0) but we can see that there is a positive intercept of 0.05 N. It appears that each value is 0.05 N too big. The reason for this could be friction. If there was friction then the actual unbalanced force acting on the trolley would be tension – friction. If this is the case then the results would imply that friction is about 0.05 N.

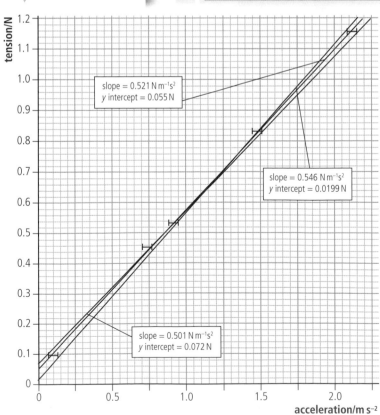

slope = 0.521 N m⁻¹s²
y intercept = 0.055 N

slope = 0.546 N m⁻¹s²
y intercept = 0.0199 N

slope = 0.501 N m⁻¹s²
y intercept = 0.072 N

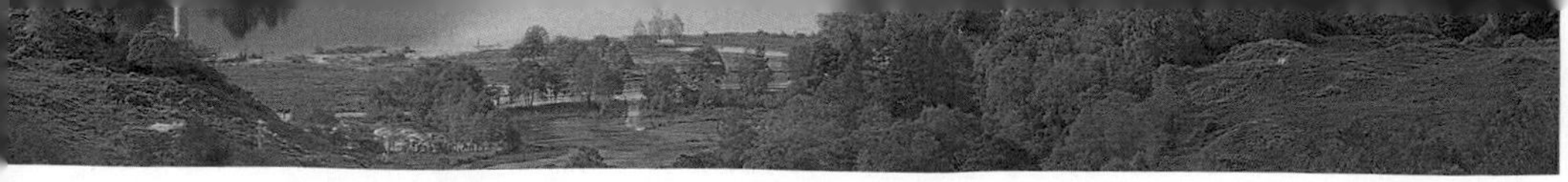

Newton's third law of motion

When dealing with Newton's first and second laws, we are careful to consider only the body that is *experiencing* the forces, not the body that is *exerting* the forces. Newton's third law relates these forces.

If body A exerts a force on body B then body B will exert an equal and opposite force on body A.

So if someone is pushing a car with a force F as shown in Figure 2.78 the car will push back on the person with a force $-F$. In this case both of these forces are the normal force.

Incorrect statements

It is very important to realise that Newton's third law is about two bodies. Avoid statements of this law that do not mention anything about there being two bodies.

Figure 2.78 The man pushes the car and the car pushes the man.

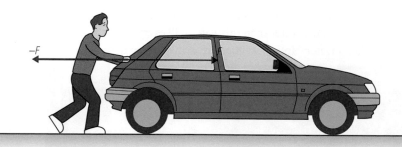

You might think that since these forces are equal and opposite, they will be balanced, and in that case how does the person get the car moving? This is wrong; the forces act on different bodies so can't balance each other.

Example 1: A falling body

A body falls freely towards the ground as in Figure 2.79. If we ignore air resistance, there is only one force acting on the body – the force due to the gravitational attraction of the Earth, that we call weight.

Figure 2.79 A falling body pulled down by gravity.

Applying Newton's third law:

If the Earth pulls the body down, then the body must pull the Earth up with an equal and opposite force. We have seen that the gravitational force always acts on the centre of the body, so Newton's third law implies that there must be a force equal to W acting upwards on the centre of the Earth as in Figure 2.80.

Figure 2.80 The Earth pulled up by gravity.

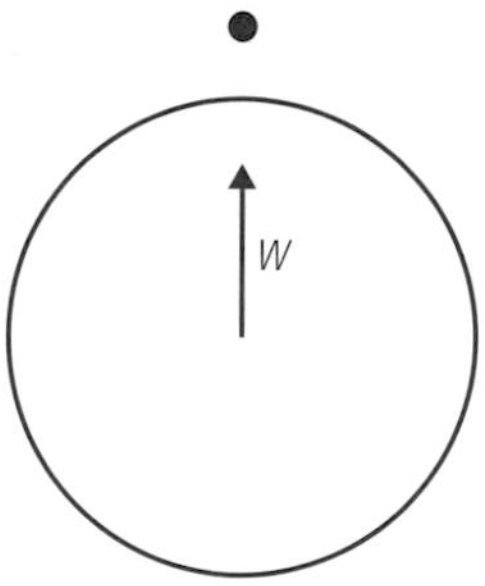

Example 2: A box rests on the floor

A box sits on the floor as shown in Figure 2.81. Let us apply Newton's third law to this situation.
There are two forces acting on the box.

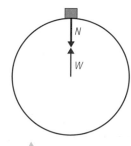

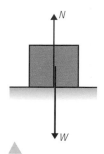

Figure 2.81 Forces acting on a box resting on the floor.

Normal force: The floor is pushing up on the box with a force N. According to Newton's third law the box must therefore push down on the floor with a force of magnitude N.

Weight: The Earth is pulling the box down with a force W. According to Newton's third law, the box must be pulling the Earth up with a force of magnitude W as shown in Figure 2.82.

Figure 2.82 Forces acting on the Earth according to Newton's third law.

Students often think that Newton's third law implies that the normal force = –weight, but *both* of these forces act on the box. If the box is at *rest* these forces are indeed equal and opposite but this is due to Newton's *first* law.

Example 3: Recoil of a gun

When a gun is fired the velocity of the bullet changes. Newton's first law implies that there must be an unbalanced force on the bullet; this force must come from the gun. Newton's third law says that if the gun exerts a force on the bullet the bullet must exert an equal and opposite force on the gun. This is the force that makes the gun recoil or 'kick back'.

Example 4: The water cannon

When water is sprayed at a wall from a hosepipe it hits the wall and stops. Newton's first law says that if the velocity of the water changes, there must be an unbalanced force on the water. This force comes from the wall. Newton's third law says that if the wall exerts a force on the water then the water will exert a force on the wall. This is the force that makes a water cannon so effective at dispersing demonstrators.

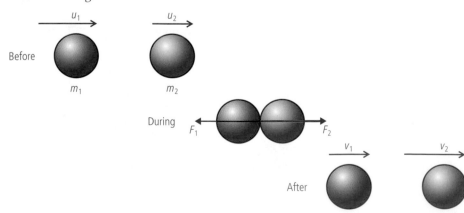

▲ A boat tests its water cannons.

Exercise

37 Use Newton's first and third laws to explain the following:

(a) When burning gas is forced downwards out of a rocket motor, the rocket accelerates up.
(b) When the water cannons on the boat in the photo are operating, the boat accelerates forwards.
(c) When you step forwards off a skateboard, the skateboard accelerates backwards.
(d) A table tennis ball is immersed in a fluid and held down by a string as shown in Figure 2.83. The container is placed on a balance. What will happen to the reading of the balance if the string breaks?

Collisions

In this section we have been dealing with the interaction between two bodies (gun–bullet, skater–skateboard, hose–water). To develop our understanding of the interaction between bodies, let us consider a simple collision between two balls as illustrated in Figure 2.84.

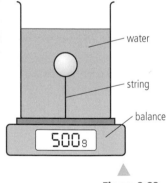

Figure 2.83.

Figure 2.84 Collision between two balls.

Let us apply Newton's three laws to this problem.

Newton's first law

In the collision the red ball slows down and the blue ball speeds up. Newton's first law tells us that that this means there is a force acting to the left on the red ball (F_1) and to the right on the blue ball (F_2).

Newton's second law

This law tells us that the force will be equal to the rate of change of momentum of the balls so if the balls are touching each other for a time Δt:

$$F_1 = \frac{m_1 v_1 - m_1 u_1}{\Delta t}$$

$$F_2 = \frac{m_2 v_2 - m_2 u_2}{\Delta t}$$

Newton's third law

According to the third law, if the red ball exerts a force on the blue ball, then the blue ball will exert an equal and opposite force on the red ball.

$$F_1 = -F_2$$
$$\frac{m_1 v_1 - m_1 u_1}{\Delta t} = \frac{-(m_2 v_2 - m_2 u_2)}{\Delta t}$$

Rearranging gives $\quad m_1 u_1 + m_2 u_2 = m_1 v_1 + m_2 v_2$

In other words the momentum at the start equals the momentum at the end. We find that this applies not only to this example but to all interactions.

The law of the conservation of momentum

For a system of isolated bodies the total momentum is always the same.

This is not a new law since it is really just a combination of Newton's laws. However it provides a useful short cut when solving problems.

Examples

In these examples we will have to pretend everything is in space isolated from the rest of the Universe, otherwise they are not isolated and the law of conservation of momentum won't apply.

1. A collision where the bodies join together

If two balls of modelling clay collide with each other they stick together as shown in Figure 2.85. We want to find the velocity, v, of the combined lump after the collision.

6 m s⁻¹
100 g

500 g

Before

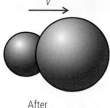

v

After

Figure 2.85 Two bodies stick together after colliding.

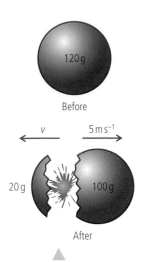

Before

v 5 m s⁻¹

20 g   100 g

After

Figure 2.86 A piece of modelling clay suddenly explodes.

If bodies are isolated then momentum is conserved so:

$$\text{momentum before} = \text{momentum after}$$
$$0.1 \times 6 + 0.5 \times 0.0 = 0.6 \times v$$
$$v = \frac{0.6}{0.6} = 1\,\text{m s}^{-1}$$

2. An explosion

A ball of clay floating around in space suddenly explodes into a big piece and a small piece, as shown in Figure 2.86. If the big bit has a velocity of 5 m s⁻¹, what is the velocity of the small bit?

Since this is an isolated system, momentum is conserved so:

$$\text{momentum before} = \text{momentum after}$$
$$0 \times 0.12 = 0.02 \times (-v) + 0.1 \times 5$$
$$0.02 \times v = 0.5$$
$$v = 25\,\text{m s}^{-1}$$

Rocket engine

The momentum of a rocket plus fuel floating in space is zero but when the engines are fired gas is expelled at high speed. This gas has momentum towards the left so in order to conserve momentum the rocket will move towards the right.

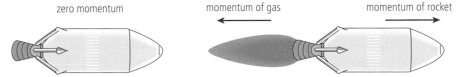

zero momentum   momentum of gas   momentum of rocket

Figure 2.87 Rocket engine expels gas to give thrust.

The momentum of the rocket will equal the momentum of the expelled gases, so increasing the rate at which the gases are expelled will increase the acceleration of the rocket. Note that the situation for a rocket about to blast off on the Earth is rather more complex since the rocket + fuel can no longer be considered isolated.

Jet engine

A passenger jet aeroplane powered by four jet engines.

A jet engine produces thrust (the force that pushes the plane forwards) by increasing the speed of air taken in at the front by passing it through a series of turbines. The fast-moving air expelled from the back of the engine has an increased momentum so if momentum is to be conserved the plane must have increased momentum in the forwards direction.

Exercise

38 Draw diagrams to represent the following collisions then use the law of conservation of momentum to find the unknown velocity. Assume all collisions are head-on, in other words they take place in one dimension.

(a) Two identical isolated balls collide with each other. Before the collision, one ball was travelling at $10\,\text{m s}^{-1}$ and the other was at rest. After the collision the first ball continues in the same direction with a velocity of $1\,\text{m s}^{-1}$. Find the velocity of the other ball.

(b) Two identical balls are travelling towards each other; each is travelling at a speed of $5\,\text{m s}^{-1}$. After they hit, one ball bounces off with a speed of $1\,\text{m s}^{-1}$. What is the speed of the other?

(c) A spaceman of mass $100\,\text{kg}$ is stranded $2\,\text{m}$ from his spaceship as shown in Figure 2.88. He happens to be holding a hammer of mass $2\,\text{kg}$ what must he do?

If he only has enough air to survive for 2 minutes, how fast must he throw the hammer if he is to get back in time? Is it possible?

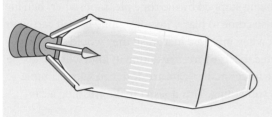
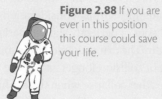

Figure 2.88 If you are ever in this position this course could save your life.

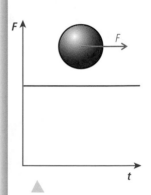

▲
Figure 2.89 Graph of force against time for constant force.

Momentum and force

If a constant unbalanced force acts on an isolated body the graph of the force against time would be as shown in Figure 2.89, force remaining constant all the time.

According to Newton's second law the bodies rate of change of momentum will be equal to force applied so $F = \frac{\Delta mv}{\Delta t}$.

Rearranging this gives $\Delta mv = F\Delta t$ where $F\Delta t$ is the area under the graph. This is the case whenever a force is applied over a time.

Now let us consider a more difficult example of a $2\,\text{kg}$ steel ball travelling at $10\,\text{m s}^{-1}$ bouncing off a concrete wall as illustrated by the graph in Figure 2.90.

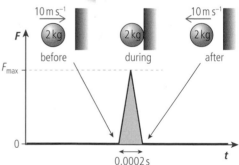

From the graph you can see that the ball is only in contact with the wall for $0.0002\,\text{s}$, the force is not constant but has its maximum value, F_{max} in the middle of the bounce.

The change in momentum (impulse) = momentum after − momentum before
$= -2 \times 10 - 2 \times 10 = -40\,\text{N s}$. This is the same as the area under the graph
$= \frac{1}{2} \times F_{max} \times 0.0002$

so $\frac{1}{2} \times F_{max} \times 0.0002 = -40\,\text{N s}$

which makes $F_{max} = -400\,\text{kN}$

▲
Figure 2.90 Graph of force against time for a hard collision.

Note that the force on the ball is *negative* because it is to the *left*.

If the same ball is thrown against a soft wall, the soft wall bends inwards as the ball hits it, resulting in a bounce lasting a much longer time as represented by the graph in Figure 2.91, let's say $0.2\,\text{s}$.

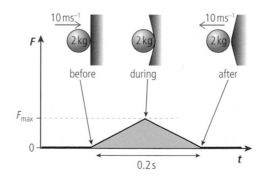

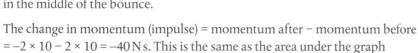

◄ **Figure 2.91** Force against time for a soft collision.

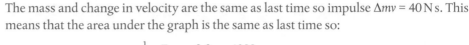

The mass and change in velocity are the same as last time so impulse $\Delta mv = 40\,\text{N s}$. This means that the area under the graph is the same as last time so:

$$\tfrac{1}{2} \times F_{max} \times 0.2 = -40\,\text{N s}$$
$$F_{max} = -400\,\text{N}.$$

From this example we can see that the amount of force required to slow down a body is related to the time of application of the force. This is very important when designing climbing ropes. If a climber fell a distance of 10 m they would be travelling at about $14\,\text{m s}^{-1}$. If the rope didn't stretch they would be brought to rest very quickly resulting in a large force applied to the climber. This sudden large force would certainly injure the climber and probably even break the rope. It is for this very reason that stretchy ropes are used, making the result of being stopped by the rope pleasant rather than life threatening. Similar considerations also come to play when designing cars. If cars were made out of perfectly rigid materials, when involved in a crash they would stop very rapidly. The driver would also subjected to large forces resulting in injury. To make the time of collision longer and hence the force smaller, cars are designed with crumple zones that collapse when the car hits something. This doesn't make crashing a car pleasant but can reduce injury.

Figure 2.92 shows some real data obtained by dropping a ball of modelling clay onto a force sensor. The negative peak is probably due to the ball sticking to the force sensor on the way back up. This graph is part of the data collected by IB student Gustav Gordon researching the relationship between temperature and maximum force experienced when a plasticine ball hits the floor for his Extended Essay.

The author testing a climbing rope.

The amount that a climbing rope stretches is related to the length of the rope. If the length is short then the stretch may not be enough to reduce the force of the fall sufficiently. In this case the person holding the rope can allow the rope to run by moving forwards. This is a little disconcerting for the climber who falls further than expected.

Figure 2.92 Force against time for a plasticine ball landing on a force sensor.

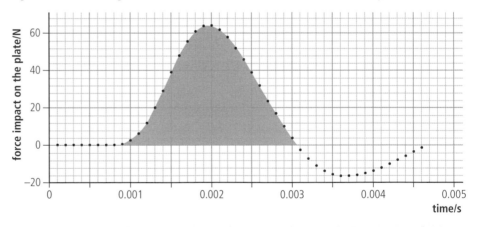

Exercises

39 (a) Calculate the impulse of the body for the motion represented in Figure 2.93.

(b) If the mass of the object is 20 g, what is the change of velocity?

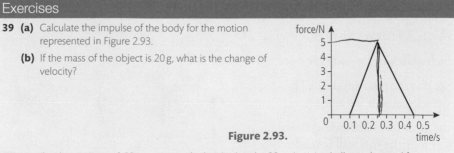

Figure 2.93.

40 Use the data in Figure 2.93 to estimate the height that the 20 g plasticine ball was dropped from.

Pressure (*P*)

If we take the example of a block resting on the ground, the bottom surface of the block is in contact with the ground so will exert a normal reaction force on the ground. The normal reaction on the ground is equal to the normal reaction on the block (Newton's third law) which, since the block is in equilibrium, is equal to the weight of the object (Newton's first law). The force on the ground will therefore be the same no matter what the area of contact is, so in Figure 2.94 the normal reaction is the same in both cases. Even though the force is the same, the *effect* of the force might be different. Imagine the block was placed on something soft like snow, mud, or sand. The block with the smallest area would then push into the soft material the most. This is because the force per unit area (*pressure*) is greater.

$$\text{pressure} = \frac{\text{force}}{\text{area}}$$

The unit pressure is the $N\,m^{-2}$. This is called a pascal (Pa).

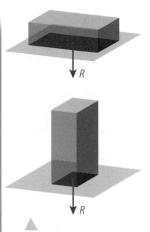

Figure 2.94 Comparing the force under two different areas.

2.4 Work, energy, and power

2.3 Work, energy, and power

Understandings, applications, and skills:

Principle of conservation of energy
• Discussing the conservation of total energy within energy transformations.
Kinetic energy
Gravitational potential energy
Elastic potential energy
• Sketching and interpreting force–distance graphs.
Work done as energy transfer
• Determining work done including cases where a resistive force acts.

   Guidance
   • *Cases where the line of action of the force and the displacement are not parallel should be considered.*
   • *Examples should include force–distance graphs for variable forces.*

Power as rate of energy transfer
• Solving problems involving power.
Efficiency
• Quantitatively describing efficiency in energy transfers.

NATURE OF SCIENCE

Scientists should remain sceptical but that doesn't mean you have to doubt everything you read. The law of conservation of energy is supported by many experiments, and is the basis of countless predictions that turn out to be true. If someone now found that energy was not conserved then there would be a lot of explaining to do. Once a law is accepted it gives us an easy way to make predictions. For example, if you are shown a device that produces energy from nowhere you know it must be a fake without even finding out how it works because it violates the law of conservation of energy.

We have so far dealt with the motion of a small red ball and understand what causes it to accelerate. We have also investigated the interaction between a red ball and a blue one and have seen that the red one can cause the blue one to move when they collide. But what enables the red one to push the blue one? To answer this question we need to define some more quantities.

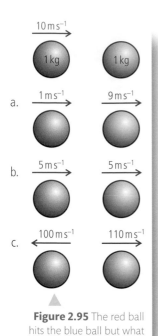

Figure 2.95 The red ball hits the blue ball but what happens?

Figure 2.96 The force acts on the orange block for a greater distance

Work

In the introduction to this book it was stated that by developing models, our aim is to understand the physical world so that we can make predictions. At this point you should understand certain concepts related to the collision between two balls, but we still can't predict the outcome. To illustrate this point let us again consider the red and blue balls. Figure 2.95 shows three possible outcomes of the collision.

If we apply the law of conservation of momentum, we realize that all three outcomes are possible. The original momentum is 10 N s and the final momentum is 10 N s in all three cases. But which one actually happens? This we cannot say (yet). All we know is that from experience the last option is not possible – but why?

When body A hits body B, body A exerts a force on body B. This force causes B to have an increase in velocity. The amount that the velocity increases depends upon how big the force is and over what distance the collision takes place. To make this simpler, consider a constant force acting on two blocks as in Figure 2.96.

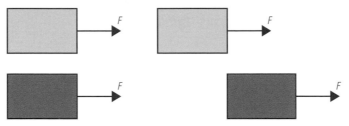

Both blocks start at rest and are pulled by the same force, but the orange block will gain more velocity because the force acts over a longer distance. To quantify this difference, we say that in the case of the orange block the force has done more work. Work is done when the point of application of a force moves in the direction of the force.

Work is defined in the following way:

Work done = force × distance moved in the direction of the force.

The unit of work is the newton metre (N m) which is the same as the joule (J).

Work is a scalar quantity.

Worked example

A tractor pulls a felled tree along the ground for a distance of 200 m. If the tractor exerts a force of 5000 N, how much work will be done?

Figure 2.97.

Solution

Work done = force × distance moved in direction of force

$$\text{Work done} = 5000 \times 200 = 1 \text{ MJ}$$

Worked example

A force of 10 N is applied to a block, pulling it 50 m along the ground as shown in Figure 2.98. How much work is done by the force?

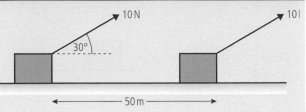

Figure 2.98.

Solution

In this example the force is not in the same direction as the movement. However, the horizontal component of the force is.

$$\text{Work done} = 10 \times \cos 30° \times 50 = 433 \text{ N}$$

Worked example

When a car brakes it slows down due to the friction force between the tyres and the road. This force opposes the motion as shown in Figure 2.99. If the friction force is a constant 500 N and the car comes to rest in 25 m, how much work is done by the friction force?

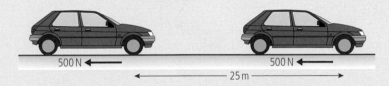

Figure 2.99 Work done against friction.

Solution

This time the force is in the opposite direction to the motion.

$$\text{Work done} = -500 \times 25 = -12\,500 \text{ J}$$

The negative sign tells us that the friction isn't doing the work but the work is being done against the friction.

Worked example

The woman in Figure 2.100 walks along with a constant velocity holding a suitcase.
How much work is done by the force holding the case?

Figure 2.100.

Solution

In this example the force is acting perpendicular to the direction of motion, so there is no movement in the direction of the force.

$$\text{Work done} = \text{zero}$$

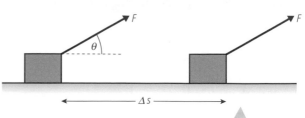

General formula

In general

$$\text{Work} = F \cos \theta \times \Delta s$$

where θ is the angle between the displacement, Δs, and force, F (see Figure 2.101).

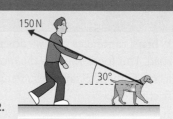

Figure 2.101.

All the previous examples can be solved using this formula.

If $\theta < 90°$, $\cos \theta$ is positive so the work is positive.

$\theta = 90°$, $\cos \theta = 0$ so the work is zero.

$\theta > 90°$, $\cos \theta$ is negative so the work is negative.

Exercises

41 Figure 2.102 shows a boy taking a dog for a walk.

   (a) Calculate the work done by the force shown when the dog moves 10 m forward.
   (b) Who is doing the work?

Figure 2.102.

42 A bird weighing 200 g sits on a tree branch. How much work does the bird do on the tree?

43 As a box slides along the floor it is slowed down by a constant force due to friction. If this force is 150 N and the box slides for 2 m, how much work is done against the frictional force?

Graphical method for determining work done

Let us consider a constant force acting in the direction of movement pulling a body a distance Δx. The graph of force against distance for this example is simply as shown in Figure 2.103. From the definition of work we know that work done = $F\Delta x$ which in this case is the area under the graph. From this we can deduce that:

work done = area under force *vs* distance graph

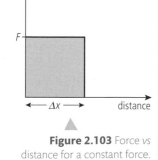

Figure 2.103 Force *vs* distance for a constant force.

Work done by a varying force

Stretching a spring is a common example of a varying force. When you stretch a spring it gets more and more difficult the longer it gets. Within certain limits the force needed to stretch the spring is directly proportional to the extension of the spring. This was first recognised by Robert Hooke in 1676, so is named 'Hooke's Law'. Figure 2.104 shows what happens if we add different weights to a spring: the more weight we add the longer it gets. If we draw a graph of force against distance as we stretch a spring, it will look like the graph in Figure 2.105. The gradient of this line, $\frac{F}{\Delta x}$ is called the spring constant, k.

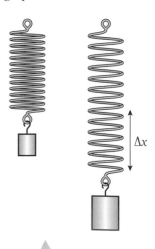

Figure 2.104 Stretching a spring.

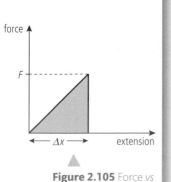

Figure 2.105 Force *vs* extension for a spring.

The work done as the spring is stretched is found by calculating the area under the graph.

$$\text{area} = \tfrac{1}{2}\text{base} \times \text{height} = \tfrac{1}{2}F\Delta x$$

So $$\text{work done} = \tfrac{1}{2}F\Delta x$$

But if $$\frac{F}{\Delta x} = k \text{ then } F = k\Delta x$$

Substituting for F gives

$$\text{work done} = \tfrac{1}{2}k\Delta x^2$$

Exercises

44 A spring of spring constant $2\,N\,cm^{-1}$ and length $6\,cm$ is stretched to a new length of $8\,cm$.

 (a) How far has the spring been stretched?
 (b) What force will be needed to hold the spring at this length?
 (c) Sketch a graph of force against extension for this spring.
 (d) Calculate the work done in stretching the spring.
 (e) The spring is now stretched a further $2\,cm$. Draw a line on your graph to represent this and calculate how much additional work has been done.

45 Calculate the work done by the force represented by Figure 2.106.

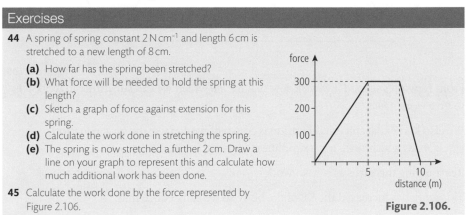

Figure 2.106.

Energy

We have seen that it is sometimes possible for body A to do work on body B but what does A have that enables it to do work on B? To answer this question we must define a new quantity, energy.

Energy is the quantity that enables body A to do work on body B.

If body A collides with body B as shown in Figure 2.107, body A has done work on body B. This means that body B can now do work on body C. Energy has been transferred from A to B.

When body A does work on body B, energy is transferred from body A to body B.

The unit of energy is the joule (J).

Energy is a scalar quantity.

Different types of energy

If a body can do work then it has energy. There are two ways that a simple body such as a red ball can do work. In the example above, body A could do work because it was moving – this is called *kinetic energy*. Figure 2.108 shows an example where A can do work even though it isn't moving. In this example, body A is able to do work on body B because of its position above the Earth. If the hand is removed, body A will be pulled downwards by the force of gravity, and the string attached to it will then drag B along the table. If a body is able to do work because of its position, we say it has *potential energy*.

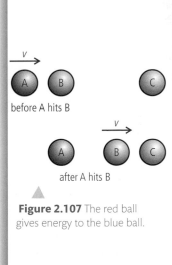

Figure 2.107 The red ball gives energy to the blue ball.

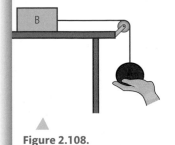

Figure 2.108.

Kinetic energy (KE)

This is the energy a body has due to its movement. To give a body KE, work must be done on the body. The amount of work done will be equal to the increase in KE. If a constant force acts on a red ball of mass m as shown in Figure 2.109, then the work done is Fs.

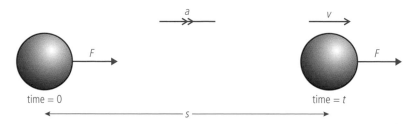

Figure 2.109.

From Newton's second law we know that $F = ma$ which we can substitute in work = Fs to give work = mas.

We also know that since acceleration is constant we can use the *suvat* equation $v^2 = u^2 + 2as$ which since $u = 0$ simplifies to $v^2 = 2as$.

Rearranging this gives $as = \frac{v^2}{2}$ so work = $\frac{1}{2}mv^2$.

This work has increased the KE of the body so we can deduce that:

$$KE = \tfrac{1}{2}mv^2$$

Gravitational potential energy (PE)

This is the energy a body has due to its position above the Earth.

For a body to have PE it must have at some time been lifted to that position. The amount of work done in lifting it equals the PE. Taking the example shown in Figure 2.110, the work done in lifting the mass, m, to a height h is mgh (this assumes that the body is moving at a constant velocity so the lifting force and weight are balanced).

If work is done on the body then energy is transferred so:

$$\text{gain in PE} = mgh$$

The law of conservation of energy

We could not have derived the equations for KE or PE without assuming that the work done is the same as the gain in energy. The law of conservation of energy is a formal statement of this fact.

Energy can neither be created nor destroyed – it can only be changed from one form to another.

This law is one of the most important laws that we use in physics. If it were not true you could suddenly find yourself at the top of the stairs without having done any work in climbing them, or a car suddenly has a speed of $200 \, \text{km h}^{-1}$ without anyone touching the accelerator pedal. These things just don't happen, so the laws we use to describe the physical world should reflect that.

Worked example

A ball of mass 200 g is thrown vertically upwards
with a velocity of $2\,\text{m s}^{-1}$ as shown in Figure 2.110.
Use the law of conservation of energy to calculate its
maximum height.

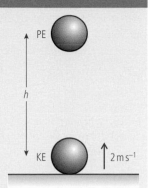

Figure 2.110 Work is done
lifting the ball so it gains PE.

Solution

At the start of its motion the body has KE. This enables the body to do work against
gravity as the ball travels upwards. When the ball reaches the top, all the KE has been
converted into PE. So applying the law of conservation of energy:

$$\text{loss of KE} = \text{gain in PE}$$

$$\tfrac{1}{2}mv^2 = mgh$$

so

$$h = \frac{v^2}{2g} = \frac{2^2}{2 \times 10} = 0.2\,\text{m}$$

This is exactly the same answer you would get by calculating the acceleration from
$F = ma$ and using the *suvat* equations.

Worked example

A block slides down the frictionless ramp shown in
Figure 2.111. Use the law of conservation of energy
to find its speed when it gets to the bottom.

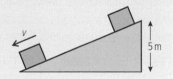

Figure 2.111 As the block slides
down the slope it gains KE.

Solution

This time the body loses PE and gains KE so applying the law of conservation of
energy:

$$\text{loss of PE} = \text{gain of KE}$$

$$mgh = \tfrac{1}{2}mv^2$$

So

$$v = \sqrt{2gh} = \sqrt{(2 \times 10 \times 5)} = 10\,\text{m s}^{-1}$$

Again, this is a much simpler way of getting the answer than using components of
the forces.

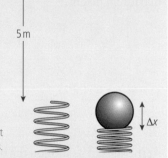

Exercises

Use the law of conservation of energy to solve the following:

46 A stone of mass 500 g is thrown off the top of a cliff with a speed of 5 m s⁻¹. If the cliff is 50 m high, what is its speed just before it hits the ground?

47 A ball of mass 250 g is dropped 5 m onto a spring as shown in Figure 2.112.

    (a) How much KE will the ball have when it hits the spring?
    (b) How much work will be done as the spring is compressed?
    (c) If the spring constant is 250 kN m⁻¹, calculate how far the spring will be compressed.

Figure 2.112 In this example the spring is compressed, not stretched, but Hooke's law still applies.

48 A ball of mass 100 g is hit vertically upwards with a bat. The bat exerts a constant force of 15 N on the ball and is in contact with it for a distance of 5 cm.

    (a) How much work does the bat do on the ball?
    (b) How high will the ball go?

49 A child pushes a toy car of mass 200 g up a slope. The car has a speed of 2 m s⁻¹ at the bottom of the slope.

    (a) How high up the slope will the car go?
    (b) If the speed of the car were doubled how high would it go now?

Forms of energy

When we are describing the motion of simple red balls there are only two forms of energy, KE and PE. However, when we start to look at more complicated systems, we discover that we can do work using a variety of different machines, such as petrol engine, electric engine, etc. To do work, these machines must be given energy and this can come in many forms, for example:

• Petrol   • Solar   • Gas   • Nuclear   • Electricity

As you learn more about the nature of matter in Chapter 3, you will discover that all of these (except solar) are related to either KE or PE of particles.

Energy conversion

Taking the example of a petrol engine, the energy stored in the petrol is converted to mechanical energy of the car by the engine. 1 litre of petrol contains 36 MJ of energy. Let's calculate how far a car could travel at a constant 36 km h⁻¹ on 1 litre of fuel; that's pretty slow but 36 km h⁻¹ is 10 m s⁻¹ so it will make the calculation easier.

The reason a car needs to use energy when travelling at a constant speed is because of air resistance. If we look at the forces acting on the car we see that there must be a constant forwards force (provided by the friction between tyres and road) to balance the air resistance or drag force.

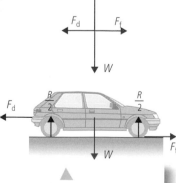

Figure 2.113 The forces acting on a car travelling at constant velocity.

So work is done against the drag force and the energy to do this work comes from the petrol. The amount of work done = force × distance travelled. So to calculate the work done we need to know the drag force on a car travelling at 36 km h⁻¹. One way to do this would be to drive along a flat road at a constant 36 km h⁻¹ and then take your foot off the accelerator pedal. The car would then slow down because of the unbalanced drag force.

This force will get less as the car slows down but here we will assume it is constant. From Newton's second law we know that $F = ma$ so if we can measure how fast the car slows down we can calculate the force. This will depend on the make of car but to reduce the speed by $1\,\mathrm{m\,s^{-1}}$ (about $4\,\mathrm{km\,h^{-1}}$) would take about $2\,\mathrm{s}$. Now we can do the calculation:

$$\text{acceleration of car} = \frac{(v - u)}{t} = \frac{(9 - 10)}{2} = -0.5\,\mathrm{m\,s^{-2}}$$

$$\text{drag force} = ma = 1000 \times -0.5 = -500\,\mathrm{N}.$$

So to keep the car moving at a constant velocity this force would need to be balanced by an equal and opposite force $F = 500\,\mathrm{N}$.

Work done = force × distance so the distance travelled by the car $= \dfrac{\text{work done}}{\text{force}}$.

So if all of the energy in 1 litre of fuel is converted to work the car will move a distance $= \frac{36 \times 10^6}{500} = 72\,\mathrm{km}$. Note that if you reduce the drag force on the car you increase the distance it can travel on 1 litre of fuel.

Efficiency

A very efficient road car driven carefully wouldn't be able to drive much further than 20 km on 1 litre of fuel so energy must be lost somewhere. One place where the energy is lost is in doing work against the friction that exists between the moving parts of the engine. Using oil and grease will reduce this but it can never be eliminated. The efficiency of an engine is defined by the equation

$$\textbf{efficiency} = \frac{\textbf{useful work out}}{\textbf{total energy in}}$$

so if a car travels 20 km at a speed of $10\,\mathrm{m\,s^{-1}}$ the useful work done by the engine

$$= \text{force} \times \text{distance} = 500 \times 20000 = 10\,\mathrm{MJ}.$$

The total energy put in = 36 MJ so the efficiency $= \frac{10}{36} = 0.28$.

Efficiency is often expressed as a percentage so this would be 28%.

Where does all the energy go?

In this example we calculated the energy required to move a car along a flat road. The car was travelling at a constant speed so there was no increase in KE and the road was flat so there was no increase in PE. We know that energy cannot be created or destroyed so where has the energy gone? The answer is that it has been given to the particles that make up the air and car. More about that in Chapter 3.

Exercises

50 A 45% efficient machine lifts 100 kg 2 m.

   (a) How much work is done by the machine?
   (b) How much energy is used by the machine?

51 A 1000 kg car accelerates uniformly from rest to $100\,\mathrm{km\,h^{-1}}$.

   (a) Ignoring air resistance and friction, calculate how much work was done by the car's engine.
   (b) If the car is 60% efficient how much energy in the form of fuel was given to the engine?
   (c) If the fuel contains 36 MJ per litre, how many litres of fuel were used?

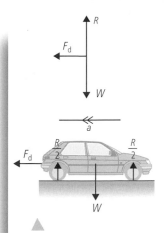

Figure 2.114 The forces on a car travelling at high speed with the foot off the accelerator pedal.

There has been a lot of research into making cars more efficient so that they use less fuel. Is this to save energy or money?

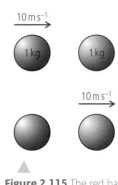

Figure 2.115 The red ball gives energy to the blue ball.

Energy and collisions

One of the reasons that we brought up the concept of energy was related to the collision between two balls as shown in Figure 2.115. We now know that if no energy is lost when the balls collide, then the KE before the collision = KE after. This enables us to calculate the velocity afterwards and the only solution in this example is quite a simple one. The red ball gives all its KE to the blue one, so the red one stops and the blue one continues, with velocity = $10\,\text{m}\,\text{s}^{-1}$. If the balls become squashed, then some work needs to be done to squash them. In this case not all the KE is transferred, and we can only calculate the outcome if we know how much energy is used in squashing the balls.

Elastic collisions

An elastic collision is a collision in which both momentum and KE are conserved.

Example: two balls with equal mass

Two balls with equal mass m collide as shown in Figure. 2.116. As you can see, the red ball is travelling faster than the blue one before and slower after. If the collision is perfectly elastic then we can show that the velocities of the balls simply swap so $u_1 = v_2$ and $u_2 = v_1$.

Figure 2.116 Collision between 2 identical balls..

If the collision is elastic then momentum and kinetic energy are both conserved. If we consider these one at a time we get:

Conservation of momentum:

$$\text{momentum before} = \text{momentum after}$$
$$mu_1 + mu_2 = mv_1 + mv_2$$
$$u_1 + u_2 = v_1 + v_2$$

Conservation of KE:

$$\text{KE before} = \text{KE after}$$
$$\tfrac{1}{2}mu_1^2 + \tfrac{1}{2}mu_2^2 = \tfrac{1}{2}mv_1^2 + \tfrac{1}{2}mv_2^2$$
$$u_1^2 + u_2^2 = v_1^2 + v_2^2$$

So we can see that the velocities are such that both their sums are equal and the squares of their sums are equal. This is only true if the velocities swap, as in Figure 2.117.

Figure 2.117 A possible elastic collision.

Collision in 2D between 2 identical balls

Anyone who has ever played pool or snooker will know that balls don't always collide in line, they travel at *angles* to each other. Figure 2.118 shows a possible collision.

Figure 2.118 A 2D collision.

In this case the blue ball is stationary so applying the conservation laws we get slightly simpler equations:

$$\vec{u} = \vec{v}_1 + \vec{v}_2$$
$$\vec{u}^2 = \vec{v}_1^2 + \vec{v}_2^2$$

Note the vector notation to remind us that we are dealing with vectors. The first equation means that the sum of the velocity vectors after the collision gives the velocity before. This can be represented by the triangle of vectors in Figure 2.119.

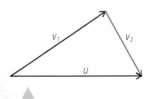

Figure 2.119 Adding the velocity vectors.

The second equation tells us that the sum of the squares of two sides of this triangle = the square of the other side. This is Pythagoras' theorem which is only true for right-angled triangles. So, after an elastic collision between two identical balls the two balls will always travel away at right angles (unless the collision is perfectly head on). This of course doesn't apply to balls rolling on a pool table since they are not isolated.

Inelastic collisions

There are many outcomes of an inelastic collision but here we will only consider the case when the two bodies stick together. We call this *totally inelastic collision*.

Pool balls may not collide like perfectly elastic isolated spheres but if the table is included their motion can be accurately modelled enabling scientists to calculate the correct direction and speed for the perfect shot. Taking that shot is another matter entirely.

Example

When considering the conservation of momentum in collisions, we used the example shown in Figure 2.120. How much work was done to squash the balls in this example?

Figure 2.120.

According to the law of conservation of energy, the work done squashing the balls is equal to the loss in KE.

KE loss = KE before − KE after = $\frac{1}{2} \times 0.1 \times 6^2 - \frac{1}{2} \times 0.6 \times 1^2$

KE loss = $1.8 - 0.3 = 1.5$ J

So   work done = 1.5 J

Explosions

Explosions can never be elastic since, without doing work, the parts that fly off after the explosion would not have any KE and would therefore not be moving. The energy to initiate an explosion often comes from the chemical energy contained in the explosive.

Example

Again consider a previous example where a ball exploded (shown again in Figure 2.121). How much energy was supplied to the balls by the explosive?

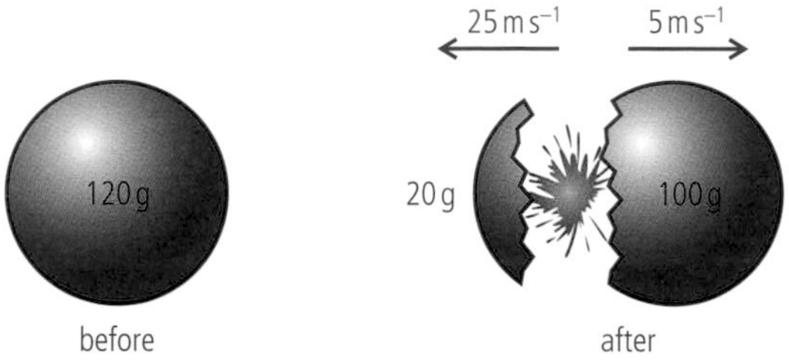

before   after

Figure 2.121.

According to the law of conservation of energy, the energy from the explosive equals the gain in KE of the balls.

$$\text{KE gain} = \text{KE after} - \text{KE before}$$

$$\text{KE gain} = (\tfrac{1}{2} \times 0.02 \times 25^2 + \tfrac{1}{2} \times 0.1 \times 5^2) - 0 = 6.25 + 1.25 = 7.5\,\text{J}$$

Sharing of energy

The result of this example is very important; we will use it when dealing with nuclear decay later on. So remember, when a body explodes into two unequal bits, the small bit gets most energy.

CHALLENGE YOURSELF

2 A 200 g red ball travelling at 6 m s^{-1} collides with a 500 g blue ball at rest, such that after the collision the red ball travels at 4 m s^{-1} at an angle of 45° to its original direction. Calculate the speed of the blue ball.

Exercises

52 Two balls are held together by a spring as shown in Figure 2.122. The spring has a spring constant of 10 N cm^{-1} and has been compressed a distance 5 cm.

Figure 2.122.

(a) How much work was done to compress the spring?
(b) How much KE will each gain?
(c) If each ball has a mass of 10 g calculate the velocity of each ball.

53 Two pieces of modelling clay as shown in Figure 2.123 collide and stick together.

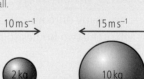

Figure 2.123.

(a) Calculate the velocity of the lump after the collision.
(b) How much KE is lost during the collision?

54 A red ball travelling at 10 m s^{-1} to the right collides with a blue ball with the same mass travelling at 15 m s^{-1} to the left. If the collision is elastic, what are the velocities of the balls after the collision?

Power

Power and velocity

If   power = $\frac{\text{work done}}{\text{time}}$

then we can also write

$$P = \frac{F\Delta s}{t}$$

so $P = F\frac{\Delta s}{t}$

which is the same as

$$P = Fv$$

where v is the velocity.

We know that to do work requires energy, but work can be done quickly or it can be done slowly. This does not alter the energy exchanged but the situations are certainly different. For example we know that to lift one thousand 1 kg bags of sugar from the floor to the table is not an impossible task – we can simply lift them one by one. It will take a long time but we would manage it in the end. However, if we were asked to do the same task in 5 seconds, we would either have to lift all 1000 kg at the same time or move each bag in 0.005 s, both of which are impossible. Power is the quantity that distinguishes between these two tasks.

Power is defined as:

power = work done per unit time.

Unit of power is the $J\,s^{-1}$ which is the same as the watt (W).

Power is a scalar quantity.

Example 1: The powerful car

We often use the term power to describe cars. A powerful car is one that can accelerate from 0 to $100\,km\,h^{-1}$ in a very short time. When a car accelerates, energy is being converted from the chemical energy in the fuel to KE. To have a big acceleration the car must gain KE in a short time, hence be powerful.

Example 2: Power lifter

A power lifter is someone who can lift heavy weights, so shouldn't we say they are strong people rather than powerful? A power lifter certainly is a strong person (if they are good at it) but they are also powerful. This is because they can lift a big weight in a short time.

Worked example

A car of mass $1000\,kg$ accelerates from rest to $100\,km\,h^{-1}$ in 5 seconds. What is the average power of the car?

Solution

$$100\,km\,h^{-1} = 28\,m\,s^{-1}.$$

The gain in KE of the car $= \frac{1}{2}mv^2 = \frac{1}{2} \times 1000 \times 28^2 = 392\,kJ$

If the car does this in $5\,s$ then

$$\text{power} = \frac{\text{work done}}{\text{time}} = \frac{392}{5} = 78.4\,kW$$

Horse power

Horse power is often used as the unit for power when talking about cars and boats.

$746\,W = 1\,hp$

So in Worked example 1, the power of the car is $105\,hp$.

Exercises

55 A weightlifter lifts $200\,kg$ $2\,m$ above the ground in $5\,s$. Calculate the power of the weightlifter in watts.

56 In $25\,s$ a trolley of mass $50\,kg$ runs down a hill. If the difference in height between the top and the bottom of the hill is $50\,m$, how much power will have been dissipated?

57 A car moves along a road at a constant velocity of $20\,ms^{-1}$. If the resistance force acting against the car is $1000\,N$, what is the power developed by the engine?

Efficiency and power

We have define efficiency by the equation:

$$\text{efficiency} = \frac{\text{useful work out}}{\text{work in}}$$

If the work out is done at the same time as the work in then we can also write:

$$\text{efficiency} = \frac{\text{useful power out}}{\text{total power in}}$$

Exercises

58 A motor is used to lift a $10\,kg$ mass $2\,m$ above the ground in $4\,s$. If the power input to the motor is $100\,W$, what is the efficiency of the motor?

59 A motor is 70% efficient. If $60\,kJ$ of energy is put into the engine, how much work is got out?

60 The drag force that resists the motion of a car travelling at $80\,km\,h^{-1}$ is $300\,N$.

    (a) What power is required to keep the car travelling at that speed?

    (b) If the efficiency of the engine is 60%, what is the power of the engine?

Practice questions

1. This question is about linear motion.

    A police car P is stationary by the side of a road. A car S, exceeding the speed limit, passes the police car P at a constant speed of $18\,\mathrm{m\,s^{-1}}$. The police car P sets off to catch car S just as car S passes the police car P. Car P accelerates at $4.5\,\mathrm{m\,s^{-2}}$ for a time of $6.0\,\mathrm{s}$ and then continues at constant speed. Car P takes a time t seconds to draw level with car S.

    (a) (i) State an expression, in terms of t, for the distance car S travels in t seconds. (1)

        (ii) Calculate the distance travelled by the police car P during the first 6.0 seconds of its motion. (1)

        (iii) Calculate the speed of the police car P after it has completed its acceleration. (1)

        (iv) State an expression, in terms of t, for the distance travelled by the police car P during the time that it is travelling at constant speed. (1)

    (b) Using your answers to (a), determine the total time t taken for the police car P to draw level with car S. (2)

    (Total 6 marks)

2. This question is about the kinematics of an elevator (lift).

    (a) Explain the difference between the gravitational mass and the inertial mass of an object. (3)

    An elevator (lift) starts from rest on the ground floor and comes to rest at a higher floor. Its motion is controlled by an electric motor. Figure 2.124 is a simplified graph of the variation of the elevator's velocity with time.

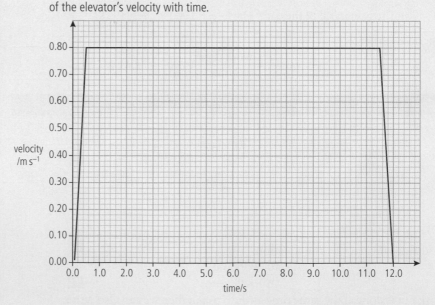

    Figure 2.124.

    (b) The mass of the elevator is $250\,\mathrm{kg}$. Use this information to calculate:

    (i) the acceleration of the elevator during the first 0.50 s. (2)

    (ii) the total distance travelled by the elevator. (2)

    (iii) the minimum work required to raise the elevator to the higher floor. (2)

    (iv) the minimum average power required to raise the elevator to the higher floor. (2)

(v) the efficiency of the electric motor that lifts the elevator, given that the input power to the motor is 5.0 kW. (2)

(c) Copy Figure 2.125 and, on the graph axes, sketch a realistic variation of velocity for the elevator. Explain your reasoning. *(The simplified version is shown as a dotted line.)*

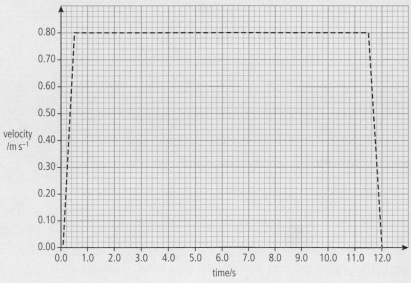

Figure 2.125.

(2)

The elevator is supported by a cable. Figure 2.126 is a free body force diagram for when the elevator is moving upwards during the first 0.50 s.

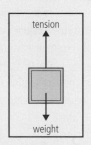

Figure 2.126.

(d) Copy Figures 2.127 and 2.128 and in the space below each box, draw free body force diagrams for the elevator during the following time intervals.

(i) 0.5 to 11.50 s

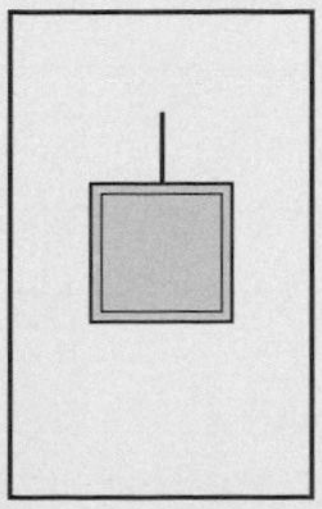

(ii) 11.50 to 12.00 s

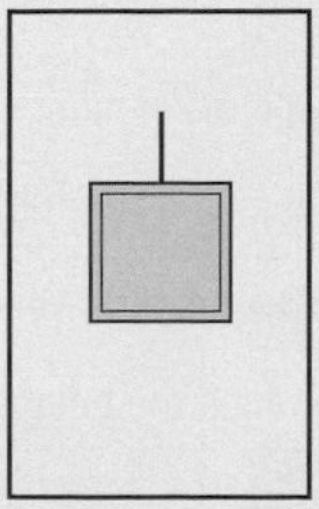

Figure 2.127.   **Figure 2.128.** (3)

A person is standing on weighing scales in the elevator. Before the elevator rises, the reading on the scales is W.

(e) Copy Figure 2.129 and on the axes, sketch a graph to show how the reading on the scales varies during the whole 12.00 s upward journey of the elevator. *(Note that this is a sketch graph – you do not need to add any values.)*

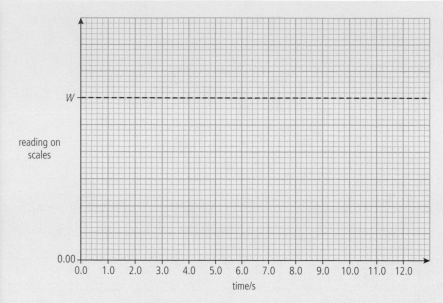

Figure 2.129.

(3)

(f) The elevator now returns to the ground floor where it comes to rest. Describe and explain the energy changes that take place during the whole up-and-down journey. (4)

(*Total 25 marks*)

3. This question is about throwing a stone from a cliff. Antonia stands at the edge of a vertical cliff and throws a stone vertically upwards.
The stone leaves Antonia's hand with a speed $v = 8.0\,\text{m s}^{-1}$.
The acceleration of free fall g is $10\,\text{m s}^{-2}$ and all distance measurements are taken from the point where the stone leaves Antonia's hand.

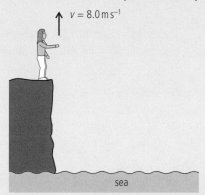

Figure 2.130.

(a) Ignoring air resistance calculate:

(i) the maximum height reached by the stone. (2)

(ii) the time taken by the stone to reach its maximum height. (1)

The time between the stone leaving Antonia's hand and hitting the sea is 3.0 s.

(b) Determine the height of the cliff. (3)

(*Total 6 marks*)

4. This question is about conservation of momentum and conservation of energy.

(a) State Newton's third law. (1)

(b) State the law of conservation of momentum. (2)

Figure 2.131 shows two identical balls A and B on a horizontal surface. Ball B is at rest and ball A is moving with speed V along a line joining the centres of the balls. The mass of each ball is M.

before collision

Figure 2.131.

During the collision of the balls, the magnitude of the force that ball A exerts on ball B is F_{AB} and the magnitude of the force that ball B exerts on ball A is F_{BA}.

(c) Copy Figure 2.132 and on the diagram, add labelled arrows to represent the magnitude and direction of the forces F_{AB} and F_{BA}.

during the collision

Figure 2.132.

(3)

The balls are in contact for a time Δt. After the collision, the speed of ball A is $+ v_A$ and the speed of ball B is $+ v_B$ in the directions shown in Figure 2.133.

after the collision

Figure 2.133.

As a result of the collision, there is a change in momentum of ball A and of ball B.

(d) Use Newton's second law of motion to deduce an expression relating the forces acting during the collision to the change in momentum of

　(i) ball B. (2)

　(ii) ball A. (2)

(e) Apply Newton's third law and your answers to (d), to deduce that the change in momentum of the system (ball A and ball B) as a result of this collision, is zero. (4)

(f) Deduce, that if kinetic energy is conserved in the collision, then after the collision ball A will come to rest and ball B will move with speed V. (3)

5. This question is about the collision between two railway trucks (carts).

(a) Define *linear momentum*. (1)

In Figure 2.134, railway truck A is moving along a horizontal track. It collides with a stationary truck B and on collision, the two join together. Immediately before the collision, truck A is moving with speed $5.0 \, \text{m s}^{-1}$. Immediately after collision, the speed of the trucks is v.

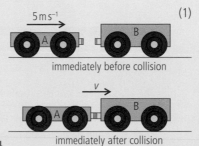

immediately before collision

immediately after collision

Figure 2.134.

The mass of truck A is 800 kg and the mass of truck B is 1200 kg.

　(b) (i) Calculate the speed v immediately after the collision. (3)

　　(ii) Calculate the total kinetic energy lost during the collision. (2)

(c) Suggest what has happened to the lost kinetic energy. (2)

(Total 8 marks)

6. This question is about estimating the energy changes for an escalator (moving staircase). Figure 2.135 represents an escalator. People step on to it at point A and step off at point B.

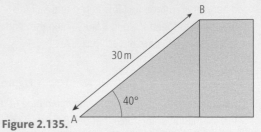

Figure 2.135.

(a) The escalator is 30 m long and makes an angle of 40° with the horizontal. At full capacity, 48 people step on at point A and step off at point B every minute.

   (i)   Calculate the potential energy gained by a person of weight 700 N in moving from A to B. (2)

   (ii) Estimate the energy supplied by the escalator motor to the people every minute when the escalator is working at full capacity. (1)

   (iii) State **one** assumption that you have made to obtain your answer to (ii). (1)

The escalator is driven by an electric motor that has an efficiency of 70%.

(b) (i) Using your answer to (a)(ii), calculate the minimum input power required by the motor to drive the escalator. (3)

    (ii) Explain why it is not necessary to take into account the weight of the escalator when calculating the input power. (1)

(c) Explain why in practice, the power of the motor will need to be greater than that calculated in (b)(i). (1)

(*Total 9 marks*)

7. This question is about collisions.

(a) State the principle of conservation of momentum. (2)

(b) In an experiment, an air-rifle pellet is fired into a block of modelling clay that rests on a table.

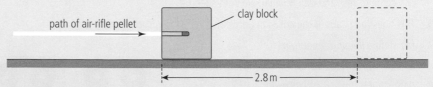

Figure 2.136. (not to scale)

The air-rifle pellet remains inside the clay block after the impact.

As a result of the collision, the clay block slides along the table in a straight line and comes to rest. Further data relating to the experiment are given below.

Mass of air-rifle pellet = 2.0 g
Mass of clay block = 56 g
Velocity of impact of air-rifle pellet = 140 m s⁻¹
Stopping distance of clay block = 2.8 m

   (i)   Show that the initial speed of the clay block after the air-rifle pellet strikes it is 4.8 m s⁻¹. (2)

(ii) Calculate the average frictional force that the surface of the table exerts on the clay block whilst the clay block is moving. (4)

(c) The experiment is repeated with the clay block placed at the edge of the table so that it is fired away from the table. The initial speed of the clay block is 4.3 m s⁻¹ horizontally. The table surface is 0.85 m above the ground.

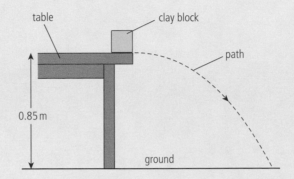

Figure 2.137.
(not to scale)

(i) Ignoring air resistance, calculate the horizontal distance travelled by the clay block before it strikes the ground. (4)

(ii) Figure 2.137 shows the path of the clay block neglecting air resistance. Copy the diagram, and on it, draw the approximate shape of the path that the clay block will take assuming that air resistance acts on the clay block. (3)

(Total 15 marks**)**

03

Thermal physics

Essential ideas

3.1
Thermal concepts
Thermal physics deftly demonstrates the links between the macroscopic measurements essential to many scientific models with the microscopic properties that underlie these models.

3.2
Modelling a gas
The properties of ideal gases allow scientists to make predictions of the behaviour of real gases.

8.2
Thermal energy transfer

NATURE OF SCIENCE

So far we have dealt with the motion of particles and, given their initial conditions, can predict their speed and position at any time. Once we realize that all matter is made up of particles we can use this knowledge to build a model of the way those particles interact with each other. So, even though we can't see these particles we can make predictions related to them.

When a gas is heated it expands making it less dense than the surrounding air. If the balloon is large enough the buoyant force it experiences will be sufficient to lift several people.

3.1 | **Thermal concepts**

3.1 Thermal concepts

Understandings, applications, and skills:

Mole, molar mass, and the Avogadro constant
Internal energy
- Describing temperature change in terms of internal energy.

  Guidance
  - *Internal energy is taken to be the total intermolecular potential energy + the total random kinetic energy of the molecules.*

Temperature and absolute temperature
- Using kelvin and Celsius temperature scales, and converting between them.

Specific heat capacity
- Applying the calorimetric techniques of specific heat capacity or specific latent heat experimentally.

  Guidance
  - *The effects of cooling should be understood qualitatively but cooling correction calculations are not required.*

Phase change
- Describing phase change in terms of molecular behaviour. Sketching and interpreting phase change graphs.

  Guidance
  - *Phase change graphs may have axes of temperature versus time or temperature versus energy.*

Specific latent heat
- Calculating energy changes involving specific heat capacity and specific latent heat of fusion and vaporisation.

8.2 Thermal energy transfer

Understandings, applications, and skills:

Conduction, convection, and thermal radiation
• Discussion of conduction and convection will be qualitative only

Guidance
• *Discussion of conduction is limited to intermolecular and electron collisions.*
• *Discussion of convection is limited to simple gas or liquid transfer via density difference.*
• *The absorption of infrared radiation by greenhouse gases should be described in terms of the molecular energy levels and the subsequent emission of radiation in all directions.*

The role of the physicist is to observe our physical surroundings, take measurements and think of ways to explain what we see. Up to this point in the course we have been dealing with the motion of bodies. We can describe bodies in terms of their mass and volume, and if we know their speed and the forces that act on them, we can calculate where they will be at any given time. We even know what happens if two bodies hit each other. However, this is not enough to describe all the differences between objects. For example, by simply holding different objects, we can feel that some are hot and some are cold.

In this chapter we will develop a model to explain these differences, but first of all we need to know what is inside matter.

The particle model of matter

Ancient Greek philosophers spent a lot of time thinking about what would happen if they took a piece of cheese and kept cutting it in half.

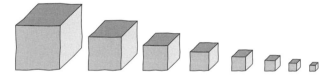

Figure 3.1 Can we keep cutting the cheese for ever?

They didn't think it was possible to keep halving it for ever, so they suggested that there must exist a smallest part – this they called the *atom*.

Atoms are too small to see (about 10^{-10} m in diameter) but we can think of them as very small perfectly elastic balls. This means that when they collide, both momentum and kinetic energy are conserved.

Elements and compounds

We might ask: 'If everything is made of atoms, why isn't everything the same?' The answer is that there are many different types of atom.

There are 117 different types of atom, and a material made of just one type of atom is called an *element*. There are, however, many more than 117 different types of material. The other types of matter are made of atoms that have joined together to form molecules. Materials made from molecules that contain more than one type of atom are called *compounds*.

How do we know atoms have different masses?

The answer to that question is thanks originally to the chemists, John Dalton in particular. Chemists make compounds from elements by mixing them in very precise

 hydrogen atom

 gold atom

Figure 3.2 Gold is made of gold atoms and hydrogen is made of hydrogen atoms.

proportions. This is quite complicated but we can consider a simplified version as shown in Figure 3.3. An atom of A joins with an atom of B to form molecule AB.

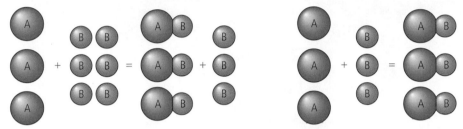

Figure 3.3 Atoms join to make a molecule.

TOK This is a good example of how models are used in physics. Here we are modelling something that we can't see, the atom, using a familiar object, a perfectly elastic ball.

We first try by mixing the same masses of A and B but find that when the reaction has finished there is some B left over; we must have had too many atoms of B. If we reduce the amount of B until all the A reacts with all the B to form AB we know that there must have been the same number of atoms of A as there were of B as shown in Figure 3.4. We can therefore conclude that the mass of an A atom is larger than an atom of B. In fact the ratio of

$$\frac{\text{mass of atom A}}{\text{mass of atom B}} = \frac{\text{total mass A}}{\text{total mass B}}.$$

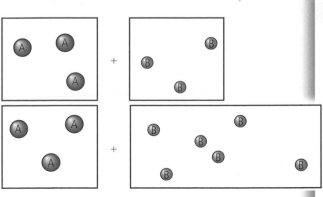

equal masses of A and B   equal number of atoms of A and B

Figure 3.4 To combine completely there must be equal numbers of atoms.

By finding out the ratio of masses in many different reactions the atomic mass of the elements relative to each other was measured. Originally everything was compared to oxygen since it reacts with so many other atoms. Later, when physicists started to measure the mass of individual atoms the standard atom was changed to carbon-12. This is taken to have an atomic mass of exactly 12 unified mass units (u), the size of 1 u is therefore equal to $\frac{1}{12}$ of the mass of a carbon-12 atom, which is approximately the mass of the smallest atom, hydrogen.

Avogadro's hypothesis

The simplified version of chemistry given here does not give the full picture: for one thing, atoms don't always join in pairs. Maybe one A joins with two Bs. Without knowing the ratio of how many atoms of B join with one atom of A we can't calculate the relative masses of the individual atoms. Amedeo Avogadro solved this problem by suggesting that equal volumes of all gases at the same temperature and pressure will contain the same number of molecules. So if one atom of A and one atom of B join to give one molecule AB then the number of molecules of AB is equal to the number of atoms of A or B and the volume of AB = $\frac{1}{2}$(A + B); but if one atom of A joins with two atoms of B then the volume of B atoms is twice the volume of the A atoms, and the volume of AB$_2$ = the volume of A. This is illustrated in Figure 3.5.

ⓘ The volume of 1 mole of any gas at normal atmospheric pressure (101.3 kPa) and a temperature of 0°C is 22.4 litres (L).

Figure 3.5 Equal volumes of gases contain the same number of molecules.

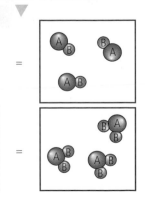

The mole and Avogadro's constant

It can be shown that 12 g of carbon-12 contains 6.02×10^{23} atoms. This amount of material is called a mole; this number of atoms is called Avogadro's constant (N_A) (named after him but not calculated by him). If we take 6.02×10^{23} molecules of a substance that has molecules that are four times the mass of carbon-12 atoms it would have relative molecular mass of 48. 6.02×10^{23} molecules of this substance would

Moles of different compounds have different masses.

therefore have a mass four times the mass of the same number of carbon-12 atoms, 48 g. So, to calculate the mass of a mole of any substance we simply express its relative molecular mass in grams. This gives us a convenient way of measuring the amount of substance in terms of the number of molecules rather than its mass.

Worked example

If a mole of carbon has a mass of 12 g, how many atoms of carbon are there in 2 g?

Solution

One mole contains 6.022×10^{23} atoms.

2 g is $\frac{1}{6}$ of a mole so contains $\frac{1}{6} \times 6.022 \times 10^{23}$ atoms $= 1.004 \times 10^{23}$ atoms

Worked example

Be careful with the units. Do all calculations using m³.

The density of iron is $7874 \, \text{kg m}^{-3}$ and the mass of a mole of iron is 55.85 g. What is the volume of 1 mole of iron?

Solution

$$\text{density} = \frac{\text{mass}}{\text{volume}}$$

$$\text{volume} = \frac{\text{mass}}{\text{density}}$$

$$\text{volume of 1 mole} = \frac{0.05585}{7874} \, \text{m}^3$$

$$= 7.093 \times 10^{-6} \, \text{m}^3$$

$$= 7.093 \, \text{cm}^3$$

The three states of matter

Solid

A solid has a fixed shape and volume so the molecules must have a fixed position.

This means that if we try to pull the molecules apart there will be a force pulling them back together. This force is called the *intermolecular force*. This force is due to a property of the molecules called *charge* which will be dealt with properly in Chapter 6. This force doesn't only hold the particles together but also stops the particles getting too close. It is this force that is responsible for the tension in a string: as the molecules are pulled apart they pull back, and the normal reaction – when the surfaces are pushed together the molecules push back.

attractive forces between molecules pulled apart

repulsive forces between molecules pushed together

Molecules of a solid are not free to move about but they can vibrate.

Liquid

A liquid does not have a fixed shape but does have a fixed volume so the molecules are able to move about but still have an intermolecular force between then. This force is quite large when you try to push the molecules together (a liquid is very difficult to compress) but not so strong when pulling molecules apart (if you throw a bucket of water in the air it doesn't stay together).

When a liquid is put into a container it presses against the sides of the container. This is because of the intermolecular forces between the liquid and the container. At the bottom of the container the molecules are forced together by the weight of liquid above. This results in a bigger force per unit area on the sides of the container; this can

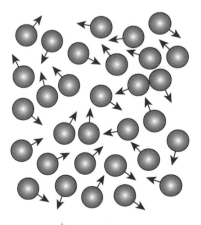

Figure 3.8 Molecules in a liquid.

be demonstrated by drilling holes in the side of the container and watching the water squirt out as shown in Figure 3.9. The pressure under a solid block also depends on the height of the block but this pressure only acts downwards on the ground not outwards or upwards as it does in a fluid.

So the force per unit area, or *pressure*, increases with depth. If you have ever been diving you may have felt this as the water pushed against your ears. The increase in pressure with depth is also the reason why submerged objects experience a buoyant force. If

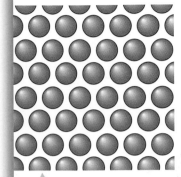

Figure 3.6 Molecules in a solid.

Figure 3.7 Intermolecular force.

The molecules of a liquid are often drawn further apart than molecules of a solid but this isn't always the case; water is an example of the opposite. When ice turns to water it contracts which is why water is more dense than ice and ice floats on water.

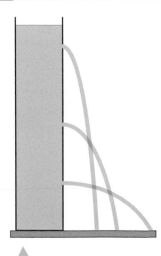

Figure 3.9 Higher pressure at the bottom of the container forces the water out further.

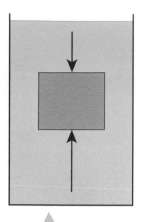

Figure 3.10 The force at the bottom is greater than at the top resulting in a buoyant force.

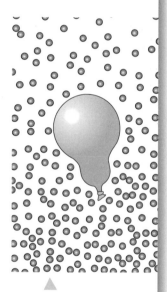

Figure 3.12 The density of air molecules is greater at the bottom of the atmosphere.

Figure 3.13 Smoke particles jiggle about.

you consider the submerged cube shown in Figure 3.10, the bottom surface is deeper than the top so experiences a greater force, resulting in a resultant upward force. Note that this is only the case if the water is in a gravitational field e.g. on the Earth, as it relies on the weight of the water pushing down on the water below.

Gas

A gas does not have fixed shape or volume, it simply fills whatever container it is put into. The molecules of a gas are completely free to move about without any forces between the molecules except when they are colliding.

Since the molecules of a gas are moving they collide with the wall of the container. The change in momentum experienced by the gas molecules means that they must be subjected to an unbalanced force resulting in an equal and opposite force on the container. This results in gas pressure. If the gas is on the Earth then the effect of gravity will cause the gas nearest the ground to be compressed by the gas above. This increases the density of the gas so there are more collisions between the gas molecules and the container, resulting in a higher pressure. The difference between the pressure at the top of an object and the pressure at the bottom results in a buoyant force is illustrated in Figure 3.12.

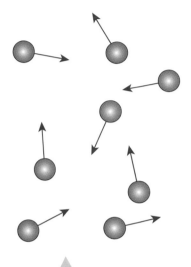

Figure 3.11 Molecules of a gas.

A car moving through air will collide with the air molecules. As the car hits the air molecules it increases their momentum so they must experience a force. The car experiences an equal and opposite force which we call air resistance or *drag*.

Brownian motion

The explanation of the states of matter supports the theory that matter is made of particles but it isn't completely convincing. More solid evidence was found by Robert Brown when, in 1827, he was observing a drop of water containing pollen grains under a microscope. He noticed that the pollen grains had an unusual movement. The particles moved around in an erratic zigzag pattern similar to Figure 3.13. The explanation for this is that they are being hit by the invisible molecules of water that surround the particles. The reason we don't see this random motion in larger objects is because they are being bombarded from all sides so the effect cancels out.

Internal energy

In Chapter 2 we considered a car moving along the road at constant velocity.

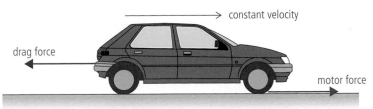

Figure 3.14 Forces on a car moving with constant velocity.

The force of the motor is applied via the friction between the tyres and the road. In this example we calculated the energy transferred from the petrol to the car so the motor is doing work but since the car is not getting any faster or going up a hill it is not gaining any kinetic or potential energy. If we consider the air to be made up of particles we can answer the question of what is happening to the energy and thus gain a better understanding of drag force.

As the car moves through the air it collides with the molecules of air as in Figure 3.15. When a collision is made the car exerts a force on the molecules so according to Newton's third law the car must experience an equal and opposite force. This is the drag force.

As the car moves forward hitting the air molecules it gives them kinetic energy; this is where all the energy is going. We call this *internal energy*, and since gas molecules have no forces between them this energy is all KE.

Another example we could consider is a block sliding down a slope at a constant speed as in Figure 3.16. As it slides down the slope it is losing PE but where is the energy going? This time it is the friction between the block and the slope that provides the answer. As the surfaces rub against each other energy is transferred to the molecules of the block and slope; the rougher the surfaces the more the molecules get bumped about. The effect of all this bumping is to increase the KE of the molecules, but solid molecules can't fly about; they can only vibrate and as they do this they move apart. This moving apart requires energy because the molecules have a force holding them together; the result is an increase in both kinetic and potential energy.

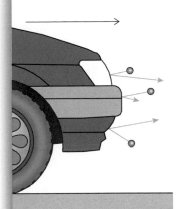

Figure 3.15 The front of the car collides with air molecules.

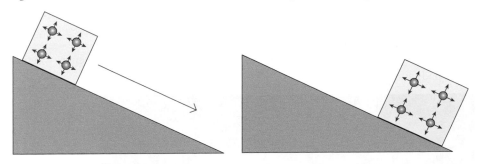

Figure 3.16 A block slides down a slope at constant speed.

Worked example

A 4 kg block slides down the slope at a constant speed of $1\,m\,s^{-1}$ as in Figure 3.17. What is the work done against friction?

Solution

The loss of PE = $mgh = 4 \times 10 \times 3 = 120\,J$.

This energy has not been converted to KE since the speed of the block has not increased. The energy has been given to the internal energy of the slope and block. The work done against friction (friction force × distance travelled in direction of the force) is therefore 120 J. The block is losing energy so this should be negative.

$$\text{Friction} \times 5 = -120\,J$$

$$\text{So friction} = -24\,N$$

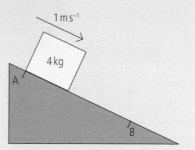
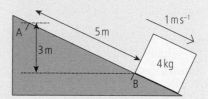

Figure 3.17 A block slides down a slope.

Worked example

A car of mass 1000 kg is travelling at $30\,m\,s^{-1}$. If the brakes are applied, how much heat energy is transferred to the brakes?

Solution

When the car is moving it has kinetic energy. This must be transferred to the brakes when the car stops.

$$KE = \tfrac{1}{2}mv^2$$

$$= \tfrac{1}{2} \times 1000 \times 30^2\,J$$

$$= 450\,kJ$$

So thermal energy transferred to the brakes = 450 kJ

When a car slows down using its brakes, KE will be converted to internal energy in the brake pads and discs.

This thermogram of a car shows how the wheels have become hot owing to friction between the road and the tyres, and the brakes pads and discs.

3   A block of metal, mass 10 kg, is dropped from a
    height of 40 m.

    (a) How much energy does the block have before it
        is dropped?

    (b) How much heat energy do the block and floor
        gain when it hits the floor?

4   If the car in the second Worked example on page
    100 was travelling at 60 m s⁻¹, how much heat energy
    would the brakes receive?

5   A 75 kg free fall parachutist falls at a constant speed of
    50 m s⁻¹. Calculate the amount of energy given to the
    surroundings per second.

6   A block, starting at rest, slides down the slope as
    shown in Figure 3.18. Calculate the amount of work
    done against friction and the size of the friction force.

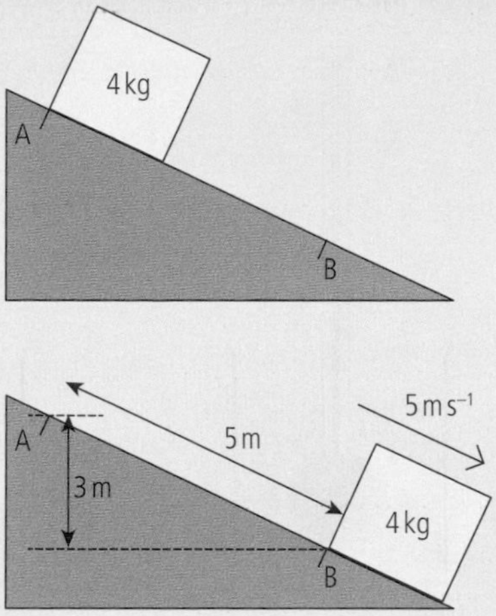

    Figure 3.18.

Internal energy and the three states of matter

Internal energy is the sum of the energy of the molecules of a body. In solids and
liquids there are forces between the molecules so to move them around requires work
to be done (like stretching a spring). The total internal energy of solids and liquids is
therefore made up of kinetic + potential energy. There is no force between molecules
of a gas so changing their position does not require work to be done. The total internal
energy of a gas is therefore only kinetic energy.

Temperature (T)

If we rub our hands together we are doing work since there is movement in the
direction of the applied force. If work is done then energy must be transferred but we
are not increasing the kinetic or potential energy of our hands; we are increasing their
internal energy. As we do this we notice that our hands get hot. This is a sensation that
we perceive through our senses and it seems from this simple experiment to be related
to energy. The harder we rub the hotter our hands become. Before we can go further
we need to define a quantity we can use to measure how hot or cold a body is.

Temperature is a measure of how hot or cold a body is.

When we defined a scale for length we simply took a known length and compared
other lengths to it. With temperature it is not so easy. First we must find some directly
measurable physical quantity that varies with temperature. One possibility is the length
of a metal rod. As the internal energy of a solid temperature increases, the molecules
move faster causing them to move apart. The problem is that the length doesn't change
very much so it isn't easy to measure. A better alternative is to use the change in volume
of a liquid. This also isn't very much but if the liquid is placed into a container with a thin
tube attached as in Figure 3.19 then the change can be quite noticeable.

To define a scale we need two fixed points. In measuring length we use the two
ends of a ruler; in this case we will measure the length of the liquid at two known
temperatures, the boiling and freezing points of pure water. But how do we know
that these events always take place at the same temperatures before we have made our
thermometer? What we can do is place a tube of liquid in many containers of freezing
and boiling water to see if the liquid always has the same lengths. If it does, then we
can deduce that the freezing and boiling temperatures of water are always the same.

TOK We perceive how hot
or cold something is
with our senses but to
quantify this we need a
measurement.

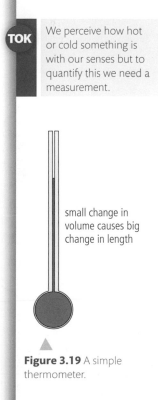

small change in
volume causes big
change in length

Figure 3.19 A simple
thermometer.

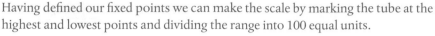

Having defined our fixed points we can make the scale by marking the tube at the highest and lowest points and dividing the range into 100 equal units.

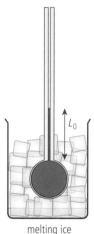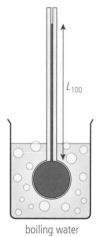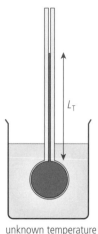

melting ice   boiling water   unknown temperature

Figure 3.20 Calibrating a thermometer.

So if we place the thermometer into water at an unknown temperature resulting in length L_T, then the temperature can be found from:

$$T = \frac{L_T - L_0}{L_{100} - L_0} \times 100$$

This is how the Celsius scale is defined.

Temperature and KE

The reason that a liquid expands when it gets hot is because its molecules vibrate more and move apart. Higher temperature implies faster molecules so the temperature is directly related to the KE of the molecules. However, since the KE of the particles is not zero when ice freezes the KE is not directly proportional to the temperature in °C. The lowest possible temperature is the point at which the KE of molecules becomes zero. This happens at −273°C.

The lowest temperature is −273.15°C, but for conversion purposes we usually find it more convenient to use −273°C.

Kelvin scale

Not all countries use the same units of temperature when describing the weather but the agreed-upon SI unit is the kelvin.

An alternative way to define a temperature scale would be to use the pressure of a constant volume of gas. As temperature increases, the KE of the molecules increases so they move faster. The faster moving molecules hit the walls of the container harder and more often, resulting in an increased pressure. As the temperature gets lower and lower the molecules slow down until at some point they stop moving completely. This is the lowest temperature possible or absolute zero. If we use this as the zero in our temperature scale then the KE is directly proportional to temperature. In defining this scale we then only need one fixed point, the other is absolute zero. This point could be the freezing point of water but the triple point is more precisely defined. This is the temperature at which water can be solid, liquid, and gas in equilibrium which in Celsius

Figure 3.21 Pressure vs temperature in Celsius and kelvin.

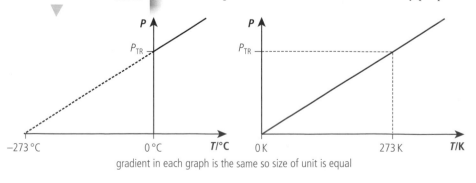

gradient in each graph is the same so size of unit is equal

is 0.01°C. If we make this 273.16 in our new scale then a change of 1 unit will be the same as 1°C. This scale is called the kelvin scale.

Because the size of the unit is the same, to convert from Celsius to kelvin we simply add 273. So

$$10°C = 283\,K$$
$$50°C = 323\,K$$

A change from 10°C to 50°C is 50 − 10 = 40°C.

A change from 283 K to 323 K is 323 − 282 = 40 K, so Δ°C = ΔK.

Temperature and molecular speed

Now we have a temperature scale that begins at absolute zero we can say that, for an ideal gas, the average KE of the molecules is directly proportional to its temperature in kelvin. The constant of proportionality is $\frac{3}{2}kT$ where k is the Boltzmann constant, $1.38 \times 10^{-23}\,m^2\,kg\,s^{-2}\,K^{-1}$.

Figure 3.22 shows the distribution of molecular velocities for different temperatures – the blue line describes molecular speed distribution of molecules in the air at about 0°C, and the red one is at about 100°C.

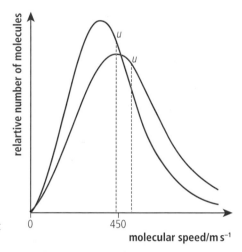

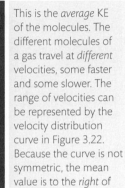

This is the *average* KE of the molecules. The different molecules of a gas travel at *different* velocities, some faster and some slower. The range of velocities can be represented by the velocity distribution curve in Figure 3.22. Because the curve is not symmetric, the mean value is to the *right* of centre.

Figure 3.22 Molecular velocity distribution for a gas.

Exercises

7 The length of a column of liquid is 30 cm at 100°C and 10 cm at 0°C. At what temperature will its length be 12 cm?

8 The average molar mass of air is 29 g mol⁻¹. Calculate:

  (a) the average KE of air molecules at 20°C.
  (b) the average mass of one molecule of air.
  (c) the average speed of air molecules at 20°C.

Heat

We know that the temperature of a body is related to the average KE of its molecules and that the KE of the molecules can be increased by doing work, for example against friction, but the internal energy of a body can also be increased by putting it in contact with a hotter body. Energy transferred in this way is called *heat*.

  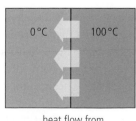 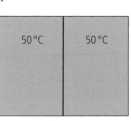

Figure 3.23 Heat travels from hot to cold until thermal equilibrium is established.

no heat flow since not in thermal contact

heat flow from hot to cold

no heat flow since thermal equilibrium

When bodies are in thermal contact heat will always flow from a high to a low temperature until the bodies are at the same temperature. Then we say they are in *thermal equilibrium*.

Heat transfer

There are three ways that heat can be transferred from one body to another; these are called conduction, convection, and radiation.

Conduction

Conduction takes place when bodies are in contact with each other. The vibrating molecules of one body collide with the molecules of the other. The fast-moving hot molecules lose energy and the slow-moving cold ones gain it.

Metals are particularly good conductors of heat because not only are their atoms well connected but metals contain some free particles (electrons) that are able to move freely about, helping to pass on the energy.

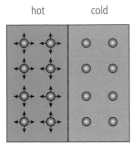

hot   cold

Figure 3.24 Energy passed from fast molecules to slow.

Figure 3.25 Electrons pass energy freely.

Gases are not very good conductors of heat because their molecules are far apart. However, heat is often transferred to a gas by conduction. This is how heat would pass from a room heater into the air of a room, for example.

Convection

This is the way that heat is transferred through fluids by fast-moving molecules moving from one place to another. When heat is given to air the molecules move around faster. This causes an increase in pressure in the hot air which enables it to expand, pushing aside the colder surrounding air. The hot air has now displaced more than its own weight of surrounding air so experiences an unbalanced upward force resulting in motion in that direction.

As the hot air rises it will cool and then come back down (this is also the way that a hot air balloon works). The circular motion of air is called a *convection current* and this is the way that heat is transferred around a room.

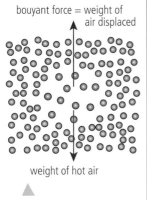

bouyant force = weight of air displaced

weight of hot air

Figure 3.26 Hot air expands.

Although the first ever engine was probably a steam turbine, cylinders of expanding gas are the basis of most engines.

Radiation

At this stage of the course we haven't really done enough to explain what radiation is but it is the way that heat can pass directly between two bodies without heating the material in between. In fact there doesn't even have to be a material between since radiation can pass through a vacuum. The name of this radiation is infrared and it is a part of the electromagnetic spectrum. The amount of radiation emitted and absorbed by a body depends on its colour. Dark, dull bodies both *emit* and *absorb* radiation better than light shiny ones. When you stand in front of a fire and feel the heat, you are feeling radiated heat.

Preventing heat loss

In everyday life, as well as in the physics lab, we often concern ourselves with minimizing heat loss. Insulating materials are often made out of fibrous matter that traps pockets of air. The air is a poor conductor and when it is trapped it can't convect. Covering something with silver-coloured paper will reduce radiation.

In cold countries houses are insulated to prevent heat from escaping. Are houses in hot countries insulated to stop heat entering?

Roof insulation in a house.

Thermal capacity (C)

If heat is added to a body, its temperature rises, but the actual increase in temperature depends on the body.

The thermal capacity (C) of a body is the amount of heat needed to raise its temperature by 1°C. Unit: $J°C^{-1}$ or JK^{-1}.

If the temperature of a body increases by an amount ΔT when quantity of heat Q is added, then the thermal capacity is given by the equation:

$$C = \frac{Q}{\Delta T}$$

This applies not only when things are given heat, but also when they lose heat.

Worked example

If the thermal capacity of a quantity of water is $5000\,J\,K^{-1}$, how much heat is required to raise its temperature from 20°C to 100°C?

Solution

Thermal capacity	$C = \frac{Q}{\Delta T}$	From definition
So	$Q = C\Delta T$	Rearranging
Therefore	$Q = 5000 \times (100 - 20)\,J$	
So the heat required	$Q = 400\,kJ$	

Worked example

How much heat is lost from a block of metal of thermal capacity $800\,J\,K^{-1}$ when it cools down from 60°C to 20°C?

Solution

Thermal capacity	$C = \frac{Q}{\Delta T}$	From definition
So	$Q = C\Delta T$	Rearranging
Therefore	$Q = 800 \times (60 - 20)\,J$	
So the heat lost	$Q = 32\,kJ$	

It is possible to buy a special shower head that uses less water. In some countries this is used to save energy; in others to save water.

105

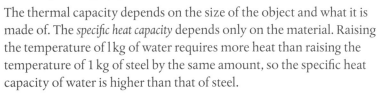

Remember, power is energy per unit time.

Specific heat capacity (*c*)

The thermal capacity depends on the size of the object and what it is made of. The *specific heat capacity* depends only on the material. Raising the temperature of 1 kg of water requires more heat than raising the temperature of 1 kg of steel by the same amount, so the specific heat capacity of water is higher than that of steel.

The specific heat capacity of a material is the amount of heat required to raise the temperature of 1 kg of the material by 1 °C. Unit: J kg⁻¹ °C⁻¹ or J kg⁻¹ K⁻¹.

If a quantity of heat Q is required to raise the temperature of a mass m of material by ΔT then the specific heat capacity (c) of that material is given by the following equation:

$$c = \frac{Q}{m\Delta T}$$

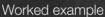

The specific heat capacity of water is quite high, so it takes a lot of energy to heat up the water for a shower.

It takes 4200 J of energy to raise the temperature of water by 1°C, this is equivalent to lifting 420 kg a height of 1 m. This makes water a good medium for transferring energy but also makes it expensive to take a shower. Oil would be cheaper to heat but not so good to wash in.

Worked example

The specific heat capacity of water is 4200 J kg⁻¹ K⁻¹. How much heat will be required to heat 300 g of water from 20°C to 60°C?

Solution

Specific heat capacity	$c = \dfrac{Q}{m\Delta T}$	From definition
So	$Q = cm\Delta T$	Rearranging
Therefore	$Q = 4200 \times 0.3 \times 40$	Note: Convert g to kg
	$Q = 50.4\,\text{kJ}$	

Worked example

A metal block of mass 1.5 kg loses 20 kJ of heat. As this happens, its temperature drops from 60 °C to 45 °C. What is the specific heat capacity of the metal?

Solution

Specific heat capacity	$c = \dfrac{Q}{m\Delta T}$	From definition
So	$c = \dfrac{20\,000}{1.5(60-45)}$	Rearranging
	$c = 888.9\,\text{J}\,\text{kg}^{-1}\,\text{K}^{-1}$	

Exercises

Use the data in Table 3.1 to solve the problems:

11 How much heat is required to raise the temperature of 250 g of copper from 20 °C to 160 °C?

12 The density of water is 1000 kg m⁻³.

   (a) What is the mass of 1 litre of water?

   (b) How much energy will it take to raise the temperature of 1 litre of water from 20 °C to 100 °C?

   (c) A water heater has a power rating of 1 kW. How many seconds will this heater take to boil 1 litre of water?

Substance	Specific heat capacity $(J\,kg^{-1}\,K^{-1})$
Water	4200
Copper	380
Aluminium	900
Steel	440

Table 3.1.

13 A 500 g piece of aluminium is heated with a 500 W heater for 10 minutes.

   (a) How much energy will be given to the aluminium in this time?

   (b) If the temperature of the aluminium was 20°C at the beginning, what will its temperature be after 10 minutes?

14 A car of mass 1500 kg travelling at 20 m s⁻¹ brakes suddenly and comes to a stop.

   (a) How much KE does the car lose?

   (b) If 75% of the energy is given to the front brakes, how much energy will they receive?

   (c) The brakes are made out of steel and have a total mass of 10 kg. By how much will their temperature rise?

15 The water comes out of a showerhead at a temperature of 50 °C at a rate of 8 litres per minute.

   (a) If you take a shower lasting 10 minutes, how many kg of water have you used?

   (b) If the water must be heated from 10 °C, how much energy is needed to heat the water?

Phase change

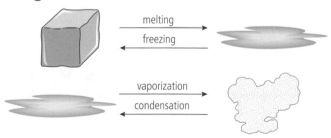

Figure 3.27 When matter changes from liquid to gas, or solid to liquid, it is changing state.

When water boils, this is called a *change of state* (or *change of phase*). As this happens, the temperature of the water doesn't change – it stays at 100 °C. In fact, we find that whenever the state of a material changes, the temperature stays the same. We can explain this in terms of the particle model.

An iceberg melts as it floats into warmer water.

Figure 3.28 Molecules gain PE when the state changes.

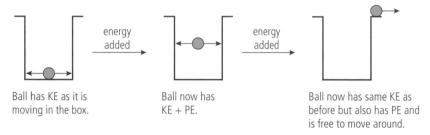

Solid molecules have KE since they are vibrating.

Liquid molecules are now free to move about but have the same KE as before.

When matter changes state, the energy is needed to enable the molecules to move more freely. To understand this, consider the example below.

Figure 3.29 A ball-in-a-box model of change of state.

Ball has KE as it is moving in the box.

Ball now has KE + PE.

Ball now has same KE as before but also has PE and is free to move around.

Boiling and evaporation

These are two different processes by which liquids can change to gases.

Boiling takes place throughout the liquid and always at the same temperature. *Evaporation* takes place only at the surface of the liquid and can happen at all temperatures.

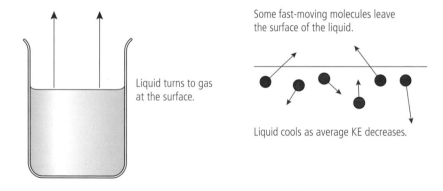

Liquid turns to gas at the surface.

Some fast-moving molecules leave the surface of the liquid.

Liquid cools as average KE decreases.

Figure 3.30 A microscopic model of evaporation.

When a liquid evaporates, the fastest-moving particles leave the surface. This means that the average kinetic energy of the remaining particles is lower, resulting in a drop in temperature.

The rate of evaporation can be increased by:

• increasing the surface area; this increases the number of molecules near the surface, giving more of them a chance to escape.
• blowing across the surface. After molecules have left the surface they form a small 'vapour cloud' above the liquid. If this is blown away, it allows further molecules to leave the surface more easily.
• raising the temperature; this increases the kinetic energy of the liquid molecules, enabling more to escape.

People sweat to increase the rate at which they lose heat. When you get hot, sweat comes out of your skin onto the surface of your body. When the sweat evaporates, it cools you down. In a sauna there is so much water vapour in the air that the sweat doesn't evaporate.

Specific latent heat (L)

The *specific latent* heat of a material is the amount of heat required to change the state of 1kg of the material without change of temperature.

Unit: $J\,kg^{-1}$

Latent means *hidden*. This name is used because when matter changes state, the heat added does not cause the temperature to rise, but seems to disappear.

If it takes an amount of energy Q to change the state of a mass m of a substance, then the specific latent heat of that substance is given by the equation:

$$L = \frac{Q}{m}$$

Worked example

The specific latent heat of fusion of water is $3.35 \times 10^5\,J\,kg^{-1}$. How much energy is required to change 500 g of ice into water?

Solution

The latent heat of fusion	$L = \dfrac{Q}{m}$	From definition
So	$Q = mL$	Rearranging
Therefore	$Q = 0.5 \times 3.35 \times 10^5\,J$	
So the heat required	$Q = 1.675 \times 10^5\,J$	

Worked example

The amount of heat released when 100 g of steam turns to water is $2.27 \times 10^5\,J$. What is the specific latent heat of vaporization of water?

Solution

The specific latent heat of vaporization	$L = \dfrac{Q}{m}$	From definition
Therefore	$L = 2.27 \times 10^5/0.1\,J\,kg^{-1}$	
So the specific latent heat of vaporization	$L = 2.27 \times 10^6\,J\,kg^{-1}$	

Exercises

Use the data about water in Table 3.2 to solve the following problems.

16 If the mass of water in a cloud is 1 million kg, how much energy will be released if the cloud turns from water to ice?

17 A water boiler has a power rating of 800 W. How long will it take to turn 400 g of boiling water into steam?

18 The ice covering a 1000 m² lake is 2 cm thick.

    (a) If the density of ice is 920 kg m⁻³, what is the mass of the ice on the lake?
    (b) How much energy is required to melt the ice?
    (c) If the Sun melts the ice in 5 hours, what is the power delivered to the lake?
    (d) How much power does the Sun deliver per m²?

Latent heat of vaporization	$2.27 \times 10^6\,J\,kg^{-1}$
Latent heat of fusion	$3.35 \times 10^5\,J\,kg^{-1}$

Table 3.2 Latent heats of water.

Solid → liquid
Specific latent heat of fusion

Liquid → gas
Specific latent heat of vaporization

This equation ($L = \frac{Q}{m}$) can also be used to calculate the heat lost when a substance changes from gas to liquid, or liquid to solid.

Before the invention of the refrigerator, people would collect ice in the winter, and store it in well-insulated rooms so that it could be used to make ice cream in the summer. The reason it takes so long to melt is because to melt 1 kg of ice requires 3.3×10^5 J of energy; in a well-insulated room this could take many months.

In this example, we are ignoring the heat given to the kettle and the heat lost.

Graphical representation of heating

The increase of the temperature of a body can be represented by a temperature–time graph. Observing this graph can give us a lot of information about the heating process.

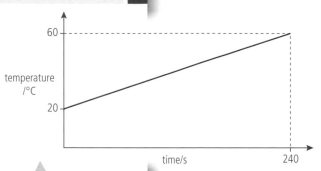

Figure 3.31 Temperature–time graph for 1 kg of water being heated in an electric kettle.

From this graph we can calculate the amount of heat given to the water per unit time (power).

$$\text{The gradient of the graph} = \frac{\text{temperature rise}}{\text{time}} = \frac{\Delta T}{\Delta t}$$

We know from the definition of specific heat capacity that

$$\text{heat added} = mc\Delta T$$

$$\text{The rate of adding heat} = P = \frac{mc\Delta T}{\Delta t}$$

So $$P = mc \times \text{gradient}$$

$$\text{The gradient of this line} = \frac{(60-20)}{240} \,°C\,s^{-1} = 0.167\,°C\,s^{-1}$$

So the power delivered $= 4200 \times 0.167\,\text{W} = 700\,\text{W}$

If we continue to heat this water it will begin to boil.

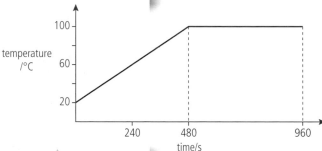

Figure 3.32 A graph of temperature vs time for boiling water. When the water is boiling, the temperature does not increase any more.

If we assume that the heater is giving heat to the water at the same rate, then we can calculate how much heat was given to the water whilst it was boiling.

$$\text{Power of the heater} = 700\,\text{W}$$

$$\text{Time of boiling} = 480\,\text{s}$$

$$\text{Energy supplied} = \text{power} \times \text{time} = 700 \times 480\,\text{J} = 3.36 \times 10^5\,\text{J}$$

From this we can calculate how much water must have turned to steam.

$$\text{Heat added to change state} = \text{mass} \times \text{latent heat of vaporization,}$$

where latent heat of vaporization of water $= 2.27 \times 10^6\,\text{J}\,\text{kg}^{-1}$.

$$\text{Mass changed to steam} = \frac{3.36 \times 10^5}{2.27 \times 10^6} = 0.15\,\text{kg}$$

The amount of heat loss is proportional to the difference between the temperature of the kettle and its surroundings. For this reason, a graph of temperature against time is actually a curve, as shown in Figure 3.33.

The fact that the gradient decreases tells us that the amount of heat given to the water gets less with time. This is because as it gets hotter, more and more of the heat is lost to the room.

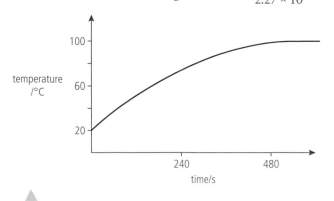

Figure 3.33 Heat loss.

Measuring thermal quantities by the method of mixtures

The method of mixtures can be used to measure the specific heat capacity and specific latent heat of substances.

Specific heat capacity of a metal

A metal sample is first heated to a known temperature. The most convenient way of doing this is to place it in boiling water for a few minutes; after this time it will be at 100 °C. The hot metal is then quickly moved to an insulated cup containing a known mass of cold water. The hot metal will cause the temperature of the cold water to rise; the rise in temperature is measured with a thermometer. Some example temperatures and masses are given in Figure 3.34.

As the specific heat capacity of water is $4180\,\mathrm{J\,kg^{-1}\,K^{-1}}$, we can calculate the specific heat capacity of the metal.

$$\Delta T \text{ for the metal} = 100 - 15 = 85\,°C$$

and

$$\Delta T \text{ for the water} = 15 - 10 = 5\,°C$$

Applying the formula $Q = mc\Delta T$ we get

$$(mc\Delta T)_{metal} = 0.1 \times c \times 85 = 8.5c$$
$$(mc\Delta T)_{water} = 0.4 \times 4180 \times 5 = 8360$$

If no heat is lost, then the heat transferred from the metal = heat transferred to the water

$$8.5c = 8360$$
$$c_{metal} = 983\,\mathrm{J\,kg^{-1}\,K^{-1}}$$

Latent heat of vaporization of water

To measure the latent heat of vaporization, steam is passed into cold water. Some of the steam condenses in the water, causing the water temperature to rise.

The heat from the steam = the heat to the water.

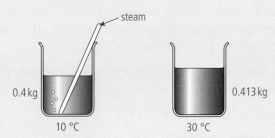

In Figure 3.35, 13 g of steam have condensed in the water, raising its temperature by 20 °C. The steam condenses then cools down from 100 °C to 30 °C.

$$\text{Heat from steam} = ml_{steam} + mc\Delta T_{water}$$
$$0.013 \times L + 0.013 \times 4.18 \times 10^3 \times 70 = 0.013L + 3803.8$$
$$\text{Heat transferred to cold water} = mc\Delta T_{water} = 0.4 \times 4.18 \times 10^3 \times 20$$
$$= 33\,440\,\mathrm{J}$$

Since

$$\text{heat from steam} = \text{heat to water}$$
$$0.013L + 3803.8 = 33\,440$$

So

$$L = \frac{33\,440 - 3803.8}{0.013}$$
$$L = 2.28 \times 10^6\,\mathrm{J\,kg^{-1}}$$

Heat loss

In both of these experiments, some of the heat coming from the hot source can be lost to the surroundings. To reduce heat loss, the temperatures can be adjusted, so you could start the experiment below room temperature and end the same amount above (e.g. if room temperature is 20 °C, then you can start at 10 °C and end at 30 °C).

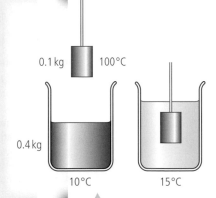

Figure 3.34 Measuring the specific heat capacity of a metal.

Measurement of the specific heat capacity of a metal by the method of mixtures

A worksheet with full details of how to carry out this experiment is available on your eBook.

Figure 3.35 By measuring the rise in temperature, the specific latent heat can be calculated.

When melting sugar to make confectionary be very careful: liquid sugar takes much longer to cool down than you might think. This is because as it changes from liquid to solid it is giving out heat but doesn't change temperature. You should wait a long time before trying to pick up any of your treats with your fingers.

To learn more about thermal concepts, go to the hotlinks site, search for the title or ISBN and click on Chapter 3.

3.2 Modelling a gas

3.2 Modelling a gas

Understandings, applications, and skills:

Kinetic model of an ideal gas

Guidance
- *Students should be aware of the assumptions which underpin the molecular kinetic theory of ideal gases.*

Pressure
Equation of state for an ideal gas
- Solving problems using the equation of state for an ideal gas and gas laws.
- Sketching and interpreting changes of state of an ideal gas on pressure–volume, pressure–temperature, and volume–temperature diagrams.
- Investigating at least one gas law experimentally.

Guidance
- *Gas laws are limited to constant volume, constant temperature, constant pressure, and the ideal gas law.*

Differences between real and ideal gases

Guidance
- *Students should understand that a real gas approximates to an ideal gas at conditions of low pressure, moderate temperature, and low density.*

The ideal gas

Of the three states of matter, the gaseous state has the simplest model; this is because the forces between the molecules of a gas are very small, so they are able to move freely. We can therefore use what we know about the motion of particles learnt in the mechanics section to study gases in more detail.

According to our simple model, a gas is made up of a large number of perfectly elastic, tiny spheres moving in random motion.

This model makes some assumptions:

- The molecules are perfectly elastic.
- The molecules are spheres.
- The molecules are identical.
- There are no forces between the molecules (except when they collide) – this means that the molecules move with constant velocity between collisions.
- The molecules are very small; that is, their total volume is much smaller than the volume of the gas.

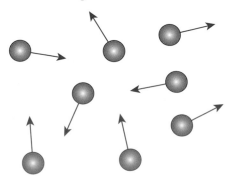

Figure 3.36 Molecules of gas in random motion.

Some of these assumptions are not true for all gases, especially when the gas is compressed (when the molecules are so close together that they experience a force between them). The gas then behaves as a liquid. However, to keep things simple, we will only consider gases that behave like our model. We call these gases *ideal* gases.

Defining the state of a gas

To define the state of an amount of matter we need to give enough information so that another person could obtain the same material with the same properties. If we were to take a 100 g cube of copper at 300 K we have stated how much and how hot it is, and even its shape, someone else would be able to take an identical piece of copper and it would behave in the same way as ours. If on the other hand we were to take 100 g of helium gas then we would also need to define its volume since this will depend on the container and different volumes cause the pressure exerted by the gas on its sides to be different.

Volume

The volume of a gas is simply the volume of the container. If we want to vary the volume we can place the gas in a cylinder with a moveable end (a piston) as in Figure 3.37.

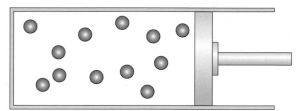

Figure 3.37 Gas molecules trapped in an adjustable container.

Temperature

Since gas molecules have no force between them it requires no work to move them around which means that there is no energy associated with their position. In other words, the molecules have no PE. The temperature of a gas in kelvin is therefore directly proportional to the average KE of a molecule.

$$KE_{mean} = \frac{3}{2}kT$$

where k is the Boltzmann constant, $1.38 \times 10^{-23}\,JK^{-1}$.

If there are N molecules then the total KE of the gas $= N \times KE_{mean} = \frac{3}{2}NkT$

A more convenient expression is $KE = \frac{3}{2}nRT$ where R is the molar gas constant, and n is the number of moles. Higher KE implies higher velocity so the molecules of a gas at high temperature will have a higher average velocity than molecules of the same gas at a low temperature, as shown in Figure 3.38.

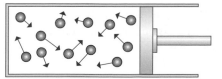
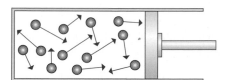

low temperature, small average KE   high temperature, large average KE

Figure 3.38.

Let us compare two gases A and B with molecules of different mass at the same temperature. Applying $KE = \frac{3}{2}nRT$ we can deduce that if temperature is the same then the average KE of the molecules will be the same. But $KE = \frac{1}{2}mv^2$ so

$$\frac{1}{2}m_A v_A{}^2 = \frac{1}{2}m_B v_B{}^2$$

$$\frac{m_A}{m_B} = \frac{v_B{}^2}{v_A{}^2}$$

This means that if A has smaller molecules the molecules in gas A must have higher velocity, as represented by the red balls in Figure 3.39.

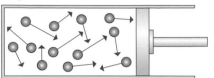
temperature = T

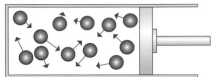
temperature = T

small molecules, high velocity

large molecules, low velocity

Figure 3.39 Same temperature, different gases.

Pressure

When gas molecules collide with the sides of the container their momentum changes. This is because they have experienced an unbalanced force from the wall. According to Newton's third law, the wall must experience an equal and opposite force so will be pushed out by the gas. This is why the piston must be held in place by the man in Figure 3.40. This is the force responsible for the pressure a gas exerts on its container (pressure $= \frac{\text{force}}{\text{area}}$).

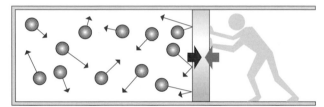

Figure 3.40 Gas pushes piston to the right so something must push it to the left.

To understand how the pressure is related to the motion of the molecules we can consider the simplified version shown in Figure 3.41 where one molecule is bouncing rapidly between the piston and the far wall of the cylinder.

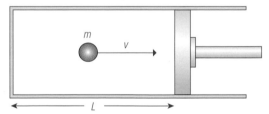

Figure 3.41 One molecule of gas.

When the molecule hits the piston it bounces off elastically. The magnitude of change in momentum is therefore $2mv$. The force exerted on the piston is equal to the rate of change of momentum which in this case = change in momentum × rate of hitting the wall. The rate at which the molecule hits the wall depends on how long it takes for the molecule to travel to the other end of the cylinder and back:

$$\text{time for molecule to travel to other end and back} = \frac{2L}{v}$$

$$\text{number of hits per unit time} = \frac{1}{\left(\frac{2L}{v}\right)} = \frac{v}{2L}$$

$$\text{rate of change of momentum} = 2mv \times \frac{v}{2L} = \frac{mv^2}{L}$$

so the pressure is directly related to the KE of the particles and therefore the temperature of the gas.

The force exerted by the gas on the piston would cause the piston to move outwards unless there was a force opposing it. In the lab this force is normally provided by the air on the outside which is also made of molecules in random motion as shown in Figure 3.42.

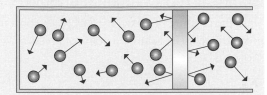

Figure 3.42 Piston pushed by trapped gas on one side and air on the other.

Relationships between *P*, *V*, and *T*

When dealing with relationships we generally are concerned with two quantities, e.g. distance and time, force and area, mass and volume. Here we have three variables, each depending on each other. To make life easier we can keep one constant and look at the relationship between the other two. This will give three different relationships which are known as the gas laws.

Boyle's law (constant temperature)

The pressure of a fixed mass of gas at constant temperature is inversely proportional to its volume.

$$P \propto \frac{1}{V}$$

As the volume of a gas is reduced the gas will become denser, because the molecules are pushed together. The molecules will therefore hit the walls more often, increasing the rate of change of momentum and hence the pressure as shown in Figure 3.43.

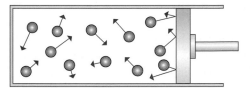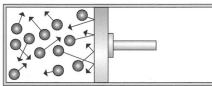

When you make changes to the state of a gas all three quantities will change unless one is kept constant. This is a rather artificial condition but makes modelling the gas easier.

Keeping the temperature constant is quite difficult because when you push in the piston you do work on the gas, increasing the KE of the molecules and hence increasing the temperature. If the compression is slow then the temperature will have time to return to the temperature of the surroundings.

Figure 3.43 Reducing the volume increases the pressure.

Experimental investigation

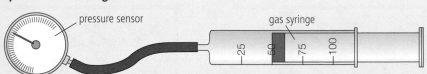

Figure 3.44.

Boyle's law apparatus.

The easiest way to test the relationship between pressure and volume is to compress a gas in a syringe that is connected via some rubber tubing to a pressure sensor as in the photo and Figure 3.44. The range of pressure will be limited to how strong you are but should be enough to show the relationship.

The relationship between the pressure and volume of a fixed mass of gas (Boyle's law)

A worksheet with full details of how to carry out this experiment is available on your eBook.

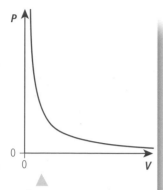

Figure 3.45 Graph of *P* vs *V.*

Figure 3.46 P vs V for different T.

When a gas is compressed work is done on it. Work done = force × distance which is the area under the *P–V* graph. This makes this graph particularly useful when investigating the energy changes that a gas undergoes when transformed. More about this if you do option B.

Figure 3.47.

Graphical representation of Boyle's law

Since the pressure of a fixed mass of gas at constant temperature is inversely proportional to its volume, a graph of pressure against volume will be a curve as shown in Figure 3.45.

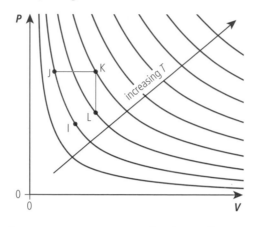

If the experiment was now repeated with the same amount of gas at different temperatures the set of blue lines shown in Figure 3.46 would be achieved. Each line is called an *isothermal*. The effect of increasing the temperature of a fixed volume of gas is to increase the pressure so we can see that the curves further away from the origin are for higher temperatures. The orange lines on the graph represent the following gas transformations:

IJ   constant temperature (isothermal)

JK   constant pressure (isobaric)

KL   constant volume (isochoric).

Pressure law (constant volume)

The pressure of a fixed mass of gas with constant volume is directly proportional to its temperature in kelvin.

$$P \propto T$$

As the temperature of a gas is increased the average KE of the molecules increases. The change in momentum as the molecules hit the walls is therefore greater and they hit the walls more often as shown in Figure 3.47. According to Newton's second law the force exerted = rate of change of momentum, so the force on the walls increases and hence the pressure increases.

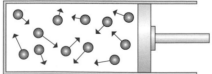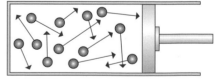

increased temperature   →   increased KE   →   increased pressure

Experimental investigation

A pressure sensor can also be used in an experiment to show the relationship between pressure and temperature. This time a flask of fixed volume is placed in a water bath as shown in the photo and Figure 3.48. A temperature sensor measures the temperature of the gas while a pressure sensor measures its pressure. The temperature of the gas is changed by heating the water, and the pressure and temperature are recorded simultaneously.

Pressure law apparatus.

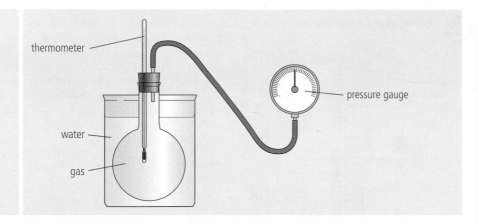

Figure 3.48 Apparatus to measure P and T.

Graphical representation of the pressure law

Since pressure is proportional to temperature a graph of pressure *vs* temperature for a fixed mass of gas at constant volume will be a straight line as shown in Figure 3.49.

If the experiment was repeated with different volumes of the same amount of gas then the set of lines shown in Figure 3.50 would be achieved, each line representing a different volume. Increasing the volume at constant temperature (line CD) will make the pressure lower so the less steep lines are for larger volumes. The orange lines on the graph represent the following gas transformations:

AB   constant volume (isochoric)

BC   constant pressure (isobaric)

CD   constant temperature (isothermal).

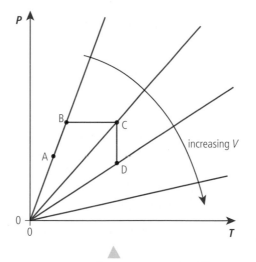

Figure 3.50 P *vs* T for different V.

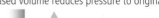

Figure 3.49 Graph of P *vs* T.

Charles' law (constant pressure)

The volume of a fixed mass of gas at a constant pressure is directly proportional to its temperature in kelvin.

$$V \propto T$$

As the temperature of a gas is increased the molecules move faster causing an increase in pressure. However, if the volume is increased in proportion to the increase in temperature the pressure will remain the same. This is shown in Figure 3.51.

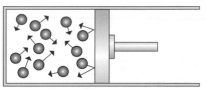 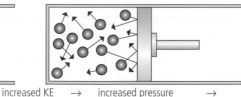

increased temperature → increased KE → increased pressure → increased volume reduces pressure to original

Figure 3.51 Constant pressure expansion.

The liquid will add a little bit to the pressure.

Experimental investigation

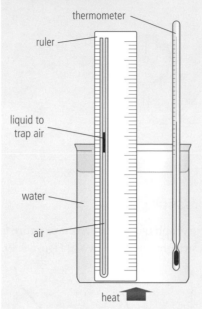

Figure 3.52 Charles' law apparatus.

To test the relationship between volume and temperature you need a narrow tube with the top end open and a small amount of liquid that traps a sample of dry air, as shown in Figure 3.52. Traditionally concentrated sulfuric acid was used to trap the air because it absorbs water. However, this might be against the safety regulations in your country. If so, oil will do the job but might not give such good results. The temperature of the sample of air is changed by placing it in a water bath which is heated. The temperature of the gas is then assumed to be the same as the temperature of the water, which is measured using a thermometer. If we assume the tube has a uniform cross-section then, as the temperature is changed, the volume is measured by measuring the length of the cylinder of gas. At the start of the experiment the pressure of the gas = the pressure of the surrounding air; as the temperature increases the pressure also increases pushing the bead up the tube increasing the volume, causing the pressure to reduce until it is again equal to the pressure of the surrounding air. We therefore assume the gas pressure is constant.

Graphical representation of Charles' law

Since volume is proportional to temperature a graph of volume *vs* temperature for a fixed mass of gas at constant pressure will be a straight line as shown in Figure 3.53.

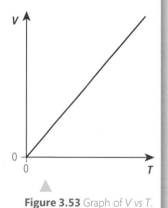

Figure 3.53 Graph of *V vs T*.

If the experiment was repeated with the gas at different constant pressures then the set of lines shown in Figure 3.54 would be achieved, each line representing a different pressure. Reducing the volume at a constant temperature (line GH) will result in a higher pressure so the less steep lines have higher pressure. The orange lines on the graph represent the following gas transformations:

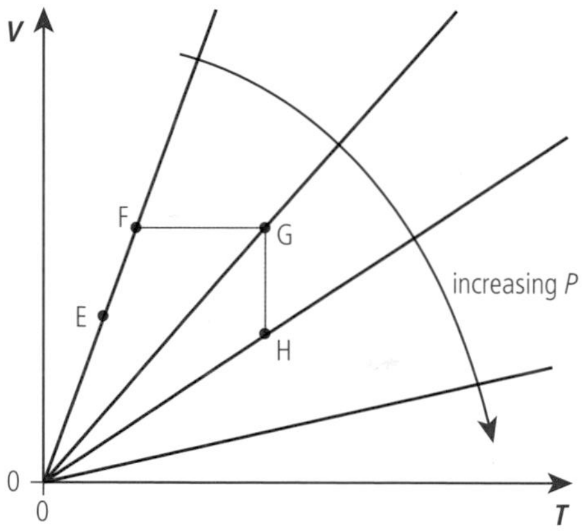

EF   constant pressure (isobaric)

FG   constant volume (isochoric)

GH   constant temperature (isothermal).

Figure 3.54 *V vs T* for different *P*.

Avogadro's hypothesis

Avogadro's hypothesis states that equal volumes of gas at the same temperature and pressure have the same number of molecules. We can now see why this is the case. To simplify the situation we will consider two cylinders each containing one molecule of a different gas with the same KE. As you can see in Figure 3.55 molecule B has a larger mass than molecule A so is travelling at a slower velocity.

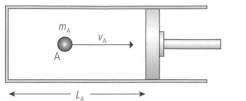
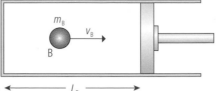

Figure 3.55 Two different gases at the same pressure and temperature.

The force exerted by each molecule is given by $\frac{mv^2}{L} = \frac{2KE}{L}$ (see page 114).

Both gases have the same KE so:

$$\text{force exerted by A} = \frac{2KE}{L_A}$$

$$\text{force exerted by B} = \frac{2KE}{L_B}$$

To make the force the same we would therefore need to make $L_A = L_B$.

In other words, equal numbers of molecules (1 in this case) with the same pressure and temperature occupy the same volume.

The ideal gas equation

The relationship between all three variables can be expressed in one equation:

$$PV = nRT$$

where n = the number of moles of gas and R = the molar gas constant ($8.31\,\text{J mol}^{-1}\,\text{K}^{-1}$).

Graphical representation of the ideal gas equation

This relationship can be represented on a graph with three axes as in Figure 3.56. The shaded area represents all the possible states of a fixed mass of gas. No matter what you do to the gas, its P, V, and T will always be on this surface. This is quite difficult to draw so the 2-dimensional views shown before are used instead.

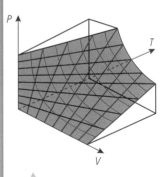

Figure 3.56.

> **Temperatures must be changed to kelvin.**

Worked example

The pressure of a gas inside a cylinder is 300 kPa. If the gas is compressed to half its original volume and the temperature rises from 27 °C to 327 °C, what will its new pressure be?

Solution

Using the ideal gas equation: $\qquad PV = nRT$

Rearranging: $\qquad\qquad\qquad \frac{PV}{T} = \text{consant}$

So $\qquad \frac{PV}{T}$ at the beginning $= \frac{PV}{T}$ at the end

$$\frac{PV}{T} \text{ at the beginning} = \frac{300\,000 \times V}{300}$$

$$\frac{PV}{T} \text{ at the end} = \frac{P \times \frac{V}{2}}{600}$$

Equating:

$$300\,000 \times \frac{V}{300} = \frac{P \times \frac{V}{2}}{600}$$

$$P = 300\,000 \times 600 \times \frac{2}{300}$$

$$P = 1200\,\text{kPa}$$

To learn more about modelling a gas, go to the hotlinks site, search for the title or ISBN and click on Chapter 3.

CHALLENGE YOURSELF

1 Two identical flasks each full of air are connected by a thin tube on a day when the temperature is 300 K and the atmospheric pressure 100 kPa. One of the flasks is then heated to 400 K while the other one is kept at 300 K. What is the new pressure in the flasks?

Exercises

19 The pressure of 10 m³ of gas in a sealed container at 300 K is 250 kPa. If the temperature of the gas is changed to 350 K, what will the pressure be?

20 A container of volume 2 m³ contains 5 moles of gas. If the temperature of the gas is 293 K:
   (a) what is the pressure exerted by the gas?
   (b) what is the new pressure if half of the gas leaks out?

21 A piston contains 250 cm³ of gas at 300 K and a pressure of 150 kPa. The gas expands, causing the pressure to go down to 100 kPa and the temperature drops to 250 K. What is the new volume?

22 A sample of gas trapped in a piston is heated and compressed at the same time. This results in a doubling of temperature and a halving of the volume. If the initial pressure was 100 kPa, what will the final pressure be?

Real gases

The assumptions we made when developing the model for an ideal gas do not fully apply to real gases except when the pressure is low and the temperature high. At high pressures the molecules can be close together so the assumption that the volume of the molecules is negligible doesn't apply, nor does the one about there being no forces between the molecules. What can also happen at low temperatures is the gas can change into a liquid which, for obvious reasons, doesn't behave like a gas. However, although no gas behaves exactly as an *ideal* gas, air at normal room temperature and pressure comes pretty close, as our experiments have shown.

Nitrogen becomes a liquid at low temperatures.

1. This question is about the change of phase (state) of ice.

A quantity of crushed ice is removed from a freezer and placed in a calorimeter. Thermal energy is supplied to the ice at a constant rate. To ensure that all the ice is at the same temperature, it is continually stirred. The temperature of the contents of the calorimeter is recorded every 15 seconds.

Figure 3.57 shows the variation with time t of the temperature θ of the contents of the calorimeter. (*Uncertainties in the measured quantities are not shown.*)

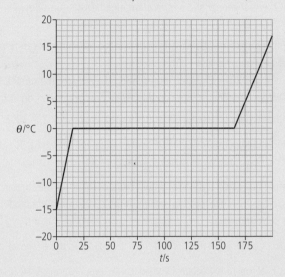

Figure 3.57.

(a) Copy Figure 3.57 and, on the graph, mark with an X the data point at which all the ice has just melted. (1)

(b) Explain, with reference to the energy of the molecules, the constant temperature region of the graph. (3)

The mass of the ice is 0.25 kg and the specific heat capacity of water is 4200 J kg^{-1}K^{-1}.

(c) Use these data and data from the graph to

   (i) deduce that energy is supplied to the ice at the rate of about 530 W. (3)

   (ii) determine the specific heat capacity of ice. (3)

   (iii) determine the specific latent heat of fusion of ice. (2)

(*Total 12 marks*)

2. This question is about thermal physics.

(a) Explain why, when a liquid evaporates, the liquid cools unless thermal energy is supplied to it. (3)

(b) State **two** factors that cause an increase in the rate of evaporation of a liquid. (2)

(c) Some data for ice and for water are given below.

Specific heat capacity of ice = 2.1×10^3 J kg^{-1}K^{-1}
Specific heat capacity of water = 4.2×10^3 J kg^{-1}K^{-1}
Specific latent heat of fusion of ice = 3.3×10^5 J kg^{-1}

A mass of 350 g of water at a temperature of 25°C is placed in a refrigerator that extracts thermal energy from the water at a rate of 86 W.

Calculate the time taken for the water to become ice at −5.0°C. (4)

(*Total 9 marks***)**

3. This question is about modelling the thermal processes involved when a person is running. When running, a person generates *thermal energy* but maintains approximately constant temperature.

    (a) Explain what *thermal energy* and *temperature* mean. Distinguish between the two concepts.

    (4)

    The following simple model may be used to estimate the rise in temperature of a runner assuming no thermal energy is lost.

    A closed container holds 70 kg of water, representing the mass of the runner. The water is heated at a rate of 1200 W for 30 minutes. This represents the energy generation in the runner.

    (b) (i) Show that the thermal energy generated by the heater is 2.2×10^6 J. (2)

    (ii) Calculate the temperature rise of the water, assuming no energy losses from the water. The specific heat capacity of water is 4200 J kg⁻¹ K⁻¹. (3)

    (c) The temperature rise calculated in (b) would be dangerous for the runner. Outline **three** mechanisms, other than evaporation, by which the container in the model would transfer energy to its surroundings. (6)

    A further process by which energy is lost from the runner is the evaporation of sweat.

    (d) (i) Describe, in terms of molecular behaviour, why evaporation causes cooling. (3)

    (ii) Percentage of generated energy lost by sweating: 50%

    Specific latent heat of vaporization of sweat: 2.26×10^6 J kg⁻¹

    Using the information above, and your answer to (b) (i), estimate the mass of sweat evaporated from the runner. (3)

    (iii) State and explain two factors that affect the rate of evaporation of sweat from the skin of the runner. (4)

    (*Total 25 marks***)**

4. This question is about the breaking distance of a car and specific heat capacity.

    (a) A car of mass 960 kg is free-wheeling down an incline at a constant speed of 9.0 m s⁻¹.

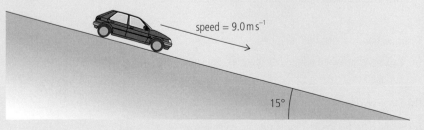

speed = 9.0 m s⁻¹

15°

Figure 3.58.

    The slope makes an angle of 15° with the horizontal.

    (i) Deduce that the average resistive force acting on the car is 2.4×10^3 N. (2)

    (ii) Calculate the kinetic energy of the car. (1)

(b) The driver now applies the brakes and the car comes to rest in 15 m. Use your answer to (a) (ii) to calculate the average braking force exerted on the car in coming to rest. (2)

(c) The same braking force is applied to each rear wheel of the car. The effective mass of each brake is 5.2 kg with a specific heat capacity of 900 J kg^{-1} K^{-1}. Estimate the rise in temperature of a brake as the car comes to rest. State one assumption that you make in your estimation. (4)

(Total 9 marks)

5. This question is about ideal gases.

(a) The atoms or molecules of an ideal gas are assumed to be identical hard elastic spheres that have negligible volume compared with the volume of the containing vessel.

  (i) State **two** further assumptions of the kinetic theory of an ideal gas. (2)

  (ii) Suggest why only the average kinetic energy of the molecules of an ideal gas is related to the internal energy of the gas. (3)

(b) An ideal gas is contained in a cylinder by means of a frictionless piston.

Figure 3.59.

At temperature 290 K and pressure 4.8 × 10^5 Pa, the gas has volume 9.2 × 10^{-4} m^3.

  (i) Calculate the number of moles of the gas. (2)

  (ii) The gas is compressed isothermally to a volume of 2.3 × 10^{-4} m^3. Determine the pressure P of the gas. (2)

  (iii) The gas is now heated at constant volume to a temperature of 420 K. Show that the pressure of the gas is now 2.8 × 10^6 Pa. (1)

(c) The gas in (b)(iii) is now expanded adiabatically so that its temperature and pressure return to 290 K and 4.8 × 10^5 Pa respectively. This state is shown in Figure 3.60 as point A.

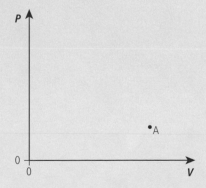

Figure 3.60.

  (i) Copy Figure 3.60 and on the axes sketch a pressure–volume (P–V) diagram for the changes in (b)(ii), (b)(iii), and (c). (3)

(Total 13 marks)

04

Circular motion and gravitation

Essential ideas

6.1 Circular motion
A force applied perpendicular to its displacement can result in circular motion.

6.2 Newton's law of gravitation
The Newtonian idea of gravitational force acting between two spherical bodies and the laws of mechanics create a model that can be used to calculate the motion of planets.

10.1 Describing fields (HL only)
Electric charges and masses each influence the space around them and that influence can be represented through the concept of field.

10.2 Fields at work (HL only)
Similar approaches can be taken in analysing electrical and gravitational potential problems.

NATURE OF SCIENCE

By applying what we know about motion in a straight line we can develop a model for motion in a circle. This is a common way that models are developed in physics: start simple and add complexity later.

4.1 Circular motion

6.1 Circular motion

Understandings, applications, and skills:

Period, frequency, angular displacement, and angular speed
● Solving problems involving centripetal force, centripetal acceleration, period, frequency, angular displacement, linear speed, and angular velocity.

Centripetal force
● Qualitatively and quantitatively describing examples of circular motion including cases of vertical and horizontal circular motion.

  Guidance
  ● *Banking will be considered qualitatively only.*

Centripetal acceleration

If a car travels around a bend at $30\,km\,h^{-1}$, it is obviously travelling at a constant speed, since the speedometer registers $30\,km\,h^{-1}$ all the way round. However, it is not travelling at constant velocity. This is because velocity is a vector quantity and for a vector quantity to be constant, both magnitude and direction must remain the same. Bends in a road can be many different shapes, but to simplify things, we will only consider circular bends taken at constant speed.

Looking at the similar patterns made by the cars and the stars it is not surprising that people used to think that the stars travelled around the Earth.

When dealing with circular motion in physics we always measure the angle in radians.

Quantities of circular motion

Consider the body in Figure 4.1 travelling in a circle radius *r* with constant speed *v*. In time Δt the body moves from A to B. As it does this the radius sweeps out an angle Δθ.

When describing motion in a circle we often use quantities referring to the angular motion rather than the linear motion. These quantities are:

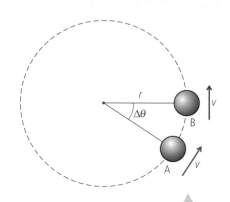

Figure 4.1.

Time period (*T*)

The time period is the time taken to complete one circle.

The unit of the time period is the second.

Angular displacement (*θ*)

The angular displacement is the angle swept out by a line joining the body to the centre.

The unit of angular displacement is the radian.

Angular velocity (*ω* – omega)

The angular velocity is the angle swept out by per unit time.

The unit of angular displacement is the radian s^{-1}.

$$\omega = \frac{\Delta\theta}{\Delta t}$$

The angle swept out when the body completes a circle is 2π and the time taken is by definition the time period *T* so this equation can also be written:

$$\omega = \frac{2\pi}{T}$$

Frequency (*f*)

The frequency is the number of complete revolutions per unit time.

$$f = \frac{1}{T}$$

So

$$\omega = 2\pi f$$

Angular velocity and speed

In a time *T* the body in Figure 4.1 completes one full circle so it travels a distance 2π*r*, the circumference of the circle. Speed is defined as the $\frac{\text{distance travelled}}{\text{time taken}}$ so $v = \frac{2\pi r}{T}$. In this time a line joining the body to the centre will sweep out an angle of 2π radians so the angular velocity $\omega = \frac{2\pi}{T}$. Substituting into the equation for *v* we get:

$$v = \omega r$$

Although the speed is constant, when a body moves in a circle its direction and hence velocity are always changing. At any moment in time the magnitude of the instantaneous velocity is equal to the speed and the direction is perpendicular to the radius of the circle.

Centripetal acceleration

From the definition of acceleration, we know that if the velocity of a body changes, it must be accelerating, and that the direction of acceleration is in the direction of the change in velocity. Let us consider a body moving in a circle with a constant speed v. Figure 4.2 shows two positions of the body separated by a short time.

To derive the equation for this acceleration, let us consider a very small angular displacement $\delta\theta$ as represented by Figure 4.3.

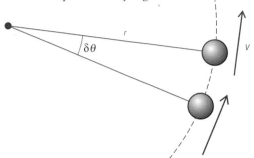

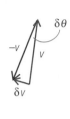

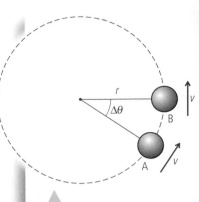

Figure 4.2 A body travels at constant speed around a circle of radius r.

Figure 4.3 A very small angular displacement.

If this small angular displacement has taken place in a short time δt then the angular velocity $\omega = \frac{\delta\theta}{\delta t}$.

From the definition of acceleration, $a = \frac{\text{change of velocity}}{\text{time}}$.

If we took only the magnitude of velocity then the change of velocity would be zero. However, velocity is a *vector* so change in velocity is found by taking the final velocity vector − initial velocity vector as in the vector addition in Figure 4.3. This triangle isn't a right-angled triangle so can't be solved using Pythagoras. However, since the angle $\delta\theta$ is small, we can say that the angle $\delta\theta$ in radians is approximately equal to $\frac{\delta v}{v}$.

Rearranging gives
$$\delta v = v\delta\theta$$
$$\text{acceleration} = \frac{\delta v}{\delta t} = \frac{v\delta\theta}{\delta t}$$

$$a = v\omega$$

But we know that $v = \omega r$ so we can substitute for v and get $a = \omega^2 r$

or substituting for
$$\omega = \frac{v}{r}$$

$$a = \frac{v^2}{r}$$

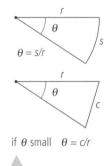

$\theta = s/r$

if θ small $\theta = c/r$

Figure 4.4 The small angle approximation.

You will *not* be asked to reproduce this derivation in the exam.

The direction of this acceleration is in the direction of δv. Now, as the angle $\delta\theta$ is small, the angle between δv, and v is approximately 90° which implies that the acceleration is perpendicular to the velocity. This makes it directed *towards* the centre of the circle; hence the name *centripetal acceleration*.

Exercise

1   A body travels with constant speed of $2\,\text{m s}^{-1}$ around a circle of radius 5 m. Calculate:

   (a) the distance moved in one revolution.
   (b) the displacement in one revolution.
   (c) the time taken for 1 revolution.
   (d) the frequency of the motion.
   (e) the angular velocity.
   (f) the centripetal acceleration.

Centripetal force

From Newton's first law, we know that if a body accelerates, there must be an unbalanced force acting on it. The second law tells us that this force is in the direction of the acceleration. This implies that there must be a force acting towards the centre. This force is called the *centripetal force*.

From Newton's second law we can also deduce that $F = ma$ so $F = \frac{mv^2}{r} = m\omega^2 r$.

$$F = m\omega^2 r$$

Circular motion and work

An alternative way of deducing that the force acts towards the centre is to consider the energy. When a body moves in a circle with constant speed it will have constant KE. This means that no work is being done on the mass. But we also know that since the velocity is changing, there must be a force acting on the body. This force cannot be acting in the direction of motion since if it was then work would be done and the KE would increase. We can therefore deduce that the force must be perpendicular to the direction of motion; in other words, towards the centre of the circle.

Examples of circular motion

All bodies moving in a circle must be acted upon by a force towards the centre of the circle. However, this can be provided by many different forces.

Mass on a string in space

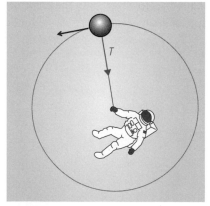

Figure 4.5 An astronaut playing with a mass on a string.

If you take a mass on the end of a string you can easily make it move in a circle but the presence of gravity makes the motion difficult to analyse. It will be simpler if we start by considering what this would be like if performed by an astronaut in deep space; much more difficult to do but easier to analyse. Figure 4.5 shows an astronaut making a mass move in a circle on the end of a string. The only force acting on the mass is the tension in the string.

In this case it is obvious that the centripetal force is provided by the tension so

$$T = \frac{mv^2}{r}.$$

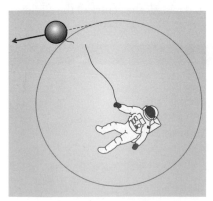

Figure 4.6 The string breaks.

From this we can predict that the force required to keep the mass in its circular motion will increase if the speed increases. This will be felt by the astronaut who, according to Newton's third law, must be experiencing an equal and opposite force on the other end of the string. If the string were to break the ball would have no forces acting on it so would travel at a constant velocity in the same direction as it was moving when the break occurred. This would be at some tangent to the circle as in Figure 4.6.

If you go over a hump back bridge too quickly your car might leave the surface of the road. This is because the force needed to keep you moving in a circle is more than the weight of the car.

In this example the astronaut has a much larger mass than the ball. If this wasn't the case the astronaut would be pulled out of position by the equal and opposite force acting on the other end of the string.

People often think that the mass will fly outwards if the string breaks. This is because they feel themselves being forced outwards so think that if the string breaks the mass will move in this direction. Applying Newton's laws we know that this is not the case. This is an example of a case where intuition gives the wrong answer.

Mass on a string on the Earth (horizontal)

When playing with a mass on a string on the Earth, there will be gravity acting as well as tension. We will first consider how this changes the motion when the mass is made to travel in a horizontal circle as in Figure 4.7.

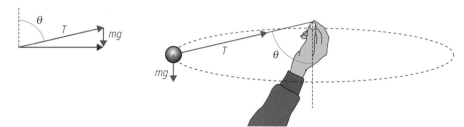

Figure 4.7 A mass swung in a horizontal circle.

For the motion to be horizontal there will be no vertical acceleration so the weight must be balanced by the vertical component of tension ($T \cos \theta = mg$). This means that the string cannot be horizontal but will always be at an angle as shown in Figure 4.7. The centripetal force is provided by the horizontal component of tension ($T \sin \theta = \frac{mv^2}{r}$), which is equal to the vector sum of the two forces.

Mass on a string on the Earth (vertical)

As a mass moves in a vertical circle the force of gravity sometimes acts in the same direction as its motion and sometimes against it. For this reason it is not possible to keep it moving at a constant speed, so here we will just consider it when it is at the top and the bottom of the circle as shown in Figure 4.8.

At the top the centripetal force $\frac{mv_t^2}{r} = T_t + mg$ so $T_t = \frac{mv_t^2}{r} - mg$

At the bottom $\frac{mv_b^2}{r} = T_b - mg$ so $T_t = \frac{mv_b^2}{r} + mg$

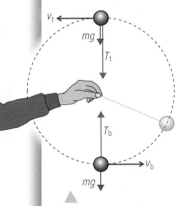

Figure 4.8 A mass swung in a vertical circle.

When the mass approaches the top of the circle its KE is converted into PE, resulting in a loss of speed. If it were to stop at the top then it would fall straight down. The minimum speed necessary for a complete circle is when the weight of the ball is enough to provide the centripetal force without any tension. So if $T_t = 0$ then $\frac{mv_t^2}{r} = mg$.

When you rotate a mass in a vertical circle you definitely feel the change in the tension as it gets less at the top and more at the bottom.

Looping the loop

When looping the loop on a rollercoaster the situation is very similar to the vertical circle example except that the tension is replaced by the normal reaction force. This also gives a minimum speed at the top of the loop when $\frac{mv_t^2}{r} = W$.

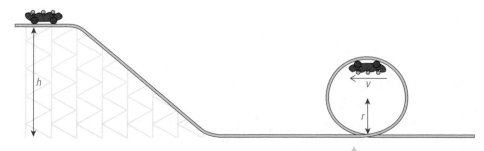

Figure 4.9 Looping the loop.

If the ride is propelled by gravity then the designer must make sure that the car has this minimum speed when it reaches the top.

Applying the law of conservation of energy to the car in Figure 4.9, if no energy is lost then the PE at the top of the hill = PE + KE at the top of the loop.

The minimum speed to complete the loop is $mg = \frac{mv^2}{r}$ so at the top of the loop $\frac{1}{2}mv^2 = \frac{1}{2}mgr$.

The height of the car at the top of the loop is $2r$ so PE = mgh = $mg2r$.

So PE at top of slope = $2mgr + \frac{1}{2}mgr$ = $2.5mgr$ which means the height of the slope = $2.5r$. In any real situation there will be energy lost due to work done against friction and air resistance so the slope will have to be a bit higher.

The wall of death

In the wall of death motorbikes and cars travel around the inside of a cylinder with vertical walls.

Wall of death.

In the wall of death shown in Figure 4.10 the centripetal force is provided by the normal reaction, R. The weight is balanced by the friction between the ball and wall which is dependent on the normal reaction $F = \mu R$. If the velocity is too slow the normal force will be small which means the friction will not be large enough to support the weight.

Figure 4.10 The wall of death with a ball rather than bike.

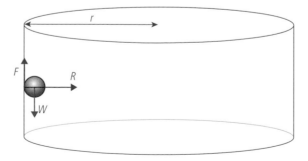

Dynamic friction is less than static friction so once a car starts to skid on a corner it will continue. This is also why it is not a good idea to spin the wheels of a car whilst going round a corner.

Car on a circular track

When a car travels around a circular track the centripetal force is provided by the friction between the tyres and the road. The faster you go, the more friction you need. The problem is that friction has a maximum value given by $F = \mu R$, so if the centripetal force required is greater than this the car will not be able to maintain a circular path. Without friction, for example on an icy road, the car would travel in a straight line. This means that you would hit the kerb on the outside of the circle, giving the impression that you've been thrown outwards. This is of course not the case since there is no force acting outwards.

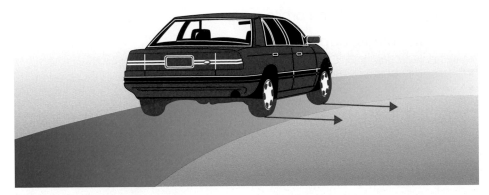

Figure 4.11 A car rounding a bend.

Car on a banked track

A banked track is a track which is angled to make it possible to go faster around the bends; these are used in indoor cycle racing. In the case shown in Figure 4.12 where the bike is represented by a ball, the centripetal force is provided by the horizontal component of the normal reaction force, so even without friction the ball can travel around the track. If the track was angled the other way then it would have the opposite effect. This is called an adverse camber; bends like this should be taken slowly.

A racing cyclist on a banked track in a velodrome.

 Centripetal **force** is not an extra force.

Remember when solving circular motion problems, centripetal force is not an extra force – it is one of the existing forces. Your task is to find which force (or a component of it) points towards the centre.

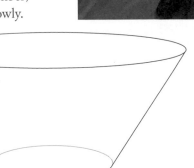

Figure 4.12 A ball on a banked track.

Exercises

2   Calculate the centripetal force for a 1000 kg car travelling around a circular track of radius 50 m at 30 km h^{-1}.

3   A 200 g ball is made to travel in a circle of radius 1 m on the end of a string. If the maximum force that the string can withstand before breaking is 50 N, what is the maximum speed of the ball?

4   A rollercoaster is designed with a 5 m radius vertical loop. Calculate the minimum speed necessary to get around the loop without falling down.

5   A 200 g ball moves in a vertical circle on the end of a 50 cm long string. If its speed at the bottom is 10 m s^{-1} calculate:

   (a) the velocity at the top of the circle.
   (b) the tension at the top of the circle.

CHALLENGE YOURSELF

1   A car of mass 1000 kg is driving around a circular track with radius 50 m. If the coefficient of friction between the tyres and road is 0.8, calculate the maximum speed of the car before it starts to slip. What would the maximum speed be if the track was banked at 45°?

4.2 Gravitational field and orbits

6.2 Gravitational field and orbits

Understandings, applications, and skills:

Newton's law of gravitation
- Describing the relationship between gravitational force and centripetal force.
- Applying Newton's law of gravitation to the motion of an object in circular orbit around a point mass.

Guidance
- *Newton's law of gravitation should be extended to spherical masses of uniform density by assuming that their mass is concentrated at their centre.*

Gravitational field strength
- Solving problems involving gravitational force, gravitational field strength, orbital speed, and orbital period.
- Determining the resultant gravitational field strength due to two bodies.

Guidance
- *Gravitational field strength at a point is the force per unit mass experienced by a small point mass at that point.*
- *Calculations of the resultant gravitational field strength due to two bodies will be restricted to points along the straight line joining the bodies.*

10.1 Describing fields

Understandings, applications, and skills:

(AHL) Gravitational fields

Guidance
- *Gravitational fields are restricted to the radial fields around point or spherical masses and the (assumed) uniform field close to the surface of massive celestial bodies and planetary bodies.*

(AHL) Field lines
- Representing sources of mass, lines of gravitational force, and field patterns using an appropriate symbolism.

Guidance
- *Gravitational fields are restricted to the radial fields around point or spherical masses, and the (assumed) uniform field close to the surface of massive celestial bodies and planetary bodies.*
- *Students should recognize that lines of force can be two-dimensional representations of three-dimensional fields.*

(AHL) Equipotential surfaces
- Describing the connection between equipotential surfaces and field lines.

Guidance
- *Students should recognize that no work is done in moving a mass on an equipotential surface.*

10.2 Fields at work

Understandings, applications, and skills:

(AHL)Potential and potential energy
- Determining the potential energy of a point mass.
- Solving problems involving potential energy.

(AHL)Potential gradient

Guidance
- *Both uniform and radial fields need to be considered.*

(AHL)Potential difference
(AHL)Escape speed
- Solving problems involving the speed required for an object to go into orbit around a planet and for an object to escape the gravitational field of a planet.

(AHL) Orbital motion, orbital speed, and orbital energy
- Solving problems involving orbital energy of masses in circular orbital motion.

Guidance
- *Orbital motion of a satellite around a planet is restricted to a consideration of circular obits.*

(AHL) Forces and inverse-square law behaviour
- Solving problems involving forces on masses in radial and uniform fields.

Guidance
- *Students should recognize that lines of force can be two-dimensional representations of three-dimensional fields.*

Gravitational force and field

We have all seen how an object falls to the ground when released. Newton was certainly not the first person to realize that an apple falls to the ground when dropped from a tree. However, he did recognize that the force that pulls the apple to the ground is the same as the force that holds the Earth in its orbit around the Sun; this was not obvious – after all, the apple moves in a straight line and the Earth moves in a circle. In this chapter we will see how these forces are connected.

Newton's universal law of gravitation

Newton extended his ideas further to say that every single particle of mass in the Universe exerts a force on every other particle of mass. In other words, everything in the Universe is attracted to everything else. So there is a force between the end of your nose and a lump of rock on the Moon.

Newton's universal law of gravitation states that:

> **every single point mass attracts every other point mass with a force that is directly proportional to the product of their masses and inversely proportional to the square of their separation.**

If two point masses with mass m_1 and m_2 are separated by a distance r then the force, F, experienced by each will be given by:

$$F \propto \frac{m_1 m_2}{r^2}$$

The constant of proportionality is the universal gravitational constant G.

$$G = 6.6742 \times 10^{-11}\, \text{m}^3\, \text{kg}^{-1}\, \text{s}^{-2}$$

Therefore the equation is

$$F = G\frac{m_1 m_2}{r^2}$$

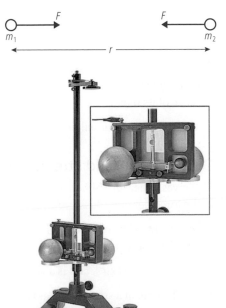

Newton universal law of gravitation suggests a very simple relationship between the mass of a body and the force between it and every other particle of mass in the Universe. However, it does not explain why matter behaves in this way.

To help us understand the way a gravitational field varies throughout space we will use the visual models of field lines and potential surfaces.

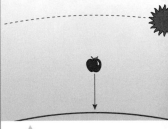

▲ **Figure 4.13** The apple drops and the Sun seems to move in a circle, but it is gravity that makes both things happen.

TOK Was it reasonable for Newton to think that his law applied to the whole Universe?

Figure 4.14 The gravitational force F between two point masses.

We often look at the applications of physics with an international perspective but perhaps we should adopt a universal perspective.

The modern equivalent of the apparatus used by Cavendish to measure G in 1798.

133

Figure 4.15 Forces between two spheres. Even though these bodies don't have the same mass, the force on them is the same size. This is due to Newton's third law – if mass m_1 exerts a force on mass m_2 then m_2 will exert an equal and opposite force on m_1.

Spheres of mass

By working out the total force between every particle of one sphere and every particle of another, Newton deduced that spheres of mass follow the same law, where the separation is the separation between their centres. Every object has a centre of mass where the gravity can be taken to act. In regularly shaped bodies, this is the centre of the object.

How fast does the apple drop?

If we apply Newton's universal law to the apple on the surface of the Earth, we find that it will experience a force given by

$$F = G\frac{m_1 m_2}{r^2}$$

where:
m_1 = mass of the Earth = 5.97×10^{24} kg
m_2 = mass of the apple = 250 g
r = radius of the Earth = 6378 km (at the Equator)

So $F = 2.43$ N

From Newton's 2nd law we know that $F = ma$.

So the acceleration (a) of the apple $= \frac{2.43}{0.25}$ m s^{-2}

$$a = 9.79 \text{ m s}^{-2}$$

This is very close to the average value for the acceleration of free fall on the Earth's surface. It is not exactly the same, since 9.82 m s^{-2} is an average for the whole Earth, the radius of the Earth being maximum at the Equator.

Exercise

6 The mass of the Moon is 7.35×10^{22} kg and the radius 1.74×10^3 km. What is the acceleration due to gravity on the Moon's surface?

Gravitational field

The fact that both the apple and the Earth experience a force without being in contact makes gravity a bit different from the other forces we have come across. To model this situation, we introduce the idea of a *field*. A field is simply a region of space where something is to be found. A potato field, for example, is a region where you find potatoes. A gravitational field is a region where you find gravity. More precisely, gravitational field is defined as a region of space where a mass experiences a force because of its mass.

So there is a gravitational field in your classroom since masses experience a force in it.

Gravitational field strength (g)

This gives a measure of how much force a body will experience in the field. It is defined as the force per unit mass experienced by a small point mass placed in the field.

So if a test mass, m, experiences a force F at some point in space, then the field strength, g, at that point is given by $g = \frac{F}{m}$.

g is measured in N kg^{-1}, and is a vector quantity.

Note: The reason a small test mass is used is because a big mass might change the field that you are trying to measure.

Field strength on the Earth's surface:

Substituting

M = mass of the Earth
= 5.97×10^{24} kg

r = radius of the Earth
= 6367 km

gives

$g = \frac{Gm_1 M}{r^2}$
= 9.82 N kg^{-1}

This is the same as the acceleration due to gravity, which is what you might expect, since Newton's 2nd law says $a = \frac{F}{m}$.

Gravitational field around a spherical object

The force experienced by the mass, m is given by;

$$F = G\frac{Mm}{r^2}$$

So the field strength at this point in space, $g = \frac{F}{m}$

So $\quad g = G\frac{M}{r^2}$

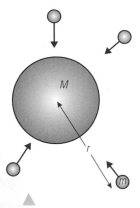

Figure 4.16 The region surrounding M is a gravitational field since all the test masses experience a force.

Exercises

7   The mass of Jupiter is 1.89×10^{27} kg and the radius 71 492 km.
    What is the gravitational field strength on the surface of Jupiter?

8   What is the gravitational field strength at a distance of 1000 km from the surface of the Earth?

Field lines

Field lines are drawn in the direction that a mass would accelerate if placed in the field – they are used to help us visualize the field.

The field lines for a spherical mass are shown in Figure 4.17.

The arrows give the direction of the field.

The field strength (g) is given by the density of the lines.

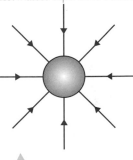

Figure 4.17 Field lines for a sphere of mass.

Gravitational field close to the Earth

When we are doing experiments close to the Earth, in the classroom for example, we assume that the gravitational field is uniform. This means that wherever you put a mass in the classroom it is always pulled downwards with the same force. We say that the field is *uniform*.

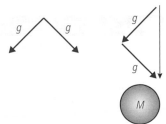

Figure 4.18 Close to the Earth the field is uniform.

The value of g is different in different places on the Earth. Do you know what it is where you live?

Addition of field

Since field strength is a vector, when we add field strengths caused by several bodies, we must remember to add them vectorially.

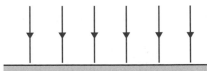

Figure 4.19 Vector addition of field strength.

In this example, the angle between the vectors is 90°. This means that we can use Pythagoras to find the resultant.

$$g = \sqrt{g_1{}^2 + g_2{}^2}$$

Worked example

Calculate the gravitational field strength at points A and B in Figure 4.20.

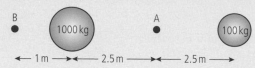

Figure 4.20.

Solution

The gravitational field strength at A is equal to the sum of the fields due to the two masses.

$$\text{Field strength due to large mass} = \frac{G \times 1000}{2.5^2} = 1.07 \times 10^{-8}\,\text{N}\,\text{kg}^{-1}$$

$$\text{Field strength due to small mass} = \frac{G \times 100}{2.5^2} = 1.07 \times 10^{-9}\,\text{N}\,\text{kg}^{-1}$$

$$\text{Field strength} = 1.07 \times 10^{-8} - 1.07 \times 10^{-9}$$
$$= 9.63 \times 10^{-9}\,\text{N}\,\text{kg}^{-1}$$

Since field strength g is a vector, the resultant field strength equals the vector sum.

Exercises

9 Calculate the gravitational field strength at point B.

10 Calculate the gravitational field strength at A if the big mass were changed for a 100 kg mass.

Gravitational potential in a uniform field

As you lift a mass m from the ground, you do work. This increases the PE of the object. As PE = mgh, we know the PE gained by the mass depends partly on the size of the mass (m) and partly on where it is (gh). The 'where it is' part is called the 'gravitational potential (V)'. This is a useful quantity because, if we know it, we can calculate how much PE a given mass would have if placed there.

Potential is PE per unit mass or:

Gravitational potential is the work done per unit mass in taking a small point mass from zero potential (the surface of the Earth) to the point in question.

In the simple example of masses in a room, the potential is proportional to height, so a mass m placed at the same height in the room will have the same PE. By joining all positions of the same potential we get a *line of equal potential*, and these are useful for visualizing the changes in PE as an object moves around the room.

Contours

Close to the Earth, lines of equipotential join points that are the same height above the ground. These are the same as contours on a map.

Worked example

Referring to Figure 4.21 what is the potential at A?

Solution

$V_A = gh$

so

potential at A = $10 \times 3 = 30\,\text{J}\,\text{kg}^{-1}$

Figure 4.21.

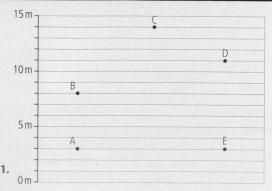

Equipotentials and field lines

If we draw the field lines in our 15 m room they will look like Figure 4.22. The field is uniform so they are parallel and equally spaced. If you were to move upwards along a field line (A–B), you would have to do work and therefore your PE would increase. On the other hand, if you travelled perpendicular to the field lines (A–E), no work would be done, in which case you must be travelling along a line of equipotential. For this reason, field lines and equipotentials are perpendicular.

The amount of work done as you move up is equal to the change in potential × mass.

$$\text{Work} = \Delta V m$$

But the work done is also equal to

$$\text{force} \times \text{distance} = mg\Delta h$$

So

$$\Delta V m = mg\Delta h$$

Rearranging gives

$$\frac{\Delta V}{\Delta h} = g$$

or the potential gradient = the field strength.

So lines of equipotential that are close together represent a strong field.

This is similar to the situation with contours as shown in Figure 4.23. Contours that are close together mean that the gradient is steep and where the gradient is steep, there will be a large force pulling you down the slope.

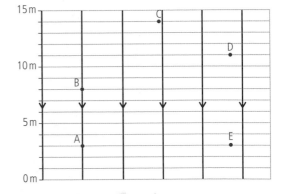

Figure 4.22 Equipotentials and field lines.

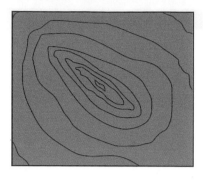
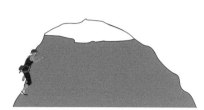

Figure 4.23 Close contours mean a steep mountain.

In this section we have been dealing with the simplified situation. Firstly we have only been dealing with bodies close to the Earth, where the field is uniform, and secondly we have been assuming that the ground is a position of zero potential. A more general situation would be to consider large distances away from a sphere of mass. This is rather more difficult but the principle is the same, as are the relationships between field lines and equipotentials.

Gravitational potential due to a massive sphere

The gravitational potential at point P is defined as:

The work done per unit mass taking a small test mass from a position of zero potential to the point P.

In the previous example we took the Earth's surface to be zero but a better choice would be somewhere where the mass isn't affected by the field at all. Since $g = \frac{GM}{r^2}$ the only place completely out of the field is at an infinite distance from the mass – so let's start there.

Figure 4.24 represents the journey from infinity to point P, a distance r from a large mass M. The work done making this journey $= -W$ so the potential $V = \frac{-W}{m}$.

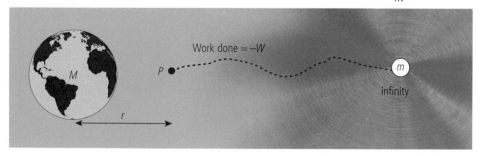

Figure 4.24 The journey from infinity to point P.

The negative sign is because the mass is being pulled to the Earth by the attractive force of gravity so you wouldn't have to pull it, it would pull you. The direction of force applied by you, holding the mass, is opposite to the direction of motion, so the work done by you would be negative.

Infinity

TOK

We can't really take a mass from infinity and bring it to the point in question, but we can calculate how much work would be required if we did. Is it OK to calculate something we can never do?

Calculating the work done

There are two problems when you try to calculate the work done from infinity to P; firstly the distance is infinite (obviously) and secondly the force gets bigger as you get closer. To solve this problem, we use the area under the force–distance graph (remember the work done stretching a spring?). From Newton's universal law of gravitation we know that the force varies according to the equation:

$F = \dfrac{GMm}{x^2}$ so the graph will be as shown in Figure 4.25.

The area under this graph can be found by integrating the function $-\dfrac{GMm}{x^2}$ from infinity to r (you'll do this in maths). This gives the result:

$$W = -\frac{GMm}{r}$$

So the potential, $V = \dfrac{W}{m} = -\dfrac{GM}{r}$

The graph of potential against distance is drawn in Figure 4.26. The gradient of this line gives the field strength, but notice that the gradient is positive and the field strength negative so we get the formula

$$g = -\frac{\Delta V}{\Delta x}$$

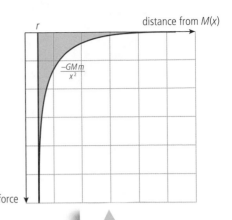

Figure 4.25 Graph of force against distance as the test mass is moved towards M.

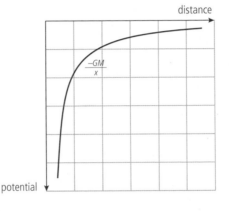

Integration

The integral mentioned here is

$$V = \int_{\infty}^{r} \frac{GM}{x^2} dx$$

Figure 4.26 Graph of potential against distance.

Equipotentials and potential wells

If we draw the lines of equipotential for the field around a sphere, we get concentric circles, as in Figure 4.27. In 3D these would form spheres, in which case they would be called *equipotential surfaces* rather the lines of equipotential.

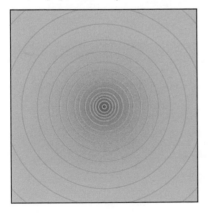

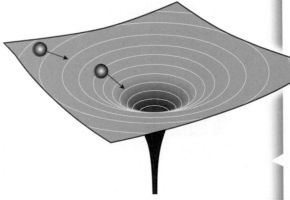

Figure 4.27 The lines of equipotential and potential well for a sphere.

An alternative way of representing this field is to draw the hole or well that these contours represent. This is a very useful visualization, since it not only represents the change in potential but by looking at the gradient, we can also see where the force is biggest. If you imagine a ball rolling into this well you can visualize the field.

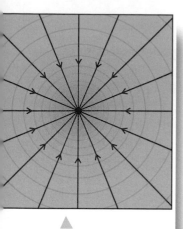

Figure 4.28 Equipotentials and field lines.

Relationship between field lines and potential

If we draw the field lines and the potential as in Figure 4.28, we see that, as before, they are perpendicular. We can also see that the lines of equipotential are closest together where the field is strongest (where the field lines are most dense). This agrees with our earlier finding that $g = -\frac{\Delta V}{\Delta x}$

Addition of potential

Potential is a scalar quantity, so adding potentials is just a matter of adding the magnitudes. If we take the example shown in Figure 4.29, to find the potential at point P we calculate the potential due to A and B then add them together.

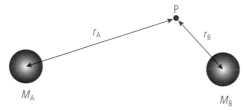

Figure 4.29 Two masses.

The total potential at $P = -\frac{GM_A}{r_A} + -\frac{GM_B}{r_B}$

The lines of equipotential for this example are shown in Figure 4.30.

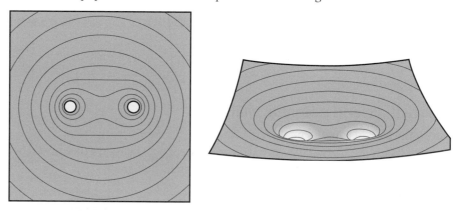

Figure 4.30 Equipotentials and potential wells for two equal masses. If you look at the potential well, you can imagine a ball could sit on the hump between the two holes. This is where the field strength is zero.

Escape speed

If a body is thrown straight up, its KE decreases as it rises. If we ignore air resistance, this KE is converted into PE. When it gets to the top, the final PE will equal the initial KE, so $\frac{1}{2}mv^2 = mgh$.

If we throw a body up really fast, it might get so high that the gravitational field strength would start to decrease. In this case, we would have to use the formula for the PE around a sphere.

$$PE = -\frac{GMm}{r}$$

So when it gets to its furthest point as shown in Figure 4.31

$$\text{loss of KE} = \text{gain in PE}$$

$$\frac{1}{2}mv^2 - 0 = -\frac{GMm}{R_2} - -\frac{GMm}{R_E}$$

If we throw the ball fast enough, it will never come back. This means that it has reached a place where it is no longer attracted back to the Earth, which we call infinity. Of course it can't actually reach infinity but we can substitute $R_2 = \infty$ into our equation to find out how fast that would be.

$$\frac{1}{2}mv^2 = -\frac{GMm}{\infty} - -\frac{GMm}{R_E}$$

$$\frac{1}{2}mv^2 = \frac{GMm}{R_E}$$

Rearranging gives:
$$v_{\text{escape}} = \sqrt{\frac{2GM}{R_E}}$$

If we calculate the escape velocity for the Earth it is about $11\,\text{km s}^{-1}$.

Why the Earth has an atmosphere but the Moon does not

The average velocity of an air molecule at the surface of the Earth is about $500\,\text{m s}^{-1}$. This is much less than the velocity needed to escape from the Earth, and for that reason the atmosphere doesn't escape.

The escape velocity on the Moon is $2.4\,\text{km s}^{-1}$ so you might expect the Moon to have an atmosphere. However, $500\,\text{m s}^{-1}$ is the *average* speed; a lot of the molecules would be travelling faster than this leading to a significant number escaping, and over time all would escape.

Black holes

A star is a big ball of gas held together by the gravitational force. The reason this force doesn't cause the star to collapse is that the particles are continuously given KE from the nuclear reactions taking place (fusion). As time progresses, the nuclear fuel gets used up, so the star starts to collapse. As this happens, the escape velocity increases until it is bigger than the speed of light. At this point not even light can escape and the star has formed a black hole.

Exercises

17 The mass of the Moon is $7.4 \times 10^{22}\,\text{kg}$ and its radius is $1738\,\text{km}$. Show that its escape speed is $2.4\,\text{km s}^{-1}$.

18 Why doesn't the Earth's atmosphere contain hydrogen?

19 The mass of the Sun is $2.0 \times 10^{30}\,\text{kg}$. Calculate how small its radius would have to be for it to become a black hole.

20 When travelling away from the Earth, a rocket runs out of fuel at a distance of $1.0 \times 10^5\,\text{km}$. How fast would the rocket have to be travelling for it to escape from the Earth? (Mass of the Earth = $6.0 \times 10^{24}\,\text{kg}$, radius = $6400\,\text{km}$.)

The solar system

The solar system consists of the Sun at the centre surrounded by eight orbiting planets. The shape of the orbits is actually slightly elliptical but to make things simpler, we will assume them to be circular. We know that for a body to travel in a circle, there must be an unbalanced force (called the centripetal force, $m\omega^2 r$) acting towards the centre. The force that holds the planets in orbit around the Sun is the gravitational force $\frac{GMm}{r^2}$.

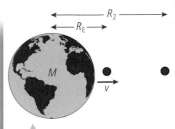

Figure 4.31 A mass m thrown away from the Earth.

Air resistance

If you threw something up with a velocity of $11\,\text{km s}^{-1}$ it would be rapidly slowed by air resistance. The work done against this force would be converted to thermal energy causing the body to vaporize. Rockets leaving the Earth do not have to travel anywhere near this fast, as they are not thrown upwards, but have a rocket engine that provides a continual force.

TOK

How can light be slowed down by the effect of gravity, when according to Newton's law, it has no mass, therefore isn't affected by gravity? This can't be explained by Newton's theories, but Einstein solved the problem with his general theory of relativity.

Equating these two expressions gives us an equation for orbital motion.

$$m\omega^2 r = \frac{GMm}{r^2} \qquad (1)$$

Now ω is the angular speed of the planet; that is, the angle swept out by a radius per unit time. If the time taken for one revolution (2π radians) is T then $\omega = \frac{2\pi}{T}$.

Substituting into equation (1) gives

$$m\left(\frac{2\pi}{T}\right)^2 r = \frac{GMm}{r^2}$$

Rearranging gives:

$$\frac{T^2}{r^3} = \frac{4\pi^2}{GM}$$

where M is the mass of the Sun.

So for planets orbiting the Sun, $\frac{T^2}{r^3}$ is a constant, or T^2 is proportional to r^3.

This is *Kepler's third law*.

From this we can deduce that the planet closest to the Sun (Mercury) has a shorter time period than the planet furthest away. This is supported by measurement:

Time period of Mercury = 0.24 years.

Time period of Neptune = 165 years.

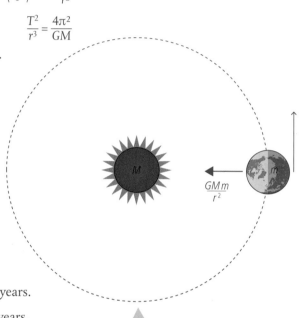

▲ **Figure 4.32** The Earth orbiting the Sun.

Exercise

21 Use a database of planetary information to make a table of the values of time period and radius for all the planets. Plot a graph to show that T^2 is proportional to r^3.

Energy of an orbiting body

As planets orbit the Sun they have KE due to their movement and PE due to their position. We know that their PE is given by the equation:

$$PE = -\frac{GMm}{r}$$

and

$$KE = \tfrac{1}{2}mv^2$$

We also know that if we approximate the orbits to be circular then equating the centripetal force with gravity gives:

$$\frac{GMm}{r^2} = \frac{mv^2}{r}$$

Rearranging and multiplying by $\frac{1}{2}$ gives

$$\tfrac{1}{2}mv^2 = \frac{GMm}{2r}$$

$$KE = \frac{GMm}{2r}$$

The total energy = PE + KE = $-\dfrac{GMm}{r} + \dfrac{GMm}{2r}$

$$\text{Total energy} = -\frac{GMm}{2r}$$

Earth satellites

The equations we have derived for the orbits of the planets also apply to the satellites that man has put into orbits around the Earth. This means that the satellites closer to the Earth have a time period much shorter than the distant ones. For example, a low-orbit spy satellite could orbit the Earth once every two hours and a much higher TV satellite orbits only once a day.

The total energy of an orbiting satellite $= -\frac{GMm}{2r}$ so the energy of a high satellite (big r) is less negative and hence bigger than a low orbit. To move from a low orbit into a high one therefore requires energy to be added (work done).

Imagine you are in a spaceship orbiting the Earth in a low orbit. To move into a higher orbit you would have to use your rocket motor to increase your energy. If you kept doing this you could move from orbit to orbit, getting further and further from the Earth. The energy of the spaceship in each orbit can be displayed as a graph as in Figure 4.33.

From the graph we can see that low satellites have greater KE but less total energy than distant satellites, so although the distant ones move with slower speed, we have to do work to increase the orbital radius. Going the other way, to move from a distant orbit to a close orbit, the spaceship needs to lose energy. Satellites in low Earth orbit are not completely out of the atmosphere, so lose energy due to air resistance. As they lose energy they spiral in towards the Earth.

There are two versions of the equation for centripetal force

Speed version:
$F = \frac{mv^2}{r}$

Angular speed version:

$F = m\omega^2 r$

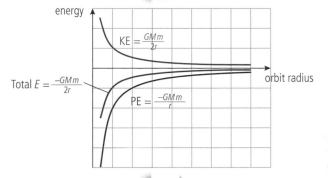

▲ **Figure 4.33** Graph of KE, PE, and total energy for a satellite with different orbital radii.

The lowest satellites orbit the Earth at a height of around 150 km. However, they are not entirely out of the atmosphere so need the occasional boost of power to keep them travelling fast enough or they would move to an even lower orbit. These satellites are mainly used for spying.

TV satellites are geostationary so must be placed about 6 Earth radii from the Earth. With the thousands of TV channels available you might expect there to be thousands of satellites but there are only about 300.

A low-orbit spy satellite.

Exercises

22 So that they can stay above the same point on the Earth, TV satellites have a time period equal to one day. Calculate the radius of their orbit.

23 A spy satellite orbits 400 km above the Earth. If the radius of the Earth is 6400 km, what is the time period of the orbit?

24 If the satellite in Exercise 23 has a mass of 2000 kg, calculate its

(a) KE
(b) PE
(c) total energy.

The orbits of spy satellites are set so that they pass over places of interest. Which countries have most spy satellites passing overhead?

Practice questions

1. This question is about the kinematics and dynamics of circular motion.

   (a) A car goes round a curve in a road at constant speed. Explain why, although its speed is constant, it is accelerating. (2)

   In Figure 4.34, a marble (small glass sphere) rolls down a track, the bottom part of which has been bent into a loop. The end A of the track, from which the marble is released, is at a height of 0.80 m above the ground. Point B is the lowest point and point C the highest point of the loop. The diameter of the loop is 0.35 m.

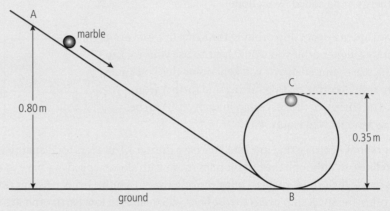

   Figure 4.34.

   The mass of the marble is 0.050 kg. Friction forces and any gain in kinetic energy due to the rotating of the marble can be ignored. The acceleration due to gravity, $g = 10 \, \text{m s}^{-2}$.
   Consider the marble when it is at point C.

   (b) (i) Copy Figure 4.34 and on the diagram, draw an arrow to show the direction of the resultant force acting on the marble. (1)

   (ii) State the names of the **two** forces acting on the marble. (2)

   (iii) Deduce that the speed of the marble is $3.0 \, \text{m s}^{-1}$. (3)

   (iv) Determine the resultant force acting on the marble and hence determine the reaction force of the track on the marble. (4)

   (*Total 12 marks*)

2. This question is about friction.

   (a) Define what is meant by *coefficient of friction*. (1)

   Figure 4.35 shows a particular ride at a funfair (sometimes called 'the fly') that involves a spinning circular room. When it is spinning fast enough a person in the room feels 'stuck' to the wall. The floor is lowered and they remain held in place on the wall. Friction prevents the person from falling.

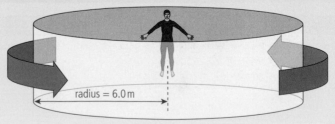

   Figure 4.35.

(b) (i) Explain whether the friction acting on the person is static, dynamic, **or** a combination of both. (2)

Figure 4.36 shows a cross-section of the ride when the floor has been lowered.

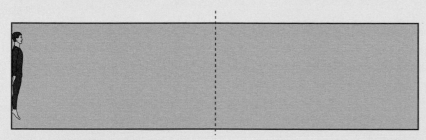

Figure 4.36.

(ii) Copy Figure 4.36 and, on your diagram, draw labelled arrows to represent the forces acting on the person. (3)

(c) Using the data given below:

mass of person = 80 kg
coefficient of friction between the person and the wall = 0.40
radius of circular room = 6.0 m

calculate each of the following.

(i) The magnitude of the minimum resultant horizontal force on the person. (2)

(ii) The minimum speed of the wall for a person to be 'stuck' to it. (2)

(*Total 10 marks*)

3. This question is about gravitation.

(a) Define *gravitational potential* at a point. (2)

(b) Figure 4.37 shows the variation of gravitational potential V of a planet and its moon with distance r from the centre of the planet. The unit of separation is arbitrary. The centre of the planet corresponds to $r = 0$ and the centre of the moon to $r = 1$. The curve starts at the surface of the planet and ends at the surface of the moon.

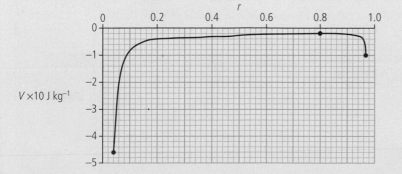

Figure 4.37.

(i) At the position where $r = 0.8$, the gravitational field strength is zero. Determine the ratio

$$\frac{\text{mass of planet}}{\text{mass of moon}}$$ (3)

(ii) A satellite of mass 1500 kg is launched from the surface of the planet. Determine the **minimum** kinetic energy at launch the satellite must have so that it can reach the surface of the moon. (3)

(Total 8 marks)

4. This question is about gravitational potential energy.

Figure 4.38 shows the variation of gravitational potential V due to the Earth with distance R from the centre of the Earth. The radius of the Earth is 6.4×10^6 m. The graph does not show the variation of potential V within the Earth.

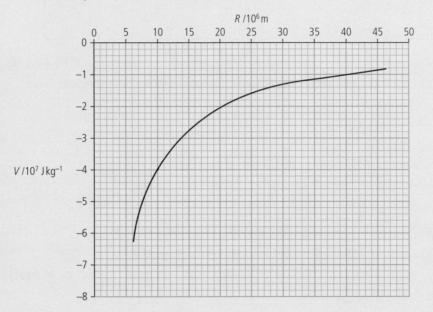

Figure 4.38.

(a) Use Figure 4.38 to find the gravitational potential

    (i) at the surface of the Earth. (1)

    (ii) at a height of 3.6×10^7 m above the surface of the Earth. (2)

(b) Use the values you have found in part (a) to determine the minimum energy required to put a satellite of mass 1.0×10^4 kg into an orbit at a height of 3.6×10^7 m above the surface of the Earth. (3)

(c) Give **two** reasons why more energy is required to put this satellite into orbit than that calculated in (b) above. (2)

(Total 8 marks)

5. This question is about a probe in orbit.

A probe of mass m is in a circular orbit of radius r around a spherical planet of mass M.

(a) State why the work done by the gravitational force during one full revolution of the probe is zero. (1)

(b) Deduce for the probe in orbit that its

   (i)   speed is $v = \sqrt{\dfrac{GM}{r}}$ (2)

   (ii) total energy is $E = -\dfrac{GMm}{2r}$ (2)

(c) It is now required to place the probe in another circular orbit further away from the planet. To do this, the probe's engines will be fired for a very short time.

State and explain whether the work done on the probe by the engines is positive, negative **or** zero. (2)

(*Total 7 marks***)**

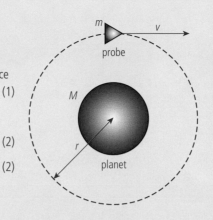

Figure 4.39.

(diagram not to scale)

6. This question is about circular motion.

A ball of mass 0.25 kg is attached to a string and is made to rotate with constant speed v along a horizontal circle of radius $r = 0.33$ m. The string is attached to the ceiling and makes an angle of 30° with the vertical.

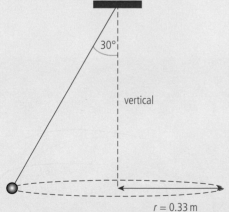

$r = 0.33$ m   **Figure 4.40.**

(a) (i) On the diagram above, draw and label arrows to represent the forces on the ball in the position shown. (2)

   (ii) State and explain whether the ball is in equilibrium. (2)

(b) Determine the speed of rotation of the ball. (3)

(*Total 7 marks***)**

05

Oscillations and waves

Essential ideas

4.1 Oscillations

A study of oscillations underpins many areas of physics with simple harmonic motion (SHM) a fundamental oscillation that appears in various natural phenomena.

4.2 Travelling waves

There are many forms of waves available to be studied. A common characteristic of all travelling waves is that they carry energy, but generally the medium through which they travel will not be permanently disturbed.

4.3 Wave characteristics

All waves can be described by the same sets of mathematical ideas. Detailed knowledge of one area leads to the possibility of prediction in another.

4.4 Wave behaviour

Waves interact with media and each other in a number of ways that can be unexpected and useful.

4.5 Standing waves

When travelling waves meet they can superpose to form standing waves in which energy may not be transferred.

9.1 Simple harmonic motion (HL only)

The solution of the harmonic oscillator can be framed around the variation of kinetic and potential energy in the system.

9.2 Single-slit diffraction (HL only)

Single-slit diffraction occurs when a wave is incident upon a slit of approximately the same size as the wavelength.

9.3 Interference (HL only)

Interference patterns from multiple slits and thin films produce accurately repeatable patterns.

9.4 Resolution (HL only)

Resolution places an absolute limit on the extent to which an optical or other system can separate images of objects.

9.5 Doppler effect (HL only)

The Doppler effect describes the phenomenon of wavelength / frequency shift when relative motion occurs.

Waves change direction due to changing depth of the water. The change in wave speed can also cause the wave to break resulting in the white foam visible in the photo.

NATURE OF SCIENCE

An oscillating body does not move in a circle but the mathematical model representing one component of circular motion is the same as that which describes a simple oscillation. In physics it is quite common that the same model can be used in different applications. As the mathematics becomes more complicated it becomes more difficult to relate the equations to the motion; this is where computer simulations and visual representations help our understanding.

5.1 Oscillations

4.1 Oscillations

Understandings, applications, and skills:

Simple harmonic oscillations
- Qualitatively describing the energy changes taking place during one cycle of an oscillation.

  Guidance
  - *Graphs describing simple harmonic motion should include displacement–time, velocity–time, acceleration–time, and acceleration–displacement.*

Time period, frequency, amplitude, displacement, and phase difference
- Sketching and interpreting graphs of simple harmonic motion examples.

Conditions for simple harmonic motion

  Guidance
  - *Students are expected to understand the significance of the negative sign in the relationship $a \propto -x$*

9.1 Simple harmonic motion

Understandings, applications, and skills:

(AHL) Defining equation of SHM
- Solving problems involving acceleration, velocity, and displacement during simple harmonic motion, both graphically and algebraically.

  Guidance
  - *Contexts for this subtopic are limited to the simple pendulum or a mass–spring system.*

(AHL) Energy changes
- Describing the interchange of kinetic and potential energy during simple harmonic motion.
- Solving problems involving energy transfer during simple harmonic motion, both graphically and algebraically.

The simple pendulum

A simple pendulum consists of a small mass, called a bob, hanging on an inextensible (non-stretchy) string. If left alone the mass will hang at rest so that the string is vertical but if pushed to one side it will oscillate about its equilibrium position. The reason that the pendulum oscillates is because there is always a force acting towards the centre as shown in Figure 5.1.

The forces drawn are the tension and weight; these forces add to give a resultant that is always directed towards the equilibrium position. Furthermore, the size of the resultant (blue arrow) gets bigger as the distance from the equilibrium position increases. Notice how the tension gets less as the pendulum swings up towards the horizontal position, and is greatest when it swings through the bottom. At the

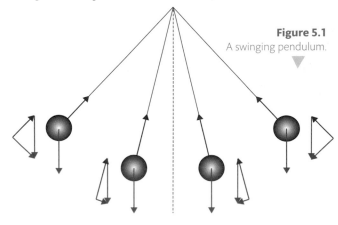

Figure 5.1
A swinging pendulum.

A swing is an example of oscillatory motion.

bottom of the swing the tension will actually be greater than the weight, causing the bob to move in a circle. Due to the changing angles, this motion is rather difficult to analyse. To make this simpler we will consider only very small displacements.

Simple harmonic motion

If the swings are kept small then force becomes directly proportional to the displacement from equilibrium. Consider the small angle shown in Figure 5.2.

Since the angle is very small we can make some approximations.

1. The displacement is horizontal (in reality the bob moves slightly up).
2. The force acting towards the equilibrium position is the horizontal component of the tension, $T \sin \theta$ (in reality it is the *resultant* of the weight and the tension).
3. The weight is approximately the same as the tension (in reality the tension is greatest at the bottom of the swing) $T = mg$ so the restoring force $= T \sin \theta = mg \sin \theta$.

Since the motion has been reduced to a one-dimensional problem we can write $F = -mg \sin \theta$ to take into account the direction of this force.

Looking at the triangle made by the string and the equilibrium position we can see that

$$\sin \theta = \frac{x}{L}$$

so

$$F = -\frac{mgx}{L}$$

Substituting for $F = ma$ from Newton's second law gives $ma = -\frac{mgx}{L}$

$$a = -\frac{gx}{L}$$

So we can deduce that for this motion the acceleration is directly proportional to the displacement from a fixed point and always directed towards that point. This kind of motion is called *simple harmonic motion*.

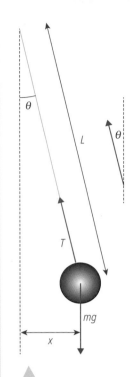

▲ **Figure 5.2** Pendulum with small displacement.

SHM and the sine function

Later in this chapter we will do a more thorough graphical analysis of SHM but by observing the motion of the pendulum we can already see that as the bob swings back and forth its displacement will be described by a sine curve. In other words, the displacement of the bob is sinusoidal. Let us analyse the motion represented by the sine curve in Figure 5.3.

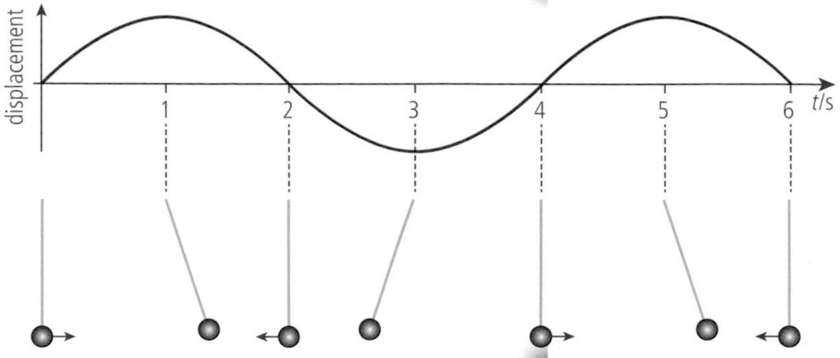

▲ **Figure 5.3** Sinusoidal motion.

0 s At the start the displacement is zero and the velocity is maximum and positive (this can be deduced from the gradient). The pendulum bob is swinging through the centre moving right.
1 s The displacement is maximum and positive and the velocity has reduced to zero. The pendulum bob is at the top of its swing to the right.
2 s The displacement is zero again and the velocity maximum and negative. The pendulum bob is swinging through the centre travelling left.
3 s The displacement is maximum and the velocity is zero.
4 s Back to the start again.

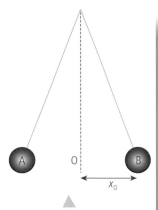

Figure 5.4 A swinging pendulum.

Terms and quantities

Before going any further we shall define the terms and quantities used to describe oscillatory motion with reference to the pendulum in Figure 5.4 swinging backwards and forwards between A and B.

Cycle

One complete 'there and back' swing, from A to B and back to A.

Amplitude (x_0)

The maximum displacement from the equilibrium position, the swing of the pendulum is symmetric so this could be the distance OA or OB.

The unit of amplitude is the metre.

Time period (T)

The time taken for one complete cycle from A to B and back to A.

The unit of time period is the second.

Frequency (f)

The number of complete cycles per second.

$$f = \frac{1}{T}$$

The unit of frequency is the hertz.

Equations for SHM

We have seen that simple harmonic motion is sinusoidal so the graph of displacement against time has the shape of a sine function but what is the equation of the line? Let us compare the displacement–time graph against a sine curve as in Figure 5.5.

The equation of the sine curve is $y = A \sin \theta$.

Comparing the two curves we can see that an angle of 2π is equivalent to one cycle of the oscillation so when $t = T$, $\theta = 2\pi$ so $\theta = \frac{2\pi t}{T}$. For the example with time period 4 s, the equivalent angle after 1 s will be

$$\theta = \frac{(2\pi \times 1)}{4} = \frac{\pi}{2}.$$

An alternative way of writing this is $\theta = 2\pi ft$

so $\qquad x = x_0 \sin (2\pi ft)$.

Angular frequency (ω)

This is the angular equivalent to frequency.

$$\omega = 2\pi f$$

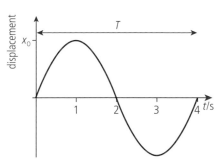

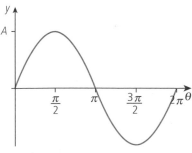

Figure 5.5 Sine curve compared to SHM.

The unit of angular frequency is radian/second (rad s^{-1}) so the equation for SHM can be written $x = x_0 \sin \omega t$.

Spreadsheet simulation

The equation for the displacement – time curve is $x = x_0 \sin(\omega t)$.

You can try plotting this in a graph plotting or spreadsheet program to see the effect of changing x_0 and f.

Set the spreadsheet up as in Table 5.1 so that you can vary the values of f and x_0.

	B2	▾	f_x	=E$3*SIN(2*PI()*E$2*A2)				
	A	B	C	D	E	F	G	H	I
1	time/s	displacement/m						
2	0.0	0.0000		frequency	1			
3	0.1	1.1756		amplitude	2			
4	0.2	1.9021						
5	0.3	1.9021						
6	0.4	1.1756						
7	0.5	0.0000						
8	0.6	-1.1756						
9	0.7	-1.9021						
10	0.8	-1.9021						
11	0.9	-1.1756						
12	1.0	0.0000						
13								
14								

displacement vs time

Notice the $ sign in the equation; this prevents the values of x_0 and f changing when you copy the equation down into all the cells.

If the time starts when the pendulum is at its highest point to the right (point B in Figure 5.4) then the equation would be $x = x_0 \cos \omega t$; this is still said to be sinusoidal.

Table 5.1 Simulation of SHM.

Because the time taken for a pendulum to complete one cycle is always the same even if the amplitude of the swing changes, pendulums used to be extensively used in clock mechanisms. Today, pendulums are not used so often but many clocks still use some sort of mechanical oscillation.

Mass on a spring

If a mass hanging on the end of a spring is lifted up and released, it will bounce up and down as in Figure 5.6. The forces acting on the mass are weight and the tension in the spring. The weight is always the same but the tension depends on how far the spring is stretched. (When you stretch a spring, the tension is proportional to the extension.)

At A, the spring is short, so the tension will be small; the weight will therefore be bigger than the tension, so the resultant force will be downwards.

As the mass passes through the middle point, the forces will be balanced.

At B, the spring is stretched, so the tension is large; the tension will therefore be greater than the weight, so the resultant for ce will be upwards.

Again we can see that the acceleration is proportional to the displacement from the central point and always directed towards it.

So this motion is also simple harmonic.

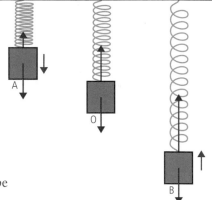

Figure 5.6 The tension increases as the spring is stretched. The resultant (orange) increases with increased distance from the centre and is always directed towards the centre.

Exercises

1 State whether the following are examples of simple harmonic motion.

   (a) A ball rolling up and down on a track (Figure 5.7a).
   (b) A cylindrical tube floating in water when pushed down and released (Figure 5.7b).
   (c) A tennis ball bouncing back and forth across the net.
   (d) A bouncing ball.

2 A pendulum completes 20 swings in 12 s. What is

   (a) the frequency?   (b) the angular frequency?

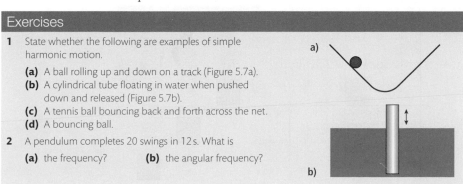

Figure 5.7

Graphical representation of SHM

When representing the motion of bodies in Chapter 2 we drew displacement–time, velocity–time, and acceleration–time graphs. Let us now do the same for the motion of a mass on a spring. The mass on the end of the spring is lifted to point A and released. In this example we will start with the mass at its highest point (maximum positive displacement) so the equation for the displacement will be $x = x_0 \cos \omega t$.

Displacement–time

As before, O is the equilibrium position and we will take this to be our position of zero displacement. Above this is positive displacement and below is negative.

At A, the mass has maximum positive displacement from O.

At O, the mass has zero displacement from O.

At B, the mass has maximum negative displacement from O.

We can see that the shape of this displacement–time graph is a cosine curve.

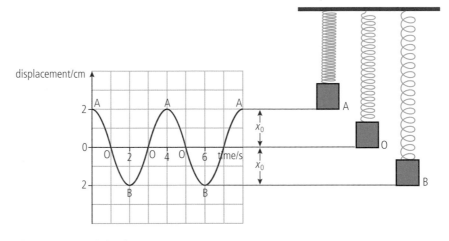

Figure 5.8 Displacement–time graph.

The equation of this line is $x = x_0 \cos \omega t$,
where x_0 is the maximum displacement and ω is the angular frequency.

Velocity–time

From the gradient of the displacement–time graph (Figure 5.8), we can calculate the velocity.

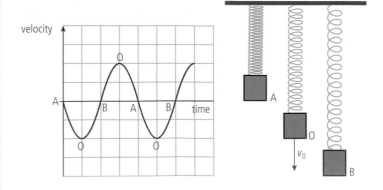

Figure 5.9 Velocity–time graph.

At A, gradient = 0 so velocity is zero.

At O, gradient is negative and maximum, so velocity is down and maximum.

At B, gradient = 0 so velocity is zero.

The equation of this line is $v = -v_0 \sin \omega t$ where v_0 is the maximum velocity.

Acceleration–time

From the gradient of the velocity–time graph (Figure 5.9) we can calculate the acceleration.

At A, the gradient is maximum and negative so acceleration is maximum and downwards.

At O, the gradient is zero so acceleration is zero.

At B, the gradient is maximum and positive so the acceleration is maximum and upwards.

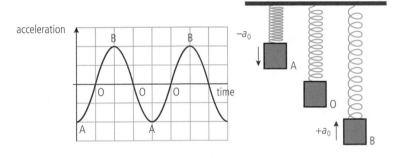

The equation of this line is $a = -a_0 \cos \omega t$ where a_0 is this maximum acceleration.

So $x = x_0 \cos \omega t$ and $a = -a_0 \cos \omega t$

When displacement increases, acceleration increases proportionally but in a negative sense; in other words: $a \propto -x$

We have confirmed that the acceleration of the body is directly proportional to the displacement of the body and always directed towards a fixed point.

Worked example

A mass on a spring is oscillating with a frequency 0.2 Hz and amplitude 3.0 cm. What is the displacement of the mass 10.66 s after it is released from the top?

Solution

$$x = x_0 \cos \omega t. \qquad \text{Since this is SHM}$$

where x = displacement

x_0 = amplitude = 3 cm

v = angular velocity = $2\pi f = 2\pi \times 0.2$

$\quad = 0.4\pi$ Hz

t = time = 10.66 s

$x = 0.03 \times \cos (0.4\pi \times 10.66)$ Substituting into the formula

$x = 0.02$ m

$\quad = 2$ cm

When calculating $\cos \omega t$, you must have your calculator set on radians.

Exercises

3 For the same mass on a spring in the Worked example on page 155, calculate the displacement after 1.55 s.

4 Draw a displacement time sketch graph for this motion.

5 A long pendulum has time period 10 s. If the bob is displaced 2 m from the equilibrium position and released, how long will it take to move 1 m?

6 As a mass on a spring travels upwards through the equilibrium position, its velocity is 0.5 m s^{-1}. If the frequency of the pendulum is 1 Hz what will the velocity of the bob be after 0.5 s?

Representing SHM with circular motion

By applying the conservation of energy to (or simply observing) a swinging pendulum it is clear that the maximum speed at which the bob swings past the equilibrium position is related to both the maximum height of the swing and the frequency, but to find exactly how these quantities are related requires some more sophisticated mathematical analysis involving calculus. An alternative method is to use the horizontal component of circular motion. If you were to observe the ball in Figure 5.11 from the side you would only see one component of the motion, so the ball would appear to be moving up and down with an amplitude equal to the radius of the circle.

Figure 5.11 When a ball moving in a circle is viewed from the side, it looks like it is moving with SHM.

Let us consider a ball travelling in a circle of radius x_0 with constant speed v. The ball starts from point O and at some time, t, it is at position A as shown in Figure 5.12. In this time the radius has swept out angle θ. From our previous study of circular motion we know that:

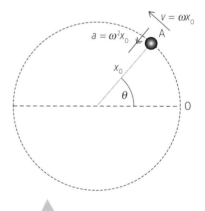

Figure 5.12 Circular analogy of SHM.

$$\text{speed} = \frac{2\pi r}{T} = \omega r \text{ so in this case } v = \omega x_0.$$

The centripetal acceleration $= \omega^2 x_0$, and is towards the centre.

We are only interested in one component of the motion, it doesn't matter which we take but this time we'll consider the horizontal component.

Displacement

As can be seen in Figure 5.13, the horizontal component of displacement $x = x_0 \cos \theta$.

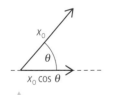

Figure 5.13 The horizontal component of displacement, $x = x_0 \cos \theta$.

Velocity

The velocity of the ball is directed perpendicular to the radius so the horizontal component of the velocity, $v_x = -\omega x_0 \sin \theta$. The negative sign is due to the fact that we are only considering one dimension, and this is in the opposite direction to the displacement, which was positive.

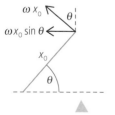

Figure 5.14

From Pythagoras' theorem we know that $\sin^2 \theta + \cos^2 \theta = 1$.

Rearranging gives $\qquad\qquad\qquad\qquad \sin \theta = \sqrt{1 - \cos^2\theta}$.

Substituting this in the equation for v_x gives $\quad v_x = -\omega x_0\sqrt{1 - \cos^2\theta} = -\omega\sqrt{x_0^2 - x_0^2 \cos^2\theta}$.

but $\qquad\qquad\qquad\qquad\qquad\qquad x_0^2\cos^2\theta = x$.

so $\qquad\qquad\qquad\qquad\qquad\qquad v_x = -\omega \sqrt{x_0^2 - x^2}$

which has its maximum value when $\qquad\qquad x = 0$.

Acceleration

The acceleration is *towards* the centre so the horizontal component $a_x = -\omega^2 x_0 \cos \theta$, again with a negative sign because of its direction.

So we have
$$x = x_0 \cos \theta$$

and
$$a_x = -\omega^2 x_0 \cos \theta$$

so
$$a_x = -\omega^2 x$$

which shows that the horizontal motion is simple harmonic. We can also see that ω^2 is the constant of proportionality relating the acceleration with displacement which implies that if the acceleration increases a lot with a small displacement then the frequency will be high. So a mass on a stiff spring will oscillate with higher frequency than a mass on a soft one, which seems to be as it is in practice.

Summary of equations

If a body is oscillating with SHM starting from a position of maximum positive displacement, then its displacement, velocity, and acceleration at any given time t can be found from the following equations:

$$x = x_0 \cos \omega t$$
$$v = -\omega x_0 \sin \omega t$$
$$a = -\omega^2 x_0 \cos \omega t$$

However, if the timing starts when the body is passing through the centre travelling in a positive direction the equations of motion are:

$$x = x_0 \sin \omega t$$
$$v = \omega x_0 \cos \omega t$$
$$a = -\omega^2 x_0 \sin \omega t$$

At a given displacement x, the velocity and acceleration can be found from the following:

$$v = \omega \sqrt{x_0^2 - x^2}$$
$$a = -\omega^2 x$$

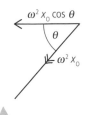

Figure 5.15

If you have done differentiation in maths then you will understand that if

displacement
$$x = x_0 \cos \omega t$$
then velocity
$$\frac{dx}{dt} = -x_0 \omega \sin \omega t$$
and acceleration,
$$\frac{d^2 x}{dt^2} = -x_0 \omega^2 \cos \omega t$$
This implies that
$$a = -\omega^2 x$$
This is a much shorter way of deriving this result!

Worked example

A pendulum is swinging with a frequency of 0.5 Hz. What is the size and direction of the acceleration when the pendulum has a displacement of 2 cm to the right?

Solution

Assuming the pendulum is swinging with SHM, then we can use the equation

$a = -\omega^2 x$ to calculate the acceleration.

$\omega = 2\pi f = 2\pi \times 0.5 = \pi$

$a = -\pi^2 \times 0.02 = -0.197 \, \mathrm{m\,s^{-2}}$ since −ve direction is to the left.

Worked example

A pendulum bob is swinging with SHM at a frequency of 1Hz and amplitude 3cm. At what position will the bob be moving with maximum velocity and what is the size of the velocity?

Solution

$v = \omega \sqrt{x_0^2 - x^2}$ Since the motion is SHM

This is maximum when $x = 0$ This is when the pendulum swings through the central position

The maximum value = ωx_0 where $\omega = 2\pi f = 2 \times \pi \times 1 = 2\pi \text{ rad s}^{-1}$

Maximum $v = 2\pi \times 0.03 = 0.188 \text{ m s}^{-1}$

Exercises

7 A long pendulum swings with a time period of 5s and an amplitude of 2m.

    (a) What is the maximum velocity of the pendulum?
    (b) What is the maximum acceleration of the pendulum?

8 A mass on a spring oscillates with amplitude 5cm and frequency 2Hz. The mass is released from its highest point. Calculate the velocity of the mass after it has travelled 1cm.

9 A body oscillates with SHM of time period 2s. What is the amplitude of the oscillation if its velocity is 1 m s^{-1} as it passes through the equilibrium position?

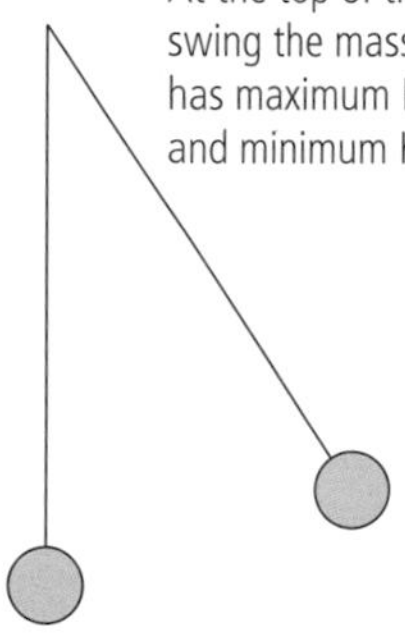

Energy changes during simple harmonic motion (SHM)

If we once again consider the simple pendulum, we can see that its energy changes as it swings.

Kinetic energy

We have already shown that the velocity of the mass is given by the equation

$$v = \omega \sqrt{x_0^2 - x^2}$$

From definition, $\text{KE} = \frac{1}{2}mv^2$

Substituting: $\text{KE} = \frac{1}{2}m\omega^2(x_0^2 - x^2)$

KE is a maximum at the bottom of the swing where $x = 0$.

So $\text{KE}_{\text{max}} = \frac{1}{2}m\omega^2 x_0^2$

At this point the PE is zero.

Total energy

The total energy at any moment in time is given by:

       total energy = KE + PE

So at the bottom of the swing:

       total energy = $\frac{1}{2}m\omega^2 x_0^2 + 0 = \frac{1}{2}m\omega^2 x_0^2$

Since no work is done on the system, according to the law of conservation of energy, the total energy must be constant.

So   total energy = $\frac{1}{2}m\omega^2 x_0^2$

At the top of the swing the mass has maximum PE and minimum KE.

At the bottom of the swing the mass has maximum KE and minimum PE.

Figure 5.16 In the simple pendulum, energy is changing from one form to another as the bob moves.

Potential energy

Potential energy at any moment = total energy – KE

So $\quad \text{PE} = \frac{1}{2}m\omega^2 x_0^2 - \frac{1}{2}m\omega^2(x_0^2 - x^2)$

$\quad\quad \text{PE} = \frac{1}{2}m\omega^2 x^2$

Graphical representation

Kinetic energy

From previous examples we know that the velocity, $v = -v_0 \sin \omega t$

So $\quad\quad\quad\quad\quad\quad\quad \frac{1}{2}mv^2 = \frac{1}{2}mv_0^2 \sin^2 \omega t$

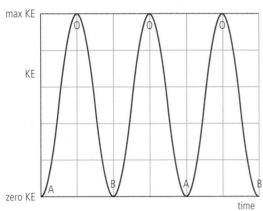

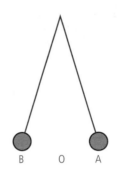

Figure 5.17 The graph of KE vs time is a sin² curve.

Potential energy

The graph of PE can be found from $\text{PE} = \frac{1}{2}m\omega^2 x^2$

Since $\quad\quad\quad\quad\quad\quad\quad x = x_0 \cos \omega t$

$\quad\quad\quad\quad\quad\quad \text{PE} = \frac{1}{2}m\omega^2 x_0^2 \cos^2 \omega t$

$\quad\quad\quad\quad\quad\quad\quad = \frac{1}{2}mv_0^2 \cos^2 \omega t$

Total energy

If these two graphs are added together it gives a constant value, equal to the total energy.

(This might remind you of Pythagoras: $1 = \cos^2\theta + \sin^2\theta$.)

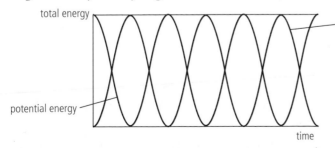

Figure 5.19 Total energy vs time.

Figure 5.18 The graph of PE vs time is a cos² curve.

Worked example

A pendulum bob of mass 200 g is oscillating with amplitude 3 cm and frequency 0.5 Hz. How much KE will the bob have as it passes through the origin?

Solution

Since the bob has SHM, $KE_{max} = \frac{1}{2}m\omega^2 x_0^2$

where $x_0 = 0.03$ m and $\omega = 2\pi f = 2\pi \times 0.5 = \pi$

$$KE_{max} = \frac{1}{2} \times 0.2 \times \pi^2 \times (0.03)^2 = 8.9 \times 10^{-4} \text{J}$$

Exercise

10 A pendulum bob of mass 100 g swings with amplitude 4 cm and frequency 1.5 Hz. Calculate:

   (a) the angular frequency of the pendulum.
   (b) the maximum KE of the bob.
   (c) the maximum PE of the bob.
   (d) the KE of the bob when the displacement is 2 cm.
   (e) the PE of the bob when the displacement is 2 cm.

Experimental investigation of the relationship between time period and length of a pendulum

At the start of this chapter we analysed the forces acting on the bob of a simple pendulum and found that, providing the displacement is small, the acceleration was given by $a = -\frac{gx}{L}$ (see Figure 5.20).

Then by comparing SHM with motion in a circle we found that the acceleration for a body moving with SHM is $a = -\omega^2 x$.

So
$$\omega^2 x = \frac{gx}{L}$$
$$\omega^2 = \frac{g}{L}.$$

Now
$$\omega^2 = \left(\frac{2\pi}{T}\right)^2 = \frac{g}{L}$$

Rearranging gives
$$T^2 = \frac{4\pi^2 L}{g} \text{ or } T = 2\pi\sqrt{\frac{L}{g}}$$

so if we measure the time period for different lengths of pendulum we should find that T^2 is proportional to L. This means that a graph of T^2 vs L would be a straight line with gradient $= \frac{4\pi^2}{g}$.

Measuring time period

The typical length of pendulum used in the lab has a time period of about 1 s so measuring one swing with a stop watch would be quite difficult. It is much better to time 10 swings then divide the time by 10 to give the time period. Alternatively the pendulum could be made to swing through a photogate and a computer used to record the time period (see Figure 5.21). The computer records every time the bob passes in and out of the photogate but if you set the software to 'pendulum timing' then it will record the time between the first time the bob enters the gate, and the third time; this will be the time period.

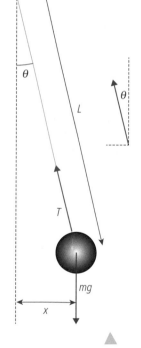

Figure 5.20.

By considering the forces on a mass hanging on a spring, it can be shown that the time period, T is given by the equation
$$T = 2\pi\sqrt{\frac{m}{k}}$$

 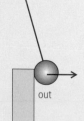 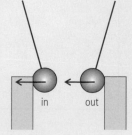 

in   out   in   out   in

Figure 5.21 Pendulum and photogate.

Phase

If we take two identical pendulum bobs, displace each bob to the right and release them at the same time, then each will have the same displacement at the same time. We say the oscillations are *in phase*. If one is pulled to the left and the other to the right, then they are *out of phase* (see Figure 5.22).

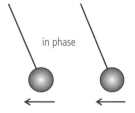
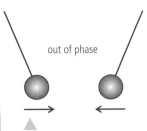

Figure 5.22 The pendulum bobs are in phase when they swing together.

This can be represented graphically:

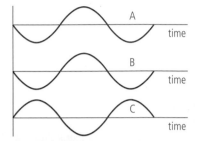

A and B represent motions that are in phase.

B and C represent motions that are out of phase.

Figure 5.23 Displacement–time graphs for bodies in and out of phase.

◀ When juggling balls they go up and down at different times – they are out of phase.

Phase difference

The phase difference is represented by an angle (usually in radians). We can see from graphs B and C in Figure 5.23 that if two oscillations are completely out of phase then the graphs are displaced by an angle π. We say the *phase difference* is π.

To learn more about oscillations, go to the hotlinks site, search for the title or ISBN and click on Chapter 5.

5.2 Waves and wave behaviour

4.2 Travelling waves

Understandings, applications, and skills:

Travelling waves
Wavelength, frequency, period, and wave speed
• Solving problems involving wave speed, frequency, and wavelength.
   Guidance
   • *Students will be expected to derive* $c = f\lambda$.
Transverse and longitudinal waves
• Explaining the motion of particles of a medium when a wave passes through it for both transverse and longitudinal cases.
• Sketching and interpreting displacement–distance graphs and displacement–time graphs for transverse and longitudinal waves.

4.3 Wave characteristics

Understandings, applications, and skills:

Amplitude and intensity
- Solving problems involving amplitude and intensity.

Superposition
- Sketching and interpreting the superposition of pulses and waves.
- Students will be expected to calculate the resultant of two waves or pulses both graphically and algebraically.

  Guidance
  - *Students will be expected to calculate the resultant of two waves or pulses both graphically and algebraically.*

Polarization
- Describing methods of polarization.

4.5 Standing waves

Understandings, applications, and skills:

The nature of standing waves
- Describing the nature and formation of standing waves in terms of superposition.
- Distinguishing between standing and travelling waves.

  Guidance
  - *Students will be expected to consider the formation of standing waves from the superposition of no more than two waves.*

Boundary conditions
- Sketching and interpreting standing wave patterns in strings.

  Guidance
  - *Boundary conditions for strings are: two fixed boundaries; fixed and free boundary; two free boundaries.*

Nodes and antinodes
- Solving problems involving the frequency of a harmonic, length of the standing wave, and the speed of the wave.

  Guidance
  - *The lowest frequency mode of a standing wave is known as the first harmonic.*
  - *The terms fundamental and overtone will not be used.*

NATURE OF SCIENCE

Complex models are often built of simple units. The complex motion of a wave becomes simple when we realize that each part is simply moving back and forth like a row of slightly out-of-step simple pendulums. In this chapter you will be learning about waves in strings and springs, water waves, sound waves, and electromagnetic waves; all completely different things but with similar characteristics. When scientists started modelling the motion of ocean waves they probably had no idea their work would one day be applied to light.

The word *wave* was originally used to describe the way that a water surface behaves when it is disturbed. We use the same model to explain sound, light, and many other physical phenomena. This is because they have some similar properties to water waves, so let's first examine the way water waves spread out.

If a stone is thrown into a pool of water, it disturbs the surface. The disturbance spreads out or *propagates* across the surface, and this disturbance is called a *wave*. Observing water waves, we can see that they have certain basic properties (in other words, they do certain things).

Reflection

If a water wave hits a wall, the waves reflect.

Refraction

When sea waves approach a beach, they change direction because of the difference in height of different parts of the sea floor. This causes the waves to bend.

Interference

When two waves cross each other, they can add together creating an extra big wave.

Diffraction

When water waves pass through a small opening, the waves spread out.

Anything that reflects, refracts, interferes, and diffracts can also be called a wave.

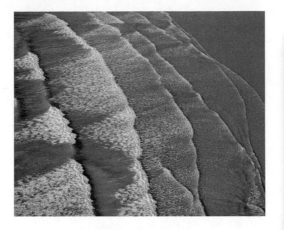

Waves change direction as they approach a beach.

Transfer of energy

Waves in the ocean are caused by winds that disturb the surface of the water. A big storm in the Atlantic Ocean can cause waves that break on the beaches of the west coast of Europe and the east coast of the Americas. The storm gives the water energy which is then spread out in the form of water waves. So a wave is the transfer of energy through the disturbance of some medium.

Although the water wave is the 'original' wave it is not the simplest one to begin with so to help understand how waves propagate we will first consider two examples of one-dimensional waves, a wave in a string and a wave in a slinky spring.

When a water wave enters a region of shallow water (near a beach) the velocity becomes less, resulting in a shorter wavelength. If the change in depth is rapid the top of the wave moves faster than the bottom causing it to be thrown over forming the tube that surfers like to get into.

Wave pulse in a string

If you take one end of a very long string and give it a flick (move it up and down once quickly) then you will see disturbance moving along the string: this is called a wave *pulse*. In lifting up the string and flicking it down you have given the string energy; this energy is now being transferred along the string at a constant speed. This speed is called the *wave speed*.

To understand how the energy is transferred consider the case where the rope is just lifted as shown in Figure 5.24. Here the string is represented by a line of balls each joined to the next by an invisible string. When the end was lifted the first ball lifted the next one which lifted the next etc. transferring energy from left to right.

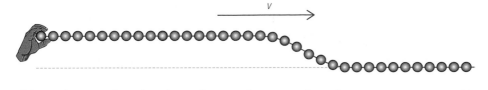

Figure 5.24 Energy transferred along the string.

If the end is moved up then down then a pulse is sent along the string as in Figure 5.25.

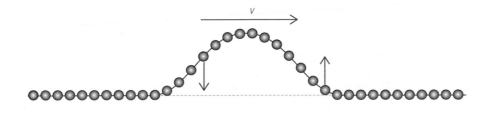

Figure 5.25 A pulse moves from left to right.

The particles at the front are moving up, and the ones at the back are moving down. As the pulse moves along the string each part of the string has the same motion, up then down, but they don't all do it at the same time; they are *out of phase* (Figure 5.25). It is like a wave going around a stadium; the crowd all stand up then sit down at different times.

Reflection of a wave pulse

If the pulse meets a fixed end (e.g. a wall), it exerts an upward force on the wall. The wall being pushed up then pushes back down on the string sending an inverted reflected pulse back along the string (Figure 5.26).

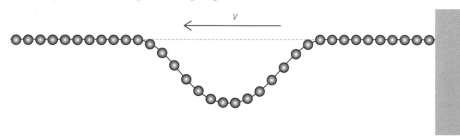

Figure 5.26 A wave pulse reflected off a fixed end.

If the end of the string is loose then you also get a reflection but this time it is reflected without phase change (Figure 5.27). It is just as if there is a hand at the end moving like the one that made the original pulse.

An upward pulse is called a peak (or crest) and a downward pulse is called a *trough*.

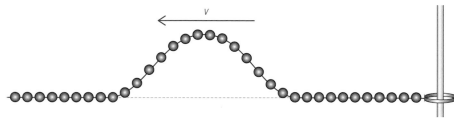

Figure 5.27 A wave pulse reflected off a free end.

A reflected wave is not only produced when the wave meets an end but whenever there is a change in the medium. If two different strings are joined together there will be a reflection at the boundary between the strings. In this case not all the wave is reflected; some is transmitted. If the second string is heavier then the reflected wave is inverted as it is off a fixed end (Figure 5.26), but if the second string is lighter then the wave is reflected as if off a free end (Figure 5.27).

Superposition of wave pulses

If two wave pulses are sent along a string from each end they will coincide in the middle. When this happens the displacements of each pulse add vectorially. This results in two peaks adding but a trough and a peak cancelling out (Figure 5.28).

Figure 5.28 Wave pulses superpose.

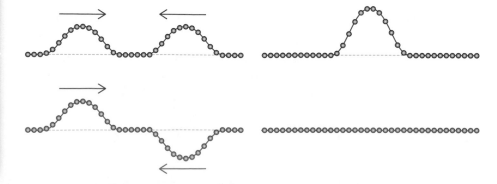

Note that when the waves cancel it appears that the energy has disappeared but if this was an animation you would see the particles are actually moving up and down so the particles have kinetic energy.

Continuous wave in a string (transverse wave)

If the end ball on the string is moved up and down with simple harmonic motion then, a short time later, the next ball along the string will also move up and down with the same motion. This motion is passed along the string until all the parts of the string are moving with SHM, each with the same amplitude and frequency but different phase. In Figure 5.29 the wave is moving from left to right as a result of the end being disturbed. The green ball is just about to move downwards, it is $\frac{3}{4}$ of a cycle $(\frac{3\pi}{2})$ out of phase with the end ball.

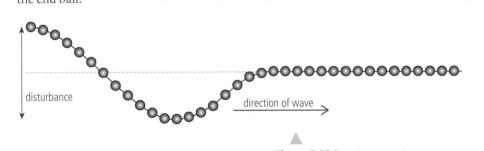

disturbance

direction of wave

Figure 5.29 Forming a continuous wave.

We can see that after the end has completed one cycle the front of the wave will be *in phase* with the original oscillation. The distance to this point depends on the speed of the wave and is called the *wavelength*, λ (Figure 5.30).

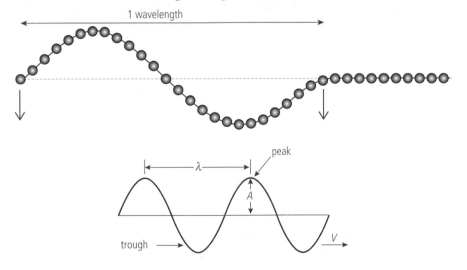

1 wavelength

Figure 5.30 One complete cycle.

peak

λ

A

trough

V

Figure 5.31 The quantities used to define a wave.

Relationship between v, f, and λ

If you observe a continuous wave moving along a string from a position at rest relative to the string then you will notice that the time between one peak passing and the next is T, the time period. In this time the wave profile has progressed a distance equal to the wavelength, λ. The velocity of the wave $= \frac{\text{distance travelled}}{\text{time taken}} = \frac{\lambda}{T}$ but $T = \frac{1}{f}$ so

$$v = f\lambda$$

Amplitude (A)

The maximum displacement of the string from the equilibrium position.

Wave speed (v)

The distance travelled by the wave profile per unit time.

Wavelength (λ)

The distance between two consecutive crests or any two consecutive points that are in phase.

Frequency (f)

The number of complete cycles that pass a point per unit time.

Period (T)

Time taken for one complete wave to pass a fixed point ($T = \frac{1}{f}$).

Change cm to m.

Worked example

The A string of a guitar vibrates at 110 Hz. If the wavelength is 153 cm, what is the velocity of the wave in the string?

Solution

$$v = f\lambda$$
$$f = 110 \text{ Hz and } \lambda = 1.53 \text{ m}$$
$$v = 110 \times 1.53 \text{ m s}^{-1}$$
$$= 168.3 \text{ m s}^{-1}$$

Worked example

A wave in the ocean has a period of 10 s and a wavelength of 200 m. What is the wave speed?

Solution

$$T = 10 \text{ s}$$
$$f = \frac{1}{T} \text{ Hz}$$
$$= 0.1 \text{ Hz}$$
$$v = f\lambda$$
$$v = 0.1 \times 200 \text{ m s}^{-1}$$
$$= 20 \text{ m s}^{-1}$$

Exercises

11 Calculate the wave velocity of a tsunami with time period 30 min and wavelength 500 km.

12 Two strings are joined together as shown in Figure 5.32.

(a) If the wave velocity in the thin string is twice its velocity in the thick string calculate the wavelength of the wave when it gets into the thick string.

(b) When the wave meets the knot, part of it will be reflected. Explain whether the reflected wave will be inverted or not.

(c) Why is the amplitude of the wave in the thick string smaller than in the thin string?

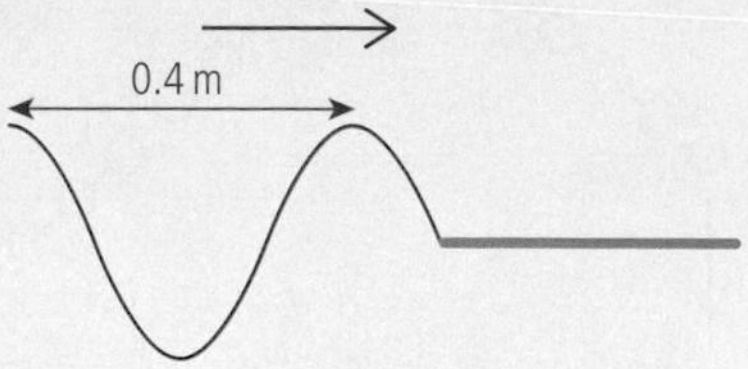

0.4 m

Figure 5.32.

13 The end of a string is moved up and down with time period 0.5 s. If the wavelength of the wave is 0.6 m what is the velocity of the wave?

A wave in which the direction of disturbance is perpendicular to the direction of the transfer of energy is called a *transverse wave*.

Polarization

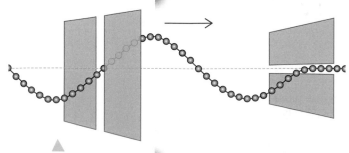

Figure 5.33 A wave in a string can be polarized by a narrow slit.

The end of a string doesn't have to be moved up and down; it can be move from side to side or at any other angle. However, if it is moved in only one plane the wave is said to be *polarized*. To make a wave in a string polarized it can be passed through a narrow slit as in Figure 5.33. If a second slit is now placed on the string it will only pass through unaffected if the slit is in the same orientation. If the second slit is at a 90° angle to the first the wave will not pass at all.

Graphical representation of a transverse wave

There are two ways we can represent a wave graphically, either by drawing a displacement–time graph for one point on the wave, or a displacement–position graph for each point along the wave.

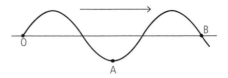

Figure 5.34 A snapshot of a transverse wave.

Displacement–time

Consider points A and B on the transverse wave in Figure 5.34.

Point A is moving up and down with SHM as the wave passes. At present, it is at its maximum negative displacement. As the wave progresses past A, this point will move up and then down (Figure 5.35).

We can also draw a graph for point B (Figure 5.36). This point starts with zero displacement then goes up.

Because the horizontal axis is time, the separation of the peaks represents the time period, not the wavelength.

The event that will happen next is to the right on the graph but the part of the wave that will arrive next is to the left on the wave.

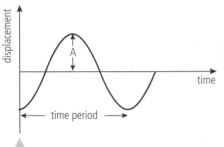

Figure 5.35 The displacement–time graph for point A.

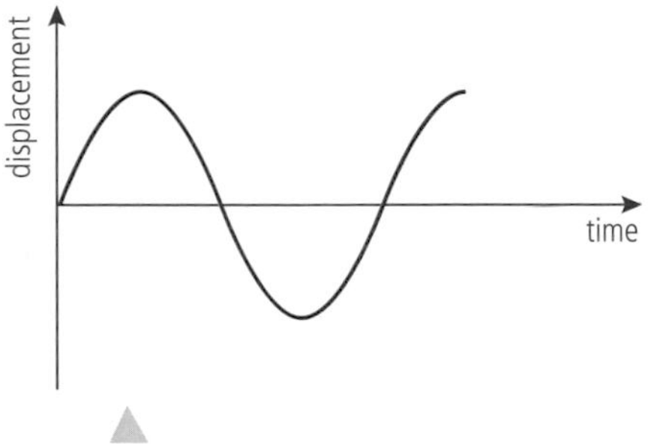

Figure 5.36 The displacement–time graph for point B.

Displacement–position

To draw a displacement–position graph, we must measure the displacements of all the points on the wave at one moment in time.

Figure 5.37 shows the graph at the same time as the snapshot in Figure 5.34 was taken. The position is measured from point O.

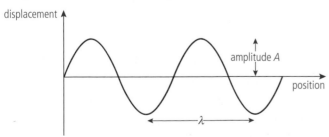

Figure 5.37 The displacement–position graph for all points at one time.

This is just like a snapshot of the wave – however, depending on the scale of the axis, it might not look quite like the wave.

The equation of a wave

For some people, seeing the equation of a wave makes the topic easier to understand. For others, it just makes it more complicated.

We have seen that each point on the wave oscillates with simple harmonic motion, so if we take the end point of the string, its displacement is related to time by the equation $y = A \sin \omega t$. If we now take a point a little bit further down the string it will also be moving with SHM but a little behind the first one, let's say an angle θ behind.

The equation for the displacement of this point is therefore $y = A \sin(\omega t - \theta)$. This phase angle depends upon how far along the string we go. In other words, θ is proportional to x or $\theta = kx$ where k is a constant.

Figure 5.38 Different parts of the wave have different phase.

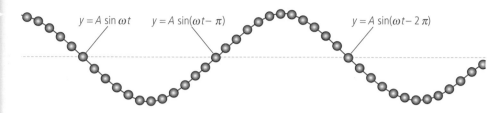

$y = A \sin \omega t$ $y = A \sin(\omega t - \pi)$ $y = A \sin(\omega t - 2\pi)$

We can now write an equation for the displacement of any point, $y = A \sin(\omega t - kx)$.

If the point is one whole wavelength from the end then the points will be in phase so $\theta = 2\pi$ or $k\lambda = 2\pi$ which means that $k = \frac{2\pi}{\lambda}$ (Figure 5.38).

The wave equation then becomes $y = A \sin\left(\omega t - \frac{2\pi x}{\lambda}\right)$.

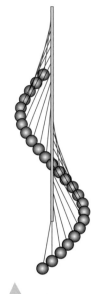

Figure 5.39 A wave profile is created when a row of pendulums are released at different times showing how a wave is made of a series of oscillations of different phase.

Figure 5.40.

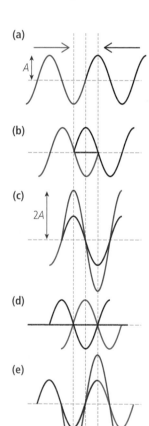

(a)

A

(b)

(c)

$2A$

(d)

(e)

antinode

(f)

node

Standing waves in strings

Consider two identical waves travelling along a string in opposite directions as shown in Figure 5.40(a). As the waves progress they cross over each other and will superpose. In Figure 5.40(b) the waves have each progressed $\frac{1}{4}\lambda$, and are out of phase so they cancel out. The green line shows the resultant wave. After a further $\frac{1}{4}\lambda$ the waves will be in phase as shown in Figure 5.40(c). Notice that even though the waves are adding, the displacement of the midpoint remains zero. Figures 5.40(a) to (e) show the waves in $\frac{1}{4}\lambda$ steps illustrating how they alternately add and cancel in such a way that the midpoint never moves: this is called a *node*. Either side of the midpoint the waves sometimes add to give a peak and sometimes a trough: these points are called *antinodes*. Figure 5.40(f) shows the two extreme positions of the resultant wave. Notice that the nodes are separated by a distance $\frac{1}{2}\lambda$.

Differences between progressive waves and standing waves

The most obvious difference between a wave that travels along the rope and the standing wave is that the wave profile of a standing wave doesn't progress and nor does the energy associated with it. Secondly, all points in between two nodes on a standing wave are in phase (think of the skipping rope) whereas points on a progressive wave that are closer than one wavelength are all out of phase (think of a Mexican wave). The third difference is related to the amplitude. All points on a progressive wave have the same amplitude, but on a standing wave some points have zero amplitude (nodes) and some points have large amplitude (antinodes).

The two ends of the skipping rope are the nodes.

Stringed instruments

Many musical instruments (guitar, violin, piano) use stretched strings to produce sound waves. When the string is plucked, a wave travels along the string to one of the fixed ends. When it gets to the end, it reflects back along the string superposing with the original wave; the result is a standing wave. The important thing to realize about the standing wave in a stretched string is that since the ends cannot move, they must become nodes, so only standing waves with nodes at the ends can be produced. Figure 5.41 shows some of the possible standing waves that can be formed in a string of length L.

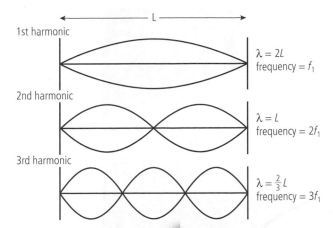

▲ **Figure 5.41** Standing waves in a string.

As shown in the diagram, each of the possible waves is called a harmonic. The first harmonic (sometimes called the fundamental) is the wave with the lowest possible frequency. To calculate the frequency, we can use the formula $f = \frac{v}{\lambda}$ so for the first harmonic:

$$f_1 = \frac{v}{2L}$$

For the second harmonic:

$$f_2 = \frac{v}{L}$$

The wave velocity is the same for all harmonics, so we can deduce that $f_2 = 2f_1$

Playing the guitar

When the guitar string is plucked, it doesn't just vibrate with one frequency but with many frequencies. However the only ones that can create standing waves are the ones with nodes at the ends (as shown in Figure 5.41). You can try this with a length of rope; get a friend to hold one end and shake the other. When you shake the end at certain specific frequencies you get a standing wave, but if the frequency isn't right, you don't. This is an example of resonance; hit the right frequency and the amplitude is big. So when the guitar string is plucked, all the possible standing waves are produced. If the signal from an electric guitar pickup is fed into a computer, the frequencies can be analysed to get a frequency spectrum. Figure 5.42 shows an example.

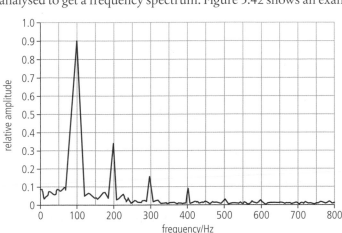

Wave speed

The speed of a wave in a string is given by the formula

$$v = \sqrt{\frac{T}{\mu}}$$

where T = tension and μ = mass per unit length.

This is why a thick guitar string is a lower note than a thin one and why the note gets higher when you increase the tension.

Sound produced by the guitar

Here we are focusing on the vibrating string. The string will cause the body of the guitar to vibrate which in turn causes the pressure of the air to vary. It is the pressure changes in the air that cause the sound wave that we hear.

Figure 5.42 Frequency spectrum for a string.

You can see from this graph that the string is vibrating at 100 Hz, 200 Hz, 300 Hz, and so on. However, the largest amplitude note is the first harmonic (100 Hz) so this is the frequency of the note you hear.

Playing different notes

A guitar has six strings. Each string is the same length but has a different diameter and therefore different mass per unit length. The wave in the thicker strings is slower than in the thin strings so, since $f = \frac{v}{\lambda}$, the thick strings will be lower notes.

To play different notes on one string, the string can be shortened by placing a finger on one of frets on the neck of the guitar. Since $f = \frac{v}{\lambda}$ the shorter string will be a higher note.

An alternative way to play a higher note is to play a harmonic; this is done by placing a finger on the node of a harmonic (e.g. in the middle for the second harmonic) then plucking the string. Immediately after the string is plucked, the finger is removed to allow the string to vibrate freely.

CHALLENGE YOURSELF

2   By adding the wave equations for two waves travelling in opposite directions show that the distance between nodes on a standing wave is $\frac{1}{2}\lambda$.

Exercises

14   The mass per unit length of a guitar string is $1.2 \times 10^{-3}\,\mathrm{kg\,m^{-1}}$. If the tension in the wire is $40\,\mathrm{N}$,

   (a) calculate the velocity of the wave.
   (b) calculate the frequency of the first harmonic if the vibrating length of the guitar string is $63.5\,\mathrm{cm}$.

15   A $30\,\mathrm{cm}$ long string of mass per unit length $1.2 \times 10^{-3}\,\mathrm{kg\,m^{-1}}$ is tensioned so that its first harmonic is $500\,\mathrm{Hz}$. Calculate the tension of a second string with half the mass per unit length but the same length that has the same first harmonic.

16   The first harmonic of a $1\,\mathrm{m}$ long stretched string is $650\,\mathrm{Hz}$. What will its first harmonic be if its length is shortened to $80\,\mathrm{cm}$ keeping the tension constant?

Waves in a slinky spring (longitudinal waves)

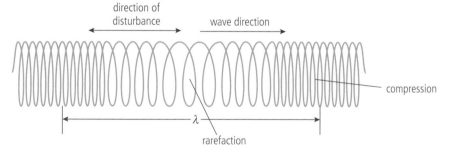

Figure 5.43 The difference between a compression wave in a spring and the transverse wave in a string is the direction of disturbance.

When a compression wave travels along a slinky spring the disturbance is parallel to the direction of energy transfer. This type of wave is called a *longitudinal wave*. Since longitudinal waves only have one direction of disturbance, they cannot be polarized.

Reflection

When the wave in a spring meets a fixed end the spring will push the wall so according to Newton's third law the wall will push back. This sends a reflected wave back along the spring (Figure 5.44).

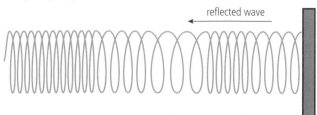

Figure 5.44 A wave in a spring is reflected off a wall.

Graphical representation of longitudinal waves

To get a better understanding of a longitudinal wave let us consider a row of balls connected by springs as in Figure 5.45.

If the ball on the left is pulled to the left then the spring connecting it to the next ball will be stretched causing the

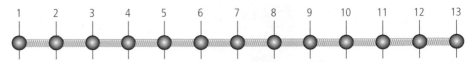

Figure 5.45.

next ball to move. In this way the displacement is passed from one ball to the next. If the ball is moved with SHM then a continuous wave is sent along the line. Each ball will move with the same frequency but a slightly different phase. The distance between two balls in phase is the wavelength; this is the same as the distance between two compressions. In Figure 5.46 it can be seen that the end balls are both at the same point in the cycle, at the equilibrium position moving left, so the distance between them is one wavelength.

The amplitude of the wave is the maximum displacement from the equilibrium position; this is marked by the letter A in Figure 5.46.

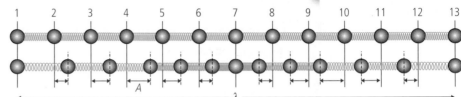

Figure 5.46 Showing the displaced positions of parts of a wave.

Displacement–time graph

A displacement–time graph shows how the displacement of one point varies with time.

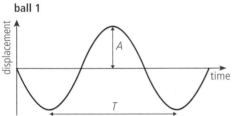
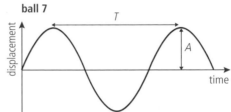

Figure 5.47.

Figure 5.47 shows two graphs for two different points. Ball 1 is about to move to the left so its displacement will become negative; ball 7 is about to move to the right so its displacement will become positive.

Displacement–position graph

A displacement–position graph represents the position of all the particles at one time. If the motion of the particles is sinusoidal then the shape of the graph will be a sine curve as shown in Figure 5.48.

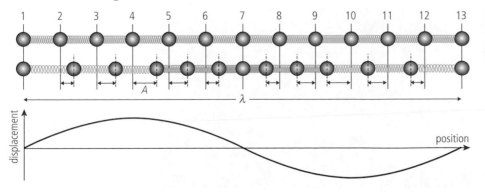

Figure 5.48.

In Figure 5.48 you can see how balls 1, 7, and 13 have zero displacement, ball 4 has maximum positive displacement, and ball 10 has maximum negative displacement.

When looking at a wave travelling to the right you must remember that the particles to the right are lagging behind those to the left so if we want to know what the displacement of particle 13 will be next we look at the particle to the left. We can therefore deduce that particle 13 is moving to the left. When looking at a graph, time progresses from left to right so you can see what will happen next by looking to the right.

To learn more about waves and wave behaviour, go to the hotlinks site, search for the title or ISBN and click on Chapter 5.

5.3 Two-dimensional waves (water waves)

4.3 Wave characteristics

Understandings, applications, and skills:

Wavefronts and rays
● Sketching and interpreting diagrams involving wavefronts and rays.

4.4 Wave behaviour

Understandings, applications, and skills:

Reflection and refraction
● Sketching and interpreting incident, reflected, and transmitted waves at boundaries between media.
● Solving problems involving reflection at a plane interface.

Snell's law
● Solving problems involving Snell's law.

Diffraction through a single-slit and around objects
● Qualitatively describing the diffraction pattern formed when plane waves are incident normally on a single-slit.

  Guidance
  ● *Students should have the opportunity to observe diffraction and interference patterns arising from more than one type of wave.*

Double-slit interference
● Quantitatively describing double-slit interference intensity patterns.

  Guidance
  ● *Students will not be expected to derive the double-slit equation.*

Path difference

If a stone is thrown into a pond then a pulse will be seen to spread out across the surface in two dimensions: energy has been transferred from the stone to the surface of the water. If the surface is disturbed continuously by an oscillating object (or the wind) a continuous wave will be formed whose profile is that of a sine wave. Viewed from directly above the wave spreads out in circles. The circles that we see are actually the peaks and troughs of the wave; we call these lines *wavefronts*. A wavefront is any line joining points that are in phase. Wavefronts are perpendicular to the direction of energy transfer, which can be represented by an arrow called a *ray*.

Ripples spreading out in circles after the surface is disturbed.

Point sources produce circular wavefronts but if the source is far away the waves will appear plane.

A plane wavefront moves towards the beach.

Wave propagation (Huygens' construction)

We can think of a wavefront as being made up of an infinite number of new centres of disturbance. Each disturbance creates its own wavelet that progresses in the direction of the wave. The wavefront is made up of the sum of all these wavelets. Figure 5.51 shows how both circular and plane wavefronts propagate according to this construction.

NATURE OF SCIENCE

The Huygens construction treats a wave front as if it is made of an infinite number of small point sources that only propagate forwards. Huygens gave no explanation for the fact that propagation is only forwards but the model correctly predicts the laws of reflection and Snell's law of refraction. Snell's law was the result of many experiments measuring the angles of light rays passing from one medium to another; the result gives the path with the shortest time, a result that is in agreement with Einstein's theory of relativity. There can be more than one theory to explain a phenomenon but they must give consistent predictions.

Reflection of water waves

When a wavefront hits a barrier the barrier now behaves as a series of wavelet sources sending wavelets in the opposite direction. In this way, a circular wavefront is reflected as a circular wavefront that appears to originate from a point behind the barrier as in Figure 5.52.

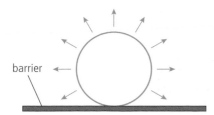

barrier becomes source of disturbance

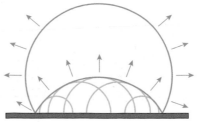

wavelets add to give reflected wavefront

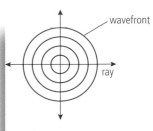

Figure 5.49 A circular wavefront spreading out from a point.

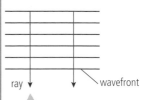

Figure 5.50 Parallel plane wavefronts.

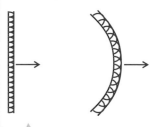

Figure 5.51 Huygens' construction used to find the new position of plane and circular wavefronts.

Figure 5.52.

A plane wavefront reflects as a plane wave making the same angle to the barrier as the incident wave, as shown in Figure 5.53.

Figure 5.53.

barrier becomes source of disturbance   wavelets add to give reflected wavefront

Refraction of water waves

Refraction is the change of direction when a wave passes from one medium to another. In the case of water waves it is difficult to change the medium but we can change the depth. This changes the speed of the wave and causes it to change direction. This can again be explained using the Huygens construction as shown in Figure 5.54, where the wave is passing into shallower water where it travels more slowly.

Figure 5.54.

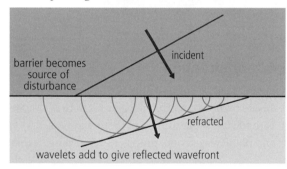

Figure 5.55.

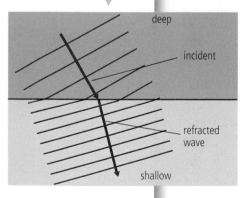

The frequency of the wave doesn't change when the wave slows down so the wavelength must be shorter ($v = f\lambda$). Note that although not drawn in Figure 5.55, when a wave meets a boundary such as this it will be reflected as well as refracted.

Snell's law

Snell's law relates the angles of incidence and refraction to the ratio of the velocity of the wave in the different media. The ratio of the sine of the angle of incidence to the sine of the angle of refraction is equal to the ratio of the velocities of the wave in the different media.

$$\frac{\sin i}{\sin r} = \frac{v_1}{v_2}$$

Note that the angles are measured to the *normal*, not to the boundary.

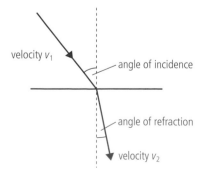

Figure 5.56 Angles of incidence and refraction.

Worked example

A water wave travelling at $20\,\text{m s}^{-1}$ enters a shallow region where its velocity is $15\,\text{m s}^{-1}$ (Figure 5.57). If the angle of incidence of the water wave to the shallow region is 50°, what is the angle of refraction?

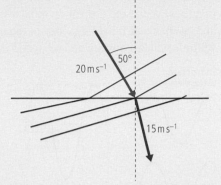

Figure 5.57.

Solution

$$\frac{\sin i}{\sin r} = \frac{v_1}{v_2} = \frac{20}{15}$$

so

$$\sin r = \frac{\sin 50°}{1.33} = 0.576 \qquad \text{Applying Snell's law}$$

$$r = 35.2°$$

Exercises

17 A water wave with wavelength 30 cm travelling with velocity 0.5 m s⁻¹ meets the straight boundary to a shallower region at an angle of incidence 30°. If the velocity in the shallow region is 0.4 m s⁻¹, calculate:

(a) the frequency of the wave.
(b) the wavelength of the wave in the shallow region.
(c) the angle of refraction.

18 A water wave travelling in a shallow region at a velocity of 0.3 m s⁻¹ meets the straight boundary to a deep region at angle of incidence 20°. If the velocity in the deep region is 0.5 m s⁻¹ calculate the angle of refraction.

Diffraction of water waves

Diffraction takes place when a wave passes through a small opening. If the opening is very small, then the wave behaves just like a point source as shown in Figure 5.58.

 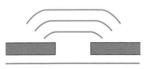

Using Huygens' construction we can explain why this happens. In the case of the very narrow slit the wavefront is reduced to one wavelet which propagates as a circle.

Waves are also diffracted by objects and edges as shown in Figure 5.59. Notice how the wave seems to pass round the very small object.

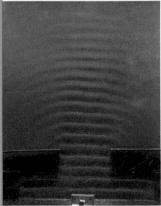

Water waves diffracting through two different sized openings. The waves are diffracted more through the narrower opening.

Figure 5.58 If the opening is a bit bigger then the effect is not so great.

Figure 5.59 Diffraction around obstacles.

Interference of water waves

If two disturbances are made in a pool of water two different waves will be formed. When these waves meet, the individual displacements will add vectorially. This is called *superposition*. If the frequency of the individual waves is equal then the resulting amplitude will be constant and related to the *phase difference* between the two waves.

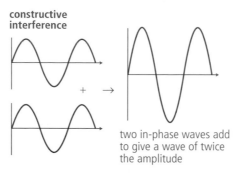

constructive interference

two in-phase waves add to give a wave of twice the amplitude

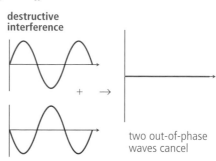

destructive interference

two out-of-phase waves cancel

Figure 5.60.

When two identical point sources produce waves on the surface of a pool of water a pattern like the one in Figure 5.61 is produced.

In Figure 5.61 we can see that there are regions where the waves are adding together (X) and regions where they cancel out (Y). If we look carefully at the waves arriving at X and Y from A and B we see that at X they are in phase and Y they are out of phase (Figure 5.62). This is because the waves have travelled the same distance to get to X but the wave from A has travelled $\frac{1}{2}\lambda$ extra to get to Y.

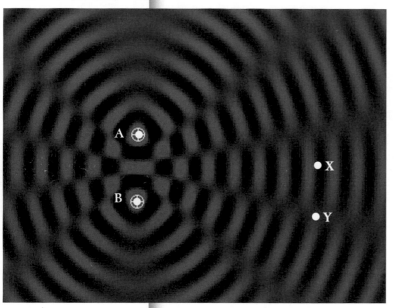

Figure 5.61 Ripple tank, a screenshot from www.paulfalstad.com.

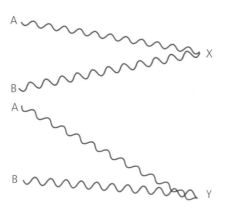

Figure 5.62 Path difference leads to phase difference.

Path difference and phase difference

We can see from the previous example that a path difference of $\frac{1}{2}\lambda$ introduces a phase difference of π so if the path difference is d then the phase difference, $\theta = \frac{2\pi d}{\lambda}$.

Worked example

Two boys playing in a pool make identical waves that travel towards each other. The boys are 10 m apart and the waves have a wavelength 2 m. Their little sister is swimming from one boy to the other. When she is 4 m from the first boy, will she be in a big wave or a small wave?

Figure 5.63 A diagram always helps, no matter how simple it is.

Solution

The waves from the boys will interfere when they meet. If the girl is 4 m from the first boy, then she must be 6 m from the other. This is a path difference of 2 m, one whole wavelength. The waves are therefore in phase and will add.

To learn more about two-dimensional waves (water waves), go to the hotlinks site, search for the title or ISBN and click on Chapter 5.

Exercise

19 Two wave sources A and B produce waves of wavelength 2 cm. What is the phase angle between the waves at:

   (a) a point C distance 6 cm from A and 6.2 cm from B?
   (b) a point D distance 8 cm from A and 7 cm from B?
   (c) a point E distance 10 cm from A and 11.5 cm from B?

5.4 Sound waves

4.2 Travelling waves

Understandings, applications, and skills:

The nature of sound waves
- Investigating the speed of sound experimentally.

4.5 Standing waves

Understandings, applications, and skills:

The nature of standing waves in pipes
- Sketching and interpreting standing wave patterns in pipes.

   Guidance
   - *For standing waves in air, explanations will not be required in terms of pressure nodes and pressure antinodes.*

Boundary conditions
- Boundary conditions for pipes are: two closed boundaries; closed and open boundary; two open boundaries

Nodes and antinodes

   Guidance
   - *The lowest frequency mode of a standing wave is known as the first harmonic. The terms fundamental and overtone will not be used.*
   - *Solving problems involving the frequency of a harmonic, length of the standing wave, and the speed of the wave.*

9.5 Doppler effect

Understandings, applications, and skills:

(AHL) The Doppler effect
- Sketching and interpreting the Doppler effect when there is relative motion between source and observer.
- Describing situations where the Doppler effect can be utilized. Solving problems involving the change in frequency or wavelength observed due to the Doppler effect to determine the velocity of the source/observer.

NATURE OF SCIENCE

The speed of sound is approximately $340 \, m \, s^{-1}$ so it proved quite difficult for early scientists to measure this accurately. The first methods assumed that light was instantaneous and measured the time difference between the light and sound arriving from an event such as a gunshot (you may have noticed this during a thunderstorm). An alternative approach is to use standing waves in pipes but with today's technology it is possible to get quite an accurate value by simply measuring the time taken for a sound to travel between two microphones on your computer.

Pitch is related to the frequency of the sound: a high pitch note has a high *frequency*.

Amplitude is related to the loudness of a sound: a loud sound has large *amplitude*.

Velocity of a sound wave travelling through air at 20°C and normal atmospheric pressure is $340 \, m \, s^{-1}$. At higher temperatures the velocity will be greater since the molecules move faster.

Properties of sound waves

When a body moves through air it compresses the air in front of it. This air then expands, compressing the next layer of air and passing the disturbance from one layer of air to the next (see Figure 5.64). If the body oscillates then a continuous wave is propagated through the air. This is called a *sound wave*.

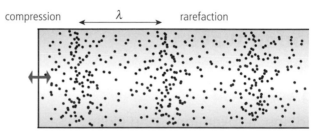

Figure 5.64 A sound wave moves along a pipe.

A sound wave is a propagation of *changing pressure*. This causes layers of gas to oscillate, but remember, the individual molecules of the gas are moving with random motion. Since the disturbance is in the same direction as the transfer of energy, sound is a longitudinal wave.

Reflection of sound

If you shout in front of a cliff, the sound reflects back as an echo. In fact any wall is a good reflector of sound, so when speaking in a room, the sound is reflected off all the surfaces This is why your voice sounds different in a room and outside.

Refraction of sound

When sound passes from warm air into cold air, it refracts. This is why sounds carry well on a still night.

The sound travels to the listener by two paths, one direct and one by refraction through the layers of air (Figure 5.63). This results in an extra loud sound.

Figure 5.63 Sound refracts through layers of air.

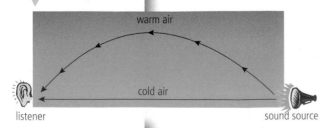

Diffraction of sound

A sound wave of frequency 600 Hz has a wavelength of about 0.5 m so will diffract when it passes through similarly sized openings like, for example, a door. However, the effect is often hidden because sound also reflects off the walls of the room causing it to travel in different directions. To do experiments on sound waves you really need a room with no reflections.

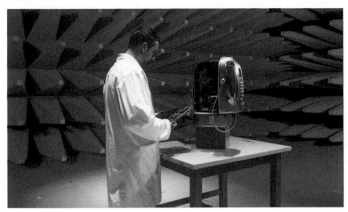

Interference of sound

If sound behaves like other waves then it should be possible to interfere two sounds to get silence. This is not often observed since the two sources of sound must have the same frequency, similar amplitude, and a constant phase relationship. If you have a computer with stereo sound you can try playing a constant frequency sound from both speakers. If you move around the room with a finger in one ear, you might be able to hear regions that are loud and quiet due to the interference of the two sound waves (Figure 5.67). This also works much better in an anechoic chamber.

Standing waves in closed pipes

When a sound wave travels along a closed pipe, it will reflect off the closed end. The reflected wave and original wave then superpose to give a standing wave. A sound wave is a propagation of disturbance in air pressure. The change in air pressure causes the air to move backwards and forwards in the direction of the propagation. If the end of the pipe is closed, then the air cannot move back and forth so a node must be formed. This limits the possible standing waves to the ones shown in Figure 5.68.

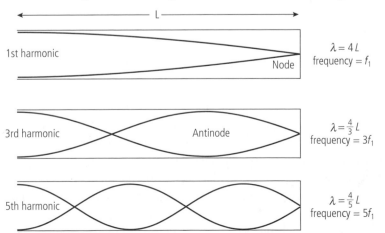

1st harmonic   Node $\lambda = 4L$ frequency $= f_1$

3rd harmonic   Antinode $\lambda = \frac{4}{3}L$ frequency $= 3f_1$

5th harmonic $\lambda = \frac{4}{5}L$ frequency $= 5f_1$

microphone

Figure 5.66 The microphone picks up sound owing to diffraction.

A room with no echo is called an anechoic chamber, and these rooms are used for experimenting with sound waves.

Sound waves cancel.   B

Sound waves add.   A

Figure 5.67 Owing to interference, the sound is loud at A but quiet at B.

Noise-cancelling headphones use interference to cancel external sounds enabling you to hear music more clearly. They work by recording the noise from the outside, electronically changing its phase by π, and then interfering it destructively with the original sound.

In these diagrams the sound waves are represented by displacement–position graphs. These make the sound look like a transverse wave but remember the displacement is in the direction of the disturbance.

Figure 5.68 Standing waves in a closed pipe.

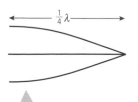

Figure 5.69 Remember this is one quarter of a wave. It can be useful to split the harmonics into quarters when determining the frequency.

These diagrams show how the displacement of the air varies along the length of the pipe, but remember, the displacement is actually along the pipe not perpendicular to it as shown. The frequency of each harmonic can be calculated using $f = \frac{v}{\lambda}$.

For the first harmonic:

$$f_1 = \frac{v}{4L}$$

For the next harmonic:

$$f_3 = \frac{v}{\frac{4}{3}L} = \frac{3v}{4L} = 3f_1 \text{ so this is the third harmonic.}$$

So when a standing wave is formed in a closed pipe, only odd harmonics are formed, resulting in the frequency spectrum shown in Figure 5.70.

Standing waves in open pipes

If a wave is sent along an open-ended pipe, a wave is also reflected. The resulting superposition of reflected and original waves again leads to the formation of a standing wave. This time there will be an antinode at both ends, leading to the possible waves shown in Figure 5.71.

This time all the harmonics are formed.

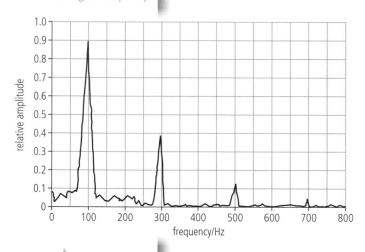

Figure 5.70 Frequency spectrum for a closed pipe.

Figure 5.71 Standing waves in an open pipe.

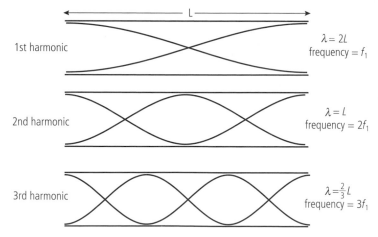

1st harmonic — $\lambda = 2L$ frequency = f_1

2nd harmonic — $\lambda = L$ frequency = $2f_1$

3rd harmonic — $\lambda = \frac{2}{3}L$ frequency = $3f_1$

In a clarinet, the reed is made to vibrate.

Wind instruments

All wind instruments (e.g. flute, clarinet, trumpet, and church organ) make use of the standing waves set up in pipes. The main difference between the different instruments is the way that the air is made to vibrate. In a clarinet a thin piece of wood (a reed) is made to vibrate, in a trumpet the lips vibrate and in a flute, air is made to vibrate, as it is blown over a sharp edge. Different notes are played by opening and closing holes; this has the effect of changing the length of the pipe. You can also play higher notes by blowing harder; this causes the higher harmonics to sound louder, resulting in a higher frequency note. If you have ever played the recorder, you might have had problems with this – if you blow too hard you get a high-pitched noise that doesn't sound so good.

Exercises

The speed of sound in air is $340\,\mathrm{m\,s^{-1}}$.

20 Calculate the first harmonic produced when a standing wave is formed in a closed pipe of length 50 cm.

21 The air in a closed pipe in Figure 5.72 is made to vibrate by holding a tuning fork of frequency 256 Hz over its open end. As the length of the pipe is increased, loud notes are heard as the standing wave in the pipe resonates with the tuning fork.

(a) What is the shortest length that will cause a loud note?

(b) If the pipe is 1.5 m long, how many loud notes will you hear as the plunger is withdrawn?

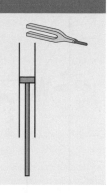

Figure 5.72.

Measuring the speed of sound

The speed of sound can be measured by sampling the sound made by a simple drinking straw whistle with your computer. In this example Audacity®, free open source software, was used. The drinking straw is turned into a whistle by cutting a notch close to one end. When blown, the noise is not very loud (more of a rush of air than a whistle) but it is enough to analyse.

The whistle was blown into the microphone of the computer and the sound recorded using Audacity® (Figure 5.74). The frequency spectrum was then analysed to find the harmonics of the sound.

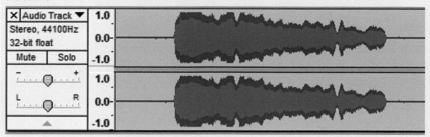

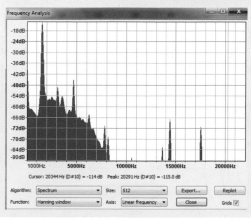

By measuring the sound from pipes of different lengths it is possible to plot a graph of f vs $\frac{1}{\lambda}$ (Figure 5.75). This should be a straight line with gradient = velocity of sound.

Measuring the speed of sound by sampling the sound from a pipe

A worksheet with full details of how to carry out this experiment is available on your eBook.

Figure 5.73 A drinking straw whistle.

Figure 5.74 Screenshot from Audacity® showing sampled sound.

When we say the source is moving we mean that it moves relative to the medium (air). The observer is at rest relative to the medium.

Figure 5.75 The frequency spectrum from Audacity®.

The Doppler effect

If you have ever stood next to a busy road or even better, a race track, you might have noticed that the cars sound different when they come towards you and when they go away. It's difficult to put this into words but the sound is something like this: 'eeeeeeeeeeeeoowwwwwwww'. The sound on approach is a higher frequency than on

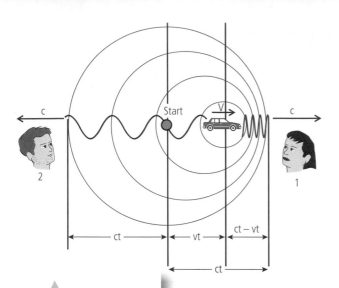

Figure 5.76 The car starts from the red spot and moves forward. The largest circle is the wavefront formed when the car began.

retreat. This effect is called the Doppler effect, and can occur when the source of the sound is moving or when the observer is moving, or when both source and observer are moving.

Moving source

The change in frequency caused when a source moves is due to the change in wavelength in front of and behind the source. This is illustrated in Figure 5.76. You can see that the waves ahead of the source have been squashed as the source 'catches up' with them. The velocity of sound is not affected by the movement of the source, so the reduction in wavelength results in an increased frequency ($v = f\lambda$).

The car in Figure 5.76 starts at the red spot and drives forwards at speed v for t seconds producing a sound of frequency f_0. In this time t the source produces $f_0 t$ complete waves ($3\frac{1}{2}$ in this example).

Ahead of the car, these waves have been squashed into a distance $ct - vt$ so the wavelength must be

$$\lambda_1 = \frac{ct - vt}{f_0 t} = \frac{c - v}{f_0}$$

The velocity of these waves is c so the observed frequency $f_1 = \frac{c}{\lambda_1}$

$$f_1 = \frac{c}{\frac{c - v}{f_0}} = \frac{cf_0}{c - v}$$

We could do a similar derivation for the waves behind the source. This time the waves are stretched out to fit into a distance $ct + vt$. The observed frequency is then

$$f_2 = \frac{cf_0}{c + v}$$

Moving observer

If the observer moves relative to a stationary source the change in frequency observed is simply due to the fact that the velocity of the sound changes. This is because the velocity of sound is relative to the air, so if you travel through the air towards a sound, the velocity of the sound will increase. Figure 5.77 illustrates the effect on frequency of a moving observer.

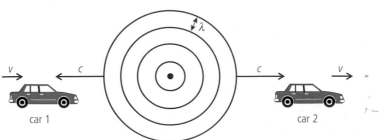

Figure 5.77.

car 1   car 2

The relative velocity of the sound coming towards car 1 approaching the source is $(c + v)$ so the frequency, $f_1 = \frac{c + v}{\lambda}$.

TOK

In this course we often explain phenomena that you have observed such as the change in frequency as an ambulance drives past. What if you have never observed such a thing?

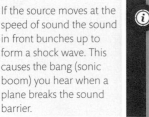

If the source moves at the speed of sound the sound in front bunches up to form a shock wave. This causes the bang (sonic boom) you hear when a plane breaks the sound barrier.

But

$$\lambda = \frac{c}{f_0}$$

so

$$f_1 = \frac{(c + v)f_0}{c} \quad \text{(approaching)}$$

For car 2, receding from the source

$$f_2 = \frac{(c - v)f_0}{c} \quad \text{(receding)}$$

Worked example

A car travelling at $30\,\mathrm{m\,s^{-1}}$ emits a sound of frequency $500\,\mathrm{Hz}$. Calculate the frequency of the sound measured by an observer in front of the car.

Solution

This is an example where the source is moving relative to the medium and the observer is stationary relative to the medium. To calculate the observed frequency, we use the equation

$$f_1 = \frac{cf_0}{c - v}$$

where

$$f_0 = 500\,\mathrm{Hz}$$
$$c = 340\,\mathrm{m\,s^{-1}}$$
$$v = 30\,\mathrm{m\,s^{-1}}$$

So

$$f_1 = \frac{340 \times 500}{340 - 30} = 548\,\mathrm{Hz}$$

The rate at which blood flows can be found by measuring the Doppler shift of ultrasound waves reflected off blood cells. In this case the blood cell is moving relative to the source and when it reflects the wave the reflected wave is moving relative to the receiver. This causes a double shift in frequency.

Exercises

22 A person jumps off a high bridge attached to a long elastic rope (a bungee jump). As they begin to fall they start to scream at a frequency of $1000\,\mathrm{Hz}$. They reach a terminal velocity of $40\,\mathrm{m\,s^{-1}}$ on the way down and $30\,\mathrm{m\,s^{-1}}$ on the way back up.

   (a) Describe what you would hear if you were standing on the bridge.
   (b) Calculate the maximum frequency you would hear from the bridge.
   (c) Calculate the minimum frequency you would hear from the bridge.
   (d) What would you hear if you were standing directly below the bungee jumper?

23 The highest frequency you can hear is $20\,000\,\mathrm{Hz}$. If a plane making a sound of frequency $500\,\mathrm{Hz}$ went fast enough, you would not be able to hear it. How fast would the plane have to go?

24 Calculate the frequency of sound you would hear as you drove at $20\,\mathrm{m\,s^{-1}}$ towards a sound source emitting a sound of frequency $300\,\mathrm{Hz}$.

To learn more about sound waves, go to the hotlinks site, search for the title or ISBN and click on Chapter 5.

5.5 Light waves

4.2 Travelling waves

Understandings, applications, and skills:

The nature of electromagnetic waves

Guidance
• Students should be aware of the order of magnitude of the wavelength ranges for radio, microwave, infrared, visible, ultraviolet, X-ray, and gamma rays.

4.3 Wave characteristics

Understandings, applications, and skills:

Amplitude and intensity
- Solving problems involving amplitude and intensity.

  Guidance
  - *Students will be expected to calculate the resultant of two waves or pulses both graphically and algebraically.*

Polarization
- Solving problems involving Malus' law.

  Guidance
  - *Methods of polarization will be restricted to the use of polarizing filters and reflection from a non-metallic plane surface.*

4.4 Wave behaviour

Understandings, applications, and skills:

Reflection and refraction (light)
- Sketching and interpreting incident, reflected, and transmitted waves at boundaries between media.
- Solving problems involving reflection at a plane interface.

Snell's law, critical angle, and total internal reflection (light)
- Solving problems involving Snell's law, critical angle, and total internal reflection.
- Determining refractive index experimentally.

  Guidance
  - *Quantitative descriptions of refractive index are limited to light rays passing between two or more transparent media. If more than two media, only parallel interfaces will be considered.*

9.2 Single-slit diffraction

Understandings, applications, and skills:

(AHL)The nature of single-slit diffraction
- Describing the effect of slit width on the diffraction pattern.
- Determining the position of interference minima.
- Qualitatively describing single-slit diffraction patterns produced from white light and from a range of monochromatic light frequencies.

  Guidance
  - *Only rectangular slits need to be considered.*
  - *Diffraction around an object (rather than through a slit) does not need to be considered in this subtopic (see Physics subtopic 4.4).*
  - *Students will be expected to be aware of the approximate ratios of successive intensity maxima for single-slit interference patterns.*
  - *Calculations will be limited to a determination of the first minimum for single-slit interference patterns using the approximation equation.*

9.3 Interference

Understandings, applications, and skills:

(AHL) Young's double-slit experiment
- Qualitatively describing two-slit interference patterns, including modulation by one-slit diffraction effect.
- Investigating Young's double-slit experimentally.
- Sketching and interpreting intensity graphs of double-slit interference patterns.

  Guidance
  - *Students should be introduced to interference patterns from a variety of coherent sources such as (but not limited to) electromagnetic waves, sound, and simulated demonstrations.*

(AHL) Modulation of two-slit interference pattern by one-slit diffraction effect

(AHL) Multiple slit and diffraction grating interference patterns

- Solving problems involving the diffraction grating equation.

  Guidance
  - *Diffraction grating patterns are restricted to those formed at normal incidence.*

(AHL) Thin film interference

- Describing conditions necessary for constructive and destructive interference from thin films, including phase change at interface and effect of refractive index.
- Solving problems involving interference from thin films.

  Guidance
  - *The treatment of thin film interference is confined to parallel-sided films at normal incidence.*

9.4 Resolution

Understandings, applications, and skills:

(AHL) The size of a diffracting aperture

Guidance
- *Calculations will be limited to a determination of the first minimum for single-slit diffraction patterns using the approximation equation*

The resolution of simple monochromatic two-source systems

- Solving problems involving the Rayleigh criterion for light emitted by two sources diffracted at a single-slit.
- Resolvance of diffraction gratings.

  Guidance
  - *Proof of the diffraction grating resolvance equation is not required.*

9.5 Doppler effect

Understandings, applications, and skills:

(AHL) The Doppler effect (light)

- Solving problems involving the change in frequency or wavelength observed due to the Doppler effect to determine the velocity of the source/observer.

  Guidance:
  - *All calculations will be required through an approximation of the equation.*
  - *Situations to be discussed should include the use of Doppler effect in radars and in medical physics, and its significance for the red-shift in the light spectra of distant galaxies.*

The electromagnetic spectrum

Light is an *electromagnetic wave*, which means that it is a propagation of disturbance in an electric and magnetic field (more about this in the next chapter). Electromagnetic (em) waves are classified according to their wavelength as represented by the spectrum shown in Figure 5.78 (on the following page). Unlike the other waves studied so far, em waves do not need to have a medium to propagate through.

NATURE OF SCIENCE

The first time thin film interference was observed in the laboratory was when Joseph Fraunhofer saw colours appearing whilst alcohol evaporated from a sheet of glass. Sometimes luck plays a part in scientific discovery but if Fraunhofer hadn't realized that the colours were interesting the discovery would have had to wait for someone else.

Some light facts

In this chapter we are particularly interested in visible light, which has wavelengths between 400 and 800 nm. Different wavelengths of visible light have different colours.

 TOK Colour is perceived but wavelength is measured.

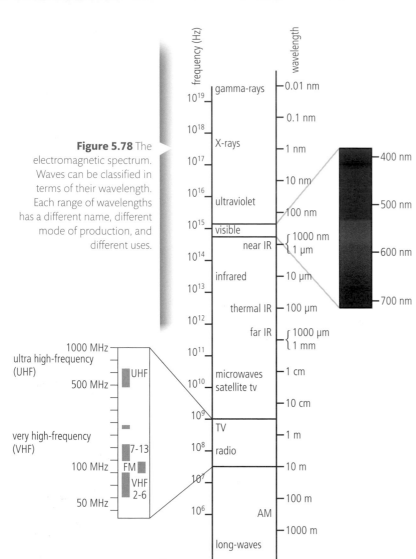

However, our perception of colour is not quite so simple. For example, red light mixed with green light gives yellow light.

The velocity of light in a vacuum is approximately $3 \times 10^8 \, \text{m s}^{-1}$.

The brightness or *intensity* of light, measured in W m^{-2}, is proportional to the square of the wave amplitude.

$$I \propto A^2$$

As you move away from a point light source its intensity gets less and less, this is because the light spreads out so the power per unit area is reduced. The light from a point source spreads out in a sphere so at a distance r the power will be spread over an area equal to $4\pi r^2$. If the power of the source is P then the intensity at this distance will be $\frac{P}{4\pi r^2}$.

Reflection of light

When light hits an object, part of it is absorbed and part reflected. It is the reflected light that enables us to see things. If the reflecting surface is uneven the light is reflected in all directions but if it is flat the light is reflected uniformly so we can see that the angle of reflection equals the angle of incidence (Figure 5.79).

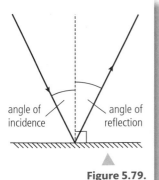

angle of incidence   angle of reflection

Figure 5.79.

Refraction of light

The velocity of light is different for different transparent media so when light passes from one medium to another it changes direction. For example, the velocity of light is greater in air than it is in glass so when light passes from air to glass it refracts as in Figure 5.80.

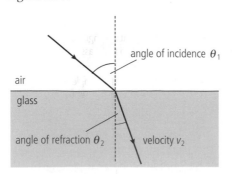

air

glass

angle of incidence θ_1

angle of refraction θ_2 velocity v_2

Figure 5.80 Light refracts from air to glass.

Applying Snell's law we get that $\frac{\sin\theta_1}{\sin\theta_2} = \frac{v_1}{v_2}$.

This can also be written $\frac{\sin\theta_1}{\sin\theta_2} = \frac{n_2}{n_1}$ where n_1 and n_2 are the *absolute refractive indices* of the two media. The bigger the difference in refractive index, the more the light ray will be deviated. We say a medium with a high refractive index is 'optically dense'.

Measurement of refractive index

To measure the refractive index of a glass block you can pass a narrow beam of light (e.g. a LASER) through it and measure the angles of incidence and refraction as the light passes from air into the glass. It is not possible to trace the ray as it passes through the block but if you place the block on a sheet of paper and mark where the ray enters and leaves the block (at B and C in Figure 5.81) then you can plot the path of the ray. If you don't have a light source you can use an alternative method with pins. Place two pins on one side of the block in positions A and B then, looking through the block, place a third pin in line with the other two. Joining the dots will give the path of a ray from A through the block.

The angles can then be measured using as protractor and the refractive index calculated.

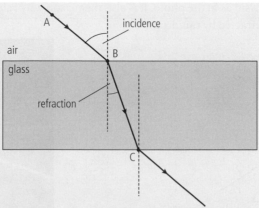

Figure 5.81 Measuring the refractive index from air to glass.

Light reflected off the straw is refracted as it comes out of the water causing the straw to appear bent.

Measuring the refractive index of a glass block

A worksheet with full details of how to carry out this experiment is available on your eBook.

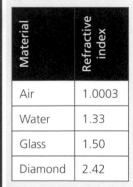

Material	Refractive index
Air	1.0003
Water	1.33
Glass	1.50
Diamond	2.42

Table 5.2 Some refractive indexes of different media.

Worked example

A ray of light travelling in air is incident on a glass block at an angle of 56°. Calculate the angle of refraction if the refractive index of glass is 1.5.

Solution

Applying Snell's law

$$\frac{\sin \theta_1}{\sin \theta_2} = \frac{n_2}{n_1}$$

where:

$$\theta_1 = 56°$$
$$n_1 = 1 \text{ (air)}$$
$$n_2 = 1.5 \text{ (glass)}$$

gives

$$\frac{\sin 56°}{\sin \theta_2} = \frac{1.5}{1}$$

$$\sin \theta_2 = \sin \frac{\sin 56°}{1.5} = 0.55$$

$$\theta_2 = 34°$$

Exercises

Use the refractive indices in the table to solve the following problems.

25 Light travelling through the air is incident on the surface of a pool of water at an angle of 40°. Calculate the angle of refraction.

26 Calculate the angle of refraction if a beam of light is incident on the surface of a diamond at an angle of 40°.

27 If the velocity of light in air is $3 \times 10^8 \text{ m s}^{-1}$, calculate its velocity in glass.

28 A fish tank made of glass contains water (and fish). Light travels from a fish at an angle of 30° to the side of the tank. Calculate the angle between the light and the normal to the glass surface as it emerges into the air.

29 Light incident on a block of transparent plastic at an angle of 30° is refracted at an angle of 20°. Calculate the angle of refraction if the block is immersed in water and the ray is incident at the same angle.

Dispersion

The angle of refraction is dependent on the wavelength of the light. If red light and blue light pass into a block of glass the blue light will be refracted more than the red causing the colours to *disperse*. This is why you see a spectrum when light passes through a prism as in the photo. It is also the reason why rainbows are formed when light is refracted by raindrops.

Figure 5.82 When white light is passed through a prism then blue light is refracted more than red.

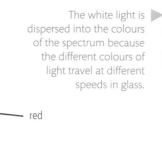

white light

prism

red

blue

The white light is dispersed into the colours of the spectrum because the different colours of light travel at different speeds in glass.

The critical angle

If light passes into an optically less dense medium, e.g. from glass to air, then the ray will be refracted away from the normal as shown in Figure 5.83.

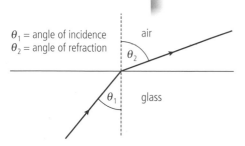

θ_1 = angle of incidence
θ_2 = angle of refraction

air

θ_2

θ_1 glass

Figure 5.83 Light refracted from glass to air.

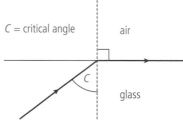

C = critical angle

air

C

glass

Figure 5.84 Light refracted at 90°.

If the angle of incidence increases, a point will be reached where the refracted ray is refracted along the boundary. The angle at which this happens is called the *critical angle*.

Applying Snell's law to this situation

$$\frac{\sin \theta_1}{\sin \theta_2} = \frac{n_2}{n_1}$$

where: $\theta_1 = c$
$\theta_2 = 90°$
$n_1 = 1.5$ for glass
$n_2 = 1$
$c = 42°$

Total internal reflection

If the critical angle is exceeded, all of the light is reflected. This is known as *total internal reflection*. Since all the light is reflected none is transmitted. This is not the case when light is reflected off a mirror when some is absorbed.

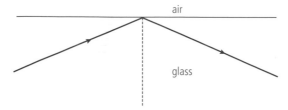

air

glass

Figure 5.85 Light totally internally reflected.

Optical fibres

An optical fibre is a thin strand of glass or clear plastic. If a ray of light enters its end at a small angle, the ray will be total internally reflected when it meets the side. Since the sides are parallel, the ray will be reflected back and forth until it reaches the other end as in Figure 5.86. Optical fibres are used extensively in communication.

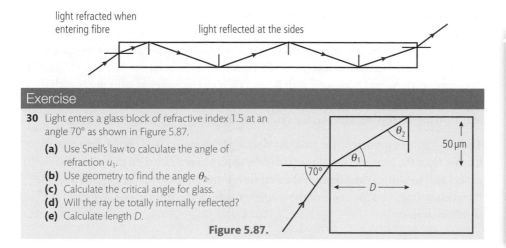

light refracted when entering fibre

light reflected at the sides

Figure 5.86 Light reflected along a fibre.

Exercise

30 Light enters a glass block of refractive index 1.5 at an angle 70° as shown in Figure 5.87.

(a) Use Snell's law to calculate the angle of refraction u_1.

(b) Use geometry to find the angle θ_2.

(c) Calculate the critical angle for glass.

(d) Will the ray be totally internally reflected?

(e) Calculate length D.

Figure 5.87.

θ_2

50 μm

θ_1

70°

D

Diffraction of light at a single slit

When light passes through a narrow slit it diffracts forming a series of bright and dark bands as shown in Figure 5.88.

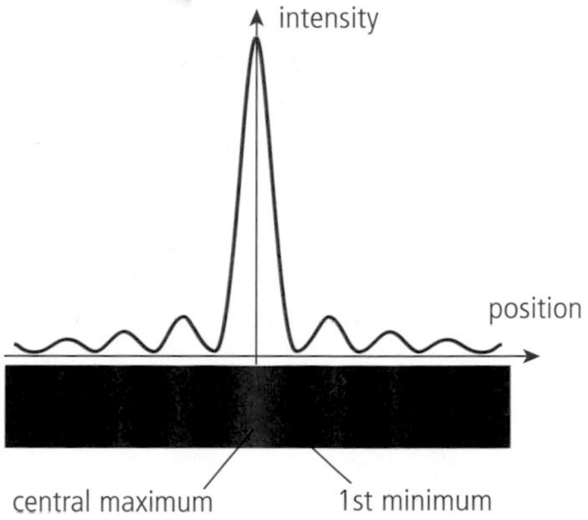

We can derive an equation for the first minima in this pattern by applying Huygens' construction.

When a wavefront passes through a narrow slit, it will propagate as if there were a large number of wavelet sources across the slit as in Figure 5.89.

The resultant intensity at some point P in front of the slit is found by summing all the wavelets. This is not a simple matter, since each wavelet has travelled a different distance so they will be out of phase when they arrive at P. To simplify the problem, we will consider a point Q a long way from the slits. Light travelling through the slit arriving at point Q is almost parallel, and if we say that it is parallel, then the geometry of the problem becomes much simpler.

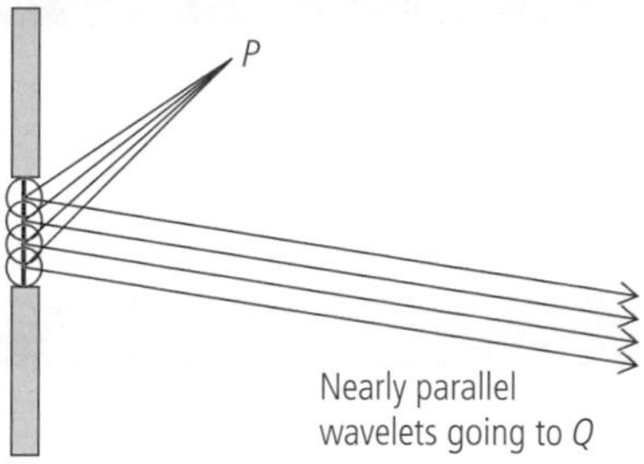

intensity

position

central maximum

1st minimum

Figure 5.88 Single-slit diffraction.

P

Nearly parallel wavelets going to Q

Figure 5.89 Wavelets add to give resultant intensity.

The central maximum

The central maximum occurs directly ahead of the slit. If we take a point a long way from the slit, all wavelets will be parallel and will have travelled the same distance, as shown in Figure 5.90. If all the wavelets have travelled the same distance they will be in phase, so will add up to give a region of high intensity (bright).

Figure 5.90 Wavelets travelling to the central maximum.

The first minimum

If we now consider wavelets travelling towards the first minimum, as in Figure 5.91, they are travelling at an angle so will not all travel the same distance. The wavelet at the top will travel further than the wavelet at the bottom. When these wavelets add together they cancel each other out to form a region of low intensity (dark).

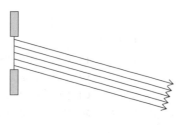

Figure 5.91 Wavelets travelling to the first minimum.

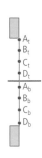

Figure 5.92 Wavelets in the top half cancel with wavelets in the bottom.

We can calculate the angle at which the first minimum is formed by splitting the slit into two halves, top and bottom, as in Figure 5.92. If all the wavelets from the top half cancel out all the wavelets from the bottom, the result will be a dark region. So if we have 8 wavelet sources, 4 in the top half (A_t, B_t, C_t, D_t) and 4 in the bottom (A_b, B_b, C_b, D_b) and if A_t cancels with A_b and B_t cancels with B_b etc., then all the wavelets will cancel with each other. For each pair to cancel, the path difference must be $\frac{1}{2}\lambda$. Figure 5.93 shows the situation for the top wavelet and the one in the middle.

The orange line cuts across the two wavelets at 90° showing that the top one travels further than the bottom one. If the path difference shown is $\frac{\lambda}{2}$ then these wavelets will cancel and so will all the others. If the first minimum occurs at an angle θ as shown, then this will also be the angle of the triangle made by the orange line. We can therefore write:

$$\sin\theta = \frac{\frac{\lambda}{2}}{\frac{b}{2}} = \frac{\lambda}{b}$$

But the angles are very small, so if θ is measured in radians, $\sin\theta = \theta$,

So:
$$\theta = \frac{\lambda}{b}$$

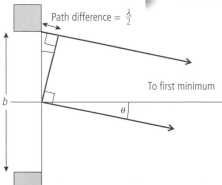

Figure 5.93 Geometric construction for the first minimum.

Knowing the position of the first minimum tells us how spread out the diffraction pattern is. From the equation we can see that if b is small then θ is big, so the pattern is spread out as shown in Figure 5.94.

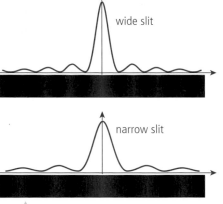

Figure 5.94 Notice that with a narrower slit the pattern is wider but less intense.

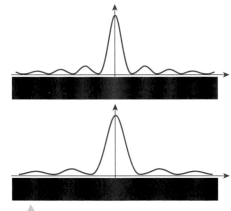

Figure 5.95 Same size slit but different wavelength light, longer wavelength gives a wider pattern.

If white light is passed through the slit, light of different wavelengths form peaks at different angles resulting in coloured fringes.

Example

A diffraction pattern is formed on a wall 2 m from a 0.1 mm slit illuminated with light of wavelength 600 nm. How wide will the central maximum be?

First draw a diagram showing the relative positions of the slit and screen.

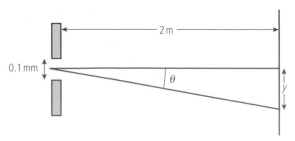

Figure 5.96.

The angle θ can be calculated from
$$\theta = \frac{\lambda}{b}$$
$$= \frac{600 \times 10^{-9}}{0.1 \times 10^{-3}}$$
$$= 0.006 \, \text{rads}$$

Since this angle is small we can say that
$$\theta = \frac{y}{2\,\text{m}} \quad \text{so} \quad y = 0.006 \times 2\,\text{m}$$
$$= 0.012\,\text{m}$$
$$= 1.2\,\text{cm}$$

This is half the width of the maximum, so   width = 2.4 cm

Exercises

31 Light of wavelength 550 nm is passed through a slit of size 0.05 mm. Calculate the width of the central maximum formed on a screen that is 5 m away.

32 Calculate the size of the slit that would cause light of wavelength 550 nm to diffract forming a diffraction pattern with a central maximum 5 cm wide on a screen 4 m from the slit.

Resolution

In the previous section we discovered that when light passes through a narrow slit it spreads out. This can cause problems for anyone using a device, such as a camera, telescope or even your eye, where light passes through a narrow opening. Try looking in the square of Figure 5.97; you should be able to see that there are two dots; we say you can *resolve* the two dots. If you move away from the page there will be a point where you can no longer resolve the two dots – they now look like one dot. The reason for this is when the light passes into your eye it diffracts; this causes the dots to appear as spots on your retina. As you move away from the page the image of the dots gets closer and closer until the two spots on your retina overlap, and the dots now look like one.

The Rayleigh criterion

The Rayleigh criterion puts a limit on the resolution of two points, based on the diffraction of light. It states that two points will just be resolved if the central maximum of the diffraction pattern formed of one point coincides with the first minimum of the other. Figure 5.98 shows this. Note that the diffraction patterns are not made of lines like those formed by slits, but are circular. This is because the aperture at the front of most optical instruments and the eye is circular, and circular apertures form circular diffraction patterns.

Figure 5.97.

> Note that the intensity of the diffraction maxima get less as you move away from the central maximum. In reality the first maximum would be smaller than shown in these diagrams (about $\frac{1}{20}$ the height of the central maximum).

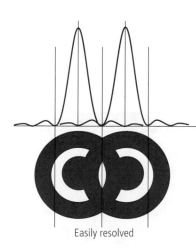
Easily resolved

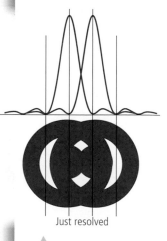
Just resolved

Figure 5.98 If the diffraction patterns overlap more than this, the two spots look like one.

From Figure 5.98 we can see that if the distance between the central maxima is less than half the width of the maxima the points will not be resolved. The width of the central maximum is defined by the position of the first minimum, which for a slit is given by the equation $\theta = \frac{\lambda}{b}$. But the central maximum for a circular aperture is 1.22 times wider than a slit, so the angular position of the first minimum is given by $\theta = \frac{1.22\lambda}{b}$ where b = diameter. Using this equation we can calculate whether two spots will be resolved or not, as long as we know the wavelength of light and the size of the aperture.

Worked example

Two small red spots 0.5 mm apart reflect light of wavelength 650 nm into a camera that has an aperture of 5 mm. What is the maximum distance between the camera and the paper if the spots are to be resolved in the photograph?

Solution

First draw a diagram:

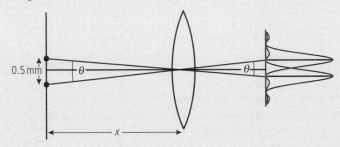

Figure 5.99.

Figure 5.99 shows two rays of light passing through the centre of the lens landing on the film. Notice these rays do not change direction since they pass through the centre of the lens. Light from each point forms a diffraction pattern on the film. If the separation of the patterns equals half the width of the central maximum of one, they will just be resolved.

$$\text{The angle } \theta \text{ on the right} = \frac{1.22\lambda}{b}$$
$$= \frac{1.22 \times 650 \times 10^{-9}}{5 \times 10^{-3}}$$
$$= 1.59 \times 10^{-4} \text{ rad}$$

The angle θ on the left is the same and since it is small

$$\theta = \frac{0.5 \times 10^{-3}}{x}$$

so

$$x = \frac{0.5 \times 10^{-3}}{1.59 \times 10^{-4}}$$
$$= 3.1 \text{ m}$$

Diffraction is not the only factor that affects the resolution of objects by optical instruments. The quality of the lens and the number of pixels in a digital camera are often the limiting factors.

Exercises

33 A telescope with aperture diameter 4 cm is used to view a collection of stars that are 4×10^{12} m away. If the stars give out light of wavelength 570 nm, what is the distance between the closest stars that can be resolved?

34 To read the headline in a newspaper you need to resolve points that are about 1 cm apart. If a spy camera is to be put in orbit 200 km above the Earth, how big must its aperture be if it is to take readable pictures of newspaper headlines? (Assume wavelength = 600 nm.)

35 The pixels on a computer screen are about 0.01 cm apart. If the aperture of your eye has diameter 5 mm should you be able to resolve the pixels at a distance of 1 m? (Assume wavelength = 600 nm.) Explain your answer.

Interference of light

For the light from two sources to interfere the light sources must be coherent. This means they have the same frequency, similar amplitude, and a constant phase difference. This can be achieved by taking one source and splitting it in two using either slits or thin films.

Two-slit interference

Light from a single source is split in two by parallel narrow slits. Since the slits are narrow the light diffracts creating an overlapping region where interference takes place. This results in a series of bright and dark parallel lines called fringes, as shown in Figure 5.100. This set up is called Young's slits.

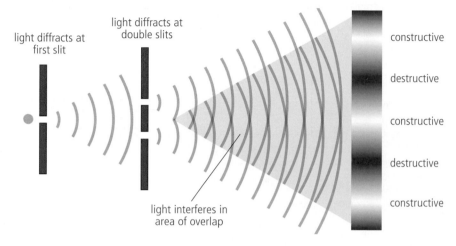

Figure 5.100 Double-slit interference.

To simplify matters let us consider rays from each slit arriving at the first maximum as shown in Figure 5.101.

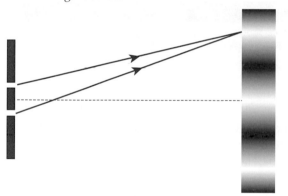

Figure 5.101.

Since this is the first interference maximum the path difference between the waves must be λ. If we fill in some angles and lengths as in Figure 5.102 we can use trigonometry to derive an equation for the separation of the fringes.

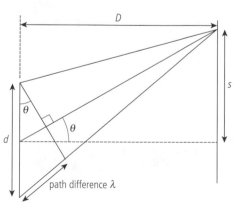

Figure 5.102 Light rays interfere at the first maximum.

Since the wavelength of light is very small, the angle θ will also be very small. This means that we can approximate θ in radians to $\frac{\lambda}{d} = \frac{s}{D}$ so the distance from the central bright fringe to the next one $s = \frac{\lambda D}{d}$. This is the fringe spacing. We can therefore conclude that if the slits are made closer together the fringes become more separated.

Interference of light using a hair

A worksheet with full details of how to carry out this experiment is available on your eBook.

Young's double-slit experiment using a human hair

It is possible to buy double slits but you can also use a human hair to split a single light source into two coherent sources. Select a hair from someone with long dark hair and mount it in a cardboard frame as shown in Figure 5.103. If using a normal light source you will have to pass it through a single slit before illuminating the hair as in Figure 5.100. The fringes will be too dim to project onto a screen but can be seen if you look towards the slits. This is not easy to set up, the single slit must be very narrow so that the light diffracts enough to pass on both sides of the hair. A lot of trial and error will be necessary. A simpler method is to use a LASER which produces an intense parallel beam of coherent light that forms interference fringes without the use of a single slit. This makes the fringes bright enough to be projected onto a screen where you can easily measure the separation of the fringes and determine the width of the hair using the formula $d = \frac{\lambda D}{s}$.

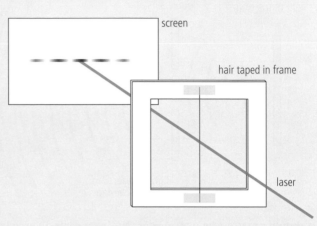

Figure 5.103.

Exercises

36 Two narrow slits 0.01 mm apart (d) are illuminated by a laser of wavelength 600 nm. Calculate the fringe spacing (y) on a screen 1.5 m (D) from the slits.

37 Calculate the fringe spacing if the laser is replaced by one of wavelength 400 nm.

Effect of diffraction

As we have seen, light is diffracted when it passes through each slit. This means that each slit will form a diffraction pattern on the screen which causes the fringes to vary in brightness as shown in Figure 5.104. Here it can also be seen how the diffraction pattern has modified the fringes.

Figure 5.104 Fringes modified by diffraction pattern.
(a) A single-slit of width b.
(b) Double slits each of width b and separation d.
(c) Double slits of width $>b$, giving a less spread diffraction pattern. The separation of the slits is d so the fringes are the same as in (b).
(d) Double slits of width b so the diffraction pattern is the same as (a). Separation of the slits $<d$ so the fringes are further apart.

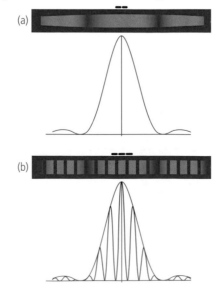

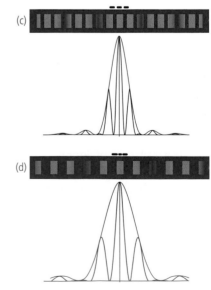

Multiple-slit diffraction

The intensity of double-slit interference patterns is very low but can be increased by using more than two slits. A diffraction grating is a series of very fine parallel slits mounted on a glass plate.

Diffraction at the slits

When light is incident on the grating it is diffracted at each slit. The slits are very narrow so the diffraction causes the light to propagate as if coming from a point source.

Interference between slits

To make the geometry simpler we will consider what would happen if the light passing through the grating were observed from a long distance. This means that we can consider the light rays to be almost parallel. So the parallel light rays diffracted through each slit will come together at a distant point. When they come together they will interfere.

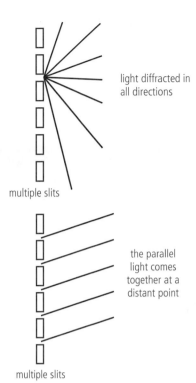

light diffracted in all directions

multiple slits

the parallel light comes together at a distant point

multiple slits

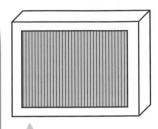

Figure 5.105 Diffraction grating (the number of lines per millimetre can be very high: school versions usually have 600 lines per millimetre).

Figure 5.106 Light diffracted at each slit undergoes interference at a distant screen.

Geometrical model

Let us consider waves that have been diffracted at an angle θ as shown in Figure 5.107 (remember light is diffracted at all angles – this is just one angle that we have chosen to consider).

We can see that when these rays meet, the ray from A will have travelled a distance x further than the ray from B. The ray from D has travelled the same distance further than C, and so on. If the path difference between neighbours is λ then they will interfere constructively, if $\frac{1}{2}\lambda$ then the interference will be destructive.

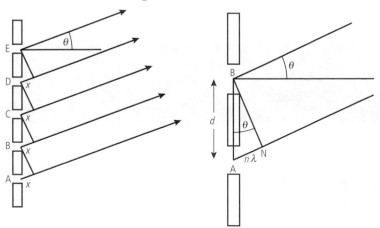

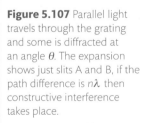

Figure 5.107 Parallel light travels through the grating and some is diffracted at an angle θ. The expansion shows just slits A and B, if the path difference is $n\lambda$ then constructive interference takes place.

The line BN is drawn perpendicular to both rays so angle N is 90°

Therefore from triangle ABN we see that $\sin \theta = \dfrac{n\lambda}{d}$

Rearranging gives $d \sin \theta = n\lambda$.

If you look at a light source through a diffraction grating and move your head around, bright lines will be seen every time $\sin \theta = \frac{n\lambda}{d}$.

Producing spectra

If white light is viewed through a diffraction grating, each wavelength undergoes constructive interference at different angles. This results in a spectrum. The individual wavelengths can be calculated from the angle using the formula $d \sin \theta = n\lambda$.

Worked example

If blue light of wavelength 450 nm and red light wavelength 700 nm are viewed through a grating with 600 lines mm^{-1}, at what angle will the first bright blue and red lines be seen?

Solution

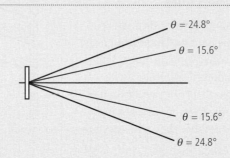

$\theta = 24.8°$

$\theta = 15.6°$

$\theta = 15.6°$

$\theta = 24.8°$

Figure 5.108 Bright lines appear at angles when $\sin \theta = \frac{n\lambda}{d}$. Red and blue lines appear at different angles.

If there are 600 lines/mm,	$d = \frac{1}{600}$ mm $= 0.001\,67$ mm
For the first lines,	$n = 1$
For blue light,	$\sin \theta = \frac{450 \times 10^{-9}}{0.001\,67 \times 10^{-3}} = 0.269$
Therefore	$\theta_{blue} = 15.6°$
For red light,	$\sin \theta = \frac{700 \times 10^{-9}}{0.001\,67 \times 10^{-3}} = 0.419$
Therefore	$\theta_{red} = 24.8°$

A CD can be used as a diffraction grating. Light reflecting off small silver lines on the CD diffract in all directions. Light from each line interferes constructively when the path difference $= n\lambda$. This takes place at different angles for different wavelengths, giving rise to the colours you see when viewing a CD in white light.

Figure 5.109 A hydrogen lamp viewed through a grating.

Diffraction grating resolvance

The width of the interference fringes produced from a diffraction grating is related to the number of lines on the grating: more lines means narrower fringes. This means that if two lines are close together they will be easier to resolve if the grating has many lines.

In Figure 5.110 two spectral lines, close together, are viewed with two gratings. The grating in B has more lines so the fringes are narrower leading to better resolution.

The resolvance R of a grating is defined as $\frac{\lambda}{\Delta\lambda}$ where λ is the wavelength of the line and $\Delta\lambda$ is the smallest difference to the next resolvable wavelength (so the next resolvable wavelength is $\lambda + \Delta\lambda$). The resolvance is related to the number of slits, N by the following equation:

$$R = \frac{\lambda}{\Delta\lambda} = mN$$

where m is the order of the spectrum.

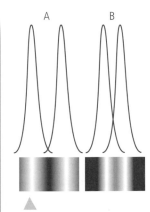

▲ **Figure 5.110** Two close spectral lines.

Exercises

38 Red light (λ = 700 nm) is shone through a grating with 300 lines mm^{-1}. Calculate:

   (a) the separation of the lines on the grating.
   (b) the diffraction angle of the first red line.

39 The spectrum of sodium light has two yellow lines known as the sodium doublet; they have wavelengths 589.0 nm and 589.6 nm. Calculate the minimum number of lines a diffraction grating must have for the spectral lines to be resolved in the first-order spectrum.

Thin film interference

The condition for observable interference between two sources of light is that the sources are coherent. This means similar amplitude, same wavelength, and a constant phase difference. We have seen how this can be achieved using a double slit to split one source in two (division of wavefront). A single source can also be split in two by reflecting half of it off a semi-reflective surface like a bubble (division of amplitude). This results in the coloured bands that we see on the surface of a soap bubble.

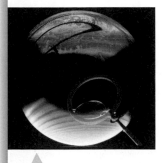

▲ Colours due to interference of light reflected off a soap bubble.

Reflection of light off thin films

When light is incident on a boundary between two different media, e.g. air and glass, part of the light reflects and part refracts. The percentage of light that reflects depends on the media; for glass in air, about 4% of the light is reflected and 96% refracted. If light is incident on a sheet of glass, 4% of the light is reflected off the front surface and then 4% of the remaining 96% off the bottom, as shown in Figure 5.111. If the glass is very thin (about 500 nm) then the two reflected waves will have about the same amplitude, so will interfere if their paths cross. A sheet of glass is too thick for this effect to be seen – however, it can be seen in soap bubbles and oil floating on water.

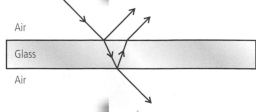

▲ **Figure 5.111.**

Interference by parallel-sided thin films

We have seen how light reflects off both surfaces of a thin film producing two coherent sources. To simplify the geometry, we will consider light that is almost perpendicular to the surface of a soap bubble as in Figure 5.112. In this case the parallel reflected rays will coincide when they are focused by the eye.

We can see from this diagram that the path difference is $2t$. This will cause a phase difference of $\frac{2t}{\lambda} \times 2\pi$.

But there will also be a phase change of π when the light reflects off the top surface, so the total phase difference = $\frac{4t\pi}{\lambda} - \pi$

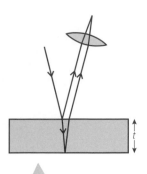

Figure 5.112 Reflected rays brought to a focus by the eye lens.

Constructive interference will take place if the phase difference is $m2\pi$ where m is an integer (0, 1, 2 …).

So for constructive interference, $\frac{4t\pi}{\lambda} - \pi = m2\pi$

This will take place when $2t = (m + \frac{1}{2})\lambda$.

Since the light is travelling in soap, we need to find the wavelength of light in soap. We know that when light passes into soap, it slows down, causing the wavelength to change. The ratio of the speed in air to the speed in soap is given by the refractive index of the air–soap boundary: $\frac{n_{\text{soap}}}{n_{\text{air}}} = \frac{c_{\text{air}}}{c_{\text{soap}}}$

but
$$n_{\text{air}} = 1$$

so
$$n_{\text{soap}} = \frac{c_{\text{air}}}{c_{\text{soap}}}$$

$$c = \frac{f}{\lambda}$$

This gives
$$n_{\text{soap}} = \frac{f\lambda_{\text{air}}}{f\lambda_{\text{soap}}} = \frac{\lambda_{\text{air}}}{\lambda_{\text{soap}}}$$

$$\lambda_{\text{soap}} = \frac{\lambda_{\text{air}}}{n_{\text{soap}}}$$

Substituting into the equation for constructive interference gives:
$$2t = \frac{(m + \frac{1}{2})\lambda_{\text{air}}}{n_{\text{soap}}}$$

And for destructive interference: $\quad 2t = \frac{m\lambda_{\text{air}}}{n_{\text{soap}}}$

Let us say that for a certain soap film, the thickness is such that green light (λ = 500 nm) satisfies this equation. If green light is reflected off the film it will interfere constructively, so the reflected light will be bright – the film looks shiny. If red light is reflected, the interference is destructive, so the film appears dull. If white light, which consists of all wavelengths, is reflected, then only the green will interfere constructively, and the film will therefore appear green.

When light reflects off a more optically dense medium it undergoes a phase change of π. This is rather like the phase change that occurs when a wave in a string reflects off a fixed end. When the reflection is off a less dense medium there is no phase change.

Camera lenses are often coated with a thin film to reduce reflection. Light reflected off each side of the film interferes destructively, removing the reflected light. Energy cannot be destroyed so this results in more light entering the lens.

Exercises

40 What is the minimum thickness of a soap film that gives constructive interference for light that has wavelength of 600 nm in soap?

41 A camera lens has an antireflective coating that appears violet when viewed in white light. If the wavelength of violet light in the coating is 380 nm, what is the minimum thickness of the coating?

42 Coloured interference fringes are viewed when white light is incident on oil floating on water. The refractive index of oil is 1.5 and the refractive index of water is 1.3.

   (a) Will there be a phase change on reflection at the oil/water boundary?

   (b) Yellow light has wavelength 580 nm in air. What is its wavelength in oil?

   (c) What is the thinnest thickness of oil that will give constructive interference for yellow light?

43 The coating shown in Figure 5.113 is applied to a lens. What thickness should the coating have to remove reflections of light that has wavelength 580 nm in air?

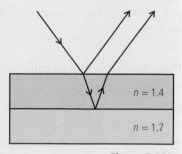

$n = 1.4$

$n = 1.7$

Figure 5.113.

The Doppler effect and EM radiation

The Doppler effect also applies to electromagnetic radiation (radio, microwaves and light). The derivation of the formula is rather more complicated since the velocity of light is not changed by the relative movement of the observer. However if the relative velocities are much smaller than the speed of light we can use the following approximation:

$$\Delta f = \frac{v}{c} f_0$$

where

Δf = the change in frequency
v = the relative speed of the source and observer
c = the speed of light in a vacuum
f_0 = the original frequency

Unlike the Doppler effect for sound, it doesn't matter whether it is the source or observer that moves.

Red shift

If a source of light is moving away from an observer, the light received by the observer will have a longer wavelength than when it was emitted. If we look at the spectrum as shown in Figure 5.114, we see that the red end of the spectrum is long wavelength and the blue end is short wavelength. The change in wavelength will therefore cause the light to shift towards the red end of the spectrum – this is called 'red shift'. This effect is very useful to astronomers as they can use it to calculate how fast stars are moving away from us. This is made possible by the fact that the spectrum of light from stars contains characteristic absorption lines from elements such as Hydrogen. The wavelength of these lines is known so their shifted position in the spectrum can be used to calculate velocity.

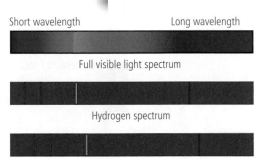

Short wavelength   Long wavelength

Full visible light spectrum

Hydrogen spectrum

Hydrogen spectrum from a receding star (red shifted)

Figure 5.114 Comparing the spectrum of hydrogen from a stationary source and a star.

Speed traps

Police speed traps use the Doppler effect to measure the speed of passing cars. When they aim the device at the car, a beam of EM radiation (microwaves or IR) is reflected off the car. The reflected beam undergoes a double Doppler shift; first the car is approaching the beam so there will be a shift due to the moving observer and secondly the reflected beam is emitted from the moving source. When the device receives the higher frequency reflected beam, the speed of the car can be calculated from the change in frequency.

Speed cameras use the Doppler effect.

Worked example

A speed trap uses a beam with a wavelength 1 cm. What is the change in frequency received by the detector if the beam reflects off a car travelling at $150\,\text{km}\,\text{h}^{-1}$?

Solution

First convert the car's speed to $\text{m}\,\text{s}^{-1}$:

$$150\,\text{km}\,\text{h}^{-1} = 42\,\text{m}\,\text{s}^{-1}$$

The frequency of the 1 cm wave $= \dfrac{c}{\lambda} = \dfrac{3 \times 10^8}{1 \times 10^{-2}} = 3 \times 10^{10}\,\text{Hz}$.

Change in f of signal received by car is given by:

$$\Delta f = \frac{v}{c} f_0$$

$$= \frac{42}{3 \times 10^8} \times 3 \times 10^{10} = 4.2 \times 10^3\,\text{Hz}.$$

This shift is then doubled since the car, now the source of the reflected wave, is travelling towards the detector; so the change in frequency $= 8.4 \times 10^3\,\text{Hz}$.

The light used to project 3D films is circularly polarized. Two images are projected, one for the left eye with light polarized anticlockwise, and one for the right eye with light polarized clockwise. The 3D glasses have polarizing filters which only allow one orientation of polarization to pass so the correct image is seen by the correct eye.

Exercises

44 A star emits light of wavelength 650 nm. If the light received at the Earth from this star has a wavelength of 690 nm, how fast is the star moving away from the Earth?

45 An atom of hydrogen travelling towards the Earth at 2×10^6 m s^{-1} emits light of wavelength 658 nm. What is the change in wavelength experienced by an observer on the Earth?

Polarization of light

As previously mentioned, light is an electromagnetic transverse wave. Variations in electric field can be in any plane parallel to the direction of energy transfer. When light is incident on a solid it is either absorbed or transmitted. Some materials absorb certain wavelengths better than others. These can be used as filters; for example, a green filter *absorbs* red and blue light but *transmits* green. There are also some materials that absorb only *one direction* of electric disturbance. Light passing through such a substance is said to be polarized.

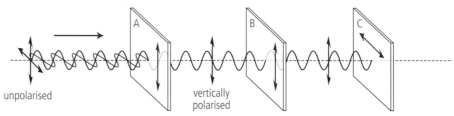

Figure 5.115.

unpolarised

vertically polarised

In Figure 5.115, unpolarized light is incident on a polarizing filter A. 50% of the light is absorbed since this filter only lets through vertical components of the electric field. The second filter, B, has no effect since the orientation of the polarizing plane is the same. However, the third filter, C, has its polarizing plane horizontal so it won't transmit any of the vertically polarized light.

When light is reflected by water and scattered by clouds it becomes polarized. Polarizing filters are used in photography to remove the glare from reflected and scattered light.

To learn more about light waves, go to the hotlinks site, search for the title or ISBN and click on Chapter 5.

Malus' law

When polarized light passes through a polarizer, only the component of amplitude of the electric field that is in the direction of the polarizing plane will pass through. From Figure 5.116, you can see that this component = $A_0 \cos \theta$

The intensity of light (I) is proportional to A^2 so if the original intensity of the polarized light was I_0, the intensity passing through the polarizer will be given by the equation

$$I = I_0 \cos^2 \theta$$

This is called Malus' law.

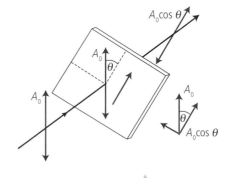

Figure 5.116 Only the component in the plane of polarization passes through.

Exercise

46 Unpolarized light of intensity I_0 is incident on a polarizer. The transmitted light is then incident on a second polarizer. The axis of the second polarizer makes an angle of 60° to the axis of the first polarizer. Calculate the fraction of intensity transmitted.

1. This question is about sound waves.
   A sound wave of frequency 660 Hz passes through air. The variation of particle displacement with distance along the wave at one instant of time is shown in Figure 5.117.

   (a) State whether this wave is an example of a longitudinal or a transverse wave. (1)

   (b) Using data from Figure 5.117, deduce for this sound wave,

   (i) the wavelength. (1)

   (ii) the amplitude. (1)

   (iii) the speed. (2)

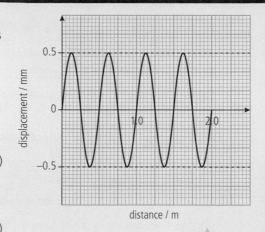

Figure 5.117.

(*Total 5 marks*)

2. This question is about waves and wave properties.

   (a) By making reference to waves, distinguish between a *ray* and a *wavefront*. (3)

   Figure 5.118 shows three wavefronts incident on a boundary between medium I and medium R. Wavefront CD is shown crossing the boundary. Wavefront EF is incomplete.

   (b) (i) Copy Figure 5.118 and, on your diagram, draw a line to complete the wavefront EF. (1)

   (ii) Explain in which medium, I or R, the wave has the higher speed. (3)

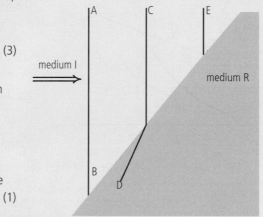

Figure 5.118.

   (iii) By taking appropriate measurements from the diagram, determine the ratio of the speeds of the wave travelling from medium I to medium R. (2)

   Figure 5.119 shows the variation with time *t* of the velocity *v* of one particle of the medium through which the wave is travelling.

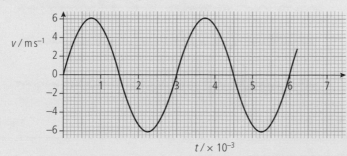

Figure 5.119.

(c) (i) Explain how it can be deduced from Figure 5.119 that the particle is oscillating. (2)

(ii) Determine the frequency of oscillation of the particle. (2)

(iii) Copy Figure 5.119 and mark on your graph with the letter M one time at which the particle is at maximum displacement. (1)

(iv) Estimate the area between the curve and the x-axis from the time $t = 0$ to the time $t = 1.5\,ms$. (2)

(v) Suggest what the area in (c) (iv) represents. (1)

(*Total 17 marks*)

3. This question is about waves and wave motion.

(a) (i) Define what is meant by the *speed of a wave*. (2)

(ii) Light is emitted from a candle flame. Explain why, in this situation, it is correct to refer to the 'speed of the emitted light', rather than its velocity. (2)

(b) (i) Define, by reference to wave motion, what is meant by *displacement*. (2)

(ii) By reference to displacement, describe the difference between a longitudinal wave and a transverse wave. (3)

The centre of an earthquake produces both longitudinal waves (P waves) and transverse waves (S waves). Figure 5.120 shows the variation with time t of the distance d moved by the two types of wave.

(c) Use Figure 5.120 to determine the speed of:

(i) the P waves. (1)

(ii) the S waves. (1)

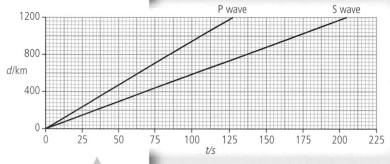

Figure 5.120.

The waves from an earthquake close to the Earth's surface are detected at three laboratories L_1, L_2, and L_3. The laboratories are at the corners of a triangle so that each is separated from the others by a distance of 900 km, as shown in Figure 5.121.

The records of the variation with time of the vibrations produced by the earthquake as detected at the three laboratories are shown in Figure 5.122. All three records were started at the same time.

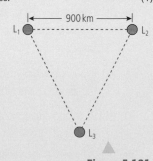

Figure 5.121.

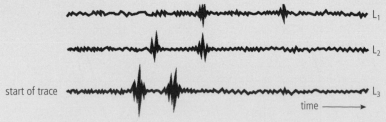

Figure 5.122.

On each record, one pulse is made by the S wave and the other by the P wave. The separation of the two pulses is referred to as the S–P interval.

(d) (i) Copy Figure 5.122 and on the trace produced by laboratory L_2 identify, by reference to your answers in (c), the pulse due to the P wave (label the pulse P). (1)

(ii) Using evidence from the records of the earthquake, state which laboratory was closest to the site of the earthquake. (1)

(iii) State **three** separate pieces of evidence for your statement in (d)(ii). (3)

(iv) The S-P intervals are 68 s, 42 s, and 27 s for laboratories L_1, L_2, and L_3 respectively. Use the figures, or otherwise, to determine the distance of the earthquake from each laboratory. Explain your working. (4)

(v) Copy Figure 5.121 and mark on the diagram a possible site of the earthquake. (1)

There is a tall building near to the site of the earthquake, as illustrated in Figure 5.123.

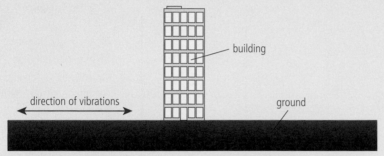

Figure 5.123.

The base of the building vibrates horizontally due to the earthquake.

(e) (i) Copy Figure 5.123 and on your diagram draw the fundamental mode of vibration of the building caused by these vibrations. (1)

The building is of height 280 m and the mean speed of waves in the structure of the building is $3.4 \times 10^3 \, \text{m s}^{-1}$.

(ii) Explain quantitatively why earthquake waves of frequency about 6 Hz are likely to be very destructive. (3)

(*Total 25 marks*)

4. This question is about the interference of waves.

(a) State the principle of superposition. (2)

A wire is stretched between two points A and B.

A ————————————————————————————— B

Figure 5.124.

A standing wave is set up in the wire. This wave can be thought of as being made up from the superposition of two waves, a wave X travelling from A to B, and a wave Y travelling from B to A. At one particular instant in time, the displacement of the wire is as shown in Figure 5.125. A background grid is given for reference and the equilibrium position of the wire is shown as a dotted line.

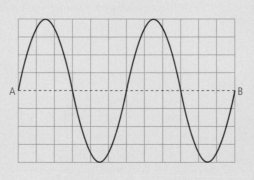

Figure 5.125.

(b) Copy the grids in Figure 5.126 and on them draw the displacements of the wire due to wave X and wave Y.

Wave X

Wave X

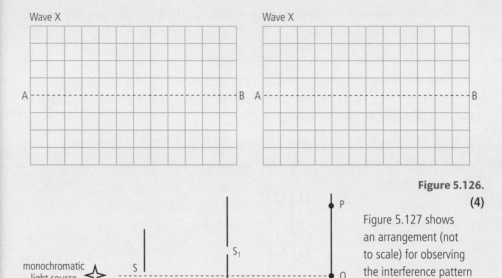

Figure 5.126.

(4)

Figure 5.127 shows an arrangement (not to scale) for observing the interference pattern produced by the superposition of two light waves.

Figure 5.127.

S_1 and S_2 are two very narrow slits. The single-slit S ensures that the light leaving the slits S_1 and S_2 is coherent.

(c) (i) Define *coherent*. (1)

(ii) Explain why the slits S_1 and S_2 need to be very narrow. (2)

The point O on the diagram is equidistant from S_1 and S_2 and there is maximum constructive interference at point P on the screen. There are no other points of maximum interference between O and P.

(d) (i) State the condition necessary for there to be maximum constructive interference at the point P. (1)

(ii) Copy Figure 5.128 and, on the axes, draw a graph to show the variation of intensity of light on the screen between the points O and P.

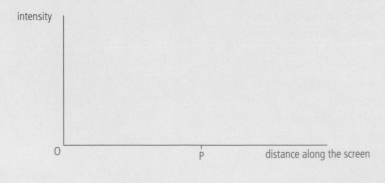

Figure 5.128.

(2)

(e) In this particular arrangement, the distance between the double slit and the screen is 1.50 m and the separation of S_1 and S_2 is 3.00×10^{-3} m.

The distance OP is 0.25 mm. Determine the wavelength of the light. (2)

(Total 14 marks)

5. This question is about wave properties and interference.

Figure 5.129 represents the direction of oscillation of a disturbance that gives rise to a wave.

Figure 5.129.

(a) Copy Figure 5.129, and add arrows to show the direction of wave energy transfer to illustrate the difference between

    (i) a transverse wave and (1)

    (ii) a longitudinal wave. (1)

A wave travels along a stretched string. Figure 5.130 shows the variation with distance along the string of the displacement of the string at a particular instant in time. A small marker is attached to the string at the point labelled M. The undisturbed position of the string is shown as a dotted line.

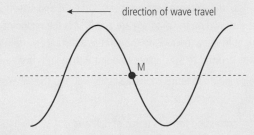

direction of wave travel

M

Figure 5.130.

(b) Copy Figure 5.130 and on the diagram:

    (i) draw an arrow to indicate the direction in which the marker is moving. (1)

    (ii) indicate, with the letter A, the amplitude of the wave. (1)

    (iii) indicate, with the letter λ, the wavelength of the wave. (1)

    (iv) draw the displacement of the string a time $\frac{T}{4}$ later, where T is the period of oscillation of the wave. Indicate, with the letter N, the new position of the marker. (2)

The wavelength of the wave is 5.0 cm and its speed is 10 cm s^{-1}.

(c) Determine

    (i) the frequency of the wave. (1)

    (ii) how far the wave has moved in $\frac{T}{4}$ s. (2)

Interference of waves

(d) By reference to the principle of superposition, explain what is meant by *constructive interference*. (4)

Figure 5.131 (not drawn to scale) shows an arrangement for observing the interference pattern produced by the light from two narrow slits S_1 and S_2.

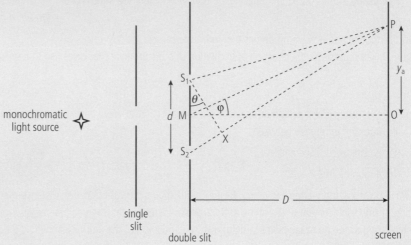

Figure 5.131.

The distance S_1S_2 is d, the distance between the double slit and screen is D and $D \gg d$ such that the angles θ and φ shown on the diagram are small. M is the midpoint of S_1S_2 and it is observed that there is a bright fringe at point P on the screen, a distance y_n from point O on the screen. Light from S_2 travels a distance S_2X further to point P than light from S_1.

(e) (i) State the condition in terms of the distance S_2X and the wavelength of the light λ, for there to be a bright fringe at P. (2)

(ii) Deduce an expression for θ in terms of S_2X and d. (2)

(iii) Deduce an expression for φ in terms of D and y_n. (1)

For a particular arrangement, the separation of the slits is 1.40 mm and the distance from the slits to the screen is 1.50 m. The distance y_n is the distance of the eighth bright fringe from O and the angle $\theta = 2.70 \times 10^{-3}$ rad.

(f) Using your answers to (e) to determine

(i) the wavelength of the light. (2)

(ii) the separation of the fringes on the screen. (3)

(*Total 24 marks*)

6. This question is about the Doppler effect.

Figure 5.132 shows wavefronts produced by a stationary wave source S. The spacing of the wavefronts is equal to the wavelength of the waves. The wavefronts travel with speed V.

(a) The source S now moves to the right with speed $\frac{1}{2}V$. In the space below, draw *four* successive wavefronts to show the pattern of waves produced by the moving source. (3)

(b) Derive the Doppler formula for the observed frequency f_0 of a sound source, as heard by a stationary observer, when the source approaches the stationary observer with speed v. The speed of sound is V and the frequency of the sound emitted by the source is f. (3)

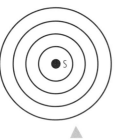

Figure 5.132.

The Sun rotates about its centre. The light from one edge of the Sun, as seen by a stationary observer, shows a Doppler shift of 0.004 nm for light of wavelength 600.000 nm.

(c) Assuming that the Doppler formula for sound may be used for light, estimate the linear speed of a point on the surface of the Sun due to its rotation. (3)

(*Total 9 marks*)

7. This question is about standing waves in pipes.
Figure 5.133 shows two pipes of the same length. Pipe A is open at both ends and pipe B is closed at one end.

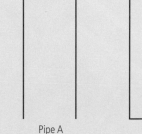

Figure 5.133.

(a) (i) Copy Figure 5.133 and on the diagrams draw lines to represent the waveforms of the fundamental (first harmonic) resonant note for each pipe. (2)

(ii) On each diagram, label the position of the nodes with the letter N and the position of the antinodes with the letter A. (2)

Pipe A   Pipe B

The frequency of the fundamental note for pipe A is 512 Hz.

(b) (i) Calculate the length of the pipe A. (Speed of sound in air = 340 m s^{-1}) (3)

(ii) Suggest why organ pipes designed to emit low frequency fundamental notes (e.g. frequency ≈ 32 Hz) are often closed at one end. (2)

(*Total 9 marks*)

8. This question is about optical resolution.

(a) Light from a point source is brought to a focus by a convex lens. The lens does not cause spherical or chromatic aberration.

(i) State why the image of the point source will not be a point image. (1)

(ii) Describe the appearance of the image. (2)

Two light receptors at the back of the eye are 4.0 μm apart. The distance of the receptors from the convex lens at the front of the eye is 17.0 mm, as shown in Figure 5.134.

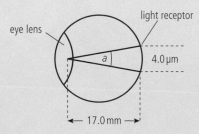

Figure 5.134.

Light of wavelength 550 nm from two point objects enters the eye. The centres of the images of the two objects are focused on the light receptors.

(b) (i) Calculate the angle *a* in radians subtended by the two receptors at the centre of the eye lens. (2)

(ii) Use the Rayleigh criterion to calculate the diameter of the pupil of the eye so that the two images are just resolved. (2)

(iii) With reference to your answer in (i), suggest why the film appears to be coloured. (2)

(*Total 9 marks*)

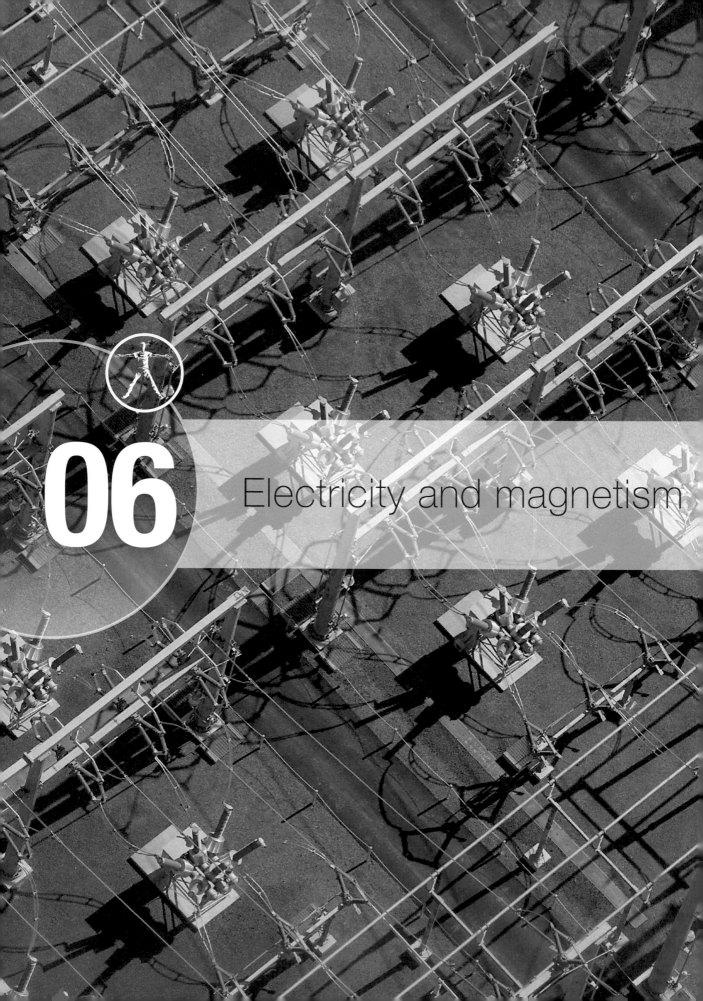

06 Electricity and magnetism

Essential ideas

5.1 **Electric fields**
When charges move an electric current is created.

5.2 **Heating effect of electric currents**
One of the earliest uses for electricity was to produce light and heat. This technology continues to have a major impact on the lives of people around the world.

5.3 **Electric cells**
Electric cells allow us to store energy in a chemical form.

5.4 **Magnetic effects of electric currents**
The effect scientists call magnetism arises when one charge moves in the vicinity of another moving charge.

10.1 **Describing fields (HL only)**
Electric charges and masses each influence the space around them, and that influence can be represented through the concept of field.

10.2 **Fields at work (HL only)**
Similar approaches can be taken in analysing electrical and gravitational potential problems.

11.1 **Electromagnetic induction (HL only)**
The majority of electricity generated throughout the world is generated by machines which were designed to operate using the principles of electromagnetic induction.

11.2 **Power generation and transmission (HL only)**
Generation an d transmission of AC electricity has transformed the globe.

11.3 **Capacitance (HL only)**
Capacitors can be used to store electrical energy for later use.

NATURE OF SCIENCE

The electric force is very similar to gravitation in that it acts over a distance and its strength is inversely proportional to the distance between affected bodies. This means that we can use the concept of field we developed for gravity to model the electric effect.

Strong electric fields can break down the air resulting in a spark. To prevent sparking between high voltage cables they must be kept far apart from each other and the Earth.

6.1 Electric fields

5.1 Electric fields/electrostatic fields

Understandings, applications, and skills:

Charge
- Identifying two forms of charge and the direction of the forces between them.

Electric field

Coulomb's law
- Solving problems involving electric fields and Coulomb's law.

  Guidance
  - *Students will be expected to apply Coulomb's law for a range of permittivity values.*

Potential difference
- Calculating work done in an electric field in both joules and electronvolts.

10.1 Describing fields

Understandings, applications, and skills:

(AHL) Electrostatic fields
- Representing sources of mass and charge, lines of electric and gravitational force, and field patterns using an appropriate symbolism.
- Mapping fields using potential.

(AHL) Electric potential

  Guidance
  - *Electrostatic fields are restricted to the radial fields around point or spherical charges, and the uniform fields between charged parallel plates.*

(AHL) Field lines
- Representing sources of charge, lines of electric force, and field patterns using an appropriate symbolism.

(AHL) Equipotential surfaces
- Mapping fields using potential.
- Describing the connection between equipotential surfaces and field lines.

  Guidance
  - *Students should recognize that no work is done in moving charge on an equipotential surface.*

10.2 Fields at work

Understandings, applications, and skills:

(AHL)Potential and potential energy
- Determining the potential energy of a point charge.
- Solving problems involving potential energy.
- Determining the potential inside a charged sphere.
- Solving problems involving orbital energy of charges in circular orbital motion.

(AHL) Potential gradient
- Solving problems involving forces on charges in radial and uniform fields.

  Guidance
  - *Students should assume that the electric field everywhere between parallel plates is uniform with edge effects occurring beyond the limits of the plates.*

(AHL) Potential difference

Electric force

If you rub a plastic ruler on a woollen sweater (or synthetic fleece) and hold it above some small bits of paper something interesting happens. The paper jumps up and sticks to the ruler. We know that to make the paper move there must have been an unbalanced force acting on it; we call this the *electric force*. To find out more about the nature of this force we need to do some more experiments. This time we will use a balloon.

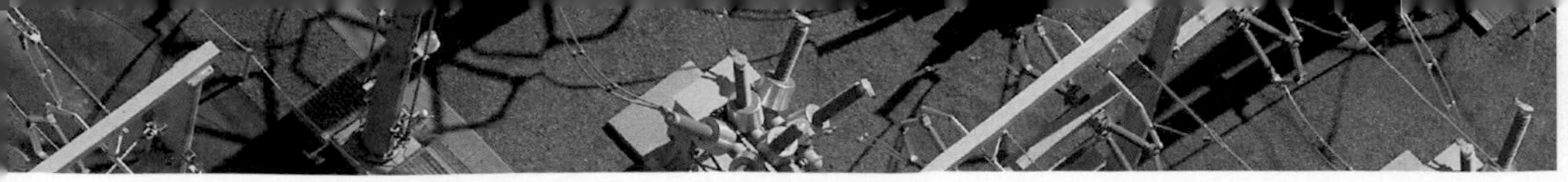

If we rub a balloon on a sweater we find that it will experience a force in the direction of the sweater as shown in Figure 6.1. The sweater is causing this force so according to Newton's third law the sweater must experience an equal and opposite force towards the balloon: the two objects are said to *attract* each other.

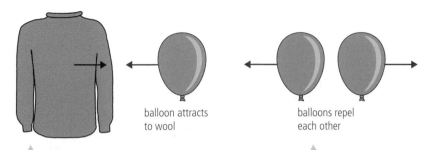

balloon attracts to wool

balloons repel each other

▲
Figure 6.1 The balloon is attracted to the wool.

▲
Figure 6.2 Balloons repel each other.

If two balloons are rubbed and held close to each other they will experience a force pushing them away from each other as shown in Figure 6.2. They are said to *repel* each other.

In some ways this effect is similar to gravity as the force acts over a distance and gets bigger as the bodies are brought closer together. In other ways it is very different to gravity. The gravitational force is always attractive whereas this force can be either attractive or repulsive. If there was repulsive gravity then some objects would fall upwards and this doesn't happen. Gravitational force is experienced by properties with mass; whatever property is responsible for this force must exist in two types. We call this property *charge*. Experimenting further, we find that the more balloons we have the greater the force, as in Figure 6.3. Also, a balloon seems to cancel out the effect of a sweater as in Figure 6.4.

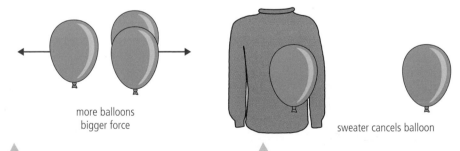

more balloons bigger force

sweater cancels balloon

▲
Figure 6.3 More balloons, bigger force.

▲
Figure 6.4 The charge on the sweater cancels the charge on the balloon.

So charges add and charges cancel. For this reason we can use positive and negative numbers to represent charge but we have to decide which will be positive and which negative. Let us say the balloon is negative and the sweater is positive.

Charge (Q)

The property of matter that causes the electrical force is charge. All bodies are either positive, negative, or neutral (zero charge). Bodies with the same charge repel each other and oppositely charged bodies attract. Charge cannot be created or destroyed so charges add or subtract.

Charge is a *scalar* quantity.

The unit of charge is the coulomb (C).

Fundamental charge (e)

Matter is made of atoms so it makes sense to suppose that the atoms are also charged. We will go more into this when we deal with atomic models in Chapter 7, but for now it is enough to say that all atoms are made of three particles: *protons* which have positive charge, *electrons* which are negative, and the aptly named *neutron* which is neutral. Each atom is made of a positive heavy nucleus consisting of protons and neutrons, surrounded by much lighter negative electrons as in Figure 6.5. The proton and electron have the same amount of charge (1.6×10^{-19} C) but the opposite sign. This is the smallest amount of charge that exists in ordinary matter, and is therefore called the *fundamental charge (e)*.

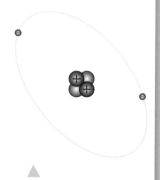

Figure 6.5 A simple model of an atom (not to scale).

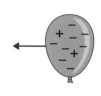

The electrons, being lighter and on the outside of the atom, are easy to move around and provide the answer to what was going on in the balloon experiment. At the start the balloon and sweater had equal numbers of positive and negative charges so were both neutral. When the balloon is rubbed on the sweater, electrons (negative charges) are rubbed from the sweater onto the balloon so the balloon becomes negative and the sweater positive as shown in Figure 6.6.

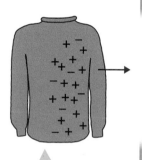

Figure 6.6 Showing the charges on the balloon and sweater.

Electric field

A region of space where an electric force is experienced is called an *electric field*. The region around the sphere of charge in Figure 6.7 is an electric field since the small positive charge placed in that region experiences a force.

When you drive around in a car on a dry day the friction between the tyres and the road causes the body of the car to become charged. The electric field inside the car is zero so you won't feel anything as long as you stay inside. When you get out of the car there will be a potential difference between you and the car resulting in a small discharge, which can be unpleasant. One way to avoid this is to ask a passer-by to touch the car for you before you get out.

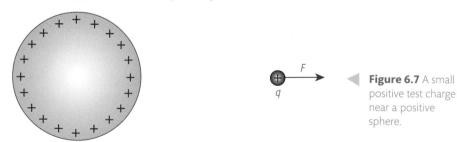

Figure 6.7 A small positive test charge near a positive sphere.

Field strength (E)

The size of the field at a given point is given by the electric field strength; this is defined as the force per unit charge experienced by a small positive test charge placed at that point. So if we consider a point some distance from a sphere of positive charge as shown in Figure 6.7, the field strength E would be $\frac{F}{q}$. Since force is a vector, field strength will also be a vector with the same direction as the force. The unit of field strength is N C^{-1}.

If the field strength at a point is E, a charge +q placed at that point will experience a force Eq in the direction of the field. A charge −q will experience the same size force but in the opposite direction.

Exercises

1   Calculate the force experienced by a charge of +5 × 10⁻⁶ C placed at a point where the field strength is 40 N C⁻¹.

2   A charge of −1.5 × 10⁻⁶ C experiences a force of 3 × 10⁻⁵ N towards the north. Calculate the magnitude and direction of the field strength at that point.

3   An electron has an instantaneous acceleration of 100 m s⁻² due to an electric field. Calculate the field strength of the field.
    electron charge = −1.6 × 10⁻¹⁹ C
    electron mass = 9.1 × 10⁻³¹ kg

Field lines

Field lines are drawn to show the direction and magnitude of the field. So for a point positive charge the field lines would be radial, showing that the force is always away from the charge as in Figure 6.8. The fact that the force gets stronger as the distance from the charge gets less can be seen from the density of the lines.

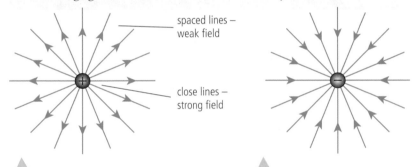

spaced lines – weak field

close lines – strong field

Figure 6.8 Field lines for a positive point charge.   **Figure 6.9** Field lines for a negative point charge.

The field between positively and negatively charged parallel plates is uniform. As can be seen in Figure 6.10, the lines are parallel and equally spaced, meaning that the force experienced by a small test charge placed between the plates will have the same magnitude and direction wherever it is placed.

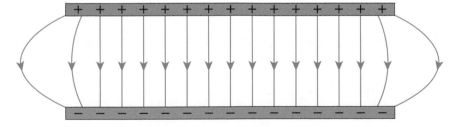

Figure 6.10 A uniform field. Note that the field is not uniform at the edges.

The field around a hollow sphere of charge is exactly the same as it would be if all the charge was placed at the centre of the sphere (Figure 6.11). This is similar to the gravitational field around a spherical mass. A point charge placed inside the sphere will experience forces in all directions due to each of the charges on the surface. The resultant of these forces is zero no matter where the point charge is placed. The electric field inside a charged sphere is therefore zero.

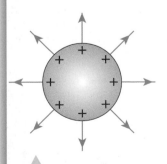

Figure 6.11 A hollow sphere.

Permittivity

The constant
$k = 9 \times 10^9 \, \text{Nm}^2\text{C}^{-2}$

This can also be expressed in terms of the permittivity of a vacuum, ε_0

$$k = \frac{1}{4\pi\varepsilon_0}$$

$\varepsilon_0 = 8.85 \times 10^{-12} \, \text{C}^2\text{N}^{-1}\text{m}^{-2}$

The permittivity is different for different media but we will usually be concerned with fields in a vacuum.

The relative permittivity (ε_r) of a material is the ratio of its permittivity to the permittivity of a vacuum.

CHALLENGE YOURSELF

1 Two small conducting spheres each of mass 10 mg are attached to two 50 cm long pieces of thread connected to the same point. This causes them to hang next to each other. A charge of 11×10^{-10} C is shared evenly between the spheres causing them to repel each other. Show that when they stabilize the spheres will be 3 cm apart.

Coulomb's law

In a gravitational field, the force between masses is given by Newton's law, and the equivalent for an electric field is Coulomb's law.

The force experienced by two point charges is directly proportional to the product of their charge and inversely proportional to the square of their separation.

The force experienced by two point charges Q_1 and Q_2 separated by a distance r in a vacuum is given by the formula

$$F = k\frac{Q_1 Q_2}{r^2}$$

The constant of proportionality $k = 9 \times 10^9 \, \text{Nm}^2\text{C}^{-2}$.

Note: Similarly to gravitational fields, Coulomb's law also applies to spheres of charge, the separation being the distance between the centres of the spheres.

This means that we can now calculate the field strength at a distance from a sphere of charge.

Worked example

A 5 µC point charge is placed 20 cm from a 10 µC point charge.

a   Calculate the force experienced by the 5 µC charge.

b   What is the force on the 10 µC charge?

c   What is the field strength 20 cm from the 10 µC charge?

Solution

a   Using the equation $\quad F = \frac{kQ_1Q_2}{r^2}$

$Q_1 = 5 \times 10^{-6}$ C, $Q_2 = 10 \times 10^{-6}$ C and $r = 0.20$ m

$$F = \frac{9 \times 10^9 \times 5 \times 10^{-6} \times 10 \times 10^{-6}}{0.20^2}\text{N}$$

$$= 11.25 \, \text{N}$$

b   According to Newton's third law, the force on the 10 µC charge is the same as the 5 µC.

c   Force per unit charge $= \frac{11.25}{5 \times 10^{-6}}$

$$E = 2.25 \times 10^6 \, \text{N C}^{-1}$$

Exercises

4   If the charge on a 10 cm radius metal sphere is 2 µC, calculate:

   (a) the field strength on the surface of the sphere.
   (b) the field strength 10 cm from the surface of the sphere.
   (c) the force experienced by a 0.1 µC charge placed 10 cm from the surface of the sphere.
   (d) Calculate the force if the space between the small sphere and the surface of the big sphere were filled with concrete of relative permittivity 4.5.

5   A small sphere of mass 0.01 kg and charge 0.2 µC is placed at a point in an electric field where the field strength is 0.5 N C^{-1}.

   (a) What force will the small sphere experience?
   (b) If no other forces act, what is the acceleration of the sphere?

Electric field and energy

Imagine taking an uncharged sphere and charging it by taking, one at a time, some small positive charges from a great distance and putting them on the sphere as illustrated in Figure 6.12. As the charge on the sphere gets bigger and bigger it would be more and more difficult to add charges as the small positive charges would be repelled from the now positive sphere. As we pushed the charges onto the sphere we would do work transferring energy to the charge. The charges on the sphere now have energy due to their position. This is *electrical potential energy* and it is equal to the amount of work done putting the charges there from a place where they had no PE (at an infinite distance from the sphere).

▲ **Figure 6.12** Charging a sphere.

Potential (*V*)

If the same amount of charge was put onto a smaller sphere the charges would be closer together. This would make it more difficult to put more charge onto it. The PE of one of the small charges on the sphere depends upon the magnitude of its charge, how much charge is on the sphere, and how big the sphere is. To quantify how much work is required per unit charge we define *potential*.

The potential of the charged sphere is defined as **the amount of work done per unit charge in taking a small positive test charge (*q*) from infinity and putting it onto the sphere.**

Because the force isn't constant we will use the area under the force–distance curve (Figure 6.13) to find the work done. This is the same method we used to find the amount of PE stored in a stretched spring.

Since this isn't linear it is not so simple to find the area under the curve. You will probably do it in maths one day but until then you just have to know that the solution is

$$\text{work done} = \frac{kQq}{r}$$

where *k* is a constant.

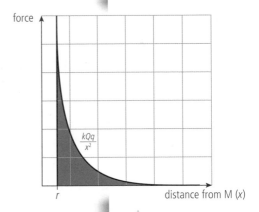

▲ **Figure 6.13** Graph of force against distance as charge +*q* approaches +*Q*.

Since energy is conserved, the electrical PE of the particle will be the same as the work done. The potential at the surface of the charged sphere = work done per unit charge:

$$V = \frac{kQ}{r}$$

The unit of potential is J C^{-1} which is the same as the volt (V).

The field inside a hollow sphere is zero so if you were to move a charge around inside the sphere no work would need to be done. Taking a point charge from infinity to the inside of a sphere would therefore require the same amount of work as it would take to bring the charge to the surface. We can therefore deduce that the potential inside the sphere equals the potential at the surface. This leads to the horizontal part of the graph in Figure 6.14.

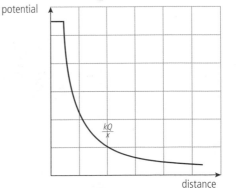

▲ **Figure 6.14** Graph of potential against distance for a positive charge.

Maybe you remember that you can find displacement from the area under a velocity–time graph and the velocity from the gradient of a displacement–time graph. Well, the same holds here: the potential is the area under the field strength–distance graph so the field strength is the gradient of the potential–distance graph. In other words:

$$E = \frac{-dV}{dx}$$

6 Calculate the electric potential a distance 20 cm from the centre of a small sphere of charge +50 μC.

7 Calculate the pd between the point in exercise 6 and a second point 40 cm from the centre of the sphere.

Figure 6.14 represents the change in potential along one dimension. We can think of this as a hill that gets steeper and steeper as we approach the top. We can extend this to two dimensions as shown in Figure 6.15: this gives a useful visual representation of the field. Moving a charge towards the sphere would be like pushing a ball up the hill: the steeper the hill becomes, the more difficult it will be to move the ball. If we draw contour lines for the hill we get a set of concentric circles. These are called lines of *equipotential*. In 3 dimensions they represent spheres called *equipotential surfaces*.

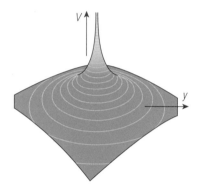
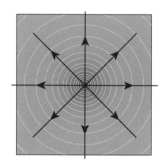

Figure 6.15 Field lines and equipotentials for a positive point charge.

Comparing the field lines and lines of equipotential we see that the field is always perpendicular to the lines of equipotential. So if a charge moves along a line of equipotential the force acting on it will be perpendicular to the direction of motion. This means no work is done so the PE of the particle doesn't change. This is what would be expected moving along a line of equipotential.

Dipoles

A dipole is a pair of opposite charges. The field lines and lines of equipotential for a dipole, along with the associated potential well and hill, are shown in Figure 6.16.

Capacitance
Capacitance is defined as the ratio of charge to potential ($C = \frac{Q}{V}$). It requires less work to place the same charge on a body with high capacitance than on one with a low capacitance. A large sphere therefore has a higher capacitance than a small one.

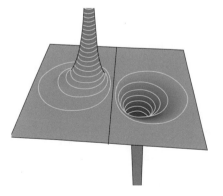
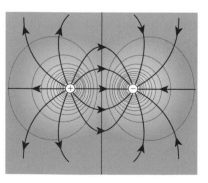

Figure 6.16 Field lines and equipotentials for a dipole.

Potential difference (pd)

The potential difference is the difference in potential between two points. This is the difference in work done per unit charge bringing a small test charge from infinity to the each of the two points. This is the same as the amount of work done per unit charge taking a test charge from one point to the other.

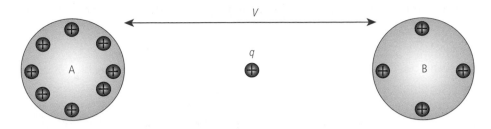

Figure 6.17 Notice how the pd is indicated with arrows showing that it is the difference between two points.

TOK Drawing potential hills and wells gives an easy-to-interpret representation of the electric field even though there are no changes in height involved.

Referring to Figure 6.17, it takes more work to move q from infinity to A than from infinity to B so A is at a higher potential than B. The potential difference between A and B (V_{AB}) is the work done per unit charge moving from B to A, so if a charge $+q$ moves from B to A it will gain an amount of PE = qV_{AB}.

Exercises

Refer to Figure 6.18 for questions 8–14.

8 **(a)** One of the charges is positive and the other is negative. Which is which?

   (b) If a positive charge were placed at A, would it move, and if so, in which direction?

9 At which point A, B, C, D, or F is the field strength greatest?

10 What is the pd between the following pairs of points?

   (a) A and C

   (b) C and E

   (c) B and E

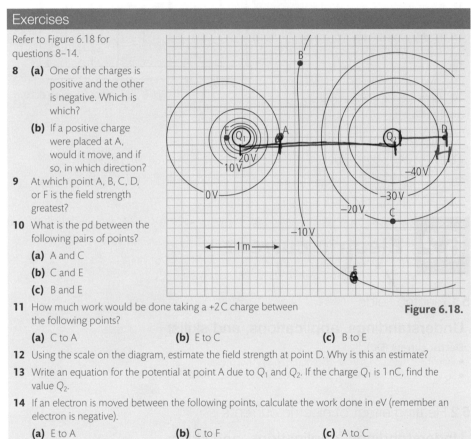

Figure 6.18.

11 How much work would be done taking a +2 C charge between the following points?

   (a) C to A   **(b)** E to C   **(c)** B to E

12 Using the scale on the diagram, estimate the field strength at point D. Why is this an estimate?

13 Write an equation for the potential at point A due to Q_1 and Q_2. If the charge Q_1 is 1 nC, find the value Q_2.

14 If an electron is moved between the following points, calculate the work done in eV (remember an electron is negative).

   (a) E to A   **(b)** C to F   **(c)** A to C

Potential in a uniform field

As mentioned previously, a uniform field can be produced between two parallel plates as shown in Figure 6.19.

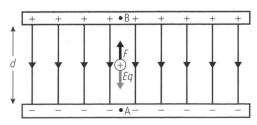

Figure 6.19.

Because this is a uniform field. The force is constant and equal to Eq, so the work done in moving a charge from A to B is force × distance moved in direction of force = Eqd. The pd is the work done per unit charge so $V_{AB} = \frac{Eqd}{q} = Ed$.

This result could also be reached by using the fact that E is the potential gradient:

$$E = \frac{V}{d}$$

The electronvolt (eV)

This is a unit of energy used in atomic physics. 1 eV = energy gained by an electron accelerated through a pd of 1 V.

To learn more about electric fields, go to the hotlinks site, search for the title or ISBN and click on Chapter 6.

Exercises

Refer to Figure 6.20 for Questions 15–22.

15 What is the potential difference (pd) between A and C?

16 What is the pd between B and D?

17 If a charge of +3 C was placed at B, how much PE would it have?

18 If a charge of +2 C was moved from C to B, how much work would be done?

19 If a charge of –2 C moved from A to B, how much work would be done?

20 If a charge of +3 C was placed at B and released

(a) what would happen to it?
(b) how much KE would it gain when it reached A?

21 If an electron was released at A and accelerated to B how much KE would it gain in eV?

22 If an electron was taken from C to D how much work would be done in eV?

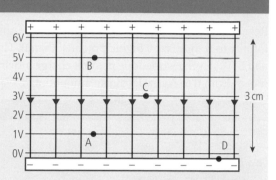

Figure 6.20.

6.2 Electric current

5.1 Electric fields

Understandings, applications, and skills:

Electric current (DC)
- Identifying sign and nature of charge carriers in a metal.
- Solving problems involving current, potential difference, and charge.

5.2 Heating effect of electric currents

Understandings, applications, and skills:

Heating effect of current and its consequences

Ohm's law and resistance expressed as $R = \frac{V}{I}$

- Identifying ohmic and non-ohmic conductors through a consideration of the $\frac{V}{I}$ characteristic graph.

   Guidance
   - *The filament lamp should be described as a non-ohmic device; a metal wire at a constant temperature is an ohmic device.*

Resistivity
- Investigating one or more of the factors that affect resistivity experimentally.

Movement of charge

If a positive charge is placed between the two spheres in Figure 6.21 it will move away from the positive sphere towards the negative one: the positive charge is moving to a position of lower potential. We can say that, if possible, a positive charge will always move from high potential to low potential in the same way as water always flows downhill. This of course can only happen if there are charges between the spheres or a material with charges that are free to move. Such a material is called a *conductor*.

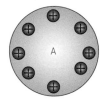 

Figure 6.21 Charges move from high to low potential.

Conductors and insulators

A conductor consists of atoms arranged in an ordered lattice with some electrons that are free to move, called 'free electrons'. Electrons are negative so when a conductor is connected between two points electrons will flow from the low potential to the high potential. Up to now we have defined everything in terms of positive charge. This gave us a helpful picture of charges flowing from high to low like water flowing down a hill. To keep this picture we will still consider the movement of positive charge even though it is actually electrons that are moving. So 'conventional current' moves from high to low potential, but electrons flow the *other* way.

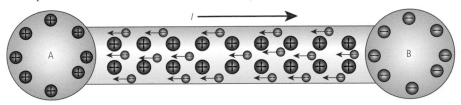

Figure 6.22 Electrons in a conductor flowing 'uphill'.

As the electrons flow they lose electrical PE which is converted momentarily to KE. However, they soon collide with the atomic lattice, transferring their energy to the atoms. This increases the vibrational KE of the atoms, resulting in an increase in temperature of the material. The motion of the electrons is rather like a ball falling down a flight of stairs, giving up energy on each bounce. Because of these interactions the electrons don't accelerate but drift through the conductor with constant velocity.

An insulator does not have free electrons so does not allow charge to flow. A semiconductor has few free electrons so doesn't let much charge flow. Metals (e.g. copper, iron, zinc) are conductors and most non-metals (e.g. plastics, glass, wood) are insulators. The free electrons also make metals good conductors of *heat* as they enable energy to be easily shared from one atom to another.

Current

Current is defined as the rate of flow of current. If a charge ΔQ flows at a constant rate in a time Δt then the current I is given by the equation:

$$I = \frac{\Delta Q}{\Delta t}$$

The unit of current is C s^{-1} or ampere (A).

Let us consider a current I flowing through a section of conductor with cross-sectional area A as shown in Figure 6.23.

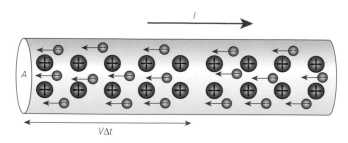

Figure 6.23 Electrons flowing
in a conductor.

When the current is in one direction, as in this case, it is termed *direct current* (DC). When it changes direction it is termed *alternating current* (AC).

If there are n electrons per unit volume that have a constant drift velocity of v then in time Δt they will travel a distance $v\Delta t$. This means that all the electrons in a volume $v\Delta tA$ will pass through the end of the section. There are n per unit volume so this is $nAv\Delta t$ electrons. Each electron has charge e so the charge passing $= nAv\Delta te$.

The current is therefore $\frac{nAv\Delta te}{\Delta t} = nAve$.

So
$$I = nAve$$

Exercise

23 Copper has a molar mass 63.5 g and density 8960 kg m^{-3}.
  (a) Calculate the volume of 1 mole of copper.
  (b) If each atom of copper contributes 1 free electron, calculate the number of free electrons per unit volume of copper.
  (c) Calculate the drift velocity of electrons along a 1 mm diameter copper wire carrying a current of 1 A.

Resistance (R)

The amount of current flowing through a particular conductor is related to the pd across it. A good conductor will allow a large current for a given pd whereas a poor conductor will only allow a small current. The ratio $\frac{V}{I}$ is defined as the *resistance*.

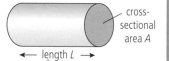

Figure 6.24 Dimensions of a conductor.

The unit of resistance is the ohm (Ω).

Resistivity

Resistance (R) is related to: cross-sectional area (A), length (L), and the material.
$$R \propto \frac{L}{A}$$

The constant of proportionality is called the *resistivity* (ρ).

So
$$R = \rho\frac{L}{A}$$

By rearranging $R = \rho\frac{L}{A}$ we get $\rho = \frac{RA}{L}$ (units Ωm).

From this we can deduce that if the length of a sample of material is 1m and the cross-sectional area is 1m^2, then $\rho = R$. You can probably imagine that the resistance of such a large piece of metal will be very small – that's why the values of resistivity are so low (e.g. for copper $\rho = 1.72 \times 10^{-8}\,\Omega$m).

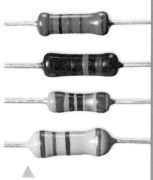

A resistor is a component with a known resistance. You can work out the resistance from the colours.

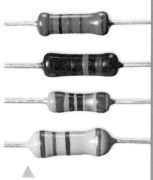

Figure 6.25 The symbol for a resistor.

Worked example

The resistivity of copper is $1.72 \times 10^{-8}\,\Omega\,m$. What is the resistance of a 1 m length of 2 mm diameter copper wire?

Solution

$$\text{Cross-sectional area} = \pi\,(0.001)^2$$
$$= 3.14 \times 10^{-6}\,m^2$$
$$R = \rho\frac{L}{A}$$
$$= 1.72 \times 10^{-8} \times \frac{1}{3.14 \times 10^{-6}}\,\Omega$$
$$= 0.0055\,\Omega$$

Area
$$= \pi r^2$$
where radius
$$= \frac{1}{2} \times 2\,mm$$
$$= 0.001\,m.$$

Exercises

24 Nichrome has a resistivity of $1.1 \times 10^{-6}\,\Omega\,m$. Calculate the diameter of a 2 m long nichrome wire with resistance $5\,\Omega$.

25 Calculate the resistance of a copper cable (resistivity $1.7 \times 10^{-8}\,\Omega\,m$) of length 2 km and diameter 0.2 cm.

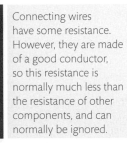

Connecting wires have some resistance. However, they are made of a good conductor, so this resistance is normally much less than the resistance of other components, and can normally be ignored.

Ohm's law

Provided that temperature remains constant, the resistance of many conductors is constant. Such conductors are said to be ohmic and obey Ohm's law:

The current through an ohmic con ductor is directly proportional to the pd across it provided that the temperature remains constant.

This means that if we know the resistance of a component we can calculate the pd V required to cause a current I to flow through it using the equation:

$$V = IR.$$

The reason that temperature affects resistance is because an increase in temperature means increased lattice vibrations resulting in more collisions between electrons and the lattice. However, increasing the temperature of a semiconductor leads to the liberation of more free electrons, which results in a *lower* resistance.

Worked example

If the pd across a 3 V resistance is 9 V what current will flow?

Solution

$V = IR$	From Ohm's law.
$I = \dfrac{V}{R}$	Rearranging.
$I = \dfrac{9}{3}A$	
$= 3\,A$	

Graphical treatment of Ohm's law

Ohmic conductor

Since $V \propto I$ for an ohmic conductor, a graph of I against V will be a straight line.

In this example, resistance $= \dfrac{V}{I} = 2\,\Omega$

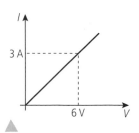

Figure 6.26.

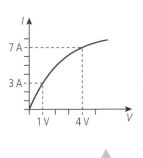

Figure 6.27.

Resistance is defined as the ratio of $\frac{V}{I}$. This can be found from the gradient of the *I–V* graph for an ohmic conductor but not for non-ohmic conductors.

Non-ohmic conductors

Not all conductors obey Ohm's law. *I–V* graphs for these conductors will not be straight. A light bulb filament is an example of a non-ohmic conductor.

In this example, the resistance at the start is $\frac{1}{3}\,\Omega$ (0.33 Ω) and at the end it is $\frac{4}{7}\,\Omega$ (0.57 Ω).

The reason for this is that as current flows through the light bulb electrical energy is converted to heat, resulting in an increased temperature and leading to an increase in resistance. Electrical energy is of course converted into heat in all resistors but if the rate of heat production is not too high it will be transferred to the surroundings rather than causing significant temperature change.

Exercises

26 If a pd of 9 V causes a current of 3 mA to flow through a wire, what is the resistance of the wire?

27 A current of 1 μA flows through a 300 kΩ resistor. What is the pd across the resistor?

28 If the pd across a 600 Ω resistor is 12 Ω, how much current flows?

29 Table 6.1 shows the pd and current through a device called a thermistor.

pd/V	Current/A
1.0	0.01
10	0.1
25	1.0

Table 6.1.

Calculate the resistance at these different potential differences.

6.3 Electric circuits

5.3 Electric cells

Understandings, applications, and skills:

Cells
- Investigating practical electric cells (both primary and secondary).
- Describing the discharge characteristic of a simple cell (variation of terminal potential difference with time).

  Guidance
  - *Students should recognize that the terminal potential difference of a typical practical electric cell loses its initial value quickly, has a stable and constant value for most of its lifetime, followed by a rapid decrease to zero.*

Internal resistance
- Determining internal resistance experimentally.

Secondary cells
- Identifying the direction of current flow required to recharge a cell.

Terminal potential difference

Electromotive force (emf)
- Solving problems involving emf, internal resistance, and other electrical quantities.

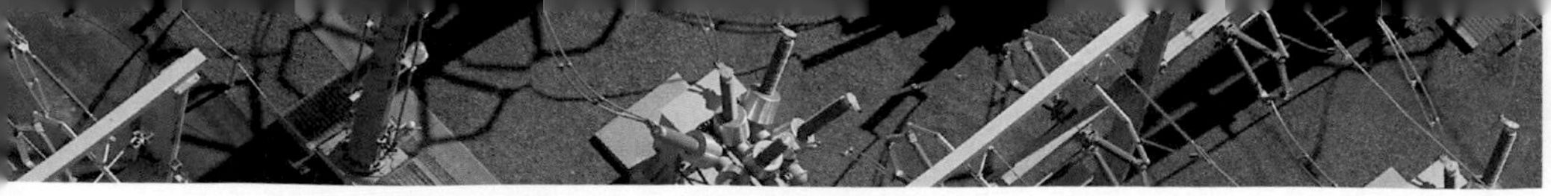

5.2 Heating effect of electric currents

Understandings, applications, and skills

Power dissipation

Circuit diagrams

- Drawing and interpreting circuit diagrams.
- Investigating combinations of resistors in parallel and series circuits.
- Describing ideal and non-ideal ammeters and voltmeters.
- Describing practical uses of potential divider circuits, including the advantages of a potential divider over a series resistor in controlling a simple circuit.

Guidance

- *The use of non-ideal voltmeters is confined to voltmeters with a constant but finite resistance.*
- *The use of non-ideal ammeters is confined to ammeters with a constant but non-zero resistance.*

Kirchhoff's circuit laws

- Solving problems involving potential difference, current, charge, Kirchhoff's circuit laws, power, resistance and resistivity.

Guidance

- *Application of Kirchhoff's circuit laws will be limited to circuits with a maximum number of two source-carrying loops.*

Electric cells and batteries

An electric cell is a device that uses the energy stored in chemicals to arrange charges in such a way that a potential difference is created which can be used to cause a current to flow in a conductor. Chemical energy is the energy associated with molecules. When chemical reactions take place this energy can be converted into other forms; for example, when coal burns the molecules of coal and oxygen recombine in a way that has less PE. This PE is converted into the KE of the new molecules, resulting in a rise in temperature. Chemical energy is actually electrical PE: molecules are simply charged bodies arranged in such a way that they do not fly apart. If they are reorganized so that their PE is less then energy is released. What is happening in a cell is that by reorganizing molecules, energy is used to separate the positive and negative charges. One way this can be done is in the so-called simple cell (Figure 6.28) which consists of zinc and copper plates dipped into acid.

When metals are put into acid (e.g. sulfuric acid) they react to give bubbles of hydrogen. Whilst this is happening the metal dissolves in the acid. When the metal atoms dissolve they don't take all their electrons with them: this leaves them positively charged (they are called *positive ions*). The electrons remaining give the metal plates a negative charge. Since zinc reacts faster than copper it gets more charge, resulting in a potential difference. The chemical energy of the metal and acid has been converted into electrical potential energy. As you can see in Figure 6.29, the zinc plate is more negative than the copper so will have a lower potential. When connecting a battery you often refer to the ends as positive and negative. However, they could be both negative as in this case. The important thing is to realize that they have different potentials, not different charge.

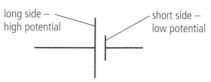

long side –
high potential
short side –
low potential

NATURE OF SCIENCE

When an ammeter or voltmeter is connected to a circuit it changes the current flowing. It is important to take this into account when analysing data from experiments.

When drawing electrical circuits we use universal symbols, with one or two alternatives, that can be understood throughout the world.

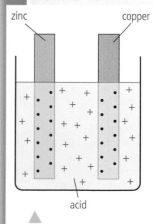

zinc
copper
acid

Figure 6.28 A simple cell.

Figure 6.29 The symbol for a cell makes a lot of sense; the side that is at the highest potential has the longest line.

A simple cell produces a potential difference of about 1 V. Even though each side is at a negative potential it is convenient to take the low side to be 0 V, called ground or *earth*, and the high side to be 1 V. A battery is a row of cells. However, the word *battery* is now used to mean anything that converts chemical energy to electrical energy. There are many different types and sizes of battery but all work on the same principle.

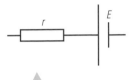

Figure 6.30 The symbol for a cell includes a resistor *r* next to the cell to show internal resistance.

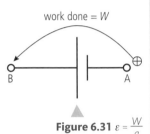

Figure 6.31 $\varepsilon = \dfrac{W}{q}$

Internal resistance

The internal components of a cell have resistance, so when current flows from the cell some energy is lost. This resistance is represented in circuit diagrams by placing a small resistor next to the symbol for a cell. In some examples we will consider cells with zero internal resistance, but this isn't possible in reality.

Emf (ε) and terminal pd

The emf of a cell is the work done per unit charge taking the charges from the low potential to the high potential. The energy to do this work has been transferred from the chemical energy so the emf of the cell is the amount of chemical energy transferred to electrical PE per unit charge.

The unit of emf is the volt (V).

If no current flows then there will be no potential drop across the internal resistance. The pd across the terminals of the battery (*terminal pd*) will equal the emf. However, if current flows the terminal pd will be *less* than the emf.

Discharge of a cell

If a simple cell is not connected to a circuit, charges will be moved to the position of high potential until the force pushing them is balanced by the repulsive force of the charges already there. This occurs at about 1 V. If the cell is now connected to a resistance, charge will flow from high potential to low. As this happens more charges will be added to the high potential, maintaining the terminal pd at 1 V. The battery is said to be discharging. This continues until all the chemical energy is used up, at which point the pd starts to get less.

As a battery discharges (runs out) its internal resistance increases, resulting in a lower terminal pd. However, if you measure the emf it might seem OK.

Discharging a battery

You can measure the terminal pd of a battery as it discharges through a resistor by using a voltmeter connected across the terminals of the battery. However, the battery should not be discharged too rapidly so the experiment might take a long time. If you use a voltage sensor and computer interface you could leave the battery to discharge on its own.

Figure 6.32 Pd *vs* time for different batteries discharging showing how the terminal pd is almost constant for the life of the battery.

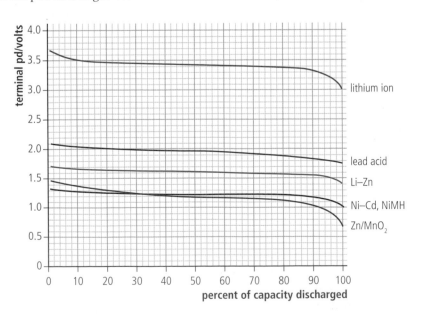

Simplest circuit

When a resistor is connected across the terminals of a battery, current will flow from high to low potential. Charges are given electrical energy by the battery which is then converted to heat in the resistor. We can think of this as being like a shopping centre with stairs and escalators. Shoppers are taken up from ground level to the first floor (given PE) by the escalators and then come down (lose PE) by the stairs.

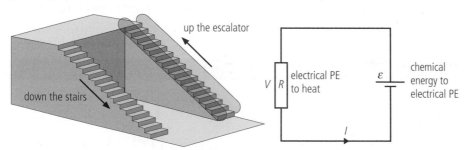

Since energy is conserved we can say that when a unit charge flows around the circuit the amount of chemical energy converted to electrical energy = the amount of electrical energy converted to heat. In other words, emf = pd. In the shopping centre this would translate to 'the height you go up by the escalator = the height you come down by the stairs'.

We can write this statement as an equation: $\varepsilon = V = IR$.

Worked example

If the emf of a battery is 9 V, how much energy is converted from chemical to electrical when 2 C of charge flow?

Solution

emf = energy converted from chemical to electrical per unit charge.

So energy converted $= 2 \times 9\,\text{J}$
$\qquad\qquad\qquad = 18\,\text{J}$

Worked example

What is the pd across a resistor if 24 J of heat are produced when a current of 2 A flows through it for 10 s?

Solution

2 A for 10 s = 2 × 10 C = 20 C of charge.

If 20 C of charge flows, then the energy per unit charge $= \dfrac{24}{20}\,\text{V} = 1.2\,\text{V}$

Figure 6.34 A circuit with internal resistance.

The not-so-simple circuit

The previous example didn't include the internal resistance of the battery. In the shopping centre, the escalator is still the same height but now there is a short stairway down before you reach the first floor. In terms of the circuit, some energy is lost as heat before the charge leaves the battery.

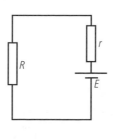

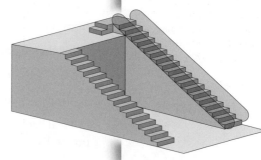

225

Applying Ohm's law to the internal resistance, the pd across it will be Ir.

From the law of conservation of energy, when a certain charge flows, the amount of energy transferred from chemical to electrical equals the amount transferred from electrical to heat.

$$\varepsilon = IR + Ir$$

Rearranging this formula, we can get an equation for the current from the battery.

$$I = \frac{\varepsilon}{R + r}$$

Worked example

A battery of emf 9 V with an internal resistance 1 Ω is connected to a 2 Ω resistor, as shown in Figure 6.35.

How much current will flow?

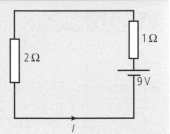

Figure 6.35 Always start by drawing a circuit showing the quantities you know and labelling the ones you want to find.

Solution

$$I = \frac{\varepsilon}{R + r}$$

$$I = \frac{9}{2 + 1}\,A = 3\,A$$

What is the pd across the 2 Ω resistor?

$$V = IR$$

$$V = 3 \times 2\,V = 6\,V$$

Exercises

30 A current of 0.5 A flows when a battery of emf 6 V is connected to an 11 Ω resistor. What is the internal resistance of the battery?

31 A 12 V battery with internal resistance 1 Ω is connected to a 23 Ω resistor. What is the pd across the 23 Ω resistor?

Electrical power

Electrical power is the rate at which energy is changed from one form to another.

Power delivered

In a perfect battery, the power is the amount of chemical energy converted to electrical energy per unit time.

If the emf of a battery is ε, then if a charge Q flows, the amount of energy converted from chemical to electrical is εQ.

If this charge flows in a time t then the power delivered $= \frac{\varepsilon Q}{t}$

But $\frac{Q}{t} =$ the current, I.

So the power delivered $= \varepsilon I$.

In a real battery, the actual power delivered will be a bit less, since there will be some power dissipated in the internal resistance.

Power dissipated

The power dissipated in the resistor is the amount of electrical energy converted to heat per unit time.

Consider a resistance R with a pd V across it. If a charge Q flows in time t then the current, $I = \dfrac{Q}{t}$.

The pd, V, is defined as the energy converted to heat per unit charge Q, so the energy converted to heat in this case $= VQ$.

Power is the energy used per unit time, so $P = \dfrac{VQ}{t}$

but $\dfrac{Q}{t} = I$, so $P = VI$.

If a current of 2 A flows through a resistor that has a pd of 4 V across it, how much power is dissipated?

Solution

$$P = VI \text{ where } V = 4\,V \text{ and } I = 2\,A$$
$$P = 4 \times 2\,W$$
$$= 8\,W$$

Worked example

What power will be dissipated when a current of 4 A flows through a resistance of 55 Ω?

Solution

Using Ohm's law $V = IR$ first we need to find out the pd across the resistor
$$= 4 \times 55\ V$$
$$= 220\,V$$

$$P = VI$$
$$= 220 \times 4\,W$$
$$= 880\,W$$

Alternative ways of writing *P = VI*

In Example 2, we had to calculate the pd before finding the power. It would be convenient if we could solve this problem in one step. We can write alternative forms of the equation by substituting for I and V from Ohm's law.

We have shown that power $P = VI$

But from Ohm's law $V = IR$

If we substitute for V we get $P = IR \times I = I^2R$

We can also substitute for $I = \dfrac{V}{R}$

Power $= V \times I = \dfrac{V \times V}{R} = \dfrac{V^2}{R}$

TOK The kilowatt hour is often wrongly called 'killowatts per hour'. This is because people are used to dealing with quantities that are rates of change like kilometres per hour.

Power

$P = VI$

$P = I^2R$

$P = \dfrac{V^2}{R}$

Exercises

32 5 A flows through a 20 Ω resistor.

  (a) How much electrical energy is converted to heat per second?

  (b) If the current flows for one minute, how much energy is released?

33 If a battery has an internal resistance of 0.5 V, how much power will be dissipated in the battery when 0.25 A flows?

34 A current of 0.5 A flows from a battery of emf 9 V. If the power delivered is 4 W, how much power is dissipated in the internal resistance?

Electric kettle (water boiler)

An electric kettle transfers the heat produced when current flows through a wire element to the water inside the kettle.

Worked example

A current of 3 A flows through an electric kettle connected to the 220 V mains. What is the power of the kettle and how long will it take to boil 1 litre of water?

Solution

The power of the kettle = $VI = 220 \times 3 = 660$ W

To calculate energy needed to boil the water, we use the formula

$$\text{heat required} = \text{mass} \times \text{specific heat capacity} \times \text{temperature change.}$$

The specific heat capacity of water is $4180 \, \text{J} \, \text{kg}^{-1} \, °\text{C}^{-1}$

The mass of 1 litre of water is 1 kg, so if we assume that the water was at room temperature, 20°C, then to raise it to 100°C the energy required is:

$$1 \times 4180 \times 80 = 334\,400 \, \text{J}$$

$$\text{power} = \frac{\text{energy}}{\text{time}}, \text{ so the time taken} = \frac{\text{energy}}{\text{power}}$$

$$= \frac{334\,400}{660}$$

$$\text{Time} = 506.67 \, \text{s}$$

$$= 8 \text{ minutes } 27 \text{ seconds}$$

This is quite a low-powered electric kettle.

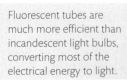

The electric circuits in a house are organized in rings. Each ring consists of 3 cables going around the house and back to the supply; sockets are connected to the live cable in parallel with each other. Each ring has its own circuit breaker which will cut the power if the current gets too big.

The light bulb

If the power dissipated in a wire is large, then a lot of heat is produced per second. When heat is added quickly, the wire doesn't have time to lose this heat to the surroundings. The result is that the temperature of the wire increases, and if the temperature is high enough, the wire will begin to glow, giving out light. Only about 10% of the energy dissipated in a light bulb is transferred to light – the rest is heat.

Fluorescent tubes are much more efficient than incandescent light bulbs, converting most of the electrical energy to light.

The electric motor

A motor converts electrical energy to mechanical energy; this could be in the form of potential energy, if something is lifted by the motor, or kinetic energy, if the motor is accelerating something like a car.

Worked example

An electric motor is used to lift 10 kg through 3 m in 5 seconds. If the pd across the motor is 12 V, how much current flows (assuming no energy is lost)?

Solution

$$\text{Work done by the motor} = mgh$$
$$= 10 \times 10 \times 3\,\text{J} = 300\,\text{J}$$
$$\text{Power} = \frac{\text{work done}}{\text{time}}$$
$$= \frac{300}{5}\text{W}$$
$$= 60\,\text{W}$$
$$\text{Electrical power, } P = IV \text{ so } I = \frac{P}{V}$$
$$= \frac{60}{12}\text{A} = 5\,\text{A}$$

Exercises

35 An electric car of mass 1000 kg uses twenty-five 12 V batteries connected together to create a pd of 300 V. The car accelerates from rest to a speed of 30 m s⁻¹ in 12 seconds.

  (a) What is the final kinetic energy of the car?
  (b) What is the power of the car?
  (c) How much electrical current flows from the battery?

36 What assumptions have you made in calculating (a)–(c)?

37 A light bulb for use with the 220 V mains is rated at 100 W.

  (a) What current will flow through the bulb?
  (b) If the bulb converts 20% of the energy to light, how much light energy is produced per second?

38 A 1 kW electric heater is connected to the 220 V mains and left on for 5 hours.

  (a) How much current will flow through the heater?
  (b) How much energy will the heater release?

A battery-powered car.

Combinations of components

In practical situations, resistors and cells are often joined together in combinations e.g. fairy lights, flashlight batteries.

There are many ways of connecting a number of components – we will consider two simple arrangements, series and parallel.

Resistors in series

In a series circuit the same current flows through each resistor.

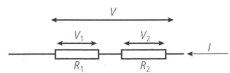

The combination could be replaced by one resistor.

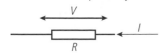

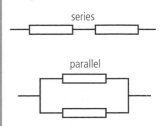

Figure 6.36 Two simple combinations of resistors.

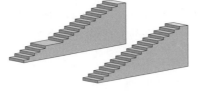

Figure 6.37 Two resistors in series are similar to two flights of stairs.

Applying the law of conservation of energy, the pd across R_1 plus the pd across R_2 must be equal to the pd across the combination.

$$V_1 + V_2 = V$$

Applying Ohm's law to each resistor: $\quad IR_1 + IR_2 = IR$

Dividing by I: $\quad\quad\quad\quad\quad\quad\quad\quad\quad R_1 + R_2 = R$

Worked example

What is the total resistance of a $4\,\Omega$ and an $8\,\Omega$ resistor in series?

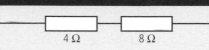

Figure 6.38.

Solution

$$\begin{aligned}\text{Total resistance} &= R_1 + R_2 \\ &= 4 + 8\,\Omega \\ &= 12\,\Omega\end{aligned}$$

Resistors in parallel

In a parallel circuit the current splits in two.

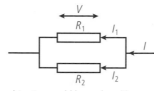

The combination could be replaced by one resistor.

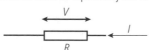

Applying the law of conservation of charge, we know that the current going into a junction must equal the current coming out.

$$I = I_1 + I_2$$

Applying Ohm's law to each resistor gives: $\dfrac{V}{R} = \dfrac{V}{R_1} + \dfrac{V}{R_2}$

Dividing by V: $\dfrac{1}{R} = \dfrac{1}{R_1} + \dfrac{1}{R_2}$

Worked example

What is the total resistance of a $4\,\Omega$ and an $8\,\Omega$ resistor in parallel?

Solution

Using

$$\frac{1}{R} = \frac{1}{R_1} + \frac{1}{R_2}$$

$$\frac{1}{R} = \frac{1}{4} + \frac{1}{8}$$

$$= \frac{2+1}{8} = \frac{3}{8}$$

so

$$R = \frac{8}{3}\,\Omega$$

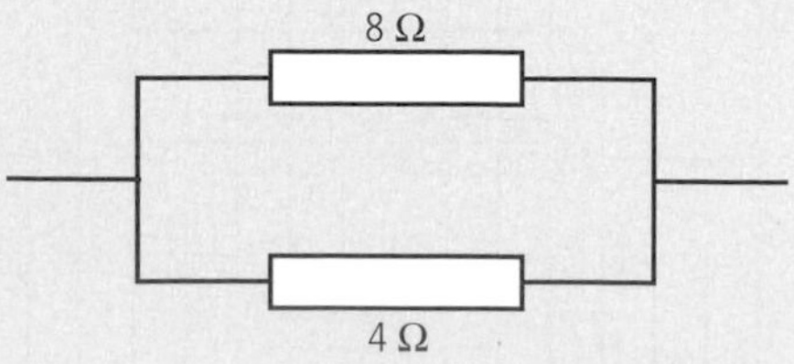

Figure 6.40.

These coloured lights are connected in series – if you take one out they all go out.

Figure 6.39 Resistors in parallel are similar to stairs side by side.

Worked example

What is the total resistance of two $8\,\Omega$ resistors in parallel?

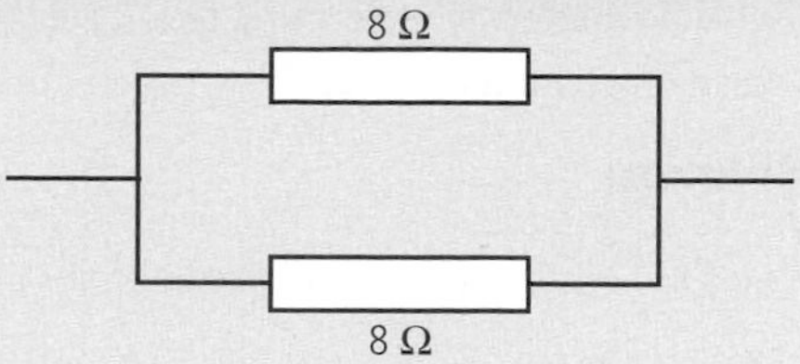

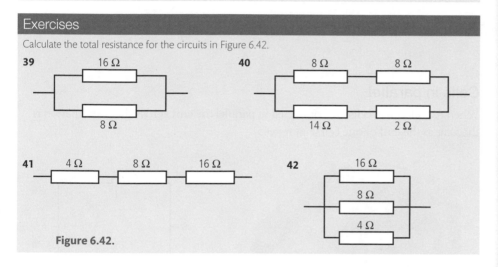

Figure 6.41 The total resistance of two equal resistors in parallel is half the resistance of one of them.

Solution

Using

$$\frac{1}{R} = \frac{1}{R_1} + \frac{1}{R_2}$$

$$\frac{1}{R} = \frac{1}{8} + \frac{1}{8} = \frac{2}{8}$$

$$R = \frac{8}{2}V = 4\,\Omega$$

Exercises

Calculate the total resistance for the circuits in Figure 6.42.

39 $16\,\Omega$ / $8\,\Omega$

40 $8\,\Omega$ / $8\,\Omega$ / $14\,\Omega$ / $2\,\Omega$

41 $4\,\Omega$ — $8\,\Omega$ — $16\,\Omega$

42 $16\,\Omega$ / $8\,\Omega$ / $4\,\Omega$

Figure 6.42.

Investigating combinations of resistors in parallel and series circuits

The simplest way to measure the electrical resistance of a component is to use a multimeter. This actually measures the current through the component when a known pd is applied to it; the resistance is then calculated and displayed. Try connecting various combinations of resistors in different combinations. Calculate the combined resistance using the equations for series and parallel resistors then check your calculation by measurement. You need to make sure that the resistors are connected properly; this is best done by soldering. If you don't have the necessary equipment then you can simulate the circuit with a custom built sim such as the PhET circuit construction kit.

Note that not all combinations of resistors can be solved using the series and parallel equations.

Cells in series

Cells are often added in series to obtain a larger emf.

$$\varepsilon = \varepsilon_1 + \varepsilon_2$$

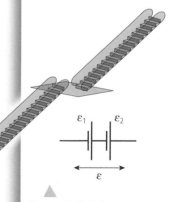

Figure 6.43 Cells in series are similar to two flights of escalators.

Worked example

Two 12 V batteries are connected in series to a 10 Ω resistor. If each battery has an internal resistance of 1 Ω, how much current will flow?

Solution

The total emf for two batteries in series

$= 12 + 12 = 24\,\text{V}$

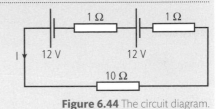

Figure 6.44 The circuit diagram.

Total resistance $= 1 + 1 + 10 = 12\,\Omega$.

Applying Ohm's law, $\qquad I = \dfrac{V}{R}$

$\qquad\qquad\qquad = \dfrac{24}{12}\,\text{A}$

$\qquad\qquad\qquad = 2\,\text{A}$

Cells in parallel

When two identical cells are connected in parallel the emf across the combination is the *same* as the emf of one cell (Figure 6.45).

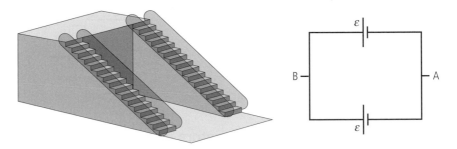

Figure 6.45 Identical cells in parallel.

If the cells are different then it is not so simple. In fact, if we were to connect two cells with different emfs and zero internal resistance we wouldn't be able to solve the problem of how you can have two different emfs depending on which battery you consider. This would be like having two different height escalators going between the same two floors, and that's not possible unless you connect a short staircase between them. That is where internal resistance comes in.

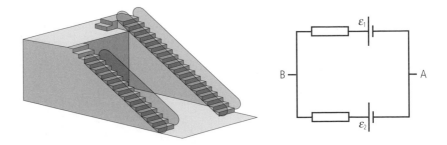

Figure 6.46 Different cells in parallel.

As can be seen in the shopping centre model in Figure 6.46, the potential drops over the internal resistance of the big escalator, and goes up over the internal resistance of the small one. This means that a current is being forced to flow into the smaller cell. This is what happens when a rechargeable battery is being recharged.

Electrical measurement

Measurement of potential difference

The pd can be measured using a voltmeter. Voltmeters can have either a numerical display (digital) or a moving pointer (analogue).

The pd is the difference in potential between two points. To measure the pd between A and B, one lead of the voltmeter must be connected to A, the other to B.

An ideal voltmeter has infinitely high resistance so that it does not take any current from the circuit.

A real voltmeter will have resistance but it is fairly high (say 10 MΩ) so when placed in parallel with a resistor it will take very little current unless the resistance of the resistor in question is of a similar size. As you can see in Figure 6.49, the voltmeter draws almost no current from the circuit so the pd across the resistor is the same with and without the voltmeter.

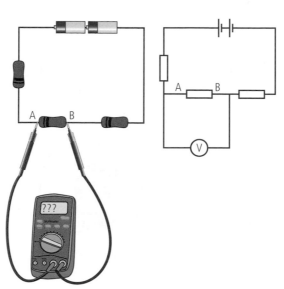

Dial used to change from voltmeter to ammeter.

Figure 6.47 A multimeter is a common instrument that can measure both pd and current. It can also measure resistance.

Figure 6.48 A voltmeter is connected from A to B.

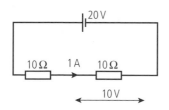

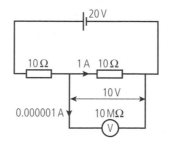

Figure 6.49 Voltmeter connected in parallel with a low resistance.

A voltmeter is probably the electrician's most useful measuring instrument. A long row of light bulbs connected in series will all go out if one of them breaks. To find the broken one you could use a voltmeter to measure the pd across each bulb: the broken one will have a pd equal to the source.

If the same meter is used to measure the pd across a 10 MΩ resistor (Figure 6.50), half of the current is diverted around the component resulting in a lower potential difference.

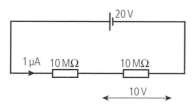

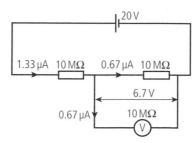

Figure 6.50 Voltmeter connected in parallel with a high resistance.

Measurement of current

To measure the current flowing through a resistor, the ammeter must be connected so that the same current will flow through the ammeter as flows through the resistor. This means disconnecting one of the wires and connecting the ammeter (Figure 6.51).

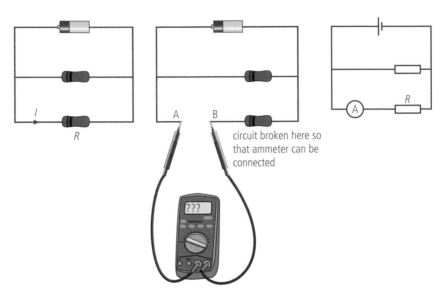

circuit broken here so that ammeter can be connected

Figure 6.51 The ammeter is connected to measure the current through *R*.

An ideal ammeter has zero resistance so that it doesn't change the current in the circuit.

A real ammeter has a small resistance so connecting it does not change the current flowing in the circuit unless the resistance of the circuit is also very small. In Figure 6.52 an ammeter of 1 Ω resistance is used to measure the current through a 10 MΩ resistor. The resistance of the ammeter makes very little difference to the circuit so the current is unchanged.

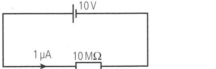
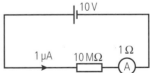

Figure 6.52 An ammeter measuring the current through a high resistance.

If the same ammeter is used to measure the current through a 1 Ω resistor, the resistance of the circuit is doubled so the current is halved, as shown in Figure 6.53.

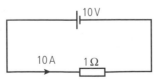
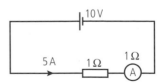

Figure 6.53 An ammeter reduces the current when in series with a low resistance.

Worked example

Calculate the current and potential difference measured by the meters in the circuit in Figure 6.54. Assume the battery has no internal resistance and that the meters are ideal.

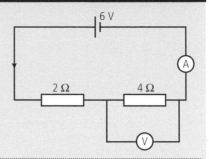

Figure 6.54.

Solution

Total resistance	$= 2 + 4\,\Omega$	
	$= 6\,\Omega$	The two resistors are in series.
	$I = \dfrac{V}{R}$	Applying Ohm's law, to find the current.
	$= \dfrac{6}{6}\,A$	
	$= 1\,A$	

So ammeter reading	$= 1\,A$	
	$V = IR$	Applying Ohm's law to the $4\,\Omega$ resistor.
	$= 1 \times 4\,V$	
	$= 4\,V$	

So the voltmeter reads 4 V.

Exercises

Find the ammeter and voltmeter readings in the circuits in Figure 6.55. All meters are ideal and the batteries have no internal resistance. (You can build them in the PhET® 'circuit construction kit' to see whether your answers agree.)

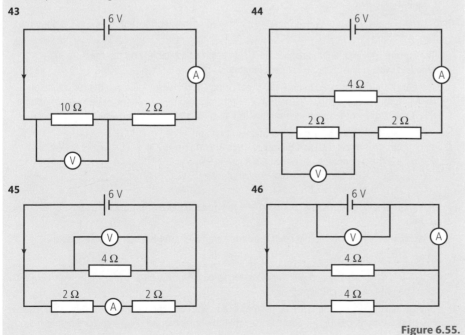

43

44

45

46

Figure 6.55.

In the following two problems the meters are not ideal (resistance is as displayed).

47 Calculate the pd across the second resistor with and without the voltmeter in Figure 6.56, and the percentage difference between these readings.

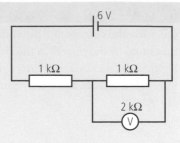

Figure 6.56.

48 Calculate the current through the resistors with and without the ammeter in Figure 6.57, and the percentage difference between these readings.

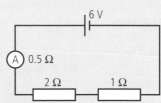

Figure 6.57.

Measuring the relationship between resistance and length for a wire

By measuring the current through and pd across a conductor it is possible to calculate its resistance. Measuring the resistance of different lengths of nichrome wire, the relationship between length and resistance can be found.

Nichrome is a metal that has a resistivity ρ of $1.5 \times 10^{-6}\,\Omega$ m. It is suitable to use in this experiment as it is a good conductor, but not so good that it will short circuit the battery. When performing this experiment one should use:

1. quite a thin wire so that the resistance isn't too small.

2. a low voltage power supply so that the current isn't too big; a high current will make the wire hot.

3. the least sensitive range on the ammeter (10 A range) should be used so that the ammeter fuse doesn't blow.

4. If the wire is in loops they shouldn't touch as this would shorten the effective length of the sample.

A length of about 1 m of wire is measured with a ruler then connected in a circuit as shown in Figure 6.58.

The current, pd, and length are recorded in an appropriate table, and the measurements repeated with at least 5 more different lengths.

The data can be processed in a spread sheet using Ohm's law to calculate the resistance of each length. The uncertainty in the resistance should also be found; the easiest way of doing this is to use the percentage uncertainties in V and I, which simply add when you calculate $\frac{V}{I}$.

> So if $V = 1.5 \pm 0.1$ V the percentage uncertainty = 7%
> and if $I = 0.54 \pm 0.01$ A the percentage uncertainty = 2%
> so the percentage uncertainty in $R = \frac{V}{I}$ is 9%.
> But $\frac{V}{I} = 2.8\,\Omega$ so the absolute uncertainty = $0.3\,\Omega$.
> The final value is $2.8 \pm 0.3\,\Omega$.

This is quite a lot of steps but you only have to write the calculation once if a spreadsheet is used.

The theoretical relationship between resistance R and length l is given by the equation:

$$R = \frac{\rho l}{A}$$

where ρ is the resistivity and A is the cross-sectional area. This means that a graph of R vs l will be a straight line with gradient $\frac{\rho}{A}$.

In this case the uncertainties are quite small but as with all experiments the results never exactly match the theoretical model. Some factors that might be worth taking into consideration are:

• the changing temperature of the wire.

• the resistance of the meters.

• the uniformity of cross-section.

The relationship between resistance and the length of a wire

A worksheet with full details of how to carry out this experiment is available on your eBook.

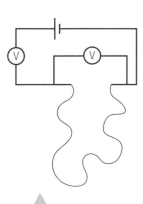

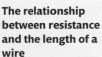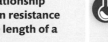

▲

Figure 6.58 Measuring the resistance of nichrome.

Circuit problems

Most circuit problems can be solved by combining components and applying three laws:

1. **Kirchhoff's first law:** the current into a junction = current out of a junction.
2. **Kirchhoff's second law:** around any closed circuit, the sum of the emfs = the sum of the pds. In the shopping centre analogy this would be like saying if you walk around the shopping centre and arrive back at the same place you must have gone up as much as you have come down.
3. **Ohms law:** V = IR.

Worked example

Find the pd across the 8 Ω resistor in the circuit shown in Figure 6.59.

Figure 6.59.

Solution

There are many ways to solve this problem but a good starting point is to find the total resistance. This is done by first adding 8 Ω and 4 Ω in series then combining this with the 4 Ω in parallel. Finally add the internal resistance of 1 Ω in series. Figure 6.60 shows how this is done.

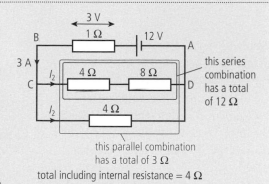

Figure 6.60.

The total current in the circuit can now be found using Ohm's law:

$$I = \frac{V}{R} = \frac{12}{4} = 3\,A.$$

Applying Ohm's law to the internal resistance: $V = IR = 3 \times 1 = 3$ V.

Applying Kirchhoff's second law to the closed loop ABCDA.

sum of emfs, 12 V = sum of pds = 3 V + V_{CD}

$12 = 3\,V + V_{CD}$

$V_{CD} = 12 - 3 = 9\,V$

(In the shopping centre; starting from A you go up a 12 V escalator, down a 3 V staircase, so to get from C to D there must be another 9 V down).

237

Applying Ohm's law again to the series combination of $4\,\Omega$ and $8\,\Omega$:

The current $I_1 = \dfrac{V}{R} = \dfrac{9}{12} = 0.75\,A$

Applying Ohm's law to the $8\,\Omega$ resistor gives $V = IR = \tfrac{3}{4} \times 8 = 6\,V$.

Once we know this we can easily find all the other values.

From Kirchhoff's first law, the current $I_2 = 3\,A - \tfrac{3}{4}A = 2\tfrac{1}{4}\,A = 2.25\,A$;
pd across the remaining $4\,\Omega$ resistor is the same as the upper combination = 9 V. To confirm this we see that from $V = IR = 2\tfrac{1}{4} \times 4 = 9\,V$.

This seems a lot but if you take it a step at a time it is not too bad.

Worked example

For the circuit shown in Figure 6.61, calculate the current flowing I and the pd V_{AB}.

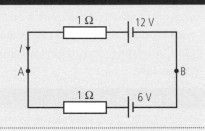

Figure 6.61.

Solution

The direction of current has already been drawn in. This was a guess (a good one) but if you guess wrong it doesn't matter. The answer will simply be negative.

Applying Kirchhoff's second law to the circuit sum of emfs = $12 - 6 = 6\,V$.

$$\text{sum of pds in this circuit} = I \times 1 + I \times 1 = 2I$$

so
$$6 = 2I.$$
$$I = 3\,A$$

Applying Ohm's law we see that the pd across each resistor is 3 V. So if we consider B to be at 0 V then if we go to A via the upper route we would go up 12 V then down 3 V, a difference of 9 V. Taking the lower route we would go up 6 V then up a further 3 V, also a total potential difference of 9 V.

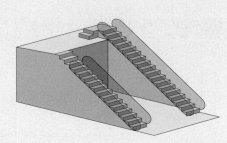

Figure 6.62 Shopping centre model of the circuit.

Exercises

49 Find the pd from A to B in Figure 6.63.

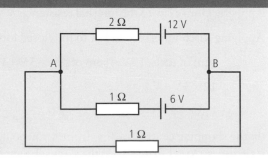

Figure 6.63.

In the IB exam this question would be split into several parts.

When solving problems like this, always draw a circuit diagram, and fill in the values of I and V as you find them.

Note that the emf of the 6 V battery is negative. This is because if you go round this circuit clockwise you would be going from high to low potential when you crossed that battery so it is not an up, it is a down.

A car battery is used to turn over the engine to get it started; to do this it must be able to deliver a large current for a short time.

50 Find the current and pd measured by the meters in Figure 6.64.

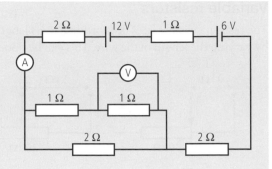

Figure 6.64.

The potential divider

Figure 6.65 shows a potential divider circuit used to give a varying pd. The battery creates a pd across the resistors equal to V_{in}

From Ohm's law we know that the current in the circuit $I = \dfrac{V}{R}$

Since the total resistance is $R_1 + R_2$

The current $I = \dfrac{V_{in}}{R_1 + R_2}$ Equation (1)

The pd across $R_2 = V_{out}$

Applying Ohm's law to R_2 gives

$V_{out} = IR_2$

Substituting from equation (1) gives

$V_{out} = V_{in} \dfrac{R_2}{R_1 + R_2}$

This is the potential divider formula.

▲ **Figure 6.65** potential divider circuit consists of two series resistors.

Worked example

Calculate the output voltage for the potential divider in Figure 6.66.

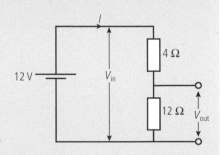

Figure 6.66.

Solution

Using the potential divider formula

$$V_{out} = V_{in} \frac{R_2}{R_1 + R_2}$$

$$V_{out} = 12 \frac{12}{4 + 12} = 9\,V$$

Variable resistors

The resistance of a wire is proportional to its length so we can make a variable resistor by varying the length of the wire. This can be done by adding a sliding contact.

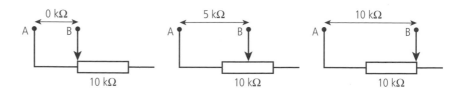

Figure 6.67 Variable resistor.

If a current is passed through the resistor then moving the slider would give a varying pd. This is a potentiometer.

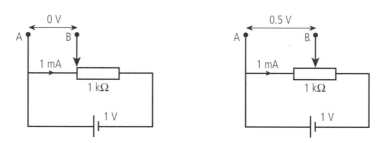

Figure 6.68 Variable potential.

This is how lights are dimmed with a dimmer switch or whenever a varying pd is required; for example, to measure the V–I characteristics of a component such as a light bulb.

Exercises

51 The slider in the circuit in Figure 6.69 is set at the middle of the variable resistor. Calculate the pd across the 2 kΩ resistor.

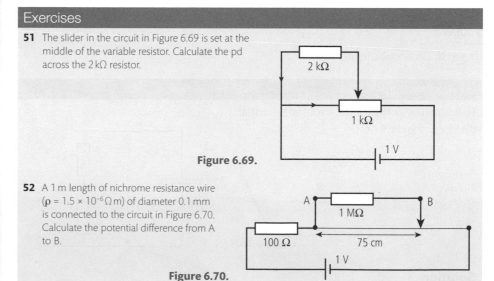

Figure 6.69.

52 A 1 m length of nichrome resistance wire ($\rho = 1.5 \times 10^{-6}\,\Omega\,\text{m}$) of diameter 0.1 mm is connected to the circuit in Figure 6.70. Calculate the potential difference from A to B.

Figure 6.70.

Figure 6.71 Circuit used to measure the characteristics of a light bulb.

Practical measurement of V and I

The circuit used to measure the current flowing through a component for different values of V is shown in Figure 6.71. Here the potential divider is providing the changing pd that is measured by the voltmeter. Note that in this circuit it is assumed that the voltmeter has a much higher resistance than the bulb so it won't draw much current.

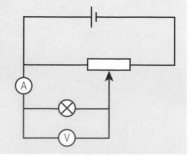

Practical measurement of ε and r

If a high-resistance voltmeter is connected across the terminals of a battery it will draw very little current so the pd across the internal resistance will be small. The terminal pd will therefore be almost equal to the emf.

To measure the internal resistance of the battery, the circuit in Figure 6.73 can be used.

The equation for this circuit is $\varepsilon = V + Ir$.

So $V = -Ir + \varepsilon$.

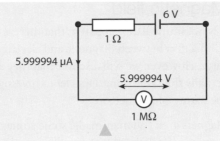

Figure 6.72 Measuring emf.

This shows that V and I are linearly related. By changing the variable resistor the pd V can be measured as the current in the circuit changes. A graph of V vs I can then be plotted. This graph should have a gradient = $-r$ and an intercept ε.

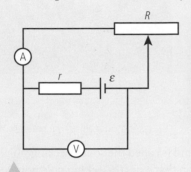

Figure 6.73 Measuring r.

As mentioned earlier, the internal resistance is due to the resistive components of the cell but there is also resistance due to the changing chemical composition. This means that the internal resistance can vary depending on how long the battery is used for.

To learn more about electric cells, go to the hotlinks site, search for the title or ISBN and click on Chapter 6.

Measuring the emf and internal resistance of a battery

A worksheet with full details of how to carry out this experiment is available on your eBook.

6.4 Magnetic effects of electric currents

5.4 Magnetic effects of electric currents

Understandings, applications, and skills:

Magnetic fields
- Sketching and interpreting magnetic field patterns.
- Determining the direction of the magnetic field based on current direction.

  #### Guidance
  - *Magnetic field patterns will be restricted to long straight conductors, solenoids, and bar magnets.*

Magnetic force
- Determining the direction of force on a current carrying conductor in a magnetic field.
- Determining the direction of force on a charge moving in a magnetic field.
- Solving problems involving magnetic forces, fields, current, and charges.

NATURE OF SCIENCE

The first recorded observation of the magnetic effect was 2500 years ago in the ancient city of Magnesia (Manisa) in what is now western Turkey. Experiment showed that one end of the magnet always pointed towards the north pole so a theory was developed related to the attraction of opposite poles. This theory gave correct predictions enabling the magnets to be used in navigation even though it wasn't entirely correct. The connection between magnetism and electricity wasn't made until a chance observation by Hans Christian Oersted in 1819.

Magnetic field

It is not immediately apparent that there is a connection between magnetic and electric force. However, we will discover that they are actually the same thing. First, let us investigate the nature of magnetism.

Magnets aren't all man-made; some stones are magnetic. If we place a small magnetic stone next to a big one it experiences forces that make it rotate. We can define a magnetic field as a region of space where a small magnet would experience a turning force. The reason that magnets turn rather than accelerate towards each other is because magnets are dipoles so one end attracts and the other repels.

Not all magnets are man-made; certain rocks (for example, this piece of magnetite) are naturally magnetic.

If one of these small magnets is placed close to the Earth we will find that it rotates so that one end always points north. Because of this, we call that end the *north-seeking pole*; the other end is called the south-seeking pole. The direction of the field is defined as the direction that a north-seeking pole points.

Magnetic field lines

In practice, a small compass can be used as our test magnet. Magnetic field lines are drawn to show the direction that the N pole of a small compass would point if placed in the field.

If we join the direction pointed out by the compass we get the field lines shown. These not only show the direction of the field but their density shows us where the field is strongest. We call the density of lines the *flux density*.

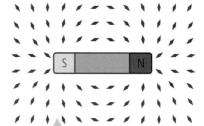

Figure 6.75 If the whole field were covered in small magnets, then they would show the direction of the field lines.

Figure 6.74 The small magnet is caused to turn, so must be in a magnetic field.

Notice that since unlike poles attract, the north-seeking pole of the small compass points to the *south* magnetic pole of the big magnet. So, if we treat the Earth like a big magnet the north-seeking end of the compass points north because there is a *south* magnetic pole there.

Figure 6.76 The Earth's magnetic field.

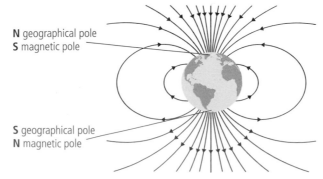

N geographical pole
S magnetic pole

S geographical pole
N magnetic pole

A uniform field can be created between two flat magnets as in Figure 6.77. As with uniform gravitational and electric fields the field lines are parallel and uniformly spaced.

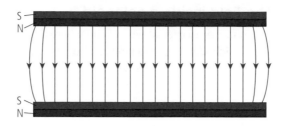

Figure 6.77 Uniform magnetic field.

Field caused by currents

If a small compass is placed close to a straight wire carrying an electric current, then it experiences a turning force that makes it always point around the wire. The region around the wire is therefore a magnetic field. This leads us to believe that magnetic fields are caused by moving charges.

We can work out the direction of the field by pretending to grip the wire with our right hand. If the thumb points in the direction of the current then the fingers will curl in the direction of the field.

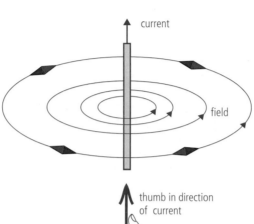

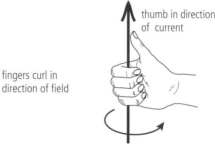

fingers curl in direction of field

thumb in direction of current

current

field

Figure 6.78 The field due to a long straight wire carrying a current is in the form of concentric circles. Notice that the field is strongest close to the wire.

When charged particles ejected from the Sun meet the Earth's magnetic field they are made to follow a helical path. As these particles move towards the poles the field becomes stronger so the helix becomes tighter until the particles turn back on themselves and head for the other pole. If the particles have enough energy they sometimes get close enough to the Earth to reach the upper atmosphere. If this happens, light is emitted as the particles ionize the air, forming the northern/southern lights.

Magnetic flux density (*B*)

From what we know about fields, the strength of a field is related to the density of field lines. This tells us that the magnetic field is strongest close to the poles. The magnetic flux density is the quantity that is used to measure how strong the field is – however it is not quite the same as field strength as used in gravitational and electric fields.

 B field

Since the letter *B* is used to denote flux density, the magnetic field is often called a *B field*.

The field inside a coil

When a current-carrying wire is made into a circular loop the field inside is due to the addition of all the field components around the loop, making the field at the centre greater (Figure 6.79). Adding more loops to form a coil will increase the field.

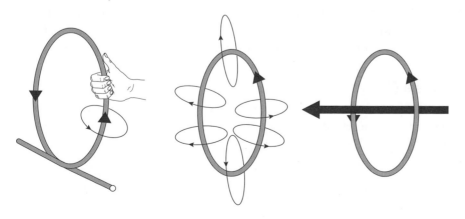

Figure 6.79 The direction of the field can be found by applying the right-hand grip rule to the wire. The circles formed by each bit of the loop add together in the middle to give a stronger field.

The field inside a solenoid

A solenoid is a a special type of coil where the loops are wound next to each other along a cylinder to form a helix as shown in Figure 6.80.

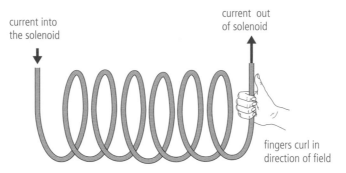

current into the solenoid

current out of solenoid

fingers curl in direction of field

Figure 6.80 The direction of the field in a solenoid can be found using the grip rule on one coil.

The magnetic field caused by each loop of the solenoid adds to give a field pattern similar to a bar magnet, as shown in Figure 6.81.

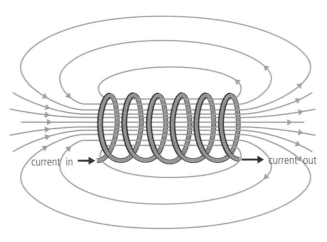

current in

current out

Figure 6.81 The field inside a solenoid.

Force on a current-carrying conductor

We have seen that when a small magnet is placed in a magnetic field, each end experiences a force that causes it to turn. If a straight wire is placed in a magnetic field, it also experiences a force. However, in the case of a wire, the direction of the force does not cause rotation – the force is in fact perpendicular to the direction of both current and field (Figure 6.82).

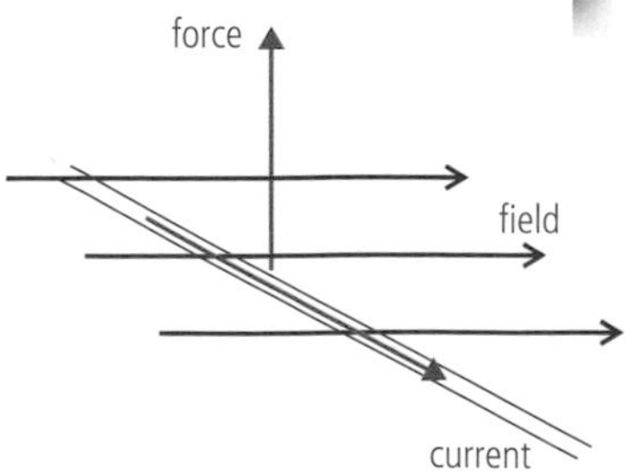

The size of the force depends upon the size of current, length of conductor, and flux density. We can therefore write that $F \propto BIL$. We can now define the unit of flux density in terms of this force to make the constant of proportionality equal to 1.

force

field

current

Figure 6.82 Force, field, and current are at right angles to each other.

The tesla (T)

A flux density of 1 tesla would cause a 1 m long wire carrying a current of 1 A perpendicular to the field to experience a force of 1 N. So if B is measured in T, $F = BIL$.

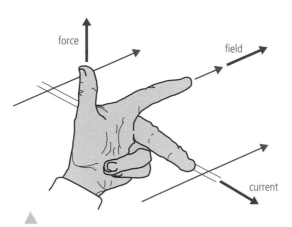

Figure 6.83 Using Fleming's left hand rule to find the direction of the force.

Figure 6.84 Field into the page can be represented by crosses, and field out by dots. Think what it would be like looking at an arrow from each end.

Definition of the ampere

Due to the difficulty in measuring the amount of charge flowing in a given time, the ampere is defined *not* in terms of charge (although there is a move to do this) but in terms of the force between two parallel conductors. Consider the two wires shown in Figure 6.85. Each wire carries a current so is creating a magnetic field around it. The wires are next to each other so each wire is in the field of the other. The magnetic field lines produced by wire X, are concentric circles which cut wire Y at right angles, as can be seen in the end view. Using Fleming's left hand rule we can determine that the direction of force is directed towards X. Likewise we can show that the force on X is directed towards Y.

One ampere is defined as the current that would cause a force of 2×10^{-7} N per metre between two long parallel conductors separated by 1 m in a vacuum.

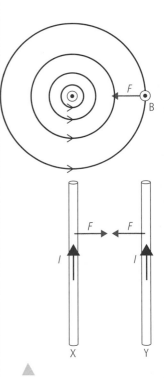

Figure 6.85 Two long wires.

Exercises

53 A straight wire of length 0.5 m carries a current of 2 A in a north–south direction. If the wire is placed in a magnetic field of 20 μT directed vertically downwards

(a) what is the size of the force on the wire?

(b) what is the direction of the force on the wire?

54 A vertical wire of length 1 m carries a current of 0.5 A upwards. If the wire is placed in a magnetic field of strength 10 μT directed towards the N geographic pole

(a) what is the size of the force on the wire?

(b) what is the direction of the force on the wire?

55 Use Fleming's left hand rule to find the direction of the force in the following examples:

(a)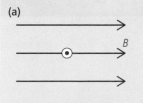

(b)

(c)

Figure 6.86.

Non-perpendicular fields

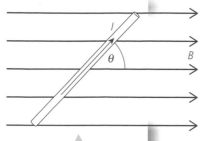

Figure 6.87 Non-perpendicular field.

If the wire is *not* perpendicular to the field then, to calculate the magnitude of the force, you need to use the component of field that is perpendicular to the wire.

So in the example shown in Figure 6.87 the component of B perpendicular to the wire = $B \sin \theta$ so the force $F = B \sin \theta \times IL = BIL \sin \theta$.

The direction of the force can be found by using Fleming's left hand rule, lining the First finger with the perpendicular component of the Field. In the case shown here that would result in a force into the page.

Charges in magnetic fields

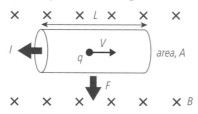

Figure 6.88 The force experienced by each electron is in the downward direction. Remember the electrons flow in the opposite direction to the conventional current.

From the microscopic model of electrical current, we believe that the current is made up of charged particles (electrons) moving through the metal. Each electron experiences a force as it travels through the magnetic field; the sum of all these forces gives the total force on the wire. $F = BIL = BnAveL = BNev$ where N is the number of electrons in this length of wire, so the force on each electron is Bev. If a free charge moves through a magnetic field, then it will also experience a force. The direction of the force is always perpendicular to the direction of motion, and this results in a circular path.

The force on each charge q is given by the formula:

$$F = Bqv.$$

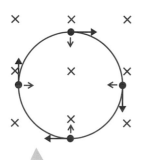

Figure 6.89 Wherever you apply Fleming's left hand rule, the force is always towards the centre.

Applying what we know about circular motion to this problem we find that the centripetal force, $\frac{mv^2}{r} = Bqv$. Rearranging gives $r = \frac{mv}{Bq}$ which means that if m, q, and B are constant then r will be proportional to v. If the particle slows down the radius will become less so the particle will follow a spiral path. As electrons travelling through air they collide with air molecules losing energy; their paths can be made visible using a cloud chamber as shown in the photo.

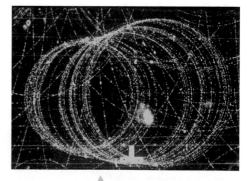

Spiral particle tracks made visible in a cloud chamber.

The charged particles travelling around the huge circular rings of the particle accelerator at CERN are also kept in a circular path using a magnetic field. These particles move so fast and have such a large mass that the field has to be very strong.

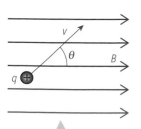

Figure 6.90 A positive particle moving in a non-perpendicular B field.

Non-perpendicular fields

If a charged particle moves through a B field at an angle then you can calculate the magnetic force experienced by it using the component of velocity perpendicular to the B field. In the example shown in Figure 6.90 this would be $B \sin \theta$ which results in a force, $F = Bqv \sin \theta$.

Using Fleming's left hand rule, this will give a force into the page (note that the charge is positive so it moves in the direction of current).

So considering the two components of the motion, perpendicular to the field the particle will travel in a circle whilst parallel to the field the velocity is uniform. The resulting motion is helical as shown in Figure 6.91.

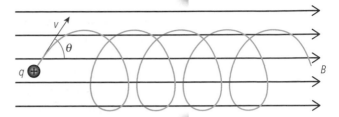

▲ **Figure 6.91** Helical path of a charge in a non-perpendicular B field.

Exercises

(Electron charge $e = 1.6 \times 10^{-19}\,\text{C}$)

56 Calculate the force experienced by an electron travelling through a B field of flux density 5 mT with velocity 500 m s⁻¹.

57 An electron is accelerated through a pd of 500 V then passed into a region of magnetic field perpendicular to its motion causing it to travel in a circular path of radius 10 cm. Calculate:

   (a) the KE of the electron in joules.

   (b) the velocity of the electron.

   (c) the flux density of the magnetic field.

58 A proton (same charge as an electron but positive) passes into a region of B field of flux density 5 mT as shown in Figure 6.92 with a velocity of 100 m s⁻¹. Calculate the force experienced by the proton.

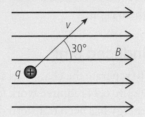

Figure 6.92.

To learn more about the magnetic effects of electric currents, go to the hotlinks site, search for the title or ISBN and click on Chapter 6.

6.5 Electromagnetic induction

11.1 Electromagnetic induction

Understandings, applications, and skills:

(AHL) Electromotive force (emf)
- Describing the production of an induced emf by a changing magnetic flux, and within a uniform magnetic field.

(AHL) Magnetic flux and magnetic flux linkage

(AHL) Faraday's law of induction
- Solving problems involving magnetic flux, magnetic flux linkage, and Faraday's law.

   Guidance
   - *Quantitative treatments will be expected for straight conductors moving at right angles to magnetic fields, and rectangular coils moving in and out of fields and rotating in fields.*

(AHL) Lenz's law
- Explaining Lenz's law through the conservation of energy.

   Guidance
   - *Qualitative treatments will be expected for fixed coils in a changing magnetic field and AC generators.*

NATURE OF SCIENCE

Having discovered that a changing current in one coil causes a current in a second unconnected coil, Faraday could have designed a simple electrical generator without any understanding of how it works. By performing experiments, changing different variables, Faraday went far beyond the initial discovery to formulate his law of electromagnetic induction.

Conductor moving in a magnetic field

We have considered what happens to free charges moving in a magnetic field, but what happens if these charges are contained in a conductor? Figure 6.93 shows a conductor of length L moving with velocity v through a perpendicular field of flux density B. We know from our microscopic model of conduction that conductors contain free electrons. As the free electron shown moves downwards through the field it will experience a force. Using Fleming's left hand rule, we can deduce that the direction of the force is to the left. (Remember, the electron is negative so if it is moving downwards the current is upwards.) This force will cause the free electrons to move to the left as shown in Figure 6.94. We can see that the electrons moving left have caused the lattice atoms on the right to become positive, and there is now a potential difference between the ends of the conductor. The electrons will now stop moving because the B force pushing them left will be balanced by an E force pulling them right.

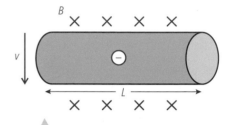

Figure 6.93 A conductor moving through a perpendicular field.

Induced emf

To separate the charges as shown in Figure 6.94 required work to be done so energy has been transferred to the charges: electrical PE. What has happened is rather like what happens in a battery; a potential difference has been created. The amount of work done per unit charge in moving the charges to the ends of the conductor is called the *induced emf*.

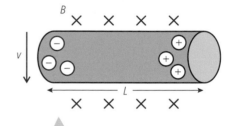

Figure 6.94 Charges gather at either end creating a potential difference.

Induced current

If the conductor is connected to a circuit then a current will flow from high potential to low potential. Connecting to a circuit is not as easy as it sounds since the circuit must not move through the field with the wire. If it did then an emf would be induced in the circuit too and no current would flow. Sliding the conductor along static rails as shown in Figure 6.95 would be one way of solving the problem.

As can be seen in Figure 6.95, the current flows anticlockwise around the circuit so it passes through the moving conductor from left to right. A current-carrying conductor experiences a force when placed in a perpendicular field so the moving conductor will now experience a force.

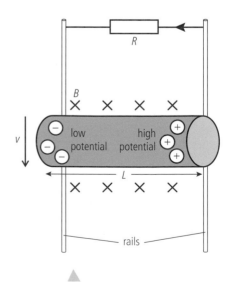

Figure 6.95 Current flows through the stationary circuit.

Using Fleming's left hand rule (shown in Figure 6.83) we can determine that the direction of this force is upwards. If the conductor is to travel at constant velocity the forces applied to it must be balanced so there must be an equal force acting downwards (Figure 6.96). This means that to keep the conductor moving with constant velocity work must be done by the person pushing the conductor. This implies that energy is transferred to the electrical PE of the electrons and the electrons in turn transfer energy to the lattice atoms of the resistor, resulting in a rise in temperature.

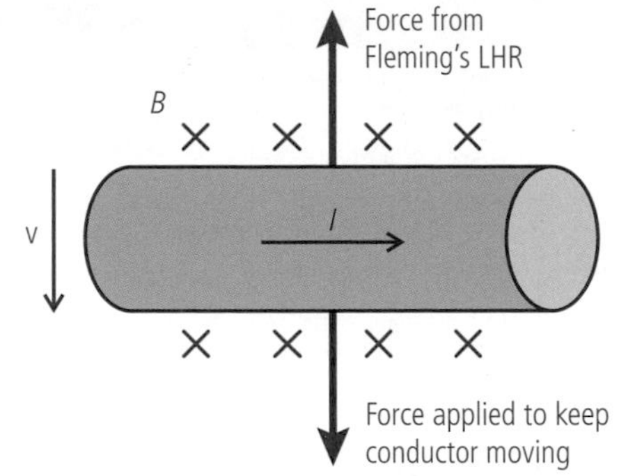

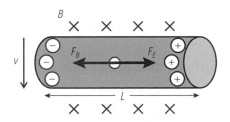

Force from Fleming's LHR

B

I

v

Force applied to keep conductor moving

Figure 6.96 If velocity is constant forces must be balanced.

Calculating induced emf

The maximum pd achieved across the conductor is when the magnetic force pushing the electrons left equals the electric force pushing them right. When the forces are balanced, no more electrons will move. Figure 6.97 shows an electron with balanced forces.

B

F_B F_E

v

L

Figure 6.97.

If F_B is the magnetic force and F_E is the electric force we can say that

$$F_B = -F_E$$

Now we know that if the velocity of the electron is v and the field strength is B then

$$F_B = Bev$$

The electric force is due to the electric field E which we can find from the equation $E = -\frac{dV}{dx}$ that we established in the section on electric potential. In this case, the field is uniform so the potential gradient $= \frac{V}{L}$

So, $$F_E = Ee = \frac{Ve}{L}$$

Equating the forces gives $$\frac{Ve}{L} = Bev$$

so $$V = BLv$$

This is the pd across the conductor, which is defined as the work done per unit charge, taking a small positive test charge from one side to the other. As current starts to flow in an external circuit, the work done by the pulling force enables charges to move from one end to the other, so the emf (mechanical energy converted to electrical per unit charge) is the same as this pd

$$\text{induced emf} = BLv$$

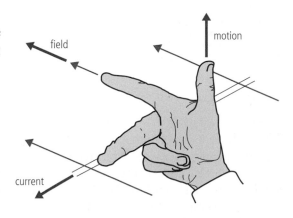

field

motion

current

Figure 6.98.

> **Fleming's right hand rule**
>
> The fingers represent the same things as in the left hand rule but it is used to find the direction of induced current if you know the motion of the wire and the field. Try using it on the example in Figure 6.96.

59 A 20 cm long straight wire is travelling at a constant $20\,\text{m s}^{-1}$ through a perpendicular *B* field of flux density $50\,\mu\text{T}$.

(a) Calculate the emf induced.
(b) If this wire were connected to a resistance of $2\,\Omega$ how much current would flow?
(c) How much energy would be converted to heat in the resistor in 1 s? (Power = I^2R)
(d) How much work would be done by the pulling force in 1 s?
(e) How far would the wire move in 1 s?
(f) What force would be applied to the wire?

Faraday's law

From the moving conductor example we see that the induced emf is dependent on the flux density, speed of movement, and length of conductor. These three factors all change the rate at which the conductor cuts through the field lines, so a more convenient way of expressing this is:

The induced emf is equal to the rate of change of flux.

So if in a time Δt the conductor sweeps over an area enclosing flux $\Delta\phi$ then $\varepsilon = \frac{\Delta\phi}{\Delta t}$.

Rate of change of flux

If flux density is related to the number of field lines per unit area then flux is related to the number of field lines in a given area. So if, as in Figure 6.99, area *A* is perpendicular to a field of flux density *B*, then flux enclosed by the area will be *BA*.

A straight conductor moving perpendicular to a *B* field will sweep through the field as shown in Figure 6.100. We can see in this diagram that the circuit encloses an amount of flux *BA*. As the wire moves the amount of flux enclosed increases so, according to Faraday's law, emf will be induced. If the conductor moves at velocity *v* then it will move a distance *v* per unit time, so the increase in area per unit time is *Lv*. Rate of change of flux is therefore *BLv*.

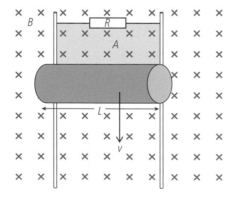
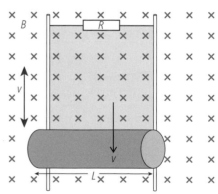

Lenz's law

We noticed that when a current is induced in a moving conductor, the direction of induced current causes the conductor to experience a force that opposes its motion. To keep the conductor moving will therefore require a force to be exerted in the opposite direction. This is a direct consequence of the law of conservation of energy. If it were not true, you wouldn't have to do work to move the conductor, so the energy given to the circuit would come from nowhere. Lenz's law states this fact in a way that is applicable to all examples:

Figure 6.99.

Figure 6.100 Flux enclosed by circuit increases as conductor moves forward distance *v* in 1 second.

The direction of the induced current is such that it will oppose the change producing it.

So Faraday's law equation can be modified by adding a − sign.

$$\varepsilon = -\frac{\Delta\phi}{\Delta t}.$$

Coils in changing *B* fields

A magnet is moved towards a coil as in Figure 6.101.

Applying Faraday's law

As the magnet approaches the coil, the *B* field inside the coil increases, and the changing flux enclosed by the coil induces an emf in the coil that causes a current to flow. The size of the emf will be equal to the rate of change of flux enclosed by the coil.

Applying Lenz's law

The direction of induced current will be such that it opposes the change producing it, which in this case is the magnet moving towards the coil. So to oppose this, the current in the coil must induce a magnetic field that pushes the magnet away; this direction is shown in Figure 6.101.

If the same magnet was pushed into a coil of N turns then each turn of the coil would enclose the same flux: the flux enclosed would then be *BAN*. If the flux enclosed changed, each turn would have an equal emf induced in it so the total emf would be given by:

$$\varepsilon = -N\frac{\Delta\phi}{\Delta t}.$$

Coil in a changing field

In Figure 6.102, the magnetic flux enclosed by coil Y is changed by switching the current in coil X on and off.

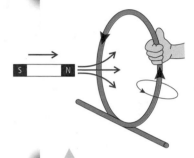

Figure 6.101 To oppose the magnet coming into the coil, the coil's magnetic field must push it out. The direction of the current is found using the grip rule.

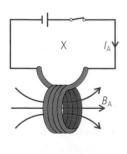 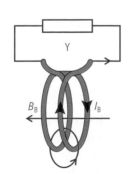

Figure 6.102 Coil X induces current in coil Y. Use the grip rule to work out the direction of the fields.

Applying Faraday's law

When the current in X flows, a magnetic field is created that causes the magnetic flux enclosed by Y to increase. This increasing flux induces a current in coil Y.

Applying Lenz's law

The direction of the current in Y must oppose the change producing it, which in this case is the increasing field from X. So to oppose this, the field induced in Y must be in the opposite direction to the field from X, as in the diagram. This is the principle behind the operation of a transformer.

To learn more about electromagnetic induction, go to the hotlinks site, search for the title or ISBN and click on Chapter 6.

CHALLENGE YOURSELF

2 When a vacuum cleaner is plugged into the mains and switched on the safety switch cuts off the current to the socket. Why does this happen, and what could be done to stop it happening?

Exercises

60 A coil with 50 turns and area $2\,cm^2$ encloses a field that is of flux density $100\,\mu T$ (the field is perpendicular to the plane of the coil).

(a) What is the total flux enclosed?

(b) If the flux density changes to $50\,\mu T$ in $2\,s$, what is the rate of change of flux?

(c) What is the induced emf?

61 A rectangular coil with sides $3\,cm$ and $2\,cm$ and 50 turns lies flat on a table in a region of magnetic field. The magnetic field is vertical and has flux density $500\,\mu T$.

(a) What is the total flux enclosed by the coil?

(b) If one side of the coil is lifted so that the plane of the coil makes an angle of $30°$ to the table, what will the new flux enclosed be?

(c) If the coil is lifted in $3\,s$, estimate the emf induced in the coil.

6.6 Power generation and transmission

11.2 Power generation and transmission

Understandings, applications, and skills:

(AHL) Alternating current (AC) generators
- Explaining the operation of a basic AC generator, including the effect of changing the generator frequency.

(AHL) Average power and root mean square (rms) values of current and voltage
- Solving problems involving the average power in an AC circuit.

  Guidance
  - *Proof of the relationship between the peak and rms values will not be expected.*

(AHL) Transformers
- Solving problems involving step-up and step-down transformers.
- Describing the use of transformers in the AC electrical power distribution.

  Guidance
  - *Calculations will be restricted to ideal transformers but students should be aware of some of the reasons why real transformers are not ideal (for example: flux leakage, joule heating, eddy current heating, magnetic hysteresis).*

(AHL) Diode bridges
- Investigating a diode bridge rectification circuit experimentally.

(AHL) Half-wave and full-wave rectification
- Qualitatively describing the effect of adding a capacitor to a diode bridge rectification circuit.

NATURE OF SCIENCE

The invention of the generator made it possible to deliver energy to homes and factories using a network of cables. Generators can be made to deliver either a current that always travels in one direction (DC) or one with changing direction (AC). In the early days of electrification there was much competition between the producers of the different generators who both wanted their system to be adopted. One advantage of AC is that it is relatively simple to step the voltage up and down using a transformer. Supporters of DC saw this as a danger and demonstrated it publicly by electrocuting an elephant called Topsy.

Coil rotating in a uniform magnetic field

Consider the coil shown in Figure 6.103. This coil is being made to rotate in a uniform magnetic field by someone turning the handle. The coil is connected to a resistor, but to prevent the wires connected to the coil twisting, they are connected via two slip rings. Resting on each slip ring is a carbon brush, which makes contact with the ring whilst allowing it to slip past.

Figure 6.103 A simple AC generator.

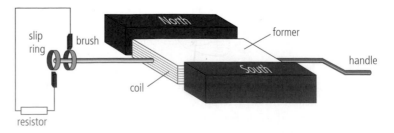

To make the operation easier to understand, a simpler 2D version with only one loop of wire in the coil is shown in Figure 6.104. As the handle is turned, the wire on the left hand side (AB) moves up through the field. As it cuts the field a current will be induced. Using Fleming's right hand rule, we can deduce that the direction of the current is from A to B as shown. The direction of motion of the right hand side (CD) is opposite so the current is opposite. The result is a clockwise current through the resistor.

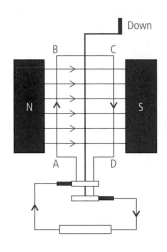

Figure 6.104 Looking at the generator from above.

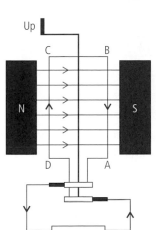

After turning half a revolution the coil is in the position shown in Figure 6.105. Side CD is now moving up through the field. Look carefully at how the slip ring has moved and you will see why, although the current is still clockwise in the coil, it is anticlockwise in the resistor circuit.

Figure 6.105 The coil after half a revolution.

The electrical energy produced by a generator comes from the work done by the person turning the coil. The more current you take from the coil the harder it is to turn. This follows from Lenz's law; the current in the coil opposes the change producing it. If you don't draw any current then it's very easy to turn the coil.

The size of the emf induced in a rotating coil

To find the size of the emf, we can use Faraday's law. This states that the induced emf will be equal to the rate of change of flux. The flux enclosed by the coil is related to the angle the coil makes with the field. Figure 6.106 shows a coil of N turns at time t. At this moment the normal to the plane of the coil makes an angle θ with the field.

Flux $\phi = BA \cos \theta$

There are N turns so total flux $\quad N\phi = BAN \cos \theta \quad\quad (1)$

This equation can be represented graphically as in Figure 6.107.

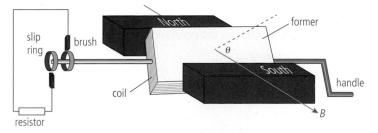

Figure 6.106.

Note that the starting point is when the angle θ is zero. This is when the coil is in the vertical position.

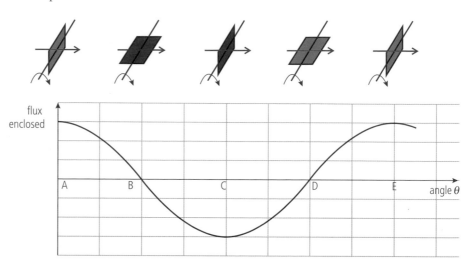

Figure 6.107 Graph of flux vs time showing position of coil.

To find the magnitude of the emf, we need the negative value of the rate of change of flux ($\varepsilon = -\frac{\Delta\varphi}{\Delta t}$). We can calculate this from the gradient of the graph in Figure 6.108. Let us consider some specific points.

A   Maximum flux enclosed but the rate of change zero (zero gradient).

B   No flux enclosed but rate of change of flux maximum (gradient negative so emf positive).

C   Maximum flux enclosed – rate of change zero.

D   No flux enclosed – rate of change maximum (positive gradient).

E   Back to the start.

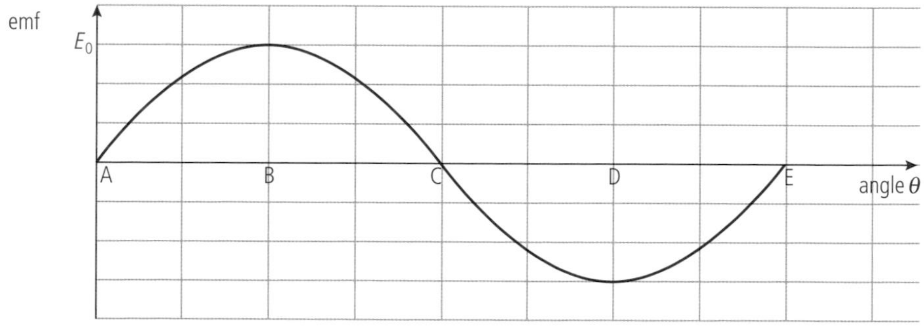

Figure 6.108 Graph of emf vs time.

The equation of this line is $\varepsilon = \varepsilon_0 \sin\theta$ where ε_0 is the maximum emf. If the coil took a time t to turn through angle θ then the angular velocity of the coil $\omega = \frac{\theta}{t}$

Rearranging gives $\theta = \omega t$

So the induced emf in terms of time is given by the equation:

$$\varepsilon = \varepsilon_0 \sin \omega t.$$

Faraday's law

If you have studied differentiation in maths you will understand that Faraday's law can be written

$$\varepsilon = \frac{-dN\varphi}{dt}$$

Then if $N\phi = BAN \cos \omega t$

$$\frac{-dN\varphi}{dt} = BAN\,\omega \sin \omega t$$

Effect of increasing angular frequency

If the speed of rotation is increased, the graph of emf against time will change in two ways, as shown in Figure 6.109. Firstly, time between the peaks will be shorter, and secondly, the peaks will be higher. This is because if the coil moves faster, then the rate of change of flux will be higher and hence the emf will be greater.

Power in AC circuits

If the output from the rotating coil is applied to a resistance (R) a current will flow. Since current is proportional to pd the current will vary at the same rate as the pd. So, if the pd across the resistor $V = V_0 \sin \omega t$, then the current $I = I_0 \sin \omega t$. This current is called *alternating current* (AC) as its direction and magnitude *vary* with time.

The power dissipated in the resistor is given by the formula $\frac{V^2}{R}$.

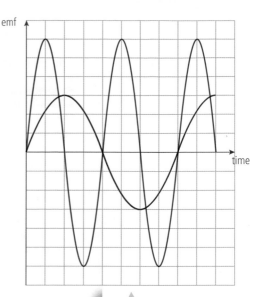

Figure 6.109 The black line is for the coil rotating at twice the angular speed of the red one.

Now
$$V = V_0 \sin \omega t \text{ so } P = \frac{V_0^2 \sin^2 \omega t}{R}$$

Over a period of time the power dissipated will go up and down but the average is given by

$$\frac{(\text{average value of } V^2)}{R} = V_0^2 \times \frac{(\text{average value of } \sin^2 \omega t)}{R}.$$

But the average value of $\sin^2 \omega t$ is $\frac{1}{2}$ so

$$P = \frac{\frac{V_0^2}{2}}{R} = \frac{\left(\frac{V_0}{\sqrt{2}}\right) \times \left(\frac{V_0}{\sqrt{2}}\right)}{R}$$

$V_0/\sqrt{2}$ is defined as the rms value of voltage (V_{rms}). The power dissipated is therefore $\frac{V_{rms}^2}{R}$. Rms stands for *root mean square*; it is the square root of the mean of the squares.

This is illustrated graphically in Figure 6.110.

Figure 6.110 Graphical mean of V_{rms}.

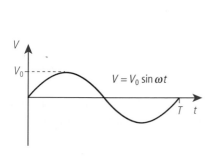

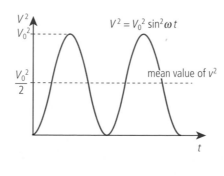

The rms voltage is defined as the voltage that would give the same power dissipation in a given resistance as an equal DC voltage. To clarify this let us consider an example:

An AC voltage of peak value 5 V is applied to a resistor of 3 Ω.

The rms voltage $= \frac{5}{\sqrt{2}} = 3.54$ V.

Power dissipated $= \frac{V_{rms}^2}{R} = 4.18$ W.

With the exception of some small communities, all countries use alternating current for domestic electrical power, but the voltage and frequency is not standardized internationally. Voltages range from 100 V (Japan) to 240 V (Malaysia) and the frequency is either 60 Hz (USA) or 50 Hz (Europe). The voltages are rms values so can be used directly to calculate power.

If a DC voltage of 3.54 V was applied to the same resistor then the power dissipated will also be 4.18 W.

This is also true for current where $I_{rms} = \left(\dfrac{I_0}{\sqrt{2}}\right)$ so $P = I_{rms}^2 R = I_{rms} \times V_{rms}$

Exercises

62 The rms voltage in the USA is 110 V. Calculate the peak voltage.

63 An electric oven designed to operate at 220 V has a power rating of 4 kW. What current flows through it when it is switched on?

64 A coil similar to the one in Figure 6.106 has an area of 5 cm² and rotates 50 times a second in a field of flux density 50 mT.

   (a) If the coil has 500 turns, calculate:
      (i) the angular velocity, ω.
      (ii) the maximum induced emf.
      (iii) the rms emf.
   (b) If the speed is reduced to 25 revolutions per second what is the new E_{rms}?

65 Calculate the resistance of a 1000 W light bulb designed to operate at 220 V.

Figure 6.111 A simple transformer.

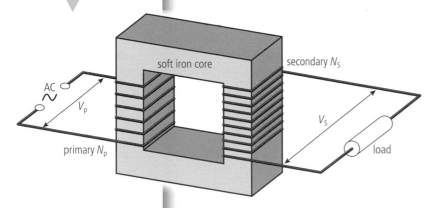

soft iron core
secondary N_S
AC
V_P
V_S
primary N_P
load

The transformer

A transformer consists of two coils wound on a common soft iron core as shown in Figure 6.111. The primary coil is connected to an AC supply. This causes a changing magnetic field inside the coil. This field is made stronger by the presence of the soft iron core which itself becomes magnetic (temporarily). Since the secondary is wound around the same former, it will have a changing magnetic field within it, which induces an emf in its coils.

The emf induced in the secondary is directly related to the number of turns. If the supply is sinusoidal then the ratio of turns in the two coils equals the ratio of the pds.

$$\frac{N_P}{N_S} = \frac{V_P}{V_S}$$

So a transformer can make a pd higher or lower depending on the ration of turns on the primary and secondary. However, since energy must be conserved, the power out cannot be bigger than the power in. Electrical power is given by $I \times V$ so if the pd goes up, the current must come down. An ideal transformer has an efficiency of 100%. This means that power in = power out.

$$V_P I_P = V_S I_S$$

where V_P, V_S, I_P, and I_S are the rms values of pd and current in the primary and secondary coils.

Warning

Figure 6.112.

The emf induced in the secondary coil depends on the rate of change of current in the primary. If you switch the current off then the change can be very big inducing a much bigger emf than you might have calculated.

Exercise

66 An ideal transformer steps down the 220 V mains to 4.5 V so it can be used to charge a mobile phone.

   (a) If the primary has 500 turns how many turns does the secondary have?
   (b) If the charger delivers 0.45 A to the phone, how much power does it deliver?
   (c) How much current flows into the charger from the mains?
   (d) The phone is unplugged from the charger but the charger is left plugged in. How much current flows into the charger now?

Power losses

Real transformers are not 100% efficient: energy is lost in several ways.

- **Joule heating:** The wires of both coils have resistance so as current flows energy will be lost as heat (I^2R). This depends on the current, which in turn depends on the resistance of the load connected to the secondary. These losses can be reduced by using low-resistance coils.
- **Eddy currents:** The changing B field in the metal core will induce currents in the core itself. These currents, called eddy currents because of their circular path, will cause the core to get hot, resulting in a loss of energy. Eddy currents can be reduced by making the core out of many insulated strips instead of a solid piece; this increases the resistance, thereby reducing the eddy currents.
- **Flux leakage:** Any flux leaking out of the transformer may also cause eddy currents in the surrounding metallic structure.
- **Magnetic hysteresis:** Magnetizing the core involves changing the direction of microscopic magnetic dipoles in the metal. This requires work to be done so energy is transferred. Using a core with easy-to-move dipoles reduces this loss.

Power transmission

As outlined previously, electrical energy can be produced by moving a coil in a magnetic field. The energy required to rotate the coil can come from many sources, for example: coal, oil, falling water, sunlight, waves in the sea, or nuclear fuel. The transformation of energy takes place in power stations that are often not sited close to the places where people live. For that reason, the electrical energy must be delivered via cables. These cables have resistance so some energy will be lost as the current flows through them. Let's take an example as illustrated in Figure 6.113.

The generators at a power station typically produce 100 MW of power at 30 kV. A small town 100 km from the power station requires electrical power which will be delivered via two aluminium cables that have a radius of 2 cm. The houses in the town cannot use such high voltage electricity so the pd must be stepped down to 220 V, using a transformer that we will assume is 100% efficient.

The first thing to do is to calculate the resistance of the cables. We can do this using the formula

$$R = \frac{\rho l}{A}$$

where r is the resistivity of aluminium ($2.6 \times 10^{-8}\,\Omega\,m$), A is the cross-sectional area and l is the length.

So
$$R = \frac{2.6 \times 10^{-8} \times 200 \times 10^3}{2\pi \times (2 \times 10^{-2})^2} = 2.1\,\Omega$$

The current that must be delivered if 100 MW is produced at a pd of 30 kV can be found using $P = IV$.

Rearranging gives
$$I = \frac{1 \times 10^8}{30 \times 10^3} = 3.3 \times 10^3\,A$$

The power loss in the cables is therefore $I^2R = (3.3 \times 10^3)^2 \times 2.1 = 22.9\,MW$

This is a lot of wasted power.

To reduce the power loss in the cables we must reduce the current. This can be done by stepping up the voltage before transmission, using a transformer as shown in Figure 6.114.

A transformer will only give an output when the input is changing, so transformers can only be used to step up alternating supplies. The voltage from a battery can be stepped up if it is repeatedly connected and disconnected from the transformer. This is the ticking that you might sometimes hear close to an electric fence.

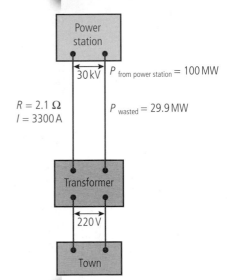

Figure 6.113.

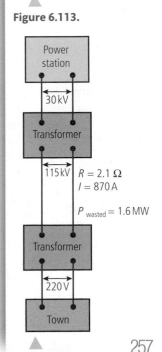

Figure 6.114.

High-voltage power lines.

The pd between the wires is typically stepped up to 115 kV. Let us now repeat the calculation, assuming all transformers are 100% efficient.

The power is now delivered at 115 kV so the current is

$$I = \frac{P}{V} = \frac{100 \times 10^6}{115 \times 10^3} = 870 \, A$$

Power loss in the cables $= I^2R = 870^2 \times 2.1 = 1.6 \, MW$.

This is still quite a lot of wasted power but much less than before.

To reduce this further, more cables could be added in parallel, thereby reducing the resistance.

Exercise

67 A power station that generates electricity at 50 kV produces 500 MW of power. This is delivered to a town through cables with a total resistance of 8 Ω. Before transmission, the pd is stepped up to 100 kV, then stepped down to 220 V at the town.

(a) How much current will flow through the cables that take the electricity away from the power station to the town?

(b) How much power is lost in the cables?

(c) What percentage of total power delivered is lost?

(d) How much power will be delivered to the town? (Assume both transformers are 100% efficient.)

(e) How much power will be available for the town to use?

(f) How much total current will flow through the town?

Rectification

One benefit of using AC for domestic electricity is that its voltage can be changed by using a transformer. However, some devices need a DC supply. Converting AC to DC is called *rectification*, and can be achieved using a diode bridge. A diode is a semiconductor device that only allows current to pass in one direction; the symbol shown in Figure 6.115 looks a bit like an arrow which points in the direction the current can go.

Figure 6.115 Symbol for a diode.

In an insulator all the electrons are fixed to individual atoms; in a conductor some electrons can move from one atom to another. For this to happen there must be some electrons that are able to move and somewhere for them to move to. A semiconductor has few free electrons so is not a good conductor, but it can be made to conduct better in two ways: either by adding impurity atoms (doping) with extra free electrons to create an N–type semiconductor or doping with an impurity with holes to accept electrons creating a P–type. This doesn't make the material charged, it only allows charges to move. A diode is made by doping one side of a semiconductor as P–type and the other N creating a PN junction where the two types meet. At the junction the electrons combine with the holes to create a region where there can be no conduction. The depletion layer is shown in Figure 6.116. This looks like the charges are the wrong way round but remember the N and P are not charged so when electrons move from the N to the P the N becomes *positive* and the P *negative*.

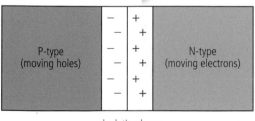

depletion layer
(electrons fill holes)

Figure 6.116 A PN junction.

When the junction is connected to a battery as shown in Figure 6.117(a) the holes flow from the P side recombining with the electrons of the depletion layer, and electrons recombine with holes on the N side. This removes the depletion layer allowing current to flow. This is called *forward bias*. If, however, the battery is connected the other way round, as in Figure 6.117(b), the depletion layer is expanded, preventing the flow of current.

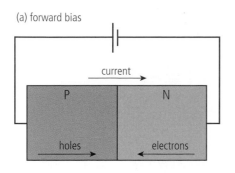

(a) forward bias

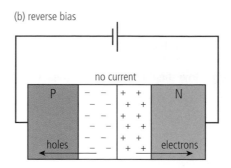

(b) reverse bias

Figure 6.117 PN junction with forward and reverse bias.

In forward bias, when electrons cross the junction from N to P they fill a hole which allows the current to flow through the P. When the electron fills a hole it loses energy. This can be released as light, which is how an LED works.

Characteristics of a PN junction

The relationship between the current flowing through a PN junction and the pd across it is represented graphically in Figure 6.118.

In forward bias there needs to be a small pd to separate the electrons and holes in the depletion layer. Once this has been exceeded the current is proportional to the pd. In reverse bias there is a small leakage of current due to the presence of some electrons in the P and some holes in the N (minority carriers) but this is negligible. When the reverse bias pd gets large the semiconductor breaks down and the diode starts to conduct.

Figure 6.118 The *I-V* characteristic curve for a diode.

Half-wave rectification

If a single diode is connected in series with a resistor as shown in Figure 6.119 the current can only pass in the direction of the arrow so only half of the cycle will be transmitted.

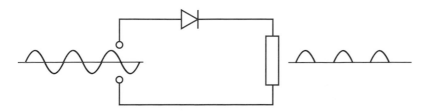

Figure 6.119 A half-wave rectifier.

Full-wave rectification

A diode bridge is a network of diodes like the one in Figure 6.120.

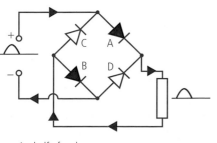

1st half of cycle

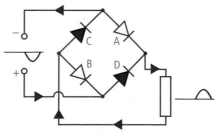

2nd half of cycle

Figure 6.120 Full-wave rectification.

To learn more about power generation and transmission, go to the hotlinks site, search for the title or ISBN and click on Chapter 6.

As can be seen in Figure 6.120, during the first half of the cycle diodes A and B conduct, and in the second half C and D. The result is that current always passes through the resistor in the same direction.

Investigation of a diode bridge circuit

To measure how the signal is changed by a diode bridge circuit you need to measure how the pd across the load changes with time. If the signal was changing slowly enough you could use a voltmeter but it is much more convenient to use a data logger to record the signal at regular intervals. If you have two voltage sensors you could directly compare the input signal with the output. When measuring alternating signals with a data logger you must pay attention to the sampling rate. This must be much greater than the frequency of the signal; if not you will not be able to see the correct waveform.

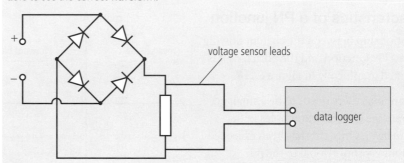

Figure 6.121 Diode bridge investigation.

NATURE OF SCIENCE

The rate at which charge flows off a capacitor is proportional to the amount of charge on the capacitor. This leads to an exponential relationship between the charge and time. This is the first time we have come across an exponential relationship but it won't be the last.

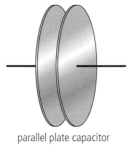

parallel plate capacitor

capacitor symbol

▲
Figure 6.122 Parallel plate capacitor and symbol.

6.7 Capacitance

11.3 Capacitance

Understandings, applications, and skills:

(AHL) Capacitance
- Solving problems involving parallel plate capacitors.
- Determining the energy stored in a charged capacitor.

   Guidance
   - *Only single parallel plate capacitors providing a uniform electric field, in series with a load, need to be considered (edge effect will be neglected).*

(AHL) Dielectric materials
- Describing the effect of different dielectric materials on capacitance.

(AHL) Capacitors in series and parallel

(AHL) Resistor–capacitor (RC) series circuits
- Solving problems involving the discharge of a capacitor at a constant current and through a fixed resistor.

   Guidance
   - *Problems involving the discharge of capacitors through fixed resistors need to be treated both graphically and algebraically.*
   - *Problems involving the charging of a capacitor will only be treated graphically.*

(AHL) Time constant
- Solving problems involving the time constant of an RC circuit for charge, voltage, and current.

   Guidance
   - *Derivation of the charge, voltage, and current equations as a function of time is not required.*

A simple capacitor can be made out of two parallel plates separated by a small air gap. The symbol for a capacitor as shown in Figure 6.122 reflects this.

When connected to a battery, charge will flow from the battery onto the plates but cannot cross the gap between them. Charge will collect on the plates until the pd between them is equal to the emf of the battery. The capacitance is defined as the ratio of the charge on the plates to the pd between them:

$$C = \frac{Q}{V}$$

The unit of capacitance is the farad (F).

Capacitance of a parallel plate capacitor

To understand how the dimensions of the plates relate to the capacitance let us consider a capacitor with movable plates connected to a battery as shown in Figure 6.123. First, let us change the separation of the plates as in Figure 6.124.

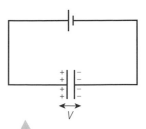

Figure 6.123 A capacitor charged by a battery.

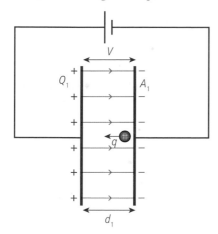 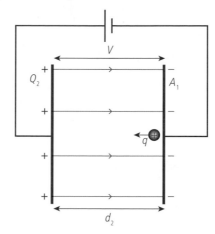

Figure 6.124 The plates of a capacitor are pulled apart.

In both cases the capacitor is connected to the same battery so the pd is the same. Pd is defined as the amount of work done per unit charge in taking a small test charge q from one plate to the other. Now, work done = force × distance but if the field between the plates is E the force is Eq so work done = Eqd.

So for each case pd,

$$W = E_1 q d_1 = E_2 q d_2$$

$$\frac{E_1}{E_2} = \frac{d_1}{d_2}$$

$$E \propto \frac{1}{d}$$

So if d is increased E must decrease.

A decrease in E implies that the field lines will be further apart which means the charge on the plates is less, as shown in Figure 6.124.

So

$$Q \propto \frac{1}{d}$$

now

$$\text{capacitance} = \frac{Q}{V}$$

so

$$C \propto \frac{1}{d}$$

In a similar way, we can show that changing the area of the plates will also result in less charge. As shown in Figure 6.125, if the pd is constant then the work done moving each charge must be the same. This means the field strength must be the same, which implies that there must be less charge on the smaller plates.

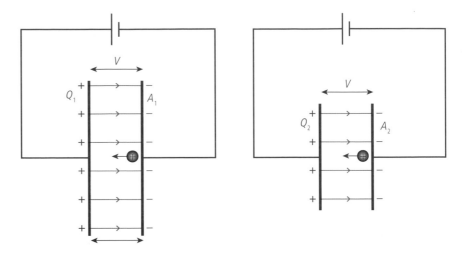

Figure 6.125 The area of the plates of a capacitor is reduced.

So we find that $C \propto \dfrac{A}{d}$.

The constant of proportionality is related to the material placed between the plates. For a vacuum it is the permittivity of a vacuum ε_0 ($8.85 \times 10^{-12}\,\text{F}\,\text{m}^{-1}$):

$$C = \frac{\varepsilon_0 A}{d}$$

Dielectric constant

Putting a dielectric material in the gap between the plates can increase the capacitance. This happens because dielectrics have polar molecules that line up with the field as shown in Figure 6.126.

This time the capacitor is charged by a battery and then isolated so the charge on the plates cannot change. When the dielectric is placed between the plates the charges line up so the negative charge moves towards the positive plate, and the positive charge moves towards the negative plate. This has the effect of reducing the potential of the positive plate and increasing the potential of the negative plate. This results in a reduction in the pd between the plates. Now $C = \dfrac{Q}{V}$ so reducing V will increase the capacitance.

The dielectric constant, ε_r is defined by the equation:

$$\varepsilon_r = \frac{\text{capacitance with dielectric}}{\text{capacitance without dielectric}} = \frac{C_2}{C_1}$$

The capacitance C of a parallel plate capacitor with dielectric is now:

$$C = \frac{\varepsilon_r \varepsilon_0 A}{d}.$$

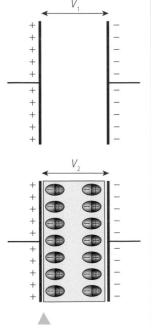

Figure 6.126 Parallel plate capacitor with and without a dielectric.

Exercises

68 Calculate the capacitance of a parallel plate capacitor made of two circular plates with 10 cm radius separated by an air gap of 0.5 cm.

69 A 1 mm thick sheet of plastic is now placed between the plates and the plates adjusted so there is no air gap between them and the plastic. If the dielectric constant of the plastic is 4, calculate the capacitance.

70 A capacitor is made by sandwiching a 0.1 mm sheet of plastic (dielectric constant 5) between two sheets of aluminium foil of size 1 cm × 200 cm which is then rolled into a cylinder. Calculate its capacitance.

71 Calculate the charge stored on a 2 µF capacitor connected to a 6 V battery.

Capacitors in series

To calculate the combined capacitance of two capacitors in series consider the situation shown in Figure 6.127.

When this circuit is connected electrons flow from the battery to the plates of the two capacitors. Notice that the right plate of C_1 and the left plate of C_2 are isolated from the battery. The only way that electrons can get onto the right plate of C_1 is if they have come from C_2, this means that the charge (Q) on each capacitor is equal.

The total charge stored on this combination is Q and the potential difference is V so the total capacitance of the combination $C_{series} = \frac{Q}{V}$.

Since energy is conserved we can say that the pd across the combination is equal to the sum of the pds across each capacitor so:

$$V = V_1 + V_2.$$

Substituting for V from the definition of capacitance gives:

$$\frac{Q}{C_{series}} = \frac{Q}{C_1} + \frac{Q}{C_2}$$

so the total capacitance is given by the formula:

$$\frac{1}{C_{series}} = \frac{1}{C_1} + \frac{1}{C_2}$$

Adding capacitors in series is rather like increasing the separation of the plates, it *reduces* the total capacitance.

Capacitors in parallel

When capacitors are placed in parallel the pd across each is the same but the charge different as shown in Figure 6.128.

The charge on each capacitor will depend on the capacitance so $Q_1 = C_1V$ and $Q_2 = C_2V$.

If the total charge is Q then the capacitance of the combination will be $C_{parallel} = \frac{Q}{V}$.

Charge is conserved so the total charge stored on the combination is equal to the sum of the charges on each:

$$Q = Q_1 + Q_2$$

Substituting for Q from the definition of capacitance gives:

$$C_{parallel}V = C_1V + C_2V$$

So the total capacitance is given by the formula:

$$C_{parallel} = C_1 + C_2$$

Adding capacitors in parallel is like increasing the surface area of the plates: it increases the capacitance.

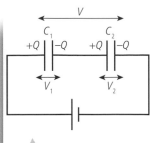

Figure 6.127.

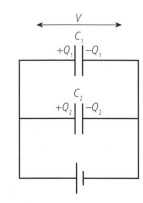

Figure 6.128.

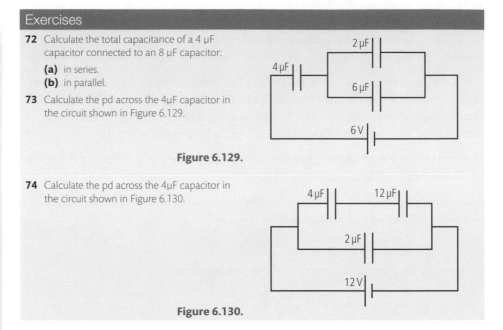

72 Calculate the total capacitance of a 4 μF capacitor connected to an 8 μF capacitor:

(a) in series.
(b) in parallel.

73 Calculate the pd across the 4μF capacitor in the circuit shown in Figure 6.129.

Figure 6.129.

74 Calculate the pd across the 4μF capacitor in the circuit shown in Figure 6.130.

Figure 6.130.

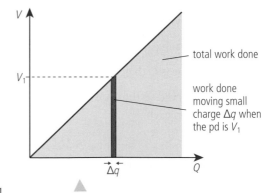

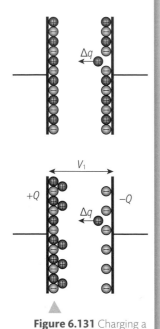

Figure 6.131 Charging a capacitor by moving charges.

Energy stored in a capacitor

To put charge on the plates of a capacitor requires work to be done so energy must be stored. To calculate the amount of work, let us consider the process of charging a capacitor by moving small charges $+\Delta q$ one at a time from one plate to the other as shown in Figure 6.131. This isn't the way charges move when a capacitor is connected to a battery but will require the same amount of energy.

At the beginning the plates are not charged so contain equal positive and negative charges. Once the first charge is moved off the plate there will be a small E field between the plates so a small amount of work will have to be done. As each charge is moved the field gets bigger so the work done is more.

If the pd between the plates is V_1 then the work done to move the small charge is $V_1\Delta q$. To calculate the total work done we can use the area under the V–Q graph.

Figure 6.132 Graph of V vs Q when charging a capacitor.

The total work done $= \frac{1}{2}QV$ which, since energy is conserved, will equal the energy stored on the capacitor.

Substituting for $Q = CV$ we get $E = \frac{1}{2}CV^2$

or substituting for $V = \frac{Q}{C}$ gives $E = \frac{Q^2}{2C}$

To summarize:

$$\text{Energy stored in a capacitor} = \frac{1}{2}QV = \frac{1}{2}CV^2 = \frac{Q^2}{2C}$$

75 Calculate the amount of energy stored in a 5 µF capacitor connected to a 9 V battery.

76 A parallel plate capacitor is made of two circular plates with 10 cm radius separated by an air gap of 0.2 cm. The plates are charged by connecting to a 6 V battery and then isolated (the battery is removed but the charge stays on the plates). Calculate:

    (a) the capacitance.

    (b) the charge on the plates.

    (c) the energy stored.

    (d) if the plates are now pulled apart so the gap becomes 0.4 cm, how much energy will be stored? Explain the change in stored energy.

77 Calculate the pd across a 100 nF capacitor with 50 electrons stored on the plates.

CHALLENGE YOURSELF

3 A 2 µF capacitor is charged by connecting to a 12 V battery. The battery is disconnected and the capacitor is connected to an uncharged 4 µF capacitor. Calculate the change in energy stored.

Charging a capacitor

We don't normally charge a capacitor by moving charges from one plate to the other, we connect it in a circuit to a battery as in Figure 6.133. Note that in order to give a true representation of a real situation the circuit has resistance.

When the switch is closed (switched on) current will flow as charge moves onto the plates of the capacitor. This can't happen instantly but takes some time. Figure 6.134 shows the situation a short time after the switch is closed.

When the switch is first closed there is no charge on the capacitor so the equation for the circuit is simply $\varepsilon = V_R = IR$.

As charge flows onto the plates of the capacitor the pd across the capacitor increases so $\varepsilon = V_R + V_c$.

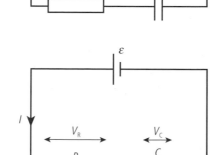

Figure 6.133 Circuit for charging a capacitor through a resistor.

Figure 6.134 The capacitor gains charge.

Here we are applying Kirchhoff's second law to the circuit:

the sum of the emfs = the sum of the pds.

This results in a smaller pd across R so the current in the circuit must be less.

As the charge on the capacitor increases, the current becomes less until the pd across the capacitor $V_c = \varepsilon$. This means that $V_R = 0$ so no current flows.

If we plot the current in the circuit against time we get an exponential decay graph as shown in Figure 6.135.

The equation of this curve is:

$$I = I_0 e^{-\frac{t}{\tau}}$$

τ is the *time constant*. If τ has a large value the charging is slow. We can see that if the resistance in the circuit is large then the initial current will be small so it will take a long time for the capacitor to reach full charge. Also, if the value of the capacitance is high then it will require a lot of charge to be transferred to the plates before the pd equals the battery emf.

In fact $\tau = RC$ which means that resistance × capacitance has the same units as time.

$R = \frac{V}{I}$ and $C = \frac{Q}{V}$ so $RC = \frac{QV}{IV} = \frac{Q}{I}$ which is time.

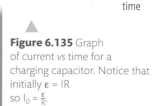

Figure 6.135 Graph of current *vs* time for a charging capacitor. Notice that initially $\varepsilon = IR$ so $I_0 = \frac{\varepsilon}{R}$.

After a time equal to RC the current flowing will be $I_0 e^{-1}$ which is about $\frac{1}{3}$ of the original current.

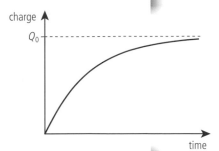

▲ **Figure 6.136** Graph of charge vs time for a charging capacitor.

Let us now consider how the charge on the capacitor varies with time. When the switch is first closed the charge on the capacitor is zero. We know that the current at the beginning is at the maximum so charge increases rapidly. As time progresses the rate at which charge increases gets less and less as it approaches its maximum value. The graph of charge against time is shown in Figure 6.136.

The equation of this line is $Q = Q_0 (1 - e^{-\frac{t}{RC}})$ where Q_0 is the charge when fully charged.

Since V is proportional to Q the graph of pd against time for charging a capacitor would have the same shape,

$$V = V_0 (1 - e^{-\frac{t}{RC}}).$$

To find out how much charge the capacitor will have after a time equal to RC we can substitute $t = RC$ into the equation. This gives that $Q = Q_0(1 - e^{-1})$, which is about $\frac{2}{3}$ of the final charge.

Discharging a capacitor

After a capacitor has been charged it can be disconnected from the battery. The charge will be stored in the capacitor until a device is connected across its terminals. In Figure 6.137 we consider a capacitor discharged through a resistor.

Immediately after the switch is closed, current will flow from the capacitor through the resistor. The initial current will be $I_0 = \frac{V_0}{R}$ where V_0 is the pd across the capacitor when fully charged.

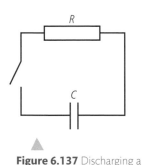

▲ **Figure 6.137** Discharging a capacitor through a resistor.

As time progresses, the charge on the capacitor will decrease resulting in a lower pd across the resistor and hence less current. From this we can deduce that the current $(\frac{dQ}{dt})$ is proportional to the charge (Q) on the capacitor which leads to an exponential relationship between charge and time.

$$Q = Q_0 e^{-\frac{t}{RC}}$$

As in the case of charging, the time taken for the capacitor to discharge is related to RC. When the time is equal to RC the charge remaining on the capacitor, $Q = Q_0 e^{-1}$ which is about $\frac{1}{3}$ of the original charge.

Applying Kirchhoff's second law to the circuit, $0 = V_R + V_C$ so $V_C = -V_R$.

But $V_c = \frac{Q}{C}$ and $V_R = IR$

so $\frac{Q}{C} = -IR$

$Q = -RCI$.

Now, I is the rate of change of charge, so

$Q = -RC\frac{dQ}{dt}$.

The solution of this equation between time, 0, when the charge was Q_0 and time t when it was Q is:

$Q = Q_0 e^{-\frac{t}{RC}}$.

At some point you will learn how to do this in maths.

▲ **Figure 6.138** Graph of charge vs time for two different values of RC.

Figure 6.138 shows the graphs of charge against time for the same 0.2 mF capacitor discharged through two different resistors, one with resistance 5 kΩ giving an RC value of 1 s and the other 10 kΩ giving an RC value of 2 s.

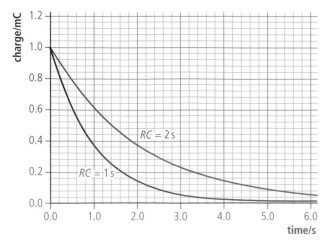

Variation of pd with time

From the definition of capacitance $Q = CV$ so substituting for Q we get:

$$CV = CV_0 e^{-\frac{t}{RC}}$$

C is constant, so

$$V = V_0 e^{-\frac{t}{RC}}$$

Taking the same values as in the previous example where a $0.2\,\text{mF}$ capacitor was discharged through a $5\,\text{k}\Omega$ resistor, we can see from the graph in Figure 6.138 that the original charge $Q_o = 1\,\text{mC}$ so the pd across the capacitance can be found from $V_0 = \frac{Q_0}{C} = \frac{1}{0.2} = 5\,\text{V}$. The graph of pd against time is shown in Figure 6.139.

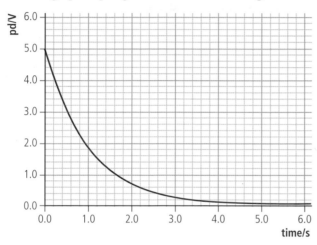

Figure 6.139.

Variation of current with time

The current in the circuit can be found from $I = \frac{V}{R}$. Since the pd is the same for R and C we can substitute for V in the equation:

$$V = V_0 e^{-\frac{t}{RC}}$$

to get

$$IR = I_0 R e^{-\frac{t}{RC}}$$

so

$$I = I_0 e^{-\frac{t}{RC}}$$

If $V_0 = 5\,\text{V}$ and $R = 5\,\text{k}\Omega$ then $I_0 = \frac{5}{5} \times 10^3 = 1\,\text{mA}$ so the graph of I against time will be as shown in Figure 6.140.

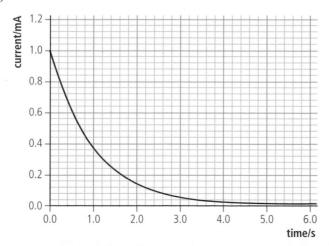

Figure 6.140 Graph of current *vs* time for a discharging capacitor.

Exercises

78 A 5 mF capacitor is charged to 10 V and then discharged through a 10 kΩ resistor. Calculate:

    (a) the time constant.
    (b) the charge on the capacitor when fully charged.
    (c) the pd across the plates after discharging for 20 s.
    (d) the initial current when starting to discharge.
    (e) the time taken for the current to get to half the initial value.

79 A 10 μF capacitor is charged through a 1 Ω resistor by a 5 V battery.

    (a) Will the capacitor be fully charged after 1 s?
    (b) If the capacitor is discharged through a 0.5 MΩ resistor what will the initial current be?
    (c) Calculate the pd after 2 s of discharging.

Simulation of discharge using a spreadsheet

It is quite difficult to visualize how changing the components will affect the time it takes to charge a capacitor. Using a spreadsheet (see Figure 6.141) we can use the equation to calculate the charge at different times, and plot graphs for varying values of R and C.

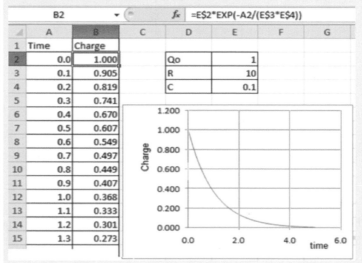

Figure 6.141.

First a table with a column for time and charge is made. Then the time column is filled with some values; in the example 0–5 in steps of 0.1 was used. To specify the values of R and C a separate table is made that just contains these values plus a value for the initial charge. In the example $Q_0 = 1$ C, $R = 10\ \Omega$, and $C = 0.1$ F. This gives a time constant of 1 s so the capacitor will lose significant charge within the 5 s time period chosen.

The charge is then calculated using the formula

$$Q = Q_0 e^{-\frac{t}{RC}}$$

Note the use of $ in the cell address. Writing E$2 means that when the formula is copied down, the number of the cell doesn't change.

Once the spreadsheet is set up the values of R and C can be varied to see what happens to the curve.

Smoothing

The idea of rectifying is to change an AC signal in to a DC one. However, the output from a full-wave rectifier is far from constant, as Figure 6.142 shows.

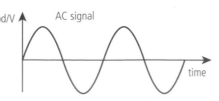
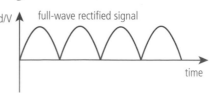

Figure 6.142 Full-wave rectified AC.

The signal can be *smoothed* by adding a parallel capacitor to the output of the rectifier as in Figure 6.143. During the first part of the cycle the capacitor becomes charged, then as the pd of the rectified signal falls, the capacitor discharges through the load. The time taken for the capacitor to discharge depends on the value of *RC* so if this is sufficiently big the time taken for the discharge will be long, maintaining the pd across the load resistor as shown by the darker red line in Figure 6.143.

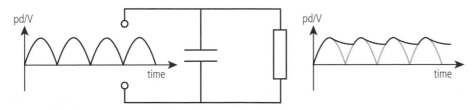

> When charging, the current doesn't flow through the resistor so the time for charging is much less than the time for discharging.

Figure 6.143 A capacitor smoothes the pd across the load resistor.

Practice questions

1. This question is about electrical energy and associated phenomena.

   Current electricity

   A cell of electromotive force (emf) *E* and internal resistance *r* is connected in series with a resistor R, as shown in Figure 6.144.

   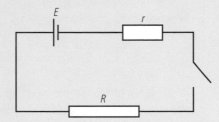

   Figure 6.144.

   The cell supplies 8.1×10^3 J of energy when 5.8×10^3 C of charge moves completely round the circuit. The current in the circuit is constant.

   (i) Calculate the emf *E* of the cell. (2)

   (ii) The resistor R has resistance $6.0\,\Omega$. The potential difference between its terminals is 1.2 V. Determine the internal resistance *r* of the cell. (3)

   (iii) Calculate the total energy transfer in the resistor R. (2)

   (iv) Describe, in terms of a simple model of electrical conduction, the mechanism by which the energy transfer in the resistor R takes place. (5)

   (Total 12 marks)

2. This question is about a filament lamp.

   (a) Copy Figure 6.145 and on the axes draw a sketch-graph to show the variation with potential difference *V* of the current *I* in a typical filament lamp (the *I–V* characteristic). (***Note:*** *this is a sketch-graph; you do not need to add any values to the axes.*) (1)

   Figure 6.145.

   (b) (i) Explain how the resistance of the filament is determined from the graph. (1)

(ii) Explain whether the graph you have sketched indicates ohmic behaviour or non-ohmic behaviour. (1)

A filament lamp operates at maximum brightness when connected to a 6.0 V supply. At maximum brightness, the current in the filament is 120 mA.

(c) (i) Calculate the resistance of the filament when it is operating at maximum brightness. (1)

(ii) You have available a 24 V supply and a collection of resistors of a suitable power rating and with different values of resistance. Calculate the resistance of the resistor that is required to be connected in series with the supply such that the voltage across the filament lamp will be 6.0 V. (2)

(Total 6 marks)

3. This question is about electric circuits.

Susan sets up the circuit shown in Figure 6.146 in order to measure the current–voltage (*I*–*V*) characteristic of a small filament lamp.

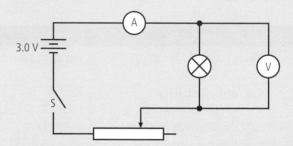

Figure 6.146.

The supply is a battery that has an emf of 3.0 V, and the ammeter and voltmeter are considered to be ideal. The lamp is labelled by the manufacturer as '3 volts, 0.6 watts'.

(a) (i) Explain what information this labelling provides about the normal operation of the lamp. (2)

(ii) Calculate the current in the filament of the lamp when it is operating at normal brightness. (2)

Susan sets the variable resistor to its maximum value of resistance. She then closes the switch S and records the following readings.

Ammeter reading = 0.18 A	Voltmeter reading = 0.60 V

She then sets the variable resistor to its zero value of resistance and records the following readings.

Ammeter reading = 0.20 A	Voltmeter reading = 2.6 V

(b) (i) Explain why, by changing the value of the resistance of the variable resistance, the potential difference across the lamp cannot be reduced to zero or be increased to 3.0 V. (2)

(ii) Determine the internal resistance of the battery. (3)

(c) Calculate the resistance of the filament when the reading on the voltmeter is

(i) 0.60 V. (1)

(ii) 2.6 V. (1)

(d) Explain why there is a difference between your answers to (c)(i) and (c)(ii). (2)

(e) Copy Figure 6.147 and on the axes, draw a sketch-graph of the *I–V* characteristic of the filament of the lamp. (***Note:*** *this is a sketch-graph; you do not need to add any values to the axis.*) (1)

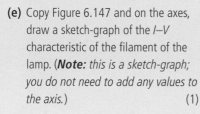

Figure 6.147.

Figure 6.148 shows an alternative circuit for varying the potential difference across the lamp.

Figure 6.148.

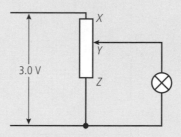

The potential divider XZ has a potential of 3.0 V across it. When the contact is at the position Y, the resistance of XY equals the resistance of YZ which equals 12 Ω. The resistance of the lamp is 4 Ω.

(f) Calculate the potential difference across the lamp. (4)

(*Total 18 marks*)

4. This question is about emf and internal resistance.
A dry cell has an emf *E* and internal resistance *r*, and is connected to an external circuit. There is a current *I* in the circuit when the potential difference across the terminals of the cell is *V* (see Figure 6.149).

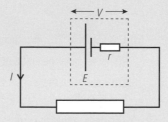

Figure 6.149.

(a) State expressions, in terms of *E*, *V*, *r*, and *I* where appropriate, for

    (i) the total power supplied by the cell. (1)

    (ii) the power dissipated in the cell. (1)

    (iii) the power dissipated in the external circuit. (1)

(b) Use your answers to (a) to derive a relationship between *V*, *E*, *I*, and *r*. (2)

Figure 6.150 shows the variation of V with I for the dry cell.

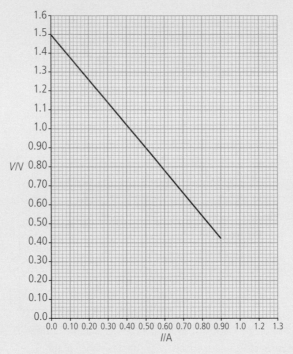

Figure 6.150.

(c) Copy and complete Figure 6.151 to show the circuit that could be used to obtain the data from which the graph in Figure 6.150 was plotted. (3)

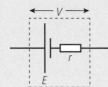

Figure 6.151.

(d) Use Figure 6.150, explaining your answers, to

  (i) determine the emf E of the cell. (2)

  (ii) determine the current in the external circuit when the resistance R of the external circuit is very small. (2)

  (iii) deduce that the internal resistance r of the cell is about $1.2\,\Omega$. (3)

(e) The maximum power dissipated in the external circuit occurs when the resistance of the external circuit has the same value as the internal resistance of the cell. Calculate the maximum power dissipation in the external circuit. (3)

(Total 18 marks)

5. This question is about the possibility of generating electrical power using a satellite orbiting the Earth.

(a) Define *gravitational field strength*. (2)

(b) Use the definition of gravitational field strength to deduce that

$$GM = g_0 R_2$$

where M is the mass of the Earth, R its radius and g_0 is the gravitational field strength at the surface of the Earth. (You may assume that the Earth is a uniform sphere with its mass concentrated at its centre.) (2)

A space shuttle orbits the Earth and a small satellite is launched from the shuttle. The satellite carries a conducting cable connecting the satellite to the shuttle. When the satellite is a distance L from the shuttle, the cable is held straight by motors on the satellite (see Figure 6.152).

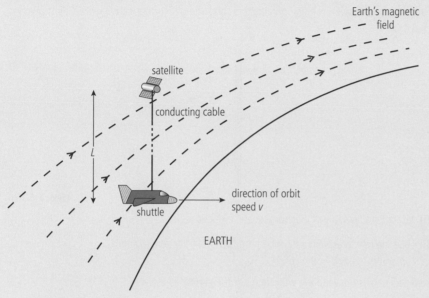

Figure 6.152.

As the shuttle orbits the Earth with speed v, the conducting cable is moving at right angles to the Earth's magnetic field. The magnetic field vector $\mathbf{B}$ makes an angle θ to a line perpendicular to the conducting cable as shown in Figure 6.153. The velocity vector of the shuttle is directed out of the plane of the paper.

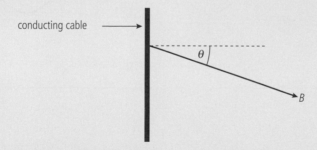

Figure 6.153.

(c) Copy Figure 6.153 and draw an arrow to show the direction of the magnetic force on an electron in the conducting cable. Label the arrow F. (1)

(d) State an expression for the force F on the electron in terms of B, v, e, and θ, where B is the magnitude of the magnetic field strength, and e is the electron charge. (1)

(e) Hence deduce an expression for the emf E induced in the conducting wire. (3)

(f) The shuttle is in an orbit that is 300 km above the surface of the Earth. Using the expression

$$GM = g_0 R_2$$

and given that $R = 6.4 \times 10^6$ m and $g_0 = 10\,\text{N kg}^{-1}$, deduce that the orbital speed v of the satellite is $7.8 \times 10^3\,\text{m s}^{-1}$. (3)

(g) The magnitude of the magnetic field strength is 6.3×10^{-6} T and the angle $\theta = 20°$.
Estimate the length L of the cable required in order to generate an emf of 1 kV. (2)

(Total 14 marks)

6. This question is about electromagnetic induction.

A small coil is placed with its plane parallel to a long straight current-carrying wire, as shown in Figure 6.154.

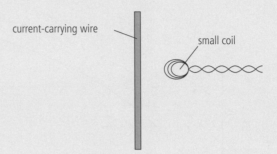

current-carrying wire

small coil

Figure 6.154.

(a) (i) State Faraday's law of electromagnetic induction. (2)

(ii) Use the law to explain why, when the current in the wire changes, an emf is induced in the coil. (1)

Figure 6.155 shows the variation with time t of the current in the wire.

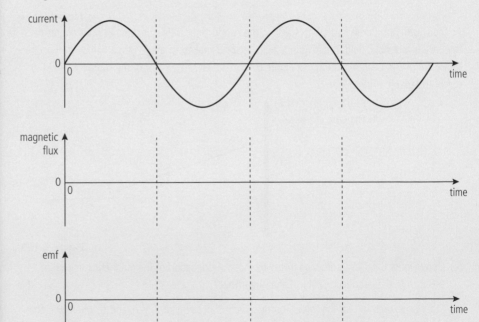

Figure 6.155.

(b) (i) Draw, copying the axes provided in Figure 6.155, a sketch-graph to show the variation with time t of the magnetic flux in the coil. (1)

(ii) Construct, copying the axes provided in Figure 6.155, a sketch-graph to show the variation with time t of the emf induced in the coil. (2)

(iii) State and explain the effect on the maximum emf induced in the coil when the coil is further away from the wire. (2)

(c) Such a coil may be used to measure large alternating currents in a high-voltage cable. Identify **one** advantage and **one** disadvantage of this method. (2)

(Total 10 marks)

7. A resistor is connected in series with an alternating current supply of negligible internal resistance. The **peak value** of the supply voltage is V_0 and the **peak value** of the current in the resistor is V_0. The average power dissipation in the resistor is

A $\dfrac{V_0 I_0}{2}$ 　　　 B $\dfrac{V_0 I_0}{\sqrt{2}}$ 　　　 C $V_0 I_0$ 　　　 D $2V_0 I_0$ (1)

8. The rms voltages across the primary and secondary coils in an ideal transformer are V_p and V_s respectively. The currents in the primary and secondary coils are I_p and I_s respectively. Which one of the following statements is always true?

A $V_s = V_p$ 　　　 B $I_s = I_p$ 　　　 C $V_s I_s = V_p I_p$ 　　　 D $\dfrac{V_s}{V_p} = \dfrac{I_s}{I_p}$ (1)

07

Atomic, nuclear, and particle physics

Essential ideas

7.1 Discrete energy and radioactivity
In the microscopic world energy is discrete.

7.2 Nuclear reactions
Energy can be released in nuclear decays and reactions as a result of the relationship between mass and energy.

7.3 The structure of matter
It is believed that all the matter around us is made up of fundamental particles called quarks and leptons. It is known that matter has a hierarchical structure with quarks making up nucleons, nucleons making up nuclei, nuclei and electrons making up atoms, and atoms making up molecules. In this hierarchical structure, the smallest scale is seen for quarks and leptons (10^{-18} m).

12.1 The interaction of matter with radiation (HL only)
The microscopic quantum world offers a range of phenomena whose interpretation and explanation require new ideas and concepts not found in the classical world.

12.2 Nuclear physics (HL only)
The idea of discreteness that we met in the atomic world continues to exist in the nuclear world as well.

NATURE OF SCIENCE

The way Thomson, Rutherford, Bohr, and Schrödinger adapted the atomic model in the light of new experimental evidence is a good example of how scientific theories develop. It also required a significant paradigm shift to think of particles as having wave-like properties. Atomic models must be consistent with other laws. It is no use having a theory that predicts correct atomic spectral lines if it disagrees with the laws of electromagnetism. The photoelectric effect cannot be explained treating light as a wave, so the results of experiments to measure the energy of photoelectrons led to a whole new theory of light. If these measurements had not been made accurately enough this pattern would not have been revealed.

7.1 Discrete energy and the interaction of matter with radiation

7.1 Discrete energy and radioactivity

Understandings, applications, and skills:

Discrete energy and discrete energy levels
• Describing the emission and absorption spectrum of common gases.
Transitions between energy levels
• Solving problems involving atomic spectra, including calculating the wavelength of photons emitted during atomic transitions.

Inside the target chamber of a fusion reactor. Although not viable yet this could be the solution to future energy needs.

12.1 The interaction of matter with radiation

Understandings, applications, and skills:

(AHL) Photons
(AHL) The photoelectric effect
- Discussing the photoelectric effect experiment and explaining which features of the experiment cannot be explained by the classical wave theory of light.
- Solving photoelectric problems both graphically and algebraically.

(AHL) Matter waves
- Discussing experimental evidence for matter waves, including an experiment in which the wave nature of electrons is evident.
- Describing a scattering experiment including location of minimum intensity for the diffracted particles based on their de Broglie wavelength.

Guidance
- *The small angle approximation is usually not appropriate to use to determine the location of the minimum intensity.*

(AHL) Pair production and annihilation
(AHL) Quantization of angular momentum in the Bohr model for hydrogen
(AHL) The wave function
(AHL) The uncertainty principle for energy and time, and position and momentum
- Stating order of magnitude estimates from the uncertainty principle.

Guidance
- *The order of magnitude estimates from the uncertainty principle may include (but are not limited to) estimates of the energy of the ground state of an atom, the impossibility of an electron existing within a nucleus and the lifetime of an electron in an excited energy state.*

(AHL) Tunnelling and potential barrier and factors affecting tunnelling probability

Guidance
- *Tunnelling to be treated qualitatively using the idea of continuity of wave functions.*

12.2 Nuclear physics

Understandings, applications, and skills:

(AHL) Rutherford scattering and nuclear radius

The arrangement of charge in the atom

We already know that matter is made up of particles (atoms) and we used this model to explain the thermal properties of matter. We also used the idea that matter contains charges to explain electrical properties. Since matter contains charge and is made of atoms, it seems logical that atoms must contain charge. But how is this charge arranged?

There are many possible ways that charges could be arranged in the atom, but since atoms are not themselves charged, they must contain equal amounts of positive and negative. Maybe half the atom is positive and half negative, or perhaps the atom is made of two smaller particles of opposite charge?

The discovery of the electron by J.J. Thomson in 1897 added a clue that helps to solve the puzzle. The electron is a small negative particle that is responsible for carrying charge when current flows in a conductor. By measuring the charge-to-mass ratio of the electron, Thomson realised that the electrons were very small compared to the whole atom. He therefore proposed a possible arrangement for the charges as shown in Figure 7.1; this model was called the 'plum pudding' model. This model was accepted for some time until, under the direction of Ernest Rutherford, Geiger and Marsden performed an experiment that proved it could not be correct.

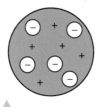

Figure 7.1 Thomson's model, positive pudding with negative plums.

What does it mean when we say we know these things? Do we know that this is true, or is it just the model that's true?

TOK

The electron is a fundamental particle with a charge of -1.6×10^{-19} C and a mass of 9.1×10^{-31} kg.

Scattering experiments

The problem with trying to find out what is inside an atom is that the atom is far too small to see, it is a bit like trying to find out what is inside a box without opening it. One way to do this would be to shoot something into the box and measure what comes out.

Imagine you have four identical boxes and each one contains one of the following: a large steel ball, a glass ball, air or sand. You have to find out what is inside the boxes without opening them. One way of doing this is to fire a bullet at each. Here are the results:

1. Shattering sound, contents – glass ball
2. Bounces back, contents – steel ball
3. Passes straight through, contents – air
4. Doesn't pass through, contents – sand

Different situations need different projectiles. If, for example, one box contained a large cube then a projectile smaller than the cube would be fine. If the big cube is made out of smaller cubes you will need a projectile so small that it can pass between the cubes or one with so much energy that it will knock some of the small cubes out of the box.

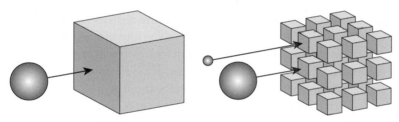

Figure 7.2 To see small detail we need to use a small projectile.

The Rutherford model

Rutherford's idea was to shoot alpha particles at a very thin sheet of gold to see what would happen. In 1909, when this was happening, very little was known about alpha particles – only that they were fast and positive. In accordance with normal scientific practice, Rutherford would have applied the model of the day so as to predict the result of the experiment. The current model was that the atom was like a small plum pudding, so a sheet of gold foil would be like a wall of plum puddings, a few puddings thick. Shooting alpha particles at the gold foil would be like firing bullets at a wall of plum puddings. If we think what would happen to the bullets and puddings, it will help us to predict what will happen to the alpha particles.

If you shoot a bullet at a plum pudding, it will pass straight through and out the other side. What actually happened was, as expected, most alpha particles passed through without changing direction, but a significant, number were deflected and a few even came right back, as shown in Figure 7.2. This was so unexpected that Rutherford said 'It was quite the most incredible event that ever happened to me in my life. It was almost as incredible as if you had fired a 15-inch shell at a piece of tissue paper and it came back and hit you.' We know from our study of collisions that you can only get a ball to bounce off another one if the second ball is much heavier than the first. This means that there must be something heavy in the atom. The fact that most alphas pass

TOK

This is an example of how scientists use experimental evidence to build models of things they can't see. Note that in these examples you don't just need a bullet, you also need a detector. What if you didn't notice the sound of breaking glass? You would have to have some idea that this was going to happen or you might not have been listening.

through means that there must be a lot of space. If we put these two findings together, we conclude that the atom must have something heavy and small within it. This small, heavy thing isn't an electron since they are too light; it must therefore be the positive part of the atom. This would explain why the alphas come back, since they are also positive and would be repelled from it.

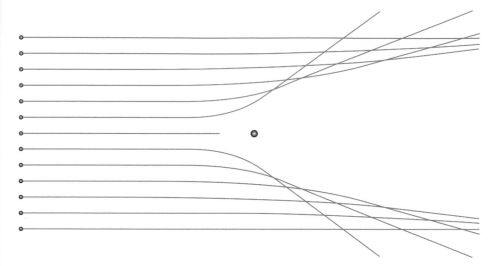

Figure 7.3 The paths of alpha particles deflected by a nucleus. At this scale it looks like most are deflected but if the nucleus was this size the next atom would be about 100 m away.

So, the atom consists of a heavy but very small positive nucleus surrounded by negative electrons. But what stops the electrons falling into the nucleus? One idea could be that the atom is like a mini solar system with electrons orbiting the nucleus, like the planets orbit the Sun. The circular motion of the electrons would make it possible for them to accelerate towards the centre without getting any closer. One problem with this model is that if an electron were to move in this way it would create a changing electric and magnetic field resulting in emission of EM radiation. This would lead to a loss of energy and the electron would spiral into the nucleus. To gain more insight into the structure of the atom we need to look more closely at the relationship between light and matter.

Very high energy alpha particles get so close to the nucleus that they become attracted by the nuclear force. This gives a different scatter pattern to that predicted.

The connection between atoms and light

There is a very close connection between matter and light. For example, if we give thermal energy to a metal, it can give out light. Light is an electromagnetic wave so must come from a moving charge; electrons have charge and are able to move, so it would be reasonable to think that the production of light is something to do with electrons. But what is the mechanism inside the atom that enables this to happen? Before we can answer that question we need to look more closely at the nature of light, in particular light that comes from isolated atoms. We must look at isolated atoms because we need to be sure that the light is coming from single atoms and not the interaction between atoms. A single atom would not produce enough light for us to see, but low-pressure gases have enough atoms far enough apart not to interact.

Atomic spectra

To analyse the light coming from an atom we need to first give the atom energy; this can be done by adding thermal energy or electrical energy. The most convenient method is to apply a high potential to a low-pressure gas contained in a glass tube (a discharge tube). This causes the gas to give out light, and already you will notice (see

Figure 7.4) that different gases give different colours. To see exactly which wavelengths make up these colours we can split up the light using a prism (or diffraction grating). To measure the wavelengths we need to know the angle of refraction; this can be measured using a spectrometer.

The hydrogen spectrum

Hydrogen has only one electron – so it is the simplest atom and the one we will consider first. Figure 7.5 shows the spectrum obtained from a low-pressure discharge tube containing hydrogen. The first thing you notice is that, unlike a usual rainbow that is continuous, the hydrogen spectrum is made up of thin lines. Light is a form of energy, so whatever the electrons do they must lose energy when light is emitted. If the colour of light is associated with different energies, then, since only certain energies of light are emitted, the electron must only be able to release certain amounts of energy. This would be the case if the electron could only have certain amounts of energy in the first place. We say the energy is *quantized*.

To help understand this, we can consider an analogous situation of buying sand. You can either buy sand loose or in 50 kg bags, and we say the 50 kg bags are quantized, since the sand comes in certain discrete quantities. So if you buy loose sand, you can get any amount you want, but if you buy quantized sand, you have to have multiples of 50 kg. If we make a chart showing all the possible quantities of sand you could buy, then they would be as shown on Figure 7.6; one is continuous and the other has lines.

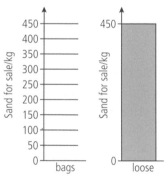

If the electron in the hydrogen atom can only have discrete energies, then when it changes energy, that must also be in discrete amounts. We represent the possible energies on an energy level diagram (Figure 7.7), which looks rather like the sand diagram.

For this model to fit together, each of the lines in the spectrum must correspond to a different energy change. Light therefore must be quantized and this does not tie in at all with our classical view of light being a continuous wave that spreads out like ripples in a pond.

The quantum nature of light

Light definitely has wave-like properties; it reflects, refracts, diffracts, and interferes. But sometimes light does things that we don't expect a wave to do, and one of these things is the photoelectric effect.

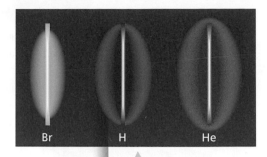

Figure 7.4 Discharge tubes containing bromine, hydrogen and helium.

Figure 7.5 The line spectrum for hydrogen.

When a metal rod is heated it first glows red but as it gets hotter it will glow white so it seems reasonable to assume that the colour of light is related to energy, red being the lowest energy and blue/violet the highest.

Figure 7.6 Ways of buying sand.

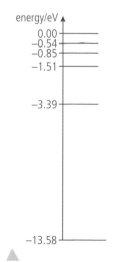

Figure 7.7 The electron energy levels of hydrogen.

The photoelectric effect

Consider ultraviolet light shining on a negatively charged zinc plate. Can the light cause the charge to leave the plate? To answer this question we can use the wave model of light, but we cannot see what is happening inside the metal, so to help us visualize this problem we will use an analogy.

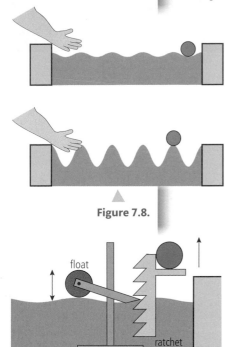

Figure 7.8.

Figure 7.9.

The swimming pool analogy

Imagine a ball floating near the edge of a swimming pool as in Figure 7.8. If you are at the other side of the swimming pool, could you get the ball out of the pool by sending water waves towards it? To get the ball out of the pool we need to lift it as high as the edge of the pool; in other words, we must give it enough PE to reach this height. We can do this by making the amplitude of the wave high enough to lift the ball. If the amplitude is not high enough, the ball will not be able to leave the pool unless we build a machine (as in Figure 7.9) that will collect the energy over a period of time. In this case, there will be a time delay before the ball gets out.

To relate this to the zinc plate, according to this model:

- electrons will be emitted only if the light source is very bright. (Brightness is related to amplitude of the wave.)
- if the source is dim we expect no electrons to be emitted. If electrons are emitted, we expect a time delay whilst the atoms collect energy from the wave.
- if we use lower frequency light, electrons will still be emitted if it is bright enough.

The zinc plate experiment

To find out if electrons are emitted or not, we can put the zinc plate on an electroscope and shine UV light on it as in Figure 7.10. If electrons are emitted charge will be lost and the electroscope leaf will fall. The results are not entirely as expected:

- the electroscope does go down indicating that electrons are emitted from the surface of the zinc plate.
- the electroscope leaf goes down even if the UV light is very dim. When very dim, the leaf takes longer to go down but there is no time delay before it starts to drop.
- if light of lower frequency is used, the leaf does not go down, showing that no electrons are emitted. This is the case even if very intense low frequency light is used.

These results can be explained if we consider light to be quantized.

Figure 7.10 UV radiation is absorbed and electrons emitted causing the gold leaf to fall.

Quantum model of light

In the quantum model of light, light is made up of packets called photons. Each photon is a section of wave with an energy E that is proportional to its frequency, f.

$$E = hf$$

where h is Planck's constant (6.63×10^{-34} J s).

The intensity of light is related to the number of photons, not the amplitude, as in the classical wave model. Using this model we can explain the photoelectric effect.

- UV light has a high frequency, so when photons of UV light are absorbed by the zinc, they give enough energy to the zinc electrons to enable them to leave the surface.
- When the intensity of light is low there are not many photons but each photon has enough energy to enable electrons to leave the zinc.
- Low frequency light is made of photons with low energy; these do not have enough energy to liberate electrons from the zinc. Intense low frequency light is simply more low energy photons, which still don't have enough energy.

If a swimming pool were like this then if someone jumped into the pool the energy they gave to the water would stay together in a packet until it met another swimmer. When this happened the other swimmer would be ejected from the pool. Could be fun!

To get a deeper understanding of the photoelectric effect we need more information about the energy of the photoelectrons.

Millikan's photoelectric experiment

Millikan devised an experiment to measure the KE of photoelectrons. He used an electric field to stop the electrons completing a circuit and used that 'stopping potential' to calculate the KE. A diagram of the apparatus is shown in Figure 7.13.

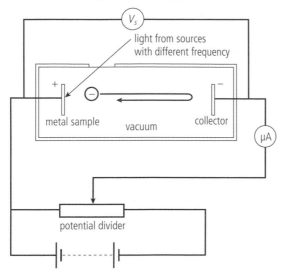

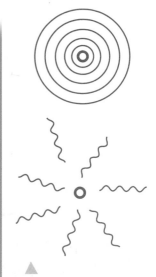

Figure 7.11 Light radiating, according to the wave model and the quantum model.

Figure 7.12 The quantum swimming pool.

Figure 7.13 The stopping potential stops the electrons from reaching the collector.

Light from a source of known frequency passes into the apparatus through a small window. If the photons have enough energy, electrons will be emitted from the metal sample. Some of these electrons travel across the tube to the collector causing a current to flow in the circuit; this current is measured by the microammeter. The potential divider is now adjusted until none of the electrons reach the collector (as in the diagram). We can now use the law of conservation of energy to find the KE of the fastest electrons.

$$\text{Loss of KE = gain in electrical PE}$$

$$\tfrac{1}{2}mv^2 = V_s e$$

So maximum KE, $$\qquad KE_{max} = V_s e$$

The light source is now changed to one with different frequency and the procedure is repeated.

The graphs in Figure 7.14 show two aspects of the results.

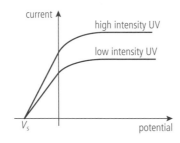
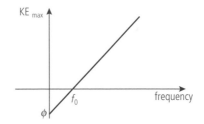

Figure 7.14 Graphs of current vs potential and maximum KE against frequency.

The most important aspect of the first graph in Figure 7.14 is that for a given potential, increasing the intensity increases the current but doesn't change the stopping potential. This is because when the intensity is increased the light contains more photons (so liberates more electrons) but does not increase the energy (so V_s is the same).

The second graph in Figure 7.14 shows that the maximum KE of the electrons is linearly related to the frequency of the photons. Below a certain value, f_0, no photoelectrons are liberated; this is called the *threshold frequency*.

Einstein's photoelectric equation

Einstein explained the photoelectric effect and derived an equation that relates the KE of the photoelectrons to the frequency of light.

Maximum photoelectron KE = energy of photon – energy needed to get photon out of metal

$$KE_{max} = hf - \varphi$$

φ is called the *work function*. If the photon has only enough energy to get the electron out then it will have zero KE, and this is what happens at the threshold frequency, f_0. At this frequency

$$KE_{max} = 0 = hf_0 - \varphi$$

so $$\qquad \varphi = hf_0$$

We can now rewrite the equation as

$$KE_{max} = hf - hf_0$$

Exercises

1 A sample of sodium is illuminated by light of wavelength 422 nm in a photoelectric tube. The potential across the tube is increased to 0.6 V. At this potential no current flows across the tube.

Calculate:

(a) the maximum KE of the photoelectrons.
(b) the frequency of the incident photons.
(c) the work function of sodium.
(d) the lowest frequency of light that would cause photoelectric emission in sodium.

2 A sample of zinc is illuminated by UV light of wavelength 144 nm. If the work function of zinc is 4.3 eV, calculate

(a) the photon energy in eV.
(b) the maximum KE of photoelectrons.
(c) the stopping potential.
(d) the threshold frequency.

3 If the zinc in Exercise 2 is illuminated by the light in Exercise 1, will any electrons be emitted?

4 The maximum KE of electrons emitted from a nickel sample is 1.4 eV. If the work function of nickel is 5.0 eV, what frequency of light must have been used?

You will find it easier to work in eV for Questions 2, 3 and 4.

The electronvolt

Remember 1 eV is the KE gained by an electron accelerated through a pd of 1 V.

1 eV = 1.6 × 10⁻¹⁹ J

Comparing energies in eV

• The average KE of an atom in air at 20 °C is about 0.02 eV

a red light photon is 1.75 eV

a blue light photon is 3.1 eV.

• The energy released by one molecule in a chemical reaction is typically 50 eV.

• The energy released by one atom of fuel in a nuclear reaction is 200 MeV.

Quantum explanation of atomic spectra

We can now put our quantum models of the atom and light together to explain the formation of atomic spectra. To summarize what we know so far:

• atomic electrons can only exist in certain discrete energy levels.
• light is made up of photons.
• when electrons lose energy they give out light.
• when light is absorbed by an atom it gives energy to the electrons.

We can therefore deduce that when an electron changes from a high energy level to a low one, a photon of light is emitted. Since the electron can only exist in discrete energy levels, there are a limited number of possible changes that can take place; this gives rise to the characteristic line spectra that we have observed. Each element has a different set of lines in its spectrum because each element has different electron energy levels. To make this clear we can consider a simple atom with electrons in the four energy levels shown in Figure 7.15.

As you can see in the diagram there are six possible ways that an electron can change from a high energy to a lower one. Each transition will give rise to a photon of different energy and hence a different line in the spectrum. To calculate the photon frequency we use the formula:

$$\text{change in energy } \Delta E = hf$$

So the bigger energy changes will give lines on the blue end of the spectrum and low energies on the red end.

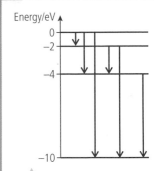

Figure 7.15.

Example

A change from the −4 eV to the −10 eV level will result in a change of 6 eV. This is $6 \times 1.6 \times 10^{-19} = 9.6 \times 10^{-19}$ J.

This will give rise to a photon of frequency given by:

$$\Delta E = hf$$

Rearranging gives
$$f = \frac{\Delta E}{h} = \frac{9.6 \times 10^{-19}}{6.63 \times 10^{-34}} = 1.45 \times 10^{15}\,\text{Hz}$$

This is a wavelength of 207 nm which is UV.

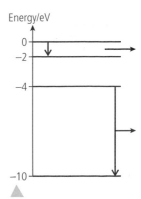

Figure 7.16.

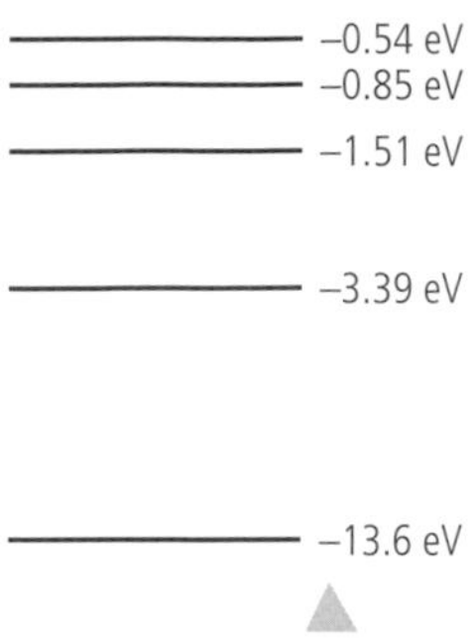

Ionization

Ionization occurs when the electrons are completely removed from an atom, leaving a charged atom called an ion. This can happen if the atom absorbs a high energy photon or the electron could be 'knocked off' by a fast moving particle like an alpha. These interactions are quite different – when a photon interacts with an atom it is absorbed but when an alpha interacts it 'bounces off'.

Absorption of light

A photon of light can only be absorbed by an atom if it has exactly the right amount of energy to excite an electron from one energy to another. If light containing all wavelengths (white light) is passed through a gas then the photons with the right energy to excite electrons will be absorbed. The spectrum of the light that comes out will have lines missing. This is called an *absorption spectrum* and is further evidence for the existence of electron energy levels.

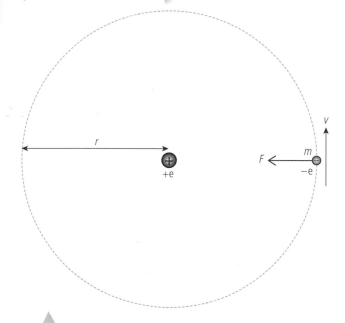

———— −0.54 eV
———— −0.85 eV
———— −1.51 eV

———— −3.39 eV

———— −13.6 eV

Figure 7.17.

A charge coupled device (CCD) is the light-sensitive part of a digital camera. It contains millions of tiny photodiodes that make up the pixels. When a photon of light is incident on a photodiode it causes an electron to be released, resulting in a pd which is converted to a digital signal.

Exercises

Use the energy level diagram of Figure 7.17 to answer the following questions.

5 How many possible energy transitions are there in this atom?

6 Calculate the maximum energy (in eV) that could be released and the frequency of the photon emitted.

7 Calculate the minimum energy that could be released and the frequency of the associated photon.

8 How much energy would be required to completely remove an electron that was in the lowest energy level? Calculate the frequency of the photon that would have enough energy to do this.

The Bohr model

We can see from the spectrum of hydrogen that the energy of atomic electrons can only have discrete values but we do not have a model for how the electrons could be arranged around the atom. In 1913 Niels Bohr proposed that if the electrons were in certain specific orbits then they would not emit EM radiation. The radii of these orbits were defined in terms of the angular momentum of the electron: this is the angular equivalent to linear momentum. If a body, mass m, is travelling in a circle radius r with constant speed v it will have angular momentum mvr. As with linear momentum, angular momentum is conserved provided no tangential forces act on the body. According to the Bohr model an electron will be in a stable orbit if $mvr = \frac{nh}{2\pi}$ where n is a whole number called the *quantum number*.

We can show how this leads to a quantization of energy by considering the orbiting electron in Figure 7.18.

The centripetal force = electrostatic attraction

so $$= \frac{mv^2}{r} = \frac{ee}{4\pi\varepsilon_0 r^2}$$ equation (1)

Rearranging and multiplying by mr gives $$m^2v^2r^2 = \frac{me^2r}{4\pi\varepsilon_0}$$

so according to Bohr $$\frac{me^2r}{4\pi\varepsilon_0} = \left(\frac{nh}{2\pi}\right)^2.$$

Figure 7.18 The Bohr atom.

This implies that

$$r = \frac{\varepsilon_o n^2 h^2}{\pi m e^2}$$

This gives the radii of all allowed orbits.

Now, the energy of the electron

$$= KE + PE = \frac{1}{2}mv^2 - \frac{e^2}{4\pi\varepsilon_o r}$$

but from equation (1) $\frac{1}{2}mv^2 = \frac{e^2}{8\pi\varepsilon_o r}$ so energy $= \frac{-e^2}{8\pi\varepsilon_o r}$.

Substituting for r gives:

$$E = \frac{-me^4}{8n^2\varepsilon_o^2 h^2} = \frac{-13.6}{n^2} \text{ eV.}$$

This predicts that the electron energies will have discrete values that get closer together as the energies increase. This closely matches the energy level diagram that was derived from spectral analysis.

Exercises

9 Calculate the radius of the lowest orbit of an electron in a hydrogen atom based on the Bohr model.

10 Use the Bohr model to calculate the frequency of EM radiation emitted when an electron in a hydrogen atom moves from the second orbit down to the first.

From close observation of spectral lines we see that they are not all the same intensity. This implies that not all transitions are equally probable. Bohr's model cannot predict this detail and although it works very nicely for hydrogen it doesn't work for any other atom. To create a more accurate model we need to look at matter in a different way.

The wave nature of matter

Rutherford used alpha particles to probe inside the atom; another particle that can be scattered by matter is the electron. Electrons are released from a metal when it is heated and can be accelerated in a vacuum through a potential difference as shown in Figure 7.20.

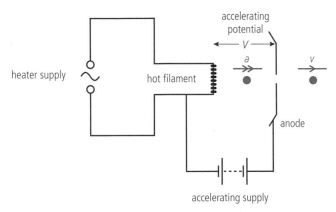

The filament, made hot by an AC supply, liberates electrons which are accelerated towards the anode by the accelerating pd. Electrons travelling in the direction of the hole in the anode pass through and continue with constant velocity.

We can calculate the speed of the electrons, using the law of conservation of energy.

$$\text{loss of electrical PE} = \text{gain in KE}$$

$$Ve = \frac{1}{2}mv^2$$

$$v = \sqrt{\frac{2Ve}{m}}$$

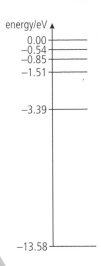

Figure 7.19 The electron energy levels of hydrogen.

Thermionic emission

In this case atomic electrons gain enough energy from thermal excitation to leave the surface of the metal.

KE in eV

The KE of the electrons in eV is numerically the same as the accelerating pd.

If pd = 200 V

KE = 200 eV

Figure 7.20 A simple electron gun.

The original TV screens were called cathode ray tubes; they consisted of an electron gun and a fluorescent screen. The picture was formed by scanning the beam across the screen many times a second. As the beam scanned across, its intensity was varied resulting in a picture. The problem with this technology is that the electron gun needs to be placed far enough from the screen so that the electrons hit all parts of it. Modern LED and plasma screens have arrays of small lights so they can be made much thinner.

Detecting electrons

You can't see electrons directly, so you need some sort of detector to find out where they go. When electrons collide with certain atoms they give the atomic electrons energy (we say the electrons are 'excited'). When the atomic electrons go back down to a lower energy level, they give out light. This is called *phosphorescence* and can be used to see where the electrons land. Zinc sulphide is one such substance; it is used to coat glass screens so that light is emitted where the electrons collide with the screen. This is how the older types of TV screens work.

The aurora borealis is caused when charged particles from the Sun excite atoms in the atmosphere causing light to be emitted.

Electron diffraction

If a beam of electrons is passed through a thin film of graphite, an interesting pattern is observed when they hit a phosphor screen. The pattern looks very much like the diffraction pattern caused when light is diffracted by a small circular aperture. Perhaps the electrons are being diffracted by the atoms in the graphite. Assuming this to be true, we can calculate the wavelength of the wave that has been diffracted.

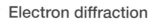

Diffraction of electrons by a graphite film.

The de Broglie hypothesis

In 1924 Louis de Broglie proposed that 'all matter has a wave-like nature' and that the wavelength of that wave could be found using the equation:

$$\lambda = \frac{h}{p}$$

where p is the momentum of the particle.

Using this equation we can calculate the wavelength of an electron accelerated through a potential difference of 50 V.

Kinetic energy gained = $50 \, eV = 50 \times 1.6 \times 10^{-19} = 8 \times 10^{-18} \, J$.

$KE = \frac{1}{2} mv^2$ so $v = \sqrt{\left(\frac{2 \times KE}{m}\right)} = \sqrt{\left(\frac{2 \times 8 \times 10^{-18}}{9.1 \times 10^{-31}}\right)} = 4.2 \times 10^6 \, m\,s^{-1}$.

Momentum = $mv = 9.1 \times 10^{-31} \times 4.2 \times 10^6 = 3.8 \times 10^{-24} \, N\,s$.

So the wavelength $\lambda = \frac{h}{mv} = 1.7 \times 10^{-10} \, m$.

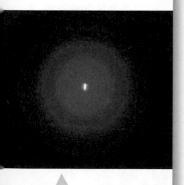

Diffraction of light by a small circular aperture.

Given this wavelength we can use the same equation that was used for the diffraction of light by a diffraction grating to calculate the angle of the first maximum in the diffraction pattern.

$$\sin \theta = \frac{\lambda}{D} \text{ where } D \text{ is the atomic spacing} \approx 2 \times 10^{-10}\,\text{m}.$$

This gives $\theta \approx 60°$ which is consistent with the observable pattern.

Exercises

11 An electron is accelerated by a pd of 100 V. Calculate its:

(a) KE in eV.
(b) KE in joules.
(c) de Broglie wavelength.

12 Calculate the de Broglie wavelength for a car of mass 1000 kg travelling at 15 m s⁻¹. Why won't you ever see a car diffract?

Probability waves

To understand the relationship between an electron and its wave let us take a fresh look at the interference of light now that we know light is made up of photons. When light is passed through two narrow slits it diffracts at each slit and then light from each slit interferes in the region of overlap as shown in Figure 7.21. This is very much the same as what happens to water waves and sound.

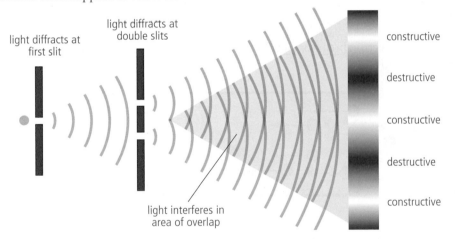

light diffracts at first slit

light diffracts at double slits

light interferes in area of overlap

constructive
destructive
constructive
destructive
constructive

Figure 7.21 Two-slit interference of light.

We now know that light is made up of photons so the bright areas in the interference pattern will be areas where there are a lot of photons and in the dark areas there will be few photons. Thus we can say that the probability of the photon landing at a particular spot is given by the intensity of the light, which is proportional to the amplitude of the wave, squared. Well, it is the same with electrons and all other particles. If electrons were to be passed through the two narrow slits in Figure 7.21 then a similar pattern would be obtained except that the slits would have to be closer together. The wave doesn't only give the probability of the particle hitting the screen, it also gives the probability of the particle being at a given position at any time. However, we only really notice the particle properties of the particle when it hits something like the screen. When electrons are fired from an electron gun we think of them as moving in straight lines; we can even see this if the region is filled with low pressure air. How can we model this with a wave? Waves spread, which would mean that the electron could be anywhere and that does not seem to be happening. The way this can be resolved is if the probability wave is thought to be made up of many waves superposed on each other such that they cancel out everywhere except in a small region of space. The probability of the particle being at a given position would then be zero almost everywhere except in the region where the waves add. This is called a *wave packet* (shown in Figure 7.22).

Figure 7.22 A wave packet.

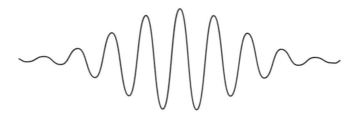

If the wave packet moves forwards then the position where the particle is most likely to be found also moves forwards. So the most probable position of an electron moving in a straight line is given by a moving wave packet which is the resultant of many guide waves which cancel each other out everywhere except in the line of flight of the electron. If a slit is placed in the electron's path then guide waves diffract, altering the probable path of the electron.

We only know where the particle is when it hits the screen. If we try to track its position we run into difficulties.

Heisenberg's uncertainty principle

Consider an electron fired from an electron gun into the open end of the large box shown in Figure 7.23.

Figure 7.23 Electrons enter an open box.

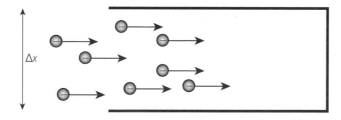

If we consider the x component of their motion, we know that the electrons are pretty much travelling in straight lines so their momentum in the x direction, as defined in the diagram, is zero; so the uncertainty in this, Δp, is quite small. However, the opening to the box is big so we are not at all certain where the electrons are, so the uncertainty in this, Δx, is large. To reduce the uncertainty in position we could make the opening to the box smaller as in Figure 7.24.

Figure 7.24 Electrons enter the box through a narrow opening.

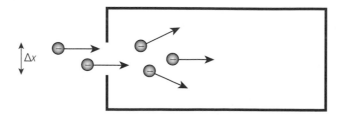

Now the uncertainty in position has been reduced but the small opening will diffract the electrons giving them momentum in the direction of x. The uncertainty in momentum Δp has now been increased.

Heisenberg proposed that it is not possible to precisely define the position and momentum of a particle at the same time; the uncertainty is expressed by the equation:

$$\Delta p \Delta x \geq \frac{h}{4\pi}$$

where h = Planck's constant.

A similar relationship exists when you try to define energy and time:

$$\Delta E \Delta t \geq \frac{h}{4\pi}$$

An alternative way of looking at this is to consider the probability wave of an electron. If this wave is a single wave, wavelength λ, spreading out like ripples in a pond, then the probability of finding the particle, given by the amplitude^2, would be the same in all directions: the electron could be *anywhere*. To confine the electron to a small region of space then, the wave would be a wave packet made of many superposed waves of different wavelengths, so by reducing the uncertainty in position we have increased the uncertainty in λ which since $\lambda = \frac{h}{p}$ has also increased the uncertainty in momentum.

Confinement

If an electron is to be held in place (*confined*) in an atom then the uncertainty in its position can't be much bigger than the atom itself so $\Delta x \approx 10^{-10}$ m.

Heisenberg's uncertainty principle implies that $\Delta p \geq \frac{h}{4\pi} \frac{1}{10^{-10}}$

So the momentum must be approximately 5×10^{-25} N s.

Now, $KE = \frac{1}{2}mv^2 = \frac{m^2v^2}{2m} = \frac{p^2}{2m}$

so the KE of the electron would be $\frac{(5 \times 10^{-25})^2}{2 \times 9.11 \times 10^{-31}} = 1.5 \times 10^{-19}$ J.

Converting this to eV gives $\frac{1.5 \times 10^{-19}}{1.6 \times 10^{-19}} \approx 1$ eV which is the same order of magnitude as the electron energy levels.

Exercise

13 Use Heisenberg's uncertainty principle to find the order of magnitude of the energy of an electron confined in the nucleus (size $\approx 10^{-15}$ m).

 TOK

It is important to realize that the uncertainty principle is not just about measurement – it is about the way things are.

Schrödinger's equation

The wave that gives the probability of finding the electron at a point in space at a given time is defined by the *wave function*. This is represented by the Greek letter ψ (psi) and can be found for different situations by solving a complicated equation called *Schrödinger's equation*. The square of the amplitude of the wave function $|\psi|^2$ gives the probability of finding the electron. Solving this equation for an electron confined by the potential well of the nucleus results in the electron having discrete energy levels in agreement with the evidence from line spectra of gases. This is similar to the way that a vibrating string can only vibrate with certain frequencies (*harmonics*) as shown in Figure 7.25.

The frequency of these waves would be given by $\frac{v}{2L} \frac{2v}{2L} \frac{3v}{2L} \ldots \ldots \ldots \frac{nv}{2L}$ where n is any whole number. So the different possible waves are defined by the number n.

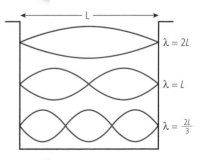

▲ **Figure 7.25.**

In solving the Schrödinger equation it is found that the wave function related to an atomic electron has 3 *quantum numbers*, the principal quantum number (n), the orbital quantum number (L), and the magnetic quantum number (m_l). Different combinations of these numbers give the different energy levels that lead to the atomic line spectra. Furthermore, the solution predicts that some energy level transitions are more likely than others, resulting in the varying line intensity that the Bohr model failed to explain.

Electron spin

Electron spin is included for completeness, you will not be tested on it in the exam.

On closer examination, some single spectral lines predicted by the wave function are actually two very close lines so it seems that we still don't have the whole picture. However, the fact that the lines move further apart in a strong magnetic field suggests that it is something to do with magnetism; maybe electrons spin on their own axis creating small magnetic dipoles. To investigate the magnetic properties of electrons isn't easy since if they were passed through a magnetic field they would be deflected due to their charge (Bqv). To get rid of the effect of charge, a neutral atom with one outer electron (such as silver) could be used. In 1921 Otto Stern and Walter Gerlach investigated the magnetic properties of electrons by passing silver atoms through a non-uniform magnetic field. If the electron acted like a small magnetic dipole then the silver atoms should be deflected by the magnetic field, the angle and direction of deflection depending on the orientation of the dipole. One would expect the orientation of these magnets to be fairly random resulting in a spread of the beam as shown in Figure 7.26.

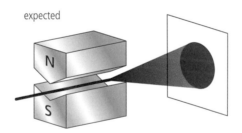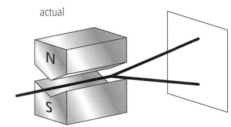

Figure 7.26 The Stern–Gerlach experiment.

The result was quite unexpected, the atoms all landed in one of two places showing that the electron magnets had only two possible orientations. This led to a new quantum number the *spin quantum number* which, for an electron, can only be $+\frac{1}{2}$ or $-\frac{1}{2}$. In 1928 Paul Dirac, using a relativistic approach, modified Schrödinger's equation to derive a wave function that predicted this 4th quantum number, as well as the existence of a positive electron!

Electron spin is a result of the wave nature of the electron and has nothing to do with spinning balls of charge. However the name has stuck.

Mass–energy equivalence

The positive electron predicted by Dirac is known as an *antiparticle*. For every particle there is an antiparticle which has the same mass but opposite charge. An antiproton, for example, is negative. Matter made of negative protons and positive electrons (positrons) is called *antimatter*. If a particle meets its antiparticle they *annihilate* each other, turning into high energy photons. An event such as this would cause a problem if you tried to solve it with classical mechanics. The particles have mass but the photons have none. However, the photons have more energy than was possessed by the original particle/antiparticle. So neither mass nor energy seem to be conserved. Einstein's theory of relativity solves this problem by showing that mass and energy are equivalent. The total energy E of a body can be expressed as:

$$E = mc^2$$

Electrons (green) and positrons (red) are formed from gamma photons. Notice how the *B* field (into page) causes them to curve in opposite directions. The bottom pair has more KE than the top pair, so the radius of their path is greater.

E = mc² is probably the most famous formula in the world – and Albert Einstein, definitely the most famous physicist.

So the mass of one electron converted to the energy of photons would give an equivalent energy of $9.1 \times 10^{-31} \times (3 \times 10^8)^2 = 8.19 \times 10^{-14}$ J.

If this is converted to eV we get $\dfrac{8.19 \times 10^{-14}}{1.6 \times 10^{-19}} = 0.511$ MeV.

If an electron annihilates a positron then the amount of energy given out as photons is 1.22 MeV.

Reversing this process, it is also possible for the energy in a 1.22 MeV photon to be transformed into the mass of an electron and a positron. This process is called *pair production*. For this to occur the photon must pass close to a nucleus which recoils, making it possible to conserve both mass/energy and momentum.

 For convenience, mass of particles is often expressed in MeV c^{-2} so the mass of an electron would be 0.511 MeV c^{-2}. This makes it very easy to calculate the equivalent energy.

Exercises

14 Calculate the mass equivalent to the increase in energy of a 1000 kg car when it accelerates from rest to 20 m s⁻¹.

15 An electron is accelerated through a pd of 500 V. Calculate:

  (a) the KE of the electron in eV.
  (b) the KE of the electron in J.
  (c) the mass equivalent in kg.
  (d) the mass equivalent to the increase in energy of the electron in eV c^{-2}.

Electron tunnelling

In one dimension we can think of an atomic electron as a wave trapped in the potential well of the nucleus, rather like a wave in a string clamped at both ends. In the case of the string, the clamps form a boundary preventing the wave progressing any further so there is no possibility of a wave beyond the string. When putting the boundary conditions of the potential well of the nucleus into the equation to find the probable positions of the electron we find that the wave function doesn't go to zero at the edge of the boundary but decreases exponentially. Therefore, if the boundary is very thin, there exists a probability that the electron could exist on the other side of it as illustrated in Figure 7.27. The probability of the electron existing on the other side of the barrier depends on the width of the barriers and the difference in energy between the electron and the height of the barrier.

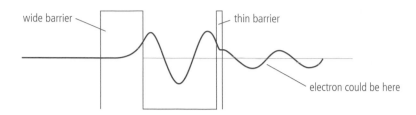

wide barrier — thin barrier

electron could be here

Figure 7.27 Electron tunnelling.

This effect is used in the tunnelling electron microscope. When a fine metal point is held close to a surface a barrier is formed between the surface atoms and the point. If the point is taken very close, the barrier becomes thin enough for electrons to tunnel from the surface to the point providing a small current. By maintaining the current as the point is tracked across the surface the surface contours can be plotted to a very high degree of accuracy, enabling single atoms to be located.

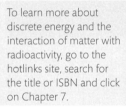

To learn more about discrete energy and the interaction of matter with radioactivity, go to the hotlinks site, search for the title or ISBN and click on Chapter 7.

Spintronics research. Coloured scanning tunnelling micrograph (STM) of a manganese atom (yellow) in a gallium arsenide semiconductor (blue).

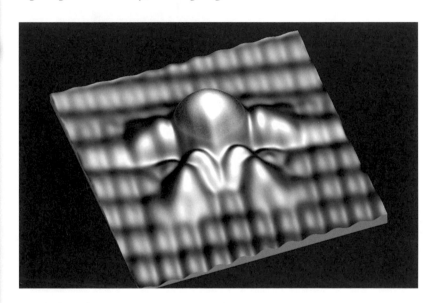

7.2 Properties of the nucleus and radioactivity

7.1 Discrete energy and radioactivity

Understandings, applications, and skills:

Radioactive decay
- Solving problems involving the energy released in radioactive decay, nuclear fission, and nuclear fusion.

Alpha particles, beta particles, and gamma rays
- Completing decay equations for alpha and beta decay

Half-life
- Determining the half-life of a nuclide from a decay curve.
- Investigating half-life experimentally (or by simulation).

  Guidance
  - *Students will be required to solve problems on radioactive decay involving only integral numbers of half-lives.*

Absorption characteristics of decay particles
Isotopes
Background radiation

7.2 Nuclear reactions

Understandings, applications, and skills:

The unified atomic mass unit

Guidance
- *Students should be aware that nuclear densities are approximately the same for all nuclei and that the only macroscopic objects with the same density as nuclei are neutron stars.*

Mass defect and nuclear binding energy
- Solving problems involving mass defect and binding energy.
- Sketching and interpreting the general shape of the curve of average binding energy per nucleon against nucleon number.

Guidance
- *Students must be able to calculate changes in terms of mass or binding energy.*
- *Binding energy may be defined in terms of energy required to separate the nucleons or the energy released when a nucleus is formed from its nucleons.*

Nuclear fission and nuclear fusion

12.2 Nuclear physics

Understandings, applications, and skills:

(AHL) Nuclear energy levels
- Describing experimental evidence for nuclear energy levels.

(AHL) The neutrino

Guidance
- *Students will be expected to include the neutrino and antineutrino in beta decay equations.*

(AHL) The law of radioactive decay and the decay constant
- Solving problems involving the radioactive decay law for arbitrary time intervals.
- Explaining the methods for measuring short and long half-lives

Charge and mass

In the 1860s chemists calculated the relative mass of many elements by measuring how they combine to form compounds. If placed in order of atomic mass, the chemical properties of the elements seemed to periodically repeat themselves. This led to the periodic table chemistry students will be familiar with. There were, however, some anomalies where the order in terms of chemical properties didn't match the order of mass. In 1911 Rutherford's scattering experiments not only revealed the existence of the nucleus but made it possible to calculate the charge of the nucleus. This was found to be the same whole number of positive electron charges for all atoms of the same element. This number is not the same as the mass number, but when the elements were placed in order of this 'charge number' then the anomalies were sorted. To summarize:

- the mass of all atoms are (approximately) multiples of the mass of a hydrogen atom, the 'mass number'.
- the charge of all atoms is a multiple of the charge of a hydrogen atom, the 'charge number'.
- the 'charge number' is not the same as the 'mass number'.

Since all nuclei are multiples of hydrogen then perhaps all nuclei are made of hydrogen nuclei. If this was the case then the charge number would be the same as the mass number, but it is not. For example, helium has a relative atomic mass of 4 but a charge of $+2e$. There appear to be two extra particles that have approximately the same mass as a hydrogen nucleus but no charge. This particle is the neutron and it was discovered by Chadwick in 1932.

NATURE OF SCIENCE

Nuclear research was undoubtedly hurried along by the strategic race to be the first to build an atom bomb; many other advancements in science have also been pushed forwards due to military, political, or financial concerns.

The unified mass unit (u) is the unit of atomic mass. 1 u is defined as the mass of $\frac{1}{12}$ of an atom of a carbon-12 atom.

So the nucleus contains two particles, shown in Table 7.1.

	Mass/kg	Mass/u	Charge
Proton	1.673×10^{-27}	1.00728	$+1.6 \times 10^{-19}$
Neutron	1.675×10^{-27}	1.00866	0

Table 7.1 The two types of nucleon.

Nucleons are the particles of the nucleus (protons and neutrons). A particular combination of nucleons is called a *nuclide*. Each nuclide is defined by three numbers:

nucleon number (A) = number of protons + neutrons (defines the *mass* of the nucleus)

proton number (Z) = number of protons (defines the *charge* of the nucleus)

neutron number (N) = number of neutrons ($A - Z$).

Isotopes are nuclides with the same proton number but different nucleon numbers.

In past IB papers these quantities have different names.

A = atomic mass number

Z = atomic number

Example

Lithium has a nucleon number of 7 and a proton number of 3, so it has 3 protons and 4 neutrons. This nuclide can be represented by the symbol $^{7}_{3}\text{Li}$.

$^{6}_{3}\text{Li}$ and $^{8}_{3}\text{Li}$ are both isotopes of lithium.

$^{6}_{3}\text{Li}$ $\qquad$ $^{7}_{3}\text{Li}$

Figure 7.28 Isotopes of lithium.

Exercises

16 How many protons and neutrons are there in the following nuclei?

   (a) $^{35}_{17}\text{Cl}$

   (b) $^{58}_{28}\text{Ni}$

   (c) $^{204}_{82}\text{Pb}$

17 Calculate the charge in coulombs and mass in kg of a $^{54}_{26}\text{Fe}$ nucleus.

18 An isotope of uranium (U) has 92 protons and 143 neutrons. Write the nuclear symbol for this isotope.

19 Describe the structure of another isotope of uranium, having the symbol $^{238}_{92}\text{U}$.

Size of the nucleus

The size of the nucleus can be determined by conducting a similar experiment to the alpha scattering experiment of Geiger and Marsden. The alpha particles that come straight back off the gold foil must have approached a nucleus head-on following a path as shown in Figure 7.29.

Figure 7.29 An alpha particle approaches a nucleus head on.

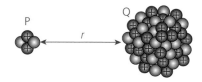

When Geiger and Marsden did their gold foil experiment they didn't have alphas with enough energy to get close enough to the gold nucleus to give a very accurate value for its radius. They did however get quite close to aluminium nuclei.

Applying the law of conservation of energy to this problem, we can deduce that at point P, where the alpha particle stops, the original KE has been converted to electrical PE.

$$\tfrac{1}{2}mv^2 = \frac{kQq}{r}$$

where Q = the charge of the nucleus ($+Ze$)

and q = the charge of the alpha ($+2e$)

The KE of the alpha can be calculated from the change in the mass of a nucleus when it is emitted (more about this later), so knowing this, the distance r can be calculated.

To determine the size of the nucleus, faster and faster alphas are sent towards the nucleus until they no longer come back. The fastest ones that return have got as close to the nucleus as possible.

This is just an estimate, especially since (as is the case for all particles) the position of the particles that make up the nucleus is determined by a probability function. This will make the definition of the edge of the nucleus rather fuzzy.

From the results of experiments like this we know that the radius of a nucleus is approximately 10^{-15} m. By measuring the radius of different nucleus it has been found that $R = R_0 A^{\frac{1}{3}}$ this implies that the volume is proportional to the mass which means the density of all nuclei is the same.

Exercise

20 It is found that alpha particles with KE 7.7 MeV bounce back off an aluminium target. If the charge of an aluminium nucleus is 12.1×10^{-18} C, calculate:

  (a) the velocity of the alpha particles (they have a mass of 6.7×10^{-27} kg).
  (b) the distance of closest approach to the nucleus.

The nuclear force

We have seen that the energy of an atomic electron is in the region of -1 eV. That means that to remove an electron from an atom requires about 1 eV of energy. This doesn't happen to air atoms at room temperature but if air is heated, colliding atoms excite electrons resulting in the emission of light. The amount of energy required to remove an electron from an atom is directly related to the strength of the force holding it around the nucleus, so the fact that it takes a million times more energy to remove a nucleon from the nucleus indicates that whatever force is holding nucleons together must be much stronger than the electromagnetic force holding electrons in position.

Unlike the gravitational and electric forces, the force between two nucleons is *not* inversely proportional to their distance apart. If it was, then all nuclei would be attracted each other. The nuclear force is in fact very short range, only acting up to distances of about 10^{-15} m; attractive when nucleons are pulled apart but repulsive when pushed together.

From data gathered about the mass and radius of nuclei it is known that all nuclei have approximately the same density, independent of the combination of protons and neutrons. This implies that the nuclear force is the same between proton–proton, proton–neutron, and neutron–neutron. If the force between neutrons was greater than that between protons you might expect nuclides with large numbers of neutrons to be more dense.

Binding energy

Pulling apart

The binding energy of a nucleus is defined as the amount of energy required to pull the nucleus apart. Since the nuclear force is very strong, the work done is relatively large,

The difference between the mass of a nucleus and its constituents is very small but when multiplied by c^2 gives a lot of energy. It is this energy that is utilized in the nuclear reactors of today and the fusion reactors of tomorrow.

297

leading to a measurable increase in the mass of the nucleons ($E = mc^2$). This difference in mass, the *mass defect*, can be used to calculate the binding energy of the nucleus. It is helpful to think of nucleons as balls in a hole as in Figure 7.30. The balls don't have energy in the hole but to get them out we would need energy to do work. Similarly, binding energy is not something that the nucleons possess; it is something that we would have to possess if we wanted to pull them apart.

Putting the nucleus together

The binding energy can also be defined as the amount of energy released when the nucleus is put together. Again, the balls in a hole might help us to understand the concept. Imagine that you have three perfectly elastic balls and a perfectly elastic hole as in Figure 7.31. If you simply throw all the balls in the hole they will probably just bounce out. To get them to stay in the hole you need to remove the energy they had before they were dropped in. One way this could happen is if the balls could collide in such a way so as to give one of the balls all of their energy. This ball would fly out of the hole very fast leaving the other two settled at the bottom; it is the same with nuclei.

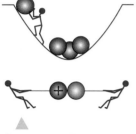

Figure 7.30 Pulling a nucleus apart (work done).

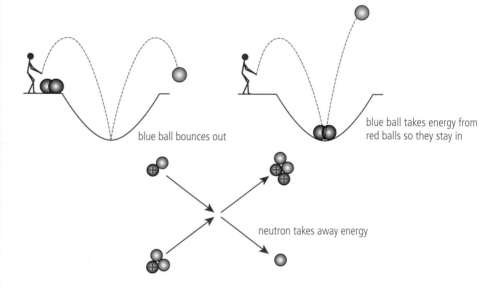

blue ball bounces out

blue ball takes energy from red balls so they stay in

neutron takes away energy

Figure 7.31 Putting a nucleus together (energy lost).

Conversion from u to MeV

The u is defined as $\frac{1}{12}$ of an atom of carbon-12. This is $1.66053878 \times 10^{-27}$ kg.

If we convert this into energy using the formula $E = mc^2$ we get

$$1.66053878 \times 10^{-27} \times (2.99792458 \times 10^8)^2 = 1.49241783 \times 10^{-10} \text{ J}.$$

To convert this to eV we divide by the charge of an electron to give

$$\frac{1.49241783 \times 10^{-10}}{1.60217653 \times 10^{-19}} = 931.494 \text{ MeV}$$

(the number of significant figures used in the calculation is necessary to get the correct answer).

This is a very useful conversion factor when dealing with nuclear masses.

Calculating binding energy

Tables normally contain atomic masses rather than nuclear masses; this is the mass of a neutral atom so it also includes Z electrons. Here, we will use atomic masses to calculate mass defect so to make sure the electron mass cancels out we use the mass of a hydrogen atom instead of the mass of a proton, as shown in Table 7.2.

The amount of energy required to split iron into its parts can be calculated from Δmc^2 where Δm is the difference in mass between the iron nucleus and the nucleons that it contains.

From Table 7.2 we can see that the iron nucleus has 26 protons and $(54 - 26) = 28$ neutrons.

> Mass defect = mass of parts − mass of nucleus
> = (mass of 26 protons + mass of 28 neutrons) − mass of iron nucleus.

But if we use atomic masses:

$$\Delta m = [(26 \times \text{mass (hydrogen atom)} - 26\, m_e) + 28\, m_n] - [\text{mass } (^{54}\text{Fe atom}) - 26\, m_e]$$

The electrons cancel so:

$$\Delta m = [26 \times \text{mass (hydrogen atom)} + 28\, m_n] - [\text{ mass } (^{54}\text{Fe atom})]$$

$$\Delta m = 26 \times 1.00782 + 28 \times 1.00866 - 53.9396 = 0.5062$$

This is equivalent to $0.5062 \times 931.5 = 471.5$ MeV.

Binding energy per nucleon

Larger nuclei generally have higher binding energy than smaller nuclei since they have more particles to pull apart. To compare one nucleus with another it is better to calculate the *binding energy per nucleon*. This gives the amount of energy required to remove one nucleon from the nucleus giving an indication of its relative stability. So for the previous

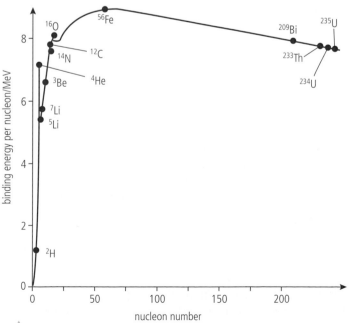

Figure 7.32 Graph of BE/nucleon vs nucleon number.

	Atomic mass/u
Hydrogen	1.00782
Neutron	1.00866
Iron ($^{54}_{26}$Fe)	53.9396

Table 7.2 Atomic masses in terms of u.

You don't need to add the electrons in every time – just use atomic masses plus the mass of hydrogen instead of the proton mass and it will all work out.

Table 7.3 The atomic mass of selected nuclides.

Atomic masses			
Z	Symbol	A	Mass/u
1	H	1	1.0078
1	D	2	2.0141
2	He	3	3.0160
3	Li	6	6.0151
4	Be	9	9.0122
7	N	14	14.0031
17	Cl	35	34.9689
26	Fe	54	53.9396
28	Ni	58	57.9353
36	Kr	78	77.9204
38	Sr	84	83.9134
56	Ba	130	129.9063
82	Pb	204	203.9730
86	Rn	211	210.9906
88	Ra	223	223.0185
92	U	233	233.0396

example, the binding energy per nucleon of ^{54}Fe is $\frac{471.5}{54}$ = 8.7 MeV/nucleon. Figure 7.32 shows the BE/nucleon plotted against nucleon number for a variety of nuclei.

From Figure 7.32 we can see that some nuclei are more stable than others: iron and nickel are in the middle so they are the most stable nuclei. If small nuclei join to make larger ones the binding energy per nucleon increases resulting in a release of energy, but to make nuclei bigger than iron, energy would have to be put in. This tells us something about how the different elements found on Earth must have been formed. Small nuclei are formed in the centre of stars as the matter gets pulled together by gravity releasing energy in the form of the light we see. When big nuclei form, energy is absorbed – this happens towards the end of a star's life. There are more details about this in Chapter 12.

Figure 7.32 is a very important graph which is used to explain almost every aspect of nuclear reactions from the energy production in stars to problems with nuclear waste.

Remember: 1u is equivalent to 931.5 MeV.

Exercises

21 Find uranium in Table 7.3.

(a) How many protons and neutrons does uranium have?
(b) Calculate the total mass, in unified mass units, of the protons and neutrons that make uranium.
(c) Calculate the difference between the mass of uranium and its constituents (the mass defect).
(d) What is the binding energy of uranium in MeV?
(e) What is the BE per nucleon of uranium?

22 Enter the data from the table into a spreadsheet. Add formulae to the spreadsheet to calculate the binding energy per nucleon for all the nuclei and plot a graph of BE/nucleon against nucleon number.

CHALLENGE YOURSELF

1 Estimate the amount of energy in joules required to break 3 g of copper (^{63}Cu) into its constituent nucleons.

Radioactive decay

To explain why a ball rolls down a hill we can say that it is moving to a position of lower potential energy. In the same way, the combination of protons and neutrons in a nucleus will change if it results in an increased binding energy. This sounds like it is the wrong way round but remember, binding energy is the energy released when a nucleus is formed so if a nucleus changes to one of higher binding energy then energy must be *released*. There are three main ways that a nucleus can change:

- **alpha emission**. Alpha particles are helium nuclei. Emission of a helium nucleus results in a smaller nucleus so according to the binding energy per nucleon curve, this would only be possible in large nuclei.

- **changing a neutron to a proton**. This results in the emission of an electron (beta minus).

- **changing a proton to a neutron**. This results in the emission of a positive electron (positron) (beta plus). This is quite rare.

Notice that all three changes result in the emission of a particle that takes energy away from the nucleus. Energy can also be lost by the emission of high energy electromagnetic radiation (gamma). The amount of energy associated with nuclear reactions is in the order of MeV so these particles are ejected at high speed. Ionizing an atom requires a few eV so one of these particles can ionize millions of atoms as they travel through the air. This makes them harmful, but also easy to detect.

Detecting radiation

A Geiger–Muller, or GM, tube is a type of ionization chamber. It contains a low pressure gas which, when ionized by a passing particle, allows a current to flow between two electrodes as in Figure 7.33.

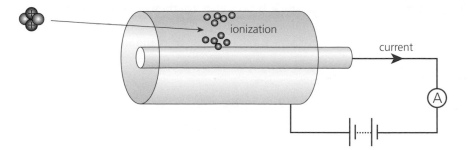

Figure 7.33 An ionization chamber.

By detecting this flow of charge we can count individual particles. However, since all of the particles are ionizing we can't tell which type of radiation it is. To do this we can use their different penetrating powers: most alpha particles, being the biggest, can be stopped by a sheet of paper; beta particles can pass through paper but are stopped by a thin sheet of aluminium; gamma rays, which are the same as high energy X-rays, are the most penetrating and will even pass through lead. For the same reason, the different radiations have varying ranges in air: alpha particles only travel a few cm, beta particles travel about 10 times further, gamma radiation travels furthest but interacts slightly differently, resulting in an inverse square reduction in intensity with increasing distance.

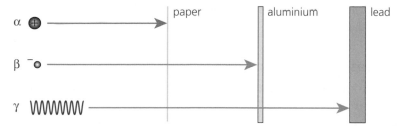

Figure 7.34 Absorption of radiation.

An alternative way of detecting radioactive particles is using a cloud chamber. This contains a vapour which turns into droplets of liquid when an ionizing particle passes through. This results in a visible line showing the path of the particle, rather like the vapour trail behind an airplane. A bubble chamber is similar but the trail is a line of bubbles.

A bubble chamber photograph from the CERN accelerator. There is a magnetic field directed out of the chamber causing positive particles to spiral clockwise.

Alpha particles leave the thickest track, betas somewhat thinner. A single gamma photon would not leave a track unless absorbed by an atomic electron which then, if given enough energy, could leave a track as it is ejected from the atom.

Table 7.4 The properties of the three types of nuclear radiation.

Particle	Mass/u	Charge/e	Stopped by
Alpha (α)	4	+2	paper
Beta (β)	0.0005	−1	aluminium
Gamma (γ)	0	0	lead

Alpha decay

When a nucleus emits an alpha particle it loses 2 protons and 2 neutrons. The reaction can be represented by a nuclear equation. For example, radium decays into radon when it emits an alpha particle.

$$^{226}_{88}\text{Ra} \rightarrow \, ^{222}_{86}\text{Rn} + \, ^4_2\text{He}$$

4 nucleons are emitted, so the nucleon number is reduced by 4.

2 protons are emitted, so the proton number is reduced by 2.

Alpha particles are emitted by large nuclei that gain binding energy by changing into smaller nuclides.

Energy released

When radium changes to radon the BE is increased. This leads to a drop in total mass, this mass having been converted to energy.

Mass of radium > (mass of radon + mass of alpha)

Energy released = {mass$_{Ra}$ − (mass$_{Rn}$ + mass$_{alpha}$)}c^2

mass$_{Ra}$ = 226.0254 u

mass$_{Rn}$ = 222.0176 u

mass$_{He}$ = 4.002602 u

Change in mass = 0.005198 u

This is equivalent to energy of 0.005198 × 931.5 MeV

Energy released = 4.84 MeV

Nuclear energy levels

When an alpha particle is ejected from a nucleus, it is like an explosion where a small ball flies apart from a big one, as shown in Figure 7.35. An amount of energy is released during the explosion, which gives the balls the KE they need to fly apart.

Applying the principle of conservation of momentum:

momentum before = momentum after

$$0 = 100 \times 1 - 800v$$
$$v = 0.125 \, \text{m s}^{-1}$$

The alpha source americium-241 is used in many smoke detectors. The alpha radiation ionizes the air between two parallel plates allowing charge to flow in a circuit. When smoke enters the gap between the plates the current falls. It is this drop in current that triggers the alarm. Even though they contain a radioisotope, smoke detectors do not present a health risk since alpha radiation will not be able to penetrate the casing of the detector.

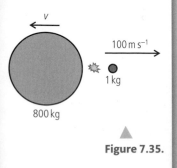

Figure 7.35.

so the kinetic energy of large ball $KE_1 = \frac{1}{2} \times 800 \times 0.125^2 = 6.25\,J$.

Kinetic energy of the small ball $KE_2 = \frac{1}{2} \times 1 \times 100^2 = 5000\,J$.

From this example we can see that the small particle gets almost all of the energy. The same is true for the alpha decay. So for the example of radium, all alphas should have a KE of 4.84 MeV. Some isotopes emit two alpha particles which differ in energy, one taking more of the energy and a second with less energy; for example, a 4.84 MeV alpha and a 4.74 MeV alpha. Emission of the lower energy alpha would leave the nucleus in an unstable excited state. The remaining 0.1 MeV of energy can be lost later through the emission of gamma radiation. This can be explained by considering the wave-like nature of the nucleons. As with all particles, the position of nucleons is given by a wave function which is limited by certain boundary conditions keeping them together in the nucleus. Solving the equations for this situation leads to a solution similar to electrons in an atom; the nucleus has energy levels too.

Alpha tunnelling

To model the forces preventing an alpha particle from leaving the nucleus we can think of a potential well created by the different forces acting on it. Drawing this would give something like Figure 7.36: a very deep well due to the strong nuclear force, with a hill on the outside to represent the electrostatic repulsion.

If we think of the alpha as a ball in a similarly shaped hole in the ground, then to get the ball out of the hole it would have to be lifted over the barrier. Once over the barrier, it would accelerate down the hill, gaining KE. The ball cannot get out without going over the barrier so at a distance from the hill the ball must have at least as much KE as the PE it had at the top of the barrier.

Applying this to the alpha particle, the KE of alphas must be at least equal to their electric PE on the outside of the nucleus ($PE = kQq/r$). In reality, this isn't the case: the alphas have less energy than required to go over the barrier. This problem can be solved by considering the wave function of the alpha particle. As illustrated in Figure 7.37, the wave function for the alpha does not disappear at the boundary but decreases exponentially. This means that if the barrier is thin there is a probability that the alpha can appear on the outside without going over the barrier. This is called *tunnelling*.

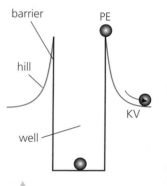

Figure 7.36 The potential well of the nucleus.

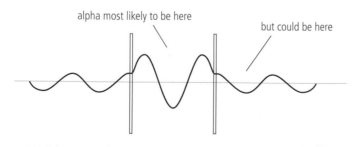

alpha most likely to be here

but could be here

Figure 7.37 Alpha tunnelling.

Exercise

23 Use Table 7.5 to calculate the amount of energy released when $^{212}_{84}Po$ decays into $^{208}_{82}Pb$.

Table 7.5 Two types of nucleon.

Nuclide	Atomic mass/u
Polonium (Po) 212	211.988842
Lead (Pb) 208	207.976627

Beta minus (β^-)

Beta minus particles are electrons. They are exactly the same as the electrons outside the nucleus but they are formed when a neutron changes to a proton. When this happens an antineutrino is also produced.

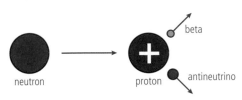

Figure 7.38 Beta minus decay.

If a neutron can change into a proton it would be reasonable to think that a neutron was a proton with an electron stuck onto it. Heisenberg's uncertainty principle tells us this is *not* possible since electrons can't be confined to the nucleus. Applying $\Delta p \Delta x = \frac{h}{4\pi}$ the uncertainty in position of an electron confined to the nucleus would have to be $\approx 10^{-15}$ m so the uncertainty in momentum would be $\frac{6.6 \times 10^{-34}}{4\pi \times 10^{-15}} = 5.3 \times 10^{-20}$ N s. This would mean the velocity of the electron $(\frac{mv}{m})$ would be approximately $\frac{5.3 \times 10^{-20}}{9.1 \times 10^{-31}} = 6 \times 10^{10}$ m s^{-1}, much greater than the speed of light and therefore not possible.

Another problem is that the electron is not affected by the nuclear force. In fact the force involved in this interaction is a whole new force called the *weak force*.

Antineutrino

An antineutrino is the antiparticle of a neutrino. All particles have antiparticles.

Effect on nucleus

When a nucleus emits a beta particle, it loses 1 neutron and gains 1 proton.

Carbon-14 decays into nitrogen-14 when it emits a beta particle.

$$^{14}_{6}\text{C} \longrightarrow \,^{14}_{7}\text{N} + e^{-1} + \bar{\nu}$$

Nuclei with too many neutrons decay by beta minus decay.

Energy released

When carbon-14 decays the BE is increased resulting in a drop in the total mass.

Energy released = $[m_{\text{Cnucleus}} - (m_{\text{Nnucleus}} + m_e)]c^2$

If using atomic masses then we should subtract the electrons.

Energy released = $[(m_{\text{Catom}} - 6m_e) - (m_{\text{Natom}} - 7m_e + m_e)]c^2$

We can see that all the electrons cancel out leaving $[m_{\text{Catom}} - m_{\text{Natom}}]c^2$.

$m_{\text{Catom}} = 14.003241$
$m_{\text{Natom}} = 14.003074$

So energy released = 0.0001×931.5 MeV = 0.16 MeV.

The size of a beta particle is much smaller than the nucleus so one would expect that the beta would take all of the energy. However, this is not the case. Beta particles are found to have a range of energies as shown by the energy spectrum in Figure 7.39.

Living organisms are constantly taking carbon either directly from the atmosphere or by eating plants that are taking it from the atmosphere. In this way the carbon content of the organism is the same as the atmosphere. The ratio of carbon-12 to carbon-14 is constant in the atmosphere so living organisms have the same ratio as the atmosphere. When organisms die the carbon is no longer replaced so as the carbon-14 starts to decay, the ratio of carbon-12 to carbon-14 increases. By measuring this ratio it is possible to determine the approximate age of dead organic material.

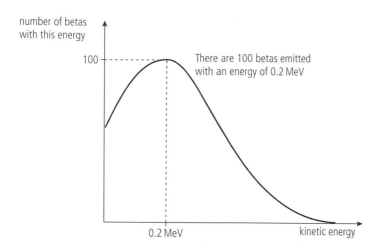

number of betas
with this energy

100 ---- There are 100 betas emitted
with an energy of 0.2 MeV

0.2 MeV kinetic energy

Figure 7.39 This graph shows the spread of beta energy. It isn't really a line graph but a bar chart with thin bars. Notice how many betas have zero KE – this is because they are slowed down by electrostatic attraction to the nucleus.

When beta radiation was first discovered the existence of the neutrino was unknown, so physicists were puzzled as to how the beta could have a range of energies; it just isn't possible if only one particle is ejected from a heavy nucleus. To solve this problem, Wolfgang Pauli suggested that there must be an 'invisible' particle coming out too. The particle was called a *neutrino* (small neutral one) since it had no charge and negligible mass. Neutrinos are not totally undetectable and were eventually discovered some 26 years later. However, they are very unreactive; they can pass through thousands of kilometres of lead without an interaction.

It was later realized that the extra particle involved in β^- decay is actually the electron antineutrino.

Exercises

24 By calculating the change in binding energy, explain why $^{213}_{84}$Po will not decay by β^- emission into $^{214}_{85}$At.

25 Use the information in Table 7.6 to calculate the maximum possible energy of the β^- radiation emitted when $^{139}_{56}$Ba decays into $^{139}_{57}$La.

Nuclide	Atomic mass /u
Polonium (Po) 213	212.992833
Astatine (At) 213	212.992911
Barium (Ba) 139	138.908835
Lanthanum (La) 139	138.906347

Table 7.6.

Beta plus (β^+) decay

A beta plus is a positive electron, or positron. They are emitted from the nucleus when a proton changes to a neutron. When this happens, a neutrino is also produced.

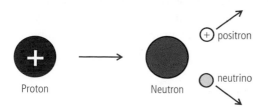

Proton → Neutron
⊕ positron
○ neutrino

Figure 7.40 Beta plus decay.

A positron has the same properties as an electron but it is positive (it is the antiparticle of an electron), so beta plus particles have very similar properties to beta minus. They penetrate paper, have a range of about 30 centimetres in air, and are weakly ionizing.

The beta plus track in a cloud chamber also looks the same as beta minus, unless a magnetic field is added. The different charged paths then curve in opposite directions as shown in the photo on page 293.

Effect on nucleus

When a nucleus emits a β^+ it loses one proton and gains a neutron. An example of a β^+ decay is the decay of sodium into neon.

$$^{22}_{11}\text{Na} \longrightarrow {}^{22}_{10}\text{Ne} + e^+ + \nu$$

In common with negative electrons, positive electrons are not affected by the nuclear force so β^+ decay is also a *weak interaction*. Once emitted, the positive electrons lose energy as they ionize atoms in the material they pass through. As they slow down they are able to annihilate with an electron resulting in gamma radiation.

Gamma radiation (γ)

Gamma radiation is electromagnetic radiation, so when it is emitted there is no change in the particles of the nucleus – they just lose energy. Each time a nucleus decays, a photon is emitted. As we have seen, the energy released from nuclear reactions is very high, so the energy of each gamma photon is also high. The frequency of a photon is related to its energy by the formula $E = hf$. This means that the frequency of gamma photons is very high. Their high energy also means that if they are absorbed by atomic electrons, they give the electrons enough energy to leave the atom. In other words they are ionizing – which means they can be detected with a GM tube, photographic paper or a cloud chamber. As they pass easily through human tissue, gamma rays have many medical applications.

Exercise

26 Americium-241 emits alpha particles with energy 5.485 MeV and 5.443 MeV. Calculate the frequency of gamma radiation that might also be emitted.

Exponential decay

As we have seen, the particles in the nucleus can be modelled by a wave function giving the probability of them being in or out of the nucleus. This makes radioactive decay a random process, meaning that we cannot predict the moment in time when a nucleus will decay. Quantum physics only applies to small-scale systems like the atom and nucleus. However, it might help understand some of the concepts by considering something we can observe more directly like bursting bubbles. If you blow a bubble with soapy water it is very difficult to predict when exactly it is going to pop. It might last only a few seconds or several minutes, so we can say that the popping of a bubble is fairly random. If we have a lot of bubbles then lots of them will be popping at any given time. The number popping each second is directly proportional to the number of bubbles.

CHALLENGE YOURSELF

2 Show that the energy released when ^{22}Na decays by β$^+$ decay is 1.82 MeV.

The decay of bubbles

When a fizzy drink (like beer or cola) is poured, bubbles form on the top. Normally you don't want too many bubbles but in this experiment you do as they are going to be measured as they pop. It would be rather difficult to count the bubbles but as they burst the level of the drink goes up so this can be used to measure how many bubbles have burst. You need a drink where the bubbles stay for a long time, like (even non-alcoholic) beer; cola is a bit too fast.

The drink is poured into a measuring cylinder and level of the drink is measured every 5 or 10 seconds until most of the foam has gone. A good way of doing this is to take a video of the foam and measure its height by analysing the frames.

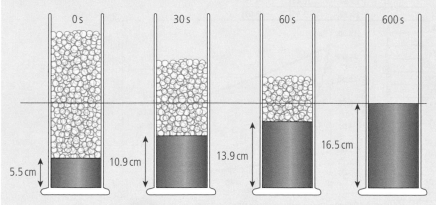

Beer bubbles.

Figure 7.41 The height of liquid is measured as the bubbles burst.

Figure 7.41 shows the drink at four different times, showing how the height of the liquid changes. However, we want to measure the amount of foam. To do this the drink is left for 10 minutes until all of the bubbles have burst. This is taken to be the zero foam level. If the liquid height is subtracted from this we get the amount of liquid that was foam.

Plotting the amount of foam *vs* time we get a curve like the one shown in Figure 7.42. The best-fit curve is an exponential decay curve with equation:

$$h = h_0 e^{-\lambda t}$$

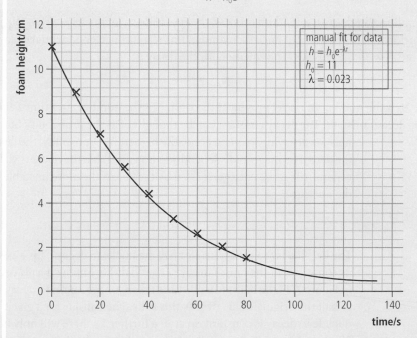

manual fit for data
$h = h_0 e^{-\lambda t}$
$h_0 = 11$
$\lambda = 0.023$

The exponential decay of bubbles

A worksheet with full details of how to carry out this experiment is available on your eBook.

Figure 7.42 The exponential decay of foam.

The special thing about an exponential curve is that the gradient is proportional to the *y* value. This means that the rate of change of height is proportional to the amount of foam. This is what we expected, since the rate at which the bubbles pop is proportional to the number of bubbles.

Decay constant λ

The value of λ gives the rate at which the bubbles decay. To understand this we can plot exponential decay curves with a spreadsheet as shown in Figure 7.43.

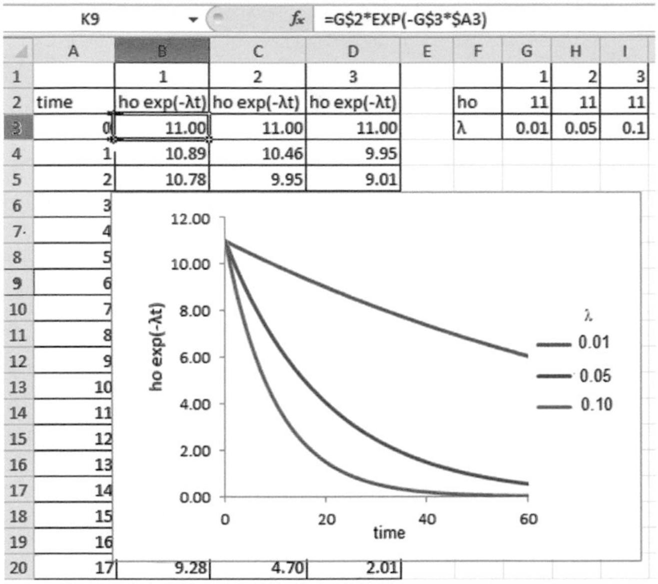

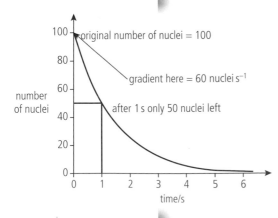

	K9		f_x	=G$2*EXP(-G$3*$A3)				
	A	B	C	D	E	F	G	H	I
1		1	2	3			1	2	3
2	time	ho exp(-λt)	ho exp(-λt)	ho exp(-λt)		ho	11	11	11
3	0	11.00	11.00	11.00		λ	0.01	0.05	0.1
4	1	10.89	10.46	9.95					
5	2	10.78	9.95	9.01					
6	3								
7	4								
8	5								
9	6								
10	7								
11	8								
12	9								
13	10								
14	11								
15	12								
16	13								
17	14								
18	15								
19	16								
20	17	9.28	4.70	2.01					

Figure 7.43 Spreadsheet to plot exponential curves.

The equation used to calculate $e^{-\lambda t}$ is shown in the formula bar. The $ sign is used so that when the formula is copied into other cells the cell locations don't change. From these curves we can see that a higher value of λ gives a faster rate of decay.

Exponential decay of radioactive isotopes

Since radioactive decay is a random process, the rate of decay of nuclei is also proportional to the number of nuclei remaining; this results in an exponential decay, the same as with the bubbles. The equation for the decay is:

$$N = N_0 e^{-\lambda t}$$

where N_0 is the number of nuclei present at the start, N is the number after time t and λ is the decay constant. The decay constant can be thought of as the probability of a nucleus decaying in one second: the higher the probability, the faster the decay. Its magnitude depends on how unstable the nucleus is. In general, the more energy released by the decay, the more unstable the nucleus.

Half-life

The half-life is the time taken for *half* the nuclei to decay. This gives us some idea of the rate of decay; a *short* half-life implies a *rapid* decay. In Figure 7.44 the half-life is the time taken for the nuclei to decay to half the original value of 100; this is 1 s. The half-life for a given nuclide to decay is constant, so after a further 1 s there will only be 25 nuclei left, and so on until there are so few nuclei that statistical approximations become invalid.

Figure 7.44 Decay curve showing half-life.

Activity

Each time a nucleus decays a radioactive particle is emitted so the rate of decay is the same as the rate of emission. This is called the *activity* of the sample and is measured in becquerel (emissions per second). Since the rate of decay is directly proportional to the number of nuclei, the graph of activity *vs* time will also be exponential. Figure 7.45 shows the activity of the sample from Figure 7.44. Notice that this is simply the gradient of the previous graph.

The equation for this line is

$$A = A_0 e^{-\lambda t}$$

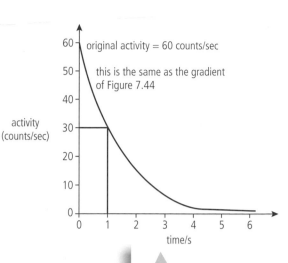

Figure 7.45 Activity *vs* time.

Background radiation

Radioactivity is a natural phenomenon as there are radioactive isotopes in rocks, building materials, the air, and even our own bodies. This all adds up to give what is known as *background radiation*. If a Geiger–Muller tube is left in a room then it will detect this radiation. This is normally in the region of 20 counts per minute. When performing experiments on radioactive decay in the laboratory we can use lead to shield our detector. This will prevent most of the radiation getting to our detector. However, some will get through resulting in a systematic error. If the background count is measured separately the count rate can be corrected accordingly. The source of this radiation is:

- the surrounding rock and soil; some rocks contain radioactive material such as uranium and thorium which decay over a long period of time.
- the air, which may contain radon gas which is emitted when radium present in some rocks decays by emitting alpha particles. Some houses built into rock particularly rich in radium can have high concentrations of radon gas. People living in these houses are advised to have good ventilation.
- the Sun, which emits fast-moving particles that arrive at the surface of the Earth; these are called cosmic rays.

Relationship between λ and half-life

The half-life, $t_{\frac{1}{2}}$ is the time taken for the number of nuclei to decay to half the original value. So if the original number of nuclei = N_0 then after $t_{\frac{1}{2}}$ seconds there will be $\frac{N_0}{2}$ nuclei. If we substitute these values into the exponential decay equation, we get:

$$\frac{N_0}{2} = N_0 e^{-\lambda t_{\frac{1}{2}}}$$

Cancelling N_0

$$\frac{1}{2} = e^{-\lambda t_{\frac{1}{2}}}$$

Taking natural logs of both sides gives

$$\ln(\tfrac{1}{2}) = -\lambda t_{\frac{1}{2}}$$

This is the same as

$$\ln 2 = \lambda t_{\frac{1}{2}}$$

So

$$t_{\frac{1}{2}} = \frac{0.693}{\lambda}$$

Measuring half-life

To find the decay constant and hence half-life of short-lived isotopes, the change in activity can be measured over a period of time using a GM tube. The activity of long-lived isotopes takes a long time to change so in this case the parent and daughter nuclei are separated. Then, knowing the number of parent nuclei and the activity of the sample, the decay constant can be found from $\frac{dN}{dt} = -\lambda N$.

So if we know the decay constant, we can find the half-life or vice versa.

If the time for decay is a whole number of half-lives then it is simply a matter of halving the original number of nuclei/activity the same number of times.

Worked example

Cobalt-60 decays by beta emission and has a half-life of approximately 5 years. If a sample of cobalt-60 emits 40 beta particles per second, how many will the same sample be emitting in 15 years time?

Solution

After 5 years the activity will be 20 particles per second.

After another 5 years it will be 10 particles per second.

Finally after a further 5 years it will emit 5 particles per second (5 Bq).

Exercises

27 ^{17}N decays into ^{17}O with a half-life of 4 s. How much ^{17}N will remain after 16 s, if you start with 200 g?

28 ^{11}Be decays into ^{11}B with a half-life of 14 s. If the ^{11}Be emits 100 particles per second, how many particles per second will it emit after 42 s?

29 A sample of dead wood contains $\frac{1}{16}$ of the amount of ^{14}C that it contained when alive. If the half-life of ^{14}C is 6000 years how old is the sample?

If the time is not a whole number of half-lives then you have to use the exponential decay equation.

Worked example

Protactinium has a half-life of 70 s. A sample has an activity of 30 Bq. Calculate its activity after 10 minutes.

Solution

We are going to use the equation $A_t = A_0 e^{-\lambda t}$. First we need to find the decay

constant $\lambda = \dfrac{0.693}{t_{\frac{1}{2}}} = 9.9 \times 10^{-3}\,\text{s}^{-1}$

The activity after 600 s is now $30 \times e^{-9.9 \times 10^{-3} \times 600} = 0.08\,\text{Bq}$

Exercises

30 A sample has activity 40 Bq. If it has a half-life of 5 mins, what will its activity be after 12 mins?

31 The activity of a sample of strontium-90 decreases from 20 Bq to 15.7 Bq in 10 years. What is the half-life of strontium 90?

32 Cobalt-60 has a half-life of 5.27 years. Calculate:

   (a) the half-life in s.
   (b) the decay constant in s^{-1}.
   (c) the number of atoms in one gram of ^{60}Co.
   (d) the activity of 1 gram of ^{60}Co.
   (e) the amount of ^{60}Co in a sample with an activity of 50 Bq.

You don't have to convert everything into seconds. If half-life is in years then the unit of γ is year^{-1}.

Nuclear fusion

Nuclear fusion is the joining up of two small nuclei to form one big one.

If we look at the BE/nucleon *vs* nucleon number curve (Figure 7.46), we see that the line initially rises steeply. If you were to add two $_1^2$H nuclei to get one $_2^4$He nucleus, then the He nucleus would have more BE per nucleon.

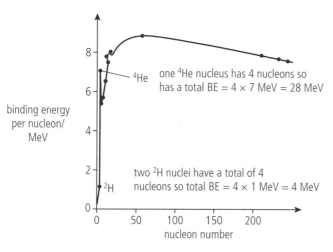

one ^{4}He nucleus has 4 nucleons so has a total BE = 4 × 7 MeV = 28 MeV

two ^{2}H nuclei have a total of 4 nucleons so total BE = 4 × 1 MeV = 4 MeV

binding energy per nucleon/ MeV

nucleon number

An artist's impression of the fusion of ^{2}H and ^{3}H to form ^{4}He.

Figure 7.46 BE/nucleon *vs* nucleon number curve, showing fusion possibility.

If we add up the total BE for the helium nucleus, it has 24 MeV more BE than the two hydrogen nuclei. This means that 24 MeV would have to be released; this could be by the emission of gamma radiation.

Worked example

Calculate the energy released by the following reaction:

$$_1^2H + _1^3H \longrightarrow _2^4He + _0^1n$$

Solution

If the masses are added, we find that the mass of the original nuclei is greater than the mass of the final ones. This mass has been converted to energy.

Mass difference = 0.018883 u

1u is equivalent to 931.5 MeV so energy released = 17.6 MeV

Each small nucleus has a positive charge so they will repel each other. To make the nuclei come close enough for the strong force to pull them together, they must be thrown together with very high velocity. For this to take place, the matter must either be heated to temperatures as high as the core of the Sun (about 13 million kelvin) or the particles must be thrown together in a particle accelerator.

The fusion reaction produces a lot of energy per unit mass of fuel and much research has been carried out to build a fusion reactor.

It wouldn't be possible to conserve both KE and momentum if two fast moving nuclei collided and fused together. That's why all the reactions result in two particles not one big one.

Exercise

33 Use the data in Table 7.7 to calculate the change in mass and hence the energy released in the following examples of fusion reactions:

(a) $_1^2H + _1^2H \longrightarrow _2^3He + _0^1n$
(b) $_1^2H + _1^2H \longrightarrow _1^3H + _1^1p$
(c) $_1^2H + _2^3He \longrightarrow _2^4He + _1^1p$

Nuclide	Mass in u
^{1}H	1.007825
^{2}H	2.014101
^{3}H	3.016049
^{3}He	3.016029
^{4}He	4.002603
^{1}n	1.008664

Table 7.7.

Nuclear fission

Looking at the right-hand side of the graph in Figure 7.47 we see that if one large nucleus is split into two smaller ones, then the total BE would again be increased. This reaction forms the basis of the nuclear reactor that you will learn more about in Chapter 8.

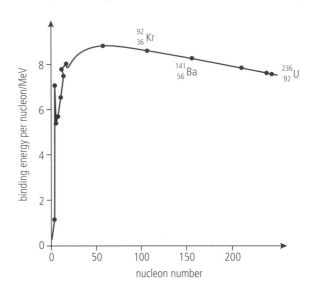

Figure 7.47 BE/nucleon *vs* nucleon number curve showing fission possibility.

Worked example

Find the energy released if uranium-236 splits into krypton-92 and barium-141.

Solution

BE of ^{236}U = 236 × 7.6

$\qquad$ = 1793.6 MeV

BE of ^{141}Ba = 141 × 8

$\qquad$ = 1128 MeV

BE of ^{92}Kr = 92 × 8.2

$\qquad$ = 754.4 MeV

Gain in BE = (1128 + 754.4) − 1793.6

$\qquad$ = 88.8 MeV

Since this leads to a release of energy, this process is possible.

To answer these questions you must find the difference in mass between the original nucleus and the products. To convert to MeV, simply multiply by 931.5.

To learn more about properties of the nucleus and radioactivity, go to the hotlinks site, search for the title or ISBN and click on Chapter 7.

Exercises

Use Table 7.8 to answer the following questions.

34 If ^{236}U splits into ^{100}Mo and ^{126}Sn, how many neutrons will be produced? Calculate the energy released in this reaction.

35 ^{233}U splits into ^{138}Ba and ^{86}Kr plus 9 neutrons. Calculate the energy released when this takes place.

Z	Symbol	A	Mass (u)
92	U	233	233.039628
92	U	236	236.045563
42	Mo	100	99.907476
50	Sn	126	125.907653
56	Ba	138	137.905233
36	Kr	86	85.910615
0	n	1	1.008664

Table 7.8 Nuclear masses.

The structure of matter

7.3 The structure of matter

Understandings, applications, and skills:

Quarks, leptons, and their antiparticles
- Describing protons and neutrons in terms of quarks.
- Describing why free quarks are not observed.

Guidance
- *A qualitative description of the standard model is required.*

Hadrons, baryons, and mesons
- Applying conservation laws in particle reactions.

The conservation laws of charge, baryon number, lepton number, and strangeness

The nature and range of the strong nuclear force, weak nuclear force, and electromagnetic force
- Comparing the interaction strengths of the fundamental forces, including gravity.

Exchange particles
- Describing the mediation of the fundamental forces through exchange particles.

Feynman diagrams
- Sketching and interpreting simple Feynman diagrams.

Confinement
- Describing protons and neutrons in terms of quarks. Describing why free quarks are not observed.

The Higgs boson

Classifying particles

If we list all the different particles that we have come across so far we get a total of 5 (plus their antiparticles):

electron
proton
neutron
neutrino
photon

These particles can be classified in term of the interactions they take part in:

The electron and proton have *charge* so take part in *electromagnetic interactions*.
The proton and neutron are nucleons so take part in *nuclear interactions*.
The neutrino only takes part in *weak interactions* (beta decay).

There is also a difference in mass; the proton and neutron have much higher mass than the other three. This leads to a first step in classifying particles. Hadrons are heavy particles that take part in nuclear interactions, leptons are light particles that don't. Photons have no mass but do have energy; they are part of another group of particles called *exchange bosons*. To see how they fit in we need to look again at the nature of fundamental forces.

NATURE OF SCIENCE

The principle of Occam's razor states that a theory should be as simple as possible. In particle physics this means that it is better to make all known particles out of as few elementary particles as possible. The standard model is elegantly simple.

New particles may be discovered when highly energetic protons collide with each other. To get high energy particles we either have to wait for one to arrive in our laboratory from the Sun (the old method) or build a particle accelerator. Particle accelerators are so expensive to construct that countries must collaborate in order to raise the money to build one.

Hadron	Lepton
proton	electron
neutron	neutrino

Table 7.9 Hadrons and leptons.

Force	Strength	range
strong	1	10^{-15} m
electromagnetic	10^{-2}	infinite
weak	10^{-6}	10^{-18} m
gravity	10^{-38}	infinite

Table 7.10 The relative strength of the fundamental forces.

Exchange forces

In 1933 Hideki Yukawa developed the theory of exchange particles. The idea is that every force is due to the exchange of a particle. Consider two canoes paddling parallel to each other. What happens if a heavy object is thrown from one canoe to the other as shown in Figure 7.48(a)? When A throws the ball, A must exert a force on the ball, according to Newton's third law. A will experience an equal and opposite force causing A to move away from B. When B catches the ball, B must exert a force on the ball in order to stop it. B will therefore experience a force away from A. The canoes repel each other.

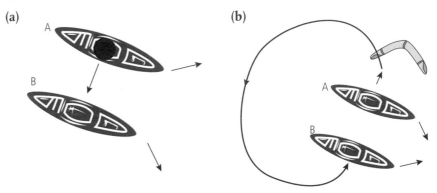

(a) **(b)**

Figure 7.48 The exchange of particles leads to repulsive or attractive forces.

To explain an attractive force, imagine what would happen if A threw a boomerang in the opposite direction to B. The boomerang spins, following a path as shown in Figure 7.48(b). When B catches the boomerang, B will be pushed towards A.

This is not the way it happens with particles but it gives an idea that it is possible. It is one thing to explain the force between two canoes in terms of the exchange of a ball, but how does this apply to the force between two electrons?

Electromagnetic force

The force between charged particles can be modelled in terms of the exchange of photons. Consider two electrons moving towards each other as shown in Figure 7.49.

If electron A emits a photon that is absorbed by electron B then the electrons will experience a force pushing them apart. But, photons have energy (hf), so to create a photon energy would have to be created, which would be against the law of conservation of energy. This would be the end of that theory if it wasn't for quantum mechanics; according to Heisenberg's uncertainty principle $\Delta E \Delta t \geq \frac{h}{4\pi}$ which implies that if the change in energy only happens for a very short time then the apparent violation is allowed. These photons cannot be measured so are called *virtual photons*. If the electrons are very close together, the time for the photon to travel from A to B is small so the energy of the photon can be big, resulting in a large force. As they move further apart the energy must be less and the force smaller. This gives $F \propto \frac{1}{r^2}$ which agrees with experiment. The model as pictured here has the electrons travelling in straight lines, then suddenly being pushed apart. In reality the particles will be pushed apart all the time resulting in a curved path. This is achieved by a continual exchange of virtual photons.

This theory is called quantum electrodynamics (QED) and was worked on by Richard Feynman in the 1950s. He developed a way of representing the interactions visually, which we call Feynman diagrams.

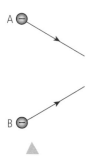

Figure 7.49 Electrons on a collision course.

Feynman diagrams

Figure 7.50 shows a Feynman diagram for the interaction between two electrons. It isn't supposed to show the paths of the particles, just the nature of the interaction. In this example, two electrons repel each other by exchanging a virtual photon. The photon moves forwards in time so it is absorbed after it is emitted.

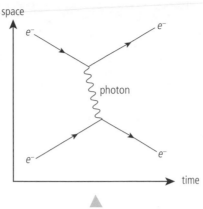

Figure 7.50.

Feynman diagrams are drawn according to simple rules:

- particles are straight lines; exchange particles are wavy lines.
- each vertex (the point where lines join) is made up of two particles and an exchange particle. Vertices represent interactions.
- time progresses from left to right (sometimes drawn vertically with time progressing upwards). So particles enter the interaction on the left and exit on the right.
- particles have arrows pointing forwards in time; antiparticles backwards (this doesn't mean they are travelling in the direction of the arrow; it is just convention).
- there is always one arrow entering a vertex and one leaving.

Feynman diagrams can be used to calculate the probability of different interactions as well as to predict new ones by rotating the arrows of known interactions. To see how this works, in Figure 7.51 we consider one of the two vertices from Figure 7.50 representing an electron emitting a photon. This would have to be either reabsorbed or absorbed by another electron but that part isn't shown.

If this diagram is rotated we can get Figures 7.52, 7.53, and 7.54.

Figure 7.51 An electron emits a photon.

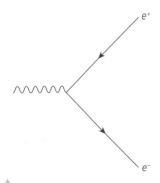

Figure 7.52 A photon enters the interaction, and a positron and electron leave. Note that the positron appears to enter the interaction but remember it is an antiparticle so the arrow is backwards. This is called *pair production*.

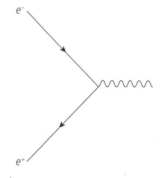

Figure 7.53 An electron and positron interact to form a photon. This is *electron–positron annihilation*.

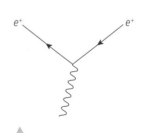

Figure 7.54 A photon is absorbed by a positron.

Exercises

36 Draw two more possible interactions by reflecting and/or rotating the arrows of Figure 7.51. Describe what they represent.

37 By rotating Figure 7.50 it is possible to get the diagrams in Figure 7.55. In each case name the particles a, b, c, d, e, and describe the interactions.

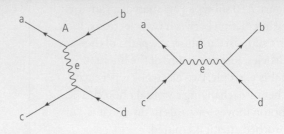

Figure 7.55.

Nuclear force

If the short range force between nucleons is also an exchange force then according to Heisenberg's uncertainty principle the exchange particle must have a relatively big mass.

The force only extends within the nucleus, so the exchange particles only live long enough to travel across a small nucleus, about 1.0×10^{-15} m.

The time taken if they are travelling near to the speed of light will be

$$\frac{1.0 \times 10^{-15}}{3 \times 10^8} \text{ s} \approx 3 \times 10^{-24} \text{ s}$$

Rearranging Heisenberg's equation gives

$$\Delta E = \frac{h}{4\pi\Delta t}$$

So

$$\Delta E = \frac{5.28 \times 10^{-35}}{3 \times 10^{-24}} = 1.76 \times 10^{-11} \text{ J}$$

To convert this to eV divide by 1.6×10^{-19} C $\quad \Delta E = 110 \text{ MeV}$

According to Einstein, energy and mass are equivalent, which leads us to believe that the exchange particle has a rest mass of about $110 \text{ MeV}c^{-2}$. This particle is called a *pion*.

Baryons and mesons

The discovery of the pion led to a whole new set of particles with masses between those of the electron and nucleons. These particles are called *mesons* and since they take part in nuclear interactions they are part of the *hadron* group of particles. This gives two categories of hadron: meson (e.g. pion) and *baryon* (e.g. proton).

By accelerating protons to very high energy then colliding them with each other, some of the energy of the collision is turned into the mass of new particles. By observing the paths of these particles using an assortment of detectors, their properties can be calculated. In this way, many new hadrons have been discovered, bringing the list of the total number of hadrons to over 200.

Quantum number and conservation

When deciding whether or not a nuclear reaction can take place, we must make sure that the nucleon number and proton number are the same on both sides of the equation. This is an example of a conservation principle, for example:

$$^{226}_{88}\text{Ra} \longrightarrow \, ^{222}_{86}\text{Rn} + \, ^{4}_{2}\text{He}$$

The proton number on the left is 88 and on the right is 86 + 2 = 88.

The nucleon number on the left is 226 and on the right is 222 + 4 = 226.

The same idea of conserving charge is used in particle physics. However, we find that simply conserving charge is not enough. For example:

$$\text{proton} \rightarrow \text{positron} + \text{gamma}$$

This interaction is fine as far as charge is concerned ($+1 = +1$) but it never happens. A baryon *can't* change into a lepton. To take this into account, baryons and leptons are assigned baryon numbers and lepton numbers which must also be conserved in all interactions.

Examples

1. $p \rightarrow n + e^+ + \nu$

   Since all are conserved, this interaction seems to be possible.

	p	$\rightarrow$	n	+	e^+	+	ν
Baryon number	1	=	1	+	0	+	0
Lepton number	0	=	0	+	⁻1	+	1
Charge	1	=	0	+	1	+	0

   > Lepton number is +1 for leptons and –1 for antileptons.
   >
   > Baryon number is +1 for baryons and –1 for antibaryons.

2. $n \rightarrow p + e^- + \overline{\nu}$

   Again, all quantum numbers are conserved so the interaction is feasible.

	n	$\rightarrow$	p	+	e^-	+	$\overline{\nu}$
Baryon number	1	=	1	+	0	+	0
Lepton number	0	=	0	+	1	+	⁻1
Charge	0	=	1	+	⁻1	+	0

3. $n + p \rightarrow e^+ + \overline{\nu}$

   Although charge is conserved, the baryon number and lepton number aren't. Therefore, this interaction is not possible.

	n	+	p	$\rightarrow$	e^+	+	$\overline{\nu}$
Baryon number	1	+	1	$\neq$	0	+	0
Lepton number	0	+	0	$\neq$	⁻1	+	⁻1
Charge	0	+	1	=	1	+	0

Tables 7.11–7.13 summarize the quantum numbers for a selection of mesons, baryons, and leptons.

Name	Symbol	Baryon number	Charge	Spin	Strangeness
Pion	π^+	0	+1	0	0
Pion	π^0	0	0	0	0
Kaon	K^+	0	+1	0	1
Kaon	K^0	0	0	0	1
Eta	η^0	0	0	0	0
Rho	ρ^+	0	+1	1	0
J/psi	J/ψ	0	0	1	0
Phi	ϕ	0	0	1	0
D	D^0	0	0	0	0

Table 7.11 Mesons.

Table 7.12 Baryons.

Name	Symbol	Baryon number	Charge	Spin	Strangeness
Proton	ρ	1	+1	$\frac{1}{2}$	0
Neutron	n	1	0	$\frac{1}{2}$	0
Delta	Δ^{++}	1	+2	$1\frac{1}{2}$	0
Delta	Δ^{+}	1	+1	$1\frac{1}{2}$	0
Delta	Δ^{0}	1	0	$1\frac{1}{2}$	0
Delta	Δ^{-}	1	−1	$1\frac{1}{2}$	0
Lambda	Λ^{0}	1	0	$\frac{1}{2}$	−1
Sigma	Σ^{0}	1	+1	$\frac{1}{2}$	−1
Sigma	Σ^{-}	1	0	$\frac{1}{2}$	−1
Sigma	Σ^{-}	1	−1	$\frac{1}{2}$	−1
Xi	Ξ^{0}	1	0	$\frac{1}{2}$	−2
Xi	Ξ^{-}	1	−1	$\frac{1}{2}$	−2
Omega	Ω^{-}	1	−1	$1\frac{1}{2}$	−3

Baryon number: baryons 1, mesons 0 (leptons 0).

Charge: the charge of the particle in multiples of e.

Spin: similar to the spin of an electron; can be either ½ or 1½ for baryons and 0 or 1 for mesons.

Strangeness: an extra quantum number that is not conserved in weak interactions.

Table 7.13 Leptons.

Name	Symbol	Lepton number	Charge	Spin
Electron	e^{-}	+1	−1	$\frac{1}{2}$
Positron (antielectron)	e^{+}	−1	+1	$\frac{1}{2}$
Electron neutrino	ν_{e}	+1	0	$\frac{1}{2}$
Electron antineutrino	$\bar{\nu}_{e}$	−1	0	$\frac{1}{2}$

(The baryon number of all leptons is 0).

Exercises

Use conservation principles to find out if the following are possible:

38 $p + e^{-} \rightarrow n + \nu$ **39** $p + p \rightarrow p + p + \bar{p}$ **40** $p + p \rightarrow p + p + \pi^{0}$ **41** $p + \bar{p} \rightarrow \pi^{0} + \pi^{0}$

42 $e^{-} + e^{+} \rightarrow \gamma + \gamma$ **43** $e^{-} + e^{+} \rightarrow n + \gamma$ **44** $p + \bar{p} \rightarrow n + \bar{\nu}$

Flavour

As far as we know, quarks don't *taste* of anything. The word flavour is used to mean the *type* of quark.

Quarks

All hadrons are made out of 6 flavours of quark (plus 6 antiquarks). Each quark has spin $\frac{1}{2}$ so a particle with spin 1 or 0 (mesons) must be made of 2 quarks and particles with spin $\frac{1}{2}$ or $1\frac{1}{2}$ (baryons) must be made of 3 quarks. To understand this we can think of the spins lining up with each other as in Figure 7.56.

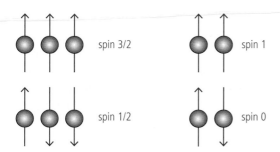

spin 3/2 — spin 1 — spin 1/2 — spin 0

Figure 7.56 Spins can be aligned or non-aligned.

All hadrons can be constructed out of combinations of the 6 quark flavours in Table 7.14.

Quark			Antiquark	
Flavour	Symbol	Charge	Symbol	Charge
Up	u	$+\frac{2}{3}$	$\bar{u}$	$-\frac{2}{3}$
Down	d	$-\frac{1}{3}$	$\bar{d}$	$+\frac{1}{3}$
Strange	s	$-\frac{1}{3}$	$\bar{s}$	$+\frac{1}{3}$
Charm	c	$+\frac{2}{3}$	$\bar{c}$	$-\frac{2}{3}$
Bottom	b	$-\frac{1}{3}$	$\bar{b}$	$+\frac{1}{3}$
Top	t	$+\frac{2}{3}$	$\bar{t}$	$-\frac{2}{3}$

Table 7.14 The six possible quarks that make up hadrons and their antiquarks. Note: to keep things simple, charm, bottom, and top quarks will not be considered in the following examples.

Baryon examples

Note that the strangeness quantum number is the given by the number of strange quarks in the particle (+1 for every antistrange and −1 for every strange).

Baryon	Quarks (and their charge)			Overall charge	Strangeness
Proton	$u\ (+\frac{2}{3})$	$u\ (+\frac{2}{3})$	$d\ (-\frac{1}{3})$	+1	0
Neutron	$d\ (-\frac{1}{3})$	$d\ (-\frac{1}{3})$	$u\ (+\frac{2}{3})$	0	0
Δ^-	$d\ (-\frac{1}{3})$	$d\ (-\frac{1}{3})$	$d\ (-\frac{1}{3})$	−1	0
Λ^0	$u\ (+\frac{2}{3})$	$d\ (-\frac{1}{3})$	$s\ (-\frac{1}{3})$	0	−1

Quarks have baryon number $\frac{1}{3}$, antiquarks have baryon number $\frac{-1}{3}$ so baryons have baryon number 1 and mesons have baryon number 0.

Table 7.15 Examples of baryons.

Meson examples

Meson	Quarks (and their charge)		Overall charge	Strangeness
π^+	$u\ (+\frac{2}{3})$	$\bar{d}\ (+\frac{1}{3})$	+1	0
K^+	$u\ (+\frac{2}{3})$	$\bar{s}\ (+\frac{1}{3})$	+1	+1

Table 7.16 Examples of mesons.

Exercises

45 Using the properties of the particles found in Tables 7.11 and 7.12, deduce the quark content of the following particles:

(a) π^- **(b)** Ω^- **(c)** Ξ^- **(d)** Ξ^0

46 During β^- decay a neutron changes to a proton. Which quark changes during this process?

Quark confinement

Quarks are held together by a very strong force so to pull them apart requires a lot of energy. In fact, so much energy is needed that it is enough to make the mass of new quarks. This means it is impossible to observe free quarks; every time one is pulled free from a particle a new quark/antiquark is formed making a meson. It is therefore not surprising that a lot of mesons are produced in high energy collision experiments, but no quarks.

Figure 7.57 Pulling apart quarks makes more quarks.

Colour force and strong interactions

Charge is the property that causes a particle to experience the electromagnetic force; *colour charge* is the property of quarks that causes them to experience the *strong* inter-quark force or *colour force*. Electric charge is conveniently two sided so we can use positive and negative numbers to represent it. Colour charge is more complex, necessitating the use of six colours. The particles are of course not really coloured but they form combinations in such a way that if they were coloured the combinations would be colourless. So, if we use the primary colours red, green, and blue, all hadrons would be made of one quark of each colour which, if this was three beams of light, would combine to be colourless. Antiquarks have anticolour which would make mesons colourless too.

Red, green, and blue light combine together to give white light.

Figure 7.58 Colourless combinations.

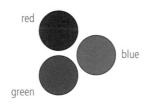
red
blue
green

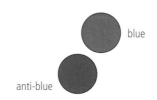
blue
anti-blue

Antiblue is drawn as yellow since yellow and blue = white.
Antired = cyan.
Antigreen = magenta.

QCD is an example where numbers cannot be used to model the physical property.

TOK

Gluons

The exchange particle of the colour force is the gluon. Gluons have a combination of colour and anticolour. When a gluon is exchanged from one quark to another the colour of the quarks change as represented by Figure 7.59. It is not at all obvious but by using this model of the force it is possible to predict which interactions will take place. This theory is called *quantum chromodynamics* or *QCD*.

Figure 7.59 A green quark emits a green/antiblue gluon so becomes blue. The blue quark absorbs a green antiblue gluon and so becomes green.

Feynman diagrams for strong interactions

Using the same rules that were used to represent electromagnetic interactions between electrons and positrons, we can represent the strong interactions between quarks. This time the exchange particles are gluons. In this case the gluons carry colour charge so the quark entering the vertex will have a different colour to the one leaving as shown in Figure 7.60. Note that although the colour of the quark changes, the flavour stays the same.

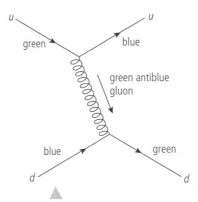

Figure 7.60 A strong interaction.

Exercise

47 Copy Figure 7.61 and fill in the missing particles X, Y, and Z (flavour and colour).

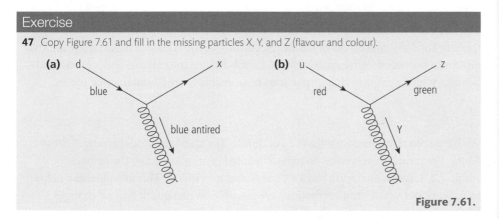

(a) **(b)**

Figure 7.61.

Weak interactions

When a nucleus decays by beta decay an electron and neutrino are produced. These are leptons so do not contain quarks and do not take part in strong reactions. The neutrino is not charged and doesn't take part in electromagnetic interactions, so there must be another type of interaction which we call the *weak interaction*. The forces involved aren't actually that weak but they are very short range (10^{-18} m), implying that the exchange bosons involved, the W and the Z, are comparatively massive. These are the only interactions in which the flavour of a particle can change. In β^- decay a neutron changes to a proton; this can be achieved if a down quark changes to an up quark as illustrated by the Feynman diagram in Figure 7.62.

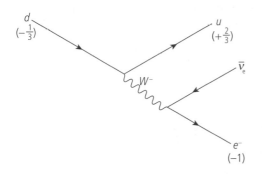

When interactions involving leptons take place the lepton number must be conserved. Here an electron (lepton number +1) is produced so an antineutrino (lepton number –1) must also be produced.

Figure 7.62 Feynman diagram for β^- decay. How is the charge conserved?

By rotating the arrows in this interaction we can predict several other interactions; for example, those shown in Figures 7.63 and 7.64.

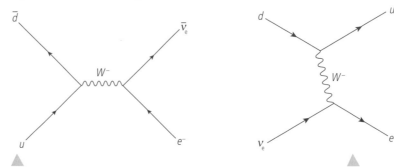

Figure 7.63 A pion decays into an electron and antineutrino.

Figure 7.64 A down quark interacts with a neutrino.

The standard model

The standard model explains how fundamental particles of matter interact under by the four fundamental forces of nature. According to the standard model there are two groups of particles: fermions, which can be subdivided into quarks and leptons, and bosons, which are the exchange particles responsible for the fundamental forces.

Quarks

We have seen that there are 6 flavours of quark. The standard model arranges these 6 into 3 generations according to mass, the third generation being the heaviest (Table 7.17). Each generation has a $+\frac{2}{3}$ quark and a $-\frac{1}{3}$ quark. This arrangement helps us to work out which transformations are possible. When quark flavour changes, for example in β^- decay, the change in charge must always be $1e$, so in all of these interactions a quark will change between the first and second row.

Charge	1st generation	2nd generation	3rd generation
$+\frac{2}{3}$	up	charm	top
$-\frac{1}{3}$	down	strange	bottom

Table 7.17 Each of these fundamental particles has an antiparticle, which can also be arranged in a similar way.

Leptons

Although we have only come across the 2 leptons so far, the electron and the neutrino, there are in fact 6 leptons. These can also be arranged into 3 generations (Table 7.18). Each generation has a separate lepton number which must be conserved during any interaction. This means that leptons only interact with other leptons in the *same* generation.

Charge	1st generation	2nd generation	3rd generation
0	electron neutrino	muon neutrino	tau neutrino
−1	electron	muon	tau

Table 7.18 Each of these fundamental particles has an antiparticle, which can also be arranged in a similar way.

Bosons

The three fundamental forces that involve fundamental particles each have an associated boson (Table 7.19). Note there are three types of boson associated with the weak force, W^+ and W^- involved in interactions where there is exchange of charge, and Z^0 involved where there is no exchange of charge.

Particle	Force
Gluon	Strong
Photon	Electromagnetic
W and Z	Weak

Table 7.19 These are the exchange particles that are responsible for the fundamental forces. Note: it is now recognized that at high energies the electric and weak forces are one and the same thing. This is called the electroweak force.

The Higgs boson

Although we haven't done all the mathematics, the particles of the standard model are all predicted by quantum mechanics. However, there is one piece that doesn't fit. According to these predictions the W and Z bosons should not have any mass, but to fit in with the observation that the interactions are short range they must have large masses. One solution to this problem would be if the mass was not a property of the particle but a property of space. This is known as the Higgs field, and if there is a field there should be a particle associated with it, which we call the Higgs boson. A particle with these properties was detected in the ATLAS and CMS experiments at CERN on 4 July 2012. The complete set of particles is now as shown in Figure 7.65.

TOK The standard model is very simple, you could say it is beautiful, but is the simplest model necessarily correct?

Why are we always trying to find the simplest solution?

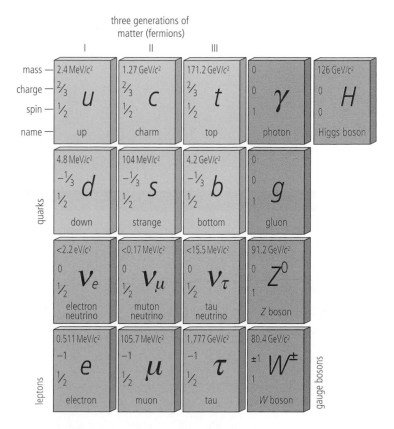

Figure 7.65 The standard model.

Problems still to be solved

The standard model is very neat but it isn't a complete model of the Universe. It does not explain gravity or the existence of the dark matter and energy which is thought to make up 96% of the Universe.

TOK Why do we have to know everything?

Isn't it best that some things are left unknown?

To learn more about the structure of matter, go to the hotlinks site, search for the title or ISBN and click on Chapter 7.

Exercises

48 Use the standard model to identify the particles X and Y in the interaction in Figure 7.66.

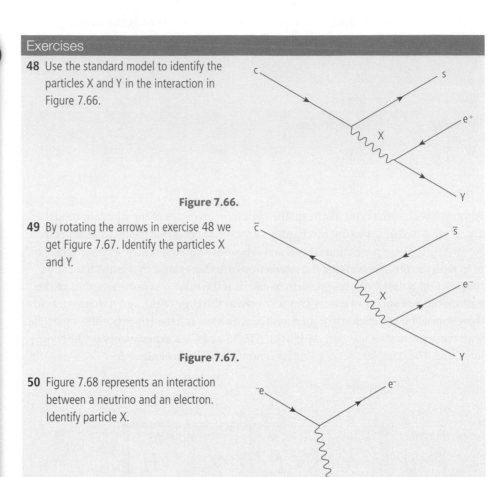

Figure 7.66.

49 By rotating the arrows in exercise 48 we get Figure 7.67. Identify the particles X and Y.

Figure 7.67.

50 Figure 7.68 represents an interaction between a neutrino and an electron. Identify particle X.

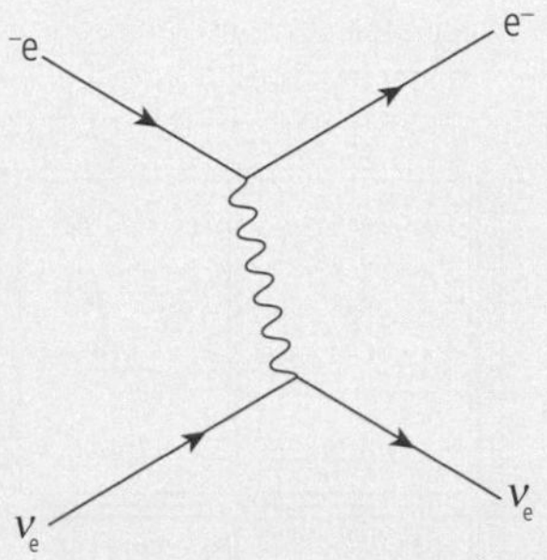

Figure 7.68.

Practice questions

1. This question considers some aspects of the atomic and nuclear physics associated with isotopes of the element helium.

   Atomic aspects

   (a) The element helium was first identified from the *absorption spectrum* of the Sun.

   (i) Explain what is meant by the term *absorption spectrum*. (2)

   (ii) Outline how this spectrum may be experimentally observed. (2)

   (b) One of the wavelengths in the absorption spectrum of helium occurs at 588 nm.

   (i) Show that the energy of a photon of wavelength 588 nm is 3.38×10^{-19} J. (2)

(ii) Figure 7.69 represents some of the energy levels of the helium atom. Use the information in the diagram to explain how absorption at 588 nm arises. (3)

Two different models have been developed to explain the existence of **atomic** energy levels. The **Bohr model** and the **Schrödinger model** are both able to predict the principal wavelengths present in the spectrum of atomic hydrogen.

(c) Outline

(i) the Bohr model, and

(ii) the Schrödinger model. (6)

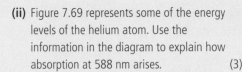

energy/10^{-19} J

0

−1.59

−2.42
−3.00

−5.80

−7.64

Figure 7.69.

Nuclear aspects

(d) The helium in the Sun is produced as a result of a nuclear reaction. Explain whether this reaction is burning, fission, or fusion. (2)

At a later stage in the development of the Sun, other nuclear reactions are expected to take place. One such overall reaction is given below.

$$^4_2\text{He} + {}^4_2\text{He} + {}^4_2\text{He} \rightarrow \text{C} + \gamma + \gamma$$

(e) (i) Identify the atomic number and the mass number of the isotope of carbon C that has been formed. (2)

(ii) Use the information below to calculate the energy released in the reaction.

Atomic mass of helium = $6.648\,325 \times 10^{-27}$ kg

Atomic mass of carbon = $1.993\,200\,0 \times 10^{-26}$ kg (3)

Another isotope of helium ^6_2He decays by emitting a β^- particle.

(f) (i) State the name of the other particle that is emitted during this decay. (1)

(ii) Explain why a sample of ^6_2He emits β^- particles with a *range of energies*. (2)

(iii) The half-life for this decay is 0.82 s. Determine the percentage of a sample of ^6_2He that remains after a time of 10 s. (3)

(iv) Describe the process of β^- decay in terms of quarks. (2)

(*Total 30 marks*)

2. This question is about nuclear reactions.

(a) Copy and complete Table 7.20, by placing a tick (✔) in the relevant columns, to show how an increase in each of the following properties affects the rate of decay of a sample of radioactive material. (2)

Property	Effect on rate of decay		
	increase	decrease	stays the same
Temperature of sample			
Pressure on sample			
Amount of sample			

Table 7.20.

Radium-226 ($^{226}_{88}$Ra) undergoes natural radioactive decay to disintegrate spontaneously with the emission of an alpha particle (α-particle) to form radon (Rn). The masses of the particles involved in the reaction are

radium:	226.0254 u
radon:	222.0176 u
α-particle:	4.0026 u

(b) (i) Copy and complete the nuclear reaction equation below for this reaction.

$^{226}_{88}$Ra → $\underline{\quad}$...... + $\underline{\quad}$Rn   (2)

(ii) Calculate the energy released in the reaction.   (3)

(c) The radium nucleus was stationary before the reaction.

(i) Explain, in terms of the momentum of the particles, why the radon nucleus and the α-particle move off in opposite directions after the reaction.   (3)

(ii) The speed of the radon nucleus after the reaction is v_R and that of the α-particle is v_α. Show that the ratio $\frac{v_\alpha}{v_R}$ is equal to 55.5.   (3)

(iii) Using the ratio given in (ii) above, deduce that the kinetic energy of the radon nucleus is much less than the kinetic energy of the α-particle.   (3)

(d) Not all of the energy of the reaction is released as kinetic energy of the α-particle and of the radon nucleus. Suggest **one** other form in which the energy is released.   (1)

Another type of nuclear reaction is a fusion reaction. This reaction is the main source of the Sun's radiant energy.

(e) (i) State what is meant by a *fusion reaction*.   (3)

(ii) Explain why the temperature and pressure of the gases in the Sun's core must both be very high for it to produce its radiant energy.   (5)

(Total 25 marks)

3. This question is about nuclear reactions.

(a) (i) Distinguish between *fission* and *radioactive decay*.   (4)

A nucleus of uranium-235 ($^{235}_{92}$U) may absorb a neutron and then undergo fission to produce nuclei of strontium-90 ($^{90}_{38}$Sr) and xenon-142 ($^{142}_{54}$Xe), and some neutrons.
The strontium-90 and the xenon-142 nuclei both undergo radioactive decay with the emission of β^- particles.

(ii) Write down the nuclear equation for this fission reaction.   (2)

(iii) State the effect, if any, on the mass number (nucleon number) and on the atomic number (proton number) of a nucleus when the nucleus undergoes β^- decay.   (2)

The uranium-235 nucleus is stationary at the time that the fission reaction occurs. In this fission reaction, 198 MeV of energy is released. Of this total energy, 102 MeV and 65 MeV are the kinetic energies of the strontium-90 and xenon-142 nuclei respectively.

(b) (i) Calculate the magnitude of the momentum of the strontium-90 nucleus.   (4)

(ii) Explain why the magnitude of the momentum of the strontium-90 nucleus is not exactly equal in magnitude to that of the xenon-142 nucleus.   (2)

In Figure 7.70, the circle represents the position of a uranium-235 nucleus before fission. The momentum of the strontium-90 nucleus after fission is represented by the arrow.

Figure 7.70.

(iii) Copy Figure 7.70 and draw an arrow to represent the momentum of the xenon-142 nucleus after the fission. (2)

(c) In a fission reactor for the generation of electrical energy, 25% of the total energy released in a fission reaction is converted into electrical energy.

(i) Using the data in (b), calculate the electrical energy, in joules, produced as a result of nuclear fission of one nucleus. (2)

(ii) The specific heat capacity of water is $4.2 \times 10^3\,\text{J kg}^{-1}\,\text{K}^{-1}$. Calculate the energy required to raise the temperature of 250 g of water from 20 °C to its boiling point (100 °C). (3)

(iii) Using your answer to (c)(i), determine the mass of uranium-235 that must be fissioned in order to supply the amount of energy calculated in (c)(ii). The mass of a uranium-235 atom is 3.9×10^{-25} kg. (4)

(*Total 25 marks*)

4. This question is about nuclear binding energy.

(a) (i) Define *nucleon*. (1)

(ii) Define *nuclear binding energy of a nucleus*. (1)

The axes in Figure 7.71 show values of nucleon number A (horizontal axis) and average binding energy per nucleon E (vertical axis). (Binding energy is taken to be a positive quantity).

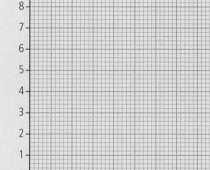

Figure 7.71.

(b) Copy Figure 7.71 and mark on the E-axis the approximate position of

(i) the isotope $^{56}_{26}$Fe (label this F). (1)

(ii) the isotope $^{2}_{1}$H (label this H). (1)

(iii) the isotope $^{238}_{92}$U (label this U). (1)

(c) Using your copy of Figure 7.71, draw a graph to show the variation with nucleon number A of the average binding energy per nucleon E. (2)

(d) Use the following data to deduce that the binding energy per nucleon of the isotope $^{3}_{2}$He is 2.2 MeV.

nuclear mass of $^{3}_{2}$He = 3.01603 u
mass of proton = 1.00728 u
mass of neutron = 1.00867 u (3)

In the nuclear reaction $_1^2H + _1^2H \rightarrow _2^3He + _0^1n$ energy is released.

(e) (i) State the name of this type of reaction. (1)

   (ii) Use your graph in (c) to explain why energy is released in this reaction. (2)

(Total 13 marks)

5. This question is about the wave nature of matter.

(a) Describe the concept of matter waves and state the de Broglie hypothesis. (3)

(b) An electron is accelerated from rest through a potential difference of 850 V. For this electron

   (i) calculate the gain in kinetic energy. (1)

   (ii) deduce that the final momentum is 1.6×10^{-23} N s. (2)

   (iii) determine the associated de Broglie wavelength. (Electron charge $e = 1.6 \times 10^{-19}$ C, Planck constant $h = 6.6 \times 10^{-34}$ J s) (2)

(Total 8 marks)

6. This question is about the Bohr model of the hydrogen atom.

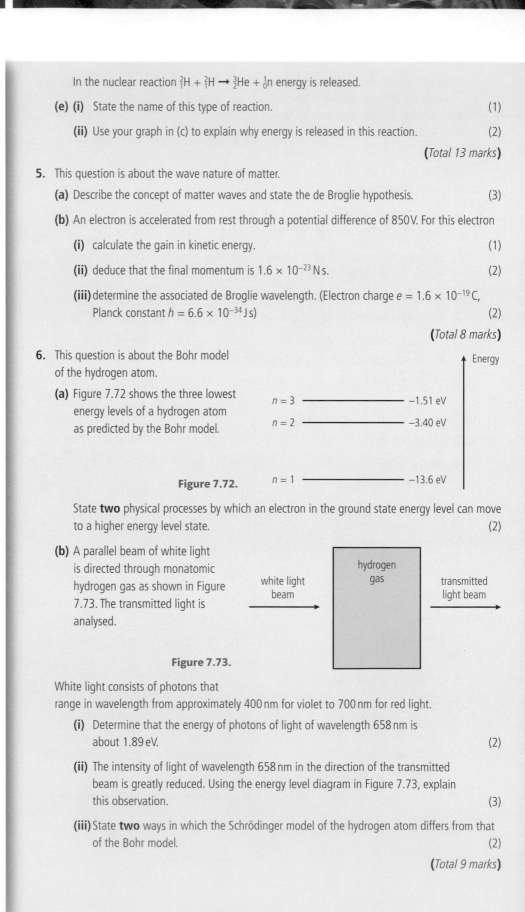

(a) Figure 7.72 shows the three lowest energy levels of a hydrogen atom as predicted by the Bohr model.

Figure 7.72.

$n = 3$ ——————— -1.51 eV

$n = 2$ ——————— -3.40 eV

$n = 1$ ——————— -13.6 eV

Energy

State **two** physical processes by which an electron in the ground state energy level can move to a higher energy level state. (2)

(b) A parallel beam of white light is directed through monatomic hydrogen gas as shown in Figure 7.73. The transmitted light is analysed.

white light beam → hydrogen gas → transmitted light beam

Figure 7.73.

White light consists of photons that range in wavelength from approximately 400 nm for violet to 700 nm for red light.

   (i) Determine that the energy of photons of light of wavelength 658 nm is about 1.89 eV. (2)

   (ii) The intensity of light of wavelength 658 nm in the direction of the transmitted beam is greatly reduced. Using the energy level diagram in Figure 7.73, explain this observation. (3)

   (iii) State **two** ways in which the Schrödinger model of the hydrogen atom differs from that of the Bohr model. (2)

(Total 9 marks)

7. This question is about the photoelectric effect.

(a) State **one** aspect of the photoelectric effect that **cannot** be explained by the wave model of light. Describe how the photon model provides an explanation for this aspect. (2)

Light is incident on a metal surface in a vacuum. Figure 7.74 shows the variation of the maximum kinetic energy E_{max} of the electrons emitted from the surface with the frequency f of the incident light.

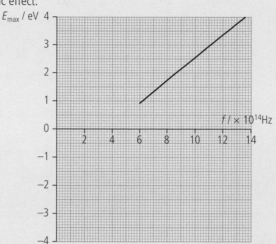

Figure 7.74.

(b) Use data from Figure 7.74 to determine

   (i) the threshold frequency (2)

   (ii) a value of the Planck constant. (2)

   (iii) the work function of the surface. (2)

The threshold frequency of a different surface is 8.0×10^{14} Hz.

(c) Copy Figure 7.74 and, draw a line to show the variation with frequency f of the maximum kinetic energy E_{max} of the electrons emitted. (2)

(*Total 10 marks*)

8. This question is about radioactive decay and the age of rocks.
A nucleus of the radioactive isotope potassium-40 decays into a stable nucleus of argon-40.

(a) Complete the equation below for the decay of a potassium-40 nucleus.

$$^{40}_{19}\text{K} \rightarrow {}^{40}_{18}\text{Ar} +$$ (2)

A certain sample of rocks contains 1.2×10^{-6} g of potassium-40 and 7.0×10^{-6} g of trapped argon-40 gas.

(b) Assuming that all the argon originated from the decay of potassium-40 and that none has escaped from the rocks, calculate what mass of potassium was present when the rocks were first formed. (1)

The half-life of potassium-40 is 1.3×10^9 years.

(c) Determine

   (i) the decay constant of potassium-40. (2)

   (ii) the age of the rocks. (2)

(*Total 7 marks*)

9. This question is about charged particles in a magnetic field.

A beam of singly ionized atoms moving at speed v enters a region of magnetic field strength B as shown in Figure 7.75.

direction of motion of ionized atoms

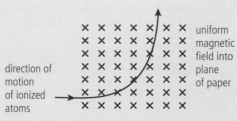

uniform magnetic field into plane of paper

Figure 7.75.

The magnetic field is directed into the plane of the paper. The ions follow a circular path,

(a) Deduce that the radius r of the circular path is given by

$$r = \frac{mv}{Bq}$$

where m and q are the mass and charge, respectively, of the ions. (2)

In one particular experiment, the beam contains singly ionized neon atoms all moving at the same speed. On entering the magnetic field, the beam divides in two. The path of the ions of mass 20 u has radius 15.0 cm.

(b) Calculate in terms of u, the mass of the ions having a path of radius 16.5 cm. (2)

The atomic number (proton number) of neon is 10.

(c) State the number of protons and neutrons in each type of neon ion. (2)

(Total 6 marks)

10. This question is about particle physics.

(a) Possible particle reactions are given below. They **cannot** take place because they violate one or more conservation laws. For each reaction identify **one** conservation law that is violated.

   (i) $\mu^- \rightarrow e^- + \gamma$ (1)

   (ii) $p + n \rightarrow p + \pi^0$ (1)

   (iii) $p \rightarrow \pi^+ + \pi^-$ (1)

(b) State the name of the exchange particle(s) involved in the strong interaction. (1)

(Total 4 marks)

11. This question is about deducing the quark structure of a nuclear particle.

When a K^- meson collides with a proton, the following reaction can take place.

   $K^- + p \rightarrow K^0 + K^+ + X$

X is a particle whose quark structure is to be determined. The quark structure of mesons is given in Table 7.21.

Particle	Quark structure
K^-	$s\bar{u}$
K^+	$u\bar{s}$
K^0	$d\bar{s}$

Table 7.21.

(a) State and explain whether the original K^- particle is a hadron, a lepton, **or** an exchange particle. (2)

(b) State the quark structure of the proton. (2)

(c) The quark structure of particle X is sss. Show that the reaction is consistent with the theory that hadrons are composed of quarks. (2)

(Total 6 marks)

12. This question is about fundamental particles and conservation laws.

Nucleons are considered to be made of quarks.

(a) State the name of

   (i) the force (interaction) between quarks; (1)

   (ii) the particle that gives rise to the force between quarks. (1)

(b) Outline in terms of conservations laws, why the interaction $\bar{v} + p = n + e^+$ is observed but the interaction $v + p = n + e^+$ has **never** been observed. (*You may assume that mass–energy and momentum are conserved in both interactions.*) (3)

(Total 5 marks)

13. This question is about quarks.

The quark content of a π^+ meson includes an up quark.
The Feynman diagram represents the decay of a π^+ meson.

(a) Identify the particles labelled A and B. (2)

(b) State, with reference to their properties, **two** differences between a photon and a W boson. (2)

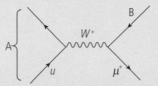

Figure 7.77.

(Total 4 marks)

14. This question is about leptons and mesons.

(a) Leptons are a class of elementary particles and each lepton has its own antiparticle. State what is meant by an

(i) elementary particle. (1)

(ii) antiparticle of a lepton. (1)

(b) The electron is a lepton and its antiparticle is the positron. The following reaction can take place between an electron and positron.

$$e^- + e^+ \longrightarrow \gamma + \gamma$$

Sketch the Feynman diagram for this reaction and identify on your diagram any virtual particles. (3)

(c) Unlike leptons, the π^+ meson is not an elementary particle. State the

(i) quark structure of the π^+ meson. (1)

(ii) reason why the following reaction does not occur.

$$p^+ + p^+ \longrightarrow p^+ + \pi^+$$ (1)

(d) State the Pauli exclusion principle. (1)

(e) Explain, with reference to your answer to (d), why quarks are assigned the property of colour. (2)

(Total 10 marks)

08

Energy production

Essential ideas

8.1 Energy sources

The constant need for new energy sources implies decisions that may have a serious effect on the environment. The finite quantity of fossil fuels and their implication in global warming has led to the development of alternative sources of energy. This continues to be an area of rapidly changing technological innovation.

8.2 Thermal energy transfer

For simplified modelling purposes, the Earth can be treated as a black-body radiator and the atmosphere treated as a grey-body.

Observing this violent explosion from a volcano it is clear that there is a lot of untapped energy right under our feet.

NATURE OF SCIENCE

Throughout this course we have been developing models that enable us to understand the relationship between physical quantities and make predictions that can be tested by experiment. Models are often simplified by only considering small angles as in the simple pendulum or ideal situations such as the gas laws. To understand the workings of a nuclear power station is a much more complicated proposition but without understanding the basic principles great technological advances would not be possible.

8.1 Energy production

8.1 Energy sources

Understandings, applications, and skills:

Specific energy and energy density of fuel sources
- Solving specific energy and energy density problems.

  Guidance
  - *Specific energy has units of J kg^{-1}; energy density has units of J m^{-3}.*

Sankey diagrams
- Sketching and interpreting Sankey diagrams.

Primary energy sources

Electricity as a secondary and versatile form of energy
- Describing the basic features of fossil fuel power stations, nuclear power stations, wind generators, pumped storage hydroelectric systems, and solar power cells.
- Solving problems relevant to energy transformations in the context of these generating systems.

Renewable and non-renewable energy sources
- Discussing safety issues and risks associated with the production of nuclear power.
- Describing the differences between photovoltaic cells and solar heating panels.

  Guidance
  - *The description of the basic features of nuclear power stations must include the use of control rods, moderators, and heat exchangers.*
  - *Derivation of the wind generator equation is not required.*
  - *Students are expected to be aware of new and developing technologies.*

Energy sources

Whenever a body is made to move, work is done and therefore energy is transferred. The very act of living implies the use of energy; without energy we couldn't move or produce the heat required to keep us warm. Since energy cannot be created or destroyed we can't simply create the energy needed, we must have a source and this is the Sun.

The Sun is our nearest star which, like other stars, was formed when the force of gravity pulled together the hydrogen and helium of a dust cloud into a ball. The gravitational force on the outer layers of the star compresses the inside increasing the density and temperature of the centre. If the total mass of the star is enough the pressure and temperature becomes sufficient for the hydrogen nuclei to fuse, resulting in the release of energy. The complete process by which hydrogen fuses to form helium is illustrated in Figure 8.1.

Figure 8.1 The energy from the proton–proton chain of the fusion reaction in the core of the Sun radiates through the other layers.

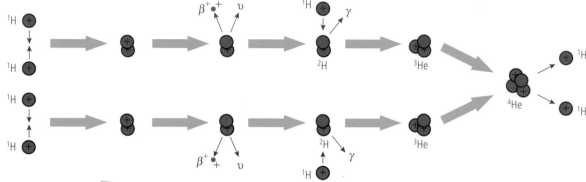

The fusion reaction increases the KE of the particles, enabling them to exert enough pressure to prevent further collapse. The high temperature (10^7 K) core of the Sun transfers energy to the cooler outer layers which also get hot (6000 K) resulting in the emission of 3.9×10^{26} watts of electromagnetic radiation into space. This radiation spreads out in an ever-expanding sphere resulting in an inverse square reduction in power per m². At the Earth's distance from the Sun the power is 1380 W m^{-2}. Approximating the Earth to a disc, this would give a total power of 1.8×10^{17} W. It is this energy that makes life on Earth possible.

Plants absorb the energy from the Sun and, through a process known as *photosynthesis*, put together molecules of carbon dioxide and water to form more complex molecules called *carbohydrates*. On a microscopic level, charges have to be pushed around. This means work is done increasing the PE of the molecules; we call this *chemical energy*. If the process is reversed by burning or eating the carbohydrate then energy is released. In this way, plants can store the energy from the Sun. The amount of energy stored per molecule is about the same as the energy needed to move an electron from one energy level to another; this is of the order of a few eV.

Fuels

Fuels are chemicals that when burnt release energy in the form of heat. Almost all of the fuels we use today are chemicals that were formed either in plants or in animals that ate the plants. It is also possible to manufacture fuels artificially but energy must be used to do this so this isn't economically viable at present.

Wood

Wood was possibly the first fuel ever to be used by man and is still used for heating in many countries. The wood must be stored and dried so it takes up a lot of space; processed wood pellets take up less space but energy must be used in the processing.

A wood-burning stove.

The process of burning wood to produce thermal energy can be represented in an energy flow, or Sankey, diagram as shown in Figure 8.2. The width of the different parts of the diagram are proportional to the amount of energy flowing, so in this case the amount of useful heat energy (heat that is transferred to the room) is greater than the wasted heat (heat that goes up the chimney). An efficient wood-burning stove would have a higher useful : wasted ratio. This can be achieved by circulating the waste gases through a system of pipes, transferring heat energy to stones that retain the thermal energy long after the fire goes out.

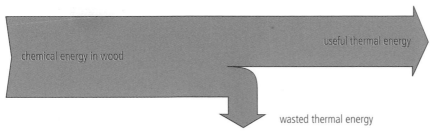

Figure 8.2 A Sankey diagram for a wood-burning stove.

$$\text{efficiency} = \frac{\text{useful energy out}}{\text{total energy in}}$$

When wood is burnt, the complex energy-storing molecules are turned back into carbon dioxide and water. Increasing the carbon dioxide in the atmosphere enhances the greenhouse effect, contributing to global warming. However, growing plants absorb carbon dioxide, so if we only burnt wood there would be no increase in carbon dioxide in the atmosphere.

The fuels mentioned here are all *primary energy sources* as they have not been processed.

Coal

Coal is composed of plants that died millions of years ago. These plants got covered by layers of sand and mud which squashed them into the hard black rock that is mined today. So, coal is made of fossilized plants – hence the name *fossil fuel*. The process of compression increases the amount of energy per kg, making coal a more efficient source of energy than wood. However, the fact that coal takes millions of years to produce means that the rate at which carbon dioxide is produced by burning coal is not matched by the rate at which it is taken out of the atmosphere as new coal is formed. The process of mining coal also uses a lot of energy although there are plans to eliminate the need for mining by burning coal underground then extracting the gas produced.

Oil and gas

Although it was coal that fuelled the industrial revolution, since the 1950s oil has overtaken coal as the most important source of energy. Oil is another fossil fuel, formed from microscopic organisms that sank to the bottom of the sea when they died. Over a long period of time this organic matter was covered in sand that turned to rock and it was pressed into oil and gas. Oil and gas are easier to extract than coal since they are fluid and can be pumped up from where they lie underground. Sometimes extraction is not simple since a lot of oil reserves are in rock that is at the bottom of the sea. However, as technology has advanced, the methods of extracting oil have become more and more ingenious and it is now possible to drill for many kilometres and even go sideways from a platform that is floating in water many kilometres deep.

Like coal, oil is non-renewable and has to be burned to turn its stored energy into heat that can be used to power an engine. This makes oil another source of greenhouse gases.

There is no data in Table 8.1 for the energy density of cow dung and household waste because the density of these is so variable.

Specific energy and energy density of fuels

Different fuels contain different amounts of energy. In Table 8.1 this is expressed in terms of the energy per unit mass (specific energy) and energy per unit volume (energy density).

Fuel	Specific energy/ MJ kg^{-1}	Energy density/ MJ L^{-1}
Crude oil	46	37
Vegetable oil	42	30
Diesel	46	36
Coal	32	72
Sugar	17	26
Wood	17	3.2
Cow dung	15	-
Household waste	10	-

Table 8.1 Energy from different fuels.

Figure 8.3 Underneath the balloon is a flame which heats the air in the balloon and this drives the engine.

Converting heat into work

The chemical energy in fuels can be converted to thermal energy by burning, but to do work we need an engine. To understand the physical principles behind the operation of engines we will consider a simple if rather impractical engine made with a hot air balloon, as shown in Figure 8.3.

When gas is burnt under the balloon, the balloon fills up with hot air which, being less dense than the surrounding cold air, results in a buoyant force greater than the weight of the balloon. The unbalanced forces on the balloon cause it to rise, pulling the string which makes the pulley turn. The chemical energy in the fuel has been transformed into work.

A hot air balloon prepares for launch.

The hot air balloon engine could be used to drive the wheels of a car or power a washing machine, but there is a problem. Once the string has unwound the balloon will have to be pulled back down to the ground to start the process again. Doing this will require as much energy as we got when the balloon went up, making the engine rather pointless. To get around this problem we could allow the balloon to get cold, then it would come down on its own giving us a net gain in energy. This would mean we would have to wait whilst the balloon came down but if we had two balloons one could be going up as the other came down, so the engine could be working all the time.

This may sound a bit contrived but it is the principle of most engines, except that instead of using a balloon the gas is contained in a piston as in Figure 8.4. The gas is heated leading to an increase in pressure that results in an unbalanced force on the piston pushing it out. The moving piston is connected to a crank that turns the linear motion into rotation rather like a pulley and string. To complete the cycle the gas must cool down, otherwise compressing it will require as much work as was done when it expanded. To increase the efficiency more cylinders can be added.

An alternative is to use the expanding gas to power a turbine. When water is turned to steam in a closed container the fast-moving gas molecules will exert pressure on the walls. If a small hole is made in the container, steam will flow through the hole due to the difference in pressure between the inside of the container and the atmospheric pressure of the surroundings. If this fast-moving jet of steam is directed onto a solid surface the change in momentum of the molecules will result in a force on the surface. This can be used to do work, as shown in Figure 8.5.

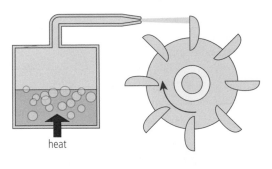

In all of these processes heat will be lost: first when the fuel burns, then when the cycle takes place, and finally due to friction.

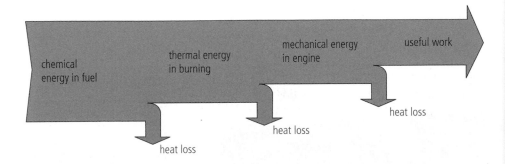

Generating electricity

Fuel can be burnt in the home to produce heat, as in a coal or wood fire, or it can be used with an engine to do work, as in a car. However, this means that fuel must be delivered to the place where it will be used, and transport uses a lot of energy. An alternative is to use the mechanical energy produced from an engine to produce electricity by turning the coils of a generator. Electrical energy can then be delivered through a wire, and this is more efficient than delivering fuel to each consumer.

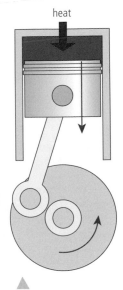

Figure 8.4 A simple single-cylinder piston engine.

Figure 8.5 A simple turbine.

Figure 8.6 A Sankey diagram for a heat engine.

CHALLENGE YOURSELF

1 A 1000 kg diesel car with a 50% efficient engine uses 3 litres of fuel to travel 100 km at a constant speed of 50 km h^{-1} on a horizontal road. If the car suddenly runs out of fuel, how far will it travel before coming to rest?

Figure 8.7 An alternator using a rotating coil. Use Fleming's right hand rule to give the direction of the current.

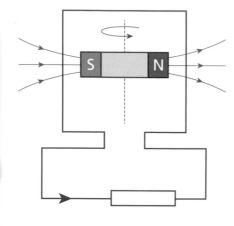

A generator as covered in chapter 6 consists of a rotating coil in a magnetic field. As the flux enclosed by the coil changes, an emf is induced that causes an alternating current to flow in an external circuit. The rotating coil is connected to the stationary circuit using slip rings and a sliding contact. This contact will wear out after time so an alternative solution is to use stationary coils and moving magnets, as in Figure 8.7.

In power stations the rotating magnet is an electromagnet rather than a permanent magnet but the principle is the same (Figure 8.8).

> Electricity is produced by processing fuel so electricity is *secondary energy*. It is also known as an energy carrier.

Figure 8.8 A Sankey diagram for electricity production.

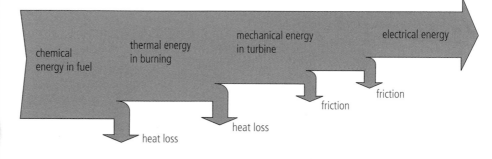

chemical energy in fuel → thermal energy in burning → mechanical energy in turbine → electrical energy

heat loss / heat loss / friction / friction

> Energy = power × time so can be expressed in terms of watts × seconds or, in the case of domestic electricity, kilowatts × hours (kWh).
> 1 kWh = 1000 × 3600 Ws
> = 3.6 × 10^6 J.

Exercises

1 Draw a Sankey diagram for an electric light bulb.
2 Draw a Sankey diagram for a bicycle dynamo producing the electricity to illuminate a light from mechanical energy.

Coal-fired power station

Figure 8.9 represents a typical coal-fired power station. The heat from the furnace boils water in the boiler that turns into steam and powers the turbine, the turbine turns a generator and produces electricity. When the steam comes out of the turbine it is cooled, causing it to condense, and this water is then returned to the boiler.

> Cooling towers are a common sight near power stations. They are used to cool down the water that cools down the steam coming out of the turbines. This waste heat could be used to heat the houses nearby, increasing the efficiency of the power station to about 70%.

The overall efficiency of a coal-fired power station is around 40% as not all of the chemical energy from the coal gets converted to electricity. The exhaust gases from the original burning take some of the heat, as does the heat given out when the steam from the turbine condenses. There is also some friction in the components of the turbine and generator.

Cooling towers.

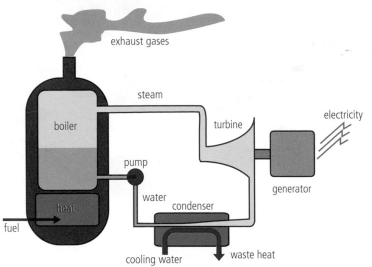

Figure 8.9 In a coal-fired power station the coal is made into dust and blown into a furnace. This produces a lot of smoke that must be cleaned before it is released into the atmosphere.

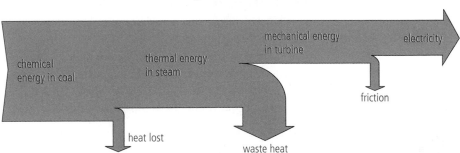

Figure 8.10 Sankey diagram for a coal-fired power station.

Finland produces 30% of its electricity from nuclear power so has a lot of nuclear waste to dispose of. To solve this problem they are constructing many km of tunnels into the very old and geologically sound rock close to Olkiluoto. The facility, known as Onkalo, will eventually contain 9000 tonnes of spent fuel.

Exercise

3 A coal-fired power station gives out 1000 MW of power.

(a) How many joules will be produced in one day?

(b) If the efficiency is 40%, how much energy goes in?

(c) The energy density of coal is 32.5 MJ kg^{-1}. How many kg are used?

(d) How many rail trucks containing 100 tonnes each are delivered per day?

Nuclear power

In chapter 7 you learnt about how, when a large nucleus splits into two smaller ones, the total binding energy increases, resulting in the release of about 100 MeV of energy. This is approximately 100 million times more energy per molecule than when coal burns so any material that does this would be a valuable source of energy.

If a uranium-235 nucleus absorbs a neutron it will undergo fission, but naturally occurring uranium only contains 0.7% ^{235}U. The remainder is mainly ^{238}U, which absorbs neutrons without undergoing fission. Before naturally occurring uranium can be used as a fuel the amount of ^{235}U must be increased to about 3%. This is called *enrichment*.

Fuel	Specific energy /MJ kg^{-1}	Energy density /MJ L^{-1}
Uranium fuel	79 500 000	1 534 000 000
Coal	32.5	72.4

Figure 8.2 Comparing energy from nuclear and fossil fuel.

The chain reaction

To split a ^{236}U nucleus requires some energy because the nucleons are held together by a strong force. This energy can be supplied by adding a neutron to a ^{235}U nucleus. This actually increases the binding energy of the nucleus, but because the nucleus cannot get rid of this energy, it splits in two. As a result there are too many neutrons and some are released. These neutrons can be captured by more ^{235}U nuclei, and so on, leading to a chain reaction.

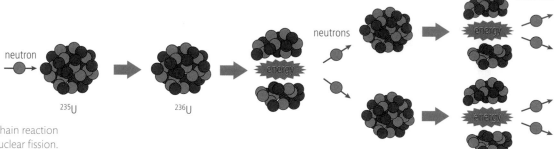

Figure 8.11 A chain reaction from nuclear fission.

Moderation

Using the word *moderation* sounds like the moderator slows down the reaction, but it doesn't. The moderator slows down the *neutrons*, enabling the chain reaction. If the moderator was removed the reaction would slow down.

The neutrons will only be absorbed if they are travelling slowly – otherwise they will pass straight through. In terms of kinetic energy, this would be about 1 eV, which is much less than the MeV they possess after being expelled during the fission process. To achieve a chain reaction we need these neutrons to be absorbed so they should be slowed down or *moderated* – this is done by introducing some small nuclei in between the ^{235}U (Figure 8.12). The neutrons collide with these nuclei and because they have a similar mass to the neutrons they receive energy and the neutrons slow down.

Figure 8.12 Only slow-moving neutrons are absorbed.

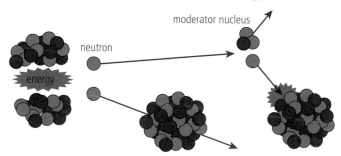

Critical mass

Another critical factor that determines whether a chain reaction can take place is the size of the piece of uranium. If it is too small, then before the neutrons have travelled far enough to be slowed down they will have left the reacting piece of uranium. The minimum mass required for a chain reaction is called the *critical mass*.

Pellets of nuclear fuel are stacked into tubes that are bundled together before being put into the reactor.

The nuclear power station

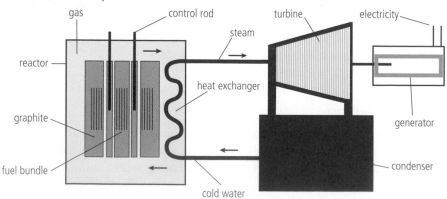

Figure 8.13 An advanced gas-cooled reactor (AGR).

Control in a nuclear reactor

The rate of reaction in a nuclear reactor is limited by the fact that the fuel contains a high proportion of ^{238}U, which absorbs neutrons. Since this cannot easily be altered it cannot be used to slow the reaction down if it goes too fast. Instead, this is done by introducing rods of a neutron-absorbing material, such as boron, in between the fuel rods (Figure 8.13).

There are many different designs of nuclear reactor but they all have a nuclear reaction at the core. The energy released when the nuclei split is given to the fission fragments (although about 10 MeV is given to neutrinos that escape). As you know from Chapter 3, the temperature of a body is related to the average KE of the atoms; this means that the temperature of the fuel increases. The hot fuel can then be used to boil water and drive a turbine as in the coal-fired power station.

The nuclear reactor is the part that produces heat and contains the fuel rods surrounded by a graphite moderator (pale orange in Figure 8.13). The control rods can be raised and lowered to control the rate of reaction. The nuclear reactor is housed in a pressure vessel in which a gas is circulating (blue). This picks up heat from the fuel rods and transfers it to water in the heat exchanger. This water turns to steam and turns the turbine. The steam cools down and turns back to water in the condenser and is recirculated.

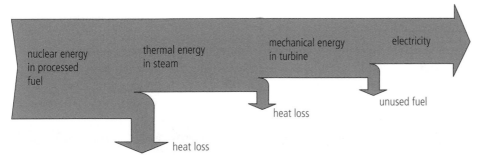

Since there is no burning of fuel involved in the nuclear reactor, no carbon dioxide is produced. This makes it favourable when compared to the use of fossil fuels to produce electricity. However, there are other problems.

Meltdown

If the nuclear reaction is not controlled properly it can overheat and the fuel rods can melt: this is called *meltdown*. When this happens the fuel cannot be removed and may cause the pressure vessel to burst, sending radioactive material into the atmosphere. A similar situation occurred in Chernobyl, Ukraine in 1986. However, it is not possible for the reactor to blow up as an atom bomb, since the fuel is not of a high enough grade.

Meltdown can be caused by a malfunction in the cooling system or a leak in the pressure vessel. It would result in severe damage to the reactor, maybe leading to complete shutdown. Further damage outside the reactor is limited by the containment building, an airtight steel construction covered in concrete which not only prevents dangerous material leaking out, but will withstand a missile attack from the outside. Improved reactor design and construction coupled with computer monitoring of possible points of weakness has reduced the possibility of any failure of the structure that might lead to meltdown. However, it is almost impossible to design a reactor that will withstand the force of a major earthquake.

Wasted energy

The efficiency of the nuclear reactor is not as high as might be expected. Firstly, the fuel has to be enriched, which takes a lot of energy. Then, it is not possible to get all the energy from the fuel because when the amount of ^{235}U falls below a certain value a chain reaction can no longer be sustained.

Figure 8.14 Sankey diagram for a nuclear reactor.

A nuclear reactor does not burn fuel so is not dependent on oxygen for it to function. This makes nuclear power particularly useful for powering submarines.

Different countries have different policies regarding the use of nuclear power. What is the policy where you live?

Low level waste

The extraction of uranium from the ground, the process of fuel enrichment and the transfer of heat from the fuel rods all leave some traces of radioactive material that must be carefully disposed of. The amount of radiation given off by this material is not great, but it must be disposed of in places away from human contact for 100–500 years.

Old reactors are another form of low level waste. They cannot simply be knocked down and recycled since most of the parts will have become radioactive. Instead, they must be left untouched for many years before demolition, or they can be encased in concrete.

High level waste

The biggest problem faced by the nuclear power industry is the disposal of spent fuel rods. Some of the isotopes they contain have a half-life of thousands of years so need to be placed in safe storage for a very long time. In the case of plutonium it would not be considered safe for at least 240 000 years. There have been many suggestions: sending it to the Sun; putting it at the bottom of the sea; burying it in the icecap; or dropping it into a very deep hole. For the moment, most of it is dealt with in one of two ways:

• stored under water at the site of the reactor for several years to cool off, then sealed in steel cylinders.

• reprocessed to separate the plutonium and any remaining useful uranium from the fission fragments. This results in waste that is high in concentrations of the very radioactive fission fragments, but the half-life of these fragments is much shorter than either uranium or plutonium, so the need for very long-term storage is reduced.

Exercises

4 Barium-142 ($^{142}_{56}$Ba) is a possible product of the fission of uranium-236. It decays by β^- decay to lanthanum (La) with a half-life of 11 months.

    (a) Write the equation for the decay of barium.

    (b) Estimate how long will it take for the activity of the barium in a sample of radioactive waste to fall to $\frac{1}{1000}$ of its original value.

5 Plutonium-239 splits into zirconium-96 and xenon-136. Use Table 8.3 to answer the following questions.

    (a) How many neutrons will be emitted?

    (b) Write the nuclear equation for the reaction.

    (c) How much energy is released when the fission takes place?

    (d) What is the mass of 1 mole of plutonium?

    (e) How many atoms are there in 1 kg of plutonium?

    (f) How much energy in eV is released if 1 kg of plutonium undergoes fission?

    (g) Convert the answer to part (f) into joules.

Isotope	Mass (U)
^{239}Pu	239.052158
^{96}Zr	95.908275
^{136}Xe	135.907213
neutron	1.008664

Table 8.3.

6 A sample of nuclear fuel contains 3% ^{235}U. If the energy density of ^{235}U is 9×10^{13} J kg^{-1}, how much energy will 1 kg of fuel release?

7 An individual uses around 10 000 kWh of energy in a year.

    (a) How many joules is this?

    (b) From your answer to Exercise 8, calculate how much nuclear fuel this amounts to.

Solar power

The energy contained in all of the fuels apart from nuclear fuel originates from the Sun, but we can also use the Sun's energy directly. There is more energy reaching the

Earth's surface from the Sun in a few hours than the total amount of energy used by mankind in a whole year.

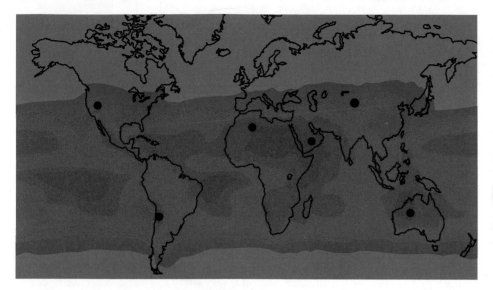

Figure 8.15 Map showing how much of the Earth's surface would have to be covered by solar panels to generate enough electricity to replace all other primary energy sources.

The town of Rjukan in Norway has installed mirrors on the top of a mountain to reflect light from the Sun so people living there can get some sunlight in winter.

Solar panels and solar lighting

One simple way of using the energy from the Sun is to build houses that make use of the Sun for lighting and heating. Not all rooms in a building can have a window but using mirrors and optical fibres, light can be reflected into the inner rooms, reducing the need for electrical lighting during the day.

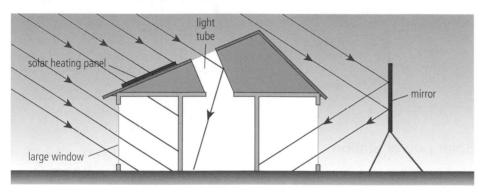

Figure 8.16 A house designed to use light from the Sun.

Solar heating panels on top of houses in Antalya. The position of solar panels depends on the amount and direction of sunlight as well as the design of the building and other considerations.

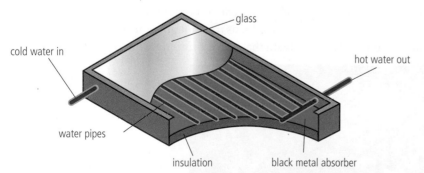

Figure 8.17 A solar heating panel allows radiation from the Sun to enter but prevents the radiation from the warm pipes escaping.

Solar heating panels can be used for central heating or for making water hot for household use. They are placed on the roofs of houses. Solar radiation enters the panel through the glass cover, is absorbed by a black metal plate which gets hot, and in turn makes the water hot by conduction. Water is continuously circulated so that, as the water gets hot, it flows out and more cold water flows in.

343

Photovoltaic cell

The photovoltaic cell is a semiconductor device based on a PN junction that converts solar energy directly into electrical energy. A PN junction is a slice of semiconductor where one side has been doped with impurities with holes and the other side impurities with electrons. At the junction between the N and P the electrons and holes migrate to give a region of electric field as shown in Figure 8.18.

depletion layer
(electrons fill holes)

Figure 8.18 A PN junction.

Light incident on the N-type semiconductor can cause more free electrons to be emitted by a process known as the *photovoltaic effect*. The electric field at the junction traps the electrons on this side, creating a potential difference across the slice. If connected to a circuit, current will flow. Figure 8.19 shows the different parts of the photovoltaic cell. Notice the top contact does not cover the whole top, leaving space for the light to get to the PN junction. Silicon is very shiny so an anti-reflective layer is added to reduce energy loss by reflection. Light reflecting off the top layer of this very thin film undergoes a phase change of π whereas light reflected off the bottom layer doesn't. The reflected light therefore interferes destructively reducing energy loss.

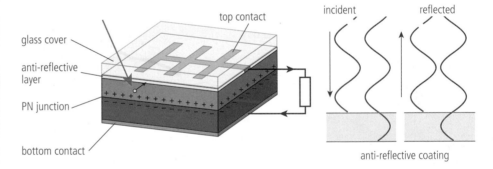

Figure 8.19 A photovoltaic cell with detail of anti-reflective coating.

Solar power station

An alternative approach to placing solar panels on houses is to build solar power stations outside cities; here solar energy is converted to electricity on a large scale, and transmitted to the users via cables. This can be done either with huge arrays of photovoltaic cells or by using mirrors to focus the sunlight onto a central boiler; here, salts are melted and used to heat steam that powers turbines as in other power stations.

Hundreds of mirrors focus sunlight onto the central boiler of this power plant in California.

Positioning of solar panels

Solar panels are positioned so that they absorb maximum sunlight in the middle of the day. On the Equator the Sun is directly overhead at midday so the panels are placed horizontally, but in other countries the position of the Sun changes with the seasons, so a compromise has to be made. In countries with less sunshine (lots of clouds) the position is not so important because the sunlight does not come from one direction (it is said to be diffuse).

Changing phase from solid to liquid requires a lot of energy (latent heat of fusion) so when a solid changes back to a liquid a lot of energy must be released. This is why molten salts are used to transfer energy in the solar power station. Furthermore, the salts will stay hot long after the Sun has gone down, making it possible for the power station to produce electricity at night.

8 A 4 m² solar heating panel is positioned in a place where the intensity of the Sun is 1000 W m⁻² .

   (a) What is the power incident on the panel?

   (b) If it is 50% efficient, how much energy is absorbed per second?

   (c) If 1 litre (1 kg) of water flows through the system in 1 minute, by how much will its temperature increase? (Specific heat capacity of water = 4 200 J kg⁻¹ °C⁻¹)

9 A photovoltaic cell of 1 cm² is placed in a position where the intensity of the Sun is 1000 W m⁻²,

   (a) If it is 15% efficient, what is the power absorbed?

   (b) If the potential difference across the cell is 0.5 V, how much current is produced? (Remember power = IV)

   (c) If 10 of these cells were placed in series, what would the total potential difference be?

   (d) If 10 of these cells were placed in parallel, what would the current be?

   (e) How many of these cells would you need to produce 100 W?

10 Draw a Sankey diagram for a photovoltaic cell.

Hydroelectric power

It may not be obvious at first, but the energy converted into electrical energy by hydroelectric power stations comes originally from the Sun. Heat from the Sun turns water into water vapour, forming clouds. The clouds are blown over the land and the water vapour turns back into water as rain falls. Rain water falling on high ground has PE that can be converted into electricity (see Figure 8.20). Some countries like Norway have many natural lakes high in the mountains and the energy can be utilized by simply drilling into the bottom of the lake. In other countries rivers have to be dammed.

The Hoover Dam in Colorado can generate 1.5 × 10⁹ watts.

The energy stored in a lake at altitude is gravitational PE. This can be calculated from the equation: PE = mgh where h is the height difference between the outlet from the lake and the turbine. Since not all of the water in the lake is the same height, the average height is used (this is assuming the lake is rectangular in cross section).

Figure 8.20 The main components in a hydroelectric power station.

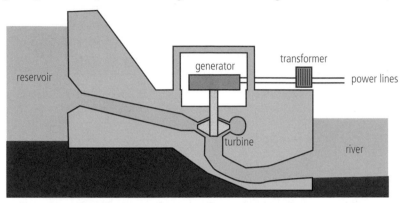

Worked example

Calculate the total energy stored and power generated in Figure 8.21 if water flows from the lake at a rate of 1 m³ per second.

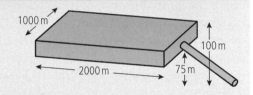

Figure 8.21.

Solution

The average height above the turbine is
$$\frac{(100 + 75)}{2} = 87.5 \, \text{m}$$

Volume of the lake = 2000 × 1000 × 25 = 5 × 10⁷ m³

Mass of the lake = volume × density = 5 × 10⁷ × 1000
$$= 5 \times 10^{10} \, \text{kg}$$

$$PE = mgh = 5 \times 10^{10} \times 9.8 \times 87.5 = 4.29 \times 10^{13} \, \text{J}$$

If the water flows at a rate of 1 m³ per second then 1000 kg falls 87.5 m per second

So the energy lost by the water = 1000 × 9.8 × 87.5 = 875 000 J s⁻¹

Power = 875 kW

Pumped storage system

There is greater demand for electricity in the daytime than at night, but it is not usually possible to shut down a power station when demand falls. For example, a coal-fired power station would cool down and you can't turn off the wind that drives a wind turbine. Some hydroelectric power plants are designed to use this excess energy to pump water up into a reservoir to be stored for use when demand is high. This process is made possible by the fact that a generator is the same as an electric motor, as shown in Figure 8.22. Feeding current into the generator of a hydroelectric power station will turn the turbine which can be used to pump water upwards. During this process energy is lost, so it is only worthwhile when there is an excess of energy being produced.

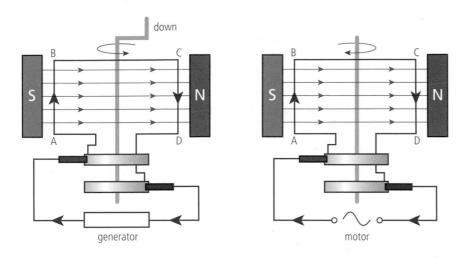

down

B   C

S   N

A   D

generator

B   C

S   N

A   D

motor

Figure 8.22 When the coil is turned current flows, but if a battery makes current flow then the coil turns in the opposite direction (note AC so direction of current changes every half revolution).

Wind power

Using the wind as a source of energy is nothing new; it is over a thousand years since the first known use in Persia was recorded. In those days windmills were used to grind (or mill) corn (hence the name); now they are used to generate electricity. The energy in the wind originates from the Sun. In simple terms the Sun heats the air which becomes less dense and rises, leaving an area of low pressure close to the Earth. Surrounding air will move into this low pressure area and this air movement is the wind. The rotation of the Earth causes this moving air to move in a circular pattern, causing the weather systems that we are familiar with.

Coastal winds

Coastal areas are particularly windy due to the different rates of heating of the land and the sea. During the day, when the Sun is shining, the land and sea absorb energy and get hot. The sea has a bigger specific heat capacity than the land so the temperature of the sea does not rise by as much as the temperature of the land ($Q = mc\,\Delta T$). The result is that the air above the land rises and this causes a low pressure that allows the air above the sea to flow in. At night the reverse happens, when the land cools down more quickly than the sea.

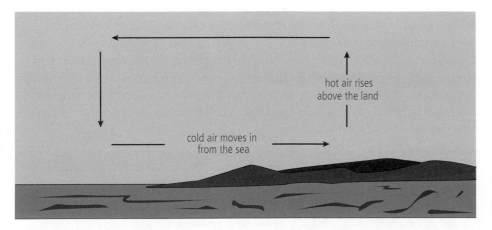

hot air rises above the land

cold air moves in from the sea

Figure 8.23 Flow of coastal winds during the day.

Katabatic winds

A katabatic wind is formed when a high pressure is caused by dense cold air pressing down at the top of a mountain, resulting in air flowing downhill. An example of this regularly takes place when cold air from the Alps and Massif Central areas in France descend towards the Mediterranean coast. Funnelling by the Rhone valley causes the air to speed up as it reaches the sea, causing a strong wind called the Mistral.

The wind turbine

Wind turbines are rather like a fan or the propeller of an aeroplane, except they are moved by the air rather than making the air move. These large turbines are often grouped together in wind farms.

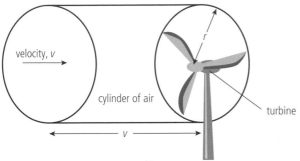

velocity, v

cylinder of air

v

turbine

r

▲
Figure 8.24 Energy from air approaching a wind turbine.

ⓘ You don't need to know this derivation for the exam, but you might have to use the equation.

Energy calculation for a wind turbine

Wind has energy in the form of KE. This enables the wind to do work against the turbine which turns a generator creating electrical energy. To calculate how much energy there is in the wind, we consider a cylinder of air with a radius the same as the radius of the turbine as shown in Figure 8.24.

If the velocity of air is v then in 1 s it will move a distance v. The volume of air passing by the turbine per second is therefore $v \times \pi r^2$ where r is the length of one of the turbine blades.

The mass of this cylinder of air, $m = \rho v \pi r^2$ where ρ is the density of air.

The KE of this air $= \frac{1}{2}mv^2 = \frac{1}{2}\rho v \pi r^2 v^2 = \frac{1}{2}\rho v \pi r^2 v^3$.

Since this is the KE of air moving past the turbine per second it gives us the power in the wind.

The wind doesn't stop after passing the turbine so not all of this energy is turned into electricity. The maximum theoretical percentage of the wind's energy that can be extracted using a turbine is 59%.

Windy places

The best place to put a wind turbine is obviously in a windy place. However, wind speed isn't the only consideration. It is also important that the wind is fairly regular so that the turbine doesn't have to keep changing its orientation. Another factor is how easy it is to lay power lines from the turbine and how easy it is to build the turbine in that position. The main problems associated with wind power are that the turbines often need to be built in areas of natural beauty and that they are unreliable – when the wind stops they produce no electricity.

Exercise

11 A turbine with a turbine blade length of 54 m is operated in a wind of speed 10 m s^{-1}. The density of air is 1.2 kg m^{-3}.

   (a) How much power is in the wind passing through the turbine?

   (b) How much electrical power can be generated if the turbine is 20% efficient?

   (c) If the wind speed increased to 15 m s^{-1}, how much power would be produced?

Wave power

Waves

If you have ever watched waves crashing into a beach on a stormy day you will have realized that there is a lot of energy transmitted in water waves. Waves in the sea are caused by winds disturbing the surface of the water; these winds can be local, in which case the waves tend to be small and with a short wavelength. The big powerful rolling waves favoured by surfers originate way out in the deep ocean. The weather map in Figure 8.25 shows the typical situation that would cause big waves to arrive at the surfing beaches of western Europe.

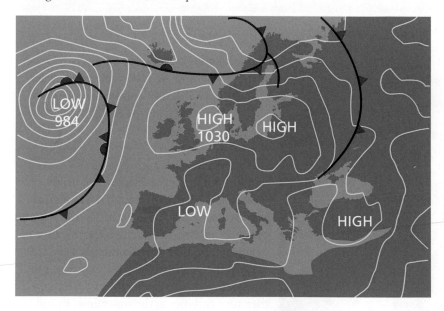

Figure 8.25 In this weather map the low pressure system in the middle of the Atlantic is a storm. This will create waves that travel towards Europe. The amount of energy carried by the waves is directly related to the duration of the storm.

Generating electricity from water waves

The oscillating water column

The principle of the oscillating water column is shown in Figure 8.26 and consists of a column that is half full of water, such that when a wave approaches it pushes water up the column. This compresses the air that occupies the top half, pushing it through a turbine which drives an electric generator. The turbine is specially designed so that it also turns when the water drops back down the column, pulling air into the chamber.

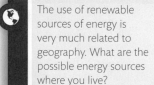

The use of renewable sources of energy is very much related to geography. What are the possible energy sources where you live?

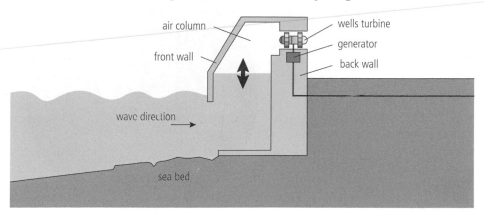

Figure 8.26 The main components of an oscillating water column generator.

349

Pelamis

The pelamis is named after a sea snake because that's what it looks like. A pelamis is made of four sections with a total length of 150 m (Figure 8.27). Each section is hinged, and when a wave passes it bends. The bending drives pumps that move fluid back and forth, powering electrical generators. A pelamis can generate 750 kW of electricity.

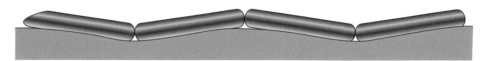

Figure 8.27 The four sections of a single pelamis.

The tidal barrage at Rance in France. After water has flowed into the estuary on the incoming sea tide it is held back and then released through 24 turbines producing 240 MW. The tidal range is up to 13.5 m.

To learn more about energy production, go to the hotlinks site, search for the title or ISBN and click on Chapter 8.

Tidal power

The gravitational attraction between the water in the oceans and the Moon causes the water to bulge outwards, not only on the side of the side of the Earth facing the Moon but also on the opposite side. As the Earth rotates these bulges travel around causing the two high tides that people living near the sea experience each day. In some areas the difference in height can be as much as 16 m. Although not as high as most hydroelectric power stations, the volume of water involved makes this a viable source of energy. There are two main methods used to harness the power of the tides. One way is to build a dam or barrage across a tidal estuary then turn turbines as the water flows in and out; the other is to fix turbines under water which are turned by the free-flowing water rather like an underwater wind turbine.

World energy usage

From the calculations on solar power we can see that there is plenty of energy available for today's needs. However, as illustrated by Figure 8.28, we are presently very much dependent on fossil fuels for our supply of energy and these are not only running out but when burnt produce carbon dioxide which when added to the atmosphere enhances the greenhouse effect resulting in global warming.

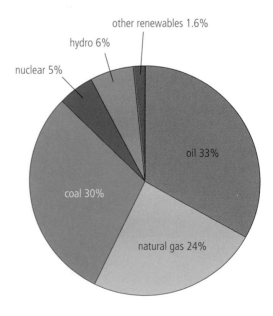

Figure 8.28 World energy use.

8.2 Thermal energy transfer

Understandings, applications, and skills:

Black-body radiation
- Sketching and interpreting graphs showing the variation of intensity with wavelength for bodies emitting thermal radiation at different temperatures.
- Solving problems involving Stefan–Boltzmann and Wien's laws.
- Describing the effects of the Earth's atmosphere on the mean surface temperature.

   Guidance
   - *The absorption of infrared radiation by greenhouse gases should be described in terms of the molecular energy levels and the subsequent emission of radiation in all directions.*

Albedo and emissivity
- Solving problems involving albedo and emissivity.

   Guidance
   - *Earth's albedo varies daily and is dependent on season (cloud formations) and latitude. The global annual mean albedo will be taken to be 0.3 (30%) for Earth.*

The solar constant
- Solving problems involving the solar constant.

The greenhouse effect
- Solving problems involving the Earth's average temperature.

   Guidance
   - *The absorption of infrared radiation by greenhouse gases should be described in terms of the molecular energy levels and the subsequent emission of radiation in all directions.*
   - *The greenhouse gases to be considered are CH_4, H_2O, CO_2, and N_2O. It is sufficient for students to know that each has both natural and man-made origins.*

Energy balance in the Earth surface–atmosphere system

Energy from the Sun

Earlier in this chapter the Sun was described as a burning ball of gas fuelled by a dense, hot core where hydrogen is fused to form helium. The Sun loses energy to its surroundings by emitting electromagnetic radiation. To understand this better, let's look at the process of radiation.

Black-body radiation

We know that a dark, dull-coloured body will emit more radiation than a light-coloured, shiny one so the best radiator will be a *black body*. We don't normally notice this but if you take two metal objects, one dark and one shiny, and heat them both to around 1000 K so they glow red hot, the dark one will glow brighter than the dark one.

Stefan–Boltzmann law

The amount of radiation emitted by a body depends on its temperature. To find out how they are related we can do an experiment using a tungsten filament bulb as a source of radiation. It is not easy to measure the temperature of the filament, but the resistance of tungsten changes with temperature. In Figure 8.29 we measure the pd across the bulb and the current through it so we can calculate the resistance and hence determine the temperature. The power radiating from the filament is measured using a thermopile. This absorbs the radiation, causing its temperature to rise and leading to a potential difference that is measured with the voltmeter.

NATURE OF SCIENCE

We can model the behaviour of a small amount of ideal gas trapped in a cylinder quite accurately but modelling the whole atmosphere is quite a different story. In this case sophisticated computer programmes are used in an attempt to make predictions. However, we can't run experiments to see if these predictions are correct.

In 1988 the Intergovernmental Panel on Climate Change (IPCC) was established by the United Nations Environmental Programme and the World Meteorological Organization to provide the decision makers of the world with a clear scientific view on the current state of knowledge in climate change and its potential environmental and socio-economic impacts.

There are certainly problems associated with the use of energy; it will be up to the imagination and creativity of future scientists to solve them.

Red hot

When a rod of metal is heated to around 1000 K it starts to glow red. Although the most intense part of the spectrum is not in the visible region, there is enough visible red light to make the rod glow.

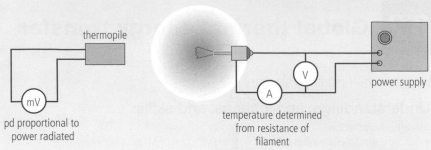

Figure 8.30 shows the results from this experiment. The pd measured across the thermopile is on the *y*-axis and the filament temperature on the *x*-axis.

The y-axis is the pd measured across the thermopile. This is proportional to the power absorbed per unit area of the sensor.

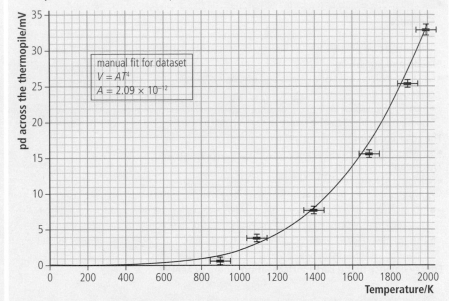

manual fit for dataset
$V = AT^4$
$A = 2.09 \times 10^{-12}$

Figure 8.30 Graph of pd across thermopile *vs* temperature.

This is obviously not a straight line but the curve $y = 2.09 \times 10^{-12}x^4$ is a good fit. Since the thermopile pd is proportional to the power absorbed per unit area, this shows that:

$$\frac{P}{A} \propto T^4.$$

By calibrating the thermopile to convert mV into W m^{-2} we find the constant of proportionality $\sigma = 5.67 \times 10^{-8}$ W m^{-2} K^{-4}. This is known as the *Stefan–Boltzmann constant*. So for a perfect black-body radiator:

$$P = A\sigma T^4.$$

Emissivity (*e*)

Not all bodies are perfect back-body radiators so they emit less radiation than predicted by this equation. The ratio of the energy radiated by a body to the energy radiated by a perfect black body at the same temperature is called the *emissivity*. So, for a body with emissivity *e* the power radiated is given by the adapted formula:

$$P = eA\sigma T^4.$$

The emissivity of a black body is 1; other materials will have emissivity less than one (see Table 8.4).

Material	Emissivity (at 0°)
Polished aluminium	0.02
Dull black paper	0.94
Brick	0.85

Table 8.4 Emissivity of different materials.

The black-body spectrum

If we view the visible spectrum of a filament lamp, we see that it is made up of a continuous spread of wavelengths as shown in Figure 8.31.

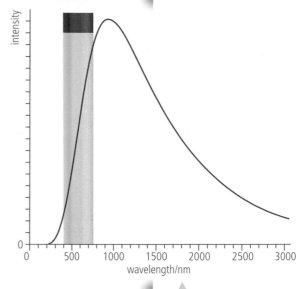

By using sensors we can measure the intensity of the different colours and also electromagnetic radiation outside the visible range to produce the complete *black-body spectrum* as shown in Figure 8.32. Notice how the peak in the spectrum is actually in the infrared region which is why a light bulb gives out more heat than light.

Wien's displacement law

A body at room at room temperature emits infrared radiation but not visible light. However, the spectrum of infrared radiation will be a similar shape to that of the tungsten bulb in Figure 8.32, except that the peak will be moved to the right and, as the total power emitted is less, the area under the graph will be smaller. Figure 8.33 shows the black-body spectra for a range of different temperatures.

Figure 8.31 The visible spectrum.

Figure 8.32 The black-body spectrum for a tungsten filament lamp.

Bodies with the same temperature but lower emissivity will emit radiation with the same peak wavelength but less power.

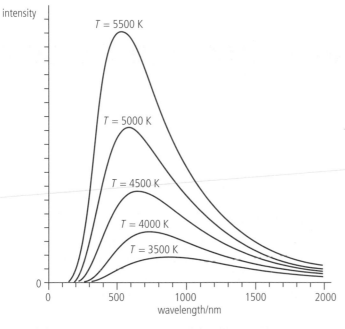

Figure 8.33 The intensity distribution for a black body at different temperatures.

The relationship between the peak wavelength and the temperature in kelvin is given by *Wien's displacement law*:

$$\lambda_{\text{peak}} = \frac{0.00289}{T}$$

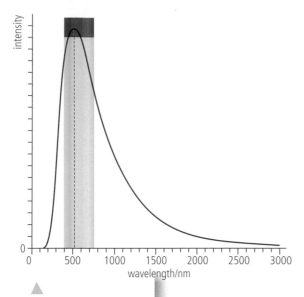

Figure 8.34 Electromagnetic spectrum of sunlight (note the vertical scale is not the same as Figure 8.32).

Although the peak is in the visible region, sunlight also contains ultraviolet (10%) and infrared (50%).

Inverse square law

The radiation from a spherical body spreads out radially in all directions so the power per unit area gets less as you get further from the source. At distance r, the radiation from a source emitting a total power P has spread out to cover a sphere of area $4\pi r^2$ so the power per unit area (I) is given by the formula:

$$I = \frac{P}{4\pi r^2}$$

Radiation from the Sun

The spectrum of light arriving at the edge of the Earth's atmosphere, as shown in Figure 8.34, has a peak value at about 500 nm. This is in the green region of the visible spectrum. Putting this value into Wien's displacement law equation gives a temperature of 5800 K.

Now we know the temperature of the Sun we can use the Stefan–Boltzmann law to calculate the power radiated per unit area:

$$P = A\sigma T^4.$$
$$\frac{P}{A} = 5.67 \times 10^{-8} \times 5800^4 = 6.42 \times 10^7 \, \text{W}.$$

The radius of the Sun = 6.9×10^8 m so the surface area = $4\pi r^2 = 6.0 \times 10^{18} \, \text{m}^2$ so the total power radiated = 3.9×10^{26} W.

The Earth is 1.5×10^{11} m from the Sun so the power per unit area at the Earth will be:

$$I = \frac{P}{4\pi r^2} = \frac{3.9 \times 10^{26}}{4\pi(1.5 \times 10^{11})^2} = 1400 \, \text{Wm}^{-2}.$$

This quantity is called the *solar constant, S*.

Exercise

12 A black ball of radius 2 cm can be considered to be a perfect black-body radiator. If the temperature of the ball is 500 K. Calculate:

(a) the peak wavelength of the spectrum of electromagnetic radiation emitted.
(b) the power per unit area emitted from the ball.
(c) the total power emitted from the ball.
(d) the intensity of radiation received at a distance of 1 m.

Interaction between solar radiation and the atmosphere

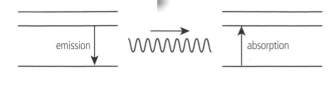

Figure 8.35 Emission and absorption of a photon.

Visible light

When an atomic electron changes from a high energy to a lower energy, a photon of electromagnetic radiation is emitted. The energy change is in the region of a few eV so the frequency of the radiation, given by $\Delta E = hf$, is in the region of the visible spectrum. If a photon of the same frequency is incident on the same atom then it can excite the electron up into a higher energy level. As light from the Sun passes through a gas the wavelengths associated with these energy transitions will be absorbed giving rise to dark lines in the spectrum.

For gases, the number of possible excitations is small which, combined with the fact that the density of gases is low, results in little absorption of visible light by the atmosphere. If this wasn't the case the atmosphere wouldn't be transparent.

Ultraviolet

Ultraviolet photons have higher energy than visible light so when they excite electrons the change in energy is bigger, sometimes resulting in electrons being liberated from the atom. This is called *ionization*. Ultraviolet radiation is absorbed by oxygen molecules (O_2), and splits them into two oxygen atoms ($2O$). The atoms can then join with O_2 molecules to form ozone (O_3), which forms a thin layer in the upper atmosphere where it again absorbs ultraviolet radiation as it splits it into O_2 and O. Most of the higher energy ultraviolet radiation is absorbed in this way. This can be represented by the absorption spectrum in Figure 8.36. 100% means that all of the radiation of that wavelength is absorbed.

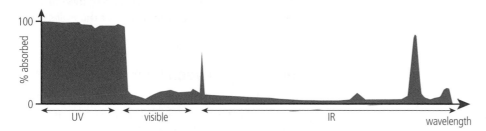

Figure 8.36 Absorption of em radiation by ozone.

Infrared

Infrared photons have lower energy than visible light so when electrons are excited the energy change is smaller. This gives fewer possibilities for absorption by atoms, but the frequency of some infrared radiation is the same as the frequency of vibration of certain molecules present in the atmosphere; e.g. carbon dioxide (CO_2), water vapour (H_2O), nitrous oxide (N_2O), and methane (CH_4). When a photon of the correct frequency is incident on the molecule it causes it to oscillate, resulting in absorption of the photon. This is called *resonance* and can be likened to someone pushing a child on a swing. If the frequency of pushing matches the natural frequency of the swing then maximum energy is transferred from the pusher to the swing. Once the molecule starts to vibrate it will re-emit the radiation in a random direction resulting in fewer photons reaching the Earth. The absorption spectrum for CO_2 is shown in Figure 8.37. Notice the 3 distinct peaks, each due to a different mode of vibration of the molecule.

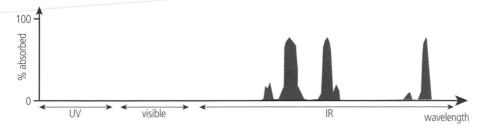

Figure 8.37 Absorption of em radiation by carbon dioxide.

Although CO_2 is the most talked about absorber of infrared radiation, water has the greatest effect. This is not only due to its absorption characteristics, shown in Figure 8.38, but also because it is more abundant in the atmosphere.

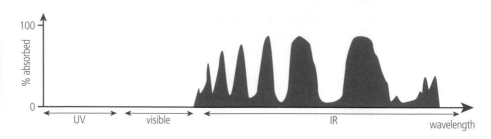

Figure 8.38 Absorption of em radiation by water.

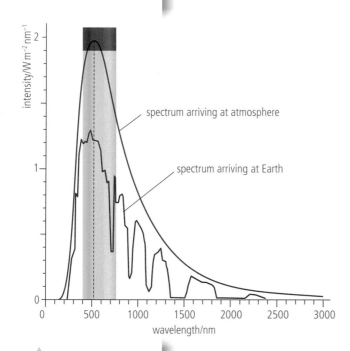

spectrum arriving at atmosphere

spectrum arriving at Earth

Figure 8.39 Spectrum of light reaching the Earth's surface.

Using the colour picker tool in photo-editing software, you can measure the amount of red, green, and blue light reflected on different surfaces in a digital photograph.

Radiation reaching the Earth

By the time the black-body radiation from the Sun reaches the surface of the Earth a lot of wavelengths have been absorbed by the different gases in the atmosphere. The spectrum now looks something like Figure 8.39. The actual amount of energy absorbed will vary with latitude since the sunlight has to pass through more atmosphere to reach the surface at the poles than at the Equator.

Interaction between light and solids

When the radiation hits the surface of the Earth, some is reflected and some is absorbed. The molecules in solids are much closer than the molecules in a gas. This results in electron energy *bands* rather than the discrete levels of a single atom. Solids can therefore emit and absorb many more wavelengths of light than low-pressure gases. When a photon is incident on a solid surface there are 3 main possibilities:

- it may be absorbed then re-emitted in the opposite direction. This is *reflection* or *scattering*.
- it may be absorbed, transferring energy to electrons which in turn pass the energy to molecular KE, resulting in an increase in temperature.
- it may not be absorbed but pass through the material.

When dealing with the surface of the Earth, we can discount the last option since no photons will pass through the Earth. Whether a particular wavelength photon is absorbed or reflected depends upon the material of the surface, it is this that makes different materials have different colours. A red object appears red because it reflects red photons but absorbs the other colours, a white object reflects all colours and a black object reflects none.

Surface heat capacity (C_s)

When heat is added to a body, the increase in temperature depends on the mass and specific heat capacity of the body ($\Delta T = \frac{Q}{mC}$). When solar energy is absorbed by 1 m^2 of the Earth's surface the rise in temperature of the surface depends upon the specific heat capacity of the material and the mass of the affected surface, which in turn depends on how deep the heat transferred penetrates, and on the density of the material. The surface heat capacity takes both of these factors into account:

$$C_s = \frac{Q}{A\Delta T}$$

so energy absorbed per unit area, $\frac{Q}{A} = C_s\Delta T$.

Average surface heat capacity of the Earth = $4 \times 10^8 \, \mathrm{J\,m^{-2}\,K^{-1}}$.

Albedo

The ratio of scattered to total incident power is called the *albedo*:

$$\text{albedo} = \frac{\text{total scattered power}}{\text{total incident power}}$$

Different surfaces have different albedo; for example, the albedo of snow is 0.9 since almost all of the light is reflected, whereas the albedo of asphalt is 0.04. If we take the whole Earth then we should also take into account the light scattered by the clouds. This gives an average albedo of 0.3.

The greenhouse effect

Since the atmosphere does not absorb much visible light, the light reflected from the Earth's surface will pass back out through the atmosphere. The absorbed light will cause the temperature of the surface to rise so it will emit radiation at a peak wavelength given by $\frac{0.0029}{T}$. The Earth isn't very hot so this peak is in the infrared region, which means that the radiation is absorbed by the carbon dioxide (CO_2), water vapour (H_2O), nitrous oxide (N_2O), and methane (CH_4) in the atmosphere. These molecules then re-emit the radiation in random directions so some of it returns to the Earth. The net result is that the energy leaving the Earth is reduced, resulting in a lower emissivity. This effect is called the *greenhouse effect* due to its similarity with the way glass traps heat in a greenhouse. The gases that cause the effect are called *greenhouse gases*.

Energy balance

Imagine we could build the solar system by taking a Sun at 5800 K and putting a 0 K Earth in orbit at a distance of 1.5×10^{11} m. The Earth would absorb energy from the Sun causing its temperature to rise. As the Earth's temperature rose above 0 K it would begin to radiate energy itself. The amount of energy radiated would increase until the amount of energy radiated equals the amount of energy absorbed and equilibrium has been reached.

Earth without atmosphere

To understand the principle of energy balance we will first consider the simplified version of a perfectly black Earth without atmosphere. We have already calculated the power received per unit area at the Earth is 1400 W m^{-2}. This radiation only lands on one side of the Earth so treating the Earth as a disc of radius 6400 km we can calculate the total power incident at the surface:

incident power = $\frac{\text{power}}{\text{area}} \times$ area of Earth = $1400 \times \pi r^2 = 1400 \times \pi \times (6.4 \times 10^6)^2$

$= 1.8 \times 10^{17}$ W.

As the temperature of the Earth increases it will emit radiation which, according to the Stefan–Boltzmann law, will be proportional to the fourth power of the temperature in kelvin. So when the temperature is T the power radiated per unit area is given by:

$$\text{power per unit area} = \sigma T^4$$

If more light is reflected from the Earth then less energy is absorbed, so the temperature will be less. One way of increasing the amount of radiation reflected would be to paint surfaces white. If asphalt was white, how much difference would that make?

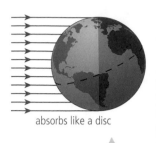

absorbs like a disc

Figure 8.41.

The radiation from the Sun hits the Earth from one direction so the Earth absorbs the same amount of radiation as if it were a disc. In this case power absorbed = $1400\pi r^2$. However, the Earth is actually a sphere so:

the power absorbed per unit area = $\frac{1400\pi r^2}{4\pi r^2} = \frac{1400}{4}$
= $350\,\mathrm{W\,m^{-2}}$.

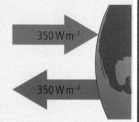

Figure 8.40 Power in = power out.

The total power radiated can be found by multiplying this value by the area of the Earth. This time we must use the total area of the sphere since energy is radiated by all parts, not just the side facing the Sun:

$$\text{power radiated from Earth} = \sigma T^4 \times 4\pi r^2$$

$$\text{power} = 2.9 \times 10^7 \times T^4\,\mathrm{W}.$$

The temperature of the Earth will rise until the power emitted = power absorbed:

$$1.8 \times 10^{17}\,\mathrm{W} = 2.9 \times 10^7 \times T^4$$

$$T = \sqrt[4]{\frac{1.8 \times 10^{17}}{2.9 \times 10^7}} = 280\,\mathrm{K}$$

Earth with atmosphere

The previous example is not realistic because not all the radiation is absorbed by the ground: some is scattered by the atmosphere (particularly clouds) and some is reflected off the surface. The average albedo of the Earth is 0.3, which means that only $\frac{7}{10}$ of the power will be absorbed by the ground. So the power absorbed = $0.7 \times 1.8 \times 10^{17} = 1.26 \times 10^{17}\,\mathrm{W}$.

Also, the power radiated is not as high because the Earth is not a black body and the greenhouse gases re-radiate some of the infrared radiation emitted by the Earth back to the ground. This results in an emissivity of around 0.6.

So power radiated from Earth = $0.6 \times 2.9 \times 10^7 \times T^4\,\mathrm{W}$
= $1.74 \times 10^7 \times T^4\,\mathrm{W}.$

Equilibrium will therefore be reached when
$1.26 \times 10^{17} = 1.74 \times 10^7 \times T^4$ which gives a value of $T = 292$ K.

We can see that the atmosphere has two competing effects: the clouds raise the albedo, resulting in less power reaching the Earth; but the greenhouse gases make the emissivity lower, resulting in a higher overall temperature.

Figure 8.42 is a very simplified picture of the energy flow. Figure 8.43 is a more complete (but still simplified) representation showing some of the detail of the exchange of energy between the ground and the atmosphere. Notice that the atmosphere absorbs energy in two ways, $358\,\mathrm{W\,m^{-2}}$ is absorbed by the greenhouse gases and $105\,\mathrm{W\,m^{-2}}$ due to convection and the energy used to turn water into water vapour.

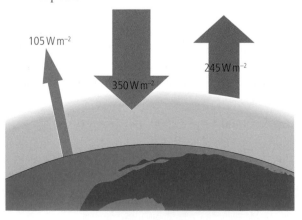

Figure 8.42 Energy flow with some reflected energy.

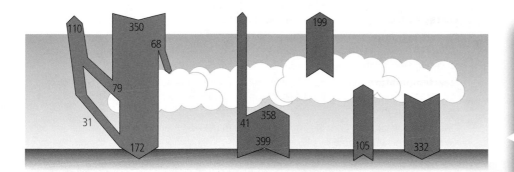

Figure 8.43 The numbers in this diagram represent power per unit area in $W\,m^{-2}$.

Exercise

13 Use Figure 8.43 to answer the following questions.

(a) What is the total power per square metre absorbed by the atmosphere?

(b) How much of the incident radiation is reflected from the surface?

(c) What is the albedo of the Earth?

(d) How much power per square metre is re-radiated by the atmosphere?

(e) What percentage of the energy radiated from the Earth passes straight through the atmosphere?

CHALLENGE YOURSELF

2 Estimate the average surface temperature of the Moon.

Excel simulation of the greenhouse effect

We can't do experiments to see the effect of changing the albedo of the Earth, but we can set up computer models to see what might happen. Using a spreadsheet we can make a simple model to predict the final temperature of the Earth given certain starting conditions. We are going to start the Earth off with an initial temperature of, say, 20 K and calculate how much the temperature will rise in a certain time interval.

The first thing we need to do is enter the variables and constants. These can be entered into a table on the side of the spreadsheet as in Table 8.5.

I	J
Solar constant S/$W\,m^{-2}$	350
Albedo α	0.3
Emissivity e	0.6
Time interval/yrs	2
Initial temp T/K	20

Table 8.5.

Next we will add some formulae to calculate the initial conditions of the Earth using the headers in Table 8.6.

	A	B	C	D	E	F	G
1	Time/yr	Energy in/$J\,m^{-2}$	Power radiated/$W\,m^{-2}$	Energy out/$J\,m^{-2}$	Energy added/$J\,m^{-2}$	Change in temp/K	New temp/K
2	0	15 452 640 000	0.005 443 2	343 313.5	1 545 229 668	38.630 741 7	20

Table 8.6. Note all energy and power values are for $1\,m^2$ of Earth.

The columns are as follows:

Time: Just a starting value, 0; subsequent times will be this plus the time interval.

Energy in: solar constant × (1 – albedo) × time interval in seconds
(= J$1*(1–J$2)*J$4*3600*24*365).

Power radiated: emissivity × σ × T^4 where T is the initial temperature, in this case 20 K
(= J$3*0.000 000 056 7*J$5^4).

Energy out: power out × time interval in seconds (= C2*J$4*3600*24*365).

Energy added: Energy in – energy out (= B2 – D2).

Change in temp: Calculated using the surface heat capacity which is 4×10^8 J m^{-2} K^{-1}. This is rather like the specific heat capacity with area instead of mass, so $\Delta T = \frac{E}{C_s}$ where E is the heat received per unit area (= $\frac{E2}{400\,000\,000}$).

New temperature: this is simply the initial temperature. Subsequent values will be calculated from the previous temperature + the change in temperature. Enter = J5 to take the temperature from the table.

Once this row has been fixed the formulae are put in the next row to calculate the heat lost at the new temperature (Table 8.7).

	A	B	C	D	E	F	G
1	Time/yr	Energy in/J m^{-2}	Power radiated/W m^{-2}	Energy out/J m^{-2}	Energy added/J m^{-2}	Change in temp/K	New temp/K
2	0	15 452 640 000	0.005 443 2	343 313.5104	15 452 296 686	38.630 741 72	20
3	2	15 452 640 000	0.402 009 08	25 355 516.7	15 427 284 483	38.568 211 21	58.630 741 72

Table 8.7.

Time: previous time + the time interval (= A2+J$4).

Energy in: solar constant × (1– albedo) × time interval in seconds (= J$1*(1–J$2)*J$4*3600*24*365).

Power radiated: emissivity × σ × T^4 where T is the new temperature, this is the temperature of the last time interval + the change in temperature (= J$3*0.0000000567*G3^4).

Energy out: power out × time interval in seconds (= C3*J$4*3600*24*365).

Energy added: energy in – energy out (= B3–D3).

Change in temperature: (= $\frac{E3}{400\,000\,000}$).

New temperature: the change in temp + the previous temp (= F2 + G2).

These formulae are now copied down for fifty rows by highlighting row 3 and dragging down. (Note: it is row 3 you copy down, not row 2 which just contains the starting values.)

To plot a graph highlight column A, then whilst pressing control highlight column G. This will leave both A and G highlighted. Now insert scatter graph, giving Figure 8.44.

Although this simulation aids our understanding of the underlying physics it is a much simplified version of reality and should not be taken to represent reality. There are, however, some much more complex computer simulations that are thought to come close.

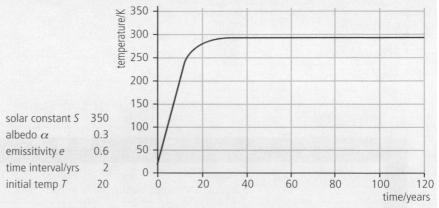

solar constant S	350
albedo α	0.3
emissitivity e	0.6
time interval/yrs	2
initial temp T	20

Figure 8.44 Graph of temperature against time.

You can now find out what happens if you change the values of albedo, emissivity, etc.

Global warming

The Excel simulation shows that if the energy in is not balanced with energy out then the average temperature of the Earth will change. A rise in average temperature is called *global warming* and can be caused by the four factors listed on the next page.

Increase in solar constant

The amount of energy reaching the Earth depends upon how much energy the Sun is giving out and the distance between the Earth and the Sun. Neither of these is constant. The Earth's orbit is elliptical so the orbital radius changes, there are also some changes due to the change of angle of the Earth's axis in relation to the Sun; these variations are called Milankovitch cycles. The Sun's surface is an ever-changing swirling mass of gas that sometimes sends out flares many tens of thousands of km high. More easily viewed from the Earth are the number of sunspots which can be seen if an image of the Sun is projected onto a screen (never look directly at the Sun). The number of sunspots present gives an indication of the amount of energy emitted; more sunspots implies more energy. This seems the wrong way round but it is the gas around the sunspot that emits the energy, not the sunspot itself.

Reduced albedo

Albedo is the ratio of reflected to total incident radiation. If the albedo is low then more energy is absorbed by the Earth resulting in a higher equilibrium temperature. Snow has a high albedo so a reduction in the amount of snow present at the poles and on glaciers would reduce the albedo.

Reduced emissivity

The emissivity is related to the greenhouse effect which reduces the amount of radiation leaving the Earth at a given temperature. Increasing the amount of greenhouse gases in the atmosphere will result in a higher equilibrium temperature.

Enhanced greenhouse effect

There is a lot of evidence that the burning of fossils fuels, that produce carbon dioxide at a faster rate than the living trees remove it, has led to an increase in the percentage of CO_2 in the atmosphere. This has enhanced the greenhouse effect, causing more energy to be radiated back to Earth. If more radiation returns to the Earth then more must be emitted, resulting in a higher average temperature. This effect is made worse by deforestation.

What can be done

To reduce the enhanced greenhouse effect, the levels of greenhouse gases must be reduced, or at the very least, the rate at which they are increasing must be slowed down. There are several ways that this can be achieved:

1 Greater efficiency of power production

In recent years the efficiency of power plants has been increasing significantly. According to the second law of thermodynamics, they can never be 100% efficient but some of the older less efficient ones could be replaced. This would mean that to produce the same amount of power would require less fuel, resulting in reduced CO_2 emission.

2 Replacing the use of coal and oil with natural gas

Gas-fired power stations are more efficient than oil and gas and produce less CO_2.

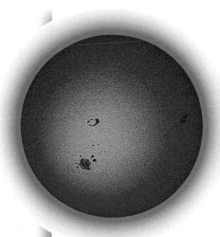

The increase in temperature as a result of many sunspots together leads to solar flares, jets of gas flying out from the Sun's surface like huge flames.

Global warming is an international problem that requires an international solution. What measures are the government and people making in the country where you live?

3 Use of combined heating and power systems (CHP)

Using the excess heat from the power station to heat homes would result in a more efficient use of fuel.

4 Increased use of renewable energy sources and nuclear power

Replacing fossil fuel burning power stations with alternative forms such as wave power, solar power, and wind power would reduce CO_2 emissions.

5 Use of hybrid vehicles

A large amount of the oil used today is used for transport, and even without global warming, there will be a problem when the oil runs out. Cars that run on electricity or a combination of electricity and petrol (hybrid) are already in production. Aeroplanes will also have to use a different fuel.

6 Carbon dioxide capture and storage

A different way of reducing greenhouse gases is to remove CO_2 from the waste gases of power stations and store it underground.

An international problem

Global warming is an international problem, and if any solution is going to work then it must be a joint international solution. Before working on the solution the international community had to agree on pinpointing the problem and it was to this end that the Intergovernmental Panel on Climate Change (IPCC) was formed.

To learn more about global thermal energy transfer, go to the hotlinks site, search for the title or ISBN and click on Chapter 8.

Practice questions

1. This question is about energy sources.

    (a) Fossil fuels are being produced continuously on Earth and yet they are classed as being non-renewable. Outline why fossil fuels are classed as non-renewable. (2)

    (b) Some energy consultants suggest that the solution to the problem of carbon dioxide pollution is to use nuclear energy for the generation of electrical energy. Identify **two** disadvantages of the use of nuclear fission when compared to the burning of fossil fuels for the generation of electrical energy. (2)

    (*Total 4 marks*)

2. This question is about solar energy.

    (a) By reference to energy transformations, distinguish between a solar panel and a solar cell. (2)

    Some students carry out an investigation on a solar panel. They measure the output temperature of the water for different solar input powers and for different rates of extraction of thermal energy. The results are shown in Figure 8.45.

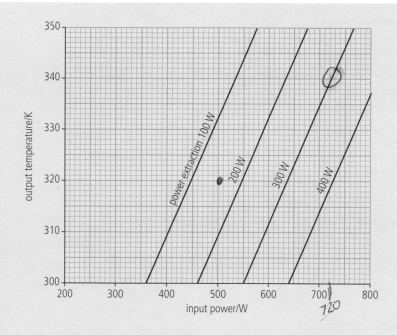

Figure 8.45.

(b) Use the data from Figure 8.45 to answer the following.

(i) The solar panel is to provide water at 340 K whilst extracting energy at a rate of 300 W when the intensity of the sunlight incident normally on the panel is 800 W m^{-2}. Calculate the effective surface area of the panel that is required. (2)

(ii) Deduce the overall efficiency of the panel for an input power of 500 W at an output temperature of 320 K. (3)

(Total 7 marks)

3. This question is about the production of electrical energy.

(a) Outline the principal energy transfers involved in the production of electrical energy from thermal energy in a coal-fired power station. (2)

(b) State and explain whether the energy sources used in the following power stations are renewable or non-renewable.

(i) Coal-fired (1)

(ii) Nuclear (1)

(c) The core of some nuclear reactors contains a moderator and control rods. Explain the function of these components.

(i) The moderator (2)

(ii) The control rods (2)

(d) Discuss **one** advantage of a nuclear power station as opposed to a coal-fired power station. (2)

(Total 10 marks)

4. This question is about wind energy.

It is required to design wind turbines for a wind farm for which the following information is available.

Total required annual electrical energy output from the wind farm = 120 TJ

Maximum number of turbines for which there is space on the farm = 20

Average annual wind speed at the site = $9.0 \, m \, s^{-1}$

(a) Deduce that the average power output required from one turbine is 0.19 MW. (3)

(b) Estimate the blade radius of the wind turbine that will give a power output of 0.19 MW. (Density of air = $1.2 \, kg \, m^{-3}$) (3)

(c) State **one** reason why your answer to (b) is only an estimate. (1)

(d) Discuss briefly **one** disadvantage of generating power from wind energy. (2)

(*Total 9 marks*)

5. This question is about the production of nuclear energy and its transfer to electrical energy.

(a) When a neutron 'collides' with a nucleus of uranium-235 ($^{235}_{92}U$) the following reaction can occur.

$$^{235}_{92}U + ^{1}_{0}n \rightarrow ^{144}_{56}Ba + ^{90}_{36}Kr + 2^{1}_{0}n$$

(i) State the name given to this type of nuclear reaction. (1)

(ii) Energy is liberated in this reaction. In what form does this energy appear? (1)

(b) Describe how the neutrons produced in this reaction may initiate a chain reaction. (1)

The purpose of a nuclear power station is to produce electrical energy from nuclear energy. Figure 8.46 is a schematic representation of the principle components of a nuclear reactor 'pile' used in a certain type of nuclear power station.

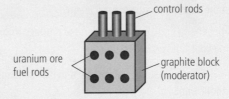

Figure 8.46.

The function of the moderator is to slow down neutrons produced in a reaction such as that described in part (a) above.

(c) (i) Explain why it is necessary to slow down the neutrons. (3)

(ii) Explain the function of the control rods. (2)

(d) Describe briefly how the energy produced by the nuclear reactions is extracted from the reactor pile and then transferred to electrical energy. (4)

(*Total 12 marks*)

6. This question is about the energy balance of the Earth.

(a) The intensity of the Sun's radiation at the position of the Earth is approximately $1400 \, W \, m^{-2}$.

Suggest why the average power received per unit area of the Earth is $350 \, W \, m^{-2}$. (2)

(b) Figure 8.47 shows a simplified model of the energy balance of the Earth's surface. The diagram shows radiation entering or leaving the Earth's surface only.

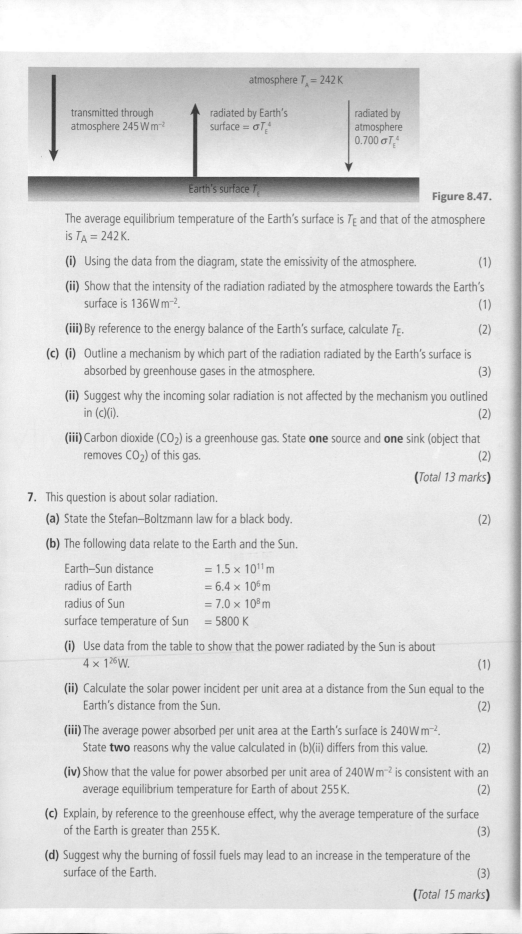

Figure 8.47.

The average equilibrium temperature of the Earth's surface is T_E and that of the atmosphere is $T_A = 242\,K$.

(i) Using the data from the diagram, state the emissivity of the atmosphere. (1)

(ii) Show that the intensity of the radiation radiated by the atmosphere towards the Earth's surface is $136\,W\,m^{-2}$. (1)

(iii) By reference to the energy balance of the Earth's surface, calculate T_E. (2)

(c) (i) Outline a mechanism by which part of the radiation radiated by the Earth's surface is absorbed by greenhouse gases in the atmosphere. (3)

(ii) Suggest why the incoming solar radiation is not affected by the mechanism you outlined in (c)(i). (2)

(iii) Carbon dioxide (CO_2) is a greenhouse gas. State **one** source and **one** sink (object that removes CO_2) of this gas. (2)

(*Total 13 marks*)

7. This question is about solar radiation.

(a) State the Stefan–Boltzmann law for a black body. (2)

(b) The following data relate to the Earth and the Sun.

Earth–Sun distance $= 1.5 \times 10^{11}\,m$
radius of Earth $= 6.4 \times 10^{6}\,m$
radius of Sun $= 7.0 \times 10^{8}\,m$
surface temperature of Sun $= 5800\,K$

(i) Use data from the table to show that the power radiated by the Sun is about $4 \times 1^{26}\,W$. (1)

(ii) Calculate the solar power incident per unit area at a distance from the Sun equal to the Earth's distance from the Sun. (2)

(iii) The average power absorbed per unit area at the Earth's surface is $240\,W\,m^{-2}$.
State **two** reasons why the value calculated in (b)(ii) differs from this value. (2)

(iv) Show that the value for power absorbed per unit area of $240\,W\,m^{-2}$ is consistent with an average equilibrium temperature for Earth of about $255\,K$. (2)

(c) Explain, by reference to the greenhouse effect, why the average temperature of the surface of the Earth is greater than $255\,K$. (3)

(d) Suggest why the burning of fossil fuels may lead to an increase in the temperature of the surface of the Earth. (3)

(*Total 15 marks*)

09

Option A: Relativity

Essential ideas

A.1 The beginnings of relativity
Einstein's study of electromagnetism revealed inconsistencies between the theory of Maxwell and Newton's mechanics. He recognized that both theories could not be reconciled and so choosing to trust Maxwell's theory of electromagnetism he was forced to change long cherished ideas about space and time in mechanics.

A.2 Lorentz transformations
Observers in relative uniform motion disagree on the numerical values of space and time coordinates for events. The Lorentz transformation equations relate the values in one reference frame to those in another. These equations replace the Galilean transformation equations which fail for speeds close to that of light.

A.3 Spacetime diagrams
Spacetime diagrams are a very clear and illustrative way to show graphically how different observers in relative motion to each other have measurements that differ from each other.

A.4 Relativistic mechanics (HL only)
The relativity of space and time requires new definitions for energy and momentum in order to preserve the conserved nature of these laws.

A.5 General relativity (HL only)
General relativity is applied to describe the fate of the Universe.

Rockets only travel close to the speed of light in science fiction and physics exams. However, at CERN relativity becomes reality.

9.1 The beginnings of relativity

A.1 The beginnings of relativity

Understandings, applications, and skills:

Reference frames
Galilean relativity and Newton's postulates concerning time and space
- Using the Galilean transformation equations.
Maxwell's equations
The constancy of the speed of light
Forces on a charge or current
- Determining whether a force on a charge or current is electric or magnetic in a given frame of reference.
- Determining the nature of the fields observed by different observers.

Guidance
- *This is a qualitative treatment of electric and magnetic fields as measured by observers in relative motion. Examples will include a charge moving in a magnetic field or two charged particles moving with parallel velocities. Students will be asked to analyse these motions from the point of view of observers at rest with respect to the particles and observers at rest with respect to the magnetic field.*

NATURE OF SCIENCE

Accepting that the velocity of light in a vacuum is $3 \times 10^8\,\text{m s}^{-1}$ even if you are travelling at $2 \times 10^8\,\text{m s}^{-1}$ towards the source requires a totally different approach than that accepted by Galilean relativity. Such a radical change is called a *paradigm shift*. Maxwell's equations turned up a result that didn't fit in with the classical view of relativity. If two theories do not predict the same outcomes then one of them must be wrong.

Reference frames

During this course we have sometimes used the term *relative*; for example, when quoting a velocity, it is very important to say what the velocity is measured relative to.

Relative velocity

Consider the example shown in Figure 9.1. **A**, **B**, and **C** measure each other's velocity but they do not agree.

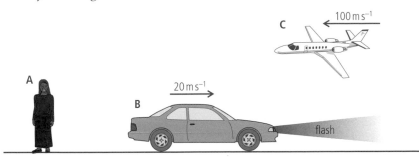

Figure 9.1 A, B, and C
measure each other's velocity.

Measured by A:

Velocity of car = 20 m s^{-1}
Velocity of plane = −100 m s^{-1}

Measured by B:

Velocity of woman = −20 m s^{-1}
Velocity of plane = −120 m s^{-1}
They don't agree because velocity is relative.

When considering an example like this there are some useful terms worth defining.

Event

An event is some change that takes place at a point in space at a particular time. If **B** were to flash his headlights, this would be an event.

Observer

An observer is someone who measures some physical quantity related to an event. In this case **A** measures the time and position when **B** flashed his lights, so **A** is an observer.

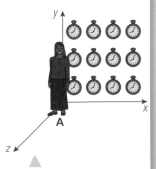

Figure 9.2 A in her frame of
reference with some of her
clocks. We won't always draw
the clocks but remember they
are there.

Frames of reference

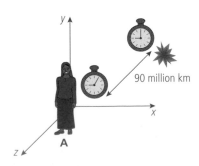

Figure 9.3 It takes 5 minutes
for the light to reach **A** from
this event. If she had used her
own clock she would have got
the wrong time.

Figure 9.2 shows a frame of reference. This is a coordinate system covered in clocks that an observer uses to measure the time and position of an event. It is covered in clocks so we can measure the time that an event took place *where* it took place. If we used our own clock we would always measure a time that was a little late, since it takes time for light to get from the event to us (Figure 9.3). An observer can only make measurements in their own frame of reference.

In the example of Figure 9.1 we have three observers with three different frames of reference. As we can see in Figure 9.4, the frames of reference are moving relative to each other with constant velocity.

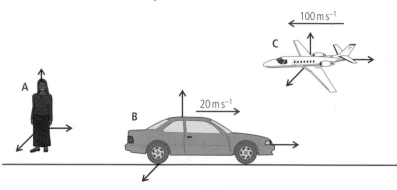

Figure 9.4 Three observers, three frames of reference.

When we look at Figure 9.4 we can see that the car and plane are moving, but the woman is standing still. This is because we often measure velocity relative to the Earth and she is stationary relative to the Earth. But, according to B, A is moving with a velocity of 20 m s⁻¹ to the left, so who is moving – A or B? Is there an experiment that we can do to prove which one of them is moving and which one is stationary?

The presence of the Earth can be confusing, since we always think of the person standing as stationary. Also the Earth's gravitational field and the fact that it is spinning complicate matters. For that reason we will now move our observers into space, as in Figure 9.5, and ask the question again: is there any experiment that A or B could do to prove who is moving and who is stationary?

Inertial frame of reference

An inertial frame of reference is a frame of reference within which Newton's laws of motion apply.

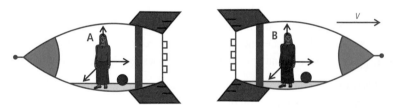

Figure 9.5 Two observers; **B** is travelling at velocity v relative to **A**.

Let's try a simple experiment. In Figure 9.5 A and B take a ball (red) and place it on the floor. If they apply a force to the ball, it will accelerate and if they don't, it will remain at rest. Newton's laws of motion apply in each frame of reference. There is in fact no experiment that A and B can do to show who is moving – they are moving relative to each other but there is no absolute movement. We call these 'inertial frames of reference'. Let us compare this to the situation in Figure 9.6 where B's rocket is accelerating.

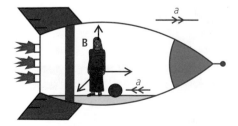

Figure 9.6 Observer **B** fires the rocket engines and accelerates.

If observer B now places a ball on the ground it will start to roll towards her even though there is no force acting on the ball, Newton's laws do not apply! Watching from the outside we can see what is happening. There is a force acting on the rocket pushing it past the ball and the ball is stationary. Newton's laws have not been broken, but inside the rocket it appears that they have. Accelerating frames of reference like this are called 'non-inertial frames of reference'.

Galilean relativity

Galileo did many experiments with both live and dead objects and came to the conclusion that the basic laws of physics are the same in all inertial frames of reference.

Coordinate transformations

If observers **A** and **B** in Figure 9.7 both measure the position of the blue balloon floating weightlessly in the spaceship of **B** then they will get different values. So if **B** were to tell **A** where the ball was, it wouldn't make sense unless **A** knew how to transform **B**'s measurement into her own frame of reference. The classical way of doing this is called a 'Galilean transformation'.

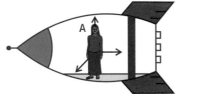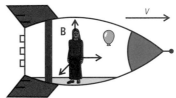

Figure 9.7 A blue balloon is at rest in **B**'s rocket.

Galilean transformations

At some time, as **A** and **B** are flying apart, the balloon bursts. **A** and **B** measure the time and position of this event. To do this they will use clocks and tape measures in their own frames of reference but to transform the measurements they need to have some reference point. So let's assume that at the time when they started their clocks, the two frames were at the same place. This isn't really possible with the rockets but we can imagine it.

If we call **A**'s frame of reference S and **B**'s S′ (S and S dash), we can then distinguish between **A** and **B**'s measurement by using a dash.

Figure 9.9 shows the moment that the balloon bursts.

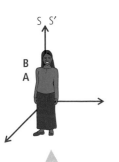

Figure 9.8 At time $t = 0$, **A** and **B** are coincident, as can be seen from the magenta dress.

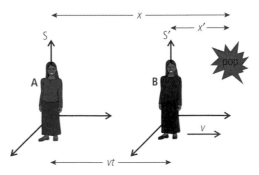

Figure 9.9 The balloon pops when **A** and **B** have moved apart.

The transforms work in both directions. Sometimes you might see examples where the event is at rest in **A**'s frame of reference rather than **B**'s.

A and **B** record the coordinates and time for this event and get the results in Table 9.1.

We can see that only the coordinate in the direction of motion (x) is changed.

Notice that the time is the same in both frames of reference.

A (S)	B (S′)	Transformation
x	x'	$x = x' + vt$
y	y'	$y = y'$
z	z'	$z = z'$
t	t'	$t = t'$

Table 9.1.

Transformation for length

A length is simply the difference between two positions so consider an object stationary in the frame of reference S' with one end at x_1' and the other at x_2'. It will have length, $L' = x_2' - x_1'$ measured in S'. An observer in S will measure the ends to be at positions x_1 and x_2 where $x_1 = x_1' + vt$ and $x_2 = x_2' + vt$, so its length measured in S will be:

$$L = x_2 - x_1 = (x_2' + vt) - (x_1' + vt) = x_2' - x_1'.$$

As you would expect, according to the Galilean transformations the length of objects are the same as measured in all inertial frames of reference.

Galilean transforms for velocity

Galilean transformations can also be used to transform velocities. Consider a small bird flying in the x direction in **B**'s spacecraft as shown in Figure 9.10.

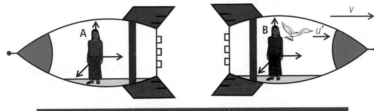

A (S)	B (S')	Transformation
u	u'	$u = u' + v$

This is the velocity of the bird as measured by B (u') minus the velocity of A's frame of reference relative to B ($-v$) = $u' - (-v) = u' + v$.

Galilean transform for acceleration

If the bird in the previous example accelerates from velocity u_1' to u_2' in a time Δt then the acceleration measured by **B** is:

$$a' = \frac{u_2' - u_1'}{\Delta t}$$

The acceleration measured by **A** will therefore be

$$a' = \frac{(u_2' + v) - (u_1' + v)}{\Delta t} = \frac{u_2' - u_1'}{\Delta t}$$

so the acceleration is the same in each frame of reference. This means that Newton's second law applies in the same way in all inertial frames of reference.

Exercise

1 A train travels through a station at a constant velocity of 8 m s^{-1}. One observer sits on the train and another sits on the platform. As they pass each other, they start their stopwatches and take measurements of a passenger on the train who is walking in the same direction as the train.

   Before starting to answer the following questions, make sure you understand what is happening; drawing a diagram will help.

   (a) The train observer measures the velocity of the passenger to be 0.5 m s^{-1}. What is the velocity to the platform observer?
   (b) After 20 s how far has the walking passenger moved according to the observer on the train?
   (c) After 20 s how far has the walking passenger moved according to the observer on the platform?

Figure 9.10 A bird flies with velocity u' as measured by **B**.

371

The nature of light

Light travels so fast that it appears to take no time at all. However, if the distances are long enough, time taken is noticeable. The first measurement of the speed of light was undertaken by Danish astronomer Ole Römer, who in 1776 observed that the timing of the eclipses of Jupiter by its moon Io were not as expected. When the Earth is at its furthest from Jupiter the eclipse is late and when the Earth is closest the eclipse occurs early. The reason for this, he concluded, was due to the time taken for light to travel from Jupiter to the Earth. Others used his measurements to calculate the velocity of light and by 1809,

James Clark Maxwell.

with improved instrumentation, the value stood at $3 \times 10^8 \, \text{m s}^{-1}$, quite close to today's value. At this time scientists knew that light had wave-like properties but not what sort of wave it was. It wasn't until 1864 that James Clerk Maxwell deduced that light was an electromagnetic wave.

Maxwell's equations

What Maxwell did was to formulate a set of four equations that modelled all aspects of electromagnetism. The mathematics is too complex for this level but it is still possible to understand what they represent – you won't be examined on these equations.

Equation 1

$$\oint E. \, \mathrm{d}A = \frac{Q}{\varepsilon_0}$$

The first equation is about how electric fields spread out from charges. To put it simply, if you take any closed surface, let's take the surface of a sphere, then the difference between the number of field lines pointing out of the sphere and the number pointing in will be proportional to the net charge inside the sphere.

If we take the example shown in Figure 9.11(a) we can see that all the field lines point outwards so the charge inside is positive. In Figure 9.11(b) the field lines point inwards so the net field pointing out is negative, meaning that there must be a negative charge inside. In Figure 9.11(c) there are as many lines pointing out as in so the net charge inside is zero.

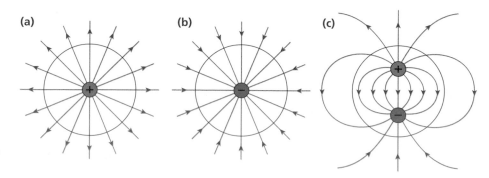

Figure 9.11 Field lines crossing a closed surface.

Equation 2

$$\oint B.\, dA = 0$$

The second equation is a similar statement but this time about magnetic fields. We have seen that whenever you have a magnet it has a north and a south pole: you can *never* get a monopole like you do with electric fields. This means that if you take a closed surface the number of magnetic field lines entering the surface will always equal the number coming out (Figure 9.12).

Equation 3

$$\oint E.\, ds = \frac{d\varphi_m}{dt}$$

This third equation is a version of Faraday's law that states that the emf induced in a closed loop is proportional to the rate of change of the magnetic flux enclosed. So a magnet moving into the loop of wire shown in Figure 9.13 will cause the charge to move. To move the charge requires an electric field so we can say that a changing B field creates an E field.

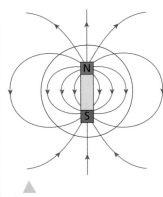

Figure 9.12 Magnetic field in and out of a closed surface.

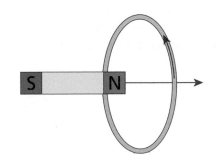

Figure 9.13 Emf is induced by a changing field.

Equation 4

$$\oint B.\, ds = \mu_0 I + \varepsilon_0 \mu_0 \frac{d\varphi_c}{dt}$$

The fourth equation relates magnetic field to the current producing it. We have seen how a current in a wire will create a B field. However, Maxwell went one step further and stated that even if there is no flow of charge a B field will still be induced by a changing E field in the same way that an E field is induced by a changing B field. So, if two parallel plates are connected to an AC supply as shown in Figure 9.14, even though no current flows between the plates the changing E field between them will produce a changing B field. The changing B field in turn produces a changing E which produces a changing B field. The result is a spreading out of changing E and B fields with no requirement for any medium.

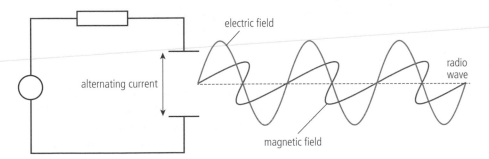

Figure 9.14 Electromagnetic wave produced from an air gap.

Frames of reference and moving charges

When charges are viewed in different frames of reference we get an apparent paradox which hints that there is something wrong with our classical view of the world.

Consider two charges moving parallel to each other as shown in Figure 9.15. According to us watching the charges move past, we can think of charge Q_1 as a flowing current and charge Q_2 as a moving charge. Charge Q_1 will produce a magnetic field which will be in the form of rings as shown in the diagram. Charge Q_2 is moving through this field so will experience a magnetic force. The resultant force between the particles will be magnetic and electric. However, according to an observer moving with the charges, charge Q_1 is not moving so produces no magnetic field; the force on Q_2 will therefore be only electric.

Figure 9.15 Moving charges.

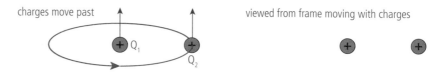

charges move past

viewed from frame moving with charges

So it seems that the magnetic force depends on the reference frame of the observer, which means that it should be possible to conduct an experiment to distinguish the two frames of reference, and this does not fit in with the idea of relativity.

When trading stocks and shares on the international market, timing is crucial. Humans can't respond fast enough so computers that can potentially make millions of trades each second are taking over. When buying and selling so quickly it is important to get the trades registered soon after the decision has been made. Information can't travel faster than the speed of light so traders setting up shop next to the markets would have an advantage. However, in an international market place being close to one market means you are far from all the others.

The speed of light

Maxwell's equations showed how light could propagate through a vacuum and also gave a value for the speed at which the changing field would travel. This turned out to be:

$$v = \frac{1}{\sqrt{\varepsilon_0 \mu_0}} = \frac{1}{\sqrt{8.85 \times 10^{-12} \times 4\pi \times 10^{-7}}} = 3.00 \times 10^8 \,\mathrm{m\,s^{-1}}$$

which is the same as the speed of light. Maxwell therefore concluded that light is an electromagnetic wave. One strange thing about this result was that there was nothing in the solution that made it possible to calculate what the velocity would be if the observer, source, or medium was moving. It seemed that the speed of light is always the same. This causes some problems when we try to transform the velocity of light using the Galilean transformations. Imagine that observer B in Figure 9.16 measured the speed of a photon of light travelling along the x-axis to be $3 \times 10^8 \,\mathrm{m\,s^{-1}}$.

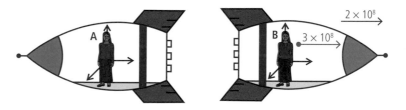

Figure 9.16.

According to the Galilean transformations (and common sense) the velocity of the photon measured by B would be $2 \times 10^8 \,\mathrm{m\,s^{-1}} + 3 \times 10^8 \,\mathrm{m\,s^{-1}} = 5 \times 10^8 \,\mathrm{m\,s^{-1}}$. This is not the case according to Maxwell's equations, which say the speed should be $3 \times 10^8 \,\mathrm{m\,s^{-1}}$. To test whether the velocity of light is indeed the same as measured by all inertial observers, many experiments have been carried out. Some involve moving light sources such as gamma rays emitted by pions travelling at $0.999c$ and others use the motion of the Earth through space. All results verify that the speed of light in a vacuum is independent of the relative motion of observers.

Momentum of light

Maxwell's equations not only predicted the velocity of light but also that a pulse of light should have momentum $= \frac{E}{c}$ where E is the energy of the pulse and c the velocity

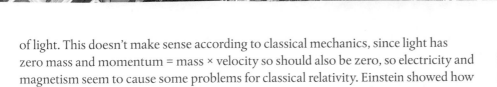

of light. This doesn't make sense according to classical mechanics, since light has zero mass and momentum = mass × velocity so should also be zero, so electricity and magnetism seem to cause some problems for classical relativity. Einstein showed how it could all fit together.

To learn more about the beginnings of relativity, go to the hotlinks site, search for the title or ISBN and click on Chapter 9.

9.2 Lorentz transformations

A.2 Lorentz transformations

Understandings, applications, and skills:

The two postulates of special relativity
Clock synchronization
The Lorentz transformations
- Using the Lorentz transformations to describe how different measurements of space and time by two observers can be converted into the measurements observed in either frame of reference.
- Using the Lorentz transformation equations to determine the position and time coordinates of various events.
- Using the Lorentz transformation equations to show that if two events are simultaneous for one observer but happen at different points in space, then the events are not simultaneous for an observer in a different reference frame.

    Guidance
    - *Problems will be limited to one-dimension.*
    - *Derivation of the Lorentz transformation equations will not be examined.*

Velocity addition
- Solving problems involving velocity addition.

Invariant quantities (spacetime interval, proper time, proper length, and rest mass)
Time dilation
- Deriving the time dilation equations using the Lorentz equations.
- Solving problems involving time dilation.

Length contraction
- Deriving the length contraction equations using the Lorentz equations.
- Solving problems involving length contraction.

The muon decay experiment
- Solving problems involving the muon decay experiment.

    Guidance
    - *Muon decay experiments can be used as evidence for both time dilation and length contraction.*

The two postulates of special relativity

Einstein's theory of relativity extends the Galilean idea that Newton's laws apply in all inertial frames of reference to take into account the nature of light. His theory is based on two statements of fact, or postulates.

First postulate
The laws of physics are the same in all inertial frames of reference.

Second postulate
The speed of light in a vacuum is the same as measured by all inertial observers.

Light clock experiments

At first the far-reaching consequences the constancy of the velocity of light may not be apparent, but a couple of interesting thought experiments will show how this simple statement will make us see the Universe in a totally different way. For this we need to

NATURE OF SCIENCE

Einstein developed the theory of relativity by applying mathematics to two clear and experimentally verifiable statements of fact. Anyone wanting to disprove the theory would need to show that the postulates were incorrect or find a fault in the mathematics.

By multiplying by a constant Einstein got the Galilean transformations to agree with Maxwell's equations, but it is no good to simply fix the equations: there must be some theoretical explanation.

consider a special type of clock called a light clock. To understand how that works, first we will consider a rubber ball clock.

A rubber ball clock is made using a perfectly elastic ball and two perfectly elastic metal plates as in Figure 9.17(a). This can't be made in reality but could be simulated with a programme such as Algodoo®.

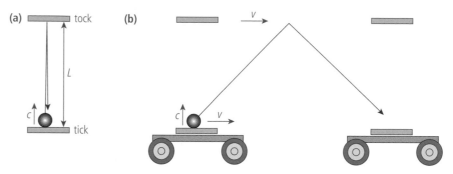

Figure 9.17 The rubber ball clock.

The rubber ball bounces back and forth between the metal plates, counting off the seconds as it ticks and tocks. If the velocity of the ball is c then the time between ticks is $\frac{2L}{c}$. Now, if the clock is rolled past us on a trolley as shown in Figure 9.17(b), the ball moves to the right as it bounces so will be seen to follow the much longer path shown. However, the clock still ticks at the same rate since although the ball is travelling further it is also travelling faster, the velocity of the ball is now the vector sum of $c + v$.

Time dilation

Now we are ready for the light clock. This is the same except that it has a photon of light bouncing between two mirrors as shown in Figure 9.18(a).

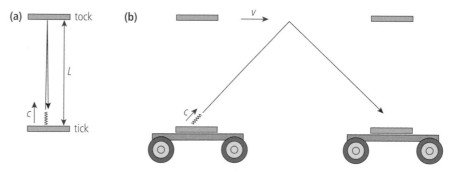

Figure 9.18 The light clock.

This time the clock will tick much more quickly but it still ticks at a constant rate. If this clock is now moved past on a trolley we see that the light also follows a longer path, but light always has the same velocity so even though the clock moves on the trolley the light will travel along this long path with the same velocity as the stationary clock. This means the moving clock must tick more slowly. The problem is that if we compared this clock with another type of clock, a wrist watch for example, we would be able to tell the difference between the moving slow-ticking clock and the stationary fast-ticking one. But according to the principle of relativity we are not supposed to be able to distinguish between inertial frames of reference, so to satisfy this condition all clocks must slow down, including the rubber ball clock that we thought wouldn't.

Proper time

Remember that an inertial frame of reference is a coordinate system covered with clocks so you have to use the clock at the position of the event. Let's say you want to measure the time between two flashes of a light. This could be done with one clock placed by the light. However, if the light was moving past on a trolley as in Figure 9.19 you would have to use two clocks, one for the first flash and one for the second. A time interval measured by a clock at the same point in space is called the *proper time*.

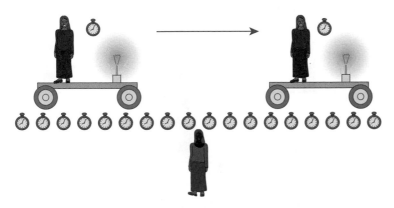

Figure 9.19 Proper time measured by woman in the red dress.

You may think that the red woman's clock is moving so how can her clock be in the same point in space? Well, in her frame of reference the clock is in the same point in space, it is the blue woman's clocks that are moving.

Length contraction

The slowing down of time has further consequences. For example, consider a space ship travelling from Earth to a distant planet at a velocity *v* as shown in Figure 9.20. Observers on Earth will see the rocket moving away at a velocity *v* and the observers on the rockets would see the Earth moving away at velocity *–v*.

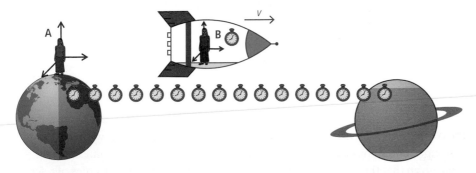

Figure 9.20 Travelling to a distant planet.

Now, if we try to measure the velocity of the rocket we could divide the distance by the time of flight. The *proper time* between take-off and landing is measured by the observer in the rocket. Since she can use the same clock to measure both leaving the Earth and arriving at the planet, she will actually see the Earth and the planet move relative to the clock which stays in the same position. This time will be shorter than the time measured by an observer on Earth who would have to use two separate clocks to measure the same event, one at the start and one at the end. The problem is that they will not agree on the velocity since they will measure the same distance but different times; that is, unless the distance measured by the astronaut is shorter. This is called *length contraction* and only happens along the direction of motion. The distance measured by an observer at rest relative to the length is called the *proper length*.

Clock synchronization

Stranger still is that events that happen at the same time for one observer don't happen at the same time for another. Imagine trying to synchronize two clocks so that they show the same time. The clocks are separated by some distance so you stand exactly in the middle and ask two friends to start the clocks when you raise your hand. When you do this light will travel from you to your helpers. Because they are the same distance from you, they will receive the light at the same time and start their watches together. As you are doing this, a third friend moves past on a trolley as shown in Figure 9.21.

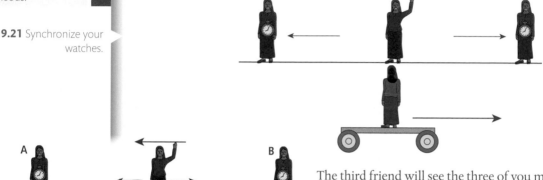

Figure 9.21 Synchronize your watches.

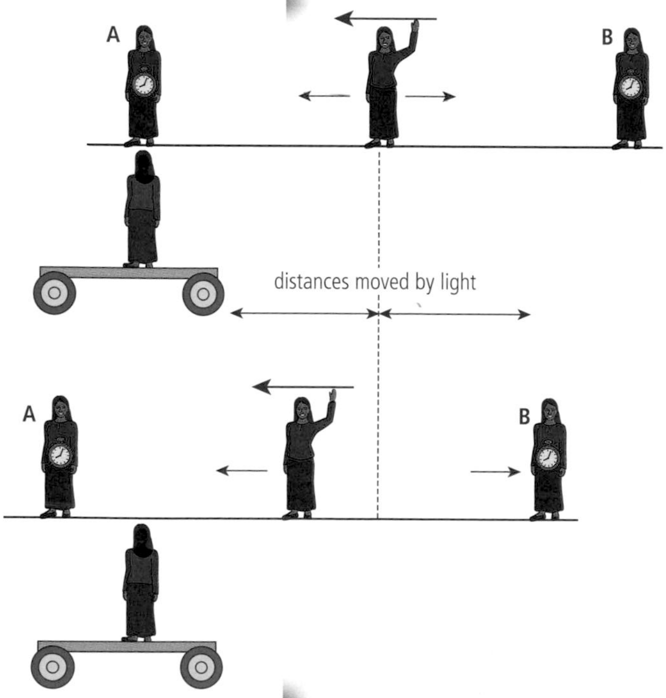

Figure 9.22 The red women move relative to the blue woman.

distances moved by light

The third friend will see the three of you moving past to the left as in Figure 9.22.

The observer on the trolley will see **A** moving away from the light beam and **B** moving towards it. This means that the light travelling to **A** has to travel further than light travelling to **B**. The light therefore arrives at **B** first, so **B** will start her clock before **A**. So according to the observer on the trolley the clocks are not synchronized.

Events at two different points in space that are simultaneous in one frame of reference are not simultaneous in all frames of reference.

Lorentz transformations

To relate the measurements in one frame of reference to another in Galilean relativity we use the Galilean transformations. These, however, do not give the correct answer when we try to transform the velocity of light. If we make the assumption that the equations can be corrected by multiplying by some constant γ then, given that the velocity of light must be the same in all inertial frames of reference, we get the following transformations between measurements taken in S and S':

$$x' = \gamma(x - vt)$$
$$y' = y$$
$$z' = z$$
$$t' = \gamma(t - \frac{vx}{c^2})$$

where

$$\gamma = \frac{1}{\sqrt{1 - \frac{v^2}{c^2}}} \quad \text{(the Lorentz factor)}$$

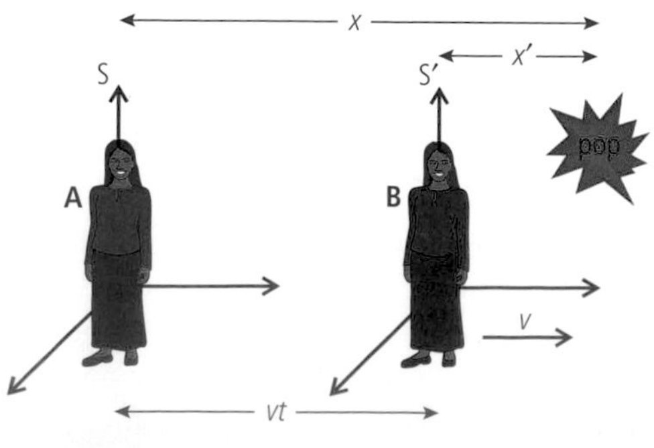

Figure 9.23 Inertial frames of reference S and S'.

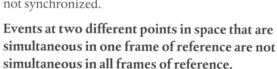

These can also be written in terms of the time interval, Δt, and the distance between two events, Δx.

$$\Delta x' = \gamma(\Delta x - v\Delta t)$$
$$\Delta t' = \gamma\left(\Delta t - \frac{v\Delta x}{c^2}\right)$$

Worked example

Two inertial frames S and S', coincident at time 0 s, move apart with relative velocity $0.9c$ as shown in Figure 9.23. An observer in S sees a balloon pop at $x = 5$ m at time 10^{-8} s. When and where did the balloon pop as measured by an observer in S'?

Solution

The relative speed of the two reference frames $= 0.9c$ so $y = \dfrac{1}{\sqrt{1 - \dfrac{v^2}{c^2}}} = \dfrac{1}{\sqrt{1 - \dfrac{0.9^2 c^2}{c^2}}} = 2.3$.

Using the Lorentz transform for x:

$$x' = \gamma(x - vt) = 2.3(5 - 0.9 \times 3 \times 10^8 \times 10^{-8}) = 5.29 \text{ m}$$

and for t:

$$t' = \gamma\left(t - \frac{vx}{c^2}\right) = 2.3\left(10^{-8} - \frac{0.9c \times 5}{c^2}\right) = -1.15 \times 10^{-8} \text{ s}.$$

This is before the clocks were started.

Exercise

2   An event takes place at a position of $x = 100$ m at a time 4×10^{-8} s as measured by an observer in frame of reference S. A second observer travelling at a speed of 2×10^8 m s^{-1} relative to the first along the line of the x-axis also measures the position and time for the event.

   (a) Calculate the Lorentz factor between the two reference frames.
   (b) Calculate the time and position measured in the second frame of reference.

Simultaneity

Using these transformations we can also show that events that are simultaneous in one frame are not simultaneous in another.

Worked example

Consider two trees observed in an inertial frame S at rest relative to the trees. One tree (an oak) is at the origin of the frame of reference. The other (a fir) is 5 km along the x-axis as shown in Figure 9.24. At a time of 4 µs both trees get hit simultaneously by lightning.

For a second observer flying past in a rocket at a speed of $0.9c$ the lightning strikes will not be simultaneous. Calculate the time between the two lightning strikes.

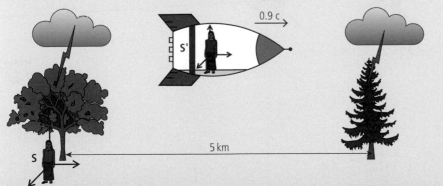

Figure 9.24 The frames of reference at the time of the lightning strikes.
At time t = 0 the two reference frames were coincident.

Solution

To calculate the time between the strikes we need to transform the time of each strike in S to S′. Taking the oak tree first:

$t' = \gamma(t - \frac{vx}{c^2})$ where $\gamma = 2.3$ as in the previous problem.

The oak tree got struck at $t_1 = 4$ μs at position $x = 0$ so $t_1' = 2.3(4 \times 10^{-6} - 0) = 9.2$ μs

The fir tree was struck at $t_2 = 4$ μs but at position $x = 5$ km

so
$$t_2' = 2.3(4 \times 10^{-6} - \frac{0.9c \times 5 \times 10^3}{c^2})$$

$$t_2' = -25.3\,\text{μs}.$$

To the observer in the rocket, the fir tree was hit 34.5 μs before the oak tree. Remember that to the observer in the rocket the trees are moving to the left, so the fir tree is moving towards the observer and the oak tree away. The light therefore travels a shorter distance from the fir tree to the red observer which is why the fir tree gets hit first.

Exercise

3 Repeat the Worked example above with the trees separated by 100 m and a speed of 0.8c.

Time dilation

To measure time between two events we can use the Lorentz transformations to transform the times of the start and finish. Let us consider two events occurring at the same place measured by an observer in frame S; for example, a light at rest relative to an observer in S flashes at time t_1 then again at time t_2 so the time between flashes measured in S is $\Delta t = t_2 - t_1$. This is the *proper time* since the two events occur at the same point in space so can be measured by the same clock. A second observer moving past at velocity v also measures the time between the flashes as t_1' and t_2' giving a time between flashes of $\Delta t' = t_2' - t_1'$. To the second observer the flashing light is moving so the two flashes do not occur at the same point in space so she will have to use different clocks to measure each flash.

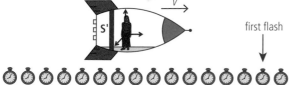

first flash   second flash

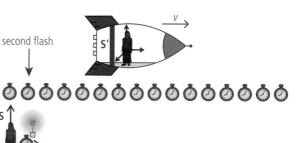

Figure 9.25 The light flashes twice as the rocket flies past. The line of clocks belong to S′ and are moving with the rocket; the clock used to measure each flash is as labelled.

Transforming these times we get:

$$t_1' = \gamma(t_1 - \frac{vx}{c^2})$$

$$t_2' = \gamma(t_2 - \frac{vx}{c^2})$$

$$t_2' - t_1' = \gamma(t_2 - \frac{vx}{c^2}) - \gamma(t_1 - \frac{vx}{c^2})$$

The position measured in S (x) is the same for each flash so:

$$t_2' - t_1' = \gamma(t_1 - t_2)$$

$$\Delta t' = \gamma \Delta t.$$

γ is always greater than 1 which means that the observer moving relative to the flashing light will measure a longer time between flashes. The time has *dilated*.

This can also be written as:

$$T = \gamma T_0$$

where T_0 = proper time (observer measures time with the same clock); T = time measured by observer who has to use two clocks to measure the time.

This can also be solved using the interval transformation
$$\Delta t' = \gamma \left(\Delta t - \frac{v \Delta x}{c^2}\right)$$
where the events in S are happening at the same place so $\Delta x = 0$.

Worked example

A woman in a rocket claps her hands once every second as she flies past an observer on the Earth at a speed of $0.8c$. What is the time between hand claps for the Earth observer?

Solution

In this example the proper time is the time measured by the woman in the rocket since she can use the same clock to measure each clap, so $T_0 = 1$ s.

The relative speed of the two frames of reference = $0.8c$ so $\gamma = \dfrac{1}{\sqrt{1 - \dfrac{v^2}{c^2}}} = \dfrac{1}{\sqrt{1 - \dfrac{0.8^2 c^2}{c^2}}} =$ 1.7.

$$T = \gamma T_0' = 1.7 \times 1 = 1.7 \text{ s}.$$

Exercises

4   Two spaceships A and B pass in space at relative velocity $0.7c$. An observer on A measures the time between swings of a pendulum he is holding to be 2 s. What will the time period be to an observer in B?

5   The half-life of the decay of some radioactive isotope is 30 s. The nucleus is accelerated to a speed of $0.99c$ relative to some observer. What will the half-life be to that observer?

6   A rocket travels between the Earth and some distant point at a constant speed of $0.8c$. The time between these events is measured by an observer on the Earth and an observer on the rocket. The rocket observer measures the time to be 2 years.

   (a) Which observer measures the proper time?
   (b) What time will the Earth observer measure?

Length contraction

The length of a body is the difference in position of its ends, so a metal rod at rest in some inertial frame S′ extending from x_1' to x_2' in the x-axis will have length $\Delta x' = x_2' - x_1'$. This is the *proper length* since the rod is not moving relative to the observer in S′. The rod and observer are moving at a velocity v relative to a second observer in frame of reference S, as shown in Figure 9.26. This observer measures the length of the rod as it passes. To do this the observer must use a method that enables her to measure each end at the same time, t. If she doesn't, the rod will move between measurements resulting in a false value. Observer A measures the length to be $x_2 - x_1$.

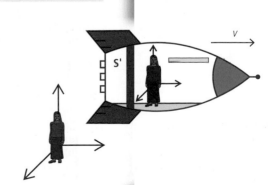

Figure 9.26 A rod at rest in inertial frame S′.

Transforming these positions we get:

$$x_1' = \gamma (x_1 - vt)$$
$$x_2' = \gamma (x_2 - vt)$$
$$x_2' - x_1' = \gamma (x_2 - vt) - \gamma (x_2 - vt)$$

but the observer in S measured both ends at the same time so:

$$x_2' - x_1' = \gamma (x_2 - x_1)$$
$$(x_2 - x_1) = \frac{1}{\gamma}(x_2' - x_1')$$

This means that the length measured by the observer moving relative to the rod is shorter than its proper length.

This can also be written:

$$L = \frac{L_0}{\gamma}$$

where:

L_0 = proper length

L = length as measured by an observer moving relative to the rod.

Worked example

A 1 m ruler is lying next to an observer on the Earth. How long will the ruler be if measured by a second observer travelling at a constant velocity of $0.9c$ along the line of the ruler?

Solution

In this case the proper length $L_0 = 1$ m.

The relative speed of the two reference frames = $0.9c$ so:

$$\gamma = \frac{1}{\sqrt{1 - \frac{v^2}{c^2}}} = \frac{1}{\sqrt{1 - \frac{0.9^2 c^2}{c^2}}} = 2.3.$$

According to the length contraction formula $L = \frac{L_0}{\gamma} = \frac{1}{2.3} = 0.43$ m.

Exercises

7 Two spaceships A and B pass in space at relative velocity $0.7c$. If an observer in B measures the length of a metal rod he is holding to be 2 m, what is the length of the rod as measured by an observer in A?

8 A nucleus decays 2×10^{-8} s (measured in the nucleus' frame of reference) after passing an observer standing on the Earth travelling at a speed of $0.99c$.

    (a) Calculate how far the nucleus travelled in the nucleus' frame of reference.
    (b) Calculate the time of flight as measured by the Earth observer.
    (c) Calculate the distance travelled measured by the Earth observer.
    (d) Which observer measured the proper time?
    (e) Which observer measured the proper distance?

9 A rocket travels to a distant point, fixed relative to the Earth, at a speed of $0.8c$. The distance to the point measured by an observer on the Earth is 5 light hours (one light hour is the distance travelled by light in 1 hour).

    (a) Calculate the time period of the flight measured by an observer on the Earth.
    (b) Calculate the distance travelled as measured by an observer on the rocket.
    (c) Calculate the time taken measured by the rocket observer.

Addition of velocity

So far we have dealt with the Lorentz transformations for position and time but there is also a transformation for velocity. So if a velocity u is measured in frame of reference S then the velocity measured in frame S′ travelling at velocity v relative to S will be given by the equation:

$$u' = \frac{u - v}{1 - \dfrac{uv}{c^2}}$$

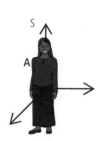 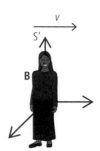 

Figure 9.27 Observer in S measures velocity of bird to be u.

Worked example

An observer in some frame of reference S measures the velocity of a particle moving along the x-axis to be $0.9c$. What would the velocity of the particle be if measured by an observer in S′ moving at $0.5c$ relative to S (along the x-axis)?

Solution

Here we can simply substitute the values into the Lorentz velocity transformation:

$$u' = \frac{u - v}{1 - \dfrac{uv}{c^2}}$$

where
$u = 0.9c$
$v = 0.5c$

$$u' = \frac{0.9c - 0.5c}{1 - \dfrac{0.9c \times 0.5c}{c^2}} = 0.7c$$

Worked example

Two rockets approach an astronaut at speeds of $0.8c$ from the left and $0.9c$ from the right. At what speed will the rockets approach one another from the frame of reference of one of the rockets?

Solution

This typical problem is slightly confusing because there are 3 possible frames of reference: 2 rockets and one floating astronaut. The velocities $0.8c$ and $0.9c$ are measured in the frame of reference of the astronaut. What you have to do is transform the velocity of one of the rockets into the frame of reference of the other. A diagram always helps (see Figure 9.28).

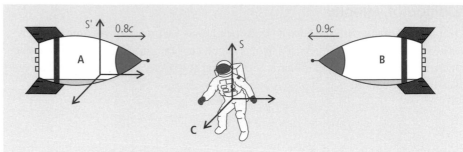

Figure 9.28 The frame of reference of rocket A (S') moves at 0.8c relative to S.

$$u' = \frac{u - v}{1 - \frac{uv}{c^2}}$$

If we substitute the values from the rocket example we get

$$u = -0.9c$$

$$v = 0.8c$$

$$u' = \frac{-0.9c - 0.8c}{1 - \frac{-0.9c \times 0.8c}{c^2}}$$

$$u' = \frac{-1.7c}{1.72}$$

$$u' = -0.988c$$

So, the rockets do not approach each other faster than the speed of light. If the velocities are small then $\frac{uv}{c^2}$ is approximately zero, so the equation will be the same as the Galilean transform, $u' = u - v$.

Measuring the speed of light

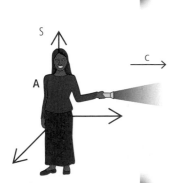

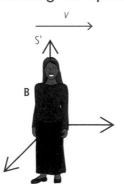

Figure 9.29 Two observers measure the speed of light.

An observer A in frame of reference S shines a light and measures the speed at which it propagates in the x-direction to be c. We can now use the Lorentz transform to find the velocity of light as measured by a second observer moving at speed v relative to A.

Using $\quad u' = \frac{u - v}{1 - \frac{uv}{c^2}}$ where $u = c$:

$$u' = \frac{c - v}{1 - \frac{cv}{c^2}}$$

$$u' = \frac{c - v}{1 - \frac{v}{c}}$$

$$u' = \frac{c(1 - \frac{v}{c})}{(1 - \frac{v}{c})} = c$$

so, as expected, the Lorentz transformations always return a value of c for the velocity of light, independent of the relative velocity of the observers.

10 Two subatomic particles are collided head on in a particle accelerator. Each particle has a velocity of 0.9c relative to the Earth. Calculate the velocity of one of the particles, as measured in the frame of reference of the other.

11 An observer on Earth sees a meteorite travelling at 0.5c on a head-on collision course with a spaceship travelling at 0.6c. What is the velocity of the meteorite as measured by the spaceship?

12 A relativistic fly flies at 0.7c in the same direction as a car travelling at 0.8c. According to the driver of the car, how quickly will the fly approach the car?

The muon experiment

Rockets travelling close to the speed of light seem a little far-fetched, so it is worth looking at some results from an actual experiment with particles that really do travel that fast. Muons are produced in the upper atmosphere as a result of the decay of pions produced by cosmic rays. They travel at 0.98c and have a half-life of 1.6 μs. They can be detected using two GM tubes, one on top of the other. They travel so fast that they appear to pass through both tubes at the same time.

Let us consider 100 muons at a height of 480 m. As they travel to the Earth they will decay, so less than 100 muons will be detected at ground level. Travelling at almost the speed of light, the muons will take 1.6 μs to travel to Earth. According to non-relativistic physics, in this time half should have decayed.

But according to special relativity the time in the muons' frame of reference is dilated so the half-life will be longer:

$$T = \gamma T_0$$

where $\gamma = 5$

T_0 = the proper time for the half-life measure in the inertial frame of the muon

T = the half-life measured from the Earth.

So the half-life measured from the Earth = 8 μs.

In travelling the 1.6 μs down to Earth, few of them will decay.

The actual number can be found using $N = N_0 e^{-\lambda t}$ which gives 87 remaining.

We can also look at this in the reference frame of the muons. They will be decaying with a half-life of 1.6 μs but the distance to the Earth will be contracted:

$$L = \frac{L_0}{\gamma}.$$

So the length measured by the muons = $\frac{480}{5}$ = 96 m.

Time taken travelling at 0.98c = 0.32 μs which is much less than one half-life.

The actual number can again be found from $N = N_0 e^{-\lambda t}$ which gives 87 remaining.

The actual results from muon experiments agree with those predicted by the Lorentz transformations.

It is obviously not possible to measure the same muons at 480 m and at ground level; what is actually measured is the *average* incidence of muons over a long period of time.

Worked example

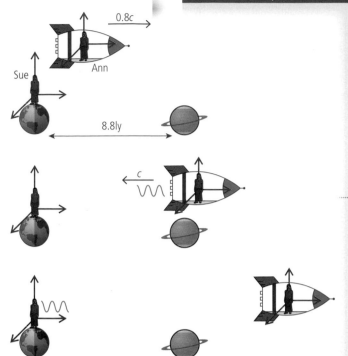

Figure 9.30.

A very common type of problem is the 'sending a signal home problem'.

Ann and Sue are twins. Sue remains on Earth. Ann travels to the star Sirius in a spaceship moving at a speed of $0.8c$ relative to Sue. The distance between Earth and Sirius is 8.8 ly, as measured by Sue. As Ann approaches Sirius, she sends a radio message back to Sue. Determine the time, as measured by Ann, that it takes for the signal to reach Sue.

Solution

The problem here is that neither Ann or Sue can measure the time for the signal to travel from the start to Earth with one clock, so what is the proper time? Sue can, however, measure the time between Ann leaving and the signal arriving with one earthbound clock so this will be the proper time.

T_0 = time for Ann to get to Sirius + time for signal to reach Earth

$T_0 = \frac{8.8}{0.8} + 8.8$ (note that $\frac{\text{distance in light years}}{\text{speed in } c} = $ time in years)

$T_0 = 19.8$ yrs.

This is the proper time measured by Sue, so the time measured by Ann will be

$\gamma T_0 = 1.67 \times 19.8 = 33$ yrs.

But this includes the time taken to get to Sirius. For Ann this was a contracted distance of $\frac{8.8}{1.67} = 5.27$ ly, so the time taken at a speed of $0.8c$ was $\frac{5.27}{0.8} = 6.6$ yrs

Time for signal to get to Earth = $33 - 6.6 = 26.4$ yrs.

Alternatively (and more easily) we can take the problem from the frame of reference of Ann.

Ann will see Sirius and Earth moving to the left at a speed of $0.8c$ so in the time taken for the signal to reach Sue the Earth has moved $0.8T$ light years further away. The total distance travelled by the Earth away from Ann is therefore $0.8T + 5.27$ which must equal the distance travelled by the signal, cT (T light years).

So $\qquad T = 0.8T + 5.27$

$\qquad (1 - 0.8)T = 5.27$

$\qquad\qquad T = 26.4$ yrs

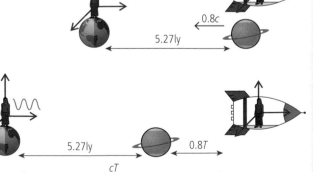

Figure 9.31.

Space–time interval

We have seen that the position and time of an event varies from one frame of reference to another, but the space–time interval doesn't; we say it is *invariant*. To understand what the space–time interval is and why it is invariant we will bring back the light clock used earlier in this chapter.

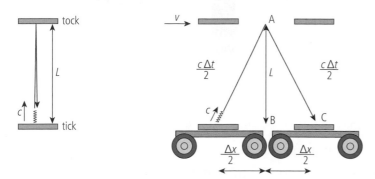

Figure 9.32.

The light clock in Figure 9.32 is moving relative to the stationary light clock so the light is following a longer path and thus will take a longer time. The interval between ticks is therefore not the same. However, the distance between the mirrors *is* the same. Applying Pythagoras to the triangle ABC:

$$L^2 = \left(\frac{c\Delta t}{2}\right)^2 - \left(\frac{\Delta x}{2}\right)^2$$

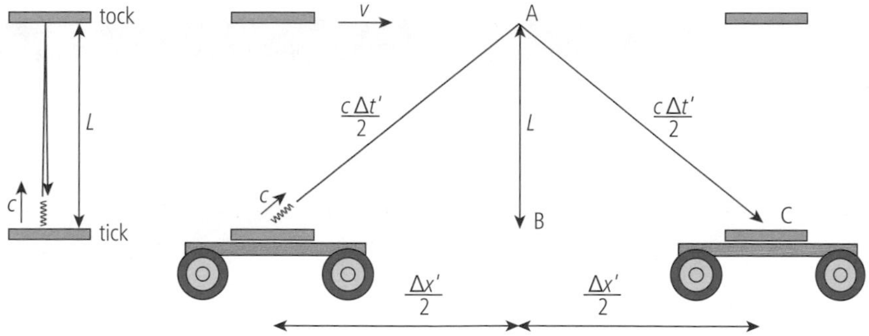

Figure 9.33.

The light clock in Figure 9.33 is travelling faster than the previous one so the distance travelled by the trolley and light is longer. Applying Pythagoras again gives:

$$L^2 = \left(\frac{c\Delta t'}{2}\right)^2 - \left(\frac{\Delta x'}{2}\right)^2$$

So

$$\left(\frac{c\Delta t}{2}\right)^2 - \left(\frac{\Delta x}{2}\right)^2 = \left(\frac{c\Delta t'}{2}\right)^2 - \left(\frac{\Delta x'}{2}\right)^2$$

$$(c\Delta t)^2 - (\Delta x)^2 = (c\Delta t')^2 - (\Delta x')^2$$

The quantity $(ct)^2 - x^2$ is invariant. This is called the *space–time interval*. Note that this is also the same for the stationary light clock where $\Delta x = 0$.

We can try this out for the example considered earlier in the chapter.

A negative space–time interval is said to be *space-like* since distance is the dominant quantity: a positive space–time interval is *time-like*.

Worked example

Two inertial frames, S and S′ coincident at time 0 s, move apart with relative velocity 0.9c as shown in Figure 9.34. An observer in S sees a balloon pop at x = 5 m at time 10^{-8} s. What is the space–time interval to the event for each observer?

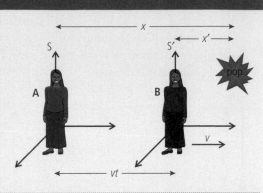

Figure 9.34.

Solution

The relative speed of the two reference frames = 0.9c so $\gamma = \dfrac{1}{\sqrt{1-\dfrac{v^2}{c^2}}} = \dfrac{1}{\sqrt{1-\dfrac{0.9^2c^2}{c^2}}} = 2.3$.

Using the Lorentz transformation for x:

$$x' = \gamma(x - vt) = 2.3(5 - 0.9 \times 3 \times 10^8 \times 10^{-8}) = 5.29\,\text{m}$$

and for t:

$$t' = \gamma\left(t - \frac{vx}{c^2}\right) = 2.3\left(10^{-8} - \frac{0.9c \times 5}{c^2}\right) = -1.15 \times 10^{-8}\,\text{s}.$$

So the space–time interval in S = $(ct)^2 - (x)^2 = (3 \times 10^8 \times 10^{-8})^2 - 5^2 = -16$

and in S′ the space–time interval = $(ct')^2 - (x')^2 = (3 \times 10^8 \times -1.15 \times 10^{-8})^2 - 5.29^2 = -16$.

To learn more about Lorentz transformations, go to the hotlinks site, search for the title or ISBN and click on chapter 9.

Exercise

13 Find the space–time interval for the two observers in Exercise 2.

9.3 Space–time diagrams

A.3 Spacetime diagrams

Understandings, applications, and skills:

Spacetime diagram
- Representing events on a spacetime diagram as points.
- Representing more than one inertial reference frame on the same spacetime diagram.
- Solving problems on simultaneity and kinematics using spacetime diagrams.
- Representing time dilation and length contraction on spacetime diagrams.

> *Guidance*
> - *Examination questions will refer to spacetime diagrams; these are also known as Minkowski diagrams.*
> - *Quantitative questions involving spacetime diagrams will be limited to constant velocity.*
> - *Spacetime diagrams can have t or ct on the vertical axis.*
> - *Examination questions may use units in which c = 1.*

Worldlines
- Representing the positions of a moving particle on a spacetime diagram by a curve (the worldline).
- Determining the angle between a worldline for specific speed and the time axis on spacetime diagram.

The twin paradox
- Describing the twin paradox.
- Resolving of the twin paradox through spacetime diagrams.

The way that space and time are connected is rather difficult to comprehend. However, things can be made easier by using space–time diagrams which give a visual representation of one dimension of space and time. To help understand what a space–time diagram represents we can start with a simple displacement time graph as in Figure 9.35. This graph is drawn the usual way with t on the x-axis and displacement on the y (slightly confusing since the y-axis represents x displacement). The gradient of the line will equal the velocity.

NATURE OF SCIENCE

A theory is not very useful if no one can understand it. Space–time diagrams provide a visual representation making difficult concepts easier to understand (hopefully).

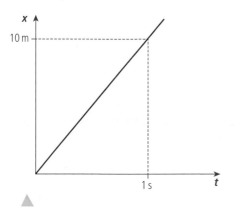

▲ **Figure 9.35** Displacement–time for a body moving at $10\,\mathrm{m\,s^{-1}}$.

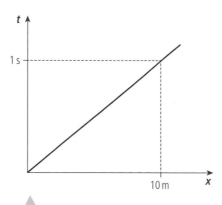

▲ **Figure 9.36** Swap the axes.

The same motion could also be represented with time t on the y-axis and displacement x on the x-axis (makes sense) as in Figure 9.36. The velocity is now $\frac{1}{\text{gradient}}$.

In this example the time is measured in seconds but we could change the scale by multiplying the time by some constant value (e.g $10\,\mathrm{m\,s^{-1}}$) to give the graph in Figure 9.37. Multiplying the time by some constant velocity turns the time into distance; $10\,\mathrm{m}$ is equivalent to $1\,\mathrm{s}$ of the body's movement.

The gradient of this graph is 1 (no units) because the body travels $10\,\mathrm{m}$ in $10\,\mathrm{m}$ worth of time. If we use the same axes to draw the graph for a body travelling at $5\,\mathrm{m\,s^{-1}}$ we get Figure 9.38. Here the body is travelling only $5\,\mathrm{m}$ in $10\,\mathrm{m}$ worth of time ($1\,\mathrm{s}$). The gradient of this line = 2 which is $\frac{10\,\mathrm{m}}{5\,\mathrm{m}}$, so we can calculate the velocity from $(\frac{1}{\text{gradient}}) \times 10\,\mathrm{m\,s^{-1}}$.

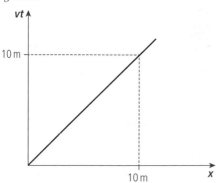

▲ **Figure 9.37** Change the scale.

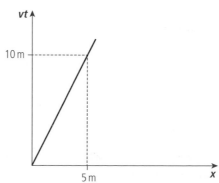

▲ **Figure 9.38.**

Space–time diagrams used in relativity are drawn in the same way except that the constant speed that is used is the speed of light, c. If we draw the position of a photon on these axes then the line will have gradient = 1 as shown in Figure 9.39.

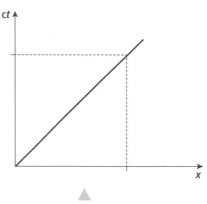

Figure 9.39.   **Figure 9.40.**

A body travelling with velocity $0.5c$ will therefore have a line that is steeper as in Figure 9.40. A line representing the position of a body at different times is called a *worldline*. The gradient of this line is 2, so we can easily calculate the velocity in multiples of c from $\frac{1}{\text{gradient}} = \frac{v}{c} = \beta$.

In a time t_1 the body will have travelled distance $= vt_1$ and the value of $ct = ct_1$ so the angle of the line is given by the equation $\tan\theta = \frac{vt_1}{ct_1} = \frac{v}{c}$

Frames of reference in space–time diagrams

Every point on a space–time diagram represents an event, e.g. the position of a moving body at different times. The axes of the graph represent the coordinate system used for the time and place of an event. A moving body is represented by a line as in Figure 9.40; if that body was an observer then the observer's frame of reference would be tilted along the same line as in Figure 9.41.

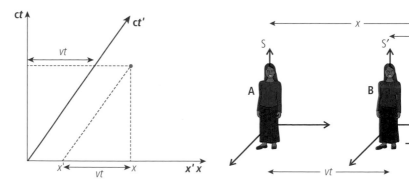

Figure 9.41 ct' represents the position axis for an observer in S'.

The yellow dot represents an event observed by both observers. To record the time of the event, a line is drawn from the event parallel to the x-axis until it coincides with the time axes ct and ct' (the black dotted line). This is the same for both observers. The position measured in S is found by taking a line parallel to the ct-axis to where it crosses the x-axis (the blue dashed line). This is the normal way you would read the position from a graph. The position measured in S' is found in a similar way but taking the line parallel to the ct'-axis (the red dashed line). This results in two different positions: x and x'. We can see from the geometry of the lines that $x' = x - vt$. This is the Galilean transformation.

We can also use the same method to transform the velocity of a moving object. The green line in Figure 9.42 represents an object moving with velocity v starting from the origin in the same direction as S'. The velocity u measured in S is $\frac{x}{t}$ and in S is $u' = \frac{x'}{t}$. Since $x' = x - vt$ we can deduce that $u' = u - v$.

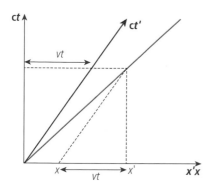

Figure 9.42.

Figure 9.43 By tilting the x'-axis we can make the gradient of the green line 1 for both sets of coordinates.

If we use the graph in Figure 9.42 to measure the speed of light we run into a problem as shown in Figure 9.43(a). The gradient of the line is different for each set of axes, meaning that light will have a different velocity for each observer. This can't be the case but it can be corrected by tilting the x-axis to match the y-axis as in Figure 9.43(b). We can now use the space–time diagrams to illustrate the consequences of relativity.

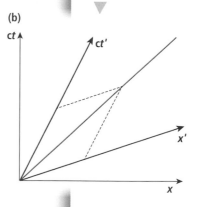

Simultaneity

Using a space–time diagram we can show that simultaneous events in one frame are not simultaneous in all frames. Consider two events occurring at time 0 in a frame of reference S. These are represented by the two lightning strikes in Figure 9.44(a). They are on either side of the origin so one occurs on the left, the other on the right. A second frame of reference travelling in a positive direction with respect to S is shown in Figure 9.44(b). If we plot the time and position of these events in S' we can clearly see that the right hand event occurred before the left hand one. This is in agreement with the previous explanation in terms of the distance travelled by light being shorter for the one where the observer is moving towards the event.

Note that if each flash occurred on the x'-axis, the observer in S' would see the two flashes simultaneously but the observer in S would not.

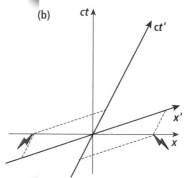

Figure 9.44 Simultaneous events in S.

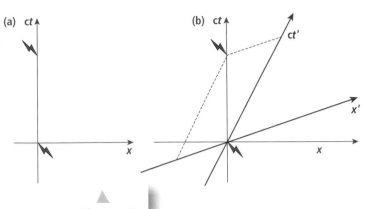

Figure 9.45.

Time dilation

Consider two events occurring at $x = 0$ in the S frame; these can be represented by the two lightning flashes on the space–time diagram Figure 9.45(a). If these flashes are observed in S', then plotting on the space–time diagram Figure 9.45(b) we can clearly see that the time between flashes is longer, time has dilated. Notice in this diagram that the position of the second flash is negative. This is because it took place to the left of the observer.

Length contraction

Consider a rod measured in S that is moving at the same velocity as the S' reference frame. The ends of the rod will have the worldlines shown by the parallel black lines in Figure 9.46(a). To measure the length of the rod, an observer will need to devise a method to simultaneously measure each end at the same time. Simultaneous events in S occur along the x-axis so the length will be L as shown.

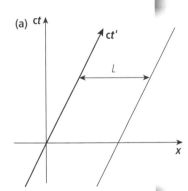

Figure 9.46.

If we now observe the rod in the reference frame S' then the rod would be stationary. Simultaneous events in S' occur along the x'-axis so the measure of length in S' would give L' as in Figure 9.46(b). This is longer than L so we can deduce that the lengths of objects contract when measured by observers moving relative to the rod (in this case the observer in S). Notice that the measurements simultaneous in one frame of reference are not simultaneous in the other.

The twin paradox

The twin paradox refers to the apparent paradox created when two twins (A and B) decide to spend some time apart when one of them (B) goes on a long and very fast journey at $0.661c$ out into space and back. Each twin will see the other's clock ticking slowly so each will think they will be the older one when the traveller (B) returns. However, they cannot both be older than each other – hence the paradox. What actually would happen is that the travelling twin would be the younger. Let's first consider twin B on the journey out as illustrated on Figure 9.47. B's frame of reference is ct' so since B is at rest in the frame she moves along the $x' = 0$ line.

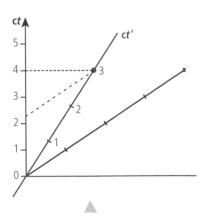

Figure 9.47 The first part of the twin's journey.

After 3 years twin B decides to turn around and go home. This will be 4 years in A's frame of reference. If it was possible for B to synchronize her clock with a clock in her frame of reference on Earth she would find that the time was a bit more than 2 years after she left: remember that all of the clocks in S′ along a line parallel to x′ will tick simultaneously. So at this point in the journey each will see the other as younger.

On the return journey, since B is travelling in the opposite direction, the space–time diagram for the return journey is tilted the other way as in Figure 9.48.

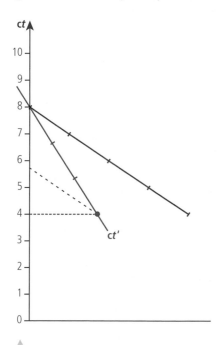

Figure 9.48 The second part of the journey.

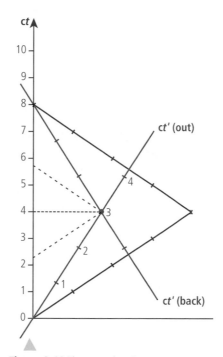

Figure 9.49 The complete journey

Once turned around the frame of reference of B has changed so if she again synchronizes her clock with a clock in the frame of reference of Earth, she will find that she has skipped about 4 years. The complete journey is shown in Figure 9.49.

From this diagram we can see that for B the journey has taken 6 years but for A it was 8 years. Of course, B can't simply turn round and come home – she must slow down then accelerate back up to cruising speed. This solves the sudden jump in years but doesn't alter the fact that B will be younger than A when she arrives home.

Faster than the speed of light

We can use a space diagram to show that it isn't possible to travel faster than the speed of light. Consider a space ship leaving planet A and travelling to planet B faster than the speed of light, as illustrated on the space–time diagram of Figure 9.50. By tracing back the axis we can see that according to an observer in S, the rocket left at time t_A and arrived some time later at t_B. However, in S′ the rocket left at time $t_A′$ and arrived some time earlier at $t_B′$ and this is not possible.

Figure 9.50 Arriving before you leave.

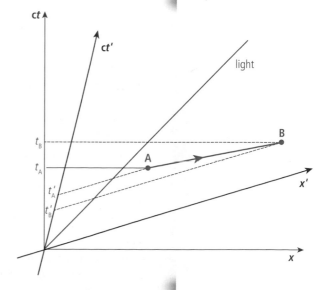

Exercises

Figure 9.51 is a space–time diagram for two frames of reference travelling at $0.5c$ relative to each other. Use it to estimate the answers to the following exercises.

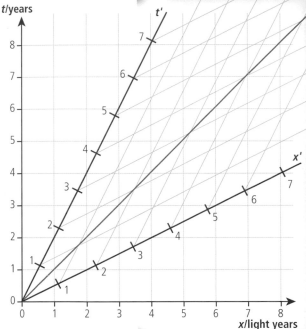

t/years

x/light years

▲
Figure 9.51.

14 Estimate the position and time in S′ of an event that takes place at a position 4 light years from the origin at a time of 6.5 years from the time when the clocks were started in S. Check your solution using the Lorentz transforms and find the space–time interval for the event in each frame.

15 Estimate the position and time in S of an event measured in S′ that takes place at a position 5 light years from the origin at a time of 1 year from the time when the clocks were started. Check your solution using the Lorentz transforms and find the space–time interval for the event in each frame.

16 Two events, stationary with respect to S, occur at a distance 4 light years from the origin at times 3 years and 6.5 years. Estimate the time between the events as measured by an observer in S′. Check your solution with the time dilation formula.

17 A very long rod at rest in the S′ frame is measured at time 0 to extend from 2 ly to 5 ly. An observer in S manages to simultaneously measure the position of each end of the rod. Estimate the length it will measure. Check your solution with the length contraction formula.

18 A rocket travels from Earth at a speed of $0.5c$. After travelling for 4 years (measured by the rocket so take the rocket as S) a radio signal is sent back to the Earth. How long after the rocket left the Earth will the Earth receive the signal (as measured on Earth)? By following the method in the earlier example, check your solution by calculation.

19 Assuming the origin represents the year 2000, a rocket leaves Earth in 2003 and travels at $4c$ for 2 years. When will the rocket depart and arrive as measured by an observer travelling at $0.5c$ relative to the Earth? What if the rocket travelled at twice the speed of light? Why can't you check this with a calculation?

To learn more about space-time diagrams, go to the hotlinks site, search for the title or ISBN and click on chapter 9.

9.4 Relativistic mechanics

A.4 Relativistic mechanics (HL only)

Understandings, applications, and skills:

(AHL) Total energy and rest energy
- Describing the laws of conservation of energy within special relativity.
- Solving problems involving relativistic energy conservation in collisions and particle decays.

  Guidance
  - *Applications will involve relativistic decays such as calculating the wavelengths of photons in the decay of a moving pion [$\pi° \rightarrow 2\gamma$].*
  - *The symbol m_0 refers to the invariant rest mass of a particle.*
  - *The concept of a relativistic mass that varies with speed will not be used.*
  - *Problems will be limited to one-dimension.*

(AHL) Relativistic momentum
- Describing the laws of conservation of momentum within special relativity.
- Solving problems involving relativistic momentum conservation in collisions and particle decays.

(AHL) Particle acceleration
- Determining the potential difference necessary to accelerate a particle to a given speed or energy.

(AHL) Photons

(AHL) MeV c^{-2} as the unit of mass and MeV c^{-1} as the unit of momentum

Relativistic momentum

According to Newton's second law of motion, the rate of change of momentum of a body is directly proportional to the unbalanced force that causes it. This means that if a constant force is applied to a body for long enough then it will continue to accelerate beyond the speed of light and this we have seen is not possible. This means that momentum must also be transformed from one frame of reference to another giving the relativistic momentum equation:

$$p = \gamma m_0 v$$

where m_0 = rest mass of the body.

So as the velocity gets bigger the momentum increases, tending towards the velocity of light. At the velocity of light the momentum would be infinite which is not achievable. The graph of Figure 9.52 shows how the classical differs from the relativistic momentum.

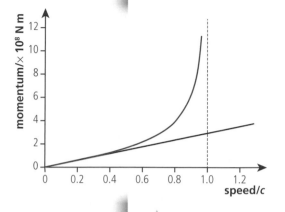

▲

Figure 9.52 Momentum calculated for different velocities using the classical (red) and relativistic (blue) formulae.

Relativistic energy

If a force acts in the direction of movement of a body then work is done on transferring energy to the body. Classically a constant force will result in an ever-increasing kinetic energy, but this would imply an eventual velocity greater than the speed of light, which isn't possible. The relativistic equation for kinetic energy is:

$$KE = (\gamma - 1)m_0 c^2$$
$$= \gamma m_0 c^2 - m_0 c^2.$$

Now, $\gamma m_0 c^2$ increases as the velocity increases but $m_0 c^2$ stays constant. This is the rest energy of the body, which is how much energy would be released if the mass was converted completely to energy. This means that $\gamma m_0 c^2$ is the total energy:

$$\text{total energy} = \text{rest energy} + \text{kinetic energy}$$

where total energy $E = \gamma m_0 c^2$ and rest energy $E_0 = m_0 c^2$.

Low velocity approximation

It is interesting to see what result the relativistic equation gives if the velocity of a body is much less than c.

$$KE = (\gamma m_0 - m_0)c^2 = \frac{m_0 c^2}{\sqrt{1 - \frac{v^2}{c^2}}} - m_0 c^2$$

Using the binomial expansion when x is small $(1 + x)^n = 1 + nx$ we can

expand the term $\qquad \left(1 - \frac{v^2}{c^2}\right)^{-\frac{1}{2}} = 1 + \frac{v^2}{2c^2}$

So $\qquad\qquad KE = \left(1 - \frac{v^2}{2c^2}\right)m_0 c^2 - m_0 c^2 = \frac{1}{2}m_0 v^2$

This is what we expected.

Energy–momentum formula

The total energy of a body with mass m travelling at speed v is given by the formula:

$$E = \gamma m_0 c^2.$$

Expanding γ gives:

$$E = \frac{m_0 c^2}{\sqrt{1 - \frac{v^2}{c^2}}}$$

Squaring gives:

$$E^2 = \frac{m_0^2 c^4}{\left(1 - \frac{v^2}{c^2}\right)} = m_0^2 c^4 \left[\frac{1}{\left(1 - \frac{v^2}{c^2}\right)} - 1\right] + m_0^2 c^4$$

$$E^2 = m_0^2 c^4 \left[\frac{\frac{v^2}{c^2}}{1 - \frac{v^2}{c^2}}\right] + m_0^2 c^4$$

$$E^2 = \frac{m_0^2 v^2 c^2}{1 - \frac{v^2}{c^2}} + m_0^2 c^4$$

but

$$p = \gamma m_0 v = \frac{m_0 v}{\sqrt{1 - \frac{v^2}{c^2}}}$$

so

$$p^2 c^2 = \frac{m_0^2 v^2 c^2}{1 - \frac{v^2}{c^2}}$$

Substituting in the equation for E^2 gives

$$E^2 = p^2 c^2 + m_0^2 c^4$$

Energy of a photon

The rest mass of a photon is zero so according to the energy–momentum equation the energy of a photon is $E = pc$. Rearranging this gives $p = \frac{E}{c}$ which agrees with the momentum of the photon calculated by Maxwell.

Simplifying the units (MeV)

Energy

In mechanics we usually use the units joule for energy, newton second for momentum, and kilogram for mass. Trains and rockets only travel at relativistic velocities (relative to Earth observers) in physics exam questions; in reality the only bodies that we can accelerate to relativistic velocities are sub-atomic particles such as electrons and protons. A particle with charge $+q$ can be accelerated in an electric field as in Figure 9.53. If the potential difference between the plates is V then the energy gained is Vq.

The energy of the particle in joules can be calculated by multiplying the potential difference in volts by the charge in coulombs, but since charge is always a multiple of the fundamental charge e it is much easier to express the energy in eV. So if an electron is accelerated through a pd of 100 V the KE = 100 eV, no calculator necessary.

Mass

When dealing with nuclei it is more convenient to use unified mass units (u) rather than kg as the unit of mass. If 1 u is converted to energy according to the equation $E = mc^2$ an amount of energy 931.5 MeV is released, so the rest energy of particle of mass 1 u is 931.5 MeV.

If 931.5 MeV $= mc^2$ then $m = 931.5 \frac{\text{MeV}}{c^2}$; we can either convert this mass to u or kg but it is much more convenient to leave it in MeV c^{-2} so we can see the equivalent energy without calculation.

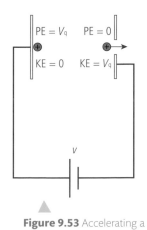

Figure 9.53 Accelerating a proton.

Momentum

When using the equation $E^2 = p^2c^2 + m_0^2c^4$ it would be convenient if all quantities were in compatible units, so with E in MeV and m_0 in MeV c^{-2} what should the units of p be? We know that $p = mv$ so we could express p in $(\text{MeV}\,c^{-2})c = \text{MeV}\,c^{-1}$.

So, if we check out the equation:

$$E^2 = p^2c^2 + m_0^2c^4$$

$$(\text{MeV})^2 = (\text{MeV}\,c^{-1})^2c^2 + (\text{MeV}\,c^{-2})c^4$$

$$(\text{MeV})^2 = (\text{MeV})^2 + (\text{MeV})^2.$$

Summary of units

The unit of energy is the MeV.
The unit of momentum is the MeV c^{-1}.
The unit of mass is the MeV c^{-2}.

The rest mass of an electron is 0.5 MeV c^{-2} and a proton 938 MeV c^{-2}.

Worked example

Calculate the momentum of an electron accelerated to a total energy of 2 MeV.

Solution

Rest mass of electron = 0.5 MeV c^{-2} so $E^2 = p^2c^2 + m_0^2c^4$

giving
$$(2\,\text{MeV})^2 = p^2c^2 + (0.5\,\text{MeV}\,c^{-2})^2c^4$$

$$p^2c^2 = 4 - 0.25 = 3.75\,\text{MeV}$$

$$p = 1.9\,\text{MeVc}^{-1}$$

Worked example

Calculate the speed of an electron that is accelerated through a pd of 1 MV.

Solution

Loss of electrical PE = gain in KE of electron

so
$$\text{KE} = 1\,\text{MeV}$$

Now
$$\text{KE} = (\gamma - 1)m_0c^2$$

where m_0c^2 is the rest energy of an electron = 0.5 MeV

So
$$1.0 = (\gamma - 1) \times 0.5$$

Rearranging gives
$$\gamma = 3.0$$

But
$$\gamma = \frac{1}{\sqrt{1 - \frac{v^2}{c^2}}} = 3.0$$

$$v = 0.94c$$

Worked example

Calculate the pd required to accelerate an electron to a velocity of 0.8c.

Solution

If $v = 0.8c$ then $\gamma = 1.67$

If the electron is travelling at 0.8c it will have a KE = $(\gamma - 1)m_0c^2$

where
$$m_0c^2 = \text{rest energy}$$
$$= 0.5\,\text{MeV}$$

$$\text{KE} = (1.67 - 1) \times 0.5 = 0.34\,\text{MeV}$$

So the pd must have been 0.34 MV.

Worked example

What is the speed of an electron with a momentum of $2\,\text{MeV}c^{-1}$

Solution

First we can find the total energy from

$$E^2 = m_0^2c^4 + p^2c^2$$

$$E^2 = 0.5^2 + 2^2$$

So

$$E = 2.06\,\text{MeV}$$

$$\text{Total } E = \gamma m_0 c^2$$

so

$$2.06 = \gamma \times 0.5$$

$$\gamma = 4.12$$

$$v = 0.97c$$

Exercises

20 Find the momentum of a particle of rest mass $100\,\text{MeV}c^{-2}$ travelling at $0.8c$.

21 A particle of rest mass $200\,\text{MeV}$ is accelerated to a KE of $1\,\text{GeV}$. Calculate its:

    (a) momentum.
    (b) velocity.

22 A particle of rest mass $150\,\text{MeV}$ is accelerated to a speed of $0.8\,c$. Calculate its:

    (a) KE.
    (b) total energy.
    (c) momentum.

23 A proton has a momentum of $150\,\text{MeV}c^{-1}$. Calculate its:

    (a) total energy.
    (b) KE.
    (c) accelerating potential.
    (d) velocity.

Neutral pion decay

When a pion decays into 2 gamma photons a particle with mass is converted into two particles with no mass. Let us consider the situation where a neutral pion (rest mass $135\,\text{MeV}\,c^{-2}$) travelling at $0.9c$ decays into two photons.

The total energy of the pion $= \gamma m_0 c^2$ where $\gamma = \dfrac{1}{\sqrt{1 - 0.9^2}} = 2.3$.

$$E = 2.3 \times 135 = 310\,\text{MeV}.$$

The two photons will therefore share this energy so if they share it equally they will have $155\,\text{MeV}$ each.

The frequency of each photon can be calculated from $E = hf$ but first we need to convert the energy into joules:

$$E = 155 \times 10^6 \times 1.6 \times 10^{-19} = 2.5 \times 10^{-11}\,\text{J}$$

$$f = \frac{E}{h} = \frac{2.5 \times 10^{-11}}{6.6 \times 10^{-34}} = 3.8 \times 10^{22}\,\text{Hz}.$$

The photons have momentum as well as energy; each photon will have momentum $= \dfrac{E}{c} = 155\,\text{MeV}\,c^{-1}$.

If both photons moved in the same direction as the original pion then the total momentum would be $310\,\text{MeV}\,c^{-1}$.

Let us now calculate the original momentum of the pion to see if momentum is conserved when the photons travel in the same direction.

For the pion:

$$E^2 = p^2c^2 + m_0{}^2c^4$$

where $E = 310\,\text{MeV}$ and $m_0 = 135\,\text{MeV}\,c^{-2}$

so

$$p = \sqrt{310^2 - 135^2} = 280\,\text{MeV}\,c^{-1}.$$

This is less than the momentum of the two photons so the photons cannot travel in the same direction. Instead they must travel at an angle to each other as in Figure 9.54.

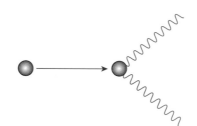

The photons could also travel in opposite directions so that their total momentum is $280\,\text{MeV}c^{-1}$ (one has momentum $380\,\text{MeV}c^{-1}$ and the other has momentum $-100\,\text{MeV}c^{-1}$).

Figure 9.54 γ photons travel at an angle to conserve momentum.

Pair production

If a gamma photon has enough energy it can decay into an electron and a positron. To enable energy and momentum to be conserved this process must take place next to a heavy nucleus which receives momentum as it recoils.

The rest masses of an electron and a positron are both $0.5\,\text{MeV}\,c^{-2}$ so the minimum energy required to form an electron–positron pair would be 1 MeV.

If a 1 MeV photon with momentum $= 1\,\text{MeV}\,c^{-1}$ then decays into an electron–positron pair the positron and electron would have only rest energy, no KE. This implies that they have no momentum so the momentum could not be conserved unless there was another particle involved, the recoiling nucleus.

Worked example

A gamma photon of energy 2.5 MeV converts into an electron–positron pair close to the nucleus of a gold atom which recoils with momentum $0.9\,\text{MeV}\,c^{-1}$ as shown in Figure 9.55. Calculate the magnitude of the momentum of the electron.

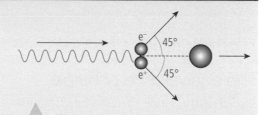

Figure 9.55.

Solution

The momentum of the photon $= \dfrac{E}{c} = 2.5\,\text{MeV}\,c^{-1}$.

Taking components of the momentum:

Vertical momentum before $= 0$ so vertical momentum of e^- is equal and opposite to e^+

Horizontal momentum $= 2.5\,\text{MeV}\,c^{-1} = p_{e+} + p_{e-} + 0.9$

$$p_{e+} + p_{e-} = 1.6\,\text{MeV}\,c^{-1}$$

The horizontal components of momentum of the positron and the electron are equal so $p_{e-} = 0.8\,\text{MeV}\,c^{-1}$.

The horizontal component is $p\cos\theta$ so the momentum of the electron

$$= \frac{0.8}{\cos 45°} = 1.1\,\text{MeV}\,c^{-1}$$

Exercises

24 An electron and a positron each with kinetic energy 1 MeV collide with each other and annihilate to form two identical photons (this is the opposite of pair production). Calculate the energy of the photons.

25 A 2.0 MeV photon converts to a positron–electron pair in as in Figure 9.55. If the electron and positron each have momentum 1.0 MeV c^{-1}, calculate the momentum of the recoiling nucleus.

26 When a photon scatters off an electron it experiences a change in momentum which leads to a change in its wavelength. This is called the *Compton effect*. If a 0.003 nm photon scatters at 60° from an electron its wavelength changes to 0.0042 nm. Calculate how much energy was given to the electron.

9.5 General relativity

A.5 General relativity (HL only)

Understandings, applications, and skills:

(AHL) The equivalence principle

> *Guidance*
> * Students should recognize the equivalence principle in terms of accelerating reference frames and freely falling frames.

(AHL) The bending of light
* Using the equivalence principle to deduce and explain light bending near massive objects.

(AHL) Gravitational redshift and the Pound–Rebka–Snider experiment
* Using the equivalence principle to deduce and explain gravitational time dilation.
* Calculating gravitational frequency shifts.
* Describing an experiment in which gravitational redshift is observed and measured.

(AHL) Schwarzschild black holes
* Calculating the Schwarzschild radius of a black hole.

(AHL) Event horizons

(AHL) Time dilation near a black hole
* Applying the formula for gravitational time dilation near the event horizon of a black hole.

(AHL) Applications of general relativity to the Universe as a whole

Figure 9.56 Two different but indistinguishable non-inertial frames of reference.

The equivalence principle

Special relativity only relates to inertial frames of reference. General relativity extends this to non-inertial frames; that is, a frame of reference within which an object will accelerate without being pushed. We have come across two examples of this, one was an accelerating rocket and the other is on the surface of the Earth. In both cases, a ball will accelerate downwards if released. The important thing to realize is that it is impossible to distinguish between these two examples; this is the starting point to general relativity.

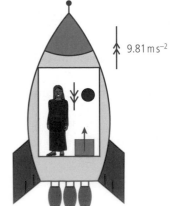

9.81 m s^{-2}

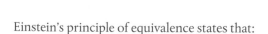

Einstein's principle of equivalence states that:

No observer can determine by experiment whether they are in an accelerating frame of reference or a gravitational field.

This may seem a bit odd, since it is very easy to tell whether you are going round a bend in a car, or falling off a cliff; so to make the point clearer we shall consider two observers in identical boxes, as in Figure 9.56. One box is sitting on the Earth, the other is accelerating with acceleration 9.81 m s^{-2} far out in space. All experiments must be done in the box and it's not allowed to look out of the window.

Whatever the two observers do they will get the same result:

The dropped red ball will fall with an acceleration g.

The blue box will sit on the floor experiencing a force, N, pushing it up. From the outside we can see they are quite different; for example the blue box on the Earth has another force acting on it, its weight, and these forces are balanced. The box in the rocket has only one force, which is unbalanced, so this box is accelerating. However, from inside the box you can't tell any difference.

Free fall

We have seen how the gravitational field g pulling our experimenter down is equivalent to an upwards acceleration of g, but if we take our earthbound experimenter's closed box to the top of a high building and drop her off the top, then as she falls to the Earth, the box and all objects inside would be falling with the same acceleration so would seem to be weightless (Figure 9.57). There would be no force between the ground and the box and the red ball would stay where it is unless pushed. In fact, it would be impossible to do any experiment that would enable the experimenter to determine whether they were in a freefalling box or floating in space. So freefalling frames of reference are equivalent to inertial frames. Of course a freefalling observer will soon know the difference, but luckily it is a soft landing.

Physicist Stephen Hawking experiencing what it is like to be weightless by taking a flight in a freefalling plane.

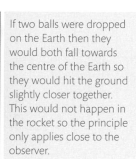

If two balls were dropped on the Earth then they would both fall towards the centre of the Earth so they would hit the ground slightly closer together. This would not happen in the rocket so the principle only applies close to the observer.

Figure 9.57.

Gravitational mass and inertial mass

In both of the frames of reference in Figure 9.56, it is possible to measure the mass of one of the objects. On the Earth the force of gravity can be used to find mass by measuring the object's weight and calculate the mass from $F = mg$. This is *gravitational mass*.

In the spaceship, the force that must be applied to make an object accelerate with the spaceship can be measured, and the mass calculated using the formula $F = ma$. This is *inertial mass*.

These two quantities are the same.

Bending of light by gravity

The principle of equivalence has some far-reaching consequences when we consider what happens to light in an accelerating frame of reference, and realize that the same thing must happen in a gravitational field. If the woman in the rocket shone a beam of light across a box accelerating at only 9.8 m s^{-2} nothing much would happen; the beam would simply go straight across the room. However, if we increased the acceleration to astronomic levels we would get a different result. So that we can see what happens at different times we will consider three glass boxes starting together and accelerating at the same rate as shown in Figure 9.58. A beam of light is shone through all three boxes as they accelerate up.

Figure 9.58 Three glass boxes photographed as the light leaves each box, The entry points would all be higher since the box has moved in the time for the light to travel across it.

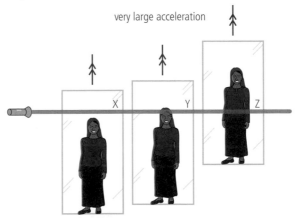

very large acceleration

As we can see from the diagram the boxes move up as the light passes through and because the boxes are accelerating, the last box has moved up more than the middle one. X, Y, and Z are the positions where the light leaves each box. According to the principle of equivalence, the same thing should happen in a gravitational field. This time we would need to take the boxes to a very large field close to a very large mass but small radius $\left(g = \frac{GM}{r^2}\right)$.

Figure 9.59 For the light to exit each box at the same place in a G field the light must have followed a curved path.

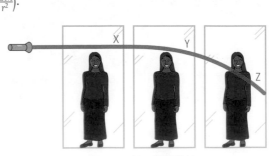

Very large field

For the same thing to happen the light must exit each box at the same point as shown in Figure 9.59.

This shows that light is bent by the large mass but this doesn't fit into our accepted theory of gravity. Gravitational force is proportional to mass and since light has no mass, how can it be attracted to the Earth in this way? However, there could be another explanation as shown in Figure 9.60.

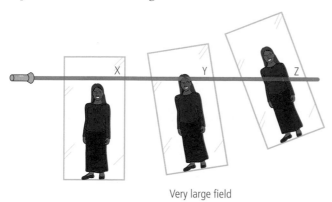

Very large field

Figure 9.60 Instead of the light bending, maybe it's the space and time that it moves through which is bent.

The solution illustrated in Figure 9.60 may seem a bit far-fetched and it isn't really correct, but it does give an idea of how Einstein's theory of general relativity tackles the problem by abandoning the idea of our coordinate system having straight lines, and considering what would happen if space–time was curved.

Large masses curve space–time.

We can also test this principle by comparing freefalling observers with observers in an inertial frame of reference. Again, light is shone across the glass boxes but this time leaves each box at the same height (Figure 9.61). For this to happen in the freefalling boxes the light must have been bent as shown in Figure 9.62.

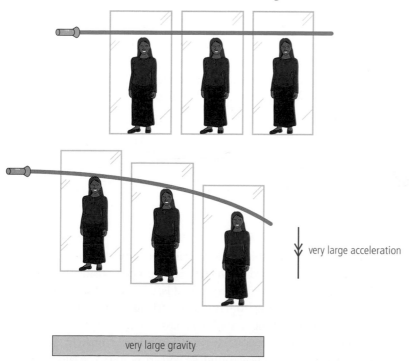

very large acceleration

very large gravity

Figure 9.61 In an inertial frame of reference the light leaves at the same height.

Figure 9.62 In a freefalling frame of reference the light leaves at the same height because it bends.

403

Bending of light by the Sun

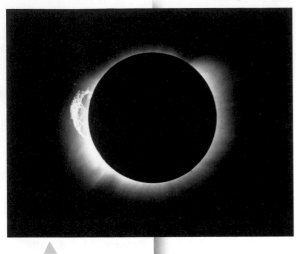

One of Arthur Eddington's original photographs from the solar eclipse in 1919.

If light is bent by objects with large mass then light should be bent as it passes the Sun. This is rather difficult to test because the Sun gives out so much light itself that you can't see light coming from behind, except during an eclipse. During a total eclipse it is possible to see stars that you normally only see at night. However, some of those stars will be behind the Sun so won't be visible. During the eclipse of 1919 Arthur Eddington found that the positions of some stars that should have been close to the Sun were shifted outwards. This could be explained if the Sun bends the light from the stars as in Figure 9.63.

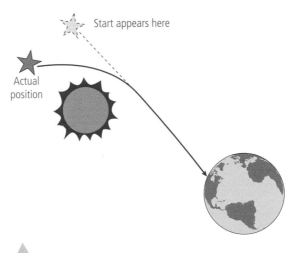

Figure 9.63 The light from a distant star is bent around the Sun. When viewed from the Earth, it appears to be to the right of its actual position.

Gravitational lensing

An Einstein ring seen with the Hubble space telescope. This is caused by gravitational lensing due to a large galaxy.

If the Sun can bend light, then whole galaxies certainly will. When two galaxies are in line with an observer, the light from the far one will bend around the near one as in Figure 9.64. When observed through a powerful telescope, the light from the distant galaxy can be seen as a ring around the close one. This is called an Einstein ring, as shown in the photo.

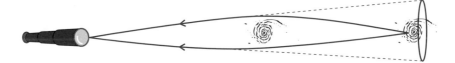

Figure 9.64 The formation of an Einstein ring by a large galaxy.

The slowing of time by large masses

If light has a constant velocity then it should always take the same time between two points. However, if a large mass is placed between the two points causing the light to follow a curved path, then it should take longer; that is, unless time slows down. To illustrate this point, consider driving from home to a friend's house in a car that travels always at 50 km h^{-1} along a straight road. You have arranged to meet at 12:30 so knowing the journey takes 30 minutes you leave at 12:00. Unfortunately there is a diversion and you have to drive a long way round, so you are going to be late ... unless, that is, you slow down your watch. Now, although you have driven further, the time taken will be the same. This doesn't work when visiting friends unless the diversion happens to be around a black hole.

Clocks near large masses tick slowly.

Gravitational red shift

Returning to the woman in a box, imagine that she has a light source on the ceiling of the box which shines light towards the floor with frequency f. We know that when the box is stationary or moving with constant velocity the light will arrive at the floor with the same frequency. However, if the box accelerates as shown in Figure 9.65(a) then the distance travelled by the light will be less which will have the effect of compressing the waves reducing their wavelength and increasing their frequency. Similarly, a light shining from the floor to the ceiling (Figure 9.65(b)) will have a longer wavelength. This effect is similar to the Doppler effect we discussed in section 5.4 on sound waves. If this happens in the accelerating box then, according to the principle of equivalence, it must also happen in the gravity box.

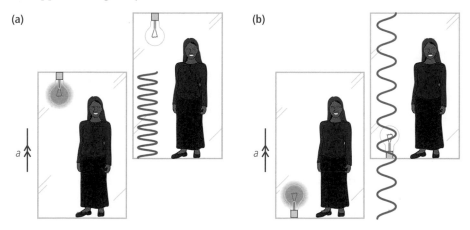

(a)

(b)

Figure 9.65 (a) Light travelling down gets squashed and (b) light travelling up gets stretched.

So if EM radiation is sent from the bottom of a high building to the top then it should have a longer wavelength when it gets to the top than it had at the bottom. But the energy of a photon = hf so if the frequency gets less it must have less energy. What is happening is the photon is losing energy as it rises to the top of the building.

The equation for the change in frequency is:

$$\frac{\Delta f}{f} = \frac{g\Delta h}{c^2}$$

where:
Δf = the change in frequency
f = original frequency
Δh = height.

In 1960 Pound, Rebka, and Snider performed an experiment at Harvard University sending gamma photons up and down a 22.6 m high tower. They found that the difference in frequency was in agreement with the predictions from general relativity.

Exercises

27 The photons used in the Pound–Rebka–Snider experiment had 14.4 keV energy, and the building was 22.6 m high. Calculate the change in frequency between the top and the bottom.

28 Two observers stand at either end of a long rocket as shown in Figure 9.66; the rocket is travelling with constant velocity. Observer **A** at the back sends an electromagnetic signal to observer **B** at the front.

(a) How does the signal received compare to the signal transmitted?

(b) The rocket engines are now turned on. Describe and explain any change in frequency of the transmitted and received signals.

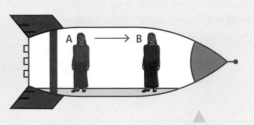

Figure 9.66.

Curvature in space–time

Newton's universal law of gravity says that all points of mass attract each other with a force that is proportional to the product of their mass and inversely proportional to their separation squared. According to this, there would be no force on something with zero mass so the path of a photon of light should not be altered by a large mass. Einstein developed an alternative approach based on the curvature of space–time.

Attraction between two masses

It is very difficult to make a visual representation of four-dimensional space–time but we can get some understanding by thinking about a two-dimensional Universe represented by a flat surface. Imagine there is a large metal ball resting on a frictionless table. Although it is not moving relative to us, it is moving through space–time so we can represent it by a ball rolling along a flat surface. If no unbalanced forces act on the ball it will continue to move along the surface in a straight line. Now a second ball is placed a few cm from the first one; it too will be moving through space. According to Newton's universal law of gravitation, there will be a force acting between the balls that will cause them to move towards each other, so as they move through space they will follow a curved path as shown in Figure 9.67.

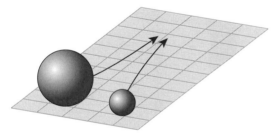

Figure 9.67 Masses in flat space.

However, there could be a different explanation for their converging paths. What if the flat surface wasn't flat at all but was part of a huge sphere as in Figure 9.68. The balls are both moving in a straight line with no force between them but because they are moving on a sphere their paths converge. Remember that we don't notice the movement through space; we just see the balls attracting each other.

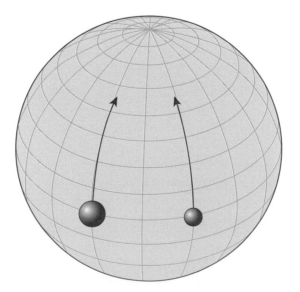

Figure 9.68 Masses in curved space.

The rate at which the two steel balls come together is related to their mass so it appears that it is their mass that curves the space as in Figure 9.69. So in curved space–time the balls will come together, even though there is *no* force acting between them.

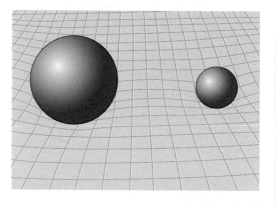

Figure 9.69 Masses curve space.

Orbits

In the 2D model a large object curves space–time like a heavy man does when he sits on a bed. A large spherical mass put in the middle of the bed would form a bowl shape around it as in Figure 9.70. A ball pushed past the bowl with constant velocity would travel in a curved path around the mass. If it had just the right velocity it could go round and round the bowl like a golf ball does just before it goes down the hole; the ball is then in orbit around the large mass. Remember, no forces are needed if the ball is travelling in curved space.

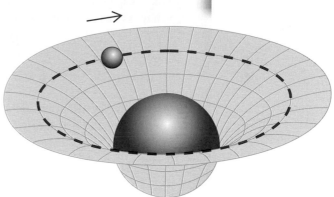

Figure 9.70 A small ball travels in a straight line in the curved space around a large mass.

Space–time diagrams

In special relativity we use space–time diagrams to represent the way events are viewed by different observers. If we represent an accelerating body on a space–time diagram we get a curve as shown in Figure 9.71(a). An observer moving at this acceleration would have a time-axis along this curve. In fact their whole coordinate system would be curved as in Figure 9.71(b).

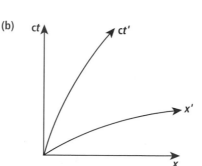

Figure 9.71 Curved space–time.

According to the principle of equivalence this frame of reference should be the same for an observer in a gravitational field, so mass must curve space–time.

Black holes

Before Einstein proposed his theory of relativity Laplace, using Newtonian mechanics, had calculated that light would not be able to escape from a very large mass with a small radius. To understand this we can imagine trying to throw a ball out of a deep hole. To get it out of the hole we need to give it enough upward speed so that its maximum height is at least the top of the hole. In terms of energy, the kinetic energy of the ball at the bottom of the hole must be at least as big as its potential energy at the top. In the case of a large mass the KE must be enough to allow the body to reach an infinite distance.

As the projectile rises loss of KE = gain in PE
(initial KE − final KE) = (final PE − initial PE).

Initial PE on the surface of the mass $= -\frac{GM}{R}$ and the final PE at infinity $= 0$

so
$$\tfrac{1}{2}mv^2 - 0 = 0 - (-\frac{GM}{R})$$

which gives:
$$v = \sqrt{\frac{2GM}{R}}$$

So the escape velocity depends on both the mass and the radius of the body. For a given mass there is a radius R_s for which the escape velocity is the speed of light:

$$c = \sqrt{\frac{2GM}{R_S}}$$

$$R_S = \frac{2GM}{c^2}$$

This is known as the Swarzschild radius, named after Karl Swarzschild who derived the same equation but from general relativity. The Earth will never be a black hole because the molecules of matter making up the Earth are held apart by intermolecular forces. The Sun also can't be a black hole as the radiation pressure from the hot core stops it collapsing. However, when a big star runs out of fuel it starts to collapse. Once its radius has reached the Swarzschild radius, no light can escape; it has become a black hole. As the star continues to collapse to smaller than the R_s the escape velocity at its surface would keep on rising but the escape velocity at a distance Rs from the centre would continue to be c. So nothing closer to the centre of the black hole than Rs could escape. From the outside it is therefore not possible to see anything closer to the centre than the Swarzschild radius. This line is therefore called the *event horizon*.

If mass curves space–time then a black hole will cause extreme curvature. This can be represented by a space–time diagram using light cones as in Figure 9.72. A light cone is a 3D space–time diagram representing the possible path of light coming from a point in space. Since nothing can travel faster than the speed of light this represents everything that can happen as a result of an event at that point; the downward pointing cone represents all past events that could affect the point. The central part of the diagram represents the edge of a star that is collapsing past the Swarzschild radius into a singularity. Light cones a long distance from the Swarszchild radius are vertical. This means that an event here can have an effect on the surrounding space. As we approach the event horizon space–time is curved causing the light cones to tip over towards the black hole. On the event horizon the light cones have tipped so far that the whole future points towards the singularity; no events taking place here can affect the surrounding space. Once beyond the event horizon anything in the future of the point will happen at the singularity, at the singularity the curvature of space–time is infinite.

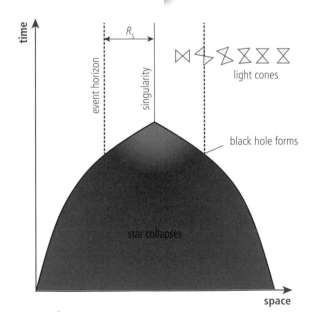

Figure 9.72 A space–time diagram showing how a black hole affects the light cones on either side of the event horizon.

Time dilation near a black hole

We have seen how curvature of space–time implies that time dilates; close to a black hole this effect is extreme. The difference between a time interval measured by a distant clock (Δt) and the same interval measured by a clock close to the event horizon (Δt_0) is given by the formula:

$$\Delta t = \frac{\Delta t_0}{\sqrt{1 - \frac{R_s}{r}}}$$

where R_s is the Schwarzschild radius and r is the distance from the singularity. We can see from this formula that as r approaches R_s the time interval measured by the distant clock tends to infinity. At the event horizon, time stands still. An observer watching something approaching a black hole would see it slowing down and stopping as it got to the event horizon where it would stay forever. For an observer travelling to the black hole (feet first) the journey would be somewhat different, extreme curvature of space–time would accelerate them rapidly towards the event horizon. For them, time would be progressing as normal. However, they are unlikely to be alive. Their feet, being closer to the black hole would accelerate faster than their head causing them to be stretched into a long line.

Exercises

29 A star of mass 2×10^{31} kg collapses to a point forming a black hole. What is the Schwarzschild radius of the black hole?

30 A spaceship with a light flashing once every minute travels towards the black hole in Exercise 29. An observer on the Earth (thankfully a long way from the black hole) watches the spaceship. Calculate time between flashes of the light when the spaceship is:

(a) 10^6 km from centre of the black hole.

(b) 100 km from the centre.

(c) 60 km from the centre.

General relativity and the Universe

If mass curves space then the mass of the Universe must curve the space of the Universe. Einstein didn't just say that space was curved, he was able to construct a mathematical model of the Universe. Using this model Alexander Friedmann derived an equation for the rate of expansion of an expanding Universe ($\frac{dR}{dt}$):

$$\left(\frac{1}{R}\frac{dR}{dt}\right)^2 = \frac{8\pi G}{3}\rho - \frac{kc^2}{R^2}$$

Basically it contains two terms: one related to the density (ρ) and the other to the curvature (k). By varying the value of k the Universe can have three possible curvatures. We can't really draw the curvature of 3-dimensional space (and time) but we can represent the idea of curvature with a 2-dimensional surface.

Figure 9.73 shows that if $k = 0$ the space is flat. This is the situation that we are most familiar with, where the 3 angles of a triangle add up to 180° and bodies travelling parallel to each other never meet.

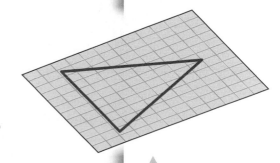

Figure 9.73 $k = 0$ flat.

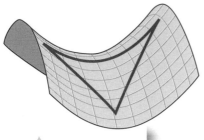

Figure 9.74 $k < 0$ negative curvature.

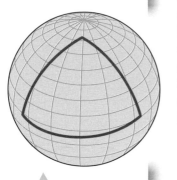

Figure 9.75 $k > 0$ positive curvature.

In Figure 9.74, with negative curvature the angles of a triangle add up to less than 180° and bodies travelling parallel move away from each other.

Figure 9.75 shows that if the curvature is positive the angles of a triangle add up to more than 180° and parallel bodies will move towards each other.

Curvature and the future of the Universe

We can't draw it but curvature applies to time as well as space, so the three different curvatures have implications for the past and future of the Universe. A positive curvature implies a *closed Universe*. Using the spherical model of Figure 9.75 you can see that if you set out walking in one direction and keep going you'll end up back at the same place. This also implies that the Universe will not have an infinite life time. After expanding for some time it will start to contract. A negative curvature (Figure 9.74) implies that the expansion will continue for ever: we call this an *open Universe*. Flat (Figure 9.73) also implies continual expansion but the expansion is continually slowing down finally stopping at infinite time. These different situations are called *Friedmann Universes* and can be represented by lines on the graph of Figure 9.76.

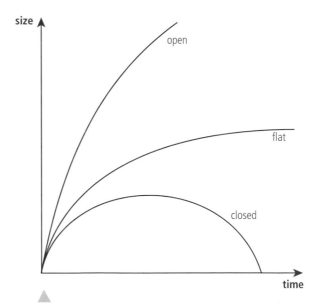

Figure 9.76 Friedmann Universes.

Astronomical observations made when these theories were being developed indicated that the Universe was static, which did not agree with the expanding models predicted by Friedmann. To fix this problem Einstein added the cosmological constant which represented a sort of negative energy. Advances in technology revealed new data which showed the Universe was in fact expanding. This made Einstein's fix unnecessary. However, more recently the constant has been reintroduced to explain why the expansion is accelerating. It seems that Einstein was even right when he was wrong!

1. This question is based upon a thought experiment first proposed by Einstein.

    (a) Define the terms *proper time* and *proper length*. (2)

    In Figure 9.77 Miguel is in a railway carriage that is travelling in a straight line with uniform speed relative to Carmen who is standing on the platform.

    Miguel is midway between two people sitting at opposite ends A and B of the carriage.

    Figure 9.77.

    At the moment that Miguel and Carmen are directly opposite each other, the person at end A of the carriage strikes a match as does the person at end B of the carriage.

    According to Miguel these two events take place simultaneously.

    (b) (i) Discuss whether the two events will appear to be simultaneous to Carmen. (4)

    (ii) Miguel measures the distance between A and B to be 20.0 m. However, Carmen measures this distance to be 10.0 m. Determine the speed of the carriage relative to Carmen. (2)

    (iii) Explain which of the *two* observers, if either, measures the correct distance between A and B? (2)

    (*Total 10 marks***)**

2. This question is about electrons travelling at relativistic speeds.

    A beam of electrons is accelerated in a vacuum through a potential difference V. Figure 9.78 shows how the speed v of the electrons, as determined by non-relativistic mechanics, varies with the potential V, (relative to the laboratory). The speed of light c is shown for reference.

    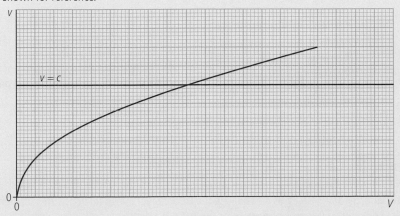

    Figure 9.78.

    (a) Copy Figure 9.78 then use the axes to draw a graph to show how the speed of the electrons varies over the same range of V as determined by relativistic mechanics. *(Note this is a sketch-graph; you do not need to add any values)* (2)

(b) Explain briefly, the general shape of the graph that you have drawn. (3)

(c) When electrons are accelerated through a potential difference of 1.50×10^6 V, they attain a speed of $0.97c$ relative to the laboratory.

Determine, for an accelerated electron,

(i) its mass. (3)

(ii) its total energy. (2)

(*Total 10 marks*)

3. This question is about time dilation.

(a) State what is meant by an ***inertial*** frame of reference. (1)

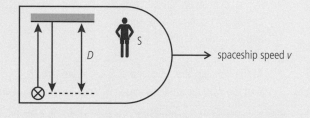

An observer S in a spacecraft sees a flash of light. The light is reflected from a mirror, distance D from the flash, and returns to the source of the flash as illustrated below. The speed of light is c.

Figure 9.79.

(b) Write down an expression, in terms of D and c, for the time T_0 for the flash of light to return to its original position, as measured by the observer S who is at rest relative to the spaceship. (1)

The spaceship is moving at speed **v** relative to the observer labelled E in Figure 9.79. The speed of light is c.

(c) (i) Copy Figure 9.79 and on your diagram draw the path of the light as seen by observer E. Label the position F from where the light starts and the position R where the light returns to the source of the flash. (1)

(ii) The time taken for the light to travel from F to R, as measured by observer E, is T. Write down an expression, in terms of the speed v of the spacecraft and T, for the distance FR. (1)

(iii) Using your answer in (ii), determine, in terms of v, T, and D, the length L of the path of light as seen by observer E. (2)

(iv) Hence derive an expression for T in terms of T_0, v, and c. (4)

(*Total 10 marks*)

4. This question is about relativistic motion.

The radioactive decay of a nucleus of actinium-228 involves the release of a β-particle that has a **total energy** of 2.51 MeV as measured in the laboratory frame of reference. This total energy is significantly larger than the **rest mass energy** of a β-particle.

(a) Explain the difference between **total energy** and **rest mass energy**. (2)

(b) Deduce that the Lorentz factor, as measured in the laboratory reference frame, for the β-particle in this decay is 4.91. (3)

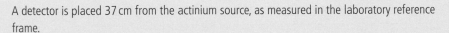

A detector is placed 37 cm from the actinium source, as measured in the laboratory reference frame.

(c) Calculate, for the laboratory reference frame,

    (i) the speed of the β-particle.   (2)

    (ii) the time taken for the β-particle to reach the detector.   (2)

    The events described in (c) can be described in the β-particle's frame of reference.

(d) For this frame,

    (i) identify the moving object.   (1)

    (ii) state the speed of the moving object.   (1)

    (iii) calculate the distance travelled by the moving object.   (2)

                                                (*Total 13 marks*)

5. This question is about the postulates of special relativity.

(a) State the **two** postulates of the special theory of relativity.   (2)

(b) Two identical spacecraft are moving in opposite directions each with a speed of $0.80c$ as measured by an observer at rest relative to the ground. The observer on the ground measures the **separation** of the spacecraft as increasing at a rate of $1.60c$.

 $0.80c$ $0.80c$

ground

Figure 9.80.

    (i) Explain how this observation is consistent with the theory of special relativity.   (1)

    (ii) Calculate the speed of one spacecraft relative to an observer in the other.   (3)

                                                (*Total 6 marks*)

6. This question is about frames of reference.

(a) Explain what is meant by a *reference frame*.   (2)

    In the diagram below, Jasper regards his reference frame to be at rest and Morgan's reference frame to be moving away from him with constant speed v in the x-direction.

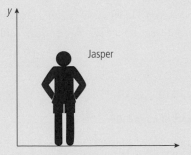
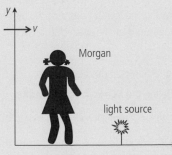

Figure 9.81.

Morgan carries out an experiment to measure the speed of light from a source which is at rest in her reference frame. The value of the speed that she obtains is *c*.

(b) Applying a Galilean transformation to the situation, state the value that Jasper would be expected to obtain for the speed of light from the source. (1)

(c) State the value that Jasper would be expected to obtain for the speed of light from the source based on Maxwell's theory of electromagnetic radiation. (1)

(d) Deduce, using the relativistic equation for the addition of velocities, that Jasper will in fact obtain a value for the velocity of light from the source consistent with that predicted by the Maxwell theory. (3)

In Morgan's experiment to measure the speed of light she uses a spark as the light source. According to her, the spark lasts for a time interval of 1.5 ms. In this particular situation, the time duration of the spark as measured by Morgan is known in the special theory of relativity as the proper time.

(e) (i) Explain what is meant by **proper time**. (1)

(ii) According to Jasper, the spark lasts for a time interval of 3.0 μs. Calculate the relative velocity between Jasper and Morgan. (3)

(*Total 11 marks*)

7. This question is about relativistic kinematics.

A spacecraft leaves Earth at a speed of 0.80*c* as measured by an observer on Earth. It heads towards, and continues beyond, a distant planet. The planet is 52 light years away from Earth as measured by an observer on Earth.

0.80*c*
Earth
52 ly

planet

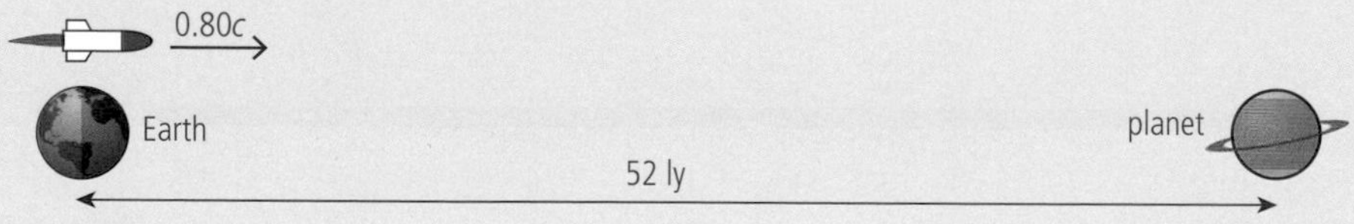

Figure 9.82.

When the spacecraft leaves Earth Amanda, one of the astronauts in the spacecraft, is 20 years old.

The Lorentz gamma factor for a speed of 0.80*c* is $\gamma = \frac{5}{3}$.

(a) Calculate

(i) the time taken for the journey to the planet as measured by an observer on Earth. (1)

(ii) the distance between the Earth and the planet, as measured by Amanda. (1)

(iii) Amanda's age as the spacecraft goes past the planet, according to Amanda. (2)

(b) As the spacecraft goes past the planet Amanda sends a radio signal to Earth. Calculate, as measured by the spacecraft observers, the time it takes for the signal to arrive at Earth. (3)

(*Total 7 marks*)

8. This question is about black holes.

(a) Define the **Schwarzschild radius**. (1)

(b) Calculate the Schwarzschild radius for an object of mass 2.0×10^{31} kg. (2)

(c) A starship is stationary just outside the event horizon of a black hole. A space station is also stationary and is located far away from the black hole and any other massive object.

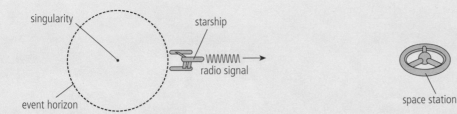

Figure 9.83.

(i) The starship transmits a radio signal to the space station. Explain why the signal received at the space station is shifted to a lower frequency than the transmitted frequency. (2)

(ii) The starship remains stationary just outside the event horizon for one hour as measured by an observer in the starship. The time elapsed, as measured by an observer in the space station, is ten hours. Determine, in terms of the Schwarzschild radius R_s of the black hole, the distance of the starship from the event horizon of the black hole. (3)

(*Total 8 marks*)

9. This question is about relativistic energy and momentum.

(a) Particle A is at rest with respect to an observer. Another identical particle B is moving with respect to the observer. Distinguish between the total energy of particle A and the total energy of particle B as measured by the observer. (2)

(b) Two protons are travelling towards each other along the same straight line in a vacuum.

Figure 9.84.

The speed of each proton, as measured in the laboratory frame of reference, is $0.960c$.

(i) Calculate the relative speed of one proton with respect to the other proton. (2)

(ii) Show that the total energy of one of the protons, according to an observer at rest in the laboratory, is 3.35 GeV. (2)

(c) The collision of the two protons results in the following reaction

$$p^+ + p^+ = p^+ + n^0 + \pi^+$$

where π^+ is a particle called a pion that has a rest mass of 140 MeV c^{-2}. The total energy of the pion is 502 MeV. Determine, according to an observer at rest in the laboratory, the

(i) total energy of the proton formed plus the total energy of the neutron formed by the collision. (2)

(ii) momentum of the pion. (2)

(d) Figure 9.85 shows the paths followed by the neutron and pion in (c).

The dotted line shows the path of the original collision of the protons in (b). Copy Figure 9.85 and on your diagram draw the direction of the proton formed in the collision. (1)

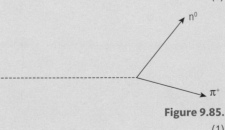

Figure 9.85.

(*Total 11 marks*)

10

Option B:
Engineering physics

Essential ideas

B.1 Rigid bodies and rotational dynamics
The basic laws of mechanics have an extension when equivalent principles are applied to rotation. Actual objects have dimensions and they require the expansion of the point particle model to consider the possibility of different points on an object to have different states of motion and/or different velocities.

B.2 Thermodynamics
The first law of thermodynamics relates together energy supplied through heat transfer and through work done. The entropy of the Universe tends to a maximum.

B.3 Fluids and their dynamics (HL only)
Fluids cannot be modelled as point particles. Their distinguishable response to compression from solids creates a set of characteristics which require an in-depth study.

B.4 Forced vibrations and resonance (HL only)
In the real world, damping occurs in oscillators and has implications that need to be considered.

NATURE OF SCIENCE

Treating bodies as if they are points is OK up to a point, but is not enough to deal with real-life examples. However, a rigid body is made up of many points so we can use what we know about point bodies. These models can then be applied to practical problems such as the design of buildings and bridges.

When water boils there are a lot of changes taking place: liquid to gas, increase in entropy, motion of a fluid, expansion of gas, exchange of energy and finally water into tea.

The Millau Viaduct in France took three years to build and is higher than the Eiffel Tower.

10.1 Rigid bodies and rotational dynamics

B.1 Rigid bodies and rotational dynamics

Understandings, applications, and skills:

Torque
- Calculating torque for single forces and couples.
- Solving problems involving moment of inertia, torque, and angular acceleration.

Moment of inertia
- Calculating the moment of inertia from mass and its distribution.
- Solving problems involving rolling without slipping.

Guidance
- *Analysis will be limited to basic geometric shapes.*
- *The equation for the moment of inertia of a specific shape will be provided when necessary.*
- *Students will only be expected to formulate moment of inertia equations using a non-calculus method.*

Rotational and translational equilibrium
- Solving problems in which objects are in both rotational and translational equilibrium.

Angular acceleration

Equations of rotational motion for uniform angular acceleration
- Solving problems using rotational quantities analogous to linear quantities.
- Sketching and interpreting graphs of rotational motion.

Guidance
- *Graphs will be limited to angular displacement–time, angular velocity–time, and torque–time.*

Newton's second law applied to angular motion

Conservation of angular momentum

Rotational motion

At the beginning of this course we dealt with the motion of a small particle (a red ball), defining quantities related to its motion, deriving relationships relating those quantities, introducing the concepts of force, momentum, and energy to investigate the interaction between bodies. These models were then used to solve problems related to larger bodies, cars, people, etc. by treating them like particles. This works fine provided all the forces act at the centre of mass, but what if they don't? Consider the two equal and opposite forces acting on the bar in Figure 10.1 (notice the bar is floating in space so no gravity is acting on it).

Figure 10.1 Forces on a bar

If the bar in Figure 10.1 was made of rubber then the problem would be even more complicated as it would also bend. Here we will only consider *rigid* bodies. These are bodies that are made of atoms that do not move relative to one another; in other words, bodies with a fixed shape.

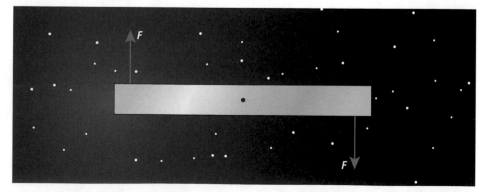

Let's apply Newton's first law to the body. The forces are balanced so the body will be at rest or moving with a constant velocity. However, if we observe what happens we find that although the centre of mass of the body remains stationary the body rotates; we need to extend our model to include this type of motion.

Torque (Γ)

(a) accelerating

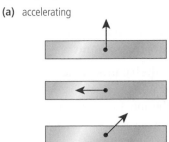

(b) accelerating and rotating

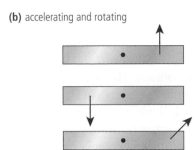

Figure 10.2 Forces don't always cause rotation.

If an unbalanced force acts on the centre of mass of a rigid body then it will have linear acceleration but it won't rotate. All the bodies in Figure 10.2(a) would have the same magnitude of acceleration. However, if the unbalanced force does not act on the centre of mass as in the examples in Figure 10.2(b), the bodies will rotate as well as accelerate. We can define the centre of mass as *the point on a body through which an unbalanced force can act without causing rotation.*

Describing forces acting on bodies floating in space is rather difficult to imagine since it is not something we deal with every day. To make things more meaningful let us consider something more down to Earth: a seesaw.

A balanced seesaw only moves when you push with your legs.

A seesaw is a rigid bar with two moveable masses. It only works in a region where the masses are under the influence of gravity e.g. on the Earth. The forces involved are as shown in Figure 10.3.

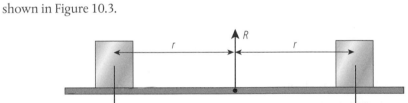

Figure 10.3 Balanced seesaw.

Here we can see that the forces up = the forces down so there will be no acceleration. There is also no rotation so the turning effect of the two children must be balanced. The normal reaction that holds the bar up does not turn the bar since it acts at the centre of mass. If, however, one child was to get off, then the bar would turn.

> The seesaw is held in position by an axle fixed to the centre of the bar. This point is called the *pivot*. The axle prevents the bar from accelerating by exerting a force that is equal and opposite to the weight of the children (assuming the bar has negligible weight), but allows it to rotate.

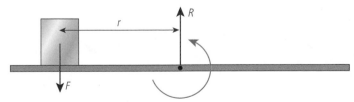

Figure 10.4 Seesaw with one child.

The bar would also turn if one child moved towards the centre or was replaced by a child with less weight.

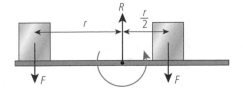
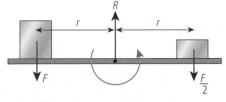

Figure 10.5 Unbalanced seesaws.

419

Balancing the forces
when two people lift a
heavy object up a flight of
stairs, one would expect
that each person would
exert a force equal to
half the weight. But if
that is the case, why is it
easiest to be at the top?
Balancing torques gives
the answer.

In this example the mass
of the bar (also called
a beam) is negligible
but even if it wasn't, we
wouldn't have to consider
it since the force at the
pivot acts in the same
place.

The turning effect of the force depends upon the force and how far the force is from the pivot. The *torque* gives the turning effect of the force.

$$\text{torque} = \text{force} \times \frac{\textbf{perpendicular distance from the line}}{\textbf{of action of the force to a point}}$$

So the torque in Figure 10.4 is $F \times r$. This torque turns the bar in an anticlockwise direction. The torques in Figure 10.3 are balanced because the clockwise torque = anticlockwise torque but in Figure 10.5(a) and (b) the anticlockwise torque ($F \times r$) is greater than the clockwise torque ($F \times \frac{r}{2}$) so the bar will rotate anticlockwise. If we take anticlockwise torques to be positive and clockwise negative we can say *the bar is balanced when the sum of torques is zero.*

Angular velocity and angular acceleration

When the bar rotates we can define the speed of rotation by the *angular velocity*. This is the angle swept out by the bar per unit time. If the torques on the bar are unbalanced then it will begin to rotate. This means there is change in the angular velocity (from zero to something); we can say that the bar has *angular acceleration*:

angular velocity (ω) is the angle swept out per unit time,
angular acceleration (α) is the rate of change of angular velocity.

Equilibrium

When dealing with point masses we say that a body is in equilibrium when at rest or moving with constant velocity. However, when we define equilibrium for larger, rigid bodies we should add that there should be no angular acceleration. This means that not only must the forces be balanced but so should the torques.

The sum of all the forces acting on the body is zero

If all the forces acting on a body are added vectorially the resultant will be zero. With many forces adding the vectors can lead to some confusing many-sided figures so it is often easier to take components in two convenient perpendicular directions, often vertical and horizontal, then sum these separately. If the total force is zero then the sum in any two perpendicular directions will also be zero.

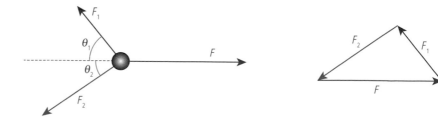

Figure 10.6 Summing vectors or taking components.

If the red ball is in equilibrium the sum of the forces must be zero so the vector sum has a zero resultant as shown by the triangle. This can be solved but it isn't a right-angled triangle so isn't simple. An easier approach is to take components:
vertical: $F_1 \sin \theta_1 - F_2 \sin \theta_2 = 0$
horizontal: $F - F_1 \cos \theta_1 - F_2 \cos \theta_2 = 0$.

In other words:

sum of the forces left = sum of the forces right

and

sum of the forces up = sum of the forces down.

The sum of all the torques acting on the body is zero

In the seesaw example we obviously considered torques about the pivot but if a body is in equilibrium then the sum of the torques about *any* point will be zero. Take the example in Figure 10.7.

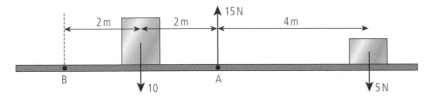

Figure 10.7.

taking torques about A:
clockwise = 5 × 4 = 20 N m
anticlockwise = 2 × 10 = 20 N m.

Taking torques about B:
clockwise = 5 × 8 + 10 × 2 = 60 N m (if B was a pivot both forces would cause a clockwise rotation).
anticlockwise = 15 × 4 = 60 N m (here we have taken the normal reaction. If this was the only force and B was a pivot it would cause the bar to rotate in an anticlockwise direction).

 When solving problems you can choose the *most convenient* place to take moments about, it doesn't have to be the pivot.

The balanced beam

There are many variations of this problem. In some cases you can ignore the weight of the beam (as in the seesaw) but in others it must be taken into account.

Worked example

Calculate the weight of the beam balanced as in Figure 10.8.

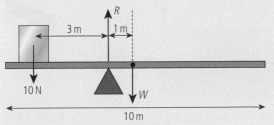

Figure 10.8.

Solution

Taking torques about the pivot we get:
clockwise torques = W × 1
anticlockwise torques = 10 × 3
since balanced, W = 30 N

Worked example

Calculate the length L between the 40 N weight and the pivot needed to balance the beam shown in Figure 10.9.

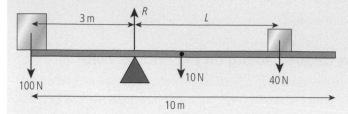

Figure 10.9.

Solution

Taking torques about the pivot:

clockwise torques	$= 10 \times 2 + 40 \times L = 20 + 40L$
anticlockwise torques	$= 100 \times 3 = 300$
since balanced	$300 = 20 + 40L$
	$280 = 40L$
	$L = 7\,\text{m}$

Exercises

1 A 1 m ruler is balanced on the 30 cm mark by placing a 300 g mass 10 cm from the end. Calculate the mass of the ruler.

2 A 100 g mass is placed at the 10 cm mark on a 20 g ruler. Where must a 350 g mass be placed so that the ruler balances at the 60 cm mark?

Levers

We have seen that the force required to balance the bar depends on how far from the pivot you apply the force. This is the principle of levers and has many applications.

Exercise

3 Calculate the unknown force F in each of the situations shown in Figure 10.10.

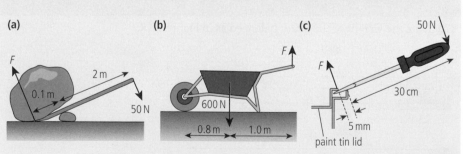

Figure 10.10.

The bridge

A simple bridge consists of a rigid construction spanning the gap between two supports. This may seem nothing to do with rotation and if built properly it isn't. However, we can use the condition for equilibrium to calculate the forces on the supports.

Worked example

A mass of 500 g is placed on the bridge as shown in Figure 10.11. If the mass of the bridge is 1 kg calculate the force on each of the supports.

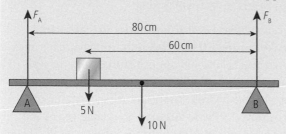

Figure 10.11.

Solution

In this case if we calculated the torques about the centre we would have two unknowns in the equation so it would be better to find torques about one of the ends; let us consider end B.

Clockwise torques $= F_A \times 0.8$
anticlockwise torques $= 5 \times 0.6 + 10 \times 0.4 = 7\,\text{N m}$

$$F_A = \frac{7}{0.8} = 8.75\,\text{N}$$

To find F_B we can now use the fact that the vertical forces must also be balanced so

$$F_A + F_B = 10 + 5$$

$$F_B = 15 - 8.75 = 6.25\,\text{N}$$

Exercises

4   A 5 m long ladder is held horizontally between two men. A third man with mass 80 kg sits on the ladder 1 m from one end. Calculate the force each man exerts if the mass of the ladder is 10 kg.

5   A 1 m long ruler of mass 200 g is suspended from two vertical strings tied 10 cm from each end. The force required to break the strings is 6 N. An 800 g mass is placed in the middle of the ruler and moved towards one end. How far can the mass move before one of the strings breaks?

Non-perpendicular forces

When a force acts at an angle to the bar as in Figure 10.12, the perpendicular distance from the line of action to the pivot is reduced so $\Gamma = F \times L \sin \theta$. This is the same component of the force perpendicular to the bar multiplied by the distance to the pivot. The parallel component does not have a turning effect since the line of action passes through the pivot.

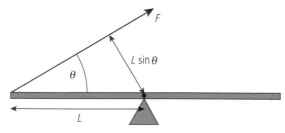

Figure 10.12.

The hanging sign

Signs and lights are often hung on brackets fixed to a wall. This can result in a lot of force on the fixings so they are often supported by a wire as shown in Figure 10.13. Note that in this case the sign hangs from the centre of the bar.

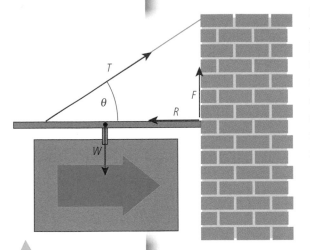

Here we can see that, because the wire is attached to the wall, it makes an angle θ with the supporting bar. This must be balanced by an equal and opposite force from the wall; this is the normal reaction R. Calculating torques around the point where the wire joins the bar we see that the bar and sign cause a clockwise torque. This is balanced by the anticlockwise torque caused by the force F at the wall. This force is provided by the fixing plate or by inserting the bar into a hole in the wall.

Figure 10.13 A hanging sign.

Exercises

6 A sign is hung exactly like the one in Figure 10.13. The sign has a mass of 50 kg and the bar 10 kg. The bar is 3 m in length and the wire is attached 50 cm from the end and makes an angle of 45° with the bar. Calculate:

  (a) the tension T in the wire.
  (b) the normal force R.
  (c) the upwards force F.

7 Repeat Exercise 6 with the sign hanging from the end of the bar.

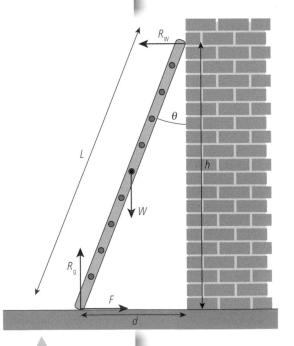

Figure 10.14 A leaning ladder.

The leaning ladder

If you have ever used a ladder to paint the wall of a house you might have wondered what angle the ladder should be: too steep and you might fall backwards, not steep enough and it might slip on the ground. By calculating torques it is possible to find out if the ladder is in equilibrium, but remember the forces change when you start to climb the ladder.

Figure 10.14 shows a ladder leaning against a frictionless wall in equilibrium. Brick walls aren't really frictionless but it makes things easier to assume that this one is. The problem is to find the friction force on the bottom of the ladder.

First we can balance the forces:
vertical forces: $R_g = W$
horizontal forces $R_w = F$

Then, calculating torques about the top of the ladder:

sum of clockwise torques = sum of anticlockwise torques

$$R_g \times d = F \times h + W \times \frac{d}{2}$$

If we were to calculate torques around the bottom of the ladder we get:

$$W \times \frac{d}{2} = R_w \times h$$

$$R_w = W \times \frac{d}{h} \times \frac{1}{2}$$

$$= W \times \frac{\tan \theta}{2}$$

but $R_W = F$ $$F = W \times \frac{\tan \theta}{2}$$

so as the angle increases the friction at the bottom (F) increases. This has a maximum value of μR_g (μ is the coefficient of friction) which limits the maximum angle of the ladder.

Exercises

8 A ladder of length 5 m leans against a wall such that the bottom of the ladder is 3 m from the wall. If the weight of the ladder is 20 kg calculate the friction between the ground and the bottom of the ladder.

9 If the ladder in Exercise 8 is moved a little bit further out it begins to slip. Calculate the coefficient of static friction between the ground and the ladder.

Constant angular acceleration

Consider a bar pivoted at one end as in Figure 10.15. As the bar rotates it sweeps out an angle $\Delta\theta$. This is the *angular displacement* of the bar and is measured in radians.

If the time taken for the bar to sweep out angle $\Delta\theta$ is Δt then the *angular velocity* of the bar ω is given by the equation:

$$\omega = \frac{\Delta\theta}{\Delta t}$$

An unbalanced torque applied to the bar will cause it to rotate faster; the rate of change of angular velocity is the *angular acceleration*, α

$$\alpha = \frac{\Delta\omega}{\Delta t}$$

These quantities are the rotational equivalents of linear displacement, velocity, and acceleration. If the angular acceleration is constant they are related in the same way giving angular equivalents of the *suvat* equations (the $\theta\,\omega_i\,\omega_f\,\alpha\,t$ equations!).

Constant angular acceleration equations

A bar rotating at an initial angular velocity of ω_i is acted upon by a torque that causes an angular acceleration α increasing the angular velocity to a final value of ω_f in t seconds. During this time the bar sweeps out an angle θ.

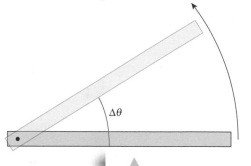

▲ **Figure 10.15.**

Figure 10.16 Uniform angular acceleration.

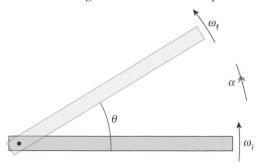

425

These quantities are related by the equations shown in Table 10.1.

Angular	Linear
$\omega_f = \omega_i + \alpha t$	$v = u + at$
$\omega_f^2 = \omega_i^2 + 2\alpha\theta$	$v^2 = u^2 + 2as$
$\theta = \omega_i t + \frac{1}{2}\alpha t^2$	$s = ut + \frac{1}{2}at^2$

Table 10.1.

These angular equations are used to solve problems in exactly the same way as the linear equations.

Worked example

A body rotating at $10\,\text{rad s}^{-1}$ accelerates at a uniform rate of $2\,\text{rad s}^{-2}$ for 5 seconds. Calculate the final angular velocity.

Solution

The data given is:
$\omega_i = 10\,\text{rad s}^{-1}$
$\alpha = 2\,\text{rad s}^{-2}$
$t = 5\,\text{s}$

we wish to find ω_f so the equation to use is $\omega_f = \omega_i + \alpha t$:

$$\omega_f = 10 + 2 \times 5 = 20\,\text{rad s}^{-1}$$

Worked example

Calculate the angle swept out by a body that starts with an angular velocity of $2\,\text{rad s}^{-1}$ and accelerates for $10\,\text{s}$ at a rate of $5\,\text{rad s}^{-2}$.

Solution

The data given is
$\omega_i = 2\,\text{rad s}^{-1}$
$\alpha = 5\,\text{rad s}^{-2}$
$t = 10\,\text{s}$

We wish to find θ so the equation to use is $\theta = \omega_i t + \frac{1}{2}\alpha t^2$:

$$\theta = 2 \times 10 + \frac{1}{2}5 \times 10^2 = 20 + 250 = 270\,\text{rad}$$

This is $\dfrac{270}{2\pi}$ revolutions.

1 revolution is 2π radians. ⓘ

Exercises

10 A wheel is pushed so that it has a uniform angular acceleration of $2\,\text{rad s}^{-2}$ for a time of $5\,\text{s}$. If its initial velocity was $6\,\text{rad s}^{-1}$ calculate:

(a) the final angular velocity.
(b) the number of revolutions made.

11 The frictional force on a spinning wheel slows it down at a constant acceleration until it stops. Initially the wheel was spinning at 5 revolutions per second. If the wheel was slowed down to stop in one revolution calculate:

(a) the angular acceleration.
(b) the time taken.

Graphical representation

As with linear motion, angular motion can be represented graphically. In the example considered previously, a bar rotating at an initial angular velocity of ω_i is acted upon by a torque that causes an angular acceleration α increasing the angular velocity to a final value of ω_f in t seconds. During this time the bar sweeps out an angle θ. This can be represented by the three graphs shown in Figure 10.17.

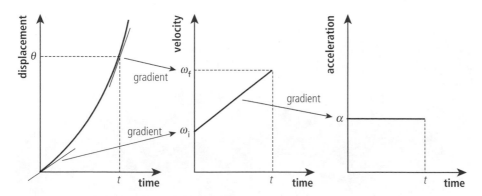

Figure 10.17 Rotational motion graphs.

As with the linear equivalents, the gradient of displacement/time $\left(\frac{\Delta\theta}{\Delta t}\right)$ gives velocity and the gradient of velocity/time $\left(\frac{\Delta\omega}{\Delta t}\right)$ gives acceleration. Working the other way around, the area under acceleration/time gives the change of velocity and the area under velocity/time gives displacement.

Relationship between angular motion and linear motion

Circular motion can be split into two components: one perpendicular to the circumference and one tangential to it. We dealt with the perpendicular component in section 4.1 (Circular motion) when we considered only bodies moving with constant speed. In this case there is acceleration towards the centre – the centripetal acceleration – but no tangential acceleration. When an unbalanced torque acts then there will be an increasing centripetal acceleration plus a tangential acceleration in the directions shown in Figure 10.18.

We know that if $\Delta\theta$ is measured in radians $\Delta\theta = \frac{\Delta s}{r}$ so $\Delta s = \Delta\theta \times r$.

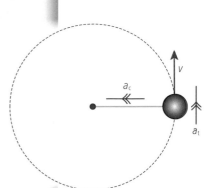

Figure 10.18.

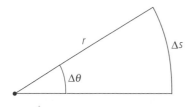

Figure 10.19.

The speed of the body is given by $\frac{\Delta s}{\Delta t} = \left(\frac{\Delta\theta}{\Delta t}\right) r = \omega r$.

If $\Delta\theta$ is a small angle then we can assume that the velocity does not change significantly so we can say that the instantaneous tangential velocity $v = \omega r$.

The tangential acceleration of the body $a_t = \frac{\Delta v}{\Delta t} = \frac{\Delta\omega r}{\Delta t} = \left(\frac{\Delta\omega}{\Delta t}\right) r$

but

$$\left(\frac{\Delta\omega}{\Delta t}\right) = \alpha$$

so

$$a_t = \alpha r$$

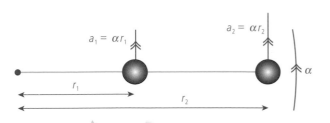

$a_1 = \alpha r_1$

$a_2 = \alpha r_2$

α

r_1

r_2

From these equations we can deduce that if a rigid body is rotating with constant angular acceleration, all points will have the same instantaneous angular velocity and angular acceleration but tangential velocity and acceleration will be greater for points furthest away from the axis of rotation as illustrated in Figure 10.20.

Figure 10.20.

The angular velocity is the same for all but the children on the outside travel faster.

Exercises

12 A 5 m long ladder is lying on the ground. One end is lifted with constant acceleration 2 m s^{-2}. Calculate:

   (a) the angular acceleration of the ladder.
   (b) the tangential acceleration of the middle of the ladder.

13 Two children, each of mass 20 kg, are enjoying a ride on a roundabout as in the photo. One is 0.5 m from the centre and the other is 2 m from the centre. If the roundabout is rotating at 0.25 revolutions per second, calculate:

   (a) the angular velocity of the roundabout.
   (b) the speed of each child.
   (c) the force required to hold each child onto the roundabout.

Newton's second law applied to angular motion

We have seen that the angular acceleration of a body is related to the torque applied. Here we will derive that relationship by considering a force acting on a particle attached to a rod of negligible mass as shown in Figure 10.21.

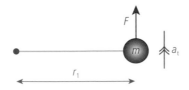

F

m

a_t

r_1

Figure 10.21 A mass on a massless rod.

If we apply Newton's second law to this particle we get

$$F = ma_t$$

but since the rod is pivoted at the end the mass will move in a circle of radius r. The angular acceleration of this body will be $\alpha = \frac{a_t}{r}$ so:

$$F = m\alpha r.$$

The rotation is caused because the force F provides a torque, F_r about the pivot. Multiplying by r gives:

$$Fr = m\alpha r^2$$

$$\Gamma = m\alpha r^2$$

A rigid body is made up of lots of particles, When a torque is applied to the body each particle experiences a small torque turning it in the direction of rotation. Let's consider the body in Figure 10.22 made of two masses joined with a massless rod rotating about the end with angular acceleration α.

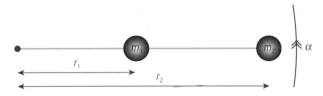

Figure 10.22.

We can apply the formula $\Gamma = m\alpha r^2$ to find the torque on each mass:

$$\Gamma_1 = m_1 \alpha r_1^2$$

$$\Gamma_2 = m_2 \alpha r_2^2$$

The total torque on the whole body is therefore:

$$\Gamma = \Gamma_1 + \Gamma_2 = m_1 \alpha r_1^2 + m_2 \alpha r_2^2$$

But the body is rigid so both masses have the same angular acceleration α.

$$\Gamma = (m_1 r_1^2 + m_2 r_2^2)\alpha$$

so the torque = the sum of $mr^2 \times \alpha$

$$I = \left(\Sigma mr^2\right) \times \alpha$$

Moment of Inertia

The value Σmr^2 is known as the moment of inertia of the body

$$\Gamma = \Sigma mr^2$$

The unit of moment of inertia is $kg\,m^2$.

For the body in Figure 10.22 this is simply $m_1 r_1^2 + m_2 r_2^2$. For more complicated bodies it can be calculated by performing an integration. This is beyond this course so we will either consider simple bodies or give the equation for the moment of inertia.

The equation for the total torque becomes:

$$\Gamma = I\alpha$$

which is the rotational equivalent of Newton's second law $F = ma$. We can think of the moment of inertia as being equivalent to the mass in linear motion. If the mass of a body is spread out a long way from the pivot then I is large so even though the two objects in Figure 10.23 have the same mass, the object in Figure 10.23(a) has the greater moment of inertia and would therefore require a bigger torque to make it rotate with the same angular acceleration.

Figure 10.23.

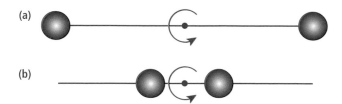

The moment of inertia of a body depends on the axis of rotation so the cylinder in Figure 10.24 will have a greater moment of inertia if rotated about its centre than if rotated about its long axis.

large I

small I

Figure 10.24.

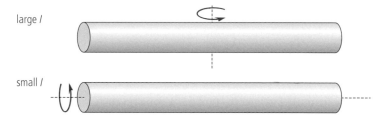

A bicycle wheel has an easy-to-calculate moment of inertia. If we assume that all of the weight is in the rim and tyre and none in the spokes or hub then all of the mass is the same distance from the centre so $I = Mr^2$ where m is the mass of the wheel.

A bicycle wheel.

Worked example

Two 1 kg masses are attached to a rod of negligible mass as shown in Figure 10.25. Calculate the moment of inertia of the body if rotated around axes A and B.

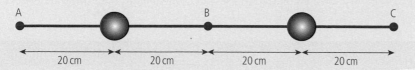

Figure 10.25.

Solution

About A, $I = 1 \times 0.2^2 + 1 \times 0.6^2 = 0.4 \, \text{kg m}^2$

About B, $I = 1 \times 0.2^2 + 1 \times 0.2^2 = 0.08 \, \text{kg m}^2$

Worked example

If a force of 100 N is applied perpendicular to the rod at point C, calculate the angular acceleration for rotation about A and B.

Solution

About A torque = $100 \times 0.8 = 80 \, \text{N m}$

$$\Gamma = I\alpha \quad \text{so} \quad \alpha = \frac{\Gamma}{I} = \frac{80}{0.4} = 200 \, \text{rad s}^{-2}$$

About B torque = $100 \times 0.4 = 40 \, \text{N m}$

$$\alpha = \frac{\Gamma}{I} = \frac{40}{0.08} = 500 \, \text{rad s}^{-2}$$

Exercises

14 Calculate the angular acceleration when a force of 20 N is applied tangentially to the tyre of a 2.5 kg bicycle wheel which has a radius of 50 cm.

15 A 2.5 kg bicycle wheel with radius 50 cm rotating at 1 revolution per second is brought to rest in 1 s by applying the brakes. Calculate the force of the brakes.

16 Two forces are applied to the body in Figure 10.26 as shown (the rod has negligible mass). Calculate the angular acceleration of the body.

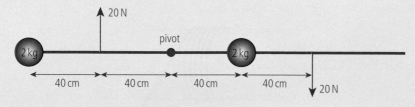

Figure 10.26.

17 The forces in Exercise 16 are moved so they act as in Figure 10.27. Calculate the angular acceleration of the body.

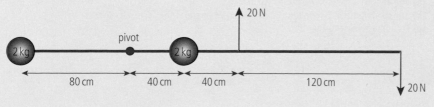

Figure 10.27.

Two identical parallel forces as in Figure 10.27 are called a *couple*. The resultant torque of a couple = one force × perpendicular distance between the forces. This is the same about any point.

Some common shapes and their moments of inertia

Although you won't have to derive the formula for the moment of inertia of anything but simple point masses on massless rods, you might come across examples in your practical work where you will need to use the moment of inertia. These are given in Table 10.2.

Table 10.2 Moments of inertia for different shapes.

Shape	Moment of inertia
![Thin hollow cylinder] **Figure 10.28** Thin hollow cylinder.	Mr^2
![Solid cylinder] **Figure 10.29** Solid cylinder.	$\frac{1}{2}Mr^2$
![Sphere] **Figure 10.30** Sphere.	$\frac{2}{3}Mr^2$ (hollow) $\frac{2}{5}Mr^2$ (solid)
![Rod] **Figure 10.31** Rod (length L).	$\frac{1}{12}ML^2$ (centre) $\frac{1}{3}ML^2$ (end)

Exercises

18 A metal cylinder is allowed to rotate along the centre of its long axis as in Figure 10.32. A string of length 1 m is wrapped around a metal cylinder and pulled with a constant force of 10 N. If the mass of the cylinder is 2 kg and its radius 2 cm, calculate:

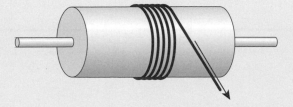

Figure 10.32.

(a) the angular acceleration of the cylinder.
(b) the total number of revolutions completed when the string comes to an end.
(c) its angular velocity after the string is pulled free.

19 The cylinder in exercise 18 spins about its central axis at 100 revolutions per second. It is slowed down by the friction of a rope that is put over the cylinder and pulled down as in Figure 10.33. If the tension in one end of the rope is 10 N and the other 15 N calculate:

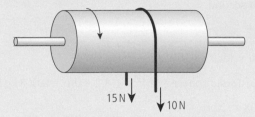

15 N   10 N

Figure 10.33.

(a) the resultant torque acting on the cylinder.
(b) the angular acceleration of the cylinder.
(c) the time taken for the cylinder to stop.

20 A 5 m long, 20 kg wooden pole lies on the ground. One end is lifted with a vertical force of 200 N. Calculate:

(a) the sum of the torques acting on the pole.
(b) the instantaneous angular acceleration of the pole.

Rotational kinetic energy

When a rigid body rotates each particle of the body is moving in a circle so although the body isn't moving forwards each particle has kinetic energy. We call this *rotational kinetic energy*. This energy was transferred to the body by the tangential force that caused the rotation. To calculate the rotational kinetic energy of a body we can again consider a point mass on a massless rod but this time it has a constant speed v as in Figure 10.34.

> For a rigid body all parts will have the same angular velocity no matter how far from the axis they are.

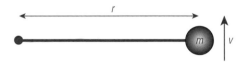

Figure 10.34.

For mass m $\qquad$ $\text{KE} = \frac{1}{2}mv^2$

but $\qquad$ $v = \omega r$

so $\qquad$ $\text{KE} = \frac{1}{2}m\omega^2 r^2 = \frac{1}{2}mr^2\omega^2$

For a body made of many particles

$$\text{KE} = \frac{1}{2}\Sigma mr^2 \times \omega^2$$

$$\text{KE} = \frac{1}{2}I\omega^2$$

Again we can see that the moment of inertia is equivalent to mass in linear motion.

Work done

When a force moves in the direction of the force, work is done. When a tangential force causes a body to have angular acceleration the direction of the force is always changing. However, if we were to consider small movements the direction is almost constant. The total work done along an arc s will be the sum of all the work done in all of these small movements.

$$\text{Work done} = Fs$$

But $\theta = \frac{s}{r}$ so work $= Fr\theta = \Gamma\theta$.

433

Worked example

Calculate the kinetic energy of a solid sphere of radius 10 cm and mass 2 kg rotating at 10 revolutions per second.

Solution

First find the angular velocity $= 10 \times 2\pi = 20\pi\,\mathrm{rad\,s^{-1}}$

moment of inertia of a solid sphere $= \frac{2}{5}Mr^2 = \frac{2}{5} \times 2 \times 0.1^2 = 0.008\,\mathrm{kg\,m^2}$

$\mathrm{KE} = \frac{1}{2}I\omega^2 = \frac{1}{2} \times 0.008 \times (20\pi)^2 = 16\,\mathrm{J}$.

Exercises

21 Calculate the rotational kinetic energy of a 3 kg metal cylinder of length 4 m and radius 2 cm rotated at 1 revolution per second:

  (a) about its centre.
  (b) about one end.
  (c) about its long axis.

22 A bicycle wheel of radius 45 cm and mass 500 g rotating at 2 revolutions per second is stopped by applying the brakes. Estimate the thermal energy transferred to the brakes and wheel.

Rolling ball

When a ball is released on an inclined plane the forces acting are as shown in Figure 10.35. The weight and normal reaction both act through the centre of mass. However, the friction doesn't so will cause rotation about the centre causing the ball to roll.

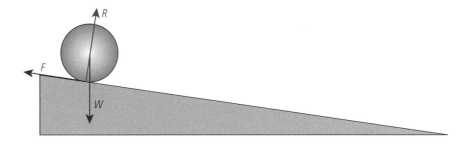

Figure 10.35.

As the ball rolls down the hill it loses gravitational potential energy and gains both rotational and translational kinetic energy. If the ball has a vertical displacement h then we can say;

$$mgh = \frac{1}{2}mv^2 + \frac{1}{2}I\omega^2$$

If a ball slips down the slope the then there will be no rotation so $mgh = \frac{1}{2}mv^2$. Comparing these two equations we can deduce that the rolling ball will travel down the hill slower than the sliding one. If the ball rolls without slipping then the tangential velocity of the edge = the translational velocity of the ball.

So $\omega = \dfrac{v}{r}$ where r is the radius of the ball. If the ball is solid then $I = \frac{2}{5}mr^2$.

So $mgh = \frac{1}{2}mv^2 + \dfrac{\frac{1}{2}(\frac{2}{5}mr^2)v^2}{r^2} = \frac{1}{2}mv^2 + \frac{2}{10}mv^2$.

$gh = \frac{7}{10}v^2$

$v = \sqrt{\dfrac{10gh}{7}}$

It is interesting to note that the velocity does not depend on either the mass or the radius.

23 Following a similar procedure as with the solid ball, derive an equation for the velocity of a rolling hollow ball after it has moved a vertical displacement h. If a hollow ball and a solid ball are rolled down the same slope which would take the less time?

24 A solid sphere of mass 500 g rolls down the slope shown in Figure 10.36. Calculate:

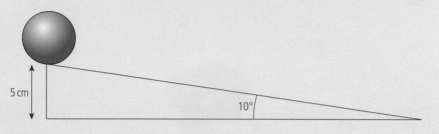

5 cm

10°

Figure 10.36.

(a) the total kinetic energy at the bottom of the slope.
(b) the velocity at the bottom of the slope.
(c) the distance travelled down the slope.
(d) the time taken to roll down the slope (assume constant acceleration).

Angular momentum (L)

Newton's law gives us the relationship $F = ma = (m \times \frac{\Delta v}{\Delta t})$ but it can also be written $F = \frac{\Delta mv}{\Delta t}$ where mv is the momentum.

In rotational motion we have a similar relationship: $\Gamma = I\alpha = (I \times \frac{\Delta \omega}{\Delta t})$.

This can be written $\Gamma = \frac{\Delta I\omega}{\Delta t}$ where $I\omega$ is the *angular momentum*.

If we consider the particle of mass rotating on a massless bar in Figure 10.37 we can see that it has instantaneous linear momentum = mv. The angular momentum of this particle would be $I\omega$. In this simple case $I = mr^2$ so angular momentum = $mr^2\omega$.

But $\omega = \frac{v}{r}$ so angular momentum = mvr which is linear momentum × r.

r

m

v

Figure 10.37.

25 Calculate the angular momentum of a 5 cm radius solid cylinder of mass 400 g rotating about its centre at 10 revolutions per second.

26 Calculate the angular momentum of a 10 cm radius solid sphere of mass 750 g rotating about its centre at 5 revolutions per second.

Conservation of angular momentum

If no external torques act then the angular momentum of a system of isolated bodies is conserved. This has some fun applications used to great effect by ballet dancers, ice-skaters, and gymnasts. A pirouette is when a ballet dancer spins around very fast as in the photo on the next page. At the start of the spin the dancer holds her arms outstretched. Her arms are then bought closer to her body reducing her moment of inertia. Since there are no external torques acting, her angular momentum is conserved resulting in an increased angular velocity. The same principle is used when gymnasts do a triple somersault. The rotation is started with the body stretched, to speed up the rotation gymnasts pull in their arms and legs to make a tight ball enabling them to make three rotations before landing.

A ballet dancer performs a pirouette.

Worked example

In Figure 10.38 a horizontal disc of radius 20 cm and mass 2 kg is rotating at 3 rotations per second. A second disc of radius 10 cm and mass 1 kg is dropped onto the first one so that the centres are coincident. Calculate the new rotational frequency.

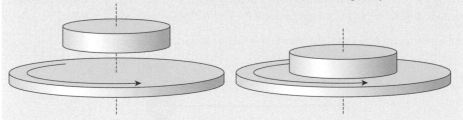

Figure 10.38.

Solution

In this example the moment of inertia of the turntable has increased so the angular velocity will decrease.

moment of inertia of turntable = $\frac{1}{2}mr^2$ = 0.5 × 2 × (0.2)² = 0.04 kg m²

moment of inertia of disc = $\frac{1}{2}mr^2$ = 0.5 × 1 × (0.1)² = 0.005 kg m²

combined moment of inertia = 0.045 kg m²

Initial angular velocity = $2\pi \times 3 = 6\pi$ rad s⁻¹

Since no external torques act, angular momentum is conserved:

$$I_i\omega_i = I_f\omega_f$$
$$0.04 \times 6\pi = 0.045 \times \omega_f$$
$$\omega_f = 5.3\pi \text{ rad s}^{-1}$$

This is 2.7 revolutions per second.

27 The body of an ice-skater can be considered to be a vertical cylinder of radius 15 cm and mass 60 kg (see Figure 10.39). The outstretched arms act like two 2 kg masses at the end of 1 m long massless rods. The ice skater is spinning with arms stretched at 1 revolution per second. The skater then pulls her arms in so she rotates with radius 25 cm. Calculate:

(a) the moment of inertia of the skater with outstretched arms.

(b) the moment of inertia with her arms pulled in.

(c) her frequency of rotation after pulling in her arms.

(d) her kinetic energy before and after.

(e) Suggest where her extra kinetic energy has come from.

Figure 10.39.

28 A turntable is a horizontal rotating disc of mass 1 kg and radius 15 cm. If the turntable rotates at 0.5 revolutions per second, calculate:

(a) the moment of inertia of the turntable.

A 100 g mass is dropped onto the turntable 10 cm from the centre. Calculate:

(b) the new moment of inertia of the turntable + mass.

(c) the angular frequency of the turntable.

29 This one is rather contrived but imagine a frictionless table with a hole in the middle. A string is threaded through the hole and a 500 g ball attached to the end. The ball is now made to travel in a circle while you hold the other end of the string (under the table).

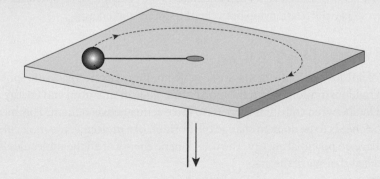

Figure 10.40.

The speed of the ball is 2 m s⁻¹ and the radius is 50 cm.

(a) Calculate the angular momentum of the ball.

(b) If the string is pulled so that it is shortened to 20 cm, calculate the new speed of the ball.

 To learn more about rigid bodies and rotational dynamics, go to the hotlinks site, search for the title or ISBN and click on Chapter 10.

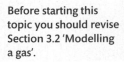

10.2 | Thermodynamics

B.2 Thermodynamics

Understandings, applications, and skills:

The first law of thermodynamics
- Describing the first law of thermodynamics as a statement of conservation of energy.
- Explaining sign convention used when stating the first law of thermodynamics as $Q = \Delta U + W$

The second law of thermodynamics
- Describing the second law of thermodynamics in Celsius form, kelvin form, and as a consequence of entropy.

Entropy
- Describing examples of processes in terms of entropy change.
- Solving problems involving entropy changes.

Cyclic processes and *P–V* diagram
- Sketching and interpreting cyclic processes.

  Guidance
  - *If cycles other than the Carnot cycle are used quantitatively, full details will be provided.*

Isovolumetric, isobaric, isothermal, and adiabatic processes
- Solving problems involving the first law of thermodynamics.
- Solving problems for adiabatic processes using $PV^{\frac{5}{3}}$ = constant.

  Guidance
  - *Only graphical analysis will be required for determination of work done on a P–V diagram when pressure is not constant.*

Carnot cycle
Thermal efficiency
- Solving problems involving thermal efficiency.

Thermodynamic systems

When work is done energy is transferred, so to do work requires a source of energy. When fuel is burnt chemical energy is converted into heat but to do work we need an engine. In this section we will consider a simple engine, an ideal gas trapped in a cylinder by a piston, but before we can understand the principle of its operation we need to investigate the relationship between the system and energy.

Internal energy of a gas (*U*)

We think of an ideal gas as being made of a large number of perfectly elastic spheres moving in random motion. When the molecules collide momentum and energy are conserved but between collisions there is no force acting between them. This means that no work needs to be done to change the position of a molecule; the molecules therefore have no potential energy. The total kinetic energy of all the molecules is called the *internal energy* of the gas.

We know that the average kinetic energy of the molecules of a gas is proportional to the temperature in kelvin.

$$\text{Average KE of a molecule} = \tfrac{3}{2}kT$$

where k = Boltzmann's constant = $1.38 \times 10^{-23}\,\text{J K}^{-1}$.

A mole of gas contains N_A (Avogadro's constant) molecules so the total KE = $\tfrac{3}{2}N_A kT$. $N_A k$ is also a constant, the universal gas constant = $8.31\,\text{J mol}^{-1}\,\text{K}^{-1}$.

So, the total KE of one mole of gas = $\frac{3}{2}RT$.

Since the internal energy of a gas is the total KE then for n moles we can say:

$$\text{internal energy } U = \frac{3}{2}nRT.$$

$U = \frac{3}{2}RT$ is only true for monatomic gases such as neon, helium, and argon.

When heat is transferred to a *fixed volume* of gas it will increase the internal energy and hence the temperature of the gas. If no heat is lost we can say that

$$Q = \Delta U.$$

Worked example

500 J of heat energy are transferred to 2 g of helium gas kept at constant volume in a cylinder. Calculate the temperature rise of the gas.

Solution

The molar mass of helium is 4 g so $n = 0.5$.

Increase in internal energy = $\frac{3}{2}nR\Delta T$ = heat added = 500 J

$$\Delta T = \frac{2 \times 500}{3 \times 0.5 \times 8.31} = 80\,\text{K}$$

Exercises

30 Calculate the internal energy of 100 g of argon (nucleon number 40) at 300 K.

31 Calculate the average kinetic energy of atoms of helium at 400 K.

Work done by a gas

Work is done when the point of application of a force moves in the direction of the force. If the pressure of a gas pushes a piston out, then the force exerted on the piston is moving in the direction of the force, so work is done. The example in Figure 10.41 is of a gas expanding at constant pressure. In this case, the force exerted on the piston = $P \times A$. The work done when the piston moved distance Δd is therefore given by:

$$\text{Work done} = P \times A \times \Delta d$$

but $A\Delta d$ is the change in volume ΔV, so

$$\text{Work done} = P\Delta V$$

Sign of work

When a gas does work, it is pushing the piston out; this is positive.

If work is done on the gas then something must be pushing the piston in. This is taken to be negative.

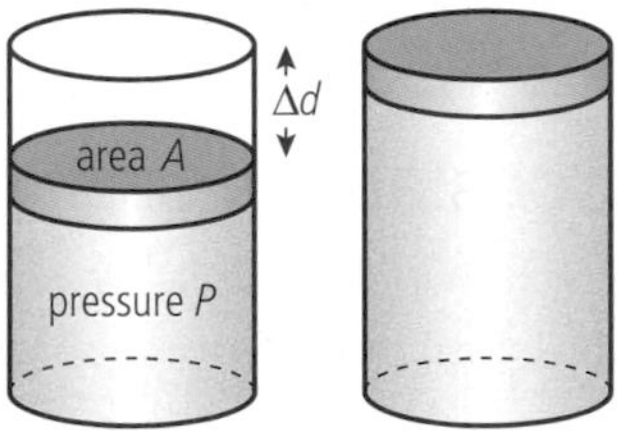

Figure 10.41 A gas expands at constant pressure.

Figure 10.42 is the P–V graph for this constant pressure expansion. From this we can see that the work done is given by the area under the graph. This is true for all processes.

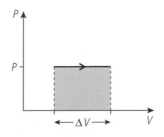

Figure 10.42.

The first law of thermodynamics

According to the law of conservation of energy, energy can neither be created nor destroyed, so the amount of heat, Q, added to a gas must equal the work done by the gas, W, plus the increase in internal energy, ΔU. This is so fundamental to the way physical systems behave that it is called the *first law of thermodynamics*. This can be written in the following way:

$$Q = \Delta U + W$$

This would be nice and easy if the only thing a gas could do is gain heat, get hot, and do work. However, heat can be added and lost, work can be done by the gas and on the gas, and the internal energy can increase and decrease. To help us understand all the different possibilities, we will use the P–V diagram to represent the states of a gas.

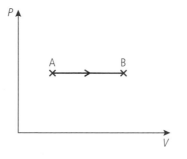

Using *P–V* diagrams in thermodynamics

We have seen how a P–V diagram enables us to see the changes in P, V, and T that take place when a gas changes from one state to another. It also tells us what energy changes are taking place. If we consider the transformation represented in Figure 10.43 we can deduce that when the gas changes from A to B:

1 since the volume is increasing, the gas is doing work (W is positive).
2 since the temperature is increasing, the internal energy is increasing (ΔU is positive).

Figure 10.43.

If we then apply the first law $Q = \Delta U + W$ we can conclude that if both ΔU and W are positive then Q must also be positive, so heat must have been added.

This is a typical example of how we use the P–V diagram with the first law; we use the diagram to find out how the temperature changes and whether work is done *by* the gas or *on* the gas, and then use the first law to deduce whether heat is added or lost.

Constant pressure compression (isobaric)

The previous example was an expansion at constant pressure. Now we will consider the constant pressure (isobaric) compression shown in Figure 10.44.

1 Temperature decrease implies that the internal energy decreases (ΔU = negative).
2 Volume decrease implies that work is done on the gas (W = negative).

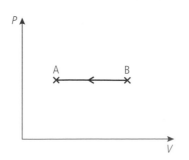

Applying the first law, $Q = \Delta U + W$, tells us that Q is also negative, so heat is lost.

Figure 10.44.

First law (simple version)

If a gas expands and gets hot, heat must have been added.

P–V graph

Remember that the P–V curve is covered in a set of curves (isotherms) representing the gas at different temperatures. A transformation from A–B will imply a rise in temperature.

Change in **volume** tells us whether work is done by the gas or on it.

Change in **temperature** tells us whether the internal energy goes up or down.

Change in **pressure** is not interesting.

Constant volume increase in temperature (isochoric)

Figure 10.45 is the P–V graph for a gas undergoing a constant volume transformation. From the graph we can deduce that:

1 The volume isn't changing, so no work is done ($W = 0$).
2 The gas changes to a higher isotherm so the temperature is increasing; this means that the internal energy is increasing (ΔU = positive).

Applying the first law $Q = \Delta U + W$ we can conclude that $Q = \Delta U$ so if ΔU is positive then Q is also positive – heat has been added.

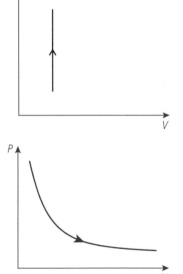

Figure 10.45 An isochoric transformation.

Isothermal expansion

For an ideal gas $PV = nRT$ so if the temperature is constant P–V = constant which implies that $P = \frac{const}{V}$ so the P–V graph follows the curve shown in Figure 10.46 ($y = \frac{k}{x}$).

From this P–V diagram we can deduce that:

1 the temperature doesn't change so there is no change in internal energy ($\Delta U = 0$)
2 the volume increases so work is done by the gas (W = positive).

Figure 10.46 An isothermal expansion.

Applying the first law, $Q = \Delta U + W$, we conclude that $Q = W$ so heat must have been added. The heat added enables the gas to do work.

Adiabatic expansion

An adiabatic process is when there is no exchange of heat between the system and the surroundings. To understand how this will be on a P–V graph let us compare an adiabatic expansion with an isothermal expansion between the same two volumes.

During an isothermal expansion work is done by the gas and the internal energy stays constant so heat must have been added. To do the same amount of work without adding heat the internal energy must go down resulting in a reduction in temperature leading to the curve in Figure 10.47.

It can be shown that for an adiabatic transformation $PV^{\frac{5}{3}}$ = constant so the shape of this curve is $y = \frac{1}{x^{\frac{5}{3}}}$.

From the P–V diagram we can deduce that:

1 the volume is increased so work is done by the gas (W = positive).
2 the temperature decreases so the internal energy is reduced (ΔU = negative).

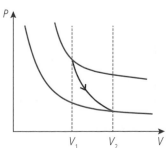

Figure 10.47.

We also know that $Q = 0$, so if we apply the first law $Q = \Delta U + W$, we get:

$$0 = -\Delta U + W$$

$$W = \Delta U$$

so the energy required for the gas to do work comes from its internal energy.

Worked example

In the following worked examples we will consider a cylinder containing 1.203×10^{-3} moles of a monatomic gas. This makes $nR = 0.01$ J K^{-1} so $\frac{PV}{T} = 10$ kPa cm^3 K^{-1}.

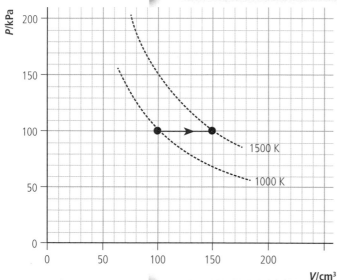

Figure 10.48 Isobaric expansion.

1. Isobaric expansion

The gas is kept at a constant pressure of 100 kPa as it expands from 100 cm^3 to 150 cm^3. As this happens the temperature rises from 1000 K to 1500 K. The process can be represented by the P–V graph shown in Figure 10.48.

When a gas expands at constant pressure work is done by the gas and it gets hot. First let us work out the work done.

$W = P\Delta V = 100 \times 10^3 \times 50 \times 10^{-6} = 5$ J.

The increase in internal energy $= \frac{3}{2}nR\Delta T = 1.5 \times 0.01 \times 500 = 7.5$ J.

Heat added = increase in internal energy + work done $(Q = \Delta U + W) = 12.5$ J.

2. Isochoric fall in temperature

The gas is now cooled at constant volume until its temperature reaches 750 K. The pressure of a gas at constant volume is proportional to the temperature so the pressure will fall to 50 kPa as shown in the P–V graph of Figure 10.49.

The volume is constant so no work is done on or by the gas. The reduction in internal energy is therefore equal to the loss of heat. $(Q = \Delta U)$.

$$\Delta U = \frac{3}{2}nR\Delta T = 1.5 \times 0.01 \times 750 = 11.25 \text{ J}$$

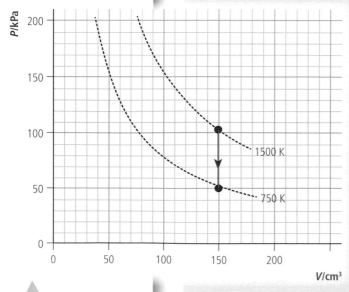

Figure 10.49 Isochoric fall in temperature.

3. Isothermal compression

The gas is compressed from 150 cm³ to 50 cm³ at a constant temperature of 750 K. The volume is reduced by $\frac{1}{3}$ so the pressure must be 3 times the original pressure shown in the P–V graph in Figure 10.50.

The volume of the gas is reduced which means work is done on the gas. However, the temperature of the gas does not increase so the work done must equal the loss of heat ($Q = W$).

The work done on the gas = the area under the curve. We can find this by counting the squares. There are approximately 82 squares: each square represents 0.1 J so work done on the gas = 8.2 J.

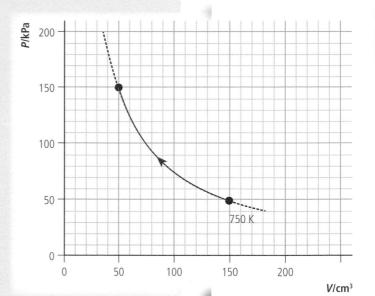

Figure 10.50 Isothermal compression.

4. Adiabatic expansion

After the previous expansion, the gas at pressure 150 kPa and volume 50 cm³ expands adiabatically until the volume is 100 cm³. For an adiabatic process $PV^{\frac{5}{3}}$ = constant so we can calculate the final pressure.

$$P_1 V_1^{\frac{5}{3}} = P_2 V_2^{\frac{5}{3}}$$

$$P_2 = P_1 \left(\frac{V_1}{V_2}\right)^{\frac{5}{3}}$$

$$P_2 = 150 \times \left(\frac{50}{100}\right)^{\frac{5}{3}} = 47 \text{ kPa}$$

The final temperature can be found from $PV = nRT$:

$$T = \frac{PV}{nR} = \frac{47 \times 100}{10} = 470 \text{ K}.$$

This process is represented by the P–V graph in Figure 10.51.

The work done on the gas can be found by counting the squares under the line.

There are approximately 42 squares each representing 0.1 J so the work done = 4.2 J.

This should be the same as the loss of internal energy of the gas which can be found from $\frac{3}{2}nR\Delta T$:

$$\Delta U = 1.5 \times 0.01 \times (750 - 470) = 4.2 \text{ J}.$$

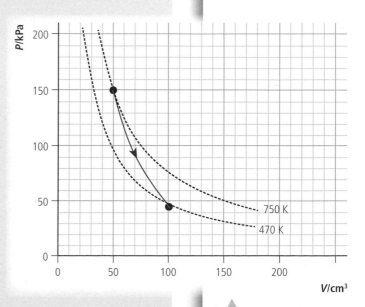

Figure 10.51 Adiabatic expansion.

Exercises

In the following exercises we will again consider a cylinder containing 1.203×10^{-3} moles of a monatomic gas, which will make $nR = 0.01$ JK^{-1}. This means you can use a simulation to confirm your answers but don't forget nR is *not* always 0.01.

32 The gas is compressed from 100 cm^3 to 50 cm^3 at a constant pressure of 70 kPa. Calculate:

    (a) the initial temperature.
    (b) the final temperature.
    (c) the change in internal energy.
    (d) the work done on the gas.
    (e) the heat lost to the surroundings.

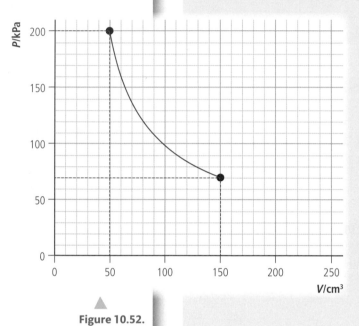

Figure 10.52.

33 The gas is compressed isothermally as illustrated by the P–V graph in Figure 10.52. Calculate:

(a) the temperature of the gas.
(b) the work done on the gas.
(c) the heat lost to the surroundings.

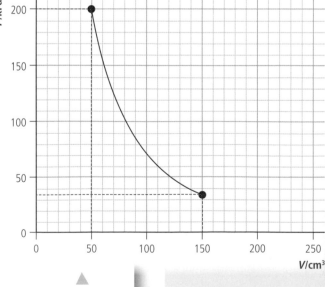

Figure 10.53.

34 The gas expands adiabatically from 52 cm^3 at a pressure of 200 kPa to a volume of 150 cm^3.

(a) Show by calculation that the new pressure is in agreement with the P–V graph of Figure 10.53.

    Calculate:

(b) the work done by the gas.
(c) the initial temperature.
(d) the final temperature.
(e) the change of internal energy.
(f) heat lost/heat gained.

Cyclic processes

A cyclic process is a series of transformations that take a gas back to its original state. When represented on a *P–V* diagram they form a closed loop such as the one shown in Figure 10.54.

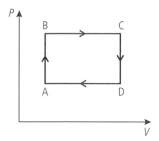

Figure 10.54 A thermodynamic cycle.

In this example the cycle is clockwise so the sequence of transformations is:

A–B isochoric temperature rise

B–C isobaric expansion

C–D isochoric temperature drop

D–A isobaric compression.

In the process of completing this cycle, work is done on the gas from D to A and the gas does work from B to C. It is clear from the diagram that the work done by the gas is greater than the work done on the gas (since the area under the graph is greater from B to C than from D to A) so net work is done. What we have here is an engine; heat is added and work is done. Let us look at this cycle more closely.

> **Net work done**
>
> The net work done during a cycle is the difference between the work done by the gas and the work done on the gas. This is equal to the area enclosed by the cycle on the *P–V* diagram.

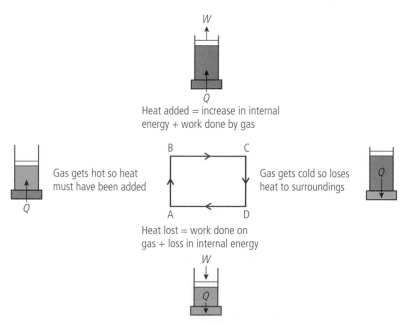

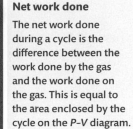

Figure 10.55 An example of a thermodynamic cycle, the red and blue rectangles placed under the piston represent hot and cold bodies used to add and take away heat.

The secret to the operation of all heat engines is that the gas is cooled down before it is compressed back to its original volume. The cold gas is easier to compress than a hot one so when the gas is hot it does work, but it's reset when it's cold.

The balloon engine from Chapter 8 operates on the same principle; when the gas is hot the balloon goes up, doing work. The balloon is then allowed to cool so that pulling it down does not use as much energy as was gained when it went up.

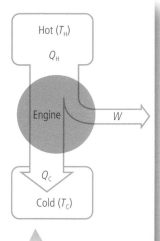

Figure 10.56 Energy flow for a heat engine.

Energy flow diagram

The principle of a heat engine can be represented by an energy flow diagram as in Figure 10.56. Heat flows from a hot source to a cold one through the engine which converts some of it into work.

The *thermal efficiency* η of an engine is defined as the ratio of the work it does to the amount of heat energy put in:

$$\eta = \frac{W}{Q_H}$$

but $W = Q_H - Q_C$ so:

$$\eta = \frac{Q_H - Q_C}{Q_H} = 1 - \frac{Q_C}{Q_H}$$

The Carnot cycle

When heat is added in the previous example the source of heat is much hotter than the gas. A more efficient process would be to transfer heat at the same temperature as the gas. The most efficient cycle possible is the Carnot cycle as represented in Figure 10.57. As Figure 10.57 shows, this consists of two isothermal transformations when heat is transferred at the same temperature as the surroundings and two adiabatic processes when the volume is changed, resulting in a change in temperature without exchanging heat to the surroundings. This is an idealized process that would have to take place very slowly but sets the limit on what is possible.

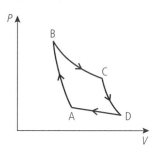

Figure 10.57 The Carnot cycle.

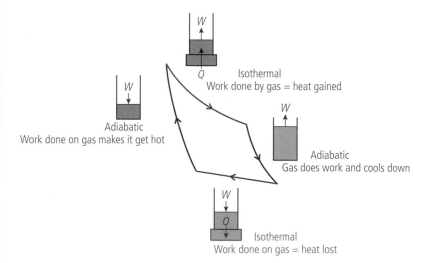

Figure 10.58 The Carnot cycle in detail. Notice that during the adiabatic transformations the cylinder is isolated from its surroundings.

The amount of heat transferred in and out of the gas during the isothermal processes is directly proportional to the temperature in kelvin, so:

$$Q_H \propto T_H \text{ and } Q_C \propto T_C$$

The efficiency of a Carnot cycle is therefore:

$$\eta = 1 - \frac{Q_C}{Q_H} = 1 - \frac{T_C}{T_H}$$

No engine can have a higher efficiency than this.

We can see that the efficiency depends on the difference between the temperatures of the hot and cold parts of the cycle. If the cold part was absolute zero (0 K) then no work would have to be done to push back the piston and the efficiency would be 1.

The reverse cycle

Let us consider what would happen if the Carnot cycle was operated in reverse. The details of this are shown in Figure 10.59.

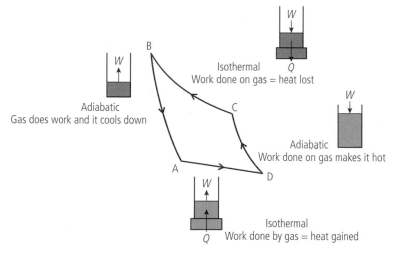

Figure 10.59 The reverse Carnot cycle.

The interesting thing about this cycle is that heat is lost to the hot body during the isothermal compression (C to B) and gained from the cold body during the isothermal expansion (A to D). So heat has been taken from something cold and given to something hot. This is what a refrigerator does – it takes heat from the cold food inside and gives it to the warm room. To make this possible, work must be done on the gas (D to C) so that it gets hot enough to give heat to the hot body.

The heat pump

A heat pump is used to extract heat from the cold air outside and give it to the inside of a house. It works in exactly the same way as a refrigerator.

Exercises

35 250 cm³ of gas at 300 K exerts a pressure of 100 kPa on its container; call this state A. It undergoes the following cycle of transformations:

 (i) an isobaric expansion to 500 cm³ (state B).

 (ii) an isochoric transformation to a pressure of 200 kPa (state C).

 (iii) an isobaric contraction back to 250 cm³ (state D).

 (iv) an isochoric transformation back to state A.

 (a) Sketch a *P–V* diagram representing this cycle, labelling the states A, B, C, and D.
 (b) Use the ideal gas equation to calculate the temperature at B, C, and D.
 (c) Calculate the amount of work done by the gas.
 (d) Calculate the amount of work done on the gas
 (e) What is the net work done during one cycle?

36 Figure 10.60 represents a Carnot cycle.
The areas of the coloured regions are as follows

A – 50 J
B – 45 J
C – 40 J
D – 35 J
E – 150 J

If the cycle is performed clockwise, how much work is done:
(a) during the isothermal expansion?
(b) during the adiabatic compression?
(c) by the gas?
(d) on the gas?
(e) in total?

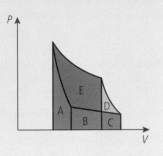

Figure 10.60.

37 The graph in Figure 10.61 shows a Carnot cycle performed with the 1.203×10^{-3} moles of a monatomic gas used in Exercises 32–34 ($nR = 0.01\,\text{J K}^{-1}$).

Use information from the graph to calculate:
(a) the temperature of the gas when expanding isothermally (T_H).
(b) the temperature of the gas when being compressed isothermally (T_C).
(c) the thermal efficiency of the engine.
(d) the net work done (W).
(e) the amount of heat added during the isothermal expansion (Q_H).
(f) Use the last two answers to get the value for the efficiency

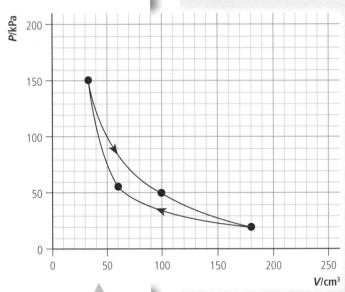

Figure 10.61.

order

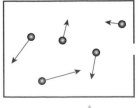

disorder

Figure 10.62.

The second law of thermodynamics

We have seen that we can use our simple thermodynamic system of a cylinder of gas to convert heat into work but to do this we must transfer heat from a hot body to a cold one. This means that we will always lose some heat. It would be even better if we could take a source of heat and transfer all the energy to work without losing any to a cold body. According to the first law of thermodynamics this should be possible since energy would be conserved. However, it can't be done. The reason for this is fundamental to the way matter behaves. To understand why, let us first consider a seemingly unconnected example in which a gas is pumped into a container as in Figure 10.62. The molecules of gas flow into the container in a nice orderly fashion through a small opening, all travelling in the same direction with the same speed (not really possible but this is a thought experiment). The molecules travel across the container and hit the other side at which point things start to get messy. The molecules hit each other; they no longer have the same energy and direction but move about in random motion, some moving fast and others moving slowly, just like the way we know the molecules of gas behave. No matter how long we wait, the molecules will never line up with the same speed again (at least it is extremely unlikely) even though, according to the law of conservation of energy, this would be perfectly OK.

Just as physical systems tend to a position of lowest potential energy, they also tend to a state where the energy is most disordered. When a metal block is held above the ground each molecule has approximately the same amount of potential energy but when it is dropped onto the floor that energy goes to increase the kinetic and potential energy of the molecules of the block and ground. Those molecules interact with neighbouring molecules as the energy is spread out. This energy will never collect together again to allow the block to return to its original position.

So an engine that, for example, took heat energy from the random motion of molecules in the air and converted it all to work to lift a mass from the ground would be creating an ordered form of energy (the PE of the mass) out of the random spread of energy in the air and that is not possible. However, if some of the energy was put into a cold body the net effect could be a more disordered form of energy overall, so this could be possible.

The second law of thermodynamics states this in a concise way:

It is not possible for a heat engine working in a cycle to absorb thermal energy and convert it all to work.

This is the Kelvin–Planck statement of the law.

Entropy

The second law of thermodynamics is about the spreading out of energy. This can be quantified by using the quantity *entropy*.

The change of entropy is ΔS, when a quantity of heat flow into a body at temperature T is equal to $\frac{Q}{T}$.

$$\Delta S = \frac{Q}{T}$$

The unit of entropy is $J\,K^{-1}$.

For example, consider the situation of a 1 kg block of ice melting in a room that is at a constant temperature 300 K. To melt the block of ice, it must gain 3.35×10^5 J of energy. Ice melts at a constant 273 K so:

The gain in entropy of the ice $= \dfrac{3.35 \times 10^5}{273} = 1.23 \times 10^3 \, J\,K^{-1}$

The loss of entropy by the room $= \dfrac{3.35 \times 10^5}{300} = 1.12 \times 10^3 \, J\,K^{-1}$

We can see from this that the entropy has increased.

Entropy always increases in any transfer of heat since heat always flows from hot bodies to cold bodies. We can therefore rewrite the second law in terms of entropy.

In any cyclic process the entropy will either stay the same or increase.

Entropy is a measure of how spread out or disordered the energy has become. Saying entropy has increased implies that the energy has become more spread out.

This statement also implies that heat cannot spontaneously flow from a cold object to a hot object. We have seen that this is possible by reversing the cycle of a heat engine but then work must be done. A third way of stating the second law is therefore:

A Stirling engine will work if you put it either on top of a mug of hot coffee or on a bowl of ice. Provided there is a temperature difference, work can be done.

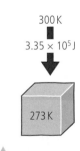

300 K

3.35×10^5 J

273 K

Figure 10.63.

It is not possible for heat to be transferred from a cold body to a warmer one without work being done.

This is the Clausius statement of the law.

To learn more about thermodynamics, go to the hotlinks site, search for the title or ISBN and click on Chapter 10.

Exercises

38 500 J of heat flows from a hot body at 400 K to a colder one at 250 K.

(a) Calculate the entropy change in
(i) the hot body
(ii) the cold body.

(b) What is the total change in entropy?

39 Use the second law to explain why heat is released when an electric motor is used to lift a heavy load.

10.3 Fluids and their dynamics

B.3 Fluids and their dynamics (HL only)

Understandings, applications, and skills:

(AHL) Density and pressure

(AHL) Buoyancy and Archimedes' principle
• Determining buoyancy forces using Archimedes' principle.

(AHL) Pascal's principle
• Solving problems involving pressure, density, and Pascal's principle.

(AHL) Hydrostatic equilibrium

(AHL) The ideal fluid

> *Guidance*
> • *Ideal fluids will be taken to mean fluids that are incompressible, non-viscous, and have steady flows.*

(AHL) Streamlines

(AHL) The continuity equation
• Solving problems using the continuity equation.

(AHL) The Bernoulli equation and the Bernoulli effect
• Explaining situations involving the Bernoulli effect.

> *Guidance*
> • *Proof of the Bernoulli equation will not be required for examination purposes.*
> • *Applications of the Bernoulli equation will involve (but not be limited to) flow out of a container, determining the speed of a plane (pitot tubes), and venturi tubes.*

(AHL) Stokes' law and viscosity
• Describing the frictional drag force exerted on small spherical objects in laminar fluid flow.
• Solving problems involving Stokes' law.

(AHL) Laminar and turbulent flow and the Reynolds number
• Determining the Reynolds number in simple situations.

> *Guidance*
> • *Laminar and turbulent flow will only be considered in simple situations.*
> • *Values of R < 10^3 will be taken to represent conditions for laminar flow.*

NATURE OF SCIENCE

In physics we often start by considering simple, ideal situations such as a body moving in space with no forces acting or the static pressure in an incompressible fluid. These simple models can then be combined to solve more complex problems.

Static fluids

In a lot of kinematics problems we imagine that there is no air. This makes the problem simpler since we don't have to take into account air resistance and buoyancy. However, if we want to model real situations then we need to include a consideration of these forces. In this section we will take a look at the way that fluids (gases and liquids) flow and how they affect the motion of bodies travelling through them, but first we will take a closer look at static fluids.

Density of a fluid

A fluid is substance that can flow. This can be either liquid or gas. The density of a fluid is defined in the same way as the density of a solid.

$$\text{density} = \frac{\text{mass}}{\text{volume}}$$

The unit of density is kg m^{-3}.

The density of a liquid can be found by finding the mass of a known volume. However, a more convenient way is to use a hydrometer (more about that later). The volume of a liquid is dependent on temperature so when quoting density we should also give the temperature. For example:

density of water at 4°C is $1.00 \times 10^3 \text{ kg m}^{-3}$.

Liquids are fairly incompressible so the volume of 1 m^3 of water cannot be changed significantly by pressing on the container. The volume of a gas is defined by the volume of the container; if the container is made smaller by pushing in the walls then the volume of the gas will get smaller. However, we know that for a given pressure and temperature the volume of a gas is constant, so when quoting gas density we need to give the pressure as well as the temperature. For example:

density of air at 0°C and 101 kPa is 1.29 kg m^{-3}.

 101.325 kPa is taken to be the 'standard atmospheric pressure' at sea level. This is an average value used to define (amongst other quantities) the density of gases.

Fluid pressure

We are familiar with the term 'pressure' as the force per unit area exerted by a gas on the walls of its container or the force per unit area exerted between two solid surfaces, but how does it apply to liquids? First let us consider a balloon containing water. If the balloon is squashed as in Figure 10.64 the liquid will push out sideways making the balloon wider. This is because the liquid is incompressible so its volume must stay the same. For the sides to move out there must be a force acting sideways.

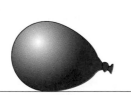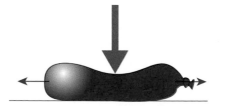

Figure 10.64 A water balloon is squashed.

To remove the complication caused by gravity we will first consider a cylinder of liquid in space as in Figure 10.65. If we push on the piston it won't move because the force will be balanced by the liquid pushing back. The liquid is exerting a force on the piston. If we now look at the disc of liquid just below the piston it has a force pushing it down (through the piston). If this was the only force acting this fluid would move down. It doesn't, so there must be a force acting upwards due the next layer of liquid. The pressure in a liquid doesn't just act in the direction of the applied force but it acts in all directions. If we consider a very small cube somewhere in the middle of the fluid then it will experience forces pushing on all sides as in Figure 10.65. These forces must be balanced, if they weren't the fluid would flow in the direction of the resultant force. So the pressure is the same *in all directions*.

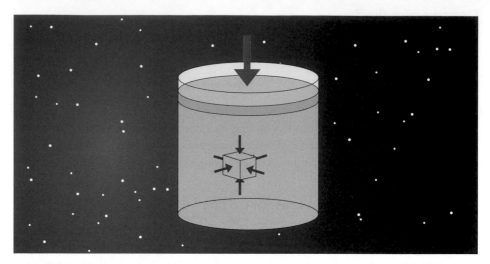

Figure 10.65 A cylinder of fluid (in space).

If the force on the piston was now increased it will increase the pressure on the surface of the piston. This would cause the fluid to flow but this doesn't happen, leading us to conclude that the pressure must have increased throughout the fluid. This leads to the Pascal principle, which states:

pressure applied to a confined fluid increases the pressure throughout the fluid.

This has many applications; for example, in the braking system of most cars which is represented by Figure 10.66.

Figure 10.66 A car braking system.

A force F_1 on the small piston causes the pressure, $P = \frac{F_1}{A_1}$ in the fluid. The fluid in the big cylinder will also have pressure P and will exert a force on the piston but this piston is much bigger so the force will be more $F_2 = PA_2 = \frac{F_1 A_2}{A_1}$.

Exercise

40 A force of 10 N is applied to the small piston of Figure 10.66. If the area of the piston is 1 cm² and the area of the big piston is 150 cm² calculate:

   (a) the pressure in the fluid.
   (b) the force on the big piston.

Hydrostatic equilibrium

On the Earth we don't have to trap liquids in cylinders with a piston since gravity holds the liquid there for us. Let us again consider a small cube of liquid, this time at the top as in Figure 10.67. The top surface has no fluid pressure acting on it (assuming no air) but the bottom surface is surrounded by liquid so will have pressure P acting on it. If the area of the bottom is A then the upward force acting on the cube will be PA. This force must be balanced by the weight of the cube or the fluid would flow. This is called *hydrostatic equilibrium.*

If the forces are balanced we can write, $PA = mg$
where m is the mass of the cube = volume × density
$= \rho Ah$.

So, $PA = \rho Ahg$, giving:

$$P = \rho gh$$

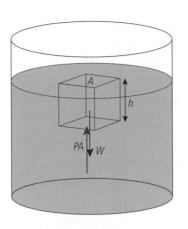

Effect of atmosphere

If there is air above the fluid it will press down
on the fluid increasing the pressure. According
to Pascal's principle the pressure will increase
throughout the fluid so if atmospheric pressure is
P_A the pressure at depth h will be:

$$P = P_A + \rho gh$$

The U-tube manometer

A U-tube manometer consists of a transparent tube containing a liquid as in Figure
10.68. It is used to measure the pressure of a gas from the difference in height of the
liquid in two sides of the tube. If the liquid is in equilibrium then the pressure at the
bottom of each column must be equal so if both sides are open to the atmosphere then
the pressure at the bottom of each will be $\rho gh + P_A$ so they have the same length as in
Figure 10.68(a). However, if the pressure on one side is higher then the height of liquid
on the other side must rise to compensate as in Figure 10.68(b).

(a)

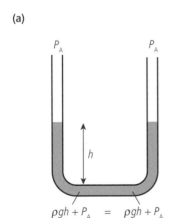

$\rho gh + P_A \quad = \quad \rho gh + P_A$

(b)

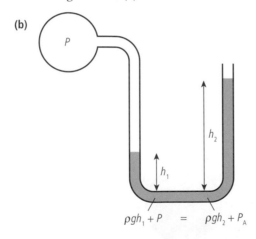

$\rho gh_1 + P \quad = \quad \rho gh_2 + P_A$

Now $\rho gh_1 + P = \rho gh_2 + P_A$
so $P = P_A + \rho g(h_2 - h_1)$

Bouyancy and Archimedes' principle

Consider a solid cube immersed in a fluid as shown in Figure 10.69. The bottom
surface of the cube is deeper than the top so the pressure will be greater.

If the top is at depth h_1 and the bottom h_2 then the difference in force will be:

$$F_2 - F_1 = \rho gh_2 A - \rho gh_1 A = \rho g A(h_2 - h_1)$$

Figure 10.67 Pressure in a
small cube of liquid at the
surface.

Gauge pressure.

Pressure sensors actually
measure the difference
between the pressure
in a container and the
atmospheric pressure.
To find the absolute
pressure inside the
container the zero has
to be adjusted by adding
the atmospheric pressure
on that day. Most labs
will have a barometer
hanging on the wall to
facilitate this.

Figure 10.68 The U-tube
manometer.

Figure 10.69.

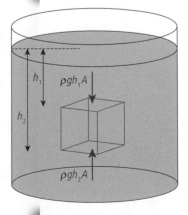

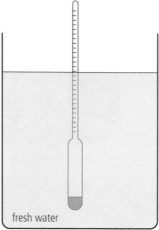

salt water

fresh water

▲
Figure 10.70 A hydrometer floats at different heights in two different liquids.

but $(h_2 - h_1)$ is the height of the cube, so $A(h_2 - h_1)$ is the volume and $\rho g A(h_2 - h_1)$ is therefore the weight of an equal volume of liquid. This is what Archimedes concluded with his principle:

The buoyant force on a body immersed in a fluid is equal to the weight of fluid displaced.

When a body floats the buoyant force must equal the weight so the part that is under the surface must displace an amount of fluid equal to the weight of the body. This implies that the density of the floating object must be less than the fluid. This principle is used to measure the density of a fluid as shown in Figure 10.70.

Worked example

The density of water is $1.0 \times 10^3 \text{ kg m}^{-3}$ and the density of iron is $7.8 \times 10^3 \text{ kg m}^{-3}$. Calculate the force required to lift a 60 kg ball of iron from the bottom of a swimming pool.

Solution

First let's draw a diagram of the forces:

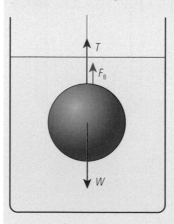

Figure 10.71.

Assuming the ball is lifted at constant velocity the forces are balanced:

$$T + F_B = W = 60 \times 9.8 = 588 \text{ N}$$

F_B = weight of fluid displaced = volume of ball × density of water × g

$$\text{volume of ball} = \frac{\text{mass}}{\text{density of iron}} = \frac{60}{7.8 \times 10^3} = 7.7 \times 10^{-3} \text{ m}^3$$

$$F_B = 7.7 \times 10^{-3} \times 1.0 \times 10^3 \times 9.8 = 75.4 \text{ N}$$

$$T = W - F_B = 588 - 75.4 = 512.6 \text{ N}$$

41 Calculate the force required to lift a 60 kg ball of gold (density 19.3×10^3 kg m^{-3}) from the bottom of a swimming pool.

42 A 1 m^3 wooden cube floats in water so that 40 cm of the cube is above the water. Calculate:

(a) the density of the wood.

(b) how much force would be required to sink the cube.

43 The density of sea water is 1.03×10^3 kg m^{-3} and the density of ice is 0.92×10^3 kg m^{-3}. Show that when ice floats in sea water 89% is under the surface.

44 A cylinder of gas with a frictionless piston has a volume of 100 cm^3 on the surface of a swimming pool. Calculate its volume at a depth of 5 m.

(atmospheric pressure = 101 kPa)

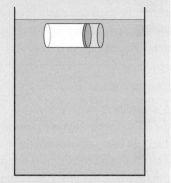

Figure 10.72.

To control their buoyancy divers wear something that looks like a life jacket called a BCD (buoyancy control device). This is inflated with air to compensate for the weight of the air tanks etc. As the diver goes deeper, the air in the BCD becomes compressed reducing its buoyancy.

Fluid dynamics

So far we have dealt with static fluids. In this section we will consider fluids in motion, flowing through pipes and past objects, with the aim of deriving mathematical models for different practical examples. To get a full understanding of the motion of a fluid we need to be able to predict where each part of the fluid will be at any time. If you have ever watched smoke rising from a fire you will be familiar with the way it swirls about as it rises. This sort of motion is very difficult to predict so we need to make some simplifications.

Ideal fluids

The volume of real fluids, particularly gases, gets less when the pressure is increased. Changes of pressure within the fluid cause unbalanced forces resulting in fluid flow that is difficult to predict. We will only consider fluids that are incompressible; this is a reasonable assumption for liquids but is only true for gases if the pressure differences are small. Another complication is that there is friction between different parts of the liquid. When a real fluid flows through a pipe the fluid in contact with the pipe is stationary. This stationary layer slows down the next layer. This internal friction is called *viscosity*.

An ideal fluid is one that is incompressible and has zero viscosity.

Steady flow

By dropping a rubber duck into a river it is possible to track the movement of the water; the path of a particle of water (or the duck) is called a *flowline*. If the duck follows the same path every time it is dropped at the same point then the flow is said to be *steady*. If the duck swirls around in an unpredictable way then the flow is *turbulent*.

Streamline

A *streamline* is a curve whose tangent at any point is in the direction of the velocity of the fluid. These could be plotted by measuring the instantaneous velocity of many ducks as they move down the river. A duck can only have one velocity at a time. If streamlines crossed then the particle would have two velocities; for this reason streamlines can't cross. We can think of a streamline as a snapshot of the velocities of all the particles at one moment of time; if the flow is steady then this will not vary with time. A *flowline* shows the path of one particle over a period of time; if the flow is steady this will be the same as the streamline.

flowline

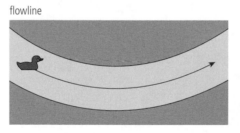

streamline

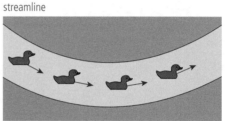

Figure 10.73 Flowline and streamline.

The continuity equation

Consider a fluid of density ρ flowing steadily through a straight wide pipe of cross-sectional area A as in Figure 10.74. If there is no viscosity, all parts of the fluid will flow at the same velocity so the whole cross section of fluid will progress a distance L in time Δt. Since the cross-sectional area is constant the volume flowing in time Δt is AL.

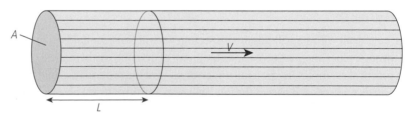

Figure 10.74.

So mass flowing per unit time = $\dfrac{\rho AL}{\Delta t}$.

But $\dfrac{L}{\Delta t}$ is the velocity of the fluid, so mass per unit time = ρAv.

If this pipe was connected to a second pipe with smaller cross-sectional area as in Figure 10.75, the mass of fluid flowing in per unit time = $\rho_1 A_1 v_1$ and the mass flowing out = $\rho_2 A_2 v_2$.

Figure 10.75 Fluid flows into a narrow section. Notice how the streamlines get closer together as the fluid speeds up.

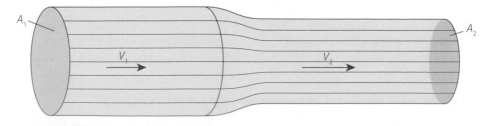

If there are no leaks then the mass flowing in per unit time = mass flowing out per unit time so:

$$\rho_1 A_1 v_1 = \rho_2 A_2 v_2.$$

If the fluid is incompressible then $\rho_1 = \rho_2$ so

$$A_1 v_1 = A_2 v_2.$$

This is called the *continuity equation* and implies that the thinner the pipe the faster the flow. If you have ever watched a river as it flows through a narrow opening or squirted water by squeezing the end of a hose pipe then you'll know about this already.

Exercises

45 A river of width 20 m and depth 3 m flows at a speed of 1 m s⁻¹. Calculate the increase in speed if the depth changes to 1 m.

46 Water flows through a pipe of diameter 1 m at a rate of 1.5 m³ s⁻¹. The pipe is connected to a second pipe a diameter of 0.5 m. Calculate the speed in the second pipe.

47 A simple water pistol is made out of a cylinder with a moveable piston as shown in Figure 10.76. The cylinder is filled with water and the piston is depressed at a constant speed in 4 seconds. Calculate the speed at which the water is squirted out.

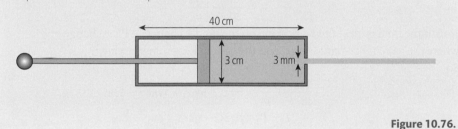

Figure 10.76.

The Bernoulli equation

When a fluid flows into a section of pipe with smaller cross-sectional area its velocity increases. This implies there must be an unbalanced force acting so the pressure on the slow-moving side must be bigger than on the fast-moving side. We also know that if a fluid flows in a vertical pipe, the pressure is greater at the bottom than at the top. So the pressure of water as it flows through the pipes will depend on the elevation and cross-sectional area of the pipes, Bernoulli's equation relates these quantities. First, let us consider water flowing in a uniform horizontal pipe as in Figure 10.77.

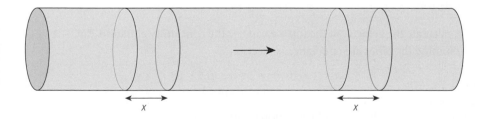

Figure 10.77 Water flowing in a horizontal pipe.

The section of water between the red markers progresses a distance x in time Δt. Since the liquid is incompressible the distance x moved by each end is the same. This is not the case with the pipe in Figure 10.78.

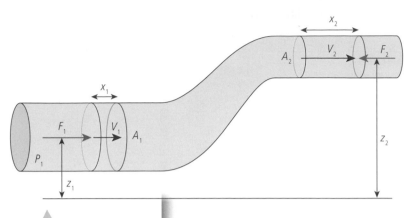

Figure 10.78 Water flowing uphill in a narrowing pipe.

In many countries water tanks are placed on hills so that the force of gravity can be used to make the water flow through pipes. What happens in flat countries? Do you know where the water in your taps comes from?

Let us again consider the section of fluid between the two red markers. The pipe at the top is narrower than at the bottom so when the fluid at the bottom advances a distance x_1 the same volume of fluid at the top will advance a greater distance x_2. As the fluid rises it gains PE and as it speeds up it gains KE, so the fluid outside the red markers must be doing work on it. The water at the bottom is being pushed by F_1 but the water at the top is pushing against F_2 so:

$$\text{net work done} = \begin{array}{c}\text{work done on the water} \\ \text{at the bottom}\end{array} - \begin{array}{c}\text{work done on the water} \\ \text{at the top}\end{array}$$

$$W = F_1x_1 - F_2x_2 = P_1A_1x_1 - P_2A_2x_2$$

$Ax = \text{volume} = \dfrac{\text{mass}}{\text{density}}$ but the mass of water (m) is the same at the top and bottom so

$$W = \frac{P_1m}{\rho} - \frac{P_2m}{\rho}$$

Now if the fluid is ideal the work done on the fluid = change in PE + change in KE where the gain in PE = $mgz_2 - mgz_1$ and the gain in KE = $\frac{1}{2}mv_2^2 - \frac{1}{2}mv_1^2$.
So

$$\frac{P_1m}{\rho} - \frac{P_2m}{\rho} = mgz_2 - mgz_1 + \frac{1}{2}mv_2^2 - \frac{1}{2}mv_1^2$$

$$P_1 - P_2 = \rho gz_2 - \rho gz_1 + \frac{1}{2}\rho v_2^2 - \frac{1}{2}v_1^2$$

$$P_1 + \frac{1}{2}\rho v_1^2 + \rho gz_1 = P_2 + \frac{1}{2}\rho v_2^2 + \rho gz_2$$

or
$$P + \frac{1}{2}\rho v^2 + \rho gz = \text{constant}$$

This is the Bernoulli equation and can be applied along any streamline.

Worked example

Water flows into the bottom of a section of pipe similar to Figure 10.78 with a pressure of 4×10^5 Pa and speed 2.0 m s^{-1}. Calculate the speed and pressure of the water at the top if the diameter of the bottom is 2.0 cm, the diameter of the top 1.0 cm, and the height difference 5 m.

Solution

To calculate the velocity at the top we can use the continuity equation $A_1v_1 = A_2v_2$
Assuming the pipes are circular cross section

$$\pi \times (1 \times 10^{-2})^2 \times 2 = \pi \times (0.5 \times 10^{-2})^2 \times v_2$$
$$v_2 = 8 \text{ m s}^{-1}$$

Now we can use the Bernoulli equation to find the pressure

$$P_1 + \frac{1}{2}\rho v_1^2 + \rho gz_1 = P_2 + \frac{1}{2}\rho v_2^2 + \rho gz_2$$

If we take the lower pipe at ground level then $z_1 = 0$

$$4 \times 10^5 + \frac{1}{2} \times 1000 \times 2^2 + 0 = P_2 + \frac{1}{2} \times 1000 \times 8^2 + 1000 \times 10 \times 5$$

$$P_2 = 400\,000 + 2000 - 32\,000 - 50\,000 = 320\,000 \text{ Pa} = 3.2 \times 10^5 \text{ Pa}$$

48 Water with speed 3 m s⁻¹ at a pressure of 500 kPa flows through a horizontal pipe that widens from diameter 2 cm to 6 cm. Assuming the fluid to be ideal, calculate:

  (a) the volume flowing per second.
  (b) the velocity of the water in the wider pipe.
  (c) the pressure in the wider pipe.

49 Water flows from a water tank at the top of a building to a washroom 20 m below. The water enters a pipe with diameter 3 cm at a pressure 100 kPa travelling at 0.5 m s⁻¹. The last metre of pipe connected to the tap in the washroom has a diameter of 1 cm. Calculate:

  (a) the volume flowing per second.
  (b) the velocity of water through the pipe connected to the tap.
  (c) the pressure in the pipe connected to the tap.

There's a hole in my bucket

Using the Bernoulli equation we can calculate the rate at which water runs out of a hole in a bucket. Consider a bucket with a small hole in the bottom as shown in Figure 10.79.

If we treat the bucket as our first section of pipe and the hole as the second, assuming these can be connected by a streamline we can apply the Bernoulli equation to get:

$$P_a + \rho g h + \tfrac{1}{2}\rho v_1^2 = P_a + \rho g \times 0 + \tfrac{1}{2}\rho v_2^2$$

Note that the pressure at the top is the same as the pressure at the bottom so the P_a terms cancel out to give:

$$\rho g h + \tfrac{1}{2}\rho v_1^2 = \tfrac{1}{2}\rho v_2^2$$

If the bucket is big and the hole small then the water level goes down so slowly that we can assume $v_1 = 0$. The equation then simplifies to:

$$\rho g h = \tfrac{1}{2}\rho v_2^2$$

So
$$v_2 = \sqrt{2gh}$$

This result is known as Torricelli's theorem. According to this equation the velocity of the fluid will be the same as if it had fallen from the same height.

The Venturi meter

The difference in pressure when a fluid flows through a constriction can be used to measure fluid flow. Consider the situation in Figure 10.80.

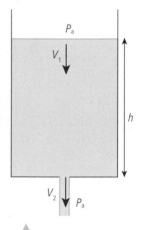

Figure 10.79 Water running out of a hole in a bucket.

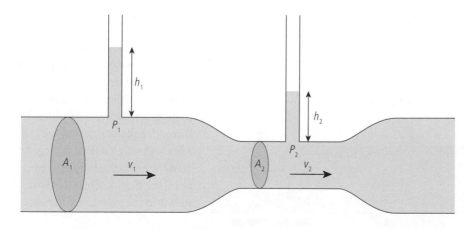

Figure 10.80 Water flowing through a constriction.

The vertical tubes (manometers) are used to measure the pressure difference. The pressure at the bottom of the tubes will be proportional to the height of fluid ($P_1 = \rho g h_1$, $P_2 = \rho g h_2$).

This tube is horizontal so the Bernoulli equation simplifies to:

$$P_1 + \tfrac{1}{2}\rho v_1^2 = P_2 + \tfrac{1}{2}\rho v_2^2$$

so the pressure difference

$$P_1 - P_2 = \tfrac{1}{2}\rho v_2^2 - \tfrac{1}{2}\rho v_1^2$$

But $\qquad P_1 - P_2 = \rho g \Delta h$ so $\rho g \Delta h = \tfrac{1}{2}\rho v_2^2 - \tfrac{1}{2}\rho v_1^2$

$$g\Delta h = \tfrac{1}{2}(v_2^2 - v_1^2)$$

Applying the continuity equation we find that $A_1 v_1 = A_2 v_2$ so $v_2 = \dfrac{A_1 v_1}{A_2}$.

So $\qquad g\Delta h = \tfrac{1}{2}v_1^2\left[\left(\dfrac{A_1}{A_2}\right)^2 - 1\right]$

If we know A_1, A_2, and Δh we can find v_1.

Stagnation pressure

According to the Bernoulli equation, when a fluid is bought to rest the pressure must increase. To see why this is the case let us consider the situation in Figure 10.81.

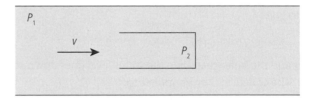

Figure 10.81.

The fluid is flowing towards a stationary closed pipe so at some point must stop. If we apply the Bernoulli equation to the fluid that stops we get:

$$P_1 + \tfrac{1}{2}\rho v^2 = P_2$$

so we can see that the pressure in the closed section of pipe (*the stagnation pressure*) is greater than in the rest of the fluid. By measuring the difference we can find the flow rate.

$$P_2 - P_1 = \tfrac{1}{2}\rho v^2$$

You may be wondering how we can apply the Bernoulli equation when the fluid doesn't all flow into the closed tube. The Bernoulli equation can be applied to *any* streamline and there is a streamline that starts in the main flow and ends in front of the closed tube.

Pitot static tube

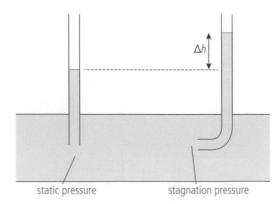

A pitot static tube uses the difference between the stagnation pressure and the pressure of the flowing fluid (static pressure) to measure the velocity of fluid through a pipe or the velocity of a body through a fluid. In Figure 10.82 the flowing fluid is used to fill the manometers used to measure the pressure difference.

Figure 10.82 The pitot static tube.

static pressure   stagnation pressure

Figure 10.83 shows the type of pitot tube that could be used to measure the speed of an airplane. The open end stops the air flowing into it and the opening at the top measures the pressure of the air moving past. Here the difference in pressure $P_2 - P_1 = \rho g \Delta h$ where ρ is the density of the liquid in the manometer.

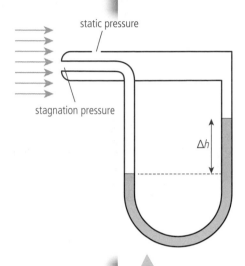

Figure 10.83 Measuring the speed of an airplane.

The pitot tube on an airplane is covered while the plane is on the ground.

Exercises

50 A pitot tube as in Figure 10.83 with a water-filled manometer is used to measure the wind speed in an air tunnel. Calculate the speed if the difference in height of the manometer columns is 3 cm.

density of air = $1.3 \, \text{kg m}^{-3}$
density of water = $1000 \, \text{kg m}^{-3}$

51 Calculate the difference in pressure in a pitot tube used to measure the speed of an airplane travelling at $600 \, \text{km h}^{-1}$.

52 Calculate the volume of water flowing through the Venturi meter shown in Figure 10.84.

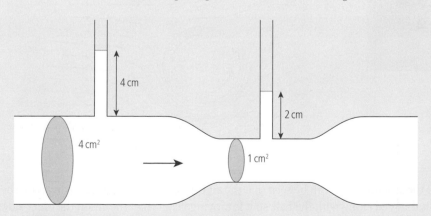

Figure 10.84 A Venturi meter.

The Venturi effect can be used to produce a fine spray used in some fuel injection systems (particularly carburettors) and perfume atomizers. Air is blown across the opening of a tube connected to a container of liquid, the fast-moving air creates a pressure difference causing the liquid to rise to the top of the tube where it is blown away in the stream of air.

Examples of the Bernoulli effect

Although Bernoulli's equation gives a neat explanation of the effects described on this page, it does not give the full picture. The lift of an airplane wing is caused more by the air deflected off the tilted wing than the pressure difference caused by different velocities of air. In the example of the spinning ball, uneven turbulence gives the reason for the sideways force. Simple is not always best (or correct).

The most obvious example of the Bernoulli effect is the wing cross section of an airplane (Figure 10.85). Air travelling over the top surface travels further so must have a higher velocity than the air on the underside. According to the Bernoulli equation, faster-moving air will have lower pressure which results in an upwards force on the wing.

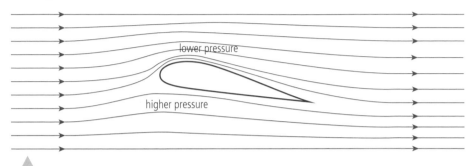

lower pressure

higher pressure

Figure 10.85 The streamlines around a wing.

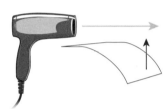

Figure 10.86 Blowing across the top of a piece of paper.

Another example which is not quite so useful but easy to try at home can be demonstrated by blowing across the top of a piece of paper as in Figure 10.86. One might think that the air would push the paper down but it is forced *up* due the low-pressure, fast-moving air on its upper surface.

If you play any ball sports you will be familiar with the way a ball can be made to change direction (swerve) by spinning it. This can also be explained in terms of the Bernoulli effect. When a spinning ball travels through the air, one side of the ball is moving in the direction of motion the other against it, as shown in Figure 10.88. Here, the ball is seen stationary with the air flowing to the left. This is equivalent to the ball moving to the right.

Figure 10.87 The falling cylinder is made to spin as the string unwinds.

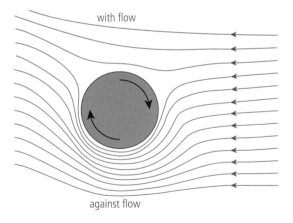

with flow

against flow

Figure 10.88 Streamlines around a spinning ball.

From the streamlines it can be seen that the air on the side of the ball moving with the flow is dragged along with the ball, so it is moving faster than the air on the other side. According to the Bernoulli principle the pressure in the fast-moving air will be lower, resulting in an unbalanced force downwards. You may not be able to make a football swerve as much as David Beckham used to be able to, but you can make a paper cylinder change direction if made to spin while falling.

Real fluids

So far, we have been dealing with ideal fluids that have no internal friction. This means that if two parallel plates are separated by an ideal fluid they can be slid past each other with no opposing force. Real fluids aren't like that; the fluid in contact with each plate will stick to the plate and move along with it. Intermolecular forces between layers of fluid result in a force opposing the relative motion of the plates. The size of this force is different for different fluids.

Viscosity

Consider two parallel plates separated by a fluid as in Figure 10.89. The fluid next to the top plate is moving to the right with the plate and the fluid at the bottom is stationary along with the bottom plate. Such flow is called *lamina flow* as the different layers (lamina) do not mix. This only happens at quite low velocities.

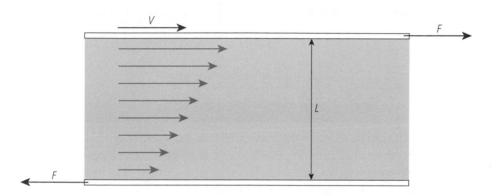

Figure 10.89 Lamina flow.

The force opposing the motion of the plates will get bigger if the plates move faster or have larger area (A) but smaller if the distance between them (L) is increased so:

$$F \propto A\frac{v}{L}$$

The other factor affecting the force is the nature of the fluid. Something like water would cause little force but a thick, sticky liquid like syrup or honey will cause a big force. This property is called the viscosity, denoted by the Greek letter η (eta):

$$F = \eta A\frac{v}{L}$$

The unit of viscosity (η) is $N\,s\,m^{-2}$.

Stoke's law

When bodies move through fluids they experience an opposing force due to the viscosity of the fluid. It follows from the definition of viscosity that the magnitude of the force on a sphere moving through a fluid is proportional to the size of the sphere and its speed. In fact it can be shown that if the flow of the fluid around the sphere is lamina, the force F on a sphere of radius r travelling at velocity v is given by the equation:

$$F = 6\pi\eta rv$$

This is known as *Stokes' law*.

Terminal velocity

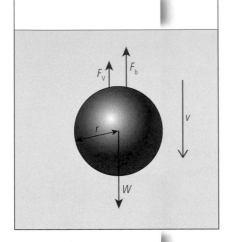

Figure 10.90 Terminal velocity.

According to Stokes' law if a sphere is falling under gravity through a viscous fluid there will be a force opposing its motion that is proportional to its velocity. This means that at some point the viscous forces on the sphere will be balanced and it will no longer accelerate. Then we say the sphere has reached its *terminal velocity*. Let us look at this in more detail: at some velocity v the forces are as shown in Figure 10.90.

There are two upward forces: buoyancy and viscous force. If the sum of these equals the weight then terminal velocity has been reached. So at terminal velocity:

$$F_v + F_b = W$$

From Stokes' law $$F_v = 6\pi\eta r v_t$$

$$\text{buoyancy} = \text{weight of fluid displaced} = \frac{4}{3} \times \pi r^3 \rho_f g \ (\rho_f \text{ is fluid density})$$

$$\text{weight} = \frac{4}{3} \times \pi r^3 \rho_s g \ (\rho_s \text{ is sphere density})$$

$$6\pi\eta r v_t + \frac{4}{3} \times \pi r^3 \rho_f g = \frac{4}{3} \times \pi r^3 \rho_s g$$

$$v_t = \frac{2}{9} \frac{g r^2}{\eta} (\rho_s - \rho_f)$$

This relationship can be tested by measuring the terminal velocity of a balloon dropped in the air or small balls dropped into a glass cylinder containing oil. The relationship does not hold for balls dropped in the air since their velocity becomes so great that the flow is no longer lamina but turbulent.

Turbulent flow

Water flowing slowly down a stream can be considered laminar but as the velocity increases the water will start to swirl about and become turbulent. The velocity at which this happens in a pipe can be found from *Reynolds number* (R_e). This defined by the equation:

$$R_e = \frac{v r \rho}{\eta}$$

where v is the average speed of the fluid and r the radius of the pipe.

Turbulence occurs when R_e exceeds 1000.

To learn more about fluids and their dynamics, go to the hotlinks site, search for the title or ISBN and click on Chapter 10.

Exercises

53 Calculate the terminal velocity of a 0.5 cm radius steel ball falling through oil.
density of oil = 900 kg m^{-3}
density of steel = 8000 kg m^{-3}
viscosity of oil = 0.2 N s m^{-2}

54 Calculate the density of a ball of radius 3 cm that has a terminal velocity of 0.5 m s^{-1} falling through the same oil as in Exercise 53.

55 Calculate the volume flow rate at which the flow of water through a 2 cm diameter pipe becomes turbulent.
viscosity of water = 0.002 N s m^{-2}

10.4 Forced vibration and resonance

B.4 Forced vibrations and resonance (HL only)

Understandings, applications, and skills:

(AHL) Natural frequency of vibration
- Qualitatively and quantitatively describing examples of under-, over-, and critically damped oscillations.
- Graphically describing the variation of the amplitude of vibration with driving frequency of an object close to its natural frequency of vibration.

(AHL) Q factor and damping
- Solving problems involving Q factor.

(AHL) Periodic stimulus and the driving frequency
- Describing the phase relationship between driving frequency and forced oscillations.

(AHL) Resonance
- Describing the useful and destructive effects of resonance.

  Guidance
  - *Only amplitude resonance is required.*

NATURE OF SCIENCE

Damping occurs when a pendulum moves through air. By combining what we know from the study of simple harmonic motion and motion through fluids we can derive a model for damped harmonic motion.

Resonance is a phenomenon related to mechanical vibrations. However, the same model can be applied to electrical circuits, molecules, atoms, and nuclei.

Damped harmonic motion

When dealing with oscillations we only considered simple harmonic motion; that is, motion where the acceleration of a body is proportional to the displacement from a fixed point and always directed towards that point; for example, a mass on the end of a stiff spring attached to the side

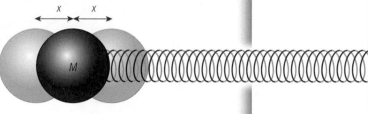

of a space ship (no gravity or air) as in Figure 10.91. When the mass moves to the left the spring gets stretched and according to Hooke's law the force will be proportional to the extension; when the mass moves to the right the spring is compressed and the force pushing back is proportional to compression.

This motion can be represented by the equation $ma = -kx$.

This implies that the displacement, $x = a \cos \omega t$. In other words, the motion is sinusoidal as represented by Figure 10.92: ω is the angular frequency, $2\pi f$, where F is the *natural frequency* of the oscillation.

Figure 10.91 A mass on a spring (in space).

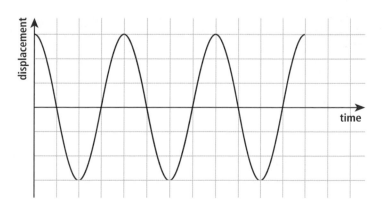

Figure 10.92 Free oscillation of a mass on a spring.

If we now add a fluid around the ball then it will experience a viscous force opposing the motion. This force is proportional to the velocity of the ball so the equation for the force becomes:

$$ma = -kx - bv \text{ where } b \text{ is some constant.}$$

Solving this equation reveals that $x = ae^{-bt/m}\cos \omega t$

so the amplitude decreases exponentially with time as shown in Figure 10.93.

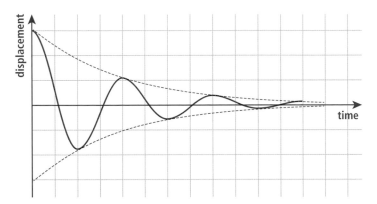

Figure 10.93 Lightly damped harmonic motion; the red line shows the exponential change of amplitude.

A car suspension is critically damped to prevent the car oscillating after it goes over a bump in the road.

The value of bm in the equation is equivalent to the decay constant in nuclear decay. If it is large, then the amplitude will decrease in a short time. b is the constant of proportionality relating the drag force with the velocity ($F_D = bv$) so if the mass was surrounded by a much more viscous fluid then the drag force would be greater resulting in heavier damping. If the fluid is very viscous the damping could be so heavy that the spring would not oscillate at all. The damping is said to be *critical* if the mass returns to the equilibrium position without crossing it as in Figure 10.94.

Figure 10.94 Critically damped harmonic motion.

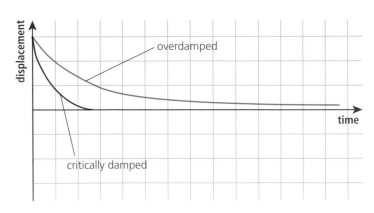

 You can see how the different constants affect the oscillation by simulating damping with Excel®.

The Q factor

The quality or Q factor of an oscillation gives us a measure of how many complete cycles will occur before the energy becomes zero. When a body oscillates there is a continual exchange of energy from one form to another. For the example of a mass on a spring; when the spring is displaced the spring has elastic potential energy; as it accelerates this is converted to kinetic energy, then back into potential energy. The total energy remains constant but it alternates between kinetic and potential. When there is damping the total energy decreases exponentially. Figure 10.95 shows the kinetic, potential, and total energy for an oscillating body.

If the damping is heavy then the energy will decrease more quickly. The Q factor is defined as:

$$Q = 2\pi \frac{\text{energy stored}}{\text{energy lost per cycle}}$$

For a mass on a spring the Q factor is given by the equation $Q = \frac{\sqrt{mk}}{b}$

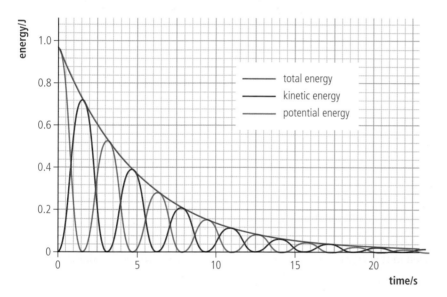

Figure 10.95.

So taking the example shown in Figure 10.95 the initial energy stored is 1.00 J. This is the same as the PE at the start. The energy after 1 cycle will be the same as the PE after one cycle which is 0.28 J. Remember that the PE is maximum every time the body has maximum displacement, so one cycle isn't the time between two maxima but the time between every other maximum in potential energy (about 6 s).

So, from the definition $Q = 2\pi \dfrac{1.00}{1.00 - 0.28} = 8.7$

If the Q factor is big then the system does not lose much energy per cycle so will go on for a long time. For large values this is approximately the number of oscillations the system will perform before it runs out of energy. A guitar string has a Q factor of about 1000 since although the vibration only lasts for a few seconds the frequency is high. An undamped oscillation will go on for ever so has an infinite Q factor. A critically damped oscillation has $Q = \frac{1}{2}$.

56 Estimate the Q factor for the damped oscillation represented in Figure 10.96 if the frequency is 0.5 Hz.

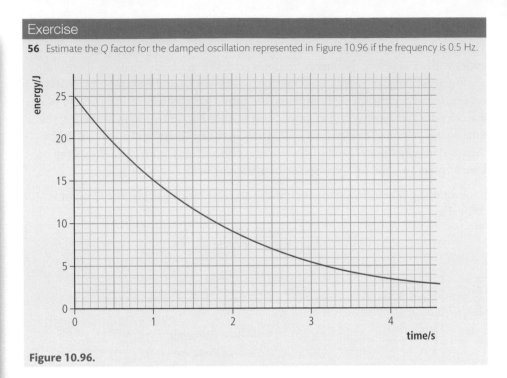

Figure 10.96.

Forced vibration

When an oscillating system such as a mass on a spring is disturbed it will oscillate at its own natural frequency $= \frac{1}{2\pi}\sqrt{\frac{k}{m}}$. The mass can also be made to vibrate at other frequencies by applying a sinusoidally varying force as in Figure 10.97. Here energy is being transferred from the motor driving the oscillating platform to the ball and spring.

When driven in this way the mass and spring will oscillate with the frequency of the driver.

Simulation of forced harmonic motion

Using a simulation programme like Algodoo® or Interactive physics® it is possible to make a simulation just like the one in Figure 10.97. By varying the speed of the wheel we can investigate how the amplitude depends upon the driving frequency. Figure 10.98 shows the results from such a simulated experiment where the natural frequency of the mass–spring system was 2 Hz.

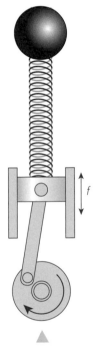

Figure 10.97 A driven oscillator.

Figure 10.98 Graph of amplitude *vs* frequency for a driven oscillator.

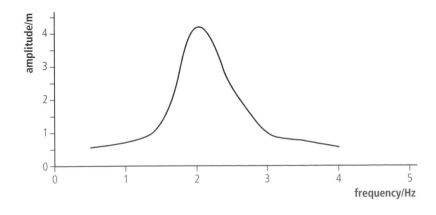

From this graph we can see that the amplitude is biggest when the driving frequency is equal to the natural frequency of the mass and spring; this is called *resonance*. You will have experienced the same phenomenon if you have ever been pushed on a swing by someone with no sense of rhythm. If the pushes are not at the natural frequency of the swing the amplitude is small. However, if the pushes are at the same frequency the amplitude becomes large.

Resonance

Resonance is an important phenomenon, both in mechanics and in other areas of physics, so is worth studying in detail.

Effect of damping

In a lightly damped system the resonant frequency is the same as the natural frequency but if the damping is heavy the resonant frequency is reduced. Figure 10.99 shows two resonance curves, one with light damping and one with heavy damping. The resonance peak for the lightly damped situation is also sharper than the heavily damped example.

It is possible to shatter a wine glass if it is made to vibrate at its own natural frequency.

Figure 10.99 Resonance curves with light and heavy damping. Notice that the resonant frequency is slightly less when the damping is heavy.

Figure 10.100 Resonance curves with different Q factors.

When a damped oscillator is driven the energy supplied by the driver is providing energy to drive the system plus doing work against the damping force. The Q factor gives us a measure of the amount of damping so an oscillation with a high Q factor will have a sharp resonance peak (Figure 10.100). The Q factor is defined by the equation:

$$Q = 2\pi \frac{\text{energy stored}}{\text{energy lost per cycle}}$$

In the case of resonance the amplitude of the oscillation is not decreasing since energy is continually supplied by the driver.

energy loss per cycle = energy loss per unit time × time for one cycle

$$= \text{power loss} \times \frac{1}{\text{resonant frequency}}$$

so

$$Q = 2\pi \times \text{resonant frequency} \times \frac{\text{energy stored}}{\text{power loss}}$$

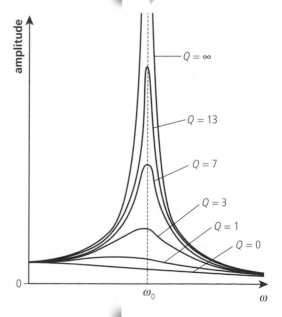

Phase difference between driver and driven

Figure 10.101 Phase difference of $\frac{\pi}{2}$ at resonance.

Figure 10.102 In phase when driver has a lower frequency than the natural frequency.

Figure 10.103 Out of phase when driver has a higher frequency than the natural frequency.

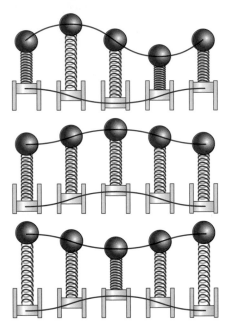

Figure 10.101 shows a mass–spring system being driven at its natural frequency. By observing the different stages in the cycle we can see that the driver is a quarter of a cycle ahead of the oscillating mass. This is equivalent to a phase difference of $\frac{\pi}{2}$. If the driving frequency is much less than the natural frequency then the mass and spring oscillate in phase with the driver as shown in Figure 10.102. If the driving frequency is higher the phase difference is π as in Figure 10.103.

Exercise

57 Figure 10.104 shows a series of pendula suspended on the same string. When pendulum A starts to swing it disturbs the suspension forcing pendulums B, C, D, E, and F to oscillate.

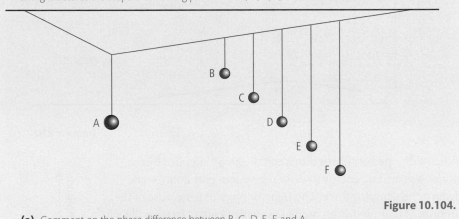

Figure 10.104.

(a) Comment on the phase difference between B, C, D, E, F, and A.
(b) Which pendulum will have the largest amplitude?

Examples of resonance

- A lorry drives past a room and makes plates rattle on a shelf.
- An opera singer shatters a wine glass by singing a note with the same frequency as its resonant frequency.
- Infrared radiation resonates with a CO_2 molecule.
- The air in a tube resonates to produce a sound when a wind instrument is blown.
- A resonating quartz crystal is the basis of many clocks.
- An engine part may break if it resonates with the frequency of the engine.
- A tall building can collapse if its natural frequency is the same as the frequency of an earthquake.

Electrical resonance

Consider a capacitor C, resistor R, and coil of wire L connected as shown in Figure 10.105.

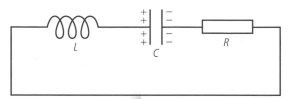

Figure 10.105 An LCR circuit.

At the present time the capacitor is charged, creating a pd across the resistance, resulting in a flow of current through the coil. The current in the coil will induce a magnetic field but the changing magnetic field in the coil induces a current in the coil that opposes the change producing it, causing current to flow back onto the capacitor. The charge oscillates back and forth, energy changing from electric to magnetic. The frequency of the oscillation depends on the size of the capacitor and coil and the resistance causes damping. If this circuit is connected to a variable frequency AC supply the current will be made to oscillate in the circuit. If the frequency is the same as the natural frequency then resonance occurs and the current flowing is a maximum. Figure 10.106 shows the resonance curves for different values of R.

This circuit is used in a radio receiver. The values of L (this is related to the coil) and C are varied to match the frequency of a radio station. An aerial picks up all radio stations but the circuit resonates with the one that has the same frequency as the natural frequency. By reducing the resistance of the circuit the peak can be made narrower (reduced bandwidth), making the circuit more selective.

> **TOK** An electrical oscillator has no moving parts but can be modelled in the same way as a mass on a spring.

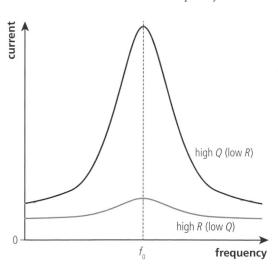

high Q (low R)

high R (low Q)

Figure 10.106 Resonance curves for different values of R.

> To learn more about forced vibrations and resonance, go to the hotlinks site, search for the title or ISBN and click on Chapter 10.

Practice questions

1. When a person lifts a suitcase, the spine experiences large extra forces. In a simplified model of the situation, the spine can be treated as a rigid rod (Figure 10.107).
   In this model, when the suitcase is lifted, three extra forces act on the spine which need to be in equilibrium.

   - The additional force due to lifting the suitcase, S.

   - The additional force from the muscles, F.

   - The additional force on the base of the spine, R.

Figure 10.107.

Figure 10.108 shows the directions and points of action of S and F, but not R.

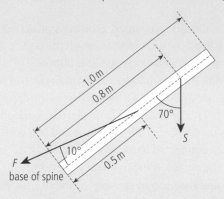

Figure 10.108.

(a) State the two conditions for S, F, and R to be in equilibrium. (2)

(b) Copy Figure 10.108 and add an arrow to show the approximate direction of R, the additional force on the base of the spine. (2)

(c) Write down an expression for the torque about the base of the spine due to the force S. (2)

(d) Show that the force F is approximately nine times the force S, i.e. the muscle force is nine times the weight of the suitcase being lifted. (2)

(*Total 8 marks*)

2. A child playing on a playground ride can be represented by a rotating disc plus a point mass as shown in Figure 10.109.

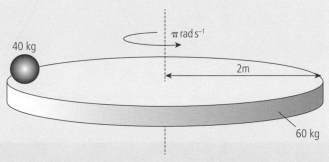

Figure 10.109.

(a) Calculate the moment of inertia of the disc plus child. (2)

(b) Calculate the angular momentum of the disc plus child. (1)

The child moves towards the centre so that he is now 1 m from the centre.

(c) Calculate the new angular velocity. (3)

(d) Calculate the change in kinetic energy when the child moves towards the centre. (3)

(e) Explain the change in kinetic energy. (2)

(*Total 11 marks*)

3. Figure 10.110 shows the variation with volume of the pressure of a system. The work done in compressing the gas from R to P is

   A 5.0×10^5 J

   B 4.5×10^5 J

   C 3.0×10^5 J

   D 0   (1)

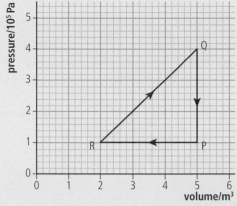

Figure 10.110.

4. This question is about the thermodynamics of a heat engine. In an idealized heat engine, a fixed mass of a gas undergoes various changes of temperature, pressure, and volume. The P–V cycle (A→B→C→D→A) for these changes is shown in Figure 10.111.

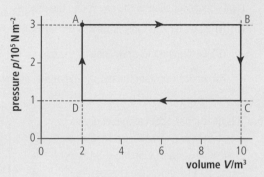

Figure 10.111.

(a) Use the information from Figure 10.111 to calculate the work done during one cycle.   (2)

(b) During one cycle, a total of 1.8×10^6 J of thermal energy is ejected into a cold reservoir. Calculate the efficiency of this engine.   (2)

(c) Copy Figure 10.112 and on the axes sketch the P–V changes that take place in the fixed mass of an ideal gas during one cycle of a *Carnot engine*. (*Note this is a sketch graph – you do not need to add any values.*)   (2)

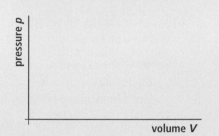

Figure 10.112.

(d) (i) State the names of the **two** types of change that take place during one cycle of a Carnot engine.   (2)

   (ii) Add labels to the above graph to indicate which parts of the cycle refer to which particular type of change.   (2)

(*Total 10 marks*)

5. This question is about thermodynamic processes.

(a) Distinguish between an **isothermal** process and an **adiabatic** process as applied to an ideal gas. (2)

An ideal gas is held in a container by a moveable piston and thermal energy is supplied to the gas such that it expands at a constant pressure of 1.2×10^5 Pa (Figure 10.113).

Figure 10.113.

The initial volume of the container is $0.050 \, \text{m}^3$ and after expansion the volume is $0.10 \, \text{m}^3$. The total energy supplied to the gas during the process is 8.0×10^3 J.

(b) (i) State whether this process is **either** isothermal **or** adiabatic **or** neither. (1)

(ii) Determine the work done by the gas. (1)

(iii) Hence calculate the change in internal energy of the gas. (2)

(*Total 6 marks*)

6. This question is about a heat engine. A certain heat engine uses a fixed mass of an ideal gas as a working substance. Figure 10.114 shows the changes in pressure and volume of the gas during one cycle ABCA of operation of the engine.

(a) For the part A → B of the cycle, explain whether

(i) work is done **by** the gas or work is done **on** the gas. (1)

(ii) thermal energy (heat) is absorbed **by** the gas or is ejected **from** the gas to the surroundings. (1)

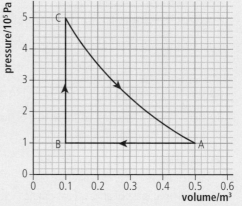

Figure 10.114.

(b) Calculate the work done during the change A → B. (2)

(c) Use Figure 10.114 to estimate the total work done during one cycle. (2)

(d) The total thermal energy supplied to the gas during one cycle is 120 kJ. Estimate the efficiency of this heat engine. (2)

(*Total 8 marks*)

7. This question is about *P–V* diagrams. Figure 10.115 shows the variation with volume of the pressure of a fixed mass of gas when it is compressed adiabatically and also when the same sample of gas is compressed isothermally.

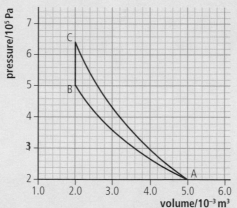

Figure 10.115.

(a) State and explain which line AB or AC represents the isothermal compression. (2)

(b) Copy Figure 10.115 and on your copy shade the area that represents the difference in work done in the adiabatic change and in the isothermal change. (1)

(c) Determine the difference in work done, as identified in (b). (3)

(d) Use the first law of thermodynamics to explain the change in temperature during the adiabatic compression. (3)

(*Total 9 marks*)

8. A domestic hot water heating system is represented by Figure 10.116.

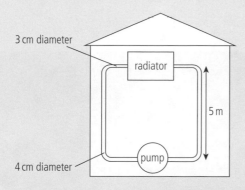

Figure 10.116.

The water is pumped at a pressure of 300 kPa with a speed of 0.5 m s^{-1}.

(a) Calculate the volume flowing per second from the pump. (1)

(b) Calculate the flow speed of the water on the second floor. (2)

(c) Calculate the pressure of the water on the second floor. (3)

(*Total 6 marks*)

9. An airplane wing of surface area 90 m^2 is shaped so that the air speed flowing over the top surface is 340 m s^{-1} and the bottom surface 290 m s^{-1}.

(a) Calculate the pressure difference between the top and the bottom. (3)

(b) Use your answer to (a) to calculate the lift force on the wing. (2)

(*Total 5 marks*)

11

Option C: Imaging

Essential ideas

C.1   Introduction to imaging
The progress of a wave can be modelled via the ray or the wavefront. The change in wave speed when moving between media changes the shape of the wave.

C.2   Imaging instrumentation
Optical microscopes and telescopes utilize similar physical properties of lenses and mirrors. Analysis of the Universe is performed both optically and by using radio telescopes to investigate different regions of the electromagnetic spectrum.

C.3   Fibre optics
Total internal reflection allows light or infrared radiation to travel along a transparent fibre. However the performance of a fibre can be degraded by dispersion and attenuation effects.

C.4   Medical imaging (HL only)
The body can be imaged using radiation generated from both outside and inside. Imaging has enabled medical practitioners to improve diagnosis with fewer invasive procedures.

11.1   Introduction to imaging

C.1 Introduction to imaging

Understandings, applications, and skills:

Converging and diverging lenses
- Describing how a curved transparent interface modifies the shape of an incident wave front.

> *Guidance*
> - *Students should treat the passage of light through lenses from the standpoint of both rays and wave fronts.*

Converging and diverging mirrors
- Solving problems involving curved mirrors by constructing scaled ray diagrams for a spherical converging mirror, a parabolic mirror, and a diverging mirror.

> *Guidance*
> - *Sign convention used in examinations will be based on real being positive (the 'real-is-positive' convention).*

Ray diagrams
- Identifying the principal axis, focal point, and focal length of a simple converging or diverging lens on a scaled diagram.
- Solving problems involving not more than two lenses/curved mirrors by constructing scaled ray diagrams.

> *Guidance*
> - *This topic is confined to knowledge of thin lens theory.*
> - *The lens-maker's formula is not required.*

Real and virtual images
Linear and angular magnification
- Solving problems involving the thin lens equation and linear and angular magnification.

Spherical and chromatic aberrations
- Explaining spherical and chromatic aberrations and describing ways to reduce their effects on images.

In the 1970s fibre optic lamps were very popular as a novel form of lighting but few people would have imagined the potential of this new technology.

NATURE OF SCIENCE

Drawing ray diagrams helps us to understand the path of rays but small errors in drawing the rays result in big errors in the final image position. Using the lens equation does not give such a visual representation but gives a more accurate result. Using the sign convention 'real-is-positive' is another example of the way the sign of a number can represent different physical situations.

Lenses

A lens is a transparent disc with curved faces used to change the path of light rays. We will consider two types of lens: a convex lens has faces curving outwards and a concave lens has faces curving inwards. To understand how a lens refracts light we will first consider a simplified version with plane sides as in Figure 11.1.

Figure 11.1 Refraction through prisms.

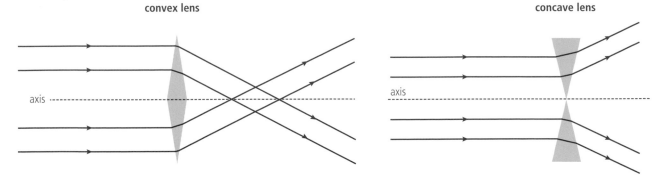

We can see how the light rays are simply refracted as they are when passing through a prism, parallel rays are refracted at the same angle so will remain parallel. A curved surface is like a prism with varying refracting angle so will refract the light at different angles. If the faces are spherical and the lens thin then the rays are refracted as in Figure 11.2.

Figure 11.2 Refraction through lenses.

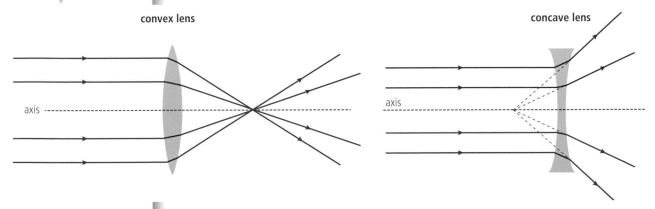

As can be seen from the ray diagrams, parallel light is brought to single *focal point* by a convex lens but *diverged* from a point by a concave lens. Light can also be represented by waves so we can draw wave fronts perpendicular to the rays as in Figure 11.3.

Figure 11.3 Showing wave fronts.

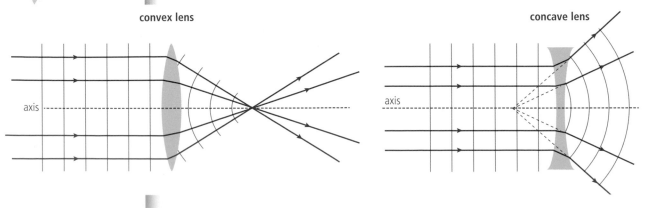

It is very difficult to draw the rays refracting at the correct angles at each surface so when drawing ray diagrams we will only change the direction of the rays at the centre of the lens, as in Figure 11.4.

Figure 11.4.

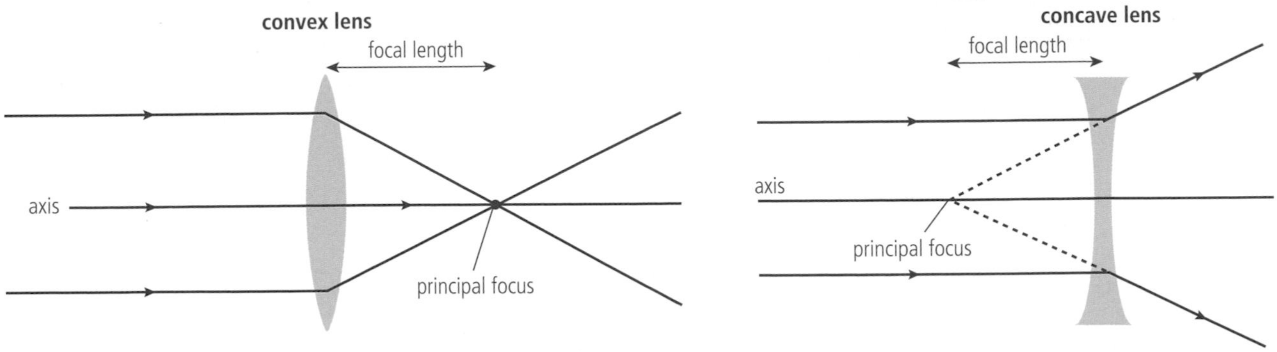

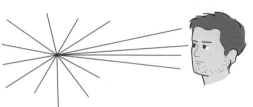

convex lens
focal length
axis
principal focus

concave lens
focal length
axis
principal focus

Note that if the focal length is shorter the rays will be deviated more by the lens. We say that the lens is more powerful where power = $\frac{1}{\text{focal length}}$. The power of a convex lens is positive and the power of a concave lens is negative.

Objects and images

The simplest object is a *point object*; this can either be a source of light or a point that reflects light in all directions.

TOK In science, words have specific meanings, but here is an exception. The power of a lens has got nothing to do with the rate at which it can do work.

Figure 11.5 Light travelling in all directions from a point object.

When a point is viewed by an observer he will see the light coming from this point. However, if the light passes through a convex lens it can be brought to a focus, crossing as in Figure 11.6. The light now appears to be coming from the point where the rays cross: this is called a *real image*. If a sheet of paper was placed at the image position the image would be seen on the paper.

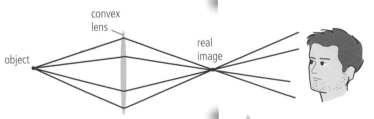

convex lens
object
real image

Figure 11.6.

If the light is passed through a concave lens it will be made to diverge away from a point as in Figure 11.7. The light now appears to be coming from a point on the other side of the lens where the rays appear to cross. This is called a *virtual image*. It is not possible to project this image on a sheet of paper as the rays do not really cross at this point.

Figure 11.7.

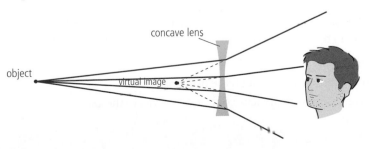

concave lens
object
virtual image

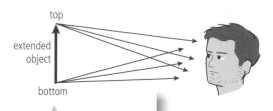

top

extended
object

bottom

Figure 11.8 An extended object.

All objects can be thought of as being made up of a collection of points. It would be rather difficult to draw rays coming from every point on an object so we just draw rays from one point at the top and one point at the bottom and assume that all the other points will be somewhere in between (Figure 11.8). An object made of more than one point is called an *extended object*. We will represent an extended object with an arrow so we can distinguish between the top and the bottom.

Image formation in convex lenses

The image of an extended object in a convex lens can be found by carefully drawing the path of two or three rays from the top of the object, the image will be formed where these rays cross or appear to cross.

In Figure 11.9 rays from the top and bottom of the object are drawn to show the top and bottom of the image. Notice how the top and bottom are the same distance from the lens. This is always the case, so we only need to find the position of the top, the bottom will be the same distance from the lens but positioned on the axis.

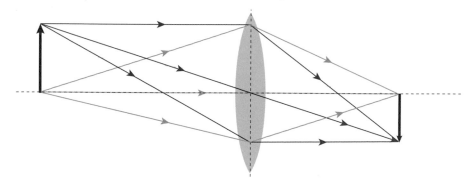

Figure 11.9.

The nature of the image

We describe the nature of an image according to whether it is:
• real or virtual.
• bigger or smaller.
• closer or further away.
• upright or upside down.

So in this case the image is:

• real (the rays actually cross).
• smaller.
• closer to the lens than the object.
• upside down (inverted).

To draw the rays in Figure 11.9 we would have to calculate the angles of refraction. Luckily we don't have to do that since there are 3 rays with known directions:

1. a ray through the centre is undeviated.
2. a ray parallel to the axis passes through the principal focus.
3. a ray coming from the principal focus continues parallel to the axis.

Drawing a ray diagram step-by-step

To see how this works, let us consider an extended object further than 2 × the focal length from a convex lens.

First draw the axis and lens, then choose an appropriate scale and mark the principal foci on either side of the lens. Now draw the object in appropriate position to the left of the lens (Figure 11.10). In this case it is simply 'more than 2F'.

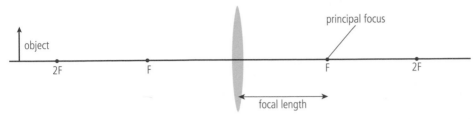

Figure 11.10.

Draw a ray from the top of the object parallel to the axis. This ray will be refracted so that it passes through the principal focus (the red ray in Figure 11.11). To find the position of the image draw a second ray through the centre of the lens. The two surfaces of the lens are parallel at the centre so the ray will pass undeflected (the blue ray in Figure 11.11).

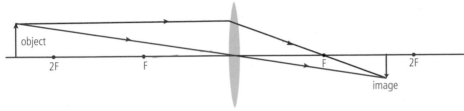

Figure 11.11 Object at more than 2F. The image is:
- real.
- smaller.
- closer.
- inverted.

The image of the top point of the object is where the rays cross and the bottom is on the axis the same distance from the lens. The position of the image can now be measured.

The nature of the image depends on how far from the lens the object is placed. The ray diagrams in Figures 11.12–11.15 show all the possibilities.

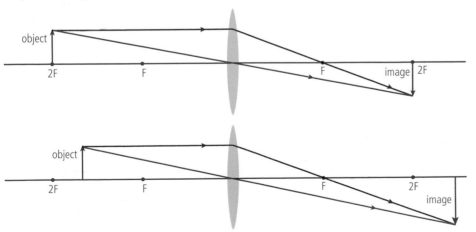

Figure 11.12 Object at a distance 2F. The image is:
- real.
- same size.
- same distance.
- inverted.

Figure 11.13 Object between F and 2F. The image is:
- real.
- larger.
- further.
- inverted.

- virtual (rays don't actually come from the point).
- larger (infinitely big).
- further (at an infinite distance).
- upright (if virtual image taken).

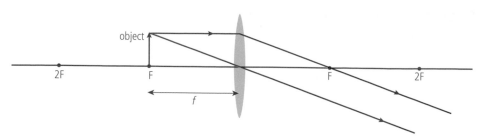

When the object is at F (Figure 11.14) there doesn't seem to be an image since the rays do not cross over. However, if viewed from the right hand side the rays appear to come from a very distant point. We can say that the image is virtual and at an infinite distance to the left of the lens. You could also argue that there was a real image an infinite distance to the right but that image cannot be viewed.

Figure 11.15 Closer than F. The image is:
- virtual.
- larger.
- further.
- upright.

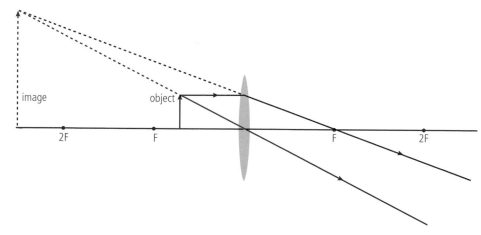

When the object is closer than F (Figure 11.15) the object is so close to the lens that the lens cannot bend the rays enough to bring them together.

Image formation in concave lenses

To find the image in a concave lens the same procedure is followed except the ray parallel to the axis (red) is drawn so that it diverges from the principal focus on the left side as in Figure 11.16. The image position is the point that the two rays appear to diverge from.

Figure 11.16. No matter where the object is placed, the image is always:
- virtual.
- smaller.
- closer.
- upright.

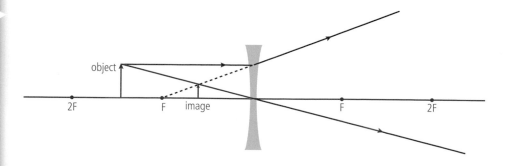

The lens formula

An alternative way of finding the image position is to use the lens formula:

$$\frac{1}{f} = \frac{1}{u} + \frac{1}{v}$$

where:

  f = focal length
  u = object distance
  v = Image distance

This formula can only be used for thin lenses and small objects where all the rays can be considered to be close to and almost parallel with the axis.

Figure 11.17 Defining u, v, and f.

To distinguish between real and virtual we use a sign convention, *real is positive, virtual negative*. This applies to any length so, since the rays don't actually cross at the focal point of a concave lens, this is taken to be a virtual length.

Worked example

An object is placed 24 cm from a convex lens of focal length 6 cm. Find the image position.

Solution

From the question:

u = 24 cm

f = 6 cm

rearranging: $\dfrac{1}{f} = \dfrac{1}{u} + \dfrac{1}{v}$ gives $\dfrac{1}{v} = \dfrac{1}{f} - \dfrac{1}{u}$

substituting values: $\dfrac{1}{v} = \dfrac{1}{6} - \dfrac{1}{24} = \dfrac{4}{24} - \dfrac{1}{24} = \dfrac{3}{24}$

so $v = \dfrac{24}{3} = 8$ cm

This is positive so the image is real. Check with a ray diagram (Figure 11.18).

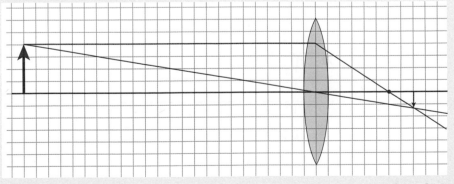

Figure 11.18.

Always draw a sketch of the relative positions of the object, image, and lens. This will help you to see what the problem involves. Then use the formula to find the thing you are asked to calculate.

Worked example

An object is placed 3 cm from a convex lens of focal length 6 cm. Find the image position.

Solution

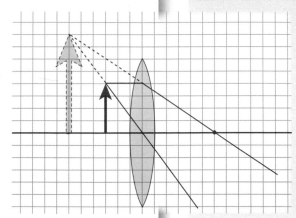

Figure 11.19.

From the question:

$u = 3\,\text{cm}$

$f = 6\,\text{cm}$

rearranging: $\dfrac{1}{f} = \dfrac{1}{u} + \dfrac{1}{v}$ gives $\dfrac{1}{v} = \dfrac{1}{f} - \dfrac{1}{u}$

substituting values: $\dfrac{1}{v} = \dfrac{1}{6} - \dfrac{1}{3} = \dfrac{1}{6} - \dfrac{2}{6} = \dfrac{-1}{6}$

so $\qquad v = \dfrac{-6}{1} = -6\,\text{cm}$

This is negative so the image is virtual.

Check with a ray diagram (Figure 11.19).

Worked example

An object is placed 3 cm from a concave lens of focal length 6 cm. Find the image position.

Solution

From the question:

$u = 3\,\text{cm}$

$f = 6\,\text{cm}$

rearranging gives: $\dfrac{1}{f} = \dfrac{1}{u} + \dfrac{1}{v}$ gives $\dfrac{1}{v} = \dfrac{1}{f} - \dfrac{1}{u}$

substituting values: $\dfrac{1}{v} = \dfrac{1}{-6} - \dfrac{1}{3} = \dfrac{-3}{6}$

So $\qquad v = -2\,\text{cm}.$

Check with a ray diagram (Figure 11.20).

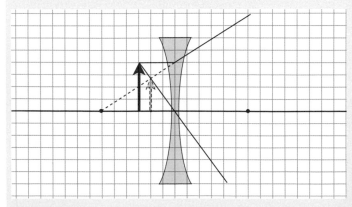

Figure 11.20.

Linear magnification (m)

Linear magnification is defined by the equation:

$$m = \frac{\text{height of image}}{\text{height of object}} = \frac{h_i}{h_o}$$

From Figure 11.21 we can see that the ray through the centre makes two similar triangles so we can also write:

$$m = -\frac{v}{u}$$

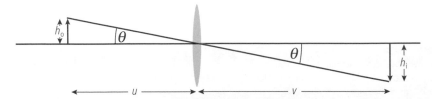

The negative sign is to be consistent with the sign conventions and help determine if the image is upright or inverted. In the previous example $m = -\left(-\frac{2}{6}\right)$ so $m = \frac{1}{2}$. Positive magnification implies the image is upright. A negative magnification means an inverted image.

Figure 11.21 Linear magnification.

Exercises

Use the lens formula to solve the following problems. You can check your answers by drawing ray diagrams too.

1 A 25 cm focal length lens is used to focus an image of the Sun onto a piece of paper. What will the distance between the lens and the paper be?

2 An object is placed 30 cm from a convex lens of focal length 10 cm.

  (a) Calculate the image distance.
  (b) Is the image real or virtual?
  (c) Calculate the magnification of the image.

3 A real image is formed 20 cm from a convex lens of focal length 5 cm. Calculate the object distance.

4 An object is placed 5 cm from a lens of focal length 15 cm.

  (a) Calculate the image distance.
  (b) Is the image real or virtual?
  (c) Calculate the magnification of the image.

5 A camera with a single lens of focal length 5 cm is used to take a photograph of a bush 5 m away. A simple camera uses a convex lens.

  (a) What is the object distance?
  (b) Calculate the distance from the lens to the film (v).
  (c) What is the linear magnification of the camera?
  (d) If the bush were 1 m high how high will the image be?

6 The camera of Exercise 5 is used to take a picture of a flower on the bush so the photographer moves towards the bush until he is 20 cm from the flower.

  (a) Calculate the image distance.
  (b) What is the linear magnification?

7 A concave lens of focal length 30 cm is used to view an object 5 m in front of the lens.

  (a) Calculate the image distance.
  (b) Calculate the linear magnification.

Virtual objects

It sounds a bit strange to have a virtual object and an actual physical object reflecting light can only be real. However, when we have combinations of lenses then the image in the first lens is taken to be the object for the second. Figure 11.22 shows a situation where the light rays passing through the first lens converges at a point beyond the second. The rays don't actually pass through this point so this is taken to be a virtual object for the second lens.

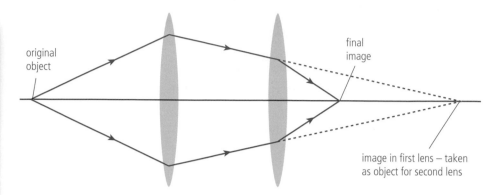

Figure 11.22.

final
image

image in first lens – taken
as object for second lens

Exercise

8 An object is placed 40 cm from two convex lenses each of focal length 20 cm separated by 10 cm. Find the position and nature of the final image.

The human eye

Inside the eye there is a convex lens. This, together with the front part of the eye, focuses light onto the retina, where millions of light-sensitive cells sense the light and send electrical signals to the brain (Figure 11.23).

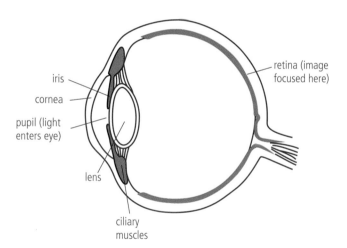

Figure 11.23 Parts of the human eye.

The eye lens is made of a rubbery substance that can be squashed; squashing the lens makes it fatter and therefore more powerful. In this way the eye can be adapted to focus on objects that are close or far away. There is a limit to how fat the lens can get. If an object is too close to the eye, then it can't focus the rays on the retina, and the image is 'out of focus'. The average closest distance is 25 cm, but this tends to get longer with age. Objects close to the eye appear bigger than distant objects because they subtend a larger angle at the eye (Figure 11.24).

Figure 11.24 A close object appears bigger.

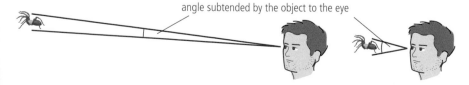

Although the wind turbines are all the same size the nearest one looks biggest.

TOK

The size of the Moon

You may have noticed that the Moon looks bigger when it is just above the horizon than it does when it is up above. This is in fact an illusion, if you measure the size of the Moon you find it never changes. Your brain decides how big something is depending on how your eyes are focused. When the Moon is on the horizon your brain thinks it is closer because of the other objects in view. This is an example of how perception sometimes doesn't agree with measurement.

The magnifying glass

We use a magnifying glass to make things look bigger; this is done by putting the object closer than the principal focus of a convex lens (Figure 11.25). Without a magnifying glass the best we can do is to put an object at our near point (25 cm in average eyes). The best we can do with a magnifying glass is with the *image* at the near point.

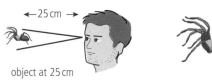

object at 25 cm

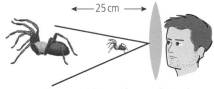

image at 25 cm with magnifying glass

Figure 11.25 Using a magnifying glass with the image at 25 cm.

The problem with looking at something so close is that it can be a bit tiring, since your eye muscles have to contract to allow the lens to become fat.

It is more relaxing to view the image at a distance, and then the eye is relaxed. This, however, doesn't give such a magnified image. If the final image is far away (we could say an infinite distance) the rays coming to the observer should be parallel. In the previous section we saw that this means the object must be at the focal point. In both cases the angle subtended when using the magnifying glass is bigger than without (see Figure 11.26).

 The natural shape of the eye lens is fat but it is kept under tension by fibres which stretch the lens into a thin shape. When the ciliary muscles contract they release the tension, allowing the lens to become fat.

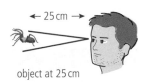

object at 25 cm

image at infinity with magnifying glass

Figure 11.26 Using a magnifying glass with the image 'at infinity'.

Angular magnification (*M*)

The angular magnification tells us how much bigger an object looks.

$$\text{Angular magnification} = \frac{\text{angle subtended by image at eye } (\theta_i)}{\text{angle subtended by object at unaided eye } (\theta_o)}$$

Angular magnification for a magnifying glass

1. Image at infinity

When the final image is an infinite distance away the object must be placed at the focal point. Looking at Figure 11.27, you can see why this image looks bigger than the image in the unaided eye.

If the angles are small (for the original object with the image at infinity) and measured in radians then

$$\theta_o = \frac{h_o}{25}$$

$$\theta_i = \frac{h_o}{f}$$

Since angular magnification $\quad M = \dfrac{\theta_i}{\theta_o} = \dfrac{h_o}{f} \times \dfrac{25}{h_o}$

So $\qquad\qquad\qquad\qquad M = \dfrac{25}{f}$

Figure 11.27 Angular magnification for an original object with image at infinity and viewed with a magnifying glass.

25 cm

h_o θ_o

object at near point

← f →

h_o θ_i

image at infinity with magnifying glass, object at f

2. Image at the near point (normal adjustment)

Figure 12.28 compares an object as close as possible to the unaided eye to the same object viewed with a magnifying glass. So that the final image is also as close as possible, the object must be placed close to the lens.

This can be shown to give an angular magnification of $1 + \frac{25}{f}$. (One more than the previous example.)

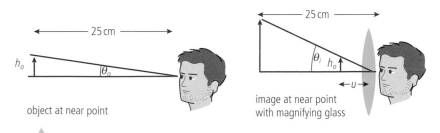

25 cm

h_o θ_o

object at near point

25 cm

θ_i h_o

← u →

image at near point with magnifying glass

Figure 11.28 Angular magnification for an image at the near point.

Derivation of $M = 1 + \dfrac{25}{f}$

Referring to Figure 11.28, if the angles are small then the angles expressed in radians are:

$\theta_o = \dfrac{h_o}{25}$

$\theta_i = \dfrac{h_o}{u}$

so $M = \dfrac{\theta_o}{\theta_i} = \dfrac{h_o}{u} \times \dfrac{25}{h_o}$

$M = \dfrac{25}{u}$ (1)

but $\dfrac{1}{f} = \dfrac{1}{u} + \dfrac{1}{v}$ so $\dfrac{1}{u} = \dfrac{1}{f} - \dfrac{1}{v}$

where $v = -25$ cm

so $\dfrac{1}{u} = \dfrac{1}{f} - \dfrac{1}{25}$

Rearranging gives

$u = \dfrac{25f}{25 + f}$

Substituting for u in equation (1) gives

$M = \left(\dfrac{25 + f}{f}\right) = 1 + \dfrac{25}{f}$

So $M = 1 + \dfrac{25}{f}$

Exercises

9. The Moon is about 3500 km in diameter and about 400 000 km away from the Earth. Estimate the angle subtended by the Moon to an observer on the Earth.

10. If a small insect 1 mm long is viewed at a distance of 25 cm from the eye, what angle will it subtend to the eye?

11. How close to a lens of focal length 5 cm should the insect of Exercise 10 be placed so that an image is formed 25 cm from the eye?

12. Use the formula to calculate the angular magnification of the insect viewed with a lens of focal length 5 cm if the final image is at the near point.

Measurement of focal length

Measuring the focal length of a convex lens is simply a matter of focusing the image of an illuminated object (such as a cross drawn on a piece of paper illuminated by a lamp) on a screen. This can be done using sticky tape and modelling clay to mount the components on a normal table or using a proper optical bench. The image distance can be measured for a range of different object distances (provided the image is real). The lens formula is used to find the focal length for each pair of lengths and the mean value calculated.

An optical bench.

To measure the focal length of a concave lens is not so straightforward since the image is virtual. However, if a virtual image is used then a real image can be projected onto a screen. Figure 11.30 shows how this can be done.

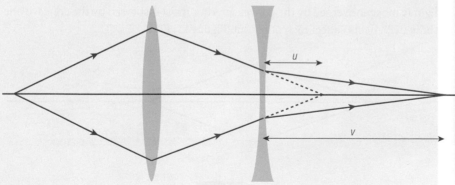

Figure 11.30.

First find the image position without the concave lens (dotted line), then position the lens and find the new image position. The value for f is again found using the lens equation, remembering that the object is *virtual*.

Remember the radian
$$= \frac{s}{f}$$
If the angle is very small then the arc, s, can be taken as a straight line.

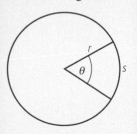

Figure 11.29.

Lens aberrations

We have assumed in all the previous examples that parallel rays of light are brought to a point when they shine through a convex lens. However, this is not the case with a real lens.

Spherical aberration

Because of the spherical curvature of a lens, the rays hitting the outer part are deviated more than the ones on the inside (see Figure 12.31).

The result is that if the image is projected onto a screen there will be a spot instead of a point. If such a lens were used to take a photograph then the picture would be blurred. To reduce this effect, the outer rays are removed by placing a card with a hole in it over the lens. This is called *stopping*.

Figure 11.31 Spherical
aberration in a convex lens.

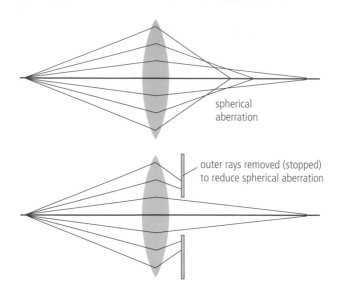

Chromatic aberration

It has been mentioned before that different wavelengths of light are refracted by
different amounts. If white light is focused with a convex lens the different colours are
focused at different points. This also causes the image to be blurred. It can be corrected
by making the lens out of two lenses of different refractive index stuck together. The
light is most converged by the convex lens but most dispersed by the concave one so
these two effects cancel each other out (Figure 11.32).

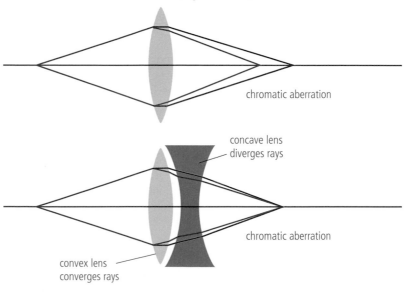

Figure 11.32 Chromatic
aberration and an achromatic
doublet. The deviation of rays
in the diagram is exaggerated
to show what is happening.

Spherical mirrors

When light is incident on a concave spherical mirror each ray is reflected according to
the laws of reflection so that the angle of reflection equals the angle of incidence. The
normal to the surface passes through the centre of curvature of the mirror resulting
in parallel rays being bought to a focus at a point half way between the centre of
curvature and the mirror as shown in Figure 11.33.

$$\text{focal length} = \tfrac{1}{2} \times \text{radius of curvature}$$

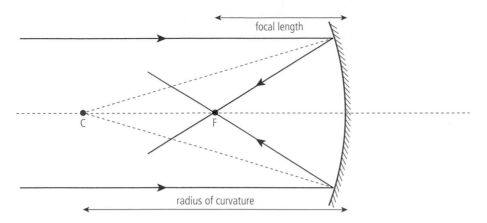

Figure 11.33 Parallel rays reflecting off a concave mirror.

Light also obeys the laws of reflection when reflected off a convex mirror but this time the light rays diverge as in Figure 11.34.

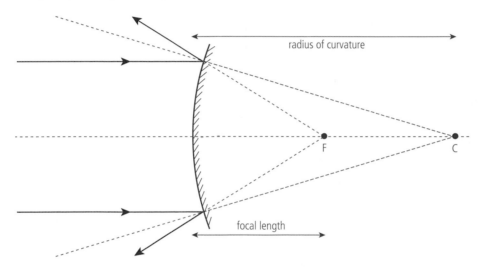

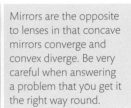

Mirrors are the opposite to lenses in that concave mirrors converge and convex diverge. Be very careful when answering a problem that you get it the right way round.

Figure 11.34 Parallel rays reflecting off a convex mirror.

Drawing ray diagrams for concave mirrors

To trace the path of a ray reflected from a concave mirror you could draw a normal to the mirror and measure the angles of incidence and reflection. However, there are certain rays that we can trace without measuring angles.

1. A ray parallel to the axis will be reflected through the principal focus.
2. A ray passing through the principal focus is reflected parallel to the axis.
3. A ray originating from the centre of curvature is reflected back along the same path.

Using these rays we can find the image of an extended object in a similar way to that used with lenses. Let us first try with an object further way than the centre of curvature (Figure 11.35).

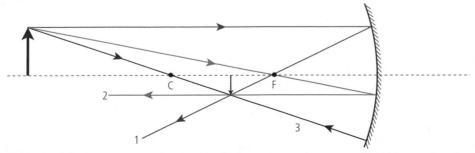

Figure 11.35 Object distance >2F. The nature of this image is:
- real.
- smaller.
- closer.
- inverted.

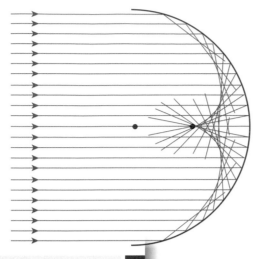

Note that the condition that rays parallel to the axis pass through the principal focus only applies to rays that are close to the axis; in other words, mirrors that are shallow. If we trace rays incident on a mirror that is half a sphere as in Figure 11.36, we can see why. The edges of the mirror curve inwards so the outer rays are not reflected to the focal point. The curved surface formed by the rays is called a *caustic curve*.

Since the ray diagrams only apply to mirrors that are quite flat we can represent the mirror in our ray diagram as a straight line with a symbolic mirror on the axis to show whether it is concave or convex.

◀ **Figure 11.36** Reflection off a hemispherical mirror forms a caustic surface.

Since the edges of a parabolic mirror do not curve inwards, the rays are focused at one point as in Figure 11.37.

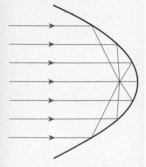

Figure 11.37.

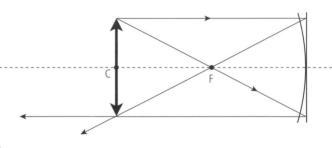

Figure 11.38 Object at C. The nature of this image is:
- real.
- same size.
- same distance.
- inverted.

Figure 11.39 Object between C and F. The nature of this image is:
- real.
- larger.
- further.
- inverted.

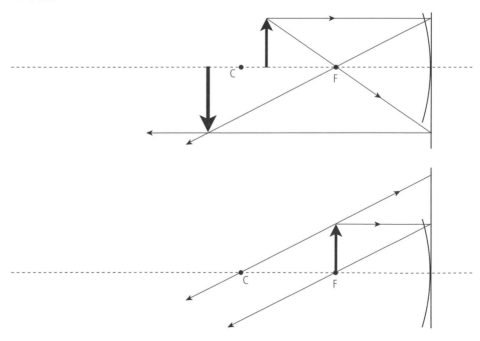

Figure 11.40 Object at F. The nature of this image is:
- virtual (on the other side of the mirror, you could also take the image to be real on the same side of the mirror as the object).
- infinitely big.
- infinity distant.
- upright.

In Figure 11.40 we can't draw the ray coming from the principal focus so we draw the ray that appears to come from the centre of curvature.

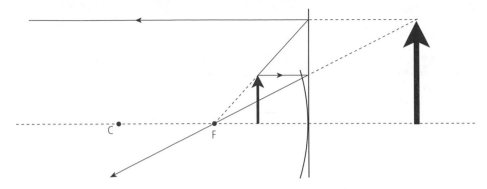

Figure 11.41 Object closer
than F. The nature of this
image is:
- virtual.
- larger.
- further.
- upright.

In Figure 11.41 the ray doesn't actually originate from F but appears to come from
that direction. This is how you would see the image of your face when looking into a
shaving/make up mirror.

Drawing ray diagrams for convex mirrors

A convex mirror diverges light so the rays are reflected away from the principal focus
as in Figure 11.42.

1. A ray travelling parallel to the axis is reflected so that it appears to originate from
    the principal focus.
2. A ray travelling towards the principal focus is reflected parallel to the axis.
3. A ray travelling towards the centre of curvature is reflected along the same path.

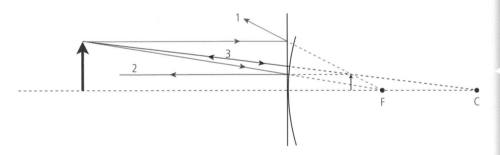

Figure 11.42. The nature of
the image is:
- virtual.
- smaller.
- closer.
- upright.

We can see from this example with the object further than the radius of curvature the
nature of the image is the same for *all* real object positions.

The mirror formula

The formula used to find the image in a spherical mirror is exactly the same as the lens
formula:

$$\frac{1}{f} = \frac{1}{u} + \frac{1}{v}$$

where:

f = focal length ($\frac{1}{2}$ radius of curvature)
u = object distance
v = Image distance

with the same sign convention that *real is positive*.

Linear magnification (*m*)

$$\text{Linear magnification} = \frac{\text{height of image}}{\text{height of object}} = -\frac{v}{u}$$

Worked example

An object is placed 25 cm from a concave mirror of focal length 10 cm. Calculate the position of the image.

Solution

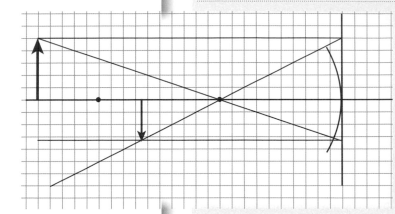

From the question:

$u = 25$ cm

$f = 10$ cm

rearranging: $\frac{1}{f} = \frac{1}{u} + \frac{1}{v}$ gives $\frac{1}{v} = \frac{1}{f} - \frac{1}{u}$

$\frac{1}{v} = \frac{1}{10} - \frac{1}{25} = \frac{1.5}{25}$

$v = 16.7$ cm. Check this with a ray diagram (Figure 11.43).

Figure 11.43.

Worked example

An object is placed 20 cm from a convex mirror of focal length 10 cm. Calculate the image position.

Solution

From the question:

$u = 20$ cm

$f = -10$ cm

rearranging gives $\frac{1}{f} = \frac{1}{u} + \frac{1}{v}$ gives $\frac{1}{v} = \frac{1}{f} - \frac{1}{u}$

$\frac{1}{v} = \frac{1}{-10} - \frac{1}{20} = \frac{-3}{20}$

$v = -6.7$ cm. Check this with a ray diagram (Figure 11.44).

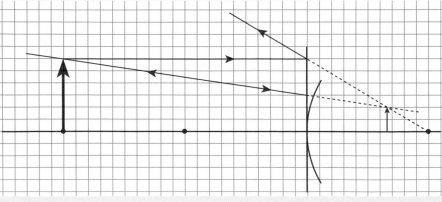

Figure 11.44.

Exercises

13 Calculate the position and size of the image when a 2 cm high object is placed 24 cm from a concave mirror of radius of curvature 20 cm. Confirm your answer with a scale diagram.

14 Calculate the position and size of the image when a 2 cm high object is placed 5 cm from a concave mirror of radius of curvature 20 cm. Confirm your answer with a scale diagram.

15 A real image of an object is formed on a screen 30 cm from a concave mirror. If the object was 20 cm from the mirror calculate the focal length of the mirror.

16 Calculate the position and size of the image when a 2 cm high object is placed 5 cm from a convex mirror of radius of curvature 20 cm. Confirm your answer with a scale diagram.

11.2 Imaging instrumentation

C.2 Imaging instrumentation

Understandings, applications, and skills:

Optical compound microscopes
- Constructing ray diagrams of optical compound microscopes at normal adjustment.
- Solving problems involving the angular magnification and resolution of optical compound microscopes.
- Investigating the optical compound microscope experimentally.

Simple optical astronomical refracting telescopes
- Constructing or completing ray diagrams of simple optical astronomical refracting telescopes at normal adjustment.
- Solving problems involving the angular magnification of simple optical astronomical telescopes.
- Investigating the performance of a simple optical astronomical refracting telescope experimentally.

Simple optical astronomical reflecting telescopes

Guidance
- *Simple optical astronomical reflecting telescope design is limited to Newtonian and Cassegrain mounting.*

Satellite-borne telescopes
- Describing the comparative performance of Earth-based and satellite-borne telescopes.

Single-dish radio telescopes and radio interferometry telescopes

Guidance
- *Radio interferometer telescopes should be approximated as a dish of diameter equal to the maximum separation of the antennae.*
- *'Radio interferometry telescopes' refer to 'array telescopes'.*

The optical compound microscope

The magnifying power of a convex lens is related to its focal length; a very short focal length lens will have a high magnifying power. However, short focal length means very curved sides; this causes distortion of the image, making it useless. A better option is to use a combination of lenses as shown in Figure 11.45. Here, the objective lens forms a magnified real image in front of the eyepiece which is used as a magnifying glass to produce a magnified virtual image at the near point of the eye (25 cm). The final image could be further away but magnification is greatest when it is as close as possible; this is called *normal adjustment*.

NATURE OF SCIENCE

An understanding that the resolution of optical microscopes is limited by the wavelength of light led to the use of shorter wavelength electrons. Scientific discoveries often precede technological advances.

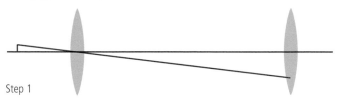

Figure 11.45 Simple ray diagram for a microscope.

objective   eyepiece

25 cm

To see how the image is magnified we need to draw a ray diagram for an extended object. This is best done in stages.

How to draw the ray diagram

Drawing this ray diagram can be tricky; if you're not careful, the final image won't fit on the page. The following instructions are a way to make it work. If asked to do this in an exam the focal points will probably be given, making the drawing easier.

1. Draw the lenses and axis then a ray through the centre of the objective to a point half way down the eyepiece. Then draw an object a short distance from the objective (Figure 11.46).

Figure 11.46 Step 1.

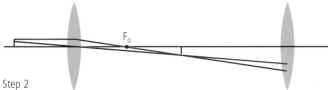

Step 1

2. Draw a ray from the object parallel to the axis. Continue this ray so that it hits the bottom of the eyepiece. Now mark F_o, it is the point where this ray crosses the axis (Figure 11.47).

Figure 11.47 Step 2.

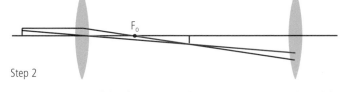

F_o

Step 2

3. To find the position of the final image draw a construction line (black dotted line) from the top of the first image through the middle of the eyepiece. The top of the image will lie on this line. Choose a point on this line beyond the objective and draw the rays coming from this point. Now add arrows to all the rays (Figure 11.48).

Figure 11.48 Step 3.

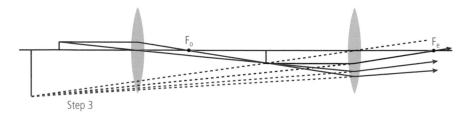

F_o F_e

Step 3

To find the focal point of the eyepiece, the red construction line can be drawn. This comes from the top of the first image and goes parallel to the axis. When it passes through the lens it appears to come from the top of the final image. The ray will pass through the focal point.

Looking at Figure 11.48 we can see that the object is placed beyond the principal focus of the objective and the image in the objective is formed closer than the principal focus of the eyepiece. In a real microscope the focal length of the objective and eyepiece are much shorter than the distance between the lenses (Figure 11.49). The lenses are separated by a tube so that the distance between the principal foci is fixed; this is called the *tube length* and is commonly 16 cm. The image is focused by changing the distance between the object and objective.

Angular magnification

$$\text{Angular magnification} = \frac{\theta_i}{\theta_o}$$

where:
θ_i = the angle subtended by the final image at the eye (25 cm from the eye).
θ_o = the angle subtended by the object without the use of the microscope also at 25 cm from the eye.

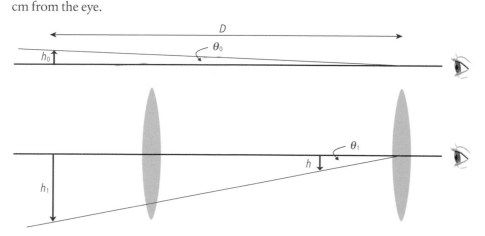

Referring to Figure 11.50 we can see that if the angles are small:

$$\theta_o = \frac{h_o}{D} \text{ and } \theta_i = \frac{h_i}{D}$$

so
$$M = \frac{\frac{h_i}{D}}{\frac{h_o}{D}} = \frac{h_i}{h_o}$$

This is the same as the linear magnification of the microscope.

Now, treating each lens separately:

magnification of the objective $m_o = \frac{h}{h_o}$ so $h_o = \frac{h}{m_o}$

magnification of the eyepiece $m_e = \frac{h_i}{h}$ so $h_i = m_e h$

substituting for h_o and h_i gives $M = m_e \times m_o$.

So the angular magnification of the microscope = the product of the linear magnifications of the eyepiece and objective. The magnification of a microscope is usually varied by changing the objective.

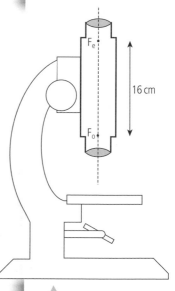

Figure 11.49 A simple microscope.

Figure 11.50.

Investigating the compound microscope

You can make a compound microscope with two lenses. The object should be placed further than the focal length of the objective, then move the eyepiece until you see a focused image. You can measure the angular magnification by comparing photographs taken with, and without, the microscope.

Worked example

A microscope has an objective of focal length 2 cm, an eyepiece of focal length 5 cm, and a tube length of 16 cm. The microscope is adjusted so that the final image is at the near point. Calculate the distance between the object and objective and the magnification of the microscope.

Solution

First we need to draw a sketch to show the relative position of the images in the different lenses. This does not need to have rays on it or to be drawn to scale.

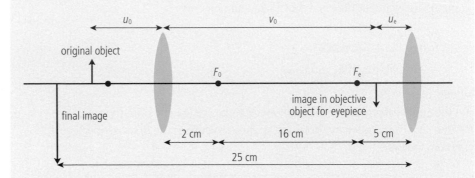

Figure 11.51.

Now we can apply the lens formula to the eyepiece to calculate the position of the intermediate image:

$v_e = -25$ cm (we know it must be virtual)

$f_e = 5$ cm

$$\frac{1}{u_e} = \frac{1}{5} - \frac{1}{-25} = \frac{6}{25}$$

$u_e = 4.2$ cm.

The distance between the lenses = 23 cm so $v_o = 23 - 4.2 = 18.8$ cm. Applying the lens formula to the objective we can now find the image distance.

$v_o = 18.8$ cm

$f_o = 2$ cm

$$\frac{1}{u_o} = \frac{1}{2} - \frac{1}{18.8} = \frac{8.4}{18.8}$$

$u_o = 2.24$ cm

The linear magnification of the objective $= \dfrac{v_o}{u_o} = \dfrac{18.8}{2.24} = 8.4$

The linear magnification of the eyepiece $= \dfrac{v_e}{u_e} = \dfrac{25}{4.2} = 5.9$

Overall angular magnification $= m_o \times m_e = 50$.

It is difficult to understand how something works without being able to see inside it. Before the invention of the microscope scientists would not have known that skin is made up of cells or that those cells had common components with fine structure. Without being able to see the parts it would have been impossible to work out their function.

Exercises

17 A microscope is constructed from an objective of focal length 1 cm and an eyepiece of focal length 5 cm. An object is placed 1.5 cm from the objective.

    (a) Calculate the distance from the objective to the first image.

    (b) If the final image is a virtual image 25 cm from the eyepiece, calculate the distance between the first image and the eyepiece.

    (c) Calculate the distance between the lenses.

18 A microscope has an objective of focal length 1 cm, an eyepiece of focal length 4 cm, and a tube length of 16 cm. Calculate the object position and the angular magnification if used in normal adjustment.

Microscope resolution

We have seen that the resolving power of an optical instrument is limited by the diffraction of light by the aperture. According to the Rayleigh criterion, the smallest resolvable angle between two objects (θ) is given by the formula:

$$\theta = \frac{1.22\lambda}{D}$$

where D = the diameter of the objective.

To produce a magnified image, the object should be close to the principal focus of the objective so if we assume the object distance = f_o then the angle subtended between two points separated by a distance d is given by $\theta = \frac{d}{f_o}$ as shown in Figure 11.52.

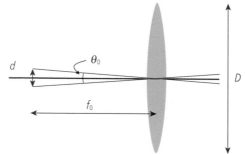

Figure 11.52.

So the closest separation such that these points will be resolved is:

$$d = f_o\theta = \frac{1.22\lambda f_o}{D} \quad (1)$$

The resolving power depends on the wavelength of light and the focal length and diameter of the objective, but it is more convenient to write this in terms of the *angle of acceptance*. This is the angle α of the cone made by all the light that enters the objective as shown in Figure 11.53.

If α is small then:

$$\sin\alpha = \frac{\frac{1}{2}D}{f_o}$$

so

$$\frac{f_o}{D} = \frac{1}{2\sin\alpha}$$

substitute into equation (1)

$$d = \frac{1.22\lambda}{2\sin\alpha} = \frac{0.61\lambda}{\sin\alpha}$$

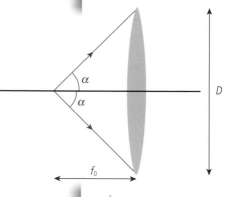

Figure 11.53.

The maximum theoretical angle of acceptance is 90°. However, in practice it is difficult to make a lens with a focal length shorter than half the diameter (as it is in Figure 11.53) which means that the highest resolution possible is approximately λ. To further increase the resolving power the wavelength of light entering the objective can be reduced. This can be achieved by introducing a medium such as oil between the object and objective. If the refractive index of the oil is n then $\lambda_{oil} = \frac{\lambda_{air}}{n}$.

Exercise

19 A microscope has an objective of diameter 1 cm and focal length 2 cm. Calculate:

(a) the smallest distance between resolvable points if light of wavelength 600 nm is used.

(b) the smallest distance between resolvable points if oil of refractive index 1.8 is introduced between the object and objective.

NATURE OF SCIENCE

Incredible advances have been made in astronomy thanks to the increased resolving power of telescopes.

The astronomical telescope

An astronomical telescope is a system of two coaxial convex lenses as in Figure 11.54, used to make distant objects look bigger. The lenses are arranged so that the final image is at an infinite distance from the eye; this is because it is more relaxing to look at distant objects than close ones. Light from a distant object can be considered parallel so an image will be formed at the principal focus of the first lens (*objective*). This image is then taken to be the object for the second lens (*eyepiece*) so to form a final image at infinity it should be at the principal focus which means that the distance between the lenses is $(f_o + f_e)$.

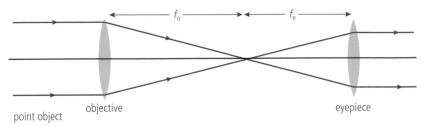

Figure 11.54 The astronomical telescope (point object).

A magnified point is still a point so to see how the image appears bigger we need to consider an extended object such as the Moon: this is shown in Figure 11.55. The three rays coming from the top of the Moon arrive at the telescope almost parallel so will converge in the focal plane of the objective. The bottom of the Moon is in line with the axis.

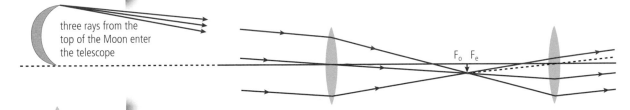

Figure 11.55 The astronomical telescope with extended object.

How to draw the ray diagram

This diagram looks difficult to draw but is okay if done in stages.

1. Draw the lenses and axis but don't draw the foci yet (Figure 11.56).

Figure 11.56 Step 1.

step 1

2. Draw a ray passing through the centre of the objective hitting the eyepiece about half way down (Figure 11.57).

Figure 11.57 Step 2.

step 2

3. Draw two more rays entering the objective at the same angle as the first. Then draw the top ray hitting the bottom of the eyepiece (Figure 11.58).

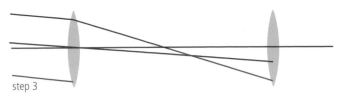

Figure 11.58 Step 3.

step 3

4. The bottom ray will cross the other two at the same place; this is just below the principal focus. You can now mark this on the axis and draw in the first image at Fo (Figure 11.59).

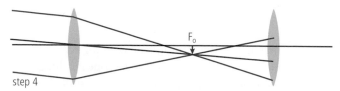

step 4

Figure 11.59 Step 4.

5. The rays emerge from the eyepiece parallel. To find the angle, draw a construction line (dotted) from the top of the image straight through the centre of the eyepiece. All the rays will be parallel to this. Add arrows to all the rays (Figure 11.60).

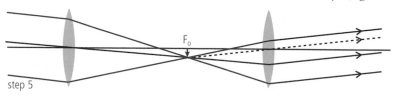

step 5

Figure 11.60 Step 5.

Angular magnification

We can see from the final ray diagram that the angle subtended by the final image at the eye is bigger than the angle subtended by the object at the telescope. Now, the length of the telescope is very small compared to the distance from the Earth to the Moon so we can take the angle subtended at the objective to be the same as the angle subtended by the Moon at the unaided eye. This means that the final image appears to be bigger than the object. The angles involved are shown in Figure 11.61.

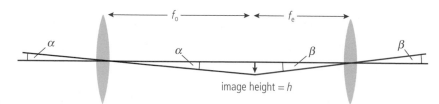

image height = h

Figure 11.61.

From the definition, the angular magnification M is given by the equation:

$$M = \frac{\text{angle subtended by image at eye}}{\text{angle subtended by object at unaided eye}} = \frac{\beta}{\alpha}$$

But if the angles are small and in radians:

$$\alpha = \frac{h}{f_o}$$

$$\beta = \frac{h}{f_e}$$

so angular magnification:

$$M = \frac{\beta}{\alpha} = \frac{h}{f_e} \times \frac{f_o}{h} = \frac{f_o}{f_e}$$

Image brightness

When you look at the Moon or planets through a telescope you see an enlarged image. Distant stars, however, still appear as points; the only difference is they are brighter and you can see more of them. This is because the telescope objective lens is bigger than the lens in your eye so it collects more light. This enables you to see stars that are too dim to see with your unaided eye. Doubling the size of the objective increases the amount

Investigating the performance of a telescope

You can make a telescope by placing two lenses a distance of $f_o + f_e$ apart. You can measure the angular magnification by comparing photographs of a distant object taken through the telescope and without the telescope.

of light collected by a factor of four so even if the magnifying power isn't increased you will be able to see more stars. The limiting factor is the difficulty in manufacturing large lenses; this is why large diameter telescopes use mirrors rather than lenses.

Resolving power

Light has wave-like properties, so when light passes through an opening it diffracts. This causes points of light to appear as spots in the image of a telescope resulting in a reduced resolution. There is no point in making a greatly enlarged image if the resolution is very low. The angle of diffraction is related to the size of the aperture so a bigger aperture will result in greater resolution, again emphasizing the importance of aperture size in telescope design.

The eye ring

When viewing an image through the eyepiece of a telescope you want as much of the light passing through the telescope to enter your eye as possible. The best position for the eye is called the *eye ring*. Figure 11.62 shows how to find the eye ring by drawing rays from the top and bottom of a distant object. If the angle subtended by these rays at the objective is too big then the rays will not be converged enough to pass through the eyepiece. The rays drawn are the widest possible. The place where they pass through the smallest area is the eye ring. This is the image of the objective in the eyepiece.

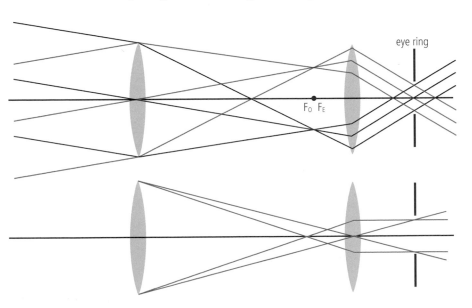

Figure 11.62 The eye ring is the image of the objective in the eyepiece.

To help the user to find the correct position, a circular aperture is positioned in front of the eyepiece (Figure 11.62).

Exercises

20 A telescope is constructed from two lenses: an objective of focal length 100 cm and an eyepiece of focal length 10 cm. The telescope is used in normal adjustment (final image at infinity):

    (a) Calculate the angular magnification.
    (b) What is the distance between the lenses?
    (c) Find the position of the eye ring.

21 A telescope has an objective of focal length 50 cm. What focal length eyepiece should be used to give a magnification of 10?

22 The Moon has a diameter of 3500 km and is 400 000 km from the Earth. Calculate the angle subtended by the Moon at an observer's eye on the Earth.

The reflecting telescope

The objective of a telescope forms a real image of the object which is then viewed with the eyepiece. Instead of using a lens to focus the light we can use a mirror; this gives the possibility to make larger apertures since it is easier to manufacture large mirrors than large lenses. There is one problem with using a mirror: when you view the image your head gets in the way of the light. To solve this you can either use a small mirror to reflect the light to the side (*Newtonian* mounting, Figure 11.63) or make a hole in the middle of the mirror and again, using a small mirror, reflect the light there (*Cassegrain* mounting, Figure 11.64). Note that the large mirrors used in these telescopes are *parabolic* rather than spherical.

The largest refracting telescopes have lenses up to 1 m in diameter, but the largest optical reflecting telescopes go up to 11 m.

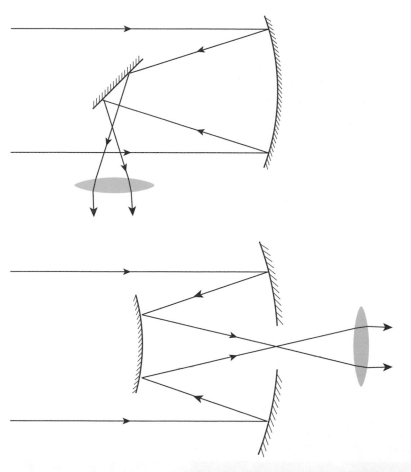

Figure 11.63 Newtonian mounting.

Figure 11.64 Cassegrain mounting.

In these telescopes the eyepiece lens can be omitted and a CCD (*charge coupled device*) placed at the focal point of the mirrors. This is the light sensitive part of a digital camera and can be used to produce a digital image of the stars which can be processed by a computer to produce an image or to do spectral analysis on the light from different objects.

An observer sitting at the prime focus of the 5 m Hale telescope, which is housed at the Palomar Observatory in California, USA.

The Hubble space telescope

'Twinkle twinkle little star how I wonder what you are'. Twinkling might inspire some people to write poetry but for astronomers it is a periodic variation in the stars' intensity caused by changes in the atmosphere, resulting in a distorted image, reducing the resolution. The effect can be minimized by building telescopes on high places. The Hale telescope in the photograph is at 1713 m above sea level in the Palomar Mountains; even then the resolving power is limited to 1 arc second. Better still is to go outside the atmosphere.

The Hubble space telescope is a Cassegrain-type reflecting telescope that orbits the Earth at a height of 569 km every 97 minutes. The 2.4 m mirror is not as big as many earthbound telescopes but the lack of atmosphere gives the possibility to resolve down to less than 0.1 arc second. Images are recorded on several different CCDs, each sensitive to a range of different wavelengths. These images are transmitted to Earth either directly or via a system of tracking and data relay satellites. Many images of the same object are recorded and processed with a computer to form a very high-resolution composite image.

Satellite telescopes can also be used to collect data from wavelengths of the electromagnetic radiation that is absorbed by the atmosphere, such as infrared and ultraviolet.

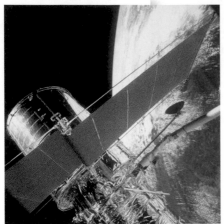

Deployment of the Hubble Space Telescope from the space shuttle Discovery on 24 April, 1990, during mission STS-31.

Single-dish radio telescopes

Stars don't just emit visible light, they also emit other forms of electromagnetic radiation including infrared, microwaves, and radio waves. The atmosphere absorbs most of the infrared, microwaves, and longer wavelength radio waves but radio waves between 1 cm and 20 cm pass through without distortion. These can be used to give us information about the stars and galaxies they originate from. The intensity of radiation coming from a distant star is very low so in order to be detected it must be collected from a wide area. This is done by a parabolic reflector with a detector either placed at the principal focus or, using a Cassegrain mounting, behind the centre of the dish. The resolving power of such a system is limited by diffraction at the aperture of the instrument; longer wavelengths are diffracted by larger apertures so to increase resolution the reflector has to be much larger than the mirror of an optical telescope. However, because of the larger wavelength, the surface of the reflector does not have to be so precisely made. This makes it possible to construct very large radio telescopes such as the Arecibo observatory in Puerto Rico with its 305 m reflector.

Aerial fisheye lens view of the Arecibo radio telescope.

The telescope is pointed at a certain object, say a distant galaxy, and the radio signal recorded. The different wavelengths in the signal can then be analysed to produce a spectrum. A radio image can be made by scanning the telescope, collecting data from each different part of the galaxy. Different colours are then used to represent the intensity of the signal, making it easier to interpret the image. By scanning many times, the image can be processed with a computer to produce a composite image.

Radio interferometer telescope

A radio telescope detects radio waves from one area of the sky. To view two stars the dish has to be rotated. A large radio telescope can resolve stars that are in the order of one arc minute apart; if they are closer than that they will appear as one. To resolve closer stars would require a telescope of wider diameter but there is a limit to how large a telescope can be. However, there is an alternative way that we can construct an image of a star using the interference between signals from two radio telescopes as in Figure 11.65. Here, two telescopes are pointing towards the same star. The distance from the star to each telescope is different so there will be a phase difference between them; as the star moves overhead the interference pattern will change. In Figure 11.65(a) the telescopes are close together so between the two angles shown there will only be one peak. Two different stars separated by a small angle will give two different patterns (red and blue) but as you can see from the diagram they will not be resolved. In Figure 11.65(b) the telescopes are further apart; there are now five peaks between the same two angles. The central peak is now much narrower enabling the two stars to be resolved.

Countries wanting to carry out astronomical research might not be well-placed geographically to build a telescope. In this case they need to cooperate with a more suitably positioned country. The European extremely large telescope is planned to be placed in Chile.

(a)

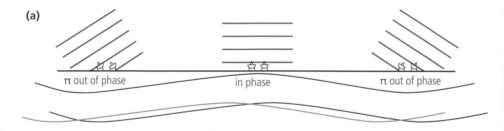

π out of phase   in phase   π out of phase

Figure 11.65 Interference between waves received at two antennae.

(b)

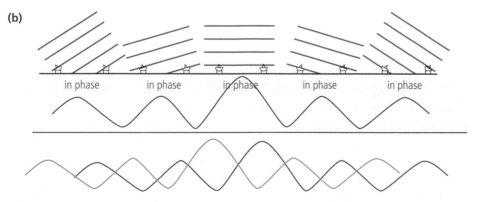

in phase   in phase   in phase   in phase   in phase

An image of the stars can be built up from the interference pattern data by a process known as *aperture synthesis*. The resulting increase in resolving power is equivalent to building one huge telescope with diameter equal to the separation of the telescopes. Using this technique, telescopes can be as wide as the Earth itself.

To learn more about imaging the Universe, go to the hotlinks site, search for the title or ISBN and click on Chapter 11.

11.3 Fibre optics

C.3 Fibre optics

Understandings, applications, and skills:

Structure of optic fibres
- Describing the advantages of fibre optics over twisted pair and coaxial cables.

Step-index fibres and graded-index fibres

Total internal reflection and critical angle
- Solving problems involving total internal reflection and critical angle in the context of fibre optics.

Waveguide and material dispersion in optic fibres
- Describing how waveguide and material dispersion can lead to attenuation and how this can be accounted for.

Guidance
- *The term waveguide dispersion will be used in examinations. Waveguide dispersion is sometimes known as modal dispersion.*

Attenuation and the decibel (dB) scale
- Solving problems involving attenuation.

Guidance
- *Quantitative descriptions of attenuation are required and include attenuation per unit length.*

Fibre optic basics

As introduced in Chapter 5, an optical fibre is a thin strand of glass or clear plastic. If a ray of light enters its end at a small angle, the ray will be total internally reflected when it meets the side. Since the sides are parallel, the ray will be reflected back and forth until it reaches the other end as in Figure 11.66. Optical fibres are used extensively in communication where digital signals are converted to light and passed along fibres.

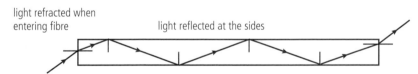

light refracted when entering fibre   light reflected at the sides

Figure 11.66 Light reflected along a fibre.

Remember that if the ray is passing from a medium with refractive index n into air then the critical angle c is given by:

$$\sin c = \frac{1}{n}$$

Worked example

Light is shone into the end of a transparent fibre with refractive index 1.8. Calculate the maximum angle of incidence such that the light will travel along the fibre.

Solution

Figure 11.67.

The maximum angle will be such that the angle of incidence at the side of the fibre (at B) will be equal to the critical angle (c) which is given by the formula $\sin c = \frac{1}{n}$.

So $c = \sin^{-1}\left(\frac{1}{1.8}\right) = 34°$.

Knowing this angle we can calculate $\theta_2 = 90° - 34° = 56°$

Applying Snell's law to the light entering the fibre at A,

$$\frac{\sin \theta_1}{\sin \theta_2} = \frac{n_2}{n_1}$$

$$\text{medium 1 is air so } n_1 = 1 \ n_2 = 1.8$$

$$\sin \theta_1 = 1.8 \times \sin 56°$$

$$\theta_1 = 42°.$$

This is called the *acceptance angle*.

The ophthalmoscope

A lens produces an image of an object by focusing the light reflected off each point on the object to the corresponding points on a screen. If a thin fibre is held in front of an object, light reflected from that point will travel along the fibre and out of the other end. If we have a bunch of fibres then each fibre will collect light from each point on the object resulting in an image at the other end.

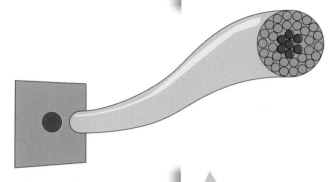

▲ **Figure 11.68** Image of an orange dot on a blue background.

Step-indexed fibre

The problem with bundling fibres is that when the fibres touch each other light could travel from one fibre to the next, messing up the image. To prevent this, fibres are made from two materials, a core and an outer layer with a lower refractive index. This sort of fibre is called a *step-indexed* fibre.

When light travels from the core to the cladding the critical angle will be less than when light travels directly to the air. Applying Snell's law to the situation in Figure 11.69 gives

$$\frac{\sin c}{\sin 90°} = \frac{n_2}{n_1}$$

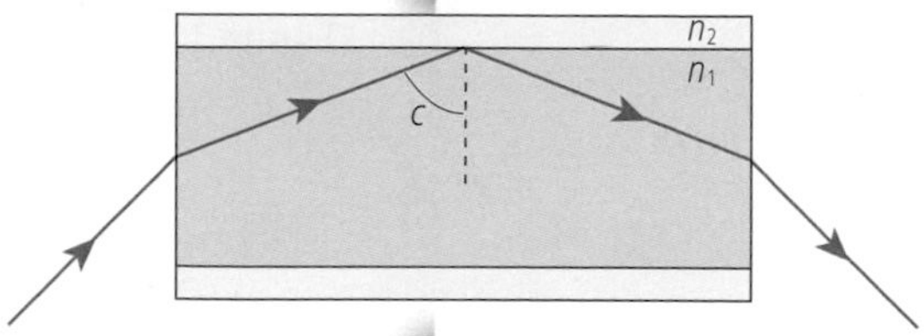

▲ **Figure 11.69** Light entering a step-indexed fibre.

Exercise

23 Calculate the maximum angle of incidence for the ray in Figure 11.69 if $n_1 = 1.8$ and $n_2 = 1.7$.

Graded-index fibre

Instead of having a sudden change from one refractive index to another at the boundary between core and cladding it is possible to construct *graded-index* fibres that have a gradual change of refractive index from the centre outwards. Figure 11.70 shows how light entering a graded-index fibre refracts in a curved path rather than reflecting at the boundary. Here the change of refractive index is such that the light follows a sine curve.

Figure 11.70 Light entering a graded-index fibre.

Optical fibres and digital communication

Digital devices such as computers operate on binary code; a series of 1s and 0s. When digital devices communicate with each other the binary code is transformed into a series of high and low voltages which can be transmitted through a wire. The problem with this form of transmission is that over a long distance the signal deteriorates due to interference caused by other electrical appliances and energy losses due to the resistance of the wire. An alternative is to convert the signal into a series of light flashes, on is a 1 and off is a 0, and then transmit the flashing light along an optical fibre. The advantage of this method is that there is no electrical interference and a fibre can be made much thinner than a wire which would have high resistance if made very thin.

Figure 11.71 A digital signal read once every 1 μs.

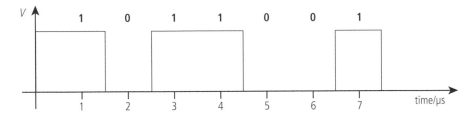

Waveguide dispersion

Light entering a fibre at angles less than the acceptance angle will pass along the fibre but not all rays will take the same path. These different paths are called *modes*. Figure 11.72 shows some of the modes for a step-indexed fibre.

Figure 11.72 Modes in a multimode step-indexed fibre.

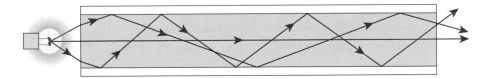

Different modes have different length paths; this means they take different times to reach the other end. If this difference is too big the flashes of light could start to overlap making the transmitted data unusable. This spreading out of the signal is called *waveguide dispersion*. This is much less of a problem in graded-index fibres due to the change in wave speed as the light moves through the regions of different refractive index. High refractive index means low wave speed, so as the light moves towards the outside of the fibre it speeds up, compensating for its longer path (Figure 11.73).

Figure 11.73. Different speeds in a graded-index fibre.

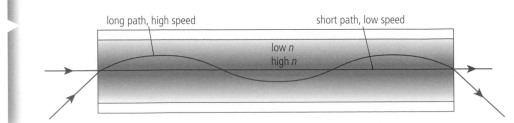

Waveguide dispersion can be reduced further by using a fibre that is so thin that only one mode is transmitted (Figure 11.74); such a fibre is called a *monomode* fibre.

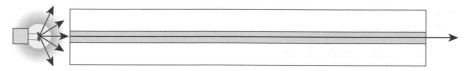

Figure 11.74 A monomode fibre.

The problem with a monomode fibre is that it is more difficult to connect light sources since the acceptance angle is so small.

Material dispersion

When light passes through a prism, different frequencies are refracted by different amounts, causing the colours to disperse. When light travels down a fibre, different frequencies have different paths, as in Figure 11.75.

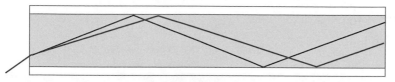

Figure 11.75 Different frequencies have different paths.

This will cause a problem if different bits of data arrive at the wrong time.

Attenuation

Attenuation is the reduction in power as light passes along a fibre due to impurities in the glass. This could be expressed as the ratio of $\frac{\text{power leaving the fibre}}{\text{power entering}}$, but this would give a very large range of values so it is more convenient to use the decibel scale which also has the advantage of being able to combine the attenuation of different sections of fibre by addition rather than multiplication.

The decibel

Attenuation in decibels is defined by the equation:

$$\text{attenuation} = 10 \log_{10}\left(\frac{P}{P_0}\right)$$

where
P = power delivered
P_0 = original power.

So if the power of a signal drops to one half of its original value:

$$\text{attenuation} = 10 \log_{10}\left(\tfrac{1}{2}\right) = -3\text{dB}$$

If the signal drops to $\frac{1}{10^6}$ of the original, the attenuation = $-60\,\text{dB}$. So although the difference in ratio is large, the difference in decibels is not. An increase in attenuation of 50 dB is equivalent to a $\frac{1}{10^5}$ change in power. The attenuation of an optical fibre is normally quoted in dB km^{-1}.

Worked example

A signal is passed along two fibres connected together. The signal into the first fibre is 100 mW and the signal out is 1 mW. The second fibre has an attenuation of −10 dB. Calculate:

(a) the attenuation of the first fibre.

(b) the attenuation of the combination.

(c) the power of the signal out of the combination.

Solution

(a) attenuation $= 10 \log_{10}\left(\dfrac{1}{100}\right) = -20$ dB

(b) Total attenuation $= -20 + -10 = -30$ dB

(c) $-30 = 10 \log_{10}\left(\dfrac{P}{100}\right)$

$10^{-3} = \dfrac{P}{100}$

$P = 0.1$ mW.

Attenuation is a negative quantity but is often expressed as positive; just remember that attenuation gives a *reduction* in power.

To learn more about fibre optics, go to the hotlinks site, search for the title or ISBN and click on Chapter 11.

Exercises

24 The power into a fibre is 1 mW. Calculate the attenuation if the power out is:

(a) 0.1 mW **(b)** 0.2 mW **(c)** 0.01 mW

25 The attenuation of light in a given fibre is 2 dB km^{-1}.

(a) What is the attenuation after 5 km of fibre?

(b) If a signal of 1 mW is sent into 5 km of fibre, what is the power of the signal that comes out?

11.4 Medical imaging

C.4 Medical imaging (HL only)

Understandings, applications, and skills:

(AHL) Detection and recording of X-ray images in medical contexts

- Explaining features of X-ray imaging, including attenuation coefficient, half-value thickness, linear/mass absorption coefficients, and techniques for improvements of sharpness and contrast.
- Solving X-ray attenuation problems.

Guidance

- *Students will be expected to compute final beam intensity after passage through multiple-layers of tissue. Only parallel plane interfaces will be treated.*

(AHL) Generation and detection of ultrasound in medical contexts

- Solving problems involving ultrasound acoustic impedance, speed of ultrasound through tissue and air, and relative intensity levels.
- Explaining features of medical ultrasound techniques, including choice of frequency, use of gel, and the difference between A and B scans.

(AHL) Medical imaging techniques involving nuclear magnetic resonance (NMR)

- Explaining the use of gradient fields in NMR.
- Explaining the origin of the relaxation of proton spin and consequent emission of signal in NMR scans.
- Discussing the advantages and disadvantages of ultrasound and NMR scanning methods, including a simple assessment of risk in these medical procedures.

NATURE OF SCIENCE

Advancements in medical imaging have enabled doctors to make more accurate diagnoses, improving the lives of millions of people. However, a doctor cannot be expected to understand how all these complicated machines work or be able to interpret the images. Hospitals employ teams of people with different specialized knowledge.

Detection and recording of X-ray images

X-rays are short-wavelength (high energy) electromagnetic radiation produced when high speed electrons collide with a metal target. When visible light photons are incident on a solid object such as the human body they are either absorbed or reflected by the surface, X-rays do not interact so readily and are able to penetrate beneath the surface. As they pass through the body they get absorbed at different rates by different materials, so if you could see the X-rays passing through a person you would see a shadow of their insides. This is the principle of X-ray imaging.

Interaction of X-rays with matter

X-rays interact with matter in two ways:

Photoelectric absorption

This is when an X-ray photon is absorbed by an atomic electron causing it to be expelled from the atom. The probability of this type of interaction between a photon with energy E and a unit mass of material with proton number Z is proportional to $\frac{Z^3}{E^3}$. This implies that higher energy X-rays are less likely to be absorbed so will penetrate further.

Compton scattering

This is the process by which an X-ray photon gives some of its energy to an atomic electron causing it to be expelled from the atom. After the interaction the X-ray photon has less energy so it therefore has a longer wavelength and a new direction. The probability of this type of interaction is directly proportional to the proton number.

Both of these interactions are related to the proton number of the material, so there will be more absorption for bone, which contains a lot of calcium (average proton number 14), than for soft tissue, which is mainly water (average proton number 7.4). The number of interactions is also related to the density; for example, the air in the lungs is less dense than the surrounding tissue so doesn't absorb as much radiation, even though the proton numbers of air and lung tissue are similar.

Attenuation of X-rays

As a beam of X-ray photons pass through a solid, some of them interact with the atoms of the solid. This leads to a reduction in intensity, or *attenuation*. As with the

Very soon after the discovery of X-rays it was found that they pass through matter enabling the inside of the body to be seen. The use of X-rays for medical diagnosis soon followed even though the dangers were not then understood. In the 1940s X-ray machines were used in shoe shops so customers could see if the shoes were a good fit.

An X-ray picture is basically a shadow of the bones, but by analysing X-rays projected at different angles it is possible to construct 3D images. Manipulating these images with a computer results in a very clear picture enabling accurate diagnosis.

attenuation of light in an optical fibre, attenuation of X-rays is measured in decibels defined by the equation:

$$\text{attenuation} = 10 \log_{10}\left(\frac{I}{I_0}\right)$$

where
I_0 = intensity going in
I = intensity coming out.

We have seen that the number of interactions depends on the energy of the X-rays and the material, but it also depends on the number of photons. If there are a lot of photons there will be a lot of interactions. As a beam passes through the material the number of photons gets less so the number of interactions also gets less. Figure 11.76 shows a graph of the number of photons in a beam against the distance travelled through the material.

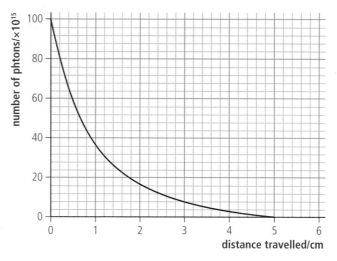

Figure 11.76 Number of photons *vs* distance travelled.

We can say that the number of photons absorbed per cm is proportional to the number of photons in the beam. This is similar to nuclear decay, where the number of decays per second is proportional to the number of nuclei which leads to an exponential relationship between number of nuclei and time. Similarly, the nature of X-ray absorption leads to an exponential relationship between beam intensity (proportional to number of photons) and absorber thickness. The intensity I passing through an absorber of thickness x is given by the equation:

$$I = I_0 e^{-\mu x}$$

where
I_0 = original intensity
μ = the linear attenuation coefficient.

The linear attenuation coefficient (μ) is the fractional decrease in intensity per cm. μ depends upon the type of material and energy of photons, so for the same energy of photons will have a bigger value for bone than it does for soft tissue. The linear attenuation coefficient (μ) depends on the chemical composition and the density (ρ) of the absorber. This means that the value for water is different to the value for ice. An alternative would be to use the *mass attenuation coefficient* which only depends on the composition. This is defined as $\frac{\mu}{\rho}$ and is the value often found in tables.

To get a better idea of how well a material absorbs radiation we can use the *half-value thickness*. This is the thickness of material that would reduce the intensity to half of the original amount.

If the thickness $= x_{\frac{1}{2}}$ then

$$I = \frac{I_0}{2} = I_0 e^{-\mu x_{\frac{1}{2}}}$$

Taking logs gives

$$x_{\frac{1}{2}} = \frac{\ln 2}{\mu} = \frac{0.693}{\mu}$$

Multiple layers

The fractional decrease in intensity when a beam of X-rays pass through an absorber is given by

$$\frac{I_0}{I_1} = e^{-\mu_1 x_1}$$

If this beam is now passed through a second absorber as in Figure 11.77 then the fractional decrease in intensity will be

$$\frac{I_1}{I_2} = e^{-\mu_2 x_2}$$

The total decrease in intensity $\dfrac{I_0}{I_2} = \dfrac{I_0}{I_1} \times \dfrac{I_1}{I_2} = e^{-\mu_1 x_1} \times e^{-\mu_2 x_2} = e^{-(\mu_2 x_2 + \mu_1 x_1)}$

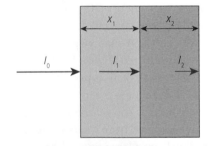

Figure 11.77.

It is easy to see bones on an X-ray picture but not so easy to see the different soft tissues and organs. The radiation emitted by excited hydrogen nuclei is slightly different for each type of tissue. This makes it possible to make detailed images of soft parts of the body like the brain.

X-rays are ionizing so they can cause damage to living cells. International organizations such as the World Health Organization and the International Atomic Energy Authority work together to produce safety guidelines for their use. Do all countries have to abide by these guidelines?

Worked example

A parallel beam of X-rays of intensity $0.2\,\mathrm{kW\,m^{-2}}$ is passed through 5 mm of a material of half-value thickness 2 mm. Calculate the intensity of the beam.

Solution

First calculate the attenuation coefficient.

$$\mu = \frac{0.693}{x_{\frac{1}{2}}} = \frac{0.693}{2}\,\mathrm{mm} = 0.35\,\mathrm{mm^{-1}}$$

Now use the attenuation equation to find I:

$$I = I_0 e^{-\mu x} = 0.2 e^{-0.35 \times 5} = 0.035\,\mathrm{kW\,m^{-2}}$$

Exercise

26 The intensity of a beam of X-rays is reduced from $0.1\,\mathrm{kW\,m^{-2}}$ to $0.08\,\mathrm{kW\,m^{-2}}$ after passing through 4 mm of a material. Calculate:

   (a) the attenuation coefficient of the material
   (b) the half-value thickness.

27 An X-ray beam of intensity $0.5\,\mathrm{kW\,m^{-2}}$ is passed through 3 mm of a material of half-value thickness 1 mm. Calculate:

   (a) the attenuation coefficient of the material.
   (b) the intensity of the beam passing through the material.

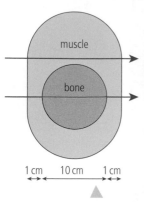

Figure 11.78.

muscle
bone

1 cm 10 cm 1 cm

28 After passing through 6 mm of material, the intensity of an X-ray beam is reduced to 40%. Calculate:

(a) the attenuation coefficient
(b) the half-value thickness.

29 Figure 11.78 shows a cross section of a leg. Calculate the percentage attenuation of a beam of 70 keV X-rays travelling along the two paths shown, given that the half-value thickness for bone is 1.8 cm and for muscle is 3.5 cm.

Producing an X-ray image

We have seen that the attenuation of an X-ray beam is different for different types of tissue so if we pass a beam of X-rays through someone's leg more X-rays will pass through the parts that are muscle than pass through the bone. Photographic plates are sensitive to X-rays so if the transmitted X-rays are incident on a photo-plate we will get a shadow of the bone. This can be seen in the photograph of the author's ankle which also shows some screws and a metal plate holding it together. These show up particularly well since metal absorbs X-rays even better than bone. Cracks in bones also show up since the cracks scatter the X-rays.

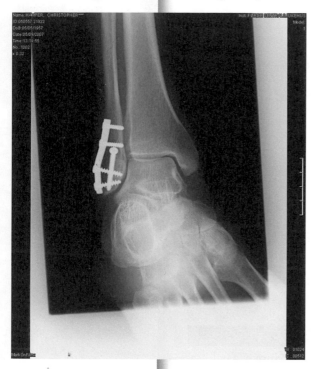

The author's repaired ankle. The light parts are the shadows.

X-Ray beam collimation

X-rays are produced by colliding high energy (10–200 keV) electrons with a metal target. This produces a wide beam of X-rays travelling in different directions. A shadow produced from such a source would be quite blurred (Figure 11.79). To improve this, the beam is made as narrow as possible by shielding the source with lead. This reduces the intensity of the beam but makes the image sharper. You get the same effect if you compare the shadow of your hand from a small source like a light bulb with the shadow from a large source like a fluorescent tube.

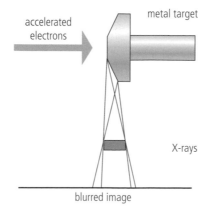

Figure 11.79 Comparing collimated and uncollimated beams.

accelerated electrons — metal target — X-rays — blurred image

shielding — clear image

Scattered radiation

When X-rays interact with matter a proportion of them are scattered. This means they continue through the material in another direction. Some of these scattered photons will reach the photographic plate, reducing the quality of the image. Reducing the beam width reduces the scatter since it reduces the total number of photons entering the sample as shown in Figure 11.80.

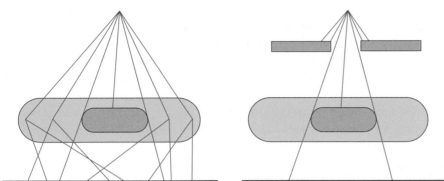

Figure 11.80 Comparing scatter from wide beam and narrow beam.

Another way of reducing scatter is to introduce a grid between the object and photo-plate as in Figure 11.81. This only allows rays that pass through the sample in a straight line from the source to arrive at the photo-plate.

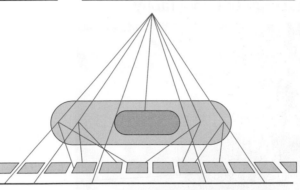

Figure 11.81 Using a grid to reduce scatter.

Further improvements

The image can be improved further by adding an image intensifier; this is a layer of material that emits visible light when X-rays are incident on it. Visible light has more of an effect on the photo-plate than X-rays so placing a layer of this material on either side of the photo-plate will give a more intense image. Bone absorbs X-rays much better than muscle so bones show up well on an X-ray image. However, organs such as the stomach do not show up well in the surrounding tissue. To produce a shadow image of the stomach it can be filled with a more dense material. This can easily be achieved by drinking a solution of barium salts (a 'barium meal') before the X-ray is taken.

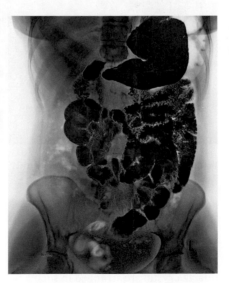

An X-ray of the stomach after swallowing a barium meal.

Digital Images

The photosensitive device (CCD) in a digital camera can't be used directly to convert X-ray photons into an electrical signal, but a fluorescent material can be used that absorbs X-rays and emits light. The light photons can then be detected using photodiodes and a digital image is produced.

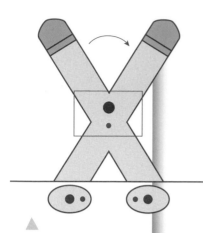

▲ **Figure 11.82** As the spotlight is moved, it is kept focused on the red ball. The circles below show the shadows produced.

▲ **Figure 11.83** The photo of the shadow.

Tomography

Sometimes a shadow picture isn't good enough, especially if the bit you are interested in is somewhere deep in the body, obscured by other bits. In these cases it would be better if you could view a slice of the body; this is made possible with tomography. The way this works can be illustrated with light. Imagine two balls fixed in a transparent block of plastic as shown in Figure 11.82. A spotlight is shone on the red ball and moved to the right. As this happens the spotlight is kept focused on the red ball. The shadow of the red ball will therefore stay in the middle of the spotlight but the blue ball's shadow will move from the left to the right. If a piece of photographic film is now moved along with the spot of light, the shadow of the red ball will form a spot in the middle but the shadow of the blue ball will be a blurred line as in Figure 11.83.

Computer tomography (CT scan)

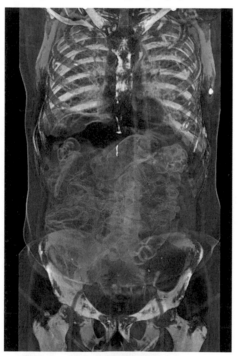

Computer tomography is a more sophisticated version of tomography, where the X-ray source and a circular array of detectors are rotated around the patient. This does not give a picture directly but by analysing the signals from the detector with a computer, a 3D picture of a slice through the patient can be put together. By moving the detectors and X-ray source along the length of the patient's body, a complete 3D image of the patient can be built up. This can be digitally manipulated and artificially coloured to show different layers and highlight specific features.

A CT scan showing the skeleton plus the position of a transplanted kidney.

Ultrasound

Ultrasound is sound that has such a high frequency that we can't hear it, i.e. greater than 20 kHz. By analysing the ultrasound reflected off different layers in the body, it is possible to build up a picture of the internal structure.

Ultrasound production and detection

When a quartz crystal is compressed or stretched a potential difference is induced across it; this is called the *piezoelectric effect*. This happens because the atoms in the quartz crystal are arranged in such a way so that when the crystal is deformed they become polarized, as illustrated in Figure 11.84.

Figure 11.84 When the crystal is stretched the dipoles line up causing a pd. If a pd is applied the crystals line up causing expansion.

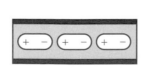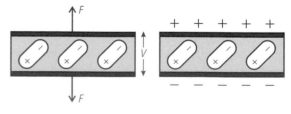

To produce ultrasound, an alternating pd of frequency >20 kHz is applied to the crystal, causing it to vibrate. To detect ultrasound, we can use the alternating pd induced when a sound wave causes a crystal to vibrate. When performing an ultrasound scan, ultrasound reflections are analysed, so to detect the reflected wave, the detector and transmitter must be in the same place. If pulsed ultrasound is used the same crystal can be used for transmission and detection; however, it is important that the pulse is short enough so that the reflected wave doesn't come back before the transmitter has finished transmitting.

Most of the organs doctors would like to see are more than a couple of millimetres under the skin so the duration of the pulse should be less than the time taken for it to travel to a depth of about 1 mm and back (Figure 11.85).

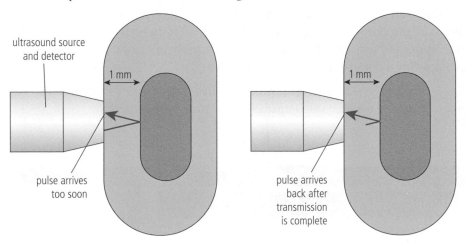

ultrasound source and detector

1 mm

pulse arrives too soon

1 mm

pulse arrives back after transmission is complete

Figure 11.85.

As the speed of sound in the body is approximately $1500\,\text{m s}^{-1}$, the time taken to travel 2 mm is 1.3×10^{-6} s so the duration of the pulse should be no longer than this. To be able to use the signal there must be at least one complete cycle of the wave so in this case the wavelength should be less than 2 mm which is equivalent to a minimum frequency of 750 kHz ($f = \frac{v}{\lambda}$).

The time between pulses must be long enough so that the next pulse isn't transmitted before the most distant reflections have been received. The most distant parts of the body are about 20 cm from the surface so the time taken for the reflection to return will be $\frac{0.4\,\text{m}}{1500\,\text{m s}^{-1}} = 0.3$ ms.

Ultrasound is a wave so will be diffracted by objects that are a similar size to its wavelength; diffraction will cause the reflected wave to spread out so that objects smaller than a few mm will not be resolved. In practice, the frequency used is between 1 and 10 MHz with a time of 1 ms between pulses (Figure 11.86).

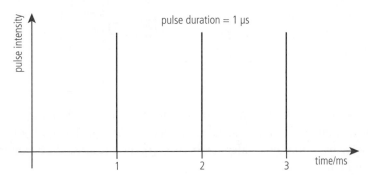

pulse intensity

pulse duration = 1 μs

time/ms

Figure 11.86 An ultrasound signal showing pulse duration and separation.

Acoustic impedance

When ultrasound waves are incident on the boundary between two media, part of the wavefront is reflected and part refracted. The percentage reflected depends upon the relative acoustic impedance of the two media, where impedance is defined by the equation

$$\text{acoustic impedance, } Z = \rho c$$

where ρ = the density of the medium
c = the velocity of the ultrasound.

The unit of Z is $\text{kg m}^{-2}\text{s}^{-1}$.

The greater the difference in acoustic impedance, the greater is the percent reflection. The difference in impedance between the air and skin is very large, so to prevent almost all the ultrasound being reflected before it enters the body, the gap between the transmitter and skin is filled with a gel. This is normally smeared over the body or the probe before the scan begins.

The intensity reflected I_r when a beam of intensity I_0 passes from a medium with impedance Z_1 to medium with impedance Z_2 is given by the equation:

$$\frac{I_r}{I_0} = \left(\frac{Z_2 - Z_1}{Z_2 + Z_1}\right)^2$$

Exercises

Material	Velocity of sound/m s^{-1}	Density/kg m^{-3}
Muscle	1540	1060
Bone	3780	1900
Fat	1480	900

Table 11.1.

30 Calculate the acoustic impedance of the different tissues in Table 11.1 above.

31 Which pair of media will give the greatest percent reflection?

32 Calculate the percentage of the beam reflected when it passes from muscle to bone.

A-scans

The most basic way to display the data is to plot a graph of the strength of the reflected beam against time. From this it is possible to see the position of any changes in medium in the body directly in front of the probe, as illustrated in Figure 11.87.

Figure 11.87 An A-scan for an organ surrounded by tissue.

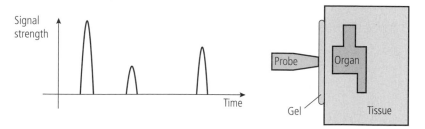

The thickness of the organ can be found from the time between the pulses. Note that due to attenuation the second pulse is smaller than the first but the third pulse is larger since there is a big impedance difference between tissue and air so the percentage reflection is high.

By sweeping the transducer, more information about the size and shape of the organ can be gathered (Figure 11.88).

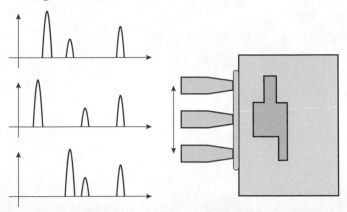

Figure 11.88 A-scans from 3 positions.

Exercise

33 The following questions relate to the A-scan shown in Figure 11.89. In this scan the ultrasound waves travelling at 1500 m s⁻¹ reflect off both sides of an organ then off a bone. The time registered is the time from the pulse leaving the transmitter to returning to the detector.

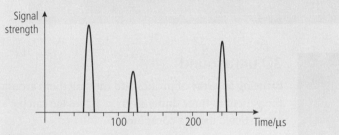

Figure 11.89.

Calculate:

(a) the depth of the organ.
(b) the thickness of the organ.

B-scan

An A-scan gives information about size of organs but doesn't give a picture. A B-scan is a picture which can be achieved by converting the signal into dots on a 2D plot that have an intensity proportional to the height of the peaks. Using an array of transducers, the dots form an image of the organ as shown in Figure 11.90.

Figure 11.90.

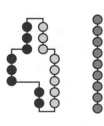 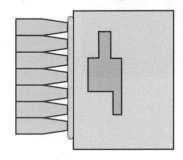

519

All these incredible ways of looking into the human body are immensely helpful in diagnosing illnesses. Unfortunately, the machines that create these images are very expensive and not available to all patients in all countries.

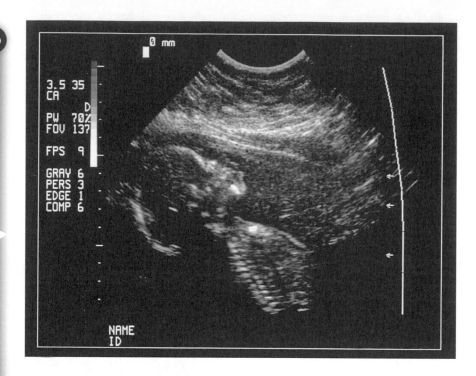

Taking an ultrasound scan of an unborn baby. The baby's backbone and head are clearly visible in the image.

A 3D scan of a fetus.

3D ultrasound

By using an array of probes and moving them around the patient in three dimensions, a 3D image can be constructed using a computer.

Nuclear magnetic resonance (NMR)

Solving a modified version of Schrödinger's wave equation to take into account relativity, it was found that electrons possess a property known as *spin* which causes them to behave like small magnets that can align either in the direction of an applied field or against it. Protons possess the same property so when hydrogen nuclei are placed in a magnetic field they either align with the field (*spin up*) or against it (*spin down*) as in Figure 11.91. These two alignments have different energies so when the nucleus changes from one level to the other EM radiation is either absorbed (up to down) or emitted (down to up), rather like the way light is emitted and absorbed when electrons change energy level.

Figure 11.91 Energy levels of a hydrogen nucleus in a magnetic field.

EM absorbed

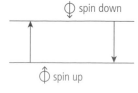

ϕ spin down

ϕ spin up

EM emitted

The difference between the two energy levels is not very high so the EM radiation associated with the change is in the radio wave part of the spectrum. Hydrogen nuclei placed in a strong magnetic field can be excited into the higher energy state (down) by absorbing radio waves of just the right frequency. This is a form of resonance. After some time the nuclei will return to the lower energy state by emitting a radio wave with the same frequency (Figure 11.91).

Magnetic resonance imaging (MRI)

The human body contains a lot of hydrogen nuclei (in water for example) which can be made to resonate if placed in a strong magnetic field. The radio waves emitted when the nuclei lose energy can be used to make an image of the inside of the body because of two important factors:

1. The frequency of radio wave is directly related to the strength of the applied magnetic field.
2. The time taken for the nucleus to return to its lower energy state (*relaxation time*) is different for different types of tissue (600 ms for muscle but only 180 ms for fat in a B field strength of 1 T).

The trick is to use a non-uniform magnetic field. Consider the field represented by Figure 11.92: if we place a hydrogen nucleus in this area its resonant frequency will depend on the field strength B.

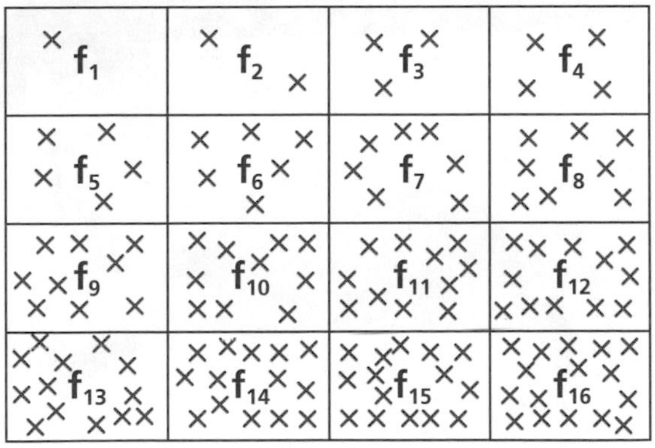

Figure 11.92.

For example, if the frequency emitted is f_1 we know that the nucleus must be in the top left hand corner.

Let's represent the human body by a cube which is half muscle and half fat and place it in the field in as shown in Figure 11.93.

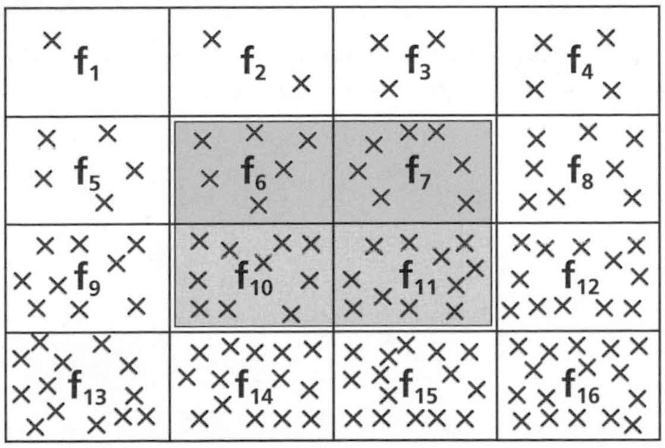

Figure 11.93 A square of tissue (pink = muscle, yellow = fat) in the non-uniform field of an MRI machine.

Radio waves are passed through the area to excite any hydrogen nuclei that might be present. The frequency of the signal is varied slowly from f_1 up to f_{16}. As the frequency increases we detect emitted radiation as hydrogen nuclei resonate at frequencies f_6, f_7, f_{10}, and f_{11} so we know that this is where the body is. If we measure the relaxation time for the different frequencies we find that the relaxation time for f_6 and f_7 is longer than for f_{10} and f_{11} telling us that areas 6 and 7 are muscle and 10 and 11 are fat. Using this technique, a complete picture of the different tissues of the body can be produced.

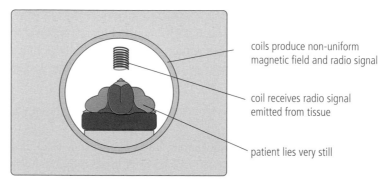

coils produce non-uniform magnetic field and radio signal

coil receives radio signal emitted from tissue

patient lies very still

Figure 11.94.

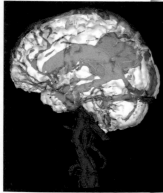

3D MRI of a brain showing a tumour in green.

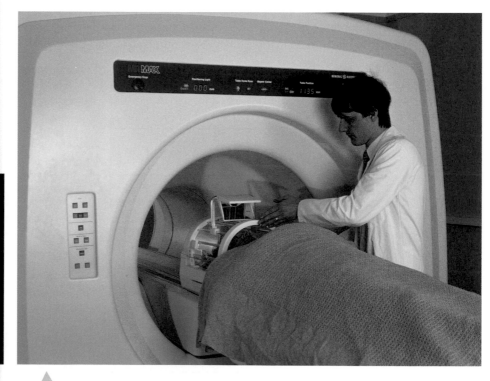

Radiographer preparing a patient for a magnetic resonance imaging (MRI) brain scan. The subject's head is surrounded by the large coils of the scanner's magnet; the smaller device above the subject's head is a radio frequency receiver.

	Advantages	Disadvantages
X-ray	high quality image quick and relatively cheap	X-rays are ionizing so over-exposure of patient or radiologist is dangerous can't be used on pregnant women not so good for viewing soft tissue
Ultrasound	not ionizing so not dangerous, can be used to view unborn babies cheap	not all organs can be viewed not very high resolution
MRI	not ionizing so not dangerous to patient or staff high-quality image bones don't get in the way of radio waves so particularly good for viewing the brain good contrast between different types of soft tissue	expensive each scan takes a long time (about 45 minutes)

▲
Table 11.2 Comparing the different methods of imaging.

To learn more about imaging the body, go to the hotlinks site, search for the title or ISBN and click on Chapter 11.

Practice questions

1. This question is about converging lenses.

   (a) Figure 11.95 shows a small object O represented by an arrow placed in front of a **converging** lens L. The focal points of the lens are labelled F.

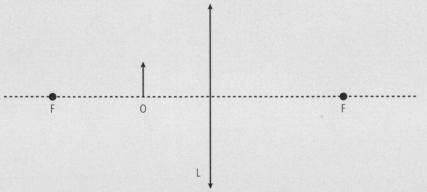

Figure 11.95.

   (i) Define the **focal point** of a converging lens. (2)

   (ii) Copy Figure 11.95 and, on your diagram, draw rays to locate the position of the image of the object formed by the lens. (3)

   (iii) Explain whether the image is real or virtual. (1)

(b) A convex lens of focal length 6.25 m is used to view an ant of length 0.80 cm that is crawling on a table. The lens is held 5.0 cm above the table.

  (i) Calculate the distance of the image from the lens. (2)

  (ii) Calculate the length of the image of the ant. (2)

(*Total 10 marks*)

2. This question is about a compound microscope.

Figure 11.96 shows two lenses of a compound microscope. L_1 is the objective lens and L_2 is the eyepiece lens.

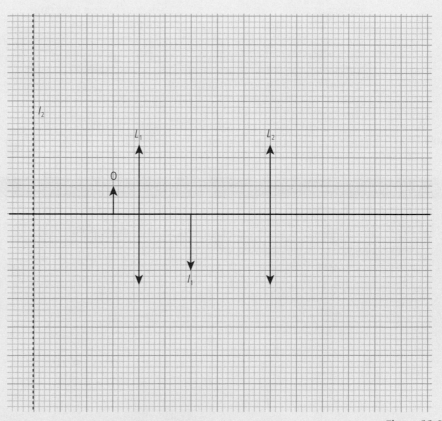

Figure 11.96.

I_1 is the image of the object O formed by the objective lens L_1. The final image formed is in the plane shown by the dotted line labelled I_2.

(a) Copy Figure 11.96 and, on the diagram, construct a ray or rays to determine the position of the principal focus of the eyepiece. Label this position with the letter F. (2)

(b) By using Figure 11.96, take measurements to determine the linear magnification of

  (i) the objective lens. (1)

  (ii) the eyepiece. (1)

(c) Use your answer to (b) to determine the total linear magnification of the microscope. (1)

(*Total 5 marks*)

3. This question is about a compound microscope.

Figure 11.97 (not to scale) is of a compound microscope.

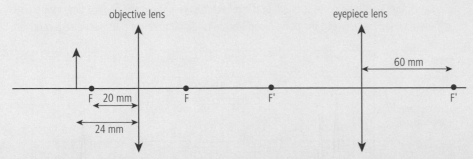

Figure 11.97.

The focal length of the objective lens is 20 mm and that of the eyepiece lens is 60 mm. A small object is placed at a distance of 24 mm from the objective lens. The microscope produces a final virtual image of the object at a distance of 240 mm from the eyepiece lens.

(a) (i) Determine, by calculation, the distance from the objective lens of the image formed by the objective lens. (2)

(ii) Explain why the image in (a)(i) is real. (1)

(iii) Determine the distance of the image formed by the objective lens from the eyepiece lens. (2)

(b) Determine the overall magnification of the microscope. (2)

(Total 7 marks**)**

4. This question is about ultrasound scanning.

(a) State a typical value for the frequency of ultrasound used in medical scanning. (1)

Figure 11.98 shows an ultrasound transmitter and receiver placed in contact with the skin.

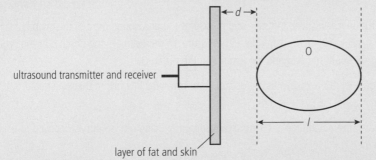

Figure 11.98.

The purpose of this particular scan is to find the depth d of the organ labelled O below the skin and also to find its length, l.

(b) (i) Suggest why a layer of gel is applied between the ultrasound transmitter/receiver and the skin. (2)

On Figure 11.99 the pulse strength of the reflected pulses is plotted against time t where t is the time lapsed between the pulse being transmitted and the time that the pulse is received.

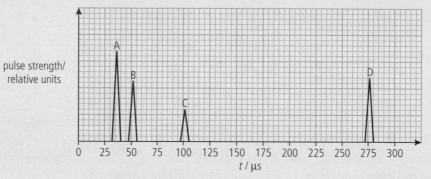

Figure 11.99.

(ii) Copy Figure 11.100 and on your diagram indicate the origin of the reflected pulses A, B, and C, and D. (2)

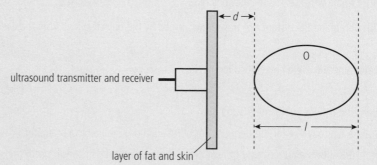

Figure 11.100.

(iii) The mean speed in tissue and muscle of the ultrasound used in this scan is $1.5 \times 10^3 \, \text{m s}^{-1}$. Using data from Figure 11.99, estimate the depth d of the organ beneath the skin and the length l of the organ O. (4)

(c) Figure 11.99 is known as an A-scan. State **one** way in which a B-scan differs from an A-scan. (1)

(d) State **one** advantage and **one** disadvantage of using ultrasound as opposed to using X-rays in medical diagnosis. (2)

(Total 12 marks)

5. This question is about medical imaging.

(a) State and explain which imaging technique is normally used

    (i) to detect a broken bone. (2)

    (ii) to examine the growth of a fetus. (2)

Figure 11.101 shows the variation of the intensity I of a parallel beam of X-rays after it has been transmitted through a thickness x of lead.

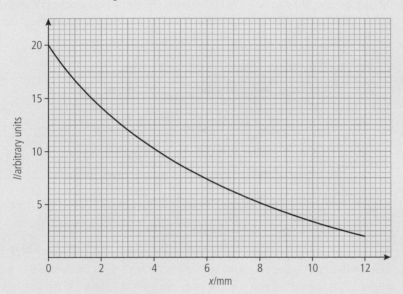

Figure 11.101.

(b) (i) Define **half-value thickness**, $x_{\frac{1}{2}}$. (2)

    (ii) Use Figure 11.101 to estimate $x_{\frac{1}{2}}$ for this beam in lead. (2)

    (iii) Determine the thickness of lead required to reduce the intensity transmitted to 20% of its initial value. (2)

    (iv) A second metal has a half-value thickness $x_{\frac{1}{2}}$ for this radiation of 8 mm. Calculate what thickness of this metal is required to reduce the intensity of the transmitted beam by 80%. (3)

(Total 13 marks)

6. This question is about X-rays.

A parallel beam of X-rays is used to investigate a broken bone. The attenuation coefficient for soft tissue (muscle) is 0.035 cm^{-1}. The X-ray half-value thickness for bone is about 150 times less than that for soft tissue.

(a) Define the term **half-value thickness**. (1)

(b) Deduce that the attenuation coefficient for bone is 5.3 cm^{-1}. (2)

(c) The parallel beam of X-rays is incident on a human leg. The leg has a bone of diameter 5.0 cm, surrounded by muscle on each side of thickness 5.0 cm. A section through the leg is shown in Figure 11.102.

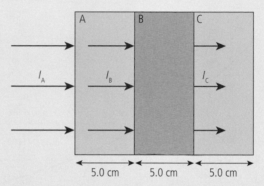

Figure 11.102.

The intensity of the X-ray beam at the surface A of the leg is I_A. At the surface B of the bone, the intensity is I_B and the intensity of the beam emerging at surface C of the bone is I_C.

Determine the ratio

(i) $\dfrac{I_B}{I_A}$ (2)

(ii) $\dfrac{I_C}{I_B}$ (1)

(d) Use your answers in (c) to explain how it is possible to obtain a shadow image of the leg and bone. (3)

(Total 9 marks)

7. This question is about ultrasound imaging.

(a) Describe

(i) what is meant by ultrasound. (1)

(ii) how ultrasound may be produced. (2)

(b) Table 11.3 gives information on the speed of sound, the density and the acoustic impedance for various materials.

Material	Speed of sound /m s^{-1}	Density / kg m^{-3}	Acoustic impedance / kg m^{-2} s^{-1}
Air	340	1.3	440
Bone	2800	1.5×10^3	
Tissue	1600	1.0×10^3	1.6×10^6

Table 11.3.

Calculate the acoustic impedance of bone and enter your answer in the table above. (1)

(c) Ultrasound of intensity I_0 is travelling in a medium of impedance Z_1 and is incident on a medium of impedance Z_2. The *reflected* ultrasound has intensity I_R given by

$$I_R = I_0 \left(\frac{Z_1 - Z_2}{Z_1 + Z_2} \right)^2$$

(i) With reference to the equation above explain why ultrasound would not be an effective method for a brain scan. (2)

(ii) Using data from the table in (b) determine the ratio $\frac{I_R}{I_0}$ of ultrasound entering tissue from air. (2)

(iii) Using your answer to (c)(ii), explain the purpose of the gel that is applied to the skin before an ultrasound scan. (2)

(d) A pulse of ultrasound is emitted from a transducer placed on a patient's skin. The pulse is reflected by the stomach and is received back at the transducer. Figure 11.103 (an A-scan) shows how the voltage due to the transmitted and the reflected pulse varies with time. The speed of sound in tissue is 1600 m s^{-1}.

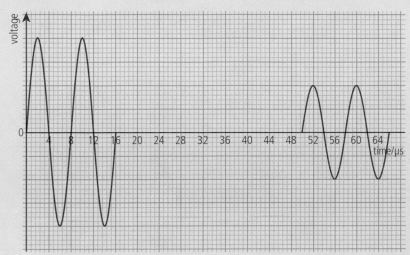

Figure 11.103.

(i) Using data from the graph determine the distance between the stomach and the transducer. (2)

(ii) Outline two differences between an A-scan and a B-scan. (2)

(Total 14 marks)

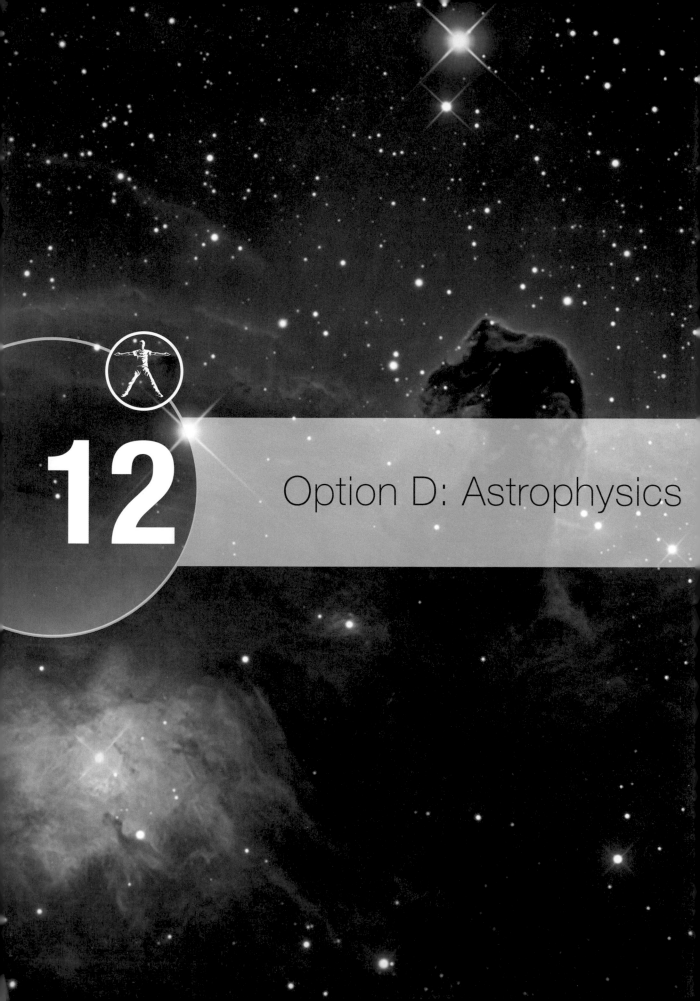

12

Option D: Astrophysics

Essential ideas

D.1 Stellar quantities
One of the most difficult problems in astronomy is coming to terms with the vast distances in between stars and galaxies and devising accurate methods for measuring them.

D.2 Stellar characteristics and stellar evolution
A simple diagram that plots the luminosity versus the surface temperature of stars reveals unusually detailed patterns that help us understand the inner workings of stars. Stars follow well-defined patterns from the moment they are created out of collapsing interstellar gas, to their lives on the main sequence and to their eventual death.

D.3 Cosmology
The hot Big Bang model is a theory that describes the expansion of the Universe and is supported by extensive experimental evidence.

D.4 Stellar evolution (HL only)
The laws of nuclear physics applied to nuclear fusion processes inside stars determine the production of all elements up to iron.

D.5 Further cosmology (HL only)
The modern field of cosmology uses advanced experimental and observational techniques to collect data with an unprecedented degree of precision and as a result very surprising and detailed conclusions about the structure of the Universe have been reached.

NATURE OF SCIENCE

All that is known about the stars has been deduced by observing the radiation emitted from them. Using this data, with the assumption that the laws of physics are the same throughout the Universe, scientists have constructed models to determine their properties and composition.

The Horse Head Nebula, a dense cloud of dust made visible by the background pink glow from the ionized gas behind. The nebula is located just south of the most easterly star of Orion's belt, but you would need to computer enhance photos from a large telescope to see it as it is in this image.

'Pillars of creation'. An image taken by the Hubble telescope showing gaseous pillars in the Eagle Nebula. These columns of dust and hydrogen act as incubators for new stars.

12.1 Stellar quantities

D.1 Stellar quantities

Understandings, applications, and skills:

Objects in the Universe
- Identifying objects in the Universe.

  Guidance
  - *For this course, objects in the Universe include planets, comets, stars (single and binary), planetary systems, constellations, stellar clusters, galaxies, clusters of galaxies, and superclusters of galaxies.*

Astronomical distances
- Using the units of light year and parsec.

  Guidance
  - *Students are expected to have an awareness of the vast changes in distance scale from planetary systems through to superclusters of galaxies and the Universe as a whole.*

Stellar parallax and its limitations
- Describing the method to determine distance to stars through stellar parallax.

Luminosity and apparent brightness
- Solving problems involving luminosity, apparent brightness, and distance.

The view from here

Astrophysics is the study of the physical properties of celestial objects (stars and other bodies in our Universe) and the interactions between them. The body of knowledge that we have about these objects has been built up over time from observations that, in the early years, were all made from the Earth. So what can we see from here?

The Sun

The Sun rises in the east and goes down in the west. It appears to be going around the Earth but we know that the movement is due to the rotation of the Earth (time period 23 hours 56 min). Ancient civilizations worshipped the Sun because it controlled the seasons; they built complicated structures to predict special events such as the longest day of the year. The Earth not only rotates but also moves around the Sun in an elliptical orbit (time period 365.35 days). The axis of rotation of the Earth is not parallel with the axis of its orbit around the Sun; this causes the position of the Sun to change slightly every day resulting in the seasons. You can see from Figure 12.1 how this causes the northern hemisphere to get more sunlight during the summer. If you were to travel to the far north during the northern summer you could see the Sun all day. The Sun emits a lot of energy in the form of electromagnetic radiation. The source of energy is nuclear fusion taking place in the core. This heats the outer layers to such a high temperature that it emits the light that we see.

Figure 12.1 The Earth rotates as it orbits the Sun but the axes of rotation are not parallel.

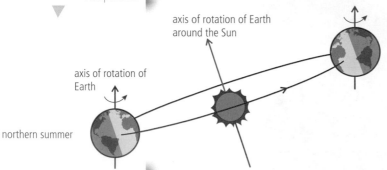

axis of rotation of Earth around the Sun

axis of rotation of Earth

northern winter

northern summer

The Moon

Due to the rotation of the Earth, the Moon also appears to move from west to east every night (and sometimes in the daytime but not so visible then). If you were to watch the Moon on several successive nights you would notice that it appears to rise slightly later each evening. This is because the Moon is orbiting the Earth with a time period of 27.3 days. The Moon is visible not because it produces light but because it reflects light from the Sun. The Sun only illuminates one side of the Moon giving rise to the varying phases (full Moon, half-Moon, and new Moon). As the Moon orbits around the Earth, the Earth orbits around the Sun with the result that periodically the Moon passes between Earth and the Sun, forming a solar eclipse.

A partial eclipse of the Sun.

Stars

The stars are very distant spherical bodies that emit light just like the Sun. The rotation of the Earth causes the stars to appear to move across the sky from east to west. The closest star visible without a telescope (not counting the Sun) is Alpha Centauri at a distance of about 3.8×10^{16} m. This is so far away that it would take light 4 years to travel from the star to Earth, hence the use of the unit *light year* (ly) when quoting astronomical distances. One light year is the distance travelled by light in one year. Deneb, one of the most distant, easily visible stars is 3200 ly from the Earth. As the Earth moves around the Sun we view the stars from different angles. This causes them to appear to move slightly with respect to one another (parallax). However, this movement is very small and not noticeable without a telescope, so with the naked eye the stars appear to have fixed positions relative to each other. By joining the dots, ancient civilizations imagined figures in the sky to give the *constellations* we use today such as Taurus and Orion.

The constellations of Orion and Taurus. Betelgeuse is Orion's left shoulder.

The stars in a constellation have no physical connection, some of them are thousands of light years apart; they just look like they are next to each other because they are so far away that they appear to be the same distance from us. Stars that are actually close together are called a *stellar cluster*. Constellations are of little interest to astrophysicists but can be useful to help locate objects of interest. For example, the star Betelgeuse is the left shoulder of Orion.

Unless you are colour blind you will notice that stars have different colours but apart from twinkling, which is caused by the atmosphere, most stars appear to have a constant brightness. On closer inspection the brightness of a lot of stars isn't constant; this can be due to pairs of orbiting stars eclipsing each other (*binary stars*) or due to changes in size (*Cepheid variables*). We can get a lot of information about stars by analysing the light we receive from them; this enables us to model their physical properties which is what most of this section will be about.

Different cultures developed different systems for defining the different patterns in the stars.

The Greeks had the 12 signs of the zodiac, the Chinese 28 xiu and the Indians 27 Nakshatra.

Planets

If you look at the night sky at exactly the same time every night for a month you will notice that the stars appear to move slightly to the west each night. This is because the period of rotation of the Earth is slightly less than 24 hours. You will also notice that almost all the stars have the same relative position (forming patterns we call the constellations). However, there are some exceptions. Some of the brightest objects move around from one day to the next; these are in fact not stars but planets. Planets are bodies like the Earth that are in orbit around the Sun. They are much closer to us than the stars and are visible because they reflect light from the Sun rather than emit light like stars. Each planet has a different orbital period. The planet closest to the Sun, Mercury, has an orbit of only 88 days whereas the furthest, Neptune, has a 164-year orbit. This means that at different times of the year they will be in different positions relative to each other, resulting in their movement when viewed from the Earth.

On 24 August 2006 the International Astronomical Union (IAU) declared the official definition of a planet:

A 'planet' is a celestial body that (a) is in orbit around the Sun, (b) has sufficient mass for its self-gravity to overcome rigid body forces so that it assumes a hydrostatic equilibrium (nearly round) shape, and (c) has cleared the neighbourhood around its orbit.

There are 8 planets in orbit around the Sun. Each planet has a different radius, time period and size.

Their order in terms of distance from the Sun is given in Table 12.1:

Planet	Orbit radius (m)	Mass (kg)	Radius (m)	Period
Mercury	5.79×10^{10}	3.30×10^{23}	2.44×10^6	88.0 days
Venus	1.08×10^{11}	4.87×10^{24}	6.05×10^6	224.7 days
Earth	1.50×10^{11}	5.98×10^{24}	6.38×10^6	365.3 days
Mars	2.28×10^{11}	6.42×10^{23}	3.40×10^6	687.0 days
Jupiter	7.78×10^{11}	1.90×10^{27}	6.91×10^7	11.86 years
Saturn	1.43×10^{12}	5.69×10^{26}	6.03×10^7	29.42 years
Uranus	2.88×10^{12}	8.66×10^{25}	2.56×10^7	83.75 years
Neptune	4.50×10^{12}	1.03×10^{26}	2.48×10^7	163.7 years

Table 12.1.

There are also over 40 dwarf planets of which Pluto is one. The reason Pluto is not a planet is because it does not dominate its neighbourhood; in fact Pluto is only twice as big as its moon Charon.

Also orbiting the Sun are *asteroids* and *comets*. Asteroids are lumps of rock up to 1000 km diameter orbiting the Sun in the Asteroid belt between Mars and Jupiter. They are rarely visible from Earth without a telescope due to their small size. A comet is a lump of rock, ice, and frozen gases with a very elongated elliptical orbit. They spend most of their time in the outer reaches of the solar system but become visible when their orbit takes them close to the Sun. Violent explosions on the Sun throw out particles forming the solar wind. When the comet moves close to the Sun the heat evaporates the frozen gases and the solar wind blows the gases and bits of ice and dust off the surface of the comet forming its characteristic tail which always points away from the Sun.

Galaxies

If we use a telescope to look at some of the distant stars we find that they are not single stars but hundreds of billions of stars called galaxies. The first of these to be discovered was the Andromeda galaxy in the photograph. Stars are grouped in galaxies which are about 10^5 ly across containing around 10^{11} stars. Almost all of the stars you see at night are in our own galaxy, the Milky Way. We are positioned two-thirds of the way out from the centre of this lens-shaped spiral galaxy; if we look towards its centre we see it as a stripe of dense stars.

Halley's comet photographed in 1986. The tail looks like it is left behind as the comet moves downwards but the comet is actually moving sideways. The tail points away from the Sun so the Sun is below the bottom of the photograph.

View of the Milky way in the sky over the William Herschel Telescope at the Roque de Los Muchachos Observatory La Palma, Canary Islands. The Andromeda galaxy is the lens shaped object at the top left of the photograph.

The distance between galaxies is about 10^6 ly so there is a lot of space between them. Galaxies are also grouped in galaxy *clusters*; our own galaxy is part of the local cluster of twenty galaxies. There are even clusters of clusters called *superclusters*.

Astronomical distances

Astronomical distances are so large that the metre is not a particularly useful unit; instead, the *light year* (ly) is often used. This is the distance travelled in a vacuum by light in 1 year:

$$1 \text{ ly} = 9.46 \times 10^{15} \text{ m}$$

The arc second

One degree can be split up into 60 arc minutes and each arc minute into 60 arc seconds, so there are 3600 arc seconds in one degree.

Another useful unit for distances on a solar system scale is the *astronomical unit* (AU). This is the average distance between the Sun and the Earth:

$$1 \text{ AU} = 1.5 \times 10^{11} \text{ m}$$

To measure astronomical distances astronomers can't measure lengths directly but instead use the angles subtended by objects as the Earth orbits the Sun. In this case, the *parsec* is a much more convenient unit to use since it can be found directly from the angle. The parsec is defined by the triangle in Figure 12.2. If the angle subtended between two points separated by 1 AU and a distant star is 1 arc second then the distance to the star is 1 parsec (pc).

Figure 12.2.

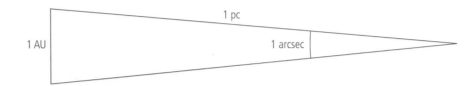

Although not developed specifically for use with telescopes, astronomers were quick to realize the potential of digital photography and have made many contributions towards the development of this technology.

So if the angle is smaller the distance is larger. The distance in pc = $\dfrac{1}{\text{angle in arc sec}}$

$$1 \text{ pc} = 3.26 \text{ ly}$$

From an early age we are taught to appreciate the relative sizes of objects by comparing them next to each other. This becomes problematic when trying to comprehend the difference in size between the Sun and the Universe. No matter how small you draw the Sun you can't get the Universe on the same page. To manage this, the Sun would have to be smaller than a proton, not that this information helps.

To get an idea of the relative size of the different structures in the Universe is very difficult as we can't draw them all on the same page. However, we can build up step by step, as in Figure 12.3. For instance, if the size of the Sun was the size of a small insect then the solar system would be the size of the great pyramid; if the solar system was the size of the insect, the Milky Way would be the size of Mount Everest, etc.

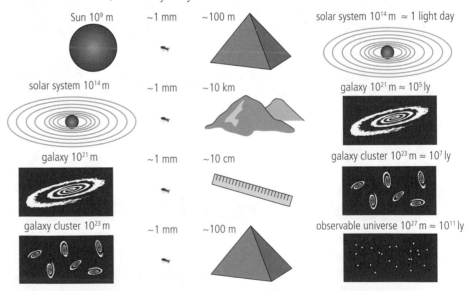

Figure 12.3 The relative sizes of different structures in the Universe.

Exercises

1 The distance to the nearest star is 4.3×10^{13} km. What is this in light years?

2 How long does it take light to travel from the Sun to the Earth?

3 How long would it take for a rocket travelling at 30 000 km h⁻¹ to travel to the nearest star from the Earth?

4 What is the distance to the nearest star in parsecs? What angle does this star subtend to the Earth when the Earth has moved a distance of 2 AU from one side of the Sun to the other? Verify that the distance in pc agrees with the angle.

Stellar parallax

As mentioned previously, astronomers can't measure distances directly but use the angle subtended by a star as the Earth moves around the Sun. This technique is known as stellar parallax. To reduce uncertainties, the biggest angle possible should be measured so the angles are measured when the Earth is on opposite sides of the Sun, which means measuring the position of a star once then again 6 months later.

Parallax is the way objects move relative to each other as you move past them. If you look straight ahead and move your head to the left then objects closer to you will move to the right relative to objects further away (assuming you are not looking at a blank wall). Very distant objects do not move at all so can be used as a reference direction when measuring the angles. Consider the simplified version in Figure 12.4. To find the distance to the red star the telescope is first lined up at position A with the distant blue star. The telescope is then rotated to the red star and the angle measured. Six months later the blue star is still in the same position but, due to parallax, the red star has moved relative to it. The angle between the stars is measured again. The distance is now:

$$d \text{ (parsec)} = \frac{1}{p \text{ (arc sec)}}$$

For distant stars the angle can be a fraction of an arcsec. This would be very difficult to measure by rotating the telescope for each star so photographs are used to measure the angles as in Figure 12.5. This can be done by first calibrating the photograph by rotating the telescope through a known angle, which will cause all the stars in the photograph to move to one side. The distance moved is proportional to the angle, so the angle subtended by the stars 6 months later can be found by measuring how far they move compared to the distant stars that don't move. Note that negatives are used to make the background transparent. This means that the photographs can be placed on top of each other making the measurements easier.

This method is limited by the smallest angle that can be measured. This is around 0.01 arcsec for a terrestrial telescope (one on the Earth) and 0.001 for a space telescope such as the Hubble space telescope. This is equivalent to a distance of 1 kpc which doesn't even extend beyond our galaxy. There are other methods for more distant stars that we will explore later.

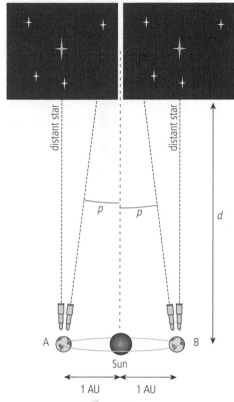

Figure 12.4 Measuring the distance to a star.

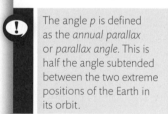

The angle p is defined as the *annual parallax* or *parallax angle*. This is half the angle subtended between the two extreme positions of the Earth in its orbit.

Figure 12.5 Using photographs to measure astronomical distances.

The star in the photograph might have changed position because it was moving. We can check if this is the case by taking a third photograph six months later to see if it is back in the original place.

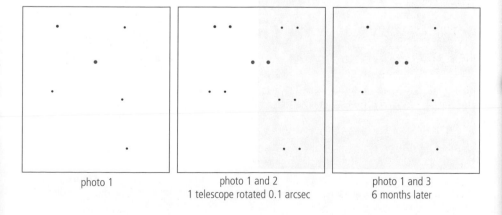

photo 1

photo 1 and 2
1 telescope rotated 0.1 arcsec

photo 1 and 3
6 months later

Exercises

5 Using the images in Figure 12.5, measure the distance from the Earth to the blue star.

6 Calculate the parallax angle for a star on the other side of our galaxy (a distance of 10^{21} m). Would the movement of this star be visible using the telescope of Exercise 5?

EM radiation from stars

All that we know about stars has been deduced by measuring the radiation they emit. This radiation has two important pieces of information: *intensity* – related to brightness – and *wavelength* – related to the colour. Knowing the distance to a star we can use this information to calculate its temperature, radius, and the amount of energy it radiates per second.

Apparent brightness (*b*)

If you look at the stars at night you will notice that some stars are brighter than others. You may also think that some look bigger than others; this is not the case. All stars except the Sun are so far away that they appear as points of light. The only objects that have size (and do not appear as point sources) are the planets, the Moon, and the occasional comet. The effect is caused by poor focus, movements of the air, and your brain telling you that brighter must be bigger. If you look at a photograph of the stars the brighter ones still look bigger. This is due to the way the camera works but gives us a useful method for measuring the relative brightness of stars and is the way brightness is indicated on a star map. In the early days of astronomy the stars were put in order of brightness from 1 to 6, 1 being the brightest, and 6 the least bright visible with the unaided eye. This number is called the *magnitude* and is still used today.

Exercise

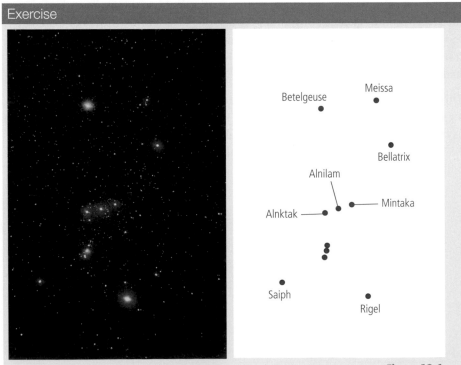

Figure 12.6.

7 Given that Rigel is a magnitude 0 star, use the photograph to estimate the magnitudes of the other stars labelled in Figure 12.6.

With today's technology it is possible to measure the brightness of a star directly using a digital photograph, the pd across each pixel being directly related to the number of photons absorbed. Brightness is the amount of power per unit area perpendicular to the direction of the radiation.

The *apparent brightness* of a star is the brightness measured from the Earth. This depends on how much power the star is emitting and how far away it is. The unit of apparent brightness is $W\,m^{-2}$.

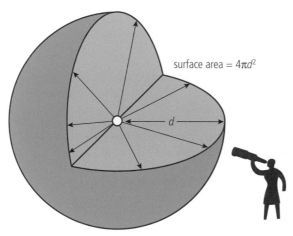

surface area = $4\pi d^2$

d

Figure 12.7 As the light travels away from the star, the energy is spread over a bigger area.

Luminosity (L)

The *luminosity* of a star is the total amount of energy emitted per unit time (power). The unit of luminosity is the watt.

The energy is radiated equally in all directions so at a distance d will be spread out over the surface of a sphere of surface area $4\pi d^2$. The apparent brightness is the power per unit area so the brightness b at distance d will be given by the equation:

$$b = \frac{L}{4\pi d^2}$$

The Sun has a luminosity $L_\odot = 3.84 \times 10^{26}$ watts. The luminosity of other stars is normally quoted as a multiple of this value $L_\odot$.

Exercises

8 The luminosity of the Sun is 3.839×10^{26} W and its distance from the Earth is 1.5×10^{11} m. Calculate its

   (a) apparent brightness.
   (b) brightness at a distance of 10 pc.

9 Sirius, the brightest star, has a luminosity 25 times greater than the Sun and is 8.61 light years from the Earth. Calculate:

   (a) its apparent brightness.
   (b) its brightness at a distance of 10 pc.

10 If the luminosity of a star is 5.0×10^{31} W and its apparent brightness is $1.4 \times 10^{-9}\,W\,m^{-2}$, calculate its distance from the Earth in ly.

To learn more about stellar quantities, go to the hotlinks site, search for the title or ISBN and click on Chapter 12.

12.2 Stellar characteristics

D.2 Stellar characteristics and stellar evolution

Understandings, applications, and skills:

Stellar spectra
- Explaining how surface temperature may be obtained from a star's spectrum.
- Explaining how the chemical composition of a star may be determined from the star's spectrum.

Hertzsprung–Russell (HR) diagram
- Sketching and interpreting HR diagrams.
- Identifying the main regions of the HR diagram and describing the main properties of stars in these regions.

> *Guidance*
> - *Main regions of the HR diagram are restricted to the main sequence, white dwarfs, red giants, super giants, and the instability strip (variable stars), as well as lines of constant radius.*
> - *HR diagrams will be labelled with luminosity on the vertical axis, and temperature on the horizontal axis.*

Mass–luminosity relation for main sequence stars
- Applying the mass–luminosity relation.

> *Guidance*
> - *Only one specific exponent (3.5) will be used in the mass–luminosity relation.*

Cepheid variables
- Describing the reason for the variation of Cepheid variables.
- Determining distance using data on Cepheid variables.

Stellar spectra

Stars are almost perfect radiators. This means the intensity distribution of electromagnetic radiation they emit is the same as the characteristic pattern of the black-body spectrum as shown in Figure 12.8.

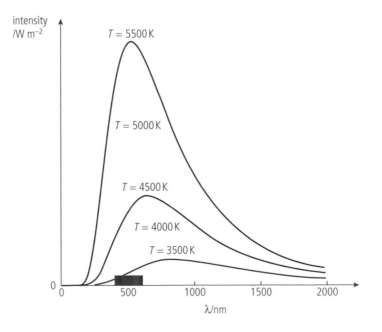

Figure 12.8 The intensity distribution for bodies of different temperature, the spectrum indicates where the visible region lies on the scale.

We can see from this set of curves that increasing the temperature reduces the average wavelength but increases the area under the graph. This means that the total power radiated per unit area has increased. The relationship between power per unit area and temperature in kelvin is given by the *Stefan–Boltzmann law* (see Chapter 8):

$$\frac{\text{power}}{\text{area}} = \sigma T^4$$

where $\sigma = 5.6 \times 10^{-8}\,\text{W m}^{-2}\text{K}^{-4}$ (the Stefan–Boltzmann constant).

The total power radiated (luminosity) by a star of surface area A is therefore:

$$L = A\sigma T^4.$$

The relationship between the peak wavelength and the temperature in kelvin is given by *the Wien displacement law*:

$$\lambda_{\text{max}} = \frac{2.9 \times 10^{-3}\,\text{m K}}{T}$$

If we plot the spectrum for a star we can calculate its temperature from the peak wavelength. This would mean measuring the intensity of light at many different wavelengths. Luckily there is a shortcut: since we know the shape of the curve is the same as a black-body spectrum we only need a few points to be able to determine which of the different temperature curves represents its spectrum. This is done by using three filters: ultra violet, blue, and green (called UBV, the V stands for *visual* but the colour is *green*).

> **!** The unit m K of the constant is *metre* kelvin.

Worked example

The maximum in the black-body spectrum of the light emitted from the Sun is at 480 nm. Calculate the temperature of the Sun and the power emitted per square metre.

Solution

Using Wien's law

$$\lambda_{\text{max}} = \frac{2.90 \times 10^{-3}}{T}$$

$$T = \frac{2.9 \times 10^{-3}}{\lambda_{\text{max}}} = \frac{2.9 \times 10^{-3}}{480 \times 10^{-9}} = 6000\,\text{K}$$

Now using the Stefan-Boltzmann law

$$\text{Power per unit area} = 5.6 \times 10^{-8} \times (6000)^4 = 7.3 \times 10^7\,\text{W m}^{-2}$$

If the radius of the Sun is 7.0×10^8 m, what is the luminosity?

$$\text{The surface area of the Sun} = 4\pi r^2 = 6.2 \times 10^{18}\,\text{m}^2$$

$$\text{The total power radiated} = 6.2 \times 10^{18} \times 7.3 \times 10^7 = 4.5 \times 10^{26}\,\text{W}$$

Exercises

11 The star Betelgeuse has a radius of 3.1×10^{11} m and a surface temperature of 2800 K. Find its luminosity.

12 The intensity peak in a star's spectrum occurs at 400 nm. Calculate:

(a) its surface temperature.

(b) the power radiated per square metre.

Absorption lines

As the black-body radiation passes through the outer layers of a star some of it is absorbed by the gases found there. This leads to dark *absorption lines* in the otherwise continuous spectrum. These lines are unique for each element and can be used to determine the chemical composition of the outer layers. The spectrum of light from the Sun includes the spectral lines of some 67 different elements. Studies show that most stars have similar composition: 72% hydrogen, 25% helium, and 3% other elements.

> The absorption lines give information about the composition of the outer layers of gas surrounding a star. However, the layers of a star are continually mixing so the outer layers have the same composition as the rest of the star.

The spectrum of the light from the Sun showing the absorption lines for many elements.

The darkness of the absorption lines are a useful indicator of the temperature of a star. To absorb a photon of radiation it must be possible for an electron to be excited from a low to high energy. Taking hydrogen as an example, if the star is very hot the hydrogen will be ionized so any further excitations will not be possible, and the light will not be absorbed so the spectral lines will be absent. At lower temperatures the number of excitations will depend on the number of electrons in the lower energy levels. Low temperature means fewer excited electrons so more excitations are possible, resulting in a darker absorption line. Consider the two transitions shown in the energy levels represented in Figure 12.9. ΔE_1 represents a high energy transition so would give an absorption line in the blue region; ΔE_2 would be in the red region. When very hot at temperature T_1 the atoms are all fully ionized so there are no possible further transitions. At temperature T_2 most electrons are in the high level so the red line will be darkest. At T_3 absorption of red light is not possible and at T_4 neither line will appear.

By measuring the intensity of absorption lines of hydrogen and other elements, the temperature of thousands of stars has been determined.

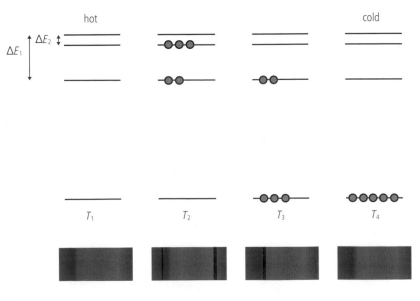

Figure 12.9 The energy of the electrons in five atoms at four different temperatures.

Spectral classification of stars

We have seen that the spectrum of a star is related to its temperature and chemical composition. This also determines its colour: if the peak is at the blue end, it will be blue, and if at the red end then it will be red. The Harvard classification classifies stars according to their colour, with each class assigned a letter OBAFGKM, as shown in Table 12.2.

Class	Temperature	Colour
O	30 000–60 000	Blue
B	10 000–30 000	Blue–white
A	7 500–10 000	White
F	6000–7500	Yellow–white
G	5000–6000	Yellow
K	3500–5000	Orange
M	2000–3500	Red

Table 12.2 The Harvard OBAFGKM classification of stars.

(!) Oh Be A Fine Girl Kiss Me (or guy or gorilla if you prefer) is a common way of remembering this unusual sequence.

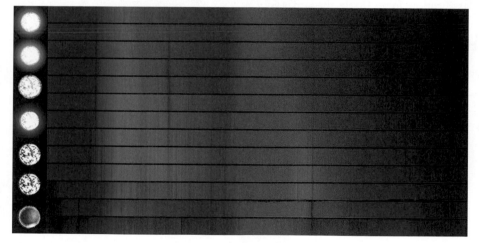

The spectra and star colour for different stars starting with O at the top ending with M at the bottom (the extra ones are sub categories). Notice the varying strength of the hydrogen absorption lines.

These classes are then split into 10 subdivisions so A5 lies halfway between A0 and F0.

 Note you won't be asked about these classifications in the exam but you might see them if you look up stars in a database.

Luminosity classification

When we observe the absorption lines for a given star we see that they are not fine lines corresponding to one particular wavelength but have a width. The broadening of the line is caused by two main effects: *Doppler broadening* and *pressure broadening*.

In Doppler broadening, the atoms of a gas move in random motion so some will be moving away from the observer and some towards. The relative movement causes Doppler shifts in wavelength towards both higher and lower wavelengths.

In pressure broadening, when we observe the spectrum of a low pressure gas we see it is made up of fine lines. Compared with the spectrum of light from a solid is continuous, because the electrons exist in bands rather than discrete energy levels. As the pressure of a gas increases the atoms become closer together resulting in a broadening of the spectral lines. The pressure of the gas at the surface of a star is related to the size of the star, large stars have lower pressures than small stars.

Stars with the same temperature will have the same amount of broadening due to the Doppler effect but the smaller ones will have more pressure broadening. The width of the spectral lines for a given class of star (same temperature) is therefore directly related to the size of the star and hence its luminosity. This leads to the Yerkes classification from I to VII as listed in Table 12.3.

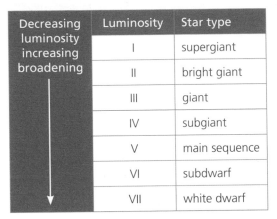

Table 12.3 The Yerkes classification of stars.

Decreasing luminosity increasing broadening	Luminosity	Star type
	I	supergiant
	II	bright giant
	III	giant
	IV	subgiant
	V	main sequence
	VI	subdwarf
	VII	white dwarf

NATURE OF SCIENCE

By plotting the position of thousands of stars on a luminosity *vs* temperature graph it is possible to see patterns that reveal the way stars are thought to evolve. Without this visual aid it would be very difficult to see any pattern in the data.

The full spectral type of a star is the spectral classification followed by the luminosity classification; for example, the Sun is G2V.

Hertzsprung–Russell (HR) diagrams

A Hertzsprung–Russell diagram is a graph on which the temperature of a star is plotted against its luminosity as shown in Figure 12.10.

When interpreting this diagram you need to be careful to look closely at the axes. The y-axis is luminosity, which is logarithmic. The x-axis is temperature which is non-linear and goes from hottest on the left to coldest on the right. A star at the top right hand corner is cold but luminous; this means it is a big star. At the other extreme, bottom left, the stars are hot but not luminous so must be small. This means that we can easily deduce the size of a star from its position on the diagram. The diagonal lines on the diagram indicate stars of equal radius.

When all the stars are plotted on the diagram we see some interesting trends. First, they are not uniformly distributed but seem to be arranged in groups.

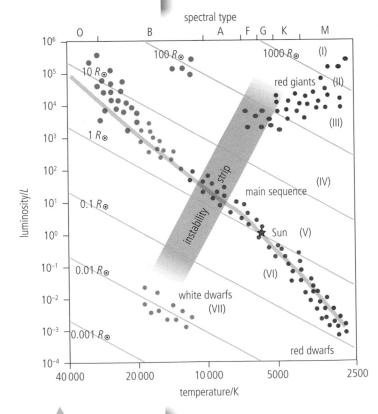

Figure 12.10 HR diagram showing position of the Sun.

Main sequence

90% of the stars are in a diagonal band called the main sequence. This band includes the Sun. The main sequence ranges from hot large blue stars on the left to small cool red stars on the right. Like the Sun, all main sequence stars have a core that is undergoing fusion from hydrogen to helium, that radiates energy causing a pressure that prevents the star from collapsing under the force of gravity. These stable stars will remain at the same point on the diagram for a long time; that's why most stars are main sequence.

Red giants

A cool star that gives out a lot of energy must be very big, so these are called giants. The coolest M class stars are called *red giants* due to their colour. The luminosity of a giant is about 100 times greater than the Sun. If they are the same temperature as the Sun, they must have an area 100 times bigger, therefore a radius 10 times bigger. If their temperature is lower they can be even larger.

Supergiants

A supergiant is a very big cool star. With luminosities 10^6 times greater than the Sun, they have radii up to 1000 times that of the Sun. These are very rare stars but one is very easy to spot: Betelgeuse is the right shoulder of Orion and you can see it in the photo on page 538.

White dwarfs

A white dwarf is a small hot star, hotter than the Sun but only the size of the Earth. They have a low luminosity so aren't possible to see without a telescope.

Variable stars

A variable star has a changing luminosity, so its position on the HR diagram is not constant. This is due to a change in size of the star. As it gets bigger its luminosity increases. This variation is sometimes cyclic as in a Cepheid variable. These stars appear in the instability strip on the HR diagram.

An understanding of the processes taking place in stars has been utilized in the development of fusion reactors.

Exercise

13 Draw a sketch of the HR diagram axis and place on it the following stars.

(a) Beta Pictoris A5V
(b) 61 Cygni A K5V
(c) Eta Arietis F5V
(d) Mira M7III
(e) 4 Cassiopeiae M1III
(f) Betelgeuse M2I
(g) Eridani K1V

Determining distance from the HR diagram

The HR diagram shows us that all stars that have been measured exist in groups (except for a few odd ones). The temperature of a star can be found from the darkness of absorption lines (or the black-body spectrum) and its luminosity class from their width. With these two bits of information the star can be placed on the HR diagram and its luminosity found. Once we know the luminosity it is possible to calculate the distance to the star.

Worked example

The maximum wavelength of a distant star is measured to be 600 nm and its apparent brightness is $1.0 \times 10^{-12} \, \text{W m}^{-2}$. What is its distance from the Earth?

Solution

First we can use Wien's law to find the star's temperature.

$$\lambda_{max} = \frac{2.90 \times 10^{-3}}{T}$$

Rearranging gives

$$T = \frac{2.9 \times 10^{-3}}{600 \times 10^{-9}} = 4800 \, \text{K}$$

Using the HR diagram we can deduce that if this is a main sequence star, its luminosity is $\quad 1 \, L_\odot = 3.84 \times 10^{26} \, \text{W}$

The apparent brightness (b) of a star is related to the luminosity by the equation

$$b = \frac{L}{4\pi d^2}$$

where d is the distance from the Earth.

Rearranging this gives

$$d = \sqrt{\frac{L}{4\pi b}} = \sqrt{\frac{3.84 \times 10^{26}}{4\pi \times 1.0 \times 10^{-12}}} = 5.5 \times 10^{18} \, \text{m}$$

$$= 584 \, \text{ly}$$

Exercises

14 The spectrum of a main sequence star has maximum intensity at 400 nm and an apparent brightness of $0.5 \times 10^{-12} \, \text{W m}^{-2}$.

   (a) Use Wien's law to find the temperature of the star.
   (b) Use the HR diagram to find the luminosity of the star.
   (c) Calculate the distance from the star to the Earth.

15 Given that Beta Pictoris A5V has an apparent brightness of $6.5 \times 10^{-10} \, \text{W m}^{-2}$ use the HR diagram to estimate its:

   (a) luminosity.   (b) radius.   (c) temperature.   (d) distance from the Earth.

The mass–luminosity relationship

We can't tell with the naked eye but by observing stars with powerful telescopes it has been found that a lot of stars are in fact two stars orbiting each other. These are called binary stars. Binary stars that are close to the Earth can actually be seen to orbit each other but most are only known to be binary because of the change in brightness as they eclipse one another, or due to the Doppler shift in their spectra as they move towards and away from the Earth. By measuring the time period on binary stars it is possible to calculate the mass of the stars. From the data received for main sequence stars it has been found that there is a relationship between the mass and luminosity:

$$L \propto M^{3.5}$$

for the Sun

$$L_\odot \propto M_\odot{}^{3.5}$$

dividing gives

$$\frac{L}{L_\odot} \propto \left(\frac{M}{M_\odot}\right)^{3.5}$$

So if we know the luminosity of a star we can find its mass in terms of the mass of the Sun.

Exercise

16 Using the information in previous exercises, estimate the ratio of the mass of Beta Pictoris to the mass of the Sun.

Cepheid variables

For stars further than 10 Mpc the amount of light received is too small to accurately determine their temperature. In this case an alternative method is used that involves measuring the time period of a flashing star.

A Cepheid variable is an unstable star that undergoes periodic expansions and contractions, leading to a periodic change in the apparent brightness of the star, as viewed from Earth. This can be represented graphically, as shown in Figure 12.11.

There are many Cepheid variables close enough to the Earth for us to use the stellar parallax method to find their distance. If we then measure their apparent brightness (*b*) it is possible to calculate their luminosity (*L*) using the equation

$$b = \frac{L}{4\pi d^2}$$

If the luminosity and period are plotted on a graph, we find that they are directly related as shown in Figure 12.12.

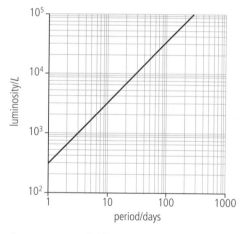

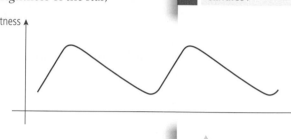

Figure 12.11 The variation of brightness with time for a Cepheid variable. Note how the increase in brightness is faster than the decrease. The star is brightest when it is biggest.

Figure 12.12 The luminosity–period relationship for a Cepheid variable. Note the logarithmic scales.

This is very useful because it means that if we know the star's period, we can use the graph to find its luminosity. Once we know the luminosity, we use the equation above to find its distance from the Earth.

Exercise

17 A Cepheid has period 20 days and brightness $8 \times 10^{-10}\,\text{W}\,\text{m}^{-2}$. Calculate its distance from the Earth.

12.3 Stellar evolution

D.2 Stellar characteristics and stellar evolution

Understandings, applications, and skills:

Balance of radiation pressure and gravitational pressure
- Describing the equilibrium of a star.

> *Guidance*
> - *The equilibrium of a star to be described qualitatively only.*

Chandrasekhar and Oppenheimer–Volkoff limits
Stellar evolution on HR diagrams
- Sketching and interpreting evolutionary paths of stars on an HR diagram.
- Describing the evolution of stars off the main sequence.

Red giants, white dwarfs, neutron stars, and black holes
- Describing the role of mass in stellar evolution.
- Describing the various end products in stellar evolution.

> *Guidance*
> - *References to electron and neutron degeneracy pressures need to be made.*

D.4 Stellar processes (HL only)

Understandings, applications, and skills:

(AHL)The Jeans criterion
- Applying the Jeans criterion to star formation.

> *Guidance*
> - *Only an elementary application of the Jeans criterion is required, i.e. collapse of an interstellar cloud may begin if M > MJ*

(AHL) Nuclear fusion and nucleosynthesis on and off the main sequence
- Describing the different types of nuclear fusion reactions taking place on and off the main sequence.
- Applying the mass–luminosity relation to compare lifetimes on the main sequence relative to that of our Sun.
- Describing the formation of elements in stars that are heavier than iron including the required increases in temperature.
- Qualitatively describe the s and r processes for neutron capture.

Type Ia and II supernovae
- Distinguishing between type Ia and II supernovae.

> *Guidance*
> - *Students should be aware of the use of type Ia supernovae as standard candles.*

The birth of a star

The life cycle of a star takes billions of years so we are never going to see the whole cycle from birth to death. However, by measuring the light emitted from stars we have discovered that stars differ in mass, temperature, radius, and composition, leading to the classifications we have plotted on the HR diagram. Trying to deduce the lifecycle of stars from this is a bit like an alien trying to make some sense of the human race from one photograph of a crowd. The alien would notice that all the humans were basically the same and although most are about the same size there are some very small ones and some thin wrinkly ones. Maybe the alien would work out that there aren't three types of creature but that these are all different stages in the life of the same thing. The alien might also deduce that, since there are more upright large ones, this is the longest part of the human's life cycle, but would be unlikely to work out where they came from or that in the end they died. Applying the same logic to the stars we deduce that the different types of star are different stages in their lifecycle. To complete the picture we can use what we know about the way matter interacts on Earth to work out how this happens.

Stars start their life inside *giant molecular clouds*; swirling clouds of gas and dust left over after the formation of a galaxy made up of mainly hydrogen but also larger elements and molecules. There are several thousand of these clouds in our galaxy, such as the Horse head nebula in the photo.

The temperature of the GMC is only about 10 K, which is why molecules are able to be present. The clouds are held together by gravity but they are kept from collapsing by the pressure of the molecules moving about in random motion. If, however, the gas is compressed by the shock wave from an exploding star or the collision between two clouds, the gravity overcomes the thermal pressure and the cloud begins to collapse. The point at which collapse takes place is given by the *Jeans criterion* which specifies the minimum mass (M_J) required for a cloud of given radius to collapse. M_J is given by the formula:

$$M_J = \frac{3kTR}{2Gm}$$

where:

> k = Boltzmann constant
> T = temperature in kelvin
> R = radius of the cloud
> G = universal gravitational constant
> m = average mass of a molecule of the cloud's contents.

TOK We can't see ultraviolet radiation but we can look at a digitally enhanced image from a UV telescope. What are we actually looking at?

When hit by a shock, wave areas of the cloud compress and collapse forming many stars of different sizes. They are difficult to see as they are inside the cloud. However, as they collapse they get hot, emitting IR radiation that can be detected with an IR telescope. Some of the bigger stars get very hot and cause strong winds to blow through the cloud, compressing more of the dust to create even more stars. Eventually, all the dust is used up.

Gravity keeps on collapsing the new star (*protostar*) until the centre becomes so dense and hot that hydrogen nuclei start to fuse to make helium. This doesn't happen in one step but through a chain of reactions called the proton–proton cycle (illustrated in Figure 12.13).

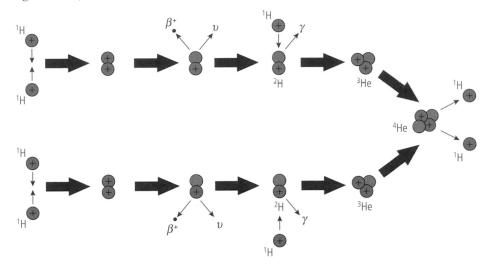

Figure 12.13 The proton–proton cycle.

This is a complicated reaction but can be summarized in the following equation:

$$4^1_1H \rightarrow ^4_2He + 2e^+ + 2v_e + 2\gamma$$

This reaction releases energy due to the fact that the mass of the products is less than the mass of the original hydrogen nuclei; this mass is converted to energy as explained in Chapter 7. The amount of energy per reaction is 26.7 MeV.

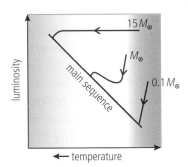

Figure 12.14 The HR diagram for three stars as they turn from protostar to main sequence. Note how the luminosity of the big ones stays constant; this is because they are getting smaller but hotter. A Sun-sized star also shrinks but its outside stays cool until the inside gets so hot that it heats the outer layers. The core of a small star never gets that hot, so it gets less and less bright as it contracts.

Once the core starts to undergo nuclear fusion the outward radiation pressure counteracts the inwards gravitation preventing further collapse. The star is now a stable main sequence star. The position of the star on the main sequence depends upon its mass. Figure 12.14 shows the changes from protostar to main sequence represented on an HR diagram.

Note that it appears that a red giant has turned into a main sequence star, but it hasn't. The large protostar was in the same region of the diagram but had very different properties to a red giant.

Main sequence

Once on the main sequence the star is stable and will remain that way until most of the hydrogen is used up. The amount of time that a star is a main sequence star depends on how much hydrogen the star contains and the rate at which it is used up. You may think that a bigger star will last longer since they have more fuel but that is not the case, remember the mass–luminosity relationship $L \propto M^{3.5}$. The luminosity is the amount of energy radiating from the star per second, which is directly related to the rate at which the hydrogen is used up; more massive stars burn faster. From this we can estimate how long a star will be main sequence compared to the Sun:

$$\text{luminosity} = \frac{\text{energy}}{\text{time}}$$

But the energy radiated is coming from the mass of the star so if we assume that all of the mass was converted to energy then the amount of energy radiated during the lifetime Δt of a star of mass M would be Mc^2:

$$L = \frac{Mc^2}{\Delta t}$$

but

$$L \propto M^{3.5}$$

so

$$\frac{Mc^2}{\Delta t} \propto M^{3.5}$$

c^2 is a constant so:

$$\Delta t \propto M^{(1-3.5)}$$

and for the Sun:

$$\Delta t_\odot \propto M_\odot^{-2.5}$$

dividing gives

$$\frac{\Delta t}{\Delta t_\odot} = \left(\frac{M}{M_\odot}\right)^{-2.5}$$

so a star with a mass 10 times bigger than the Sun will be a main sequence star for $10^{-2.5}$ (i.e. $\frac{1}{300}$) times the time for the Sun.

Exercise

18 Calculate how long Beta Pictoris will be a main sequence star compared to the Sun.

After the main sequence

A star will stay on the main sequence until it uses up almost all of the hydrogen in the core. This is only about 10% of the total amount of hydrogen in the star so the mass of the star doesn't change a great deal. This means that its position on the HR diagram stays almost the same as at its point of entry. As the hydrogen fuses to helium, the heavier helium sinks to the centre of the core which is the densest hottest part of the star. Hydrogen fusion continues outside this central core until the pressure and temperature are no longer great enough and the fusion slows. It is the pressure caused by the fusion that stops the star from collapsing so when the rate of fusion gets less the core starts to collapse resulting in an increase in core temperature. This heats the outer layers of the star causing them to expand and changing the main sequence star into a red giant as represented on the HR diagram in Figure 12.15.

What happens next depends on the mass of the star; we will start by considering roughly Sun-sized stars.

Sun-sized stars

According to the Pauli exclusion principle, electrons cannot occupy the same quantum mechanical state so as the core is compressed by the gravitational attraction of the surrounding matter it reaches a point when the electrons cannot get any closer. This is called *electron degeneracy* and gives the maximum density of the core. After this point is reached the core cannot get any smaller but continues to get hotter. When the core temperature exceeds 10^8 K helium can fuse to form beryllium:

$$^4_2\text{He} + {}^4_2\text{He} \rightarrow {}^8_4\text{Be} + \gamma$$

A star smaller than about 0.25 $M_\odot$ will never get to the point where fusion starts, it would simply cool down into a lump of matter called a *brown dwarf*.

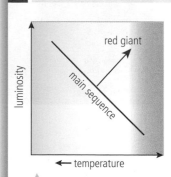

Figure 12.15 HR diagram representing the change from main sequence to red giant.

Beryllium then fuses with more helium to form carbon:

$$^8_4Be + {}^4_2He \rightarrow {}^{12}_6C + \gamma$$

which in turn fuses with more helium to form oxygen:

$$^{12}_6C + {}^4_2He \rightarrow {}^{16}_8O + \gamma$$

This is called the *triple alpha process* as it involves three helium nuclei (alpha particles). During this stage in the star's life the outer layers are very far from the central core so the force of gravity holding them together is not very strong. Any increased activity in the core can cause these outer layers to blow away. This happens over a period of time leaving the core surrounded by the remains of the outer layers. The core is no longer producing energy so contracts until electron degeneracy prevents it getting any smaller. It is now called a *white dwarf*. The whole process is represented on the HR diagram in Figure 12.16. The interesting thing about white dwarfs is that they get smaller as their mass gets larger. Electron degeneracy sets a limit on how small a white dwarf can be, which puts a maximum value on the mass of a core that can form a white dwarf. This is called *the Chandrasekhar limit*:

$$\text{Chandrasekhar limit} = 1.4\,M_\odot$$

The core makes up about $\frac{1}{3}$ of the mass of a star, so stars with mass greater than about $4\,M_\odot$ will not form white dwarfs.

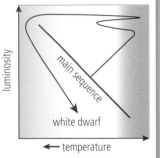

Figure 12.16 The evolutionary path of a Sun-sized star.

If the white dwarf is part of a binary system of stars its large gravitational field can attract matter from its partner causing the mass of the white dwarf to increase. If the mass exceeds the Chandrasekhar limit the white dwarf will collapse violently causing the fusion of heavier elements to occur resulting in a massive release of energy. The resulting explosion is called a *type Ia supernova*.

Type Ia supernovae all occur when a white dwarf mass increases to larger than $1.4\,M_\odot$ which results in a peak luminosity of about $10^{10}\,L_\odot$. This means that not only can they be seen from a very great distance but since we know their luminosity, they can be used as *standard candles* to determine their distance from the Earth (this is the same idea used with Cepheid variables). Since they have much higher luminosity they can be seen from much further away, extending the range of distance measurement to about 500 times further than is possible using Cepheids.

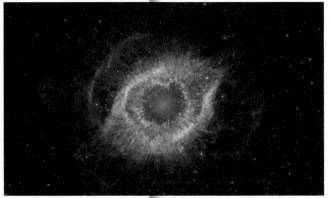

The helix nebula. This object is a planetary nebula, a dying star ejecting its dusty outer layers. The image was obtained by combining infrared (yellow, green, and red) and ultraviolet (UV, blue) data from NASA's Spitzer Space Telescope and Galaxy Evolution Explorer (GALEX). The ejected layers are glowing due to the intense UV radiation from the collapsed stellar core, a white dwarf (not visible at this scale).

Exercise

19 Calculate the distance from the Earth to a type Ia supernova that has an apparent brightness of $2.3 \times 10^{-16}\,W\,m^{-2}$.

Large stars

The pressure generated in the core by stars with masses over $4\,M_\odot$ is enough to enable the carbon and oxygen to fuse into larger elements such as neon and magnesium. For example:

$$^{12}_6C + {}^{12}_6C \rightarrow {}^{20}_{10}Ne + {}^4_2He$$

$$^{12}_6C + {}^{12}_6C \rightarrow {}^{24}_{12}Mg + \gamma$$

As this happens the heavier elements sink to the centre of the core. For larger stars with masses over $8\,M_\odot$ this process continues until iron is produced. If you remember the BE/nucleon *vs* nucleon number curve you will know that iron is at the top of the peak, so fusing iron with other elements to produce larger nuclei will not liberate energy. This makes iron the end of the road as far as energy production in stars is concerned. However, as the core runs out of nuclear fuel it collapses resulting in an increase in temperature. This allows iron to fuse resulting in the absorption of energy. This reduces the outward pressure preventing the core from collapsing – so the core collapses. Since the core mass is larger than the Chandrasekhar limit the size will not be limited by electron degeneracy but will collapse causing electrons to combine with protons to form neutrons.

$$p^+ + e^- \rightarrow n^0 + v_e$$

This continues until the core contains only neutrons, which are also bound by the Pauli exclusion principle preventing them getting too close (*neutron degeneracy*). This collapse takes only about 0.25 s so leaves a gap between the core and the outer layers. The outer layers fall into the gap resulting in a rapid rise in temperature causing a huge explosion that blows away everything except the core. This is called a *type II supernova* and what remains of the core is a *neutron star*. Type II supernovae can be distinguished from type I by their different spectra; type I are made from an exploding white dwarf so contain all the elements fused in the core whereas type II are the outer layers which are mainly hydrogen. The way the brightness changes with time is also different as can be seen from the light curves of Figure 12.17.

Another process taking place in red giants and supernovae is the capture of neutrons by other nuclei. This results in neutron-rich nuclei that decay by β^- emission. If the neutrons are absorbed quicker than they decay this is known as rapid or *r-process* and if the neutron decays before the next one is added it is a slow or *s-process*. This is how the heavy elements such as gold and uranium are formed. So all elements on Earth that have proton numbers above iron were formed in supernova explosions.

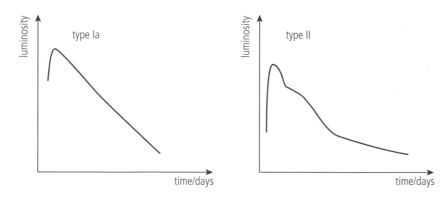

Figure 12.17 Supernova light curves.

For main sequence stars greater than about $20\,M_\odot$ the core that remains contains so much mass that not even neutron degeneracy can stop it collapsing to a point (a *singularity*). This will happen if the mass of the core is greater than the *Oppenheimer–Volkhoff* limit:

$$\text{Oppenheimer–Volkhoff limit} = 3\,M_\odot$$

This results in a gravitational field that is so strong that not even light can escape: a *black hole* is formed.

The final stage of a large star depends on how massive it is, but the initial stages off the main sequence are similar to that represented by the path on the HR diagram of Figure 12.18.

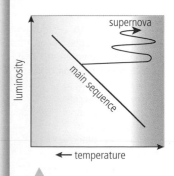

Figure 12.18 The evolutionary path of a large star.

Exercise

20 Using the HR diagram (Figure 12.10) estimate whether the star Phi Orionis B0V could possibly end its life as a black hole.

12.4 Cosmology

D.3 Cosmology

Understandings, applications, and skills:

The Big Bang model
• Describing both space and time as originating with the Big Bang.

Hubble's law

The accelerating Universe and redshift (z)
• Solving problems involving z, R, and Hubble's law.
• Estimating the age of the Universe by assuming a constant expansion rate.

The cosmic scale factor (R)

Cosmic microwave background (CMB) radiation
• Describing the characteristics of the CMB radiation.
• Explaining how the CMB radiation is evidence for a hot Big Bang.

> *Guidance*
> • *CMB radiation will be considered to be isotropic with T = 2.73 K.*
> • *For CMB radiation a simple explanation in terms of the Universe cooling down or distances (and hence wavelengths) being stretched out is all that is required.*

D.5 Further cosmology (HL only)

Understandings, applications, and skills:

The cosmological principle
• Describing the cosmological principle and its role in models of the Universe.

Rotation curves and the mass of galaxies, dark matter
• Describing rotation curves as evidence for dark matter.
• Deriving rotational velocity from Newtonian gravitation.

> *Guidance*
> • *Students are expected to be able to refer to rotation curves as evidence for dark matter and must be aware of candidates for dark matter.*

Fluctuations in the CMB
• Describing and interpreting the observed anisotropies in the CMB.

> *Guidance*
> • *Students must be familiar with the main results of COBE and WMAP and the Planck space observatory.*

The cosmological origin of redshift

> *Guidance*
> • *Students are expected to show that the temperature of the Universe varies with the scale factor as* $T \propto \dfrac{1}{R}$

Critical density
• Deriving critical density from Newtonian gravitation.

Dark energy
• Describing qualitatively the cosmic scale factor in models with and without dark energy.

The cosmological principle

Cosmology is the study of the Universe: how big it is, how old it is, where it came from, and how it will end. Any model we have of the Universe must explain what we observe. In Newton's time observations showed that the Universe was static so he tried to explain how this could be. The problem is that Newton's universal law of gravity states that all particles of mass must attract all other particles so the edges of the Universe should be attracted towards the centre causing the Universe to contract. This wasn't observed so the model called for an infinitely large, infinitely old Universe. There are several problems with this model: if the Universe is infinite then there are an infinite number of stars and if it is infinitely old the light from every star will have reached the Earth. This means the sky would be completely filled with stars. So even if the Universe is infinitely large it can't be infinitely old.

If we are to develop a model for the Universe based on our view from the Earth then we must assume that it is the same in every place, so the Earth is not a special place but just the same as anywhere else (*homogeneous*) and looks the same in every direction (*isotropic*). We can see that this isn't true on a small scale since the sky doesn't look the same in all directions but on a big scale the Universe is uniform. These conditions are known as the *cosmological principle*. Another assumption is that the laws of physics that apply on the Earth must apply everywhere else; if this isn't true, we have a big problem.

According to Newton's universal law of gravity all particles with mass attract all others with a force that is proportional to the product of their mass and inversely proportional to their separation squared. We have seen how this can be applied to the orbit of the planets around the Sun to predict the different time periods and explain why an apple falls to the Earth from a tree. Newton also developed laws of motion which stated that if the same force was applied to different bodies the acceleration produced would be inversely proportional to the mass of the body. So mass is responsible for two effects, the size of the gravitational force and the magnitude of acceleration. Einstein took things further by suggesting that these effects were equivalent. If this is the case then light should follow a curved path in a gravitational field (see Chapter 9 for more details).

This cannot be explained using Newton's Universal law since light, having no mass, is not affected by gravity. To overcome this problem, Einstein developed the general theory of relativity which explains the acceleration of objects in gravitational fields by considering space and time to be curved by mass.

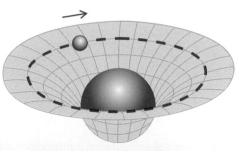

By its very nature it is not easy to utilize the advancements in astrophysics and cosmology here on Earth. However, the greater understanding that is gained as a result of this work helps mankind to put itself in perspective.

Figure 12.19 A massive object curves space.

This photo of galactic cluster 0024 + 1654 by the Hubble space telescope shows the effect of the curvature of space on the light travelling past a large mass. The blue rings are the light from a more distant galaxy bent by the nearer cluster. This is called *gravitational lensing*.

If mass curves space–time then the mass of the Universe must curve the space of the Universe. This curvature can take three forms: flat, negative, or positive, as shown in Figure 12.20.

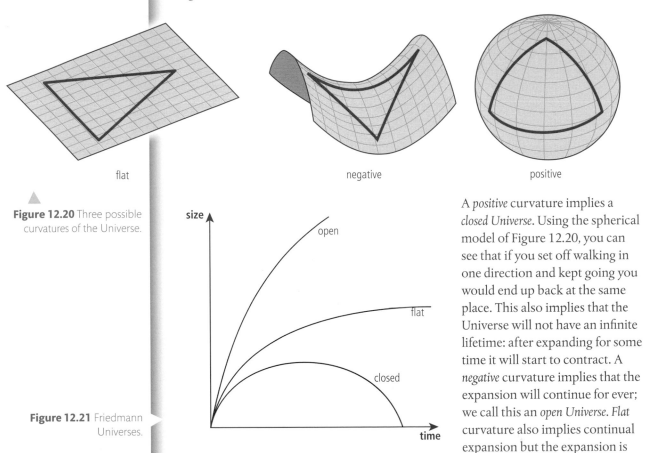

flat   negative   positive

Figure 12.20 Three possible curvatures of the Universe.

Figure 12.21 Friedmann Universes.

A *positive* curvature implies a *closed Universe*. Using the spherical model of Figure 12.20, you can see that if you set off walking in one direction and kept going you would end up back at the same place. This also implies that the Universe will not have an infinite lifetime: after expanding for some time it will start to contract. A *negative* curvature implies that the expansion will continue for ever; we call this an *open Universe*. *Flat* curvature also implies continual expansion but the expansion is continually slowing down, approaching a finite size at infinite time. These different situations are called *Friedmann Universes* and can be represented by the three lines on the graph of Figure 12.21.

Critical density (ρ_c)

Whether the Universe is open, closed, or flat depends on its density. We can get an understanding of this by applying Newton's Universal law of gravitation. If the density is large then the different parts of the Universe would be pulled back together. If the density is small they would keep moving apart; and if just the right size the Universe would stop expanding at infinite time. The density required to create a flat Universe is called the *critical density* and can be calculated by applying Newton's law to an expanding spherical cloud of matter with mass M. If at some time it has size R then the total energy of the cloud will equal PE + KE:

$$\text{PE} = \frac{-GMm}{R}; \text{KE} = \frac{1}{2}mv^2$$

As the cloud expands the PE will increase and the KE will decrease until, when the cloud reaches infinite size, both PE and KE will be zero. Applying the law of conservation of energy we know that the loss of KE must equal the gain in PE so:

$$\frac{1}{2}mv^2 = \frac{GMm}{R}$$

This can be rewritten in terms of the cloud density, which since the cloud is spherical is given by:

$$\rho_c = \frac{M}{\frac{4}{3}\pi R^3}$$

$$\frac{1}{2}v^2 = \frac{G\frac{4}{3}\pi R^3 \rho_c}{R}$$

$$\rho_c = \frac{3v^2}{8\pi G R^2}$$

The expanding Universe

In the early 1920s Albert Einstein developed his theory of general relativity, and while Einstein and Friedmann were developing their theories Vesto Slipher and Edwin Hubble were taking measurements. Slipher was measuring the line spectra from distant galaxies and Hubble was measuring how far away they were. Slipher discovered that the spectral lines from *all* the galaxies were shifted towards the red end of the spectrum. If this was due to the Doppler shift it would imply that *all* of the galaxies were moving away from the Earth. Given the change in wavelength Hubble then calculated the velocity of the galaxies using the Doppler formula:

$$\frac{v}{c} = \frac{\Delta\lambda}{\lambda_{em}} = z$$

where

v = the recessional velocity
c = the speed of light
$\Delta\lambda$ = the change in wavelength
λ_{em} = the wavelength originally emitted from the galaxy
z = the fractional increase or z parameter (no units).

Exercises

21 A spectral line from a distant galaxy of wavelength 434.0 nm is red-shifted to 479.8 nm. Calculate the recession speed of the galaxy.

22 The same line from a second galaxy is shifted to 481.0 nm. Calculate its recession speed. Is this galaxy closer or further away?

Hubble's law

In 1929 Hubble published his discovery that there appeared to be a linear relationship between the recessional velocity and distance to the galaxy. This can be illustrated by plotting the data on a graph as shown in Figure 12.22.

The recessional velocity of a distant galaxy is directly proportional to its distance.

In other words, the further away a galaxy is, the faster it moves away from us.

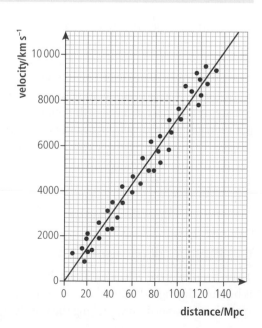

Figure 12.22 Graph of recession speed of galaxies against their distance from the Earth.

557

This can be expressed in terms of the formula

$$v \propto d$$

or

$$v = H_0 d$$

where H_0 is the *Hubble constant*. This is the gradient of the line and has the value 72 km s^{-1} Mpc^{-1}. This gives a measure of the rate of expansion of the Universe. This is probably not a constant rate since the effect of gravity might slow down the rate over time. H_0 is the current value.

Exercises

23 Use Hubble's law to estimate the distance from the Earth to a galaxy with a recessional velocity of 150 km s^{-1}.

24 If a galaxy is 20 Mpc from Earth, how fast will it be receding?

Expanding space

There is a problem with the Doppler explanation. At very large distances, the recessional velocity will be faster than the speed of light. However, there is another explanation; according to Einstein's general relativity an expanding Universe will have expanding space, so the galaxies aren't moving apart through space; it is the space they are in that is expanding. This also explains why the further galaxies recede faster. Imagine the Universe is a rubber strip with some galaxies drawn on it as in Figure 12.23.

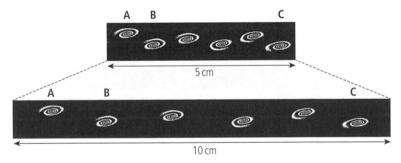

Figure 12.23 Galaxies move apart as the Universe expands.

As we can see, when the rubber is doubled in length the galaxies move further apart. Comparing galaxies B and C to A, the distance between A and B has increased from 1 cm to 2 cm, an increase of 1 cm, but the distance from A to C has increased from 5 cm to 10 cm an increase of 5 cm. If the expansion takes place in 1 second then the recessional velocity of B is 1 cm s^{-1} and the velocity of C is 5 cm s^{-1}. The most distant galaxies recede fastest. It is worth noting that in the real Universe it is only the space between galaxies that gets bigger, not the galaxies themselves. This is because the mass in galaxies and their relatively compact nature (compared to cosmological distances) keeps them gravitationally bound. It also doesn't matter which galaxy we choose, they all move away from each other. This is an important point as it shows that this result is in accordance with the cosmological principle. So galaxies don't fly apart, it is the space between them that increases.

Cosmological redshift

The reason why the wavelength of light from distant galaxies is increased (Figure 12.24) is because during the time taken for the light to travel from the galaxy to the Earth the space has expanded, so stretching the wavelength. This is called *cosmological redshift*.

Figure 12.24 As space expands wavelength expands.

Scale factor *R*

It is difficult to say how big the Universe is, so it is convenient to use a *scale factor* which gives a measure not of how big it is but of how big it is relative to today. So if the scale factor is 4 it means that the Universe is 4 times bigger than today. In an expanding Universe this would imply sometime in the future. A scale factor of 1 means the present time. Red-shifted light from distant galaxies is shifted because of the expansion on the Universe so we can calculate the scale factor of the Universe at the time the light was emitted from the change in wavelength.

If $R_{(tobs)}$ is the scale factor at the time of observing the light (now) and $R_{(tem)}$ is the scale factor when emitted then the ratio of wavelengths will equal the ratio of scale factor:

$$\frac{R_{(tobs)}}{R_{(tem)}} = \frac{\lambda_{(tobs)}}{\lambda_{(tem)}}$$

but

$$z = \frac{\lambda_{(tobs)} - \lambda_{(tem)}}{\lambda_{(tem)}} = \frac{\lambda_{(tobs)}}{\lambda_{(tem)}} - 1 = \frac{R_{(tobs)}}{R_{(tem)}} - 1$$

so

$$z + 1 = \frac{R_{(tobs)}}{R_{(tem)}}$$

but the scale factor now = 1 so $R_{(tobs)} = 1$

$$z + 1 = \frac{1}{R_{(tem)}}$$

Worked example

If $z = 3$ then the scale factor at the time that the light was emitted $R_{(tem)} = \frac{1}{4}$ so the Universe has expanded by a factor of 4 in the time since the light left the galaxy.

The BIG Bang

With space constantly expanding, there must have been a time in the past when all the material and energy of the observable Universe was so concentrated that space can be imagined as originating from one single point, as if the Universe started from some sort of gigantic explosion or 'Big Bang'. If we go to the very beginning then we would get to an infinitely small point where all the material eventually making up the entire Universe resides in a singularity. This caused a problem for the theory when it was first suggested and it wasn't until the work of Hawking and Penrose in the 1960s that it became more accepted that if a star can collapse into a singularity (a black hole) then the Universe could start from something similar. We now know that the Universe is very much bigger than the bit that we can see, in fact it could well be infinite, if this is the case then even though the observable Universe was once very small the whole Universe would have been infinite. Even if the Universe isn't infinite the curvature of space–time makes it possible for the Universe to continually expand into itself. So the Universe didn't start with a Big Bang but is continually expanding. If we go back in time there is a point when the observable Universe is, compared to today, the size of a small point. At this time the Universe was so dense and hot that none of today's physics applies. We can think of this as the beginning of the Universe as we know it.

The age of the Universe

At the time of the Big Bang all parts of the Universe were in the same place, so if we know how fast any two parts are moving apart and how far apart they are now, we can calculate the age of the Universe.

$$\text{Age of Universe} = \frac{\text{separation distance}}{\text{recessional velocity}}$$

This is the same as $\frac{1}{H_0}$

So the age of the Universe $= \frac{1}{H_0}$

To calculate this in seconds we first need to convert the distance into km.

$$H_0 = \frac{72}{3.09 \times 10^{19}} = 2.33 \times 10^{-18}\,\text{s}^{-1}$$

So $\quad \frac{1}{H_0} = 4.29 \times 10^{17}\,\text{s}$

Now converting this into years

$$\frac{1}{H_0} = \frac{4.29 \times 10^{17}\,\text{s}}{3.16 \times 10^7} = 1.36 \times 10^{10}\,\text{years}$$

This calculation assumes that the velocity is constant. However, we know that gravitational attraction will slow the galaxies down; the recessional velocity we measure today is therefore smaller than it was. This makes our value too large, so according to these measurements, the Universe can't be older than 1.36×10^{10} years.

Estimating critical density

Earlier we derived the following equation for the critical density

$$\rho_c = \frac{3v^2}{8\pi G R^2}$$

Now the Hubble constant, $H_0 = \frac{v}{d}$ which is the same as $\frac{v}{R}$ so substituting gives:

$$\rho_c = \frac{3H_0{}^2}{8\pi G}$$

Exercise

25 Estimate the critical density of the Universe and calculate how many hydrogen atoms per m³ this is equivalent to.

The early development of the Universe

Before the stars and galaxies formed, the Universe was an expanding cloud of gas. As it expanded adiabatically the particles gained PE and lost KE, resulting in a reduction of temperature. This would imply that at the time of the Big Bang the temperature was very high, so high that the particles we see today could not have existed; they would have knocked each other apart. This leads to a model of the Universe split into different stages.

1. Before 10^{-43} s we have no model of the Universe. This is called the Planck time.
2. The Universe was a sea of quarks and leptons, both particles and antiparticles.

3. Protons and neutrons form. Particles and antiparticles annihilate each other forming photons that in turn produce more pairs of particles.

4. As the wavelength of the photons becomes stretched by the expansion of space they no longer have enough energy to form protons or neutrons, which continue annihilating with their antiparticles. The result is a lot of photons and not so many hadrons.

5. Nuclei form, but electrons are not able to combine with the nuclei to form atoms because of the abundance of high energy photons that would ionize any atom that formed. These photons were continually interacting with the ions so the Universe was completely opaque. Radiation from such a body would have the same spectrum as a black body. This is really important so worthy of further explanation:

    A black body is a body that perfectly absorbs all wavelengths of light. The best way to make a near-perfect black body is to make a small hole in a hollow object as in Figure 12.25. Light entering the hole would be reflected off the walls so many times that all light entering would be absorbed; in other words, the inside would appear totally black.

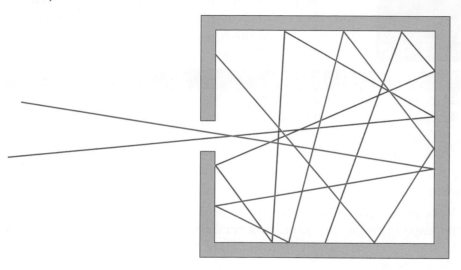

Figure 12.25 A cavity absorbs all radiation entering it.

    If heated, the cavity would emit radiation with a spectrum the same as any other black body. The cavity situation is very similar to the early Universe with so many ions that photons would be continually absorbed.

6. As the Universe expands and cools, a point will be reached when the photons no longer have enough energy to ionize the atoms allowing electrons to combine with nuclei. We know from experiment that this happens at a KE of about 0.26 eV. This is equivalent to a temperature of 3000 K. Since the photons can no longer interact with the atoms the Universe will become transparent, allowing photons to fly through space until they interact with something. Some of these photons should still be around today except they will have a longer wavelength due to the expansion of space.

Cosmic microwave background (CMB)

In 1964 two radio astronomers, Arno Penzias and Robert Wilson, made a chance discovery that no matter which direction they pointed their microwave antenna they detected a uniform signal of wavelength of around 1 mm. This radiation had some interesting features:

- It was the same in every direction. If the source was in our galaxy it would be stronger when the antenna pointed towards the centre. The homogeneous, isotropic nature of the radiation makes it look like something much bigger.
- By measuring the intensity of the radiation at different wavelengths it was found to follow the black-body spectrum almost perfectly as shown by the graph in the photograph. (Note how small the error bars are.)
- Using Wein's law:

$$\lambda_{max} = \frac{2.9 \times 10^{-3}}{T}$$

We can calculate the temperature of the black-body radiation to be 2.73 K.

From this equation we can see that $T \propto \frac{1}{\lambda}$ but as the Universe expands the wavelength will be proportional to the scale factor R so:

$$T \propto \frac{1}{R}$$

There seems to be a lot of evidence to suggest that the CMB is the leftover black-body radiation that filled the Universe just before it became transparent. This is very strong supporting evidence for the Big Bang model of the Universe.

Dr John Cromwell Mather, talking at a press conference about the work for which he was awarded a share of the 2006 Nobel Prize in Physics. The graph in the background presents data from the COBE (Cosmic Background Explorer) probe, which was launched in 1989.

Exercises

26 Calculate the peak in the black-body radiation curve from a black body of temperature 2.73 K.

27 Given that the temperature of the Universe when it became transparent was 3000 K, calculate the original peak in the black-body curve and hence the value of the z parameter.

28 Calculate the scale factor for the Universe at the time that it became transparent.

Measuring density

To find out how the Universe will evolve we need to know the Hubble constant and the density of the Universe. To make the numbers more manageable, scientists refer to the density parameter Ω rather than the density. This is the ratio of the density to the critical density

$$\Omega = \frac{\rho}{\rho_c}$$

If the density equals the critical density and the Universe is flat $\Omega = 1$. If the Universe is open $\Omega < 1$ and the Universe is closed if $\Omega > 1$.

To measure the density of the Universe we need to measure the mass in a given volume. We would need to take a big volume so it would represent the homogeneous nature of the Universe. This volume would contain many galaxies so we need to know the mass of a galaxy. This could be done by estimating the number of stars that a galaxy such as the Milky Way contains then multiplying by the mass of an average-sized star like the Sun. Calculations like this give a value of Ω much less than 1, implying an open Universe. However, if we look more closely at the galaxies we find something is wrong.

Rotation curves

A big spiral galaxy such as the NGC 6744 looks very much like it is rotating and that is because it is. It is not possible to see this rotation but if viewed edge on, one side of the galaxy will be coming towards the Earth, and the other moving away. This causes a different Doppler shift in spectral lines from light coming from the two sides enabling astronomers to calculate the speed of rotation and from the speed it is possible to calculate the mass.

Choosing stars at different distances from the centre of the galaxy, we expect that once we get beyond the central part of the galaxy the speed of the stars should get less as distance increases. We can show why this is using Newton's law of gravitation. Consider the star orbiting the massive centre of a galaxy as shown in Figure 12.26.

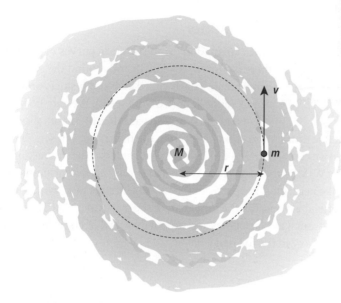

Figure 12.26 A star rotates with a rotating galaxy.

The star is moving with circular motion where the centripetal force is provided by the gravitational attraction of the part of the galaxy inside the orbit (the effect of the outside part will cancel out). Applying Newton's law gives:

$$\frac{GMm}{r^2} = \frac{mv^2}{r}$$

so

$$v = \sqrt{\frac{GM}{r}}$$

But assuming the density of the galaxy is constant, the mass of the inside part will be

$$M = \frac{4}{3}\pi r^3 \rho$$

This gives:

$$v = \sqrt{\frac{4\pi G\rho}{3}}\,r$$

so within the galaxy the stars will move faster as you increase the distance from the centre:

$$v_{in} \propto r$$

If we go towards the edge of the galaxy and beyond, any orbiting stars will simply be attracted to the central mass which will not change as the orbit radius is increased:

$$v = \sqrt{\frac{GM}{r}}$$

$$v_{out} \propto \frac{1}{\sqrt{r}}$$

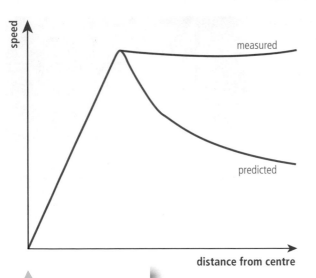

Figure 12.27 Rotation curves for a galaxy: predicted, and measured.

This can be represented by drawing a graph of the velocity against distance from the centre. This is called a rotation curve and is shown by the blue line in Figure 12.27.

By measuring the Doppler shift for stars that are in the main part of the galaxy and beyond it is found that the velocities do not match this prediction. The velocity of stars on the outside are far too big suggesting that there is a lot more mass there than we can see.

Dark matter

One explanation for the rotation curves of galaxies is that there is a lot more mass in and around the galaxy than can be seen. This is called *dark matter* since, unlike stars, it doesn't emit light (we can't see it). We can, however, see its effects on the stars and gas. Measurements show that there must be about five times more dark matter than the matter we can see. The problem is that, because we can't see it, it is difficult to say what it is. Two interestingly named possibilities are WIMPs and MACHOs. Wimps are *weakly interacting massive particles*. These, rather like neutrinos, are particles that hardly interact at all with the regular particles of matter, baryons. On the other end of the size scale, MACHOs are *massive compact halo objects* such as black holes and brown dwarfs that could be present around the outside of a galaxy in the form of a halo.

Accelerating expansion

Improvements in technology have enabled astronomers to view dimmer objects, increasing their range of measurement. One such object is the type Ia supernova which, as discussed previously, can be used as a standard candle for the measurement of distance. Extending Hubble's graph from 140 Mpc to 10 000 Mpc, the red shift of the light from the supernovae tell us how far back in time the explosion took place. Based on the assumption that the Universe has been expanding at a constant rate, we can use Hubble's law to calculate what the red shift should be. Now, we would expect this to give us the wrong answer since the effect of gravity should be slowing down the expansion. However, we actually find the opposite. The rate of expansion is increasing.

Dark energy

It is the increase of potential energy that reduces the kinetic energy of parts of the Universe, causing the expansion to slow down, so if there was some sort of negative energy then it would have the opposite effect. This is called *dark energy*. The density of dark energy can also be expressed in terms of a density parameter Ω_Λ. So the density parameter Ω is made of two components: Ω_m represents the contribution from matter (including dark matter) and Ω_Λ the contribution from dark energy. The condition for a flat Universe is that $\Omega = 1$.

The Wilkinson Microwave Anisotropy Probe (WMAP)

In 2001 the Wilkinson Microwave Anisotropy Probe (WMAP) was launched to make accurate measurements of the cosmic microwave radiation. At first sight the radiation appeared to be uniform in every direction but when analysed more closely it was

Within the field of astrophysics one development often leads to another; for example, the study of supernovae led to the possibility to determine the recessional velocity of distant galaxies.

found that there are very small variations of less than 10^{-4} K. Variations in temperature represent original variations in the density of the expanding Universe just before it became transparent. This can be explained if we go back to an earlier time when the Universe was a lot smaller. Small-scale phenomena such as atoms and nuclei are governed by quantum mechanics so the position of a particle is given by a probability distribution rather than a definite point. This makes it difficult to have a perfectly uniform gas of particles so at this very small scale there would have been *quantum mechanical fluctuations* resulting in variations in density. If this stage was followed by a rapid *inflation* these small-scale fluctuations would be expanded into large-scale variations in density that would form the centres for large-scale structures containing clusters of galaxies.

An explanation for dark energy could be what is also called *vacuum energy*, where space itself, due to quantum effects, has an underlying background energy that exists in all space throughout the entire Universe. As space expands, so does the amount of vacuum energy, which might push the Universe apart. Yet, according to Einstein, energy and mass are related ($E = mc^2$). This empty space energy should also generate a gravitational effect. Understanding this discrepancy and the nature of dark energy could help us to determine the fate of the entire Universe.

Cosmic and galactic microwave background, whole sky projection from the WMAP (Wilkinson Microwave Anisotropy Probe) satellite. The Milky Way galaxy is the red band crossing the sky, while the cosmic microwave background (CMB) fills the rest of the sky. The colours show tiny temperature variations (plus or minus 200 millionths of a kelvin) in the background radiation (average is 3 kelvin).

The early Universe behaved much like a fluid so, based on knowledge of the way fluids behave, it is possible to make a mathematical model of the early Universe that predicts the variations in CMB temperature represented by the power spectrum in Figure 12.28.

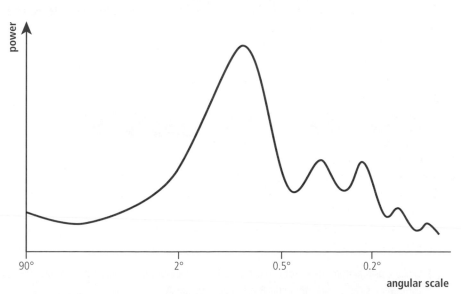

Figure 12.28 The power spectrum showing the variations in CMB with angle. Notice the angular scale is not linear.

The mathematical model has various parameters (including Ω_{m}, Ω_{Λ}, and H_0) that, if changed, will result in a different power spectrum. By varying these parameters to find the best fit between the theoretical and experimental power spectrum it is

To learn more about cosmology, go to the hotlinks site, search for the title or ISBN and click on Chapter 12.

possible to determine the most likely values of Ω_m, Ω_Λ, and H_0. This has resulted in the following values:

$\Omega_m = 0.27$
$\Omega_\Lambda = 0.73$
So $\Omega_m + \Omega_\Lambda = 1$

So the Universe is flat.

Practice questions

1. This question is about the nature of certain stars on the Hertzsprung–Russell diagram and determining stellar distance.

   Figure 12.29 shows the grid of a Hertzsprung–Russell (HR) diagram on which the positions of the Sun and four other stars **A**, **B**, **C**, and **D** are shown.

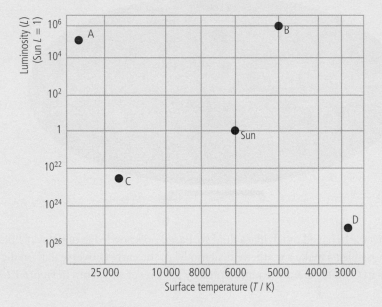

Figure 12.29.

   (a) State an alternative labelling of the axes:

   (i) *x*-axis. (1)

   (ii) *y*-axis. (1)

   (b) Complete Table 12.4.

Star	Type of star
A	
B	
C	
D	

Table 12.4.

(4)

   (c) Explain, using information from Figure 12.29, and without making any calculations, how astronomers can deduce that star **B** is larger than star **A**. (3)

(d) Using the following data and information from Figure 12.29, show that star **B** is at a distance of about 700 pc from Earth.

Apparent visual brightness of the Sun $= 1.4 \times 10^3\,\text{Wm}^{-2}$
Apparent visual brightness of star **B** $= 7.0 \times 10^{-8}\,\text{Wm}^{-2}$
Mean distance of the Sun from Earth $= 1.0\,\text{AU}$
1 parsec $= 2.1 \times 10^5\,\text{AU}$ (4)

(e) Explain why the distance of star **B** from Earth cannot be determined by the method of stellar parallax. (1)

(*Total 14 marks*)

2. This question is about some of the properties of Barnard's star.
Barnard's star, in the constellation Ophiuchus, has a **parallax angle** of 0.549 arc second as measured from Earth.

(a) With the aid of a suitable diagram, explain what is meant by **parallax angle** and outline how it is measured. (6)

(b) Deduce that the distance of Barnard's star from the Sun is 5.94 ly. (2)

(c) The ratio $\dfrac{\text{apparent brightness of Barnard's star}}{\text{apparent brightness of the Sun}}$ is 2.6×10^{-14}.

   (i) Define the term **apparent brightness**. (2)

   (ii) Determine the value of the ratio $\dfrac{\text{luminosity of Barnard's star}}{\text{luminosity of the Sun}}$ $(1\,\text{ly} = 6.3 \times 10^4\,\text{AU})$. (4)

(d) The surface temperature of Barnard's star is about 3 500 K. Using this information and information about its luminosity, explain why Barnard's star cannot be:

   (i) a white dwarf. (1)

   (ii) a red giant. (1)

(*Total 16 marks*)

3. This question is about Cepheid variables.

(a) Define

   (i) **luminosity**. (1)

   (ii) **apparent brightness**. (1)

(b) State the mechanism for the variation in the luminosity of the Cepheid variable. (1)

The variation with time t, of the apparent brightness b, of a Cepheid variable is shown in Figure 12.30.

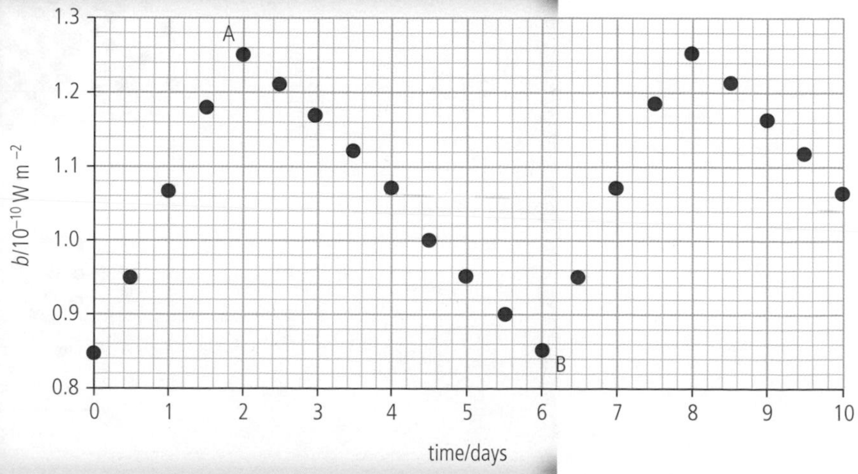

Figure 12.30.

Two points in the cycle of the star have been marked A and B.

(c) (i) Assuming that the surface temperature of the star stays constant, deduce whether the star has a larger radius after two days or after six days. (2)

(ii) Explain the importance of Cepheid variables for estimating distances to galaxies. (3)

(d) (i) The maximum luminosity of this Cepheid variable is 7.2×10^{29} W. Use data from Figure 12.30 to determine the distance of the Cepheid variable. (3)

(ii) Cepheids are sometimes referred to as 'standard candles'. Explain what is meant by this. (2)

(Total 13 marks)

4. This question is about the mean density of matter in the Universe.

(a) Explain the significance of the **critical density** of matter in the Universe with respect to the possible fate of the Universe. (3)

The critical density ρ_0 of matter in the Universe is given by the expression

$$\rho_0 = \frac{3H_0^2}{8\pi G}$$

where H_0 is the Hubble constant and G is the gravitational constant.

An estimate of H_0 is 2.7×10^{-18} s^{-1}.

(b) (i) Calculate a value for ρ_0. (1)

(ii) Hence determine the equivalent number of nucleons per unit volume at this critical density. (1)

(Total 5 marks)

5. A partially completed Hertzsprung–Russell (HR) diagram for some stars in the Milky Way galaxy is shown in Figure 12.31.

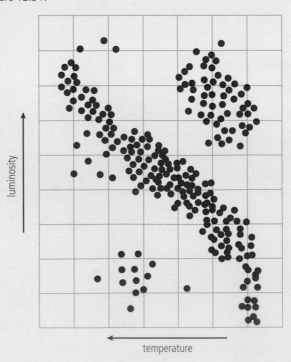

temperature

Figure 12.31.

(a) Copy Figure 12.31 and on your diagram,

    (i) identify the regions associated with red giants (label the region R) and white dwarfs (label the region W). (1)

    (ii) mark with the letter S the approximate present position of the Sun. (1)

    (iii) draw the evolutionary path of the Sun from its present position to its ultimate position. (2)

(b) At the end of its main sequence lifetime, a star of approximately ten times the mass of the Sun will start to produce energy at a much higher rate and its surface will become cooler. Outline how it is possible for the star to be producing more power and yet its surface is cooling. (2)

6. This question is about cosmic microwave background radiation.
Figure 12.32 shows the spectrum of the cosmic microwave background radiation.

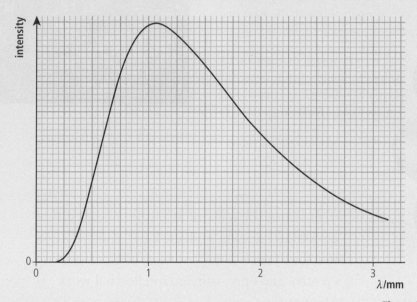

Figure 12.32.

The shape of the graph suggests a black-body spectrum, i.e. a spectrum to which the Wien displacement law applies.

(a) Use Figure 12.32 to estimate the black-body temperature. (2)

(b) Explain how your answer to (a) is evidence in support of the Big Bang model. (2)

(c) State and explain another piece of experimental evidence in support of the Big Bang model. (2)

(Total 6 marks)

Theory of Knowledge

> 66 The task is not to see what has never been seen before, but to think what has never been thought before about what you see every day. 99
> Erwin Schrödinger

In the Theory of Knowledge course you will be asked to analyse and discuss the different ways of knowing and areas of knowledge. Physics is one of the areas of knowledge that you have been introduced to, but what makes it different from other subjects such as art or languages? In this chapter we will look at the way that you gain knowledge in physics, so that you can compare this with the ways of knowing in your other subjects.

What is the role of imagination in physics? Can physics be beautiful? Is physics all logic and maths or is there a place for feelings?

Figure 13.1 Are these particle physics equations beautiful? Can you use your imagination to work out what they represent?

> 66 It is not the *result* of scientific research that ennobles humans and enriches their nature, but the *struggle to understand* while performing creative and open-minded intellectual work. 99
> Albert Einstein

Is this what an atom looks like?

Is this sunset more beautiful to people who understand Einstein's theory of general relativity?

The scientific method

The scientific method is the way that physicists work to invent new theories and to discover new laws, and it is also the way that you will have been working in the practical program. There are actually many variations to this process and many exceptions, where new theories have come about without following any strict procedure. However, to make things simple, we will consider just one four-step version.

1 Observation

Physics is all about making models to help us understand the universe. Before we can make a model, we must observe what is happening. In physics, the observations are often of the form

How does one thing affect another?

2 Hypothesis

Having made an observation, the next step is to use your knowledge to develop an idea of what is causing the event you have observed. What factors cause this thing to happen and what factors are not involved? Having made a hypothesis, it is possible to predict the outcome of a change in one of the variables.

Franklin's lightning experiment. If Franklin had had a full understanding of electricity, he wouldn't have done this. He was lucky that the kite did not get struck by lightning, and in fact many people died repeating this experiment.

Galileo makes observations using a telescope.

3 Experiment

The experiment is designed to test the hypothesis. It is important to change only the quantity that you think is responsible for the event. You must keep the other variables constant.

If the experiment does not prove the hypothesis then you must go back to the observations and think of a new one (this is often helped by the outcome of the experiment). If the experiment supports the hypothesis then you can go on to the next step.

4 Theory

If experiment supports the hypothesis, you can make a theory that relates the variables involved. A theory is a set of related statements that can be used to make predictions and explain observations.

66 The secret of genius is to carry the spirit of childhood into maturity. 99
T. H. Huxley

All experiments are conducted to test hypotheses.

Example – the simple pendulum

Observation

A student watches a simple pendulum swinging and wonders what factors affect the frequency of the swing.

Hypothesis

The student hadn't studied the motion of the pendulum so used his intuition to come up with an idea related to the mass of the bob. He thought that since the bigger mass had more weight, then the force pulling it down would be greater, causing it to swing faster. So the hypothesis was that the frequency of the bob was proportional to the mass of the bob.

Experiment

An experiment was carried out measuring the frequency of bobs with different mass. The length of the string, the height of release and all other variables were kept constant. The result showed that there was no change; the hypothesis was therefore wrong.

Back to observations

On observing the pendulum further, the student noticed that if its length were increased, it appeared to swing more slowly. This led to a second hypothesis and the process continued.

Theories must be falsifiable

For a theory to be accepted it must be possible to think of a way that it can be proved wrong. For example: Newton's gravitational theory would be proved wrong if an object with mass was seen to be repelled from the Earth.

However, the theory that the Earth is inhabited by invisible creatures with eyes on each finger is not falsifiable since you cannot see the creatures to tell if they have eyes on their fingers or not.

Occam's razor

A razor is a strange name for a principle. Its name arises because it states that a theory should not contain any unnecessary assumptions – it should be shaved down to its bare essentials.

> ❝ There are children playing in the street who could solve some of my top problems in physics, because they have modes of sensory perception that I lost long ago. ❞
>
> Robert Oppenheimer

This is the same as the KIS principle , 'keep it simple'.

For example, a theory for gravitational force could be that there is a force between all masses that is proportional to the product of their mass and is caused by invisible creatures with very long arms. The last bit about the invisible creatures is unnecessary so can be cut out of the theory (using Occam's razor).

'Just a theory'

If someone says 'The theory of special relativity is just a theory', what do they mean?

The use of the word *theory* in the English language can cause some problems for scientists. The word is sometimes used to mean that something isn't based on fact. For instance, you could say that you have a theory as to why your friend was annoyed with you last night. In physics, a theory is based on strong experimental evidence.

Serendipity

Discoveries aren't always made by following a rigorous scientific method – sometimes luck plays a part. Serendipity is the act of finding something when you were looking for something else. For example, someone could be looking for their car keys but find their sunglasses. There are some famous examples of this in physics.

Hans Christian Oersted discovered the relationship between electricity and magnetism when he noticed the needle of a compass moving, during a lecture on electric current.

Arno A. Penzias and Robert Woodrow Wilson discovered radiation left over from the Big Bang, whilst measuring the microwave radiation from the Milky Way. They at first thought their big discovery was just annoying interference.

These serendipitous discoveries were all made by people who had enough knowledge to know that they had found something interesting. If they weren't expert physicists, would they have realized that they had discovered something new?

Previous knowledge

When you do practical work for the IB diploma, is the principle behind what you are doing the same as that used by leading physicists working in research departments of universities around the world?

What you are doing is using the knowledge learnt in class to develop your hypothesis. You should find out that, if you apply your knowledge correctly, your experiment will support your hypothesis. At the cutting edge of science, the scientists are developing new theories so the experiment is used to test the theory, not to test if they have applied accepted theory correctly. To find a new way of relating quantities requires imagination, but what you are being asked to do in your physics lab is to use accepted theory and not to use imagination. How can students trained to apply strict physical laws be expected to make imaginative new theories?

Paradigm shifts

A paradigm is a set of rules that make up a theory that is accepted by the scientific community. Having completed this course, you will have accepted certain paradigms. We see and interpret the world by virtue of paradigms and theories. Newtonian mechanics is

▲ Hans Christian Oersted experimenting with magnets and current after a chance observation.

a paradigm – we apply Newton's laws of motion to balls, electrons, planes, and cars. The theory works well and is accepted by the scientific community. The way we treat almost everything as a particle is another paradigm. This paradigm is so much a part of the way that we think that it is almost impossible to think of matter not being made of particles. How could you have a gas that was continuous? Before anyone thought of matter being made of particles, this wouldn't have been a problem, but now it is. To change your way of thinking requires a big leap of imagination, and this is called a paradigm shift. Throughout the development of physics there have been many paradigm shifts.

Copernicus

In 1543, when Copernicus suggested that the Sun was the centre of the solar system, it went against a theory that had been accepted for over a thousand years. Furthermore, it not only went against scientific theory it went against common sense, for how can we be going around the Sun when we are quite obviously standing still? It required a totally new way of thinking to accept this new idea. At the time the evidence was not strong enough to be convincing and the old paradigm remained. It was not until Galileo provided more evidence and later Newton developed an explanation, that the shift took place.

Einstein's theory of relativity

Before Einstein, it was accepted that time is the same everywhere, the length of a body is the same as measured by everyone and the mass of a body is constant. Einstein showed that time, length, and mass all depend on the relative velocity of two observers. After this discovery it wasn't possible to carry on as if nothing had happened; what was required was a new way of thinking and a new set of laws. However, when a paradigm shift takes place, the old laws don't suddenly become obsolete; they just obtain limits. Newtonian mechanics is still fine when relative velocities are much less than the speed of light, and that is why it is still included in physics courses such as this.

The next paradigm shift

Will there be another paradigm shift? Can physics advance without one? Because there have been paradigm shifts in the past, does that mean that there has to be another one to advance physics further? In 1900 Lord Kelvin famously said 'There is nothing new to be discovered in physics now, all that remains is more and more precise measurement.' He was certainly wrong. Does that mean that if someone said the same thing today they'd also be wrong? One problem is that, as students go through the process of education, they get entrenched in the ways of thinking of their teachers, so the leap in imagination to make that new paradigm shift becomes bigger and bigger as time goes on.

The battleship and a bucket of water

Can a battleship float in a bucket of water? To solve this problem, you use Archimedes' principle that tells you that a body will float if it displaces it own weight of water. You might therefore conclude that the ship can't float in a bucket of water, because it has to displace (move out of the way) its own weight of water and there isn't that much water in the bucket. However, this is a misinterpretation of the theory. What Archimedes meant is that, when a boat is floating, if you filled the space in the water taken up by the boat with water, then it would be the same weight as the boat. This still might not make sense – that's why physicists use so many diagrams.

This demonstrates again how important it is to understand the language.

Use of language

In physics, we use language in a very precise way; every time a quantity is named, it is given a specific definition. For example *velocity* means one thing and one thing only, the rate of change of displacement. In normal use of language, words can mean more than one thing; this is often used in jokes, poems and literature but not in physics.

Sometimes the other meanings of a word can lead to confusion. *Potential energy* sounds like a body could possibly have energy but it actually means the energy a body has owing to its position. *Electron spin* sounds like the electron is actually a little ball spinning; a spinning charge would indeed have the properties exhibited by the electron; however these properties do not arise because it's spinning.

To get around this problem, physicists sometimes use words that can't be confused with other meanings, who would think that a charm quark was actually charming, for instance?

Opinions

If you see a painting, read a book or watch the news on the television, you will probably formulate some opinion about it. In many subjects that you study you are actively encouraged to formulate opinions and discuss them in class. For example, you could think a painting is beautiful or you could think that it is horrible. Either way is fine, because it's your opinion and you can have whatever opinion you like when it comes to such things.

Can you have an opinion in physics? Is it OK to say that in your opinion Newton was wrong when he said that force was proportional to rate of change momentum and that you think that they are independent? In physics, opinions don't count for much, although they can sometimes be the beginning of the formulation of a testable hypothesis.

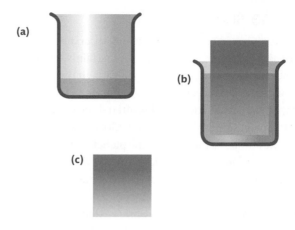

Figure 13.2 (a) Bucket with a bit of water. (b) Large object floating in bucket. The bucket is now almost full because the object is taking the place of the water. The object displaces the water. (c) Archimedes says that the weight of fluid displaced equals the weight of the object. So this amount of water will have the same weight as the object.

Laws

In Physics we use the term *law* quite a lot; for example, Newton's laws of motion, the law of conservation of energy and Ohm's law. The laws are generalized descriptions of observations that are used to solve problems and make predictions. If we want to know what height a ball will reach when thrown upwards, then we can use the law of conservation of energy to find the answer. When you use a law to solve a problem, you have a solid foundation for your solution. If someone were to disagree with your solution then they are disagreeing not only with you, but the law (assuming you applied it correctly). Laws sometimes give easy answers to difficult problems. If someone comes to you with a design of a machine that is 100% efficient, you don't need to study the details, because you can simply apply the second law of thermodynamics and say it won't work.

How much water do you need to float this huge oil tanker?

▼

Universal laws

Some of the laws in physics are called universal laws; for example, Newton's universal law of gravitation. A universal law applies to the whole universe, but it is possibly naïve (or arrogant) to think that we can write laws that apply to the whole universe, when we can only make measurements from one very small part of it. Today, scientists are more modest in their claims and accept that there are probably parts of the universe that do not behave in the same way as things in our solar system.

“ All truths are easy to understand once they are discovered; the point is to discover them. ”
Galileo Galilei

Sense and perception

Physics is based on observation and observations are made with our senses. This was certainly true hundreds of years ago but today, although the information finally arrives into our brain via our senses, the observation itself is often done via some instrument. Copernicus had difficulty convincing anyone about his theory that the planets orbited the Sun, because he didn't have any convincing observations. He had predicted that Venus would have phases like the Moon, but couldn't observe this. Galileo used the telescope to observe that Venus did indeed have phases like the Moon. At first, this was still not accepted, since people didn't trust the telescope – they wanted to 'see it with their own eyes'.

Deceptive pictures

A camera operates on the same physical principle as the human eye. Visible light is reflected from an object and focused by a lens onto a screen. It is reasonable to think that a picture is a good record of what we see. Using digital technology, it is now possible to recreate pictures from light that we can't see. Is this seeing? Can we say that we have seen a distant galaxy when we look at a picture constructed from radio waves? Can we say that we have seen the face of a flea when the picture was constructed from the diffraction pattern of electrons?

Can you see a hidden face in this picture? Apparently those with 'physical brains' take a long time. See below for a hint.

The face of a flea. Can you really say that this is what it looks like since you can never see it directly?

Hint: Look between 3 o'clock and 5 o'clock.

Galaxy cluster MS0735.6+7421. The red part of this image is radio, the blue X-ray and the yellow is light. You could never see this.

Seeing is believing?

During the IB physics course you will have been asked to make observations and devise research questions; is this easier when you have studied the topic already or when it's something totally new? When you already know what you are supposed to be looking for, it is often easier to get started. However, if you have no preconceived ideas, you might have more chance of spotting something new.

Children use their imagination all the time when playing. What happens to this skill in later life?

Imagination

Have you made use of your imagination during this course? Maybe not, but it is important that physicists have imagination, as Einstein famously said;

> 66 I am enough of an artist to draw freely upon my imagination. Imagination is more important than knowledge. Knowledge is limited. Imagination encircles the world. 99

Without imagination, the huge leaps that have brought about the paradigm shifts in the way we perceive the world would never have been made. In learning basic physics, following rules tends to be emphasized more than using imagination, but at the cutting edge it is imagination that enables scientists to forge their way forward.

The Moon illusion

Have you ever noticed that the Moon looks bigger when it's close to the horizon? If you know some physics, you might have thought of an explanation. Maybe it's due to the refraction of the light by the atmosphere, or the elliptical orbit of the Moon causing it to sometimes be closer to the Earth. These theories would be based on the observation that you have made using your senses. However, if you were actually to measure the size of the Moon you'd find that it doesn't change as it moves from overhead to the horizon; it's an illusion. Physical theories are based on measurement not perception.

Physics or intuition?

One of the problems with studying physics is that we all live in the physical world and have all seen how bodies interact. We all know that if you drop something it falls to Earth and if you push someone on a swing they will move back and forth. These observations give us a feeling for what is going to happen in other instances; we call this feeling intuition, the ability to sense or know what is going to happen without reasoning. In physics, we create models to help give a reason for what is happening. This all works fine until intuition gives us a different answer to the laws of physics. Here's an example:

Consider a metal bar floating in space, where the gravitational field strength is zero. If you apply two forces to the bar as shown in Figure 13.3, what happens?

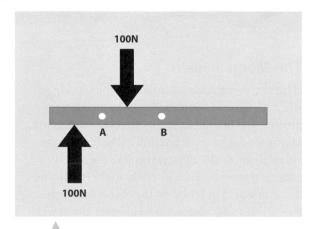

▲ **Figure 13.3** What happens when the bar experiences these forces?

Intuition will probably tell you that the bar will rotate about point A. This is because if you do this yourself that is what will happen. However that answer is wrong. Let's now apply Newton's laws of motion to the problem.

Newton's first law states that a body will remain at rest or with uniform motion in a straight line unless acted upon by an unbalanced force. The forces in this example are balanced, so the centre of mass of the bar (B) will not move.

We can see however that the turning effect (torque) of these forces is not balanced, so the rod will turn.

If the rod turns but point B doesn't move, then the rod must turn about B. And that is what happens.

The reason for the difference in these two predictions is that this rod is not in a gravitational field. When we try to do this with a rod on Earth, there are other forces acting.

Intuition was wrong; physics was right. The laws of physics can tell you what happens even if you can't do it or see it yourself.

Peer review

One of the strengths of modern scientific practice is that every new discovery goes through a rigorous process of peer review. Before a theory is published, it is sent to other scientists working in the same field. They give feedback to the research team before the theory is published. In this way mistakes can be spotted and problems ironed out. It also gives the possibility for other groups working in the same field to think of experiments that could be conducted to prove the theory wrong. Scientists are continually looking for ways to prove theories wrong, so when a theory is accepted by the scientific community one can be sure that it has been rigorously tested.

> 66 There are many hypotheses in science which are wrong. That's perfectly all right; they're the aperture to finding out what's right. 99
>
> Carl Sagan

> 66 The most exciting phrase to hear in science, the one that heralds new discoveries, is not 'Eureka!' (I found it!) but 'That's funny…' 99
>
> Isaac Asimov

Ethics and physics

Ethics is the study of right and wrong. It is sometimes not easy to decide when a course of action is right or wrong, and in these cases it is useful to have a moral code or set of guidelines to refer to. In physics, there are two areas where ethical considerations are important:

1 the way physicists work in relation to other physicists; for example, they shouldn't copy each other's work or make up data.

2 the way their actions affect society; for example, physicists shouldn't work on projects that will endanger human life.

Whether a particular piece of research is ethical or not can be difficult to determine, especially when you do not know what the results of the experiment might lead to.

Should Rutherford have performed his experiments in nuclear physics, since the discovery of the nucleus led to the invention of the atom bomb?

Can it be ethical to work in the weapons industry?

Who should decide whether a piece of research is carried out: physicists or governments?

If you left your body to science, would it be OK if it were used to test car seat belts? How about if it were used to test how far different types of bullets penetrate flesh?

Is it ethical to spend billions to carry out an experiment to test someone's hypothesis?

Internal assessment

Internal Assessment in physics consists of one scientific investigation of around 6–12 pages which is worth 20% of the final assessment. It will be marked by your teacher and externally moderated by the IB. The level of work should be in line with the other practical work done during the course so should have the same level of analysis and requirement for detailed evaluation of results. There are various different tasks that could be completed for this.

A hands-on laboratory investigation

These are similar to the practical work that you will be doing throughout the course as outlined in the different chapters of this book. However, simply repeating a standard laboratory experiment like measuring the acceleration due to gravity by measuring the time for a ball to drop a measured distance will *not* be enough to earn full marks. You need to be a bit more inventive so maybe you could extend the investigation by measuring the acceleration of different-sized balls to investigate the effect of air resistance, or turn the investigation upside down and measure the upward acceleration of a helium balloon.

Research question

The investigation should start with research question such as:

'What is the relationship between the radius of a ball and its terminal velocity when falling freely through air?'

Research questions in physics are usually of the form 'what is the relationship between *x* and *y*?' Try to keep it simple by only considering one research question in your investigation. If you really want to consider more than one aspect then split the report into two sections.

Variables

The variables should then be clearly stated.

Independent variable

- Radius of the ball (this is the variable you are going to change).

Dependent variable

- Terminal velocity of the ball (this is the variable that changes because of the independent variable you changed).

Controlled variables

- Mass and material of ball.
- Air temperature, density, and humidity.

(These are things that could be changed but you are not going to change them.)

Hypothesis

A hypothesis is your prediction as to the outcome of your experiment. This shouldn't be a wild guess. Try to use the physics you have learnt in class to make a mathematical model of the situation that you are investigating. It doesn't have to give the correct answer but you should apply what you know correctly. Having a mathematical model will make the analysis of the data easier but it is not essential. It is also possible to find the relationship from your data by analysing the graph.

Method

The method should contain all the details of how you did the experiment including:

- how the independent variable was changed.
- how the dependent variable was measured.
- how the controlled variables were kept constant.

It is always important to collect sufficient data. This means a wide range of many different values for the independent variable and many repeats of each measurement of the dependent variable. This might be limited by the materials on hand but try to get as much data as possible. If you have different ways of testing your hypothesis it will strengthen your conclusion.

Data collection

- Data is always organized in a table which should include units and uncertainties in the headers.
- If your data is coming from video analysis or some 'data logger' graph then include an example in the report.
- Follow the usual procedure outlined in Chapter 1 with regard to uncertainties and significant figures.
- Don't forget to comment on how you arrived at the uncertainties in your table.
- Include any relevant observations.

Data processing

Processing of data will first involve finding the mean of your repeated measurements. If you have predicted the relationship between the variables then you might be able to process the data so that you can plot a straight-line graph. This makes the interpretation easier since you will only have the gradient and intercept to explain.

It is usual to use a spreadsheet to process tables of data but make sure that you explain the calculation performed.

Graphing

As in the other experiments performed throughout the course:

- the graph should be correctly labelled including units.
- the equation of the line should be clearly displayed.
- there should be error bars on the points.
- if relevant, the gradient of the line should be displayed.
- the uncertainty in the gradient should be found either by plotting steepest and least steep lines or using the inbuilt function of the software used.

If you can't linearize the relationship between your variables then you can plot a curve. However, you should have some idea of which curve to plot. Just because the line touches the points doesn't mean that you have found the relationship: a polynomial best fit will fit almost anything.

Conclusion

The conclusion should be based on the results of your experiment so look at your graph of results and interpret what you see. This is much easier if you have a linear relationship since you only have to explain the relevance of the gradient and the intercept.

If there was some known value that could be calculated from the gradient or intercept then quote it here (with uncertainties) and compare it to the accepted/expected value.

Try to justify any statements made here by referring to the spread of data along the best fit line and how close the intercept is to the origin (or expected value).

If there is an outlier you could try leaving it out and plotting the graph again but don't just delete outliers to make the line fit. Be honest about your data.

Evaluation

When writing an evaluation, think like a detective. You must have evidence for any statements you make. The idea is to explain the deviation of your results from what you expected in terms of what you did in the experiment. You shouldn't say that there were big random errors in the results if the data points lie almost perfectly on the best fit line. Don't blame friction if there is no evidence in your results that friction was a problem.

If your results are not what you expected don't assume that this is because your experimental technique was in some way flawed. It might be that your original hypothesis was incorrect. Maybe you forgot to include something in your derivation of the formula. You will often find that the theory learnt in class does not apply exactly to practical situations.

If your gradient is bigger than expected try to explain what could have made it bigger. If the intercept is negative then make sure your explanation would cause a negative intercept.

In the case of outliers go back to your original data table to see if you can see what caused the point to lie outside the best fit line.

- Do your error bars reflect the spread of data?
- Did you control all of the controlled variables or were there things you forgot to consider?

Discussion

Here you can discuss possible ways of improving the experimental method or elaborate on deviations from the theory that you might have highlighted in the evaluation. Any improvements must relate to problems that were mentioned in the evaluation. There is no point in repeating measurements to reduce random errors if the points were lying almost exactly on the best fit line.

If possible do a small experiment to support observations that you made in the evaluation.

Explain fully any modifications you might make to the apparatus. Diagrams are often useful here.

Rather than repeating the experiment it might be better to try a simulation to support your evaluation. A simulation will show you what result the theory predicts so might help to highlight any deviations from the expected.

Spreadsheet analysis and modelling

An investigation does not necessarily have to have any 'actual hands-on' measurements; it could be based entirely on a mathematical model that you develop using a spreadsheet. There are several examples in this book where this has been done.

Modelling waves

In Chapter 5 a spreadsheet was set up to model simple harmonic motion. A wave is made up of a series of points oscillating with slightly different phase. By incorporating this into your spreadsheet it is possible to model a wave but you should work out the details for yourself. Once you have modelled one wave you can add two waves together to investigate superposition, standing waves, and beats. To animate waves in Excel® a slider can be added that changes time as it is moved.

The greenhouse effect

Very sophisticated spreadsheets are used to model the greenhouse effect but you can make your own like the one in Chapter 8. However, it is not enough to simply copy the formulae from the book; you need to develop your own way of doing it. How might you introduce the effect of the concentration of greenhouse gases, for example?

Radioactive decay

Modelling the exponential decay of a radioactive isotope would be fairly straight forward using a spreadsheet but how about modelling a decay chain where isotope A decays into isotope B which decays into C, etc.?

If you undertake a spreadsheet investigation you need to be sure that you show how this is connected to the real world. Combining a spreadsheet model with a hands-on lab would be a good way to do this.

Databases

A database is a computer program that enables you to store related data making it relatively easy to find the connections between different parts. Schools often use databases to connect student information to class lists, rooms, grades, and reports. There are many scientific databases that can be used as the basis of an investigation; for example, databases containing the physical properties of materials such as Engineering Toolbox are used by engineers to look up data on building materials and elements. Astronomical data and images are also stored in databases such as SIMBAD which includes a star map. This is not particularly easy to use so you will need to read the user guide and have some idea of what it is you want to find out. A lot of the databases you will find on the web are for use by professionals so it might be difficult to understand what the data represents. If you don't understand it then don't use it!

Simulations

There are many excellent simulations on the web but they are programmed so that they follow the theoretical models. There would be no point in investigating whether a gas represented by a simulation obeys the gas laws because it is programmed to do just that. What would be more interesting would be to build your own simulation using Geogebra®, Interactive Physics®, Algodoo®, or something similar. In Geogebra® you can plot graphs from equations so you could set up sliders to vary the pressure volume and temperature of a gas and plot P–V curves. Using Algodoo® or Interactive Physics® you could model a gas by putting a large number of perfectly elastic balls into a container. Try compressing the gas and see what happens. By building your own simulations you have much more control of the underlying mathematical model so will have a better chance of making your own personal input. If you do use a readymade simulation make sure that it has many controls. Search 'ripple tank applet' and you will find an example which has many possibilities for some interesting investigations.

There is no set format for the writing of your investigation report; this is just an example of one way of doing it.

A wingsuit.

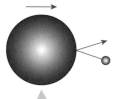

Figure IA.1 A moving ball collides with an air molecule.

Example investigation

In this example a traditional hands-on practical is combined with a simulation.

Introduction

When studying motion I performed an experiment to determine the acceleration due to gravity by measuring the time taken for a small steel ball to fall from different heights. The results obtained were in fairly close agreement with the expected result of 9.81 m s^{-2}, showing that for the range of heights involved (from 20 cm to 120 cm) the motion was indeed constant acceleration, implying that air resistance was negligible. The following week our class was shown videos of free fall parachutists wearing wing suits to demonstrate the way that air resistance opposes the force of gravity resulting in terminal velocity. This gave me the idea to try to investigate the effect of air resistance on falling bodies.

Theory

When a body moves through the air it collides with air molecules changing their velocity. According to Newton's first law this implies that there must be an unbalanced force acting on the molecules. This unbalanced force is exerted by the moving body so according to Newton's third law there must be an equal and opposite force acting on the moving body. Applying Newton's second law we can deduce that the size of the force acting on the molecules is equal to their rate of change of momentum. This situation can be likened to hitting a tennis ball with a racket. The moving racket hits the ball resulting in a change of momentum of the ball. The faster the racket moves, the greater is the change in momentum of the ball meaning that the force on the racket must be greater. So we can see that if the body moves faster the force on it due to the air will be greater. This force is called *drag*.

The drag force on a body depends on the shape of the body, how fast the body is moving, and the properties of the air it is moving through. To simplify matters we will consider only spherical bodies moving through the air. If the velocity is low then the drag force can be modelled by Stokes' law so the force would be given by the equation

$$F = 6\pi\eta vr$$

where

η = viscosity of the fluid
v = velocity of the body
r = radius

If the motion is faster, then the force is proportional to the velocity squared

$$F = \frac{1}{2}A\rho Cv^2$$

(http://hyperphysics.phy-astr.gsu.edu/hbase/airfri.html)

where

C = drag coefficient (related to the shape of the body)

A = cross-sectional area

v = velocity

In this investigation a balloon will be dropped and allowed to fall until it reaches its terminal velocity. A balloon displaces the air around it so will also experience a buoyant force equal to the weight of the air displaced. If we take the balloon to be spherical then

$$F_{buoyant} = \frac{4}{3}\pi r^3 \rho$$

When it reaches terminal velocity the forces will be balanced so

$$mg = F_{drag} + F_{bouyant}$$

So $\quad F_{drag} = mg - \frac{4}{3}\pi r^3 \rho$

If we consider spheres of equal radius but different mass we can deduce that a sphere with a greater mass will need a larger drag force to balance its weight and hence will reach a higher terminal velocity. To see if this was the case I built a simple simulation using Interactive Physics®.

In this simulation I made two spheres of equal radius but different masses: the red sphere has a mass of 10 kg and the blue one 1 kg. In Interactive Physics® the air resistance has two settings, low speed with F_{drag} proportional to v and high speed where it is proportional to v^2. With the low speed setting the heavier mass took a long time to reach terminal velocity so I chose the high speed option. In Figure IA.2(a) the red 10 kg body in reaches a higher terminal velocity than the lighter 1 kg body in Figure IA.2(b).

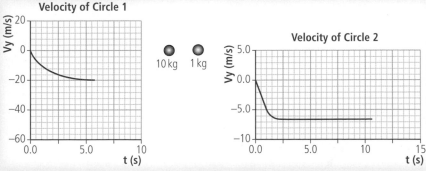

Figure IA.2 Graphs produced from Interactive Physics® showing how two falling balls reach their terminal velocity.

This simulation, however, does not include the buoyant force so I added this by giving each ball an equal upward force. The force was chosen to be 5 N so that both balls would still accelerate downwards. Figure IA.3 shows that the terminal velocity is less in both cases but that the lighter mass is most affected since the buoyant force is half of the weight.

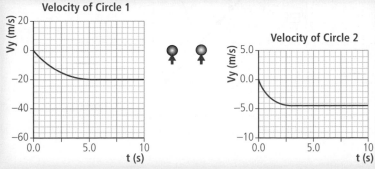

Figure IA.3 Simulation graphs showing the effect of buoyancy on the terminal velocity of two masses.

To learn more, go to the hotlinks site, search for the title or ISBN and click on Chapter Internal Assessment.

Research question

There are two different equations used to model the drag force of a spherical body moving through the air. I decided to investigate which of these equations better models the motion of a balloon falling through air.

What is the relationship between the drag force experienced by a falling balloon and its velocity?

To measure the drag force I will allow the balloon to reach terminal velocity. At that point I know that the forces are balanced so I can find the drag force from $F_{drag} = mg - \frac{4}{3}\pi r^3 \rho$. I will then change the mass of the balloon and repeat the experiment. By increasing the mass of the balloon it will achieve a higher terminal velocity so my independent variable is the mass and my dependent variable is the terminal velocity.

Preliminary experiments

From my experience with other practical work in physics I realized that there were several possible ways of measuring the terminal velocity of the balloon. First I tried dropping the balloon onto a motion sensor. This device reflects a sound wave off the balloon and the computer calculates the distance of the balloon from the sensor by recording the time for the reflected sound to come back. I had problems getting the balloon to fall in a straight line so the method was abandoned. To solve the line-of-fall problem I tried tying the balloon onto a string that was passed over a smart pulley. A small mass tied to the other end of the string kept the string tight but this also added an upward force to the balloon. However, this force was known so could be added into the equation. After a few trials I realized that this method also had its problems: the added weight reduced the velocity of the balloon by so much that terminal velocity was not reached before the balloon hit the floor. The method that I finally decided to use was filming the falling balloon with my webcam and analysing the video with LoggerPro®.

Video analysis

Using my webcam I filmed the balloon falling from a height of approximately 2 m. Analysing the video with LoggerPro® I found that the velocity of the balloon becomes constant after a very short distance. This can be seen in the displacement–time graph in Figure IA.4. The gradient appears constant and the best fit straight line is very close to all the points. If this had not been the case I would have dropped the balloon from a greater height.

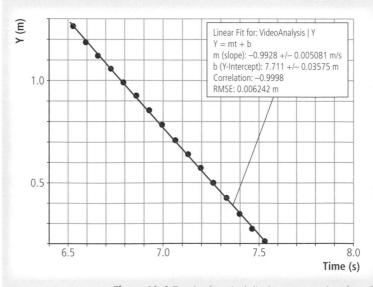

Linear Fit for: VideoAnalysis | Y
Y = mt + b
m (slope): −0.9928 +/− 0.005081 m/s
b (Y-Intercept): 7.711 +/− 0.03575 m
Correlation: −0.9998
RMSE: 0.006242 m

Figure IA.4 Graph of vertical displacement vs time for a falling balloon.

To change the weight I added small pieces of blutac® to the end of the balloon. To reduce time used between runs I decided to prepare seven 1 g pieces that could be quickly added to the balloon. The mass of the balloon was found to be just under 3 g so I increased this to 3 g by adding a small piece of blutac®. The balloon I used was black (with a pirate flag on it) so to make this show up on the video I chose a white background and set up the webcam. I made four runs of 8 different masses and then I held a metre rule at the same place as the line of fall of the balloon so that I would have a reference length on the video. I used the same balloon throughout the experiment and did all the runs in 10 minutes, thereby ensuring that the atmospheric conditions and properties of the balloon were the same for all drops.

To find the velocity of the balloon LoggerPro® was used. This software has a video analysis option that allows graphs of displacement against time to be plotted by simply marking the position of the balloon on each frame of the video. I chose to mark the middle of the balloon as the edges were so blurred (see Figure IA.5).

To find the velocity I displayed y-displacement against time graphs for each drop then used the linear fit tool to find the gradient of the best fit line for each run. One set of these lines is shown in Figure IA.6.

▲
Figure IA.5 A video still from the video analysis option of LoggerPro®.

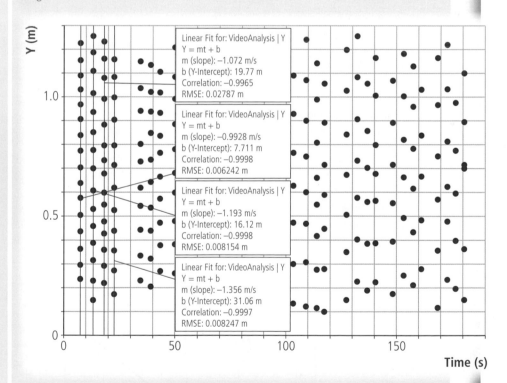

Figure IA.6 Data from the analysed video showing the gradients for one set of runs for the same height.

The gradient of each run was then entered into a spreadsheet for further processing, giving the results in Table IA.1.

Table IA.1 Analysis of the results from Figure IA.6.

Mass/g ± 0.1	Velocity(v)/m s⁻¹ ±0.001				Mean v/m s⁻¹	Unc. in mean v/m s⁻¹
3.0	1.025	1.141	0.943	1.300	1.10	0.18
4.0	1.384	1.507	1.528	1.543	1.49	0.08
5.0	1.700	1.697	1.695	1.959	1.76	0.13
6.0	2.100	2.105	2.138	2.122	2.12	0.02
7.0	2.368	2.347	2.151	2.337	2.30	0.11
8.0	2.595	2.575	2.524	2.302	2.50	0.15
9.0	2.636	2.721	2.719	2.791	2.72	0.08
10.0	3.110	2.914	2.907	2.811	2.94	0.15

One value was found to be a long way from the others in the run. Looking at the points on the graph it was apparent that two of the dots were on the same point. The video was analysed again; this time a much closer value was found.

The uncertainty in mass is the smallest reading of the digital balance and the uncertainty in the velocity is nominally set at the last digit of the value given by LoggerPro®. This is clearly an underestimate since the spread of data is much greater. For plotting error bars the $\frac{(max - min)}{2}$ is used.

Data processing

The object of this experiment was to find the relationship between the drag force and the velocity of the balloon. Since the balloon was travelling at constant velocity we can assume that the forces are balanced so F_{drag} = weight – buoyant force. However, the mass of the inflated balloon was measured on a top pan balance so the buoyant force will have been present then too. The weight measured will therefore be weight – buoyant force.

So $\qquad mg = F_{drag}$

where m is the balance reading.

To test the relationship between F_{drag} and velocity we can plot a graph of m vs v and if this is linear then F_{drag} is proportional to v.

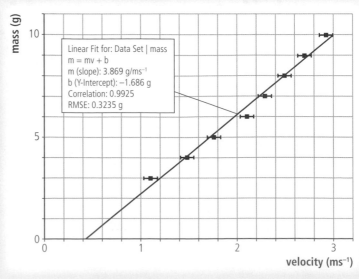

Linear Fit for: Data Set | mass
m = mv + b
m (slope): 3.869 g/ms⁻¹
b (Y-Intercept): −1.686 g
Correlation: 0.9925
RMSE: 0.3235 g

Figure IA.7 Graph of mass vs velocity for the falling balloon.

Looking at Figure IA.7 it can be seen that the best fit line almost passes through all the error bars missing just one point. However, the line does not pass through the origin and there is a clear curve in the points. I next tried fitting a quadratic (Figure IA.8).

This is a better fit but to test the relationship further I plotted mass vs v^2. Before I could do that I needed to find the uncertainties in v^2. To do this I found the maximum and minimum values of v^2 from the data and then calculated $\frac{(max - min)}{2}$, as in Table IA.2.

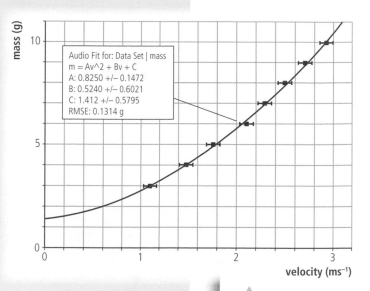

Figure IA.8 Graph of mass vs velocity with quadratic fit.

Table IA.2 Calculating velocity^2 and uncertainties from the results in Figure IA.8.

Mass/g ± 0.1	Velocity (v)/m s^{-1} ±0.001				Mean v/m s^{-1}	Unc. v/m s^{-1}	mean v^2/m^2 s^{-2}	Unc. v^2/m^2 s^{-2}
3.0	1.025	1.141	0.943	1.300	1.10	0.18	1.21	0.40
4.0	1.384	1.507	1.528	1.543	1.49	0.08	2.22	0.23
5.0	1.700	1.697	1.695	1.959	1.76	0.13	3.11	0.48
6.0	2.100	2.105	2.138	2.122	2.12	0.02	4.48	0.08
7.0	2.368	2.347	2.151	2.337	2.30	0.11	5.29	0.49
8.0	2.595	2.575	2.524	2.302	2.50	0.15	6.25	0.72
9.0	2.636	2.721	2.719	2.791	2.72	0.08	7.38	0.42
10.0	3.110	2.914	2.907	2.811	2.94	0.15	8.62	0.89

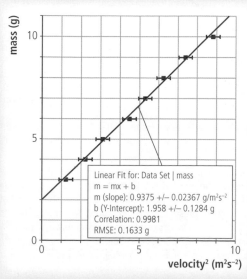

Figure IA.9 Graph of mass vs velocity^2.

589

This appears to be a better fit than the linear fit of the mass *vs* velocity graph so it seems that at the speed that the balloon is travelling the drag force is related to the square of the velocity. However, there is a significant positive intercept of 2 g which will need to be explained.

Discussion

Since it is possible to fit a straight line through the points on the mass *vs* velocity^2 graph it appears that the drag force experienced by the balloon is proportional to v^2 rather than v. Theory predicts that $F_{drag} = \frac{1}{2}A\rho Cv^2$ so if the measured mass m is proportional to the drag force at terminal velocity, then the best fit line should pass through the origin but it doesn't: the intercept with the y-axis is 2 g which is quite significant. The points lie quite close to the line of best fit so this does not seem to be due to random errors. The graph could be corrected by subtracting 2 g from every value of m. A systematic measurement error of +2 g would explain this but it seems unlikely. The weight of the balloon was checked on another balance which agreed with previous value of 3.0 g. It is more likely that there was a systematic error in the velocity measurement. This could be due to incorrect calibration when analysing the video but this would mean that all the values of v would be changed by the same factor which would change the gradient, not the intercept. There were other factors that could also have affected the result: the balloon didn't always fall straight down and although it was always dropped in the same way it didn't fall in the same orientation each time. However, I would expect these factors to introduce a random error which was not evident from the results. In fact, the error bars on the graph appear to be *overestimated* as the data is not as spread out as the size of the error bars.

According to the graph the drag force is equivalent to 2 g even when the velocity is zero. This looks very much like the buoyant force. However, this was taken into account with the way the balloon was weighed (with air in it). To investigate this I went back to the simulation. With spheres of different mass falling in air with v^2 drag, a graph of m *vs* v^2 gave a straight line passing very close to the origin as in Figure IA.10(a). With a small force acting upwards on the sphere the intercept was positive as shown in Figure IA.10(b).

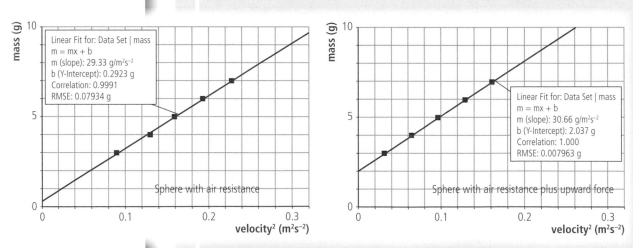

Figure IA.10 Graphs showing the effect of a constant force on the relationship between mass and velocity^2 (obtained from a simulation).

As stated in the introduction, there are two models for drag force. At low speeds when the flow is streamlined, the force is due to the air flowing around the body ($F \propto v$) but at higher speeds it is due to the air molecules bouncing off the body ($F \propto v^2$). The results suggest that the latter is the case but that there is another force present. Using the simulation I investigated what the results would look like if both forces were present at the same time. To achieve this I took the already prepared equations for the high and low speed forces in Interactive Physics® and added them together to give a customized force. Spheres of different mass were again dropped and their terminal velocity recorded. The results are as shown in Figure IA.11.

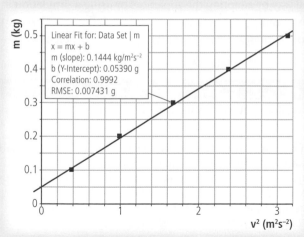

Figure IA.11 Graph of mass *vs* velocity^2 for a simulated experiment with combined drag force.

Although there is a slight curve to the points the relationship appears almost linear with a positive *y* intercept rather like the results from my experiment.

Conclusion

The results support the theory that at low speeds the drag force experienced by a falling balloon is linearly related to the velocity but at high speeds it is related to the velocity squared.

Further investigation

One problem of using a falling balloon to measure the drag force is that terminal velocity must be reached. This limited the possible range. The lowest value possible is with no mass attached to the balloon; for lower speeds a helium-filled balloon could be used.

An alternative that would allow a bigger range and give better control of the balloon's orientation is to measure the force experienced by the balloon as it moves through the air at constant speed. One possible way to do this would be to suspend the balloon inside a wooden frame with elastic bands as shown in Figure IA.12.

As the frame is moved through the air the elastic bands would be stretched enabling the force to be measured. For low speeds the frame could be mounted on a dynamics track trolley and for higher speeds the roof of a car. Measurements could be made by photographing the balloon then measuring the length of the elastic bands from the photograph. If the setup is calibrated by measuring the force needed to stretch the bands by different amounts, the force on the balloon could be found.

Figure IA.12 A balloon mounted in a frame.

Assessment criteria

Before you start your investigation you must know how it is going to be assessed. There are five criteria weighted according to Table IA.3.

Table IA.3 The five assessment criteria and marks allocated to each.

Personal engagement	Exploration	Analysis	Evaluation	Communication	Total
2 (8%)	6 (25%)	6 (25%)	6 (25%)	4 (17%)	24 (100%)

Personal engagement

This criterion assesses your engagement with the topic. It might be the case that you have an interest in a certain sport or play a musical instrument that led to the idea of undertaking the investigation. This would give you a personal attachment to the topic but is not essential so don't pretend. What is more important is that you develop your investigation in a personal way by adapting the apparatus or using a simulation in an interesting and novel way. Simply following a standard procedure won't score top marks here but thinking of an interesting way to solve a practical problem will.

Table IA.4 Allocation of marks for personal engagement.

Mark	Descriptor
0	The student's report does not reach a standard described by the descriptors below.
1	**The evidence of personal engagement with the exploration is limited with little independent thinking, initiative, or insight.** The justification given for choosing the research question and/or the topic under investigation does not demonstrate personal significance, interest, or creativity. There is little evidence of personal input and initiative in the designing, implementation, or presentation of the investigation.
2	**The evidence of personal engagement with the exploration is clear with significant independent thinking, initiative, or insight** The justification given for choosing the research question and/or the topic under investigation demonstrates personal significance, interest, or curiosity. There is evidence of personal input and initiative in the designing, implementation, or presentation of the investigation.

In the example experiment the student showed personal engagement by both developing the experimental technique and customizing the Interactive Physics® simulation to test whether the theory would give the results achieved.

Exploration

This criterion assesses the extent to which you establish the scientific context for the work. The research question must be about some physical phenomenon or the relationship between physical quantities. This is not an extended essay so you are not expected to use theories beyond the level of the course. However, any theory used should be used in the appropriate way. Throughout the course you will be performing many different experiments, learning ways to handle apparatus, using computer models, processing data, and evaluating results. You should use the same skills in your investigation.

Table IA.5 Allocation of marks for exploration.

Mark	Descriptor
0	The student's report does not reach a standard described by the descriptors below.
1–2	The topic of the investigation is identified and a research question of some relevance is **stated but it is not focused**. The background information provided for the investigation is **superficial** or of limited relevance and does not aid the understanding of the context of the investigation. The methodology of the investigation is only appropriate to address the research question to a very limited extent since it takes into consideration few of the significant factors that may influence the relevance, reliability, and sufficiency of the collected data. The report shows evidence of limited awareness of the significant **safety,** ethical, or environmental issues that are **relevant to the methodology of the investigation***.

Mark	Descriptor
3–4	The topic of the investigation is identified and a relevant but not fully focused research question is described. The background information provided for the investigation is mainly appropriate and relevant and aids the understanding of the context of the investigation. The methodology of the investigation is mainly appropriate to address the research question but has limitations since it takes into consideration only some of the significant factors that may influence the relevance, reliability, and sufficiency of the collected data. The report shows evidence of some awareness of the significant **safety,** ethical, or environmental issues that are **relevant to the methodology of the investigation*.**
5–6	The topic of the investigation is identified and a relevant and fully focused research question is clearly described. The background information provided for the investigation is entirely appropriate and relevant and enhances the understanding of the context of the investigation. The methodology of the investigation is highly appropriate to address the research question because it takes into consideration all, or nearly all, of the significant factors that may influence the relevance, reliability, and sufficiency of the collected data. The report shows evidence of full awareness of the significant **safety,** ethical, or environmental issues that are **relevant to the methodology of the investigation.***

* This indicator should only be applied when appropriate to the investigation.

Studying the relationship between the velocity of a balloon and the drag force is an appropriate and focused research question. The theory described is relevant to the research question and the explanation acceptable for a student at this level. The use of video analysis is an acceptable way to measure the terminal velocity of the balloon. The Interactive Physics® simulations added an interesting dimension to the investigation. In any investigation it is difficult to control all the variables but the student understands the limitations of the method.

Analysis

This criterion assesses the extent to which your report provides evidence that you have selected, recorded, processed, and interpreted the data in ways that are relevant to the research question and can support a conclusion. Firstly, you must have devised an experimental method or found a source that will enable you to collect sufficient data to be able to test your hypothesis. If you can only find data about three different types of golf ball then it is not a good idea to do your investigation on golf balls. If your uncertainties are too big then you won't be able to support a conclusion so careful measurement and reliable sources are required. Any processing of data must be done correctly with no mathematical mistakes and uncertainties must be propagated in the usual way. Processed data is often presented in a graphical form to enable interpretation; the graphs should be relevant to the original research question and plotted in an acceptable fashion to support the conclusion.

Table IA.6 Allocation of marks for analysis.

Mark	Descriptor
0	The student's report does not reach a standard described by the descriptors below.
1–2	The report includes **insufficient relevant** raw data to support a valid conclusion to the research question. Some basic data processing is carried out but is either too **inaccurate or too insufficient to lead to a valid** conclusion. The report shows evidence of little consideration of the impact of measurement uncertainty on the analysis. The processed data is incorrectly or insufficiently interpreted so that the conclusion is invalid or very incomplete.
3–4	The report includes relevant but incomplete quantitative and qualitative raw data that could support a simple or partially valid conclusion to the research question. Appropriate and sufficient data processing is carried out that could lead to a broadly valid conclusion but there are significant inaccuracies and inconsistencies in the processing. The report shows evidence of some consideration of the impact of measurement uncertainty on the analysis. The processed data is interpreted so that a broadly valid but incomplete or limited conclusion to the research question can be deduced.
5–6	The report includes sufficient relevant quantitative and qualitative raw data that could support a detailed and valid conclusion to the research question. Appropriate and sufficient data processing is carried out with the accuracy required to enable a conclusion to the research question to be drawn that is fully **consistent** with the experimental data. The report shows evidence of full and appropriate consideration of the impact of measurement uncertainty on the analysis. The processed data is correctly interpreted so that a completely valid and detailed conclusion to the research question can be deduced.

The research question *'what is the relationship between the drag force experienced by a falling balloon and its velocity?'* was investigated by measuring the terminal velocity of balloons of different mass, in this way, sufficient relevant data was collected to determine whether the force was proportional to v or v^2. To support the conclusion a simulation was used to compare the theoretical model with reality. Data was analysed in an appropriate way leading to graphs that facilitated interpretation. Errors were included where appropriate. Plotting a graph of mass *vs* v^2 was an appropriate way of determining if force was proportional to v^2 since the drag force is equal to the measured weight at terminal velocity.

Evaluation

This criterion assesses the extent to which your report provides evidence of evaluation of the investigation and the results with regard to the research question and the accepted scientific context. Your conclusion does not have to support your hypothesis but it does have to be related to the research question. The conclusion should also involve some theoretical background. It is much more difficult to explain what actually happened than what the theory predicted should happen. Your conclusion should be based on the evidence from your experiment or data; if you can't give evidence then it shouldn't be in your conclusion. Don't assume that any deviation from the expected result is due to experimental error; maybe the theoretical model needs adjusting. Your data will also hold clues as to the areas of weakness in your experiment or data: refer to these clues when evaluating your procedure. Even if your experiment worked well there is always room for improvement. However, make sure that any improvements would address the weaknesses.

Table IA.7 Allocation of marks for evaluation.

Mark	Descriptor
0	The student's report does not reach a standard described by the descriptors below.
1–2	A conclusion is **outlined** which may not be relevant to the research question or may not be supported by the data presented. The conclusion makes superficial comparison to the accepted scientific context. Strengths and weaknesses of the investigation, such as limitations of the data and sources of error, are outlined but are restricted to an **account of the practical** or **procedural issues** faced. The student has **outlined** very few realistic and relevant suggestions for the improvement and extension of the investigation.
3–4	A conclusion is **described** which is relevant to the research question and supported by the data presented. A conclusion is described which makes some relevant comparison to the accepted scientific context. Strengths and weaknesses of the investigation, such as limitations of the data and sources of error, are **described** and provide evidence of some awareness of the **methodological issues** involved in establishing the conclusion. The student has **described** some realistic and relevant suggestions for the improvement and extension of the investigation.
5–6	A detailed conclusion is **described and justified** which is entirely relevant to the research question and fully supported by the data presented. A conclusion is correctly **described and justified** through relevant comparison to the accepted scientific context. Strengths and weaknesses of the investigation, such as limitations of the data and sources of error, are **discussed** and provide evidence of a clear understanding of the **methodological issues** involved in establishing the conclusion. The student has **discussed** realistic and relevant suggestions for the improvement and extension of the investigation.

The results for the balloon drop investigation were not as expected but there is detailed discussion of what might have caused the deviations. Simulations have been used to support the explanation based on the original theoretical model. During the planning stage many different methods were experimented with and in conclusion some interesting suggestions were made as to how the range could be increased.

Communication

This criterion assesses whether your investigation is presented and reported in a way that supports effective communication of the focus, process, and outcomes. It is not easy to explain things you don't understand so don't be too ambitious. Always keep in mind your research question. Use sub-headings to organize the report. The introduction should introduce the research question, the theory should be relevant to the research question, the hypothesis should attempt to apply theory to answer the research question, the experiment should address the research question, and the conclusion should attempt, if possible, to answer the research question.

Table IA.8 Allocation of marks for communication.

Mark	Descriptor
0	The student's report does not reach a standard described by the descriptors below.
1–2	**The presentation of the investigation is unclear, making it difficult to understand the focus, process, and outcomes.** The report is not well structured and is unclear: the necessary information on focus, process, and outcomes is missing or is presented in an incoherent or disorganized way. The understanding of the focus, process, and outcomes of the investigation is obscured by the presence of inappropriate or irrelevant information. There are many errors in the use of subject specific terminology and conventions.
3–4	**The presentation of the investigation is clear. Any errors do not hamper understanding of the focus, process, and outcomes**. The report is well structured and clear: the necessary information on focus, process, and outcomes is present and presented in a coherent way. The report is relevant and concise thereby facilitating a ready understanding of the focus, process, and outcomes of the investigation. The use of subject specific terminology and conventions is appropriate and correct. Any errors do not hamper understanding.

The balloon investigation is clearly about the drag force experienced by a falling balloon, the drag force at different velocities is measured by experiment and simulated with Interactive Physics®. The results are analysed and a conclusion made regarding the nature of the force. The report could hardly be described as lacking focus.

Extended essay

The Extended Essay is a 4000 word piece of independent research on an IB topic of your choice. Tackling an Extended Essay in physics can be a daunting prospect, but your physics teacher will supervise your research and will be on hand to give guidance and help solve any practical problems that you might come across. Your supervisor will also give you a booklet, 'The Extended Essay guide', giving guidance on how to construct the essay with some specific recommendations for physics.

Choosing a topic

If you have chosen a good topic, then writing an Extended Essay in physics can be quite straightforward. Your supervisor will help you but here are some additional guidelines:

- Don't be too ambitious; simple ideas often lead to the best essays. Students often don't believe that they can write 4000 words on something as simple as a ball of plasticine being dropped on the floor, but end up struggling to reduce the number of words.
- Make sure your topic is about physics. Avoid anything that overlaps with chemistry or biology and keep well away from metaphysics or bad science.
- Although the essay does not have to be something that has never been done before, it must not be something lifted straight from the syllabus.
- Avoid a purely theoretical essay unless you have specialist knowledge. The essay must include some personal input; this is very difficult if you write about some advanced topic like black holes or superstrings.
- It is best if you can do whatever experiments you require in the school laboratory under the supervision of your supervisor. If you do the experiments at home during the holiday, keep in contact with your supervisor, so your research is kept on the right track.
- Choose a topic that interests you; it will be easier to keep motivated when the going gets tough.
- Sports offer a wide range of interesting research questions but sometimes it is very difficult to perform experiments. Roberto Carlos' famous free kick is a fascinating topic for an Extended Essay, but not even he can do it every time, let alone with different amounts of spin. If you are keen to do this sort of research try to think how you can simplify the situation so it can be done in the laboratory not on the football pitch.
- You must not do anything dangerous or unethical.

The research question

Once a topic has been decided upon, you will have to think of a specific research question. This normally involves some experimental trials and book research. The title of the essay often poses a question that could be answered in many ways; the research question focuses on the way that you are going answer the question. It is important that as you write the essay you refer back to the original topic and don't get lost in the intricacies of your experimental method.

Examples of topics and research questions

Does the depth of a swimming pool affect the maximum speed achieved by a swimmer?

Rather than trying to measure the speed of swimmers in different depth pools, experiments were performed in the physics lab pulling a floating ball across a ripple tank. This led to the research question 'What is the relationship between the depth of water and the drag experienced by a body moving across the surface?'

Why isn't it possible to charge a balloon that isn't blown up?

This topic led to the research question 'What is the relationship between the electron affinity of rubber and the amount that the rubber is stretched'. To perform the experiment a machine was built that could rub different samples of stretched rubber in the same way.

Why does my motorbike lean to the left when I turn the handle bars to the right?

Rather than experimenting on a motorbike, experiments were performed in the lab with a simple gyroscope. The research question was 'How is the rate of precession of a spinning wheel related to the applied torque?'

Giovanni Braghieri (IB physics student and EE writer) riding his motorbike.

Performing the practical work

Most Extended Essays will involve some practical work and you should start this as early as possible. If it doesn't work or you find you don't have the right equipment, you might want to change the research question. You don't have to spend hours and hours on the experiment (although some students do). The whole essay is only supposed to take 40 hours, so keep things in perspective. Make sure the experiments are relevant to the research question and that you consider possible sources of error, as you would in any other piece of practical work. If you get stuck ask your supervisor for help. They can't do the essay for you but can help you solve problems.

Research

Remember that you're doing research, not a piece of Internal Assessment. This means that you should find out what other people have done and compare their findings with your own. This might be difficult if you have chosen a particularly novel topic but most things have been done before. You can try the internet but science journals found in university libraries are often the best source of good information.

Writing the essay

Once you have done some research and conducted your experiment, you are ready to write the essay. Remember you are trying to answer a research question, so get straight to the point. There is no need to tell a story such as how this has been your greatest interest since you were a small child. Make a plan of how you want your essay to be; the thread running through it is the research question – don't lose sight of this. Here is a plan of the essay mentioned above about the balloon:

• Introduction of the topic and research question – how the electron affinity of rubber is connected to the charging of a balloon.

• The theory of charging a balloon and electron affinity.

- Hypothesis based on the theory.
- How I am going to test the hypothesis.
- Details of experimental technique.
- Results of experiment.
- Interpretation of results including evaluation of method.
- Conclusion – how my results support my hypothesis and the findings of others.
- Why a balloon that is inflated cannot be charged.

What can go wrong

In the real world things are rarely as simple as they first appear and you might find that your data does not support your original hypothesis. This can be disappointing but shouldn't ruin your chances of writing a good essay. First make sure that you haven't made any mistakes in your initial assumptions or analysis of data, then try to think what why the experiment doesn't match the theory and write this in the conclusion. Don't pretend that it does match if it doesn't.

Extended Essay assessment

The Extended Essay is marked by experienced physics teachers against five criteria. It is important that you understand the criteria, since if your essay does not satisfy them it will not score well, even if it is a good essay. You can read the full criteria in the official IB Extended Essay guide. Here is some advice on how to get the most from your Extended Essay.

A) Focus and Method (Topic research question and methodology) 6 marks

The essay title should be a statement saying what the essay is about, for example, 'A practical investigation into the effect of pool depth on swimming times'. The essay title is fairly self-explanatory, however, it is not the research question. The research question must be posed as a question that is introduced and put into context in the introduction to the essay. You may have come up with the idea that the drag on a swimmer's body is dependent on the depth of the pool, and that this in turn might affect swimming times. The research question is then: 'What is the relationship between the depth of a swimming pool and the drag experienced by a body moving across the surface?'

The whole essay should be an attempt to answer the research question, which, once it has been formulated in the introduction, should be followed with some background information to put it into context. You must then apply physical theory to develop a hypothesis. The theory you use does not have to be beyond the syllabus, but its application should be an extension of it. The experimental method should be appropriate given the constraints of a school lab, with attempts made to control all other variables apart from those mentioned in the research question and careful measurement of independent and dependent variables. The conclusion should explain how the results answer the research question, or if they don't, you should include an explanation as to why. At the end of the essay there is room for a discussion, which can bring in other angles. Remember that the examiner will only mark the first 4000 words of the essay.

B) Knowledge and understanding (Context and terminology) 6 marks

When scientists do research they first find out what else has been done. This is known as 'book research', and you are expected to do the same for your Extended Essay. At university the main source of information is likely to be scientific papers and journals, but you are more likely to find appropriate information in text books and on websites. Make sure that websites are published by a reliable source, such as a university. Bookmark the pages you have used so that you can add appropriate citations and a bibliography when you come to write the essay. Don't copy and paste text into your draft.

Similar research may have been done by someone else before you. If you find that someone has already derived an equation, for example for the relationship between pool depth and drag, then it is acceptable to use their equation as long as you quote the source.

This is a physics essay so you must use the language of physics. Make sure you understand what all the words mean and use them in the right context. If you write about something you do not understand, your examiner will be able to tell. There will probably be some maths in the essay so make sure you get it right, including the units.

C) Critical thinking (Research, analysis, discussion and evaluation) 12 marks

Critical thinking doesn't mean that you have to question every piece of knowledge. So, for example, don't waste time justifying the law of conservation of energy, but do be careful when quoting the results of other experimenters – what did they do to justify their results? Keep an open mind when analysing and drawing conclusions from your results. Don't try to justify results that clearly don't support your hypothesis. Cast a critical eye over your method and try to work out what its weaknesses were. However, bear in mind that the theory could be wrong, not your method.

Graphs are very useful when testing relationships between two quantities. If the graph is straight then the relationship is linear, a quadratic relationship gives a parabola, and so on. Simply drawing the closest fitting curve to the data is meaningless unless you have some idea of the relationship you are testing. For example, if your theory predicts that the relationship is sinusoidal then it would not be useful to plot a best fit parabola, even if it was a perfect fit. If you can find the equation of the line then you will also find the values of any constants. If possible, use known values to test the validity of the graph.

D) Presentation (Structure and layout) 4 marks

The general structure of the essay should follow a logical progression from introduction to theory, hypothesis, method, results, conclusion, evaluation and discussion. Each of these sections can include subsections with individual subtitles.

Equations should be numbered, axes labelled, and all measurements should include uncertainties as well as units. You don't have to include all of your raw data, just enough to make sense. Make sure labels on diagrams and graphs are readable.

Learn how to use your word processor, graphics, spreadsheet and graph plotting programmes properly. If you use an image from the internet make sure you reference it. A title page, contents page, page numbers and a bibliography are all essential.

E) Engagement (Process and research) 6 marks

During the process of writing your essay you will meet with your supervisor to reflect on the process. You will be asked to make a written reflection on three occasions: at the start, in the middle and at the end. The nature of your reflections, together with the final essay, will be used to gauge your engagement with the writing process. This means that leaving everything to the night before the final deadline will not score well. The sort of thing you might reflect upon are difficulties you faced in finding information, sources you found particularly useful, things you learnt along the way and skills you needed to develop, such as using a particular piece of software.

Set yourself realistic deadlines and try to stick to them. Work with your supervisor and respond to the advice that you receive. To ensure timely feedback, keep to the schedule you have agreed upon. Writing an Extended Essay is an opportunity to do some in depth research into a subject you are interested in, so enjoy the process.

Index

Page numbers in *italics* refer to boxes and diagrams.

Index

Index

Index

Index

Index